VOLUME **59**

# SCREEN WORLD™

THE FILMS OF
## 2007

VOLUME **59**

# SCREEN WORLD™

THE FILMS OF
**2007**

## JOHN WILLIS
## and BARRY MONUSH

**APPLAUSE**
**THEATRE & CINEMA BOOKS**

AN IMPRINT OF HAL LEONARD CORPORATION
NEW YORK

Published in 2008 by Applause Theatre & Cinema Books
An Imprint of Hal Leonard Corporation
7777 West Bluemound Road
Milwaukee, WI 53213

Trade Book Division Editorial Offices
19 West 21st Street, New York, NY 10010

Printed in the United States of America

Book design by Damien Castaneda
Book composition by Kristina Rolander

ISBN: 978-1-55783-741-7
ISSN: 1545-9020

www.applausepub.com

TO
# MICHAEL CAINE

One of the most exciting and original talents to emerge from the British New Wave of the 1960's; a tremendously persuasive and gifted actor whose dramatic skills and infinite charms have made him an enduring star.

**US Theatrical Releases: 1957:** Blonde Sinner/Yield to the Night; Panic in the Parlor/Sailor Beware; **1958:** The Steel Bayonet; How to Murder a Rich Uncle; The Key; **1959:** The Two-Headed Spy; Room 43/Passport to Shame; **1960:** Danger Within; **1961:** A Foxhole in Cairo; **1962:** The Day the Earth Caught Fire; **1963:** The Wrong Arm of the Law; **1964:** Zulu; **1965:** The Ipcress File; **1966:** Alfie (*Oscar nomination*); The Wrong Box; Gambit; Funeral in Berlin; **1967:** Hurry Sundown; Woman Times Seven; Billion Dollar Brain; **1968:** Deadfall; The Magus; **1969:** Play Dirty; The Italian Job; The Battle of Britain; **1970:** Too Late the Hero; **1971:** The Last Valley; Get Carter; Kidnapped; **1972:** X, Y & Zee/Zee & Company; Pulp; Sleuth (*Oscar nomination*); **1974:** The Black Windmill; The Destructors/The Marseilles Contract; **1975:** Peeper; The Wilby Conspiracy; The Romantic Englishwoman; The Man Who Would Be King; **1976:** Harry and Walter Go to New York; **1977:** The Eagle Has Landed; A Bridge Too Far; **1978:** Silver Bears; The Swarm; California Suite; **1979:** Ashanti; Beyond the Poseidon Adventure; **1980:** The Island; Dressed to Kill; **1981:** The Hand; Victory; **1982:** Deathtrap; **1983:** Educating Rita (*Oscar nomination*); Beyond the Limit/The Honorary Consul; **1984:** Blame it on Rio; The Jigsaw Man; **1985:** The Holcroft Covenant; **1986:** Water; Hannah and Her Sisters (*Academy Award Winner for Best Supporting Actor*); Sweet Liberty; Mona Lisa; Half Moon Street; **1987:** The Whistle Blower; The Fourth Protocol (also exec. prod.); Jaws the Revenge; Surrender; **1988:** Without a Clue; Dirty Rotten Scoundrels; **1990:** A Shock to the System; Mr. Destiny; **1992:** Noises Off; The Muppet Christmas Carol; **1994:** On Deadly Ground; **1997:** Blood and Wine; **1998:** Little Voice; **1999:** The Cider House Rules (*Academy Award Winner for Best Supporting Actor*); **2000:** Get Carter; Quills; Miss Congeniality; **2001:** Last Orders; **2002:** Austin Powers in Goldmember; The Quiet American (*Oscar nomination*); **2003:** Secondhand Lions; The Statement; **2004:** Around the Bend; **2005:** Batman Begins; Bewitched; The Weather Man; **2006:** The Prestige; Children of Men. **2007:** Sleuth; **2008:** Flawless; The Dark Knight

# CONTENTS

# PREFACE
## THE YEAR OF THE RAT

Looking at the very top of the 2007 box office list, I'm dismayed to see an abundance of sequels, but these days it's never a good idea to start at the top when searching for originality or durability. As I glance further down the chart, however, I find some noteworthy cinema—for instance, the most charming animated feature yet to come from Pixar, *Ratatouille*, which manages the feat of making rats lovable; the most fully realized of Judd Apatow's growing number of rude-but-human comedies, *Knocked Up*; one of the smartest teen-oriented films in years, *Juno*, written in a fresh and witty voice by Oscar-winner Diablo Cody; and a smashing celluloid transition of one of Broadway's most dynamic modern musicals, *Hairspray*.

Any year in which a musical can find a spot in the box office top 25 is okay with me, and the fact that there was also a darkly satisfying adaptation of *Sweeney Todd: The Demon Barber of Fleet Street* on hand; a visually striking compendium of Beatles tunes, *Across the Universe*; a sprinkling of musical numbers inserted into the popular Disney fantasy *Enchanted*; and a more subdued Irish import that centers around creating music, *Once*, proved that there was plenty to be pleased about in 2007.

Audiences were also privileged to see the Coen Brothers shake off their customary winking humor and play it pretty much straight with the grippingly successful *No Country for Old Men*, the 2007 Academy Award winner for Best Picture. Equally as worthwhile was Oscar nominee *Atonement*, an adaptation of the marvelous novel by Ian McEwan. Also in the drama category was *Michael Clayton*, the George Clooney thriller that harkens back to a time when front- rank mainstream entertainment was still smart, and *Charlie Wilson's War*, which brings out the best in its star trio, Tom Hanks, Julia Roberts, and Philip Seymour Hoffman. For moviegoers who wanted to skip the visceral booms and pay attention to characterization and words, there were several choices, including another Hoffman offering, *The Savages*, which pits him against Oscar nominee Laura Linney with terrific results; *Breach*, an unsettling exposé of an American traitor; *Freedom Writers*, which celebrates the importance of education; *Zodiac*, which uses the true story of a serial killer to explore the nature of obsession; and *The Great Debaters*, which presented traditional moviemaking at its very best by charting an unsung moment in black history. Jack Nicholson and Morgan Freeman gave their emotional all in *The Bucket List*, as did many other actors in 2007, such as Tommy Lee Jones in *In the Valley of Elah*; Meryl Streep, Tom Cruise, and Robert Redford in *Lions for Lambs*; Daniel Day Lewis in *There Will Be Blood*; and Emile Hirsch and Hal Holbrook in *Into the Wild*. And Marion Cotillard's electrifying portrayal of tortured songstress Edith Piaf in *La Vie en Rose* was so impressive, the Motion Picture Academy had to defy their inclination to vote for non-foreign language performances and give her the Oscar.

When it came to family entertainment, some films aimed higher than others, as was the case with Dreamwork's *Bee Movie*, which features the wit of Jerry Seinfeld; *The Simpsons Movie*, a worthy extension of television's longest running animated series; and *Bridge to Terabithia*, which emphasizes emotion and humanity over CGI.

On the western front, *3:10 to Yuma* not only does the genre proud but manages to be a rare quality remake of a good film that stands on its own merits.

As for bang-for-your-buck cinema, if you wanted noise delivered with gusto, there was a thundering adaptation of *Transformers*; a one-of-a-kind double feature, *Grindhouse*, complete with mock coming attractions; a visually unparalleled take on old gladiator movies with *300*; and *The Bourne Ultimatum*, which seemed determined to grab the record for fastest edits in film history.

Documentaries flooded the fringe market at an alarming rate, though most failed to find public interest. One that did have success was a highly important one, as the ever-dependable Michael Moore shook us up with *Sicko*, shedding light on some of America's health care system disgraces.

Of course, anybody who really appreciates movies knows that motion pictures found *way* off the Top 100 Box Office charts are also deserving of ample rewards. Often, these films are neglected by the public, made marginally accessible by the fact that most multiplexes won't even consider booking them, or are just plain difficult to track down because of film distribution issues. The terrible pattern film distribution has fallen into recently often leaves plenty of good movies dumped on the market in tiny venues for a quick one-week run before being relegated to the DVD format. Just a fraction of a long list of films that deserve to be seen by a wider audience includes *Seraphim Falls*, *Starter for Ten*, *The Namesake*, *Black Book*, *Year of the Dog*, *Hot Fuzz*, *Away from Her*, *Bug*, *You Kill Me*, *Talk to Me*, *Goya's Ghosts*, *Sunshine*, *The Ten*, *2 Days in Paris*, *Romance & Cigarettes*, *Gone Baby Gone*, *Starting Out in the Evening*, *The Diving Bell and the Butterfly*, and *The Kite Runner*.

All of these movies, and many others, are featured in what I refer to as the "A" section of *Screen World*, which hopes to bring attention and pay tribute to those releases that had pedigree and quality, along with those that had box office power, some of which did not forsake quality while pleasing substantial portions of the public. Because every cinematic year is bursting with releases—far more than the average citizen might even be aware of— there is simply not enough room to feature all of them upfront. Therefore, the less significant offerings, in consideration of quality, status, or photo availability, are summarized in a more compact format. The foreign releases are organized in the same manner.

This volume, to the best of my knowledge, presents a complete documentation of the movies released in the United States during 2007. If I've inadvertently left you out, you know where to find me.

— BARRY MONUSH

# ACKNOWLEDGMENTS

Anthology Film Archives, ArtMattan Films, Artistic License, Balcony Releasing, James Barnett, Thomas Buxereau, Damien Castaneda, Pearl Chang, David Christopher, The Cinema Guild, Cinema Libre, Columbia Pictures, DreamWorks, Brian Durnin, Emerging Pictures, Film Forum, First Look, First Run Features, First Run-Icarus, Focus Features, Fox Searchlight, Freestyle Releasing, Stephen Geoffreys, IFC Films, International Film Circuit, Tim Johnson, Marybeth Keating, Kino International, Koch Lorber Films, Lionsgate Films, Tom Lynch, MGM, Mangolia Pictures, Michael Messina, Miramax Films, Daniel Munro, David Munro, New Line Cinema, New Yorker Films, Newmarket Films, Outsider Pictures, Palm Pictures, Paramount Pictures, Paramount Vantage, Picturehouse, Picture This!, Regent Releasing, Roadside Attractions, Rogue Pictures, Kristina Rolander, Greg Rossi, Screen Gems, Seventh Art Releasing, Samuel Goldwyn Films, Slowhand Releasing, Sony Pictures Classics, Sony Pictures Entertainment, Strand Releasing, Tartan Films, ThinkFilm, TriStar, Truly Indie, Twentieth Century Fox, United Artists, Universal Pictures, Walt Disney Pictures, Warner Bros., Warner Independent Pictures, The Weinstein Company, Yari Film Group

# DOMESTIC FILMS

## 2007 RELEASES
### JANUARY 1–DECEMBER 31

# FREEDOM WRITERS

(PARAMOUNT) Producers, Danny DeVito, Michael Shamberg, Stacey Sher; Executive Producers, Hilary Swank, Tracey Durning, Nan Morales, Dan Levine; Director/Screenplay, Richard LaGravenese; Based on the book *The Freedom Writers Diary* by the Freedom Writers and Erin Gruwell; Photography, Jim Denault; Designer, Laurence Bennett; Costumes, Cindy Evans; Music, Mark Isham, will.i.am; Music Supervisor, Mary Ramos; Casting, Margery Simkin; a Jersey Films/Double Feature Films production, presented in association with MTV Films; Dolby; Rated PG-13; 123 minutes; Release date: January 5, 2007.

Jaclyn Ngan, April Lee Hernandez © PARAMOUNT PICTURES

## Cast

Erin Gruwell **Hilary Swank**
Scott Casey **Patrick Dempsey**
Eva Benitez **April Lee Hernandez**
Steve Gruwell **Scott Glenn**
Margaret Campbell **Imelda Staunton**
Andre Bryant **Mario**
Gloria Munez **Kristin Herrera**
Marcus **Jason Finn**
Ben Daniels **Hunter Parrish**
Jamal Hill **Deance Wyatt**
Brandy Ross **Vanetta Smith**
Brian Gelford **John Benjamin Hickey**
Miep Gies **Pat Carroll**
Sindy **Jaclyn Ngan**
Alejandro Santiago **Sergio Montalvo**
Tito **Gabriel Chavarria**
Miguel **Antonio García**
Victoria **Giovonnie Samuels**
Dr. Carl Cohn **Robert Wisdom**
Paco **Will Morales**
Grant Rice **Armand Jones**
Eva's Father **Ricardo Molina**
Eva's Mother **Angela Alvarado**
Sindy's Boyfriend **Anh Nguyen**
and Liisa Cohen (Brandy's Mother); Brian Bennett (Brandy's Father); Horace Hall (Himself); Tim Halligan (Principal Banning); Lisa Banes (Karin Polachek); Giselle Bonilla (Young Eva); Earl Williams (Young Marcus); Blake Hightower (Clive); Angela Sargeant (Marcus' Mother); Robin Skye (PTA Mom); Chil Kong (Store Owner); Juan Garcia (Defense Attorney); Larry Cahn (Prosecutor); Sharaud Moore (Hall Monitor); Abel Soto (Gang Member); Dan Warner, Randy Hall, Carl Paoli (Cops); Dominic Daniel (Drug Dealer); Cody Chappel (Bookstore Clerk); DJ Motiv8 (DJ); Renee Firestone, Eddie Zlam, Elisabeth Mann, Gloria Ungar (Holocaust Survivors)

Mario, Deance Wyatt, Hilary Swank

In an effort to reach her racially charged and deeply troubled students, idealistic teacher Erin Gruwell encourages them to keep a journal of their everyday thoughts and experiences.

Patrick Dempsey, Hilary Swank

## ALPHA DOG

(UNIVERSAL) Producers, Sidney Kimmel, Chuck Pacheco; Executive Producers, Marina Grasic, Andreas Grosch, Jan Körbelin, Andreas Schmid, Steve Markoff, Robert Geringer, Avram Butch Kaplan; Director/Screenplay, Nick Cassavetes; Photography, Robert Fraisse; Designer, Dominic Watkins; Costumes, Sara Jane Slotnick; Music, Aaron Zigman; Music Supervisor, Spring Aspers; Editor, Alan Heim; Casting, Matthew Barry, Nancy Green-Keyes; a Sidney Kimmel Entertainment presentation of a VIP Medienfonds 2/A-Mark Entertainment production; Dolby; J-D-C Scope; Deluxe color; Rated R; 122 minutes; Release date: January 12, 2007.

### Cast

| | |
|---|---|
| Jake Mazursky | **Ben Foster** |
| Elvis Schmidt | **Shawn Hatosy** |
| Johnny Truelove | **Emile Hirsch** |
| Keith Stratten | **Christopher Marquette** |
| Olivia Mazursky | **Sharon Stone** |
| Frankie Ballenbacher | **Justin Timberlake** |
| Zack Mazursky | **Anton Yelchin** |
| Sonny Truelove | **Bruce Willis** |
| Julie Beckley | **Amanda Seyfried** |
| Sabrina Pope | **Charity Shea** |
| Susan Hartunian | **Dominique Swain** |
| Butch Mazursky | **David Thornton** |
| Cosmo Gadabeeti | **Harry Dean Stanton** |
| Buzz Fecske | **Lukas Haas** |
| Angela Holden | **Olivia Wilde** |
| Elaine Holden | **Janet Jones Gretzky** |
| Douglas Holden | **Alan Thicke** |
| Pick Giaimo | **Vincent Kartheiser** |
| Interviewer | **Matt Barry** |
| Tiko "TKO" Martinez | **Fernando Vargas** |
| Bobby "911" | **Alex Solowitz** |
| P.J. Truelove | **Alec Vigil** |
| Adrian Jones | **Frank Cassavetes** |

and Nicole Dubos (Neighborhood Girl on Couch); Regina Rice ("Dance Bitch" Girl); Laura Nativo (Party Girl); Heather Wahlquist (Wanda Haynes); Jesse Erwin (Employee); Paul Johansson (Himself); Danny Abeckaser, James A. Molina (Latino Youths); Nancy DeMayo (Dale Dierker); Xan Cassavetes (Jonna Kirshner); Chuck Pacheco (Chucky Mota); Frank Peluso (Gay "Lumpy" Yeager); Shera Danese (Abby); Greg Williams (De Rosa); Joshua Alba (Klemash); Shirley Kurata (Lu); Patrick Nguyen (V.C.); Chris Kinkade (Juergen Ballenbacher); Alex Kingston (Tiffany Hartunian); Bobby Cooper (Bob Nolder); Stephanie Fowler (Delores Stratten); Natasha Elliott (Bathroom Party Girl); Amber Heard (Alma); Rick Salomon (Salesman); Adrianna Belan (Leigh Fecske); Holt McCallany (Det. Tom Finnegan).

When Jake Mazursky cannot come up with the money he owes drug dealer Johnny Truelove, the latter retaliates by ordering the kidnapping of Jake's kid brother.

Alma Heard, Anton Yelchin, Amanda Seyfried

Bruce Willis, Harry Dean Stanton, Emile Hirsch

Emile Hirsch, Justin Timberlake, Olivia Wilde © UNIVERSAL STUDIOS

# STOMP THE YARD

Columbus Short

(SCREEN GEMS) Producer, Will Packer; Executive Producer, Rob Hardy; Director, Sylvain White; Screenplay, Robert Adetuyi; Based on a screenplay by Gregory Anderson; Photography, Scott Kevan; Designer, Jonathan Carlson; Costumes, Keith G. Lewis; Music, Sam Retzer, Tim Boland; Music Supervisors, Ali Muhammad, Akinah Rahmaan; Choreographer, Dave Scott; Stunts, Gus Williams; Casting, Tracy "Twinkie" Byrd; a Rainforest Films production; Dolby; Arri Widescreen; Deluxe color; Rated PG-13; 114 minutes; Release date: January 12, 2007.

## Cast

DJ **Columbus Short**
April **Meagan Good**
Rich Brown **Ne-Yo**
Grant **Darrin Henson**
Sylvester **Brian J. White**
Zeke **Laz Alonso**
Jackie **Valarie Pettiford**
Noel **Jermaine Williams**
Dr. Palmer **Allan Louis**
Nate **Harry Lennix**
Duron **Chris Brown**
Easy **Oliver Ryan Best**
Mark **Richmond Duain Martyn**
and Justin Hires (Byron); Sahr Ngaujah (Harold); Roderick Thomas (Paul); Christopher "Lil C" Toler (Theata #2); Pedro Coiscou (Bambino, Theata #2); April Clark (Maya); Sean Riggs (Mu Gamma #1); Debra Nelson (Assistant); Tony Vaughn (Dr. Wilson); DJ Drama, Sway (Themselves); Roxanne Mims (Secretary); Ayesha T. Ngaujah (Girl in Line); Khalid Freeman (Stomp Dancer, Artist); Gordie Bernard Holt (Mu Gamma Stepper 9); Jonathan "Legacy" Perez (Sphere's Crew Dancer); Ivan "Flipz" Velez (DJ's Crew Dancer)

Columbus Short, Meagan Good

To avoid juvenile hall, DJ is sent to Truth U, where his dance prowess earns him a place at Theta Nu Theta fraternity, who hope to win the national stepping championship.

Chris Brown © SCREEN GEMS

# THE HITCHER

Zachary Knighton, Sophia Bush © ROGUE PICTURES

(ROGUE) Producers, Michael Bay, Andrew Form, Brad Fuller, Charles Meeker, Alfred Haber; Director, David Meyers; Screenplay, Jake Wade Wall, Eric Bernt; Based on the film written by Eric Red; Photography, James Hawkinson; Designer, David Lazan; Costumes, Leeann Radeka; Music, Steve Jablonsky; Music Supervisor, Jojo Villanueva; Editor, Jim May; Casting, Lisa Fields; a Platinum Dunes production, an Indiepro Pictures presentation in association with Michael Bay; Dolby; Super 35 Widescreen; Color; Rated R; 84 minutes; Release date: January 19, 2007.

## Cast

John Ryder **Sean Bean**
Grace Andrews **Sophia Bush**
Jim Halsey **Zachary Knighton**
Lt. Esteridge **Neal McDonough**
and Kyle Davis (Buford's Store Clerk); Skip O'Brien (Sheriff Harlan Bremmer, Sr.); Travis Schuldt (Deputy Harlan Bremmer, Jr.); Danny Bolero (Officer Edwards); Jeffrey Hutchinson (Young Father); Yara Martinez (Beth); Lauren Cohn (Marlene); Joseph Michael Self, Mike Fisher (Transport Guards); Kurt Grossi (Officer Franklin); Kurt Bryant (Paramedic); Richard Hancock (Ryder's Guard); Jesse De Luna (Officer Jessup); George McLain (Officer George); Kurt Soderling (Helicopter Co-Pilot); Lance Strumpf (Helicopter Pilot); Damon Carney (Negotiator)

Grace and Jim live to regret their decision to give a lift to hitchhiker John Ryder when their enigmatic passenger proceeds to terrorize the young couple.

# EPIC MOVIE

(20TH CENTURY FOX) Producer, Paul Schiff; Executive Producers, Arnon Milchan, Jason Friedberg, Aaron Selzer, Rodney Liber; Director/Screenplay, Jason Friedberg; Photography, Shawn Maurer; Designer, William A. Elliott; Costumes, Frank Helmer; Music, Ed Shearmur; Music Supervisors, Dave Jordan, Jojo Villanueva; Editor, Peck Prior; Visual Effects Supervisor, Ariel Velasco Shaw; Casting, Amanda Harding, Amanda Koblin; a Regency Enterprises presentation of a New Regency/Schiff production; Dolby; Deluxe color; Rated PG-13; 86 minutes; Release date: January 26, 2007.

## Cast

Edward **Kal Penn**
and Adam Campbell (Peter); Jennifer Coolidge (The White Bitch); Jayma Mays (Lucy); Faune Chambers (Susan); Crispin Glover (Willy); Fred Willard (Aslo); Hector Jiminez (Mr. Tumnus); Darrell Hammond (Capt. Jack Swallows); Carmen Electra (Mystique); David Carradine (Museum Curator); Tony Cox (Bink); Kevin McDonald (Harry Potter); George Alvarez (Ron); Crista Flanagan (Hermione); Dana Seltzer (Flight Attendant); Dane Farwell (Dumbledore); Tad Hilgenbrinck (Cyclops); Jim Piddock (Magneto); Groovy (Wolverine); Kahshanna Evans (Storm); Lindsey Kraft (Rogue); Jareb Dauplaise (Nacho Libre); Rico Rodriguez (Chanchito); Danny Jacobs (Borat/Pirate with Eye Patch); David Lehre (Ashton Kutcher Look-Alike); James Walker, Sr. (Samuel Jackson Look-Alike); Cordele Taylor (Kanye West Look-Alike); Alla Petrou (Paris Hilton Look-Alike); Gregory Jbara (Mel Gibson Look-Alike); Jill Latiano (Singing Pirate Girl); Abe Spigner (Flavor Flav Look-Alike); Shawn McDonald (P. Diddy Faun); Lauren Conrad (Herself); Katt M. Williams (Voice of Harry Beaver); Nick Steele (Lead Archer); Brennan Thomas (Woodsman); David J. Catching, Jesse Hughes, Brian O'Connor, Gene Trautmann (Aslo's Camp Band); Kenny Yates (Pirate with Heart); Daniel Joseph, Taran Killam, Jeremy Rowley (Pirates); Anwar Burton (Michael Jackson Look-Alike); Scott L. Schwartz (Hagrid); Heather Storm (Aslo's Girl); Irina Voronina (Jogging Girl); Audra Lynn (Wardrobe Girl); Darko Belgrade (James Bond); Brooklyn Freed, Michelle Misty Lang (Bond Girls); Sabi Dorr (Blacksmith); Kevin Hart (Monk); Mike Grief (Prison Guard); Mary Castro (Breast Bite Woman); Ron Léroy (Nose Bite guy); Thomas Van Tassel (Crotch Bite Guy); Paul Zies (Thug); Roscoe Lee Browne (Narrator)

Four orphans find themselves on a series of adventures bearing striking resemblances to several recent film epics.

Kal Penn, Darrell Hammond © 20TH CENTURY FOX

# SMOKIN' ACES

(UNIVERSAL) Producers, Tim Bevan, Eric Fellner; Executive Producers, Robert Graf, Liza Chasin; Director/Screenplay, Joe Carnahan; Photography, Mauro Fiore; Designer, Martin Whist; Costumes, Mary Zophres; Music, Clint Mansell; Music Supervisor, Nick Angel; Editor, Robert Frazen; Stunts, Ben Bray; Casting, Amanda Mackey, Cathy Sandrich Gelfond; a Working Title production in association with StudioCanal and Relativity Media and Scion Films; Dolby; Panavision; Technicolor; Rated R; 109 minutes; Release date: January 26, 2007.

Andy Garcia, Ray Liotta, Ryan Reynolds © UNIVERSAL STUDIOS

## Cast

Jack Dupree **Ben Affleck**
Stanley Locke **Andy Garcia**
Georgia Sykes **Alicia Keys**
Agent Donald Carruthers **Ray Liotta**
Buddy "Aces" Israel **Jeremy Piven**
Agent Richard Messner **Ryan Reynolds**
"Pistol" Pete Deeks **Peter Berg**
Sharice Watters **Taraji Henson**
Darwin Tremor **Chris Pine**
Hollis Elmore **Martin Henderson**
Rupert "Rip" Reed **Jason Bateman**
Pasqual Acosta ("S.A. Gerald Diego") **Nestor Carbonell**
Sir Ivy **Common**
Primo Sparazza **Joseph Ruskin**
Serna **Alex Rocco**
Himself **Wayne Newton**
Beanie **Christopher Holley**
Freeman Heller **Mike Falkow**
FBI Aid **Joe Drago**
Top-Coated Gunman **Jeff Habberstad**
Loretta Wyman **Davenia McFadden**
Jeeves Tremor **Kevin Durand**
and Maury Sterling (Lester Tremor); George Fisher (McGarey); Tommy Flanagan (Lazlo Soot); Curtis Armstrong (Morris Mecklen); Vladmir Kulich (The Swede); Janet Edwards (Naked Prostitute); Joel Edgerton (Hugo Croop); David Proval (Victor Padiche); Suzanne Stover (Prostitute #1); Scott Halberstadt (Pimply Casino Employee); Lorna Scott (Hotel Receptionist); Matthew Fox (Bill Security Super); Lonnie Moore (Gary the Security Guard); Patrick St. Espirit (Moustache); Steve Florian, Robert J. Weir (Security Members); Zach Cumer (Warren); Ken Rudulph (CS Team Member); Christopher Murray (Sergeant/Chief); Michael Murphy (Sheriff Badger); Marianne Muellerleile (Margie Turlock); Stefanie Cruz, John Alston (Reporters); Brian Bloom (Agent Baker); Paul Wilson (Magician); Scott Bloom, Alfred Woodley (FBI Agents); James Conkle (Young Buddy); Clare Carey (Laverne); David "Goldy" Goldsmith (Stage Manager)

Alicia Keys, Common

FBI agents Carruthers and Messner must nab high-profile Vegas entertainer Buddy "Aces" Israel before the mob rubs him out.

Jeremy Piven

# CATCH AND RELEASE

(COLUMBIA) Producer, Jenno Toppin; Executive Producers, B. Casey Grant, Ryan Cavanaugh, Lynwood Spinks; Director/Screenplay, Susannah Grant; Photography, John Lindley; Designer, Brent Thomas; Costumes, Tish Monaghan; Music, BT and Tommy Stinson; Editor, Anne V. Coates; Casting, Deborah Aquila, Tricia Wood, Jennifer Smith; a Relativity Media presentation of a Jenno Topping production; Dolby; Super 35 Widescreen; Color; Rated PG-13; 110 minutes; Release date: January 26, 2007.

### Cast

Gray Wheeler **Jennifer Garner**
Fritz **Timothy Olyphant**
Dennis **Sam Jaeger**
Sam **Kevin Smith**
Maureen **Juliette Lewis**
Mattie **Joshua Friesen**
Mrs. Douglas **Fiona Shaw**
Eve **Tina Lifford**
Persephone **Georgia Craig**
Flower Delivery Guy **Christopher Redman**
Housekeeper **Joyce Krenz**
Caterer **Sonja Bennett**
Co-Worker **Yorgo Constantine**
Deadhead Singers **Dan Parker, Nancy Hower**
and Jennifer Spence, Kyla Anderson, Leanna Nash, Wendy Noel (Comforting Friends); Leslie McMichaels (Jogstroller); Michael Adamthwaite (Cowboy); John B. Destry (Paint Salesman); Nancy Wetzel (Cyclist); Dillard Brinson (Michael Soltman); Sacha Levin (Drummer); Terence Kelly (Mr. Wheeler); Gabrielle Rose (Mrs. Wheeler).

Devastated by the death of her fiancé, grieving Gray Wheeler is surprised to discover that her late lover had been paying money to support a child borne from a fling with a massage therapist.

Joshua Friesen, Juliette Lewis © COLUMBIA PICTURES

Timothy Olyphant, Jennifer Garner

Timothy Olyphant, Jennifer Garner

Kevin Smith, Sam Jaeger

# SERAPHIM FALLS

Liam Neeson (center)

Anjelica Huston

(GOLDWYN/DESTINATION) Producers, Bruce Davey, David Flynn; Executive Producer, Stan Wlodkowski; Director, David Von Ancken; Screenplay, David Von Ancken, Abby Everett Jaques; Photography, John Toll; Designer, Michael Hanan; Costumes, Deborah L. Scott; Music, Harry Gregson-Williams; Editor, Conrad Buff; Special Effects Supervisor, Peter Chesney; Stunts, Bud Davis; Casting, Mali Finn; an Icon production; Dolby; Panavision; Deluxe color; Rated R; 115 minutes; Release date: January 26, 2007.

## Cast

Carver **Liam Neeson**
Gideon **Pierce Brosnan**
Hayes **Michael Wincott**
Parsons **Ed Lauter**
The Kid **John Robinson**
Pope **Robert Baker**
Virgil **Jimmi Simpson**
Cousin Bill **Nate Mooney**
Evan **James Jordan**
Henry **Kevin O'Connor**
Madame Louise Fair **Anjelica Huston**
Charlotte **Shannon Zeller**
Minister Abraham **Tom Noonan**
and Angie Harmon (Rose); Xander Berkeley (Railroad Foreman); Adam Houlton, Darren Gibson (Irish Henchmen); Hugh Elliot (Railroad Camp Pimp); George Anton, Richard Barela, Harp Corrigan, Scott Flick (Railroad Workers); Wes Studi (Charon, Water Man); Robert Nathan Gleason, Tom B. Gleason (Mountain Men); Justin Tade (Lt. DeButts); Johnny Radlcliff, Henry Herman (Cavalry Solders); Argos MacCallum (Wizened Christian); Zachary Sears (Young Christian); Janelle Sperow (Christian Woman); Adon Cravens (Nathaniel); Christopher Andrews (Carver's Son); Boots Southerland (Big Henchman); Bill Dufault (Gospel Singer)

Gideon must use his wiles to escape Carver and his relentless posse, who are determined to make him pay for an atrocity for which Carver holds him responsible.

Michael Wincott, Liam Neeson, Robert Baker, Ed Lauter, John Robinson

Pierce Brosnan © SAMUEL GOLDWYN FILMS

# BECAUSE I SAID SO

Diane Keaton, Mandy Moore, Lauren Graham, Piper Perabo © UNIVERSAL STUDIOS

(UNIVERSAL) Producers, Paul Brooks, Jessie Nelson; Executive Producers, Scott Niemeyer, Norm Waitt, Michael Flynn; Director, Michael Lehmann; Screenplay, Karen Leigh Hopkins, Jessie Nelson; Photography, Julio Macat; Designer, Sharon Seymour; Costumes, Shay Cunliffe; Music, David Kitay; Music Supervisor, Dana Sano; Editors, Paul Seydor, Troy Takaki; Co-Producer, Wendy Rhoads; Casting, Eyde Belasco; a Gold Circle Films presentation; Dolby; Color; Rated PG-13; 102 minutes; Release date: February 2, 2007.

## Cast

Daphne Wilder  **Diane Keaton**
Milly  **Mandy Moore**
Johnny  **Gabriel Macht**
Jason  **Tom Everett Scott**
Maggie  **Lauren Graham**
Mae  **Piper Perabo**
Joe  **Stephen Collins**
Lionel  **Ty Panitz**
Eli  **Matt Champagne**
Derek  **Colin Ferguson**
Stuart  **Tony Hale**
Milly's Staff #1, Matisse  **Sophina Brown**
Milly's Staff #2, Charlie  **Karen Leigh Hopkins**
and Emily Maisano (Milly's Staff #3); Gerald Downey (Cousin Dougy's Friend); Ingrid Sanai Buron (Singing Bride); Satya Lee (Daphne's Masseuse); Alexis Rhee (Maggie's Masseuse); Shu Lan Tuan (Milly's Masseuse); Steve Little (Bad Teeth Guy); John Ross Bowie (Cute Food Spewing Guy); Parvesh Cheena (Foreign Guy); Doug Budin (Sneezer); William Belli (Transsexual); Carlo Michael Mancini (Arnold); Mary Pat Gleason (Iris); Judi Barton (Jason's Mother); Rudolph Willrich (Jason's Father); David Purdham (Uncle Philip); P.J. Byrne (Photographer); Edith Jefferson (Senator); Holly Western (Catering Staff); Nate Petre (Bleached Teeth Guy); Allison Caetano; Chris Monberg (Roller Bladers)

Worried that her daughter Milly will end up making the same mistakes she has, meddlesome single mom Daphne Wilder tries to set her up with someone from the online personals.

# THE MESSENGERS

(SCREEN GEMS) Producers, Sam Raimi, Rob Tapert, William Sherak, Jason Shuman; Executive Producers, Nathan Kahane, Joe Drake; Co-Producers, J.R. Young, Kelli Konop, Jimm Miller, Lou Arkoff; Directors, Danny Pang, Oxide Pang; Screenplay, Mark Wheaton; Photography, David Geddes; Designer, Alicia Keywan; Costumes, Mary Hyde-Kerr; Music, Joseph LoDuca; Editors, John Axelrod, Armen Minasian; Visual Effects Supervisor, Bruce Jones; a Screen Gems/Ghost House Pictures/Columbia Pictures presentation of a Blue Star Pictures production; Dolby; Deluxe color/Black and white; Rated PG-13; 90 minutes; Release date: February 2, 2007.

## Cast

Jess Solomon  **Kristen Stewart**
Roy Solomon  **Dylan McDermott**
Denise Solomon  **Penelope Ann Miller**
Burwell Rollins  **John Corbett**
Ben Solomon  **Evan Turner, Theodore Turner**
Bobby  **Dustin Milligan**
Colby Price  **William B. Davis**
Plume  **Brent Briscoe**
Michael Rollins  **Jodelle Ferland**
and Michael Daingerfield (Police Officer); Tatiana Maselany (Lindsay Rollins); Shirley McQueen (Mary Rollins); Anna Hagan (Doctor); Blaine Hart (Charlie); Graham Bell (Jim); Kaitlyn McMillan (Nurse); Peter Scoular (Deputy)

In dire financial straits, the Solomon family moves to a rundown North Dakota farm, which is inhabited by the ghosts of a previous family who were brutally slaughtered on the property.

Kristen Stewart © SCREEN GEMS

# NORBIT

Cuba Gooding Jr., Thandie Newton

Thandie Newton, Eddie Murphy

(PARAMOUNT/DREAMWORKS) Producers, John Davis, Eddie Murphy; Executive Producers, Mike Tollin, Brian Robbins, David Householter; Director, Brian Robbins; Screenplay, Eddie Murphy, Charles Murphy, Jay Scherick, David Ronn; Story, Eddie Murphy, Charles Murphy; Photography, Clark Mathis; Designer, Clay A. Griffith; Costumes, Molly Maginnis; Music, David Newman; Editor, Ned Bastille; Makeup, Debra Coleman; Prosthethic Makeup Supervisor, Kazuhiro Tsuji; Special Makeup Effects, Rick Baker; Visual Effects Supervisors, Leandro H. Visconti, Michael Owens; Choreographers, Fatima Robinson, Aakomon "AJ" Jones; Casting, Juel Bestrop, Seth Yanklewitz; a Paramount release of a DreamWorks presentation of a John Davis production; Dolby; Deluxe color; Rated PG-13; 103 minutes; Release date: February 9, 2007.

## Cast

Norbit/Rasputia/Mr. Wong  **Eddie Murphy**
Kate Thomas  **Thandie Newton**
Big Jack Latimore  **Terry Crews**
Earl Latimore  **Clifton Powell**
Blue Latimore  **Lester "Rasta" Speight**
Deion Hughes  **Cuba Gooding, Jr.**
and Eddie Griffin (Pope Sweet Jesus); Katt Williams (Lord Have Mercy); Floyd Levine (Abe the Tailor); Anthony Russell (Giovanni); Pat Crawford Brown (Mrs. Henderson); Jeanette Miller (Mrs. Coleman); Michael Colyar (Morris the Barber); Marlon Wayans (Buster); Alexis Rhee (Mrs. Ling Ling Wong); Khamani Griffin (Norbit, age 5); Austin Reid (Norbit, age 9); Lindsey Sims-Lewis (Rasputia, age 10); China Anderson (Kate, age 5); Kristen Schaal (Event Organizer); Rob Huebel (Excited Man on TV); Michael Vossler, Travis Vossler (Bullies); Mason Knight (Boy at Schoolyard); Jonathan Robinson (Norbit, age 17); Yves Lola St. Vil (Rasuptia, age 17); Richard Gant (Preacher); Susan Beaubain (Shop Owner); John Gatins (Attendant); Laura Ortiz (Teen Attendant); Miles Robbins (Kid at Water Park); Charlie Murphy (Voice of Floyd the Dog); Hayley Marie Norman, Sara Sanderson, Smith Cho (Ex-Wives); Esther Friedman, Lonnie L. Henderson, Carmen Rojas (Beauticians); Marianne Muellerleile (Helga); Frank Langley IV (Puppeteer); Donald Johnson (Charlie); Greta Bommerlje (Kid); Jesse Mendel (Little Girl in the Pool); Kayren Wallace (Orphan Girl); Kendra McCulty, Amanda Sawyer, Cameron Ur (Moonbounce Kids); Lisa Marie Fernandez (Kissing Booth Girl); Taylor Kennedy, Hakeem Washington (Basketball Kids); Fumi Desalu (Booty Shaker Girl); Sammy B. Wills (Rib Shack Waitress); Shyann Shane Lee, Richard Corgiat, Marc De'Antone, Vince Micelli (Giovanni Staff); Ollie Rasbury, Donald Bell (Vocalists); Ron Cole, Eurydice Davis (Wedding Guests); George Angelo, Anthony Vela (Bar Patrons)

Eddie Murphy, Marlon Wayans © DREAMWORKS

Timid Norbit hopes to free himself of his domineering, 500-lb. wife Rasputia when his childhood friend Kate returns to town.

This film received an Oscar nomination for Makeup.

## MUSIC AND LYRICS

(WARNER BROS.) Producers, Martin Shafer, Liz Glotzer; Executive Producers, Nancy Juvonen, Hal Gaba, Bruce Berman; Co-Producers, Scott Elias, Melissa Wells; Director, Marc Lawrence; Screenplay, Xavier Perez Grobet; Designer, Jane Musky; Costumes, Susan Lyall; Music, Adam Schlesinger; Editor, Susan E. Morse; Casting, Ilene Starger; Songs: "Pop! Goes My Heart" by Andrew W. Blakemore and Alanna Vicente, "Way Back to My Heart" by Adam Schlesinger; a Castle Rock Entertainment presentation in association with Village Roadshow Pictures of a Reserve Room production; Dolby; Technicolor; Rated PG-13; 106 minutes; Release Date: February 14, 2007.

Scott Porter, Hugh Grant © WARNER BROS.

### Cast

Alex Fletcher **Hugh Grant**
Sophie Fisher **Drew Barrymore**
Chris Riley **Brad Garrett**
Rhonda **Kristen Johnston**
Cora Corman **Haley Bennett**
Khan **Aasif Mandvi**
Sloan Cates **Campbell Scott**
Greg Antonsky **Jason Antoon**
Ray **Matthew Morrison**
Colin Thompson **Scott Porter**
Willy **Daniel Stewart Sherman**
Charlie **Jeremy Karson**
Lucy Fisher **Emma Lesser**
Gary Fisher **Adam Grupper**
Barbara **Charlotte Maier**
Tricia **Toni Trucks**
Mia **Lanette Ware**
Pop Bass Player **Nick Bacon**
Pop Guitar Player **Andrew Wyatt Blakemore**
Pop Drummer **Dan McMillan**
Has-Beens Promo Announcer **Tom Foglino**
David Newbert, TV Executive **Zak Orton**
Janice Stern, TV Executive **Brooke Tansley**
Derek **Billy Griffith**
Gloria **Kathleen McNenny**
Maitre D' **Stevie Ray Dallimore**
Beth Riley **Spenser Leigh**
Security Guard **Lou Torres**
Stage Manager **Kali R. Harrison**
Reunion Classmate **Ken Sladyk**
Guitar Player: Cora's Band **Ben Butler**
Sitar Player **Rachel Golub**
Bass Player **Conrad Korsch**
and Seth Matthew Faulk (Drummer); Daniel Mintseris (Keyboard Player); Zak Soulam (Heavy Metal Guitar Player)

Drew Barrymore, Hugh Grant

Hoping to make his comeback by writing a tune for pop queen Cora Corman, former boy band member Alex Fletcher finds an unexpected collaborator in the woman who has come to water his plants, Sophie Fisher.

Hugh Grant, Haley Bennett

# BREACH

Ryan Phillippe, Chris Cooper

Laura Linney, Ryan Phillippe

Caroline Dhavernas, Ryan Phillippe © UNIVERSAL STUDIOS

Kathleen Quinlan

(UNIVERSAL) Producers, Bobby Newmyer, Scott Strauss, Scott Kroopf; Executive Producers, Adam Merims, Sidney Kimmel, William Horberg; Director, Billy Ray; Screenplay, Adam Mazer, William Rotko, Billy Ray; Story, Adam Mazer, William Rotko; a Sidney Kimmel Entertainment presentation of an Outlaw/Intermedia production; Dolby; Technicolor; Rated PG-13; 110 minutes; Release date: February 16, 2007.

## Cast

Robert Hanssen **Chris Cooper**
Eric O'Neill **Ryan Phillippe**
Kate Burroughs **Laura Linney**
Juliana O'Neill **Caroline Dhavernas**
Rich Garces **Gary Cole**
Dean Plesac **Dennis Haysbert**
Bonnie Hanssen **Kathleen Quinlan**
John O'Neill **Bruce Davison**
Geddes **Jonathan Watton**
Jim Olsen **Tom Barnett**
D.I.A. Suit **Jonathan Potts**
and David Huband (Photographer); Catherine Burdon (Agent Nece); Scott Gibson (Agent Sherin); Courtenay Stevens (Agent Loper); Clare Stone (Lisa Hanssen); Jonathan Keltz (Greg Hanssen); Richard Fitzpatrick (Michael Rochford); Melissa Thomson (Jane); Craig Eldridge (Gene Connors); Jonathan Whittaker (Tim Bereznay); Reagan Pasternak (Beautiful Reporter); Mary Jo Deschanel (Vivian O'Neill); Elie Gemael (Libyan Man); Oula Boubkraoui (Libyan Wife); Chris Owens (Trunk Cataloguer); Jonathan Ruckman (SWAT Agent); Stan Coles (Father McKee); Bart Bedford (Information Center Manager); David Frisch (Agent Pack); Scott McCulloch (Director Louis Freeh); Mathew Lyons (Richard); Greg Campbell (Special Agent in Charge); David O'Neill (Man in Car); Guido Rossi (Latin-Speaking Man at Church)

Agent-in-training Eric O'Neill is transferred to FBI headquarters in order to investigate the claim that longtime operative Robert Hanssen is guilty of treason.

# BRIDGE TO TERABITHIA

Terabithia © WALT DISNEY PICTURES

Zooey Deschanel

(WALT DISNEY PICTURES) Producers, Hal Lieberman, Lauren Levine, David Paterson; Executive Producer, Alex Schwartz; Director, Gabor Csupo; Screenplay, Jeff Stockwell, David Paterson; Based on the book by Katherine Paterson; Photography, Michael Chapman; Designer, Rob Gillies; Costumes, Barbara Darragh; Music, Aaron Zigman; Music Supervisor, George Acogny; Editor, John Gilbert; Co-Producers, Kevin Halloran, Tim Coddington; Visual Effects Supervisor, Matt Aitken; Visual Effects, Weta Digital; Stunts, Allan Poppleton; Casting, Stephanie Corsalini; a Walden Media presentation of a Hal Lieberman Co. and Lauren Levine production; Distributed by Buena Vista; Dolby; Color; Rated PG; 94 minutes; Release date: February 16, 2007.

## Cast

Jess Aarons  **Josh Hutcherson**
Leslie Burke  **AnnaSophia Robb**
Jack Aarons  **Robert Patrick**
Ms. Edmunds  **Zooey Deschanel**
May Belle Aarons  **Bailee Madison**
Mary Aarons  **Kate Butler**
Brenda Aarons  **Devon Wood**
Ellie Aarons  **Emma Fenton**
Joyce Aarons  **Grace Brannigan**
Bill Burke  **Latham Gaines**
Judy Burke  **Judy McIntosh**
Grandma Burke  **Patricia Aldersley**
Janice Avery  **Lauren Clinton**
Carla  **Isabelle Rose Kircher**
Scott Hoager  **Cameron Wakefield**
and Elliot Lawles (Gary Fulcher); Carly Owen (Madison); Jen Wolfe (Mrs. Myers); James Gaylyn (Principal Turner); Ian Harcourt (Kenny, Bus Driver); Brandon Cook (First Grade Boy); Tyler Atfield (Eighth Grade Boy); Maisy McLeod-Riera (First Grade Girl); Hudson Mills (Willard Hughes); Matt Gibbons (Dark Master); Philip Grieve (Mr. Bailey)

Josh Hutcherson, AnnaSophia Robb

Josh Hutcherson

Jess Aarons, a shy, ten-year-old misfit, forms a bond with his impulsive, free-spirited new neighbor Leslie, the two of them creating their own magical kingdom to escape from the world around them.

# GHOST RIDER

(COLUMBIA) Producers, Avi Arad, Steven Paul, Michael De Luca, Gary Foster; Executive Producers, E. Bennett Walsh, Ari Arad, Stan Lee, Norm Golightly, David S. Goyer, Lynwood Spinks; Director/ScreenStory/Screenplay, Mark Steven Johnson; Based on the Marvel comic; Photography, Russell Boyd; Designer, Kirk M. Petruccelli; Costumes, Lizzy Gardiner; Music, Christopher Young; Music Supervisor, Dave Jordan; Editor, Richard Francis-Bruce; Visual Effects Supervisor, Kevin Mack; Casting, Juel Bestrop, Jeanne McCarthy, Christine King; Presented in association with Crystal Sky Pictures, in association with Relativity Media; Dolby; Panavision; Deluxe color; Rated PG-13; 110 minutes; Release date: February 16, 2007.

Ghost Rider © COLUMBIA PICTURES

### Cast

Johnny Blaze (Ghost Rider)  **Nicolas Cage**
Roxanne Simpson  **Eva Mendes**
Blackheart  **Wes Bentley**
Caretaker  **Sam Elliott**
Mack  **Donal Logue**
Young Johnny Blaze  **Matt Long**
Mephistopheles  **Peter Fonda**
Barton Blaze  **Brett Cullen**
Young Roxanne  **Raquel Alessi**
Gressil  **Laurence Breuls**
Wallow  **Daniel Frederiksen**
Abigor  **Mathew Wilkinson**
Amy Page  **Kirstie Hutton**
Stuart  **Gibson Nolte**
Team Blaze  **Tony Ghosthawk, Hugh Sexton, Marcus Jones, Matt Norman**
TV Reporter  **Kenneth Ransom**
X Games Announcer  **Cameron Steele**
Motorcycle Gang Member  **Eddie Baroo**
Broken Spoke Waitress  **Jessica Napier**
Makeup Artist  **Alexis Porter**
Waiter  **Ryan Johnson**
Motorcycle Cop  **Jonathan Oldham**
Station Master  **Peter Callan**
and Rebel Wilson (Girl in Alley); Peter Barry (The Mugger); Bruce Hughes (Penance Stare Pharmacist); Rita Kalnejais (Penance Stare Mugger's Girlfriend); David Roberts (Captain Dolan); Arthur Angel (Officer Edwards); Jason Raftopoulos (Forensics Inspector); Brett Swain (Guard); Duncan Young (Skinhead); Joel Tobeck (Redneck); Jacob Vanderpuije (Innocent Young Man); Fabio Robles (Priest); Marty Fields (Surveillance Guard); Troy Planet (Impound Worker); Charlie Garber (Officer Mackie); Vittorio Scalise (Window Cleaner); Richard Cox (Helicopter Pilot); Sandy Kerr (Miss Zamitt); Ling-Hsueh Tang (News Reporter); Estefanie Sousa (Street Person)

Daniel Frederikson, Laurence Breuls, Wes Bentley, Mathew Wilkinson

Eva Mendes, Nicolas Cage

Johnny Blaze, a daredevil motorcyclist who sold his soul to the Devil in order to save his father's life, must face Satan's vengeful son Blackheart and prevent him from world domination.

# TYLER PERRY'S DADDY'S LITTLE GIRLS

(LIONSGATE) Producers, Tyler Perry, Reuben Cannon; Executive Producer, Michael Paseornek; Co-Producers, Roger M. Bobb, D. Scott Lumpkin; Director/Screenplay, Tyler Perry; Photography, Toyomichi Kurita; Designer, Ina Mayhew; Costumes, Keith G. Lewis; Music, Brian McKnight; Music Supervisor, Joel C. High; Editor, Maysie Hoy; Casting, Kim Williams; a Tyler Perry Studios/Reuben Cannon Prods./Lionsgate production; Dolby; Color; Rated PG-13; 99 minutes; Release date: February 16, 2007.

### Cast

| | |
|---|---|
| Julia | **Gabrielle Union** |
| Monty | **Idris Elba** |
| Willie | **Louis Gossett, Jr.** |
| Jennifer | **Tasha Smith** |
| Cynthia | **Tracee Ellis Ross** |
| Maya | **Malinda Williams** |
| Brenda | **Terri J. Vaughn** |
| China James | **China McClain** |
| Joseph | **Gary Strugis** |
| Rita | **Cassi Davis** |
| Lauryn James | **Lauryn McClain** |
| Sierra | **Sierra McClain** |
| Katheryn | **Juanita Jennins** |
| Wife | **Maria Howell** |
| Miss Rochelle | **Rochelle Dewberry** |
| Councilman | **L. Warren Young** |
| Doorman | **Steve Coulter** |
| Civil Lawyer | **Sharyn Shields** |
| District Attorney | **Leland Jones** |
| Byron | **Craig Robinson** |
| Waiter | **Daniel Kim** |
| Nurse | **Minnie Tee** |
| Social Worker | **Donna Biscoe** |

and Bishop Eddie L. Long (Pastor); Bennet Guillory (Principal); Mark Oliver (Jennifer's Lawyer); Hajji Golightly (Member); LaVan Davis (Lester); Katie Kneeland (Waitress); Chantell D. Christopher, Sasha the Diva (Club Ladies); Arron Momon (Young Monty); Joey Nappo, Arvell Poe (Players); Greyson Chadwick (Amanda); Jasmine Burke (Girl); Ric Reitz (Dad); Guila Pagano (Criminal Judge); Bob Banks (Mr. Jones); Sharron Cain (Civil Court Bailiff); Dan Albright, George Bryant (Judges); Sharan Mansfield (Mrs. Mansfield); Gabriel McClain (Boy); Demetria "Dee Dee" McKinney (Club Lady #1); Javon Johnson (Brenda's Husband); Richmond Duain Martyn (Gang Member); Marshall Middletown (Young Man); E. Roger Mitchell (Joe's Criminal Lawyer); Judy Peterson (Choir Soloist); Gordon Daniels (Probation Officer); John Beasley (125 Family Court Judge); Monica Kaufman (Announcer); Joan Pringle (Civil Court Judge); Robert Hatch (Restaurant Patron); June Letourneau (Attorney); Brian J. White (Christopher)

Divorced dad Monty is devastated when the courts award custody of his three daughters to his irresponsible ex and her drug-dealing boyfriend.

Sierra McClain, Lauryn McClain, Idris Elba, China Anne McClain

Terri J. Vaughn, Tracee Ellis Ross, Gabrielle Union

Malinda Williams, Idris Elba, Cassi Davis © LIONSGATE

# THE NUMBER 23

Virginia Madsen, Danny Huston, Jim Carrey

(NEW LINE CINEMA) Producers, Beau Flynn, Tripp Vinson; Executive Producers, Mike Drake, Toby Emmerich, Richard Brener, Keith Goldberg, Brooklyn Weaver, Eli Richbourg; Director, Joel Schumacher; Co-Producer/Screenplay, Fernley Phillips; Photography, Matthew Libatique; Designer, Andrew Laws; Costumes, Daniel Orlandi; Music, Harry Gregson-Williams; Visual Effects Supervisor, Jamie Hallett; Visual Effects, Intelligent Creatures; Casting, Mali Finn; a Contrafilm/Firm Films production; Dolby; Panavision; Deluxe color; Rated R; 97 minutes; Release date: February 23, 2007.

## Cast

Walter Sparrow/Fingerling **Jim Carrey**
Agatha Sparrow/Fabrizia **Virginia Madsen**
Robin Sparrow **Logan Lerman**
Isaac French/Dr. Miles Phoenix **Danny Huston**
Suicide Blonde/Mrs. Dobkins/Young Fingerling's Mother **Lynn Collins**
Laura Tollins **Rhona Mitra**
Sybil **Michelle Arthur**
Kyle Flinch **Mark Pellegrino**
Young Fingerling/Young Walter **Paul Butcher**
Hotel Clerk **David Stifel**
Sergeant Burns **Corey Stoll**
Father Sebastian **Ed Lauter**
Barnaby **Troy Kotsur**
Chinese Restaurant Owner **Walter Soo Hoo**
Dr. Alice Mortimer **Patricia Belcher**
Dr. Nathaniel **Rudolph Willrich**
and Bud Cort (Dr. Sirius Leary); John Fink (Young Walter's Father/Young Fingerling's Father); Julie Remala (Mail Clerk); Tara Karsian (Box Company Clerk); Kerry Hoyt (Suicide Blonde's Father); Jennifer Lee Grafton (Suicide Blonde's Mother); Tom Lenk (Bookstore Salesperson); Ka'ramuu Kush (Fingerling's Sergeant); Helen Jordan (Lady Walking Dog); Eddie Rouse (Building Super); Lesli Margherita (Attractive Co-Ed); Maile Flanagan (Charades Friend); Bob Zmuda (Desk Clerk); Susan Kitchen, Coier Amerson (Partygoers); Michael Hurley, Donna G. Earley (Agatha's Friends); Shannon Gayle (Lucinda)

Dog catcher Walter Sparrow starts to lose his grip when he comes to believe that he is being overshadowed by the number 23, much like the protagonist of a mystery novel he is reading.

Danny Huston, Logan Lerman © NEW LINE CINEMA

Virginia Madsen, Jim Carrey, Logan Lerman

# THE ASTRONAUT FARMER

Billy Bob Thornton, Virginia Madsen, Max Thieriot, Jasper Polish, Logan Polish

(WARNER BROS.) Producers, Mark Polish, Michael Polish, Len Amato, Paula Weinstein; Executive Producer, J. Geyer Kosinski; Co-Producer, Robert Benjamin; Director, Michael Polish; Screenplay, Mark Polish, Michael Polish; Photography, M. David Mullen; Designer, Clark Hunter; Costumes, Danny Glicker; Editor, James Haygood; Music, Stuart Matthewman; Visual Effects Supervisor, Jason Piccioni; Second Unit Director, Mark Polish; Casting, Victoria Thomas; a Spring Creek Pictures and Polish Brothers Construction production; Dolby; Panavision; Color; Rated PG; 104 minutes; Release date: February 23, 2007.

Bruce Dern, Virginia Madsen © WARNER BROS.

## Cast

Charlie Farmer **Billy Bob Thornton**
Audie Farmer **Virginia Madsen**
Hal **Bruce Dern**
Jacobson **J.K. Simmons**
Kevin Munchak **Tim Blake Nelson**
Shepard Farmer **Max Thieriot**
FBI Agent Kilborne **Jon Gries**
FBI Agent Mathis **Mark Polish**
Stanley Farmer **Jasper Polish**
Sunshine Farmer **Logan Polish**
Col. Doug Masterson **Bruce Willis**
Pepe Garcia **Sal Lopez**
Phyllis **Kiersten Warren**
Arnold "Arnie" Millard **Rick Overton**
Chopper Miller **Richard Edson**
Madison Roberts **Elise Eberle**
Beth Goode **Julie White**
Frank **Graham Beckel**
Judge Miller **Marshall Bell**
Mrs. Harder **Kathleen Arc**
Mrs. Graham **Lois Geary**
Reporters **Dianne Anderson Mathis, William Lawrence Allen, Deborah Martinez, Richard Holcomb, Joan Findley, John Burke**
NASA Committee Member **Gregory Chase**
State Senator **Forrest Fyre**
State Congresswoman **Janelle Sperow**
Will Beacon **Robert E. Fleischer**
and Kathy Lamkin (Jodie); Charlie Brown (Phil); Gary Houston (Dr. Livingston); Adam Taylor, David House, John Lawrence Page (FBI Agents); Mark Mathis (ABC News Reporter); Matthew Kimbrough (Henry Malone); Richard McClarkin (Karl); Brian McCallister (Student); Jay Leno (Himself); Doris Hargrave (Gretchen Boyd); George McKelvey (Doug); Steve Cormier (Appraiser); Scarlett McAlister (Local News Reporter); Ben Petry, Cheyenne Serano, Hannah Wiggins, David Marcilla (Children); Robyn Reede (Secretary); Olive Gallagher (Morning Show Host); Kevin Wiggins (Rocket Expert); Mary Sue Evans (NASA Expert); Ida Darvish (Italian Anchorwoman); Eugene Nomura (Japanese Anchorman); Vik Shah (Hindu Anchorman); Yvans Jourdain (French Anchorman); Jennfier Chu (Chinese Anchorwoman); Dallas Raines (National Anchorman); Roy Costley (Astro "Nut" Local); Esodie Geiger (CNN News Reporter); J.D. Garfield (Sky Copter Reporter); J. Michael "Yak" Oliva (Balloon Game Carnie); Richard Gunn, Joey Solis (Square Dance Callers); Marc Miles (Rocket Ride Operator); Jenny Gabrielle (Vanessa); Mark DeLisle (Mission Control #1); Robert Michael Lee (MP #1); David Sullivan (Young Man)

Charlie Farmer, a one-time astronaut-in-training who missed his chance to become part of the space race, hopes to fulfill his dream by building and launching a rocket on his own property.

# RENO 911!: MIAMI

(20TH CENTURY FOX) Producers, Danny DeVito, Stacey Sher, Michael Shamberg, John Landgraf; Executive Producers, Thomas Lennon, Robert Ben Garant, Kerri Kenney-Silver, Peter Principato, Paul Young; Co-Producer, Penny Adams; Director, Robert Ben Garant; Screenplay, Robert Ben Garant, Thomas Lennon, Kerri Kenney-Silver; Photography, Joe Kessler; Editor, John Refoua; Music, Craig Wedren; Set Decorator, Robinson Royce; Costumes, Maryann Bozek; Casting, Julie Ashton-Barson; a High Sierra Carpeting/Jersey Films/Double Feature Films production, presented in association with Comedy Central; Dolby; Deluxe color; Rated R; 80 minutes; Release date: February 23, 2007.

### Cast

Deputy James Garcia  **Carlos Alazraqui**
Deputy Cherisha Kimball  **Mary Birdsong**
Deputy Travis Junior  **Robert Ben Garant**
Deputy Trudy Wiegel  **Kerri Kenney-Silver**
Lieutenant Jim Dangle  **Thomas Lennon**
Deputy Clementine Johnson  **Wendi McLendon-Covey**
Deputy Raineesha Williams  **Niecy Nash**
Deputy S. Jones  **Cedric Yarbrough**
Chief of Police  **Lenny Loftin**
Ethan the Druglord  **Paul Rudd**
District Attorney  **Danny DeVito**
Miss Acapulco  **Alejandra Gutierrez**
Jeff Spoder  **Patton Oswalt**
Bus Driver  **Michael H. Clark**
Kevlar Guy  **Brandon Molale**
Cheyenne the Helicopter Model  **Kathryn Fiore**
Persnickety Desk Worker  **Dave Holmes**
Glen the Desk Clerk  **Toby Huss**
Spring Break Dream Girl  **Cathy Shim**
Captain Rogers, DHS  **Ian Roberts**
Alligator Expert  **Chris Tallman**
and Tamara Fox Meyerson (Tammy); David Koechner (Sheriff of Aspen); Kyle Dunnigan (Drug Lord's First Hostage); David Wain (Breen the Plumber); Todd Holoubek (Tattooed Guy); Michael Patrick Jann, Joe Lo Truglio (Tattoo Shop Owners); Nick Swardson (Terry); Brian T. Finney (Decontamination Guy); Irina Voronina (Russian Model); Steve Little (Drug Lord's Second Hostage); Ken Marino (Deaf Tattoo Artist); Kevin Allison (Tattoo Victim); Eric Price (Wrestling Referee); Kathryn Smith (Jello Wrestler); Michael Ian Black (Ron of Ron's Tattoo); Michael Showalter (Paul); Shanti Hall (Hot Paramedic); Mindy Sterling (Spoder's Mom); Matthew Budds (Clapping Cop); Michael Hoback (Barry Baum); Paul Reubens (Sir Terrence); Jack Plotnick (Steve Marmella); Oscar Nuñez (Jose Jose Jose); Floyd Van Buskirk (Proctologist); Dwayne Johnson (Rick Smith, S.W.A.T.)

Members of Reno's police force are called to duty when a mishap during a Miami police convention makes them the only law enforcement officials available.

Wendi McLendon-Covey, Kerri Kenney-Silver, Carlos Alazraqui, Thomas Lennon, Niecy Nash, Robert Ben Garant

Cedric Yarbrough, Carlos Alazraqui, Paul Rudd

Kerri Kenney-Silver, Robert Ben Garant, Thomas Lennon © 20TH CENTURY FOX

# ZODIAC

Mark Ruffalo © PARAMOUNT PICTURES

(PARAMOUNT) Producers, Mike Medavoy, Arnold W. Messer, Bradley J. Fischer, James Vanderbilt, Cean Chaffin; Executive Producer, Louis Phillips; Director, David Fincher; Screenplay, James Vanderbilt, based on the book by Robert Graysmith; Photography, Harris Savides; Designer, Donald Graham Burt; Costumes, Casey Storm; Editor, Angus Wall; Music, David Shire; Music Supervisors, George Drakoulias, Randall Poster; Visual Effects, Digital Domain, Matte World Digital, Mar Vista Ventures, Ollin Studio; Visual Effects Supervisor, Eric Barba; Casting, Laray Mayfield; a Phoenix Pictures production; Dolby; HD; Widescreen; Technicolor; Rated R; 156 minutes; Release date: March 2, 2007.

Elias Koteas, Anthony Edwards, Mark Ruffalo, John Carroll Lynch

## Cast

Inspector David Toschi  **Mark Ruffalo**
Robert Graysmith  **Jake Gyllenhaal**
Paul Avery  **Robert Downey Jr.**
Inspector William Armstrong  **Anthony Edwards**
Melvin Belli  **Brian Cox**
Bob Vaughn  **Charles Fleischer**
Mel Nicolai  **Zach Grenier**
Sherwood Morrill  **Philip Baker Hall**
Sgt. Jack Mulanax  **Elias Koteas**
Captain Ken Narlow  **Donal Logue**
Arthur Leigh Allen  **John Carroll Lynch**
Captain Marty Lee  **Dermot Mulroney**
Melanie  **Chloë Sevigny**
Al Hyman  **Ed Setrakian**
Templeton Peck  **John Getz**
Charles Thieriot  **John Terry**
Carol Fisher  **Candy Clark**
Duffy Jennings  **Adam Goldberg**
Officer George Bawart  **James Le Gros**
Zodiac 1 and 2  **Richmond Arquette**
Zodiac 3  **Bob Stephenson**
Zodiac 4  **John Lacy**
Mrs. Toschi  **June Raphael**
Darlene Ferrin  **Ciara Hughes**
Young Mike Mageau  **Lee Norris**
Bryan Hartnell  **Patrick Scott Lewis**
Cecilia Shepard  **Pell James**
Father  **David Lee Smith**
Lab Tech Dagitz  **Jason Wiles**
Cabbie, Paul Stine  **Charles Schneider**
Shorty  **James Carraway**
Jim Dunbar  **Tom Verica**
Mike Mageau  **Jimmi Simpson**
Belli's Housekeeper  **Doan Ly**
Woman  **Karina Logue**
Inspector Kracke  **Joel Bissonnette**
Riverside Captain  **John Mahon**
John Allen  **Matt Winston**
Catherine Allen  **Jules Bruff**
Terry Pascoe  **John Ennis**
and J. Patrick McCormack (Police Commissioner); Clea DuVall (Linda del Buono); Paul Schulze (Sandy Panzarella); Adam Trese (Detective #1); Penny Wallace (Mulanax's Secretary); John Hemphill (Donald Cheney); Michel Francoeur (Man on Marquee); Thomas Kopache, Barry Livingston, Christopher Fields (Copy Editors)

The true story of how a series of unexplained murders in the San Francisco Bay Area became an obsession with several reporters and detectives determined to solve the puzzling crimes.

Jake Gyllenhaal, Chloë Sevigny

Brian Cox

Anthony Edwards

# WILD HOGS

(TOUCHSTONE) Producers, Mike Tollin, Brian Robbins, Todd Lieberman; Executive Producers, Sharla Sumpter Ridgett, Amy Sayres; Director, Walt Becker; Screenplay, Brad Copeland; Photography, Robbie Greenberg; Designer, Michael Corinblith; Costumes, Penny Rose; Editors, Christopher Greenbury, Stuart Pappe; Music, Teddy Castlellucci; Visual Effects, Digital Dream; Casting, Anne McCarthy, Jay Scully; a Tollin/Robbins production; Dolby; Panavision; Color; Rated PG-13; 99 minutes; Release date: March 2, 2007.

Marisa Tomei, William H. Macy

## Cast

Doug Madsen **Tim Allen**
Woody Stevens **John Travolta**
Bobby Davis **Martin Lawrence**
Dudley Frank **William H. Macy**
Jack **Ray Liotta**
Maggie **Marisa Tomei**
Red **Kevin Durand**
Murdock **M. C. Gainey**
Kelly Madsen **Jill Hennessy**
Billy Madsen **Dominic Janes**
Karen Davis **Tichina Arnold**
Charley **Stephen Tobolowsky**
Earl Dooble **Jason Sklar**
Buck Dooble **Randy Sklar**
Highway Patrolman **John C. McGinley**
Damien Blade **Peter Fonda**
Haley Davis **Drew Sidora**
Claire Davis **Cymfenee**
Dana **Margaret Travolta**
Mr. Putnam **Vic Izay**
Paul **Paul Teutul, Sr.**
Mike **Paul Teutul, Jr.**
Kent, B.I. Biker **Michael Hitchcock**
Doctor **Drew Pinsky**
Mother-in-Law **Bebe Drake**
Family Dad **Patrick O'Neal**
Family Mom **Jessica Tuck**
Family Kid **Taylor Warden**
Huge Tattooed Biker **Art Aitken**
Mrs. Putnam **Cynthia Frost**
and Héctor Jiménez (Clerk); Stephanie Skewes (Selma); Kyle Gass (Lead Singer); Shane Baumel (Toby); Ty Pennington (Himself); Liezl Carstens (Del Fuegos Biker Chick); James Johnstone, Jonathan Rau (Diner Patrons); Nick Loren (Chili Pepper); Marcel Becker (Softball Booth Vendor); Sam Travolta (Festival Goer); Sterling Rice (Chili Booth Vendor); Steve Landesberg (Accountant); Arnold Chon (Really Tiny Biker); Anthony Schmidt (Truck Driver)

Tim Allen, John Travolta, William H. Macy, Martin Lawrence

M.C. Gainey, Kevin Durand, Ray Liotta © TOUCHSTONE PICTURES

Four middle-class friends, disillusioned with their lives, decide to hop upon their motorcycles and take a road trip in hopes of finding some fulfillment.

# BLACK SNAKE MOAN

Christina Ricci

S. Epatha Merkerson

(PARAMOUNT VANTAGE) Producers, John Singleton, Stephanie Allain; Executive Producer, Ron Schmidt; Director/Screenplay, Craig Brewer; Photography, Amy Vincent; Designer, Keith Brian Burns; Costumes, Paul Sims; Editor, Billy Fox; Music, Scott Bomar; Casting, Kim Hardin, Winsome Sinclair; a New Deal/Southern Cross the Dog production; Dolby; Panavision; Deluxe color; Rated R; 115 minutes; Release date: March 2, 2007.

## Cast

Lazarus **Samuel L. Jackson**
Rae **Christina Ricci**
Ronnie **Justin Timberlake**
Angela **S. Epatha Merkerson**
Reverend R.L. **John Cothran**
Tehronne **David Banner**
Gill **Michael Raymond-James**
Rose Woods **Adriane Lenox**
Jesse **Amy Lavere**
Sandy, Rae's Mother **Kim Richards**
Lincoln **Neimus K. Williams**
Deke Woods **Leonard L. Thomas**
Mayella **Ruby Wilson**
Bojo **Claude Phillips**
Kell **Clare Grant**
and Jeff Pope (Batson); Skip Pitts (Charlie); Willie Hall (Pinetop); John Malloy (Gene); T.C. Sharpe (Archie); John Still (Herman); Jared Hopkins (Auto Worker); Tosh Newman (Conner); Cody Block (Bryan); Benjamin Rednour (Guardsman); Carnell Pepper (Melvin); David Chapman (Red); Jolynne Palmer (Ella Mae); Raymond Neal (Hershel); John Pickle (Arty); Kim Justis (Waitress); Cedric Burnside, Kenny Brown (Themselves)

Justin Timberlake, Christina Ricci

Having allowed her sexual activities to spiral out of control since her lover has left for Iraq, Rae is found bloodied and unconscious by Lazarus, who chains the girl to a radiator, making it his mission to cure her of her wanton ways.

Christina Ricci, Samuel L. Jackson © PARAMOUNT VANTAGE

# 300

Kelly Craig

(WARNER BROS.) Produced by Gianni Nunnari, Mark Canton, Bernie Goldmann, Jeffrey Silver; Executive Producers, Deborah Snyder, Frank Miller, Craig J. Flores, Thomas Tull, William Fay, Benjamin Waisbren; Co-Producers, Steve Barnett, Josette Perrotta; Director, Zack Snyder; Screenplay, Zack Snyder, Kurt Johnstad, Michael B. Gordon, based on the graphic novel by Frank Miller; Photography, Larry Fong; Designer, James Bissell; Costumes, Michael Wilkinson; Editor, William Hoy; Music, Tyler Bates; Visual Effects Supervisor, Chris Watts; Digital Visual Effects, Hybride; Visual Effects, Animal Logic/Hydraulx/Pixel Magic/Scanline/Buzz Image Group/Screaming Death Monkey/At the Post/Lola VFX/Technicolor-Toronto and Montreal; Visual Effects Art Director, Grant Freckelton; Special Effects Supervisor, Louis Craig; Makeup and Creature Effects, Shaun Smith, Mark Rappaport; Stunts/Fight Choreographers, Damon Caro, Chad Stahelski; Stunts, Stephane Lefebvre; Associate Producers, Wesley Coller, Silenn Thomas, Nathalie Peter-Contesse; Casting, Carrie Hilton; a Mark Canton/Gianni Nunnari production, presented in association with Legendary Pictures and Virtual Studios; Dolby; Panavision; Technicolor; Rated R; 116 minutes; Release date: March 9, 2007.

Andrew Tiernan © WARNER BROS.

## Cast

King Leonidas **Gerard Butler**
Queen Gorgo **Lena Headey**
Theron **Dominic West**
Dilios **David Wenham**
Captain **Vincent Regan**
Stelios **Michael Fassbender**
Astinos **Tom Wisdom**
Daxos **Andrew Pleavin**
Ephialtes **Andrew Tiernan**
Xerxes **Rodrigo Santoro**
Pleistarchos **Giovani Antonio Cimmino**
Messenger **Peter Mensah**
Loyalist **Stephen McHattie**
Oracle Girl **Kelly Craig**
Leonidas at 7/8 years **Eli Snyder**
Leonidas at 15 years **Tyler Neitzel**
Leonidas' Father **Tim Connolly**
Leonidas' Mother **Marie-Julie Rivest**
Fighting Boy **Sebastian St. Germain**
Spartan Baby Inspector **Dennis St. John**
Spartan with Stick **Neil Napier**
Spartan Generals **Robert Paradis, Jere Gillis**
Sentries **Dylan Scott Smith, Maurizio Terrazzano**
Ephors **Greg Kramer, Alex Ivanovici, Tom Rack, David Francis, James Bradford**
Persian **Kwasi Songui**
Burned Village Child **Alexandra Beaton**
Statesman **Frédéric Smith**
Spartan Babies **Loucas Minchillo, Nicholas Minchillo** and Andrew Shaver (Free Greek, Potter); Robin Wilcock (Free Greek, Blacksmith); Marcel Jeannin (Free Greek, Baker); Jeremy Thibodeau (Spartan Boy); Tyrone Benskin (Persian Emissary); Robert Maillet (Uber Immortal Giant); Patrick Sabongui, Stewart Myiow (Persian Generals); Leon Laderach (Executioner); Dave Lapommeray (Persian General Slaughtered); Vervi Mauricio (Armless Concubine); Charles Papasoff (Blacksmith); Isabelle Champeau (Mother at Market); Veronique-Natale Szalankiewicz (Daughter at Market); Maéva Madon (Girl at Market); David Thibodeau (Boy #1 at Market); David Schaap (Potter); Jean Michel Paré (Other Council Guard); Andreanne Ross, Sara Giacalone (Concubines); Ariadne Bourbonnière, Isabelle Fournel (Kissing Concubines); Sandrine Merette-Attiow (Contortionist); Elisabeth Etienne, Danielle Hubbard, Ruan Vibegaard (Dancers); Genevieve Guilbault, Bonnie Mak, Amélie Sorel, Caroline Aspirot, Gina Gagnon, Tania Trudell, Stéphanie Aubry, Mercedes Leggett, Stephanie Gambarova, Chanelle Lamothe, Sabrina-Jasmine Guilbault (Slave Girls); Atif Siddiqi (Arabian Transsexual); Manny Cortez Tuazon (Asian Transsexual); Camille Rizkallah (Giant with Arrow); Trudi Hanley (Long Neck Woman); Neon Cobran (Litter Bearer); Gary A. Hecker (Ubermortal Vocals)

Gerard Butler

Leonidas leads 300 Spartans into battle with the invading Persian army, resulting in a bloody three-day siege that proves crucial in preventing an enemy takeover of the Hellenic lands. Previous film on the event was *The 300 Spartans* (20th, 1962) starring Richard Egan and David Farrar.

Robert Maillet

Gerard Butler, Rodrigo Santoro

Lena Headey, Dominic West

# THE NAMESAKE

(FOX SEARCHLIGHT) Producers, Lydia Dean Pilcher, Mira Nair; Executive Producers, Yasushi Kotani, Taizo Son, Ronnie Screwvala; Co-Producers, Lori Keith Douglas, Yukie Kito, Zarina Screwvala; Director, Mira Nair; Screenplay, Sooni Taraporevala, based on the novel by Jhumpa Lahiri; Photography, Frederick Elmes; Editor, Allyson C. Johnson; Music, Nitin Sawhney; Music Supervisor, Linda Cohen; Designer, Stephanie Carroll; Costumes, Arjun Bhasin; Casting, Cindy Tolan; India Casting, Tess Joseph; a Fox Searchlight Pictures/Entertainment Farm/UTV Motion Pictures presentation of a Mirabi Films and Cine Mosaic production; Dolby; Deluxe color; Rated 122 minutes; Release date: March 9, 2007.

Kal Penn, Irrfan Khan, Sahira Nair, Tabu

## Cast

Gogol Ganguli **Kal Penn**
Ashima Ganguli **Tabu**
Ashoke Ganguli **Irrfan Khan**
Maxine Ratliff **Jacinda Barrett**
Mr. Lawson **Linus Roche**
Sonia Ganguli **Sahira Nair**
Lydia Ratliff **Glenne Headly**
Gerald Ratliff **Daniel Gerroll**
Pamela **Amy Wright**
Sally **Brooke Smith**
Ghosh **Jagannath Guha**
Ashoke's Mother **Ruma Guha Thakurta**
Music Teacher **Sandip Deb**
Rini **Sukanya**
Ashima's Mother **Tanushree Shankar**
Ashima's Father **Sabyasachi Chakraborty**
Ashoke's Father **Tamal Roy Choudhury**
and Dhruv Mookerji (Rana); Supriya Devi (Ashima's Grandmother); Stuart Rudin (Homeless Man); Heather MacRae (Nurse Patty); Sumitra Kanti (Calcutta House Staff); Michael Countryman (Mr. Wilcox); Kousik Bhowal (Dr. Gupta); Rupak Ginn (Uncle); Soham Chatterjee (Gogol, age 4); Gargi Mukherjee (Mira Mashi); Pallavi Shah (Kajol Mashi); Jhumpa Lahiri (Jhumpa Mashi); Noor Lahiri Vourvoulias (Baby Sonia); Josh Grisetti (Jerry); Justin Rosini (Marc); Dan McCabe (Bart); Bobby Steggert (Jason); B.C. Parikh (Mr. Mazumdar); Sibani Biswas (Mrs. Mazumdar); Zuleikha Robinson (Moushumi Mazumdar); Lakhan Das (Baul Singer); Kharaj Mukherjee (Chotu); Christie Moreau (Phone Operator); Jo Yang (Ms. Lu); Krishna Dikshit (Funeral Priest); Kartik Das (Boat Man); Gary Cowling (Hotel Manager); Sudipta Bhawmik (Subroto Mesho); Gretchen Egolf (Astrid); Baylen Thomas (Blake); Jeb Brown (Oliver); Jessica Blank (Edith); Mia Yoo (Viola); Benjamin Bauman (Donald); Sebastian Roché (Pierre); Maximiliano Hernández (Ben); Partha Chatterjee (Reformed Hindoo); Mitali Bhawmik (Singing Voice); Marcus Collins (Graham); Sandi DeGeorge (Moshumi's Friend)

Kal Penn, Jacinda Barrett

American-raised Gogol Ganguli, disenchanted with his Indian heritage and a name he considers unappealing, begins to explore his familial roots, taking him on a journey of self-discovery.

Tabu © FOX SEARCHLIGHT PICTURES

# PREMONITION

Julian McMahon, Sandra Bullock

Shyann McClure, Courtney Taylor Burness, Sandra Bullock

(TRISTAR/MGM) Producers, Ashok Amritraj, Jon Jashni, Adam Shankman, Jennifer Gibgot, Sunil Perkash; Executive Producers, Andrew Sugerman, Nick Hamson, Lars Sylvest; Director, Mennan Yapo; Screenplay, Bill Kelly; Photography, Torsten Lippstock; Designer, Dennis Washington; Costumes, Jill Ohanneson; Editor, Neil Travis; Music, Klaus Badelt; Music Supervisor, Buck Damon; a Hyde Park Entertainment presentation of an Ashok Amritraj/ Offspring production; Dolby; Color; Rated PG-13; 97 minutes; Release date: March 16, 2007.

Kate Nelligan, Sandra Bullock

### Cast

Linda Hanson **Sandra Bullock**
Jim Hanson **Julian McMahon**
Annie **Nia Long**
Joanne **Kate Nelligan**
Claire **Amber Valletta**
Dr. Norman Roth **Peter Stormare**
Bridgette Hanson **Courtney Taylor Burness**
Megan Hanson **Shyann McClure**
Mrs. Quinn **Irene Ziegler**
Sheriff Reilly **Marc Macaulay**
Father Kennedy **Jude Ciccolella**
Model Home Salesman **E.J. Stapleton**
Doug Caruthers **Mark Famiglietti**
School Aide **Laurel Whitsett**
Receptionist **Kristin Ketterer**
Bob **Marcus Lyle Brown**
Emergency Room Doctor **Jason Douglas**
and Dave Shaffer (Doctor's Assistant); Floriana Tullio (Nurse); Phillip DeVona, Ritchie Montgomery (Funeral Attendant); Matt Moore (Young Priest)

Traumatized by the news that her husband has been killed in a car accident, Linda Hanson is stunned to awaken one morning to discover that he is very much alive, leading her to wonder if she has become unstuck in time and is experiencing the week of his death in random order.

Amber Valletta © TRISTAR/MGM

# I THINK I LOVE MY WIFE

(FOX SEARCHLIGHT) Producers, Chris Rock, Lisa Stewart, Ronnie Screwvala; Co-Producer, Zarina Screwvala; Director, Chris Rock; Screenplay, Chris Rock, Louis C.K.; Based on the motion picture *Chloe in the Afternoon* by Eric Rohmer; Photography, William Rexer II; Designer, Sharon Lomofsky; Costumes, Suzanne McCabe; Music, Marcus Miller; Music Supervisor, Dave Jordan; Editor, Wendy Greene Bricmont; Casting, Victoria Thomas; a UTV Motion Picture presentation of a Zahrlo production; Dolby; Deluxe color; Rated R; 94 minutes; Release date: March 16, 2007.

**Cast**

Richard Cooper **Chris Rock**
Nikki Tru **Kerry Washington**
Brenda Cooper **Gina Torres**
George **Steve Buscemi**
Mr. Landis **Edward Herrmann**
Mary **Welker White**
Tracy **Samantha Ivers**
Teddy **Michael K. Williams**
Jennifer **Cassandra F. Freeman**
Allan **Stephen A. Smith**
Sean **Wendell Pierce**
Kelly Cooper **Milan Howard**
Landlady **Roz Ryan**
Candy **Christina Vidal**
Lisa **Eliza Coupe**
Cologne-Spraying Salesman **André Blake**
Department Store Salesmen **Ian Brennan, Matthew Morrison**
Therapist **Linda Powell**
Maitre D' **Adam LeFevre**
Hope **Eva Pigford**
Pam **Hazel J. Medina**
Ron **Divine T. Cox**
Mr. Yuni **James Saito**
Mr. Yakamoto **Ron Nakahara**
Irresistible Fantasy Women **Pearl Veldwijk, Elizabeth Mathis, Krista Coyle**
Irresistible Fantasy Screw You Woman **Jenny Powers**
Convenience Store Cashier **Julie Halston**
Hot Waitress **Dani Marco**
D.C. TV Reporter **Paul Messina**
and Bambadjan Bamba (Rapper on Elevator); Kimberly Hebert Gregory (Babysitter); Susan E. McCallum (Lady on Elevator); Michael Tenaglia, Daniel Stewart Sherman (D.C. Cops); GQ (White Rapper); Orlando Jones (Nelson)

Bored with his comfortable but unremarkable marriage of eight years, Richard Cooper finds himself deeply attracted to the ex-girlfriend of one of his buddies, who has come to him for advice and assumes their relationship will be kept on a platonic basis. Remake of the 1972 film *Chloe in the Afternoon.*

Steve Buscemi, Chris Rock

Chris Rock, Kerry Washington, Gina Torres

Kerry Washington, Chris Rock © FOX SEARCHLIGHT

# REIGN OVER ME

Jada Pinkett Smith, Don Cheadle © COLUMBIA PICTURES

(COLUMBIA) Producers, Jack Binder, Michael Rotenberg; Executive Producers, Jack Giarraputo, Lynwood Spinks; Co-Producer, Rachel Zimmerman; Director/Screenplay, Mike Binder; Photography, Russ Alsobrook; Designer, Pipo Wintter; Costumes, Deborah L. Scott; Editors, Steve Edwards, Jeremy Roush; Music, Rolfe Kent; Music Supervisor, Dave Jordan; Casting, Sharon Bialy; a Mr. Madison/Sunlight production, presented in association with Relativity Media; Dolby; Color; HD-to-35mm; Rated R; 128 minutes; Release date: March 23, 2007.

## Cast

| | |
|---|---|
| Charlie Fineman | **Adam Sandler** |
| Alan Johnson | **Don Cheadle** |
| Janeane Johnson | **Jada Pinkett Smith** |
| Angela Oakhurst | **Liv Tyler** |
| Donna Remar | **Saffron Burrows** |
| Judge Raines | **Donald Sutherland** |
| Jonathan Timpleman | **Robert Klein** |
| Ginger Timpleman | **Melinda Dillon** |
| Bryan Sugarman | **Mike Binder** |
| Stetler | **Jonathan Banks** |
| Adell Modell | **Rae Allen** |
| Melanie | **Paula Newsome** |
| Nigel Pennington | **John de Lancie** |
| George Johnson | **Paul Butler** |
| Cherie Johnson | **Camille LaChe-Smith** |
| Jocelyn Johnson | **Imani Hakim** |
| Psychiatric Hospital Therapist | **Denise Dowse** |
| William Johnson | **Anthony Chisholm** |
| Mr. Fallon | **B.J. Novak** |
| Night Club Comic | **Jessica Golden** |
| Peter Savarino | **Ted Raimi** |
| Kemp | **Harris Peet** |
| Becky Fishman | **Molly Binder** |

and Tommy Nohilly (Patty); Robert Harvey (Dental Partner); Nick Taylor (Taxi Driver); M.D. Walton, Chad R. Brigockas (New York Police Officers); Elizabeth Andrews (Sugarman's Secretary); Neal Robert Young (New Dental Patient); Lela Loren (Dental Hygenist); Diana Gettinger (Doreen Fineman); Karen Huie (News Reporter)

Manhattan dentist Alan Johnson tries to reach out to his college roommate Charlie Fineman, who is so traumatized by the death of his family in the terrorist attacks of 9/11 that he has cut himself off from human contact.

Adam Sandler

Saffron Burrows, Liv Tyler, Adam Sandler, Don Cheadle

# SHOOTER

(PARAMOUNT) Produced by Lorenzo di Bonaventura, Ric Kidney; Executive Producers, Erik Howsam, Mark Johnson; Director, Antoine Fuqua; Screenplay, Jonathan Lemkin, based on the novel *Point of Impact* by Stephen Hunter; Photography, Peter Menzies Jr.; Designer, Dennis Washington; Costumes, Ha Nhuyen; Editors, Conrad Buff, Eric Sears; Music, Mark Mancina; Visual Effects Supervisors, Deak Ferrand, Erik Liles; Visual Effects, HY*DRAU*LX; Special Effects Coordinators, Joel Whist, Michael Frechette (U.S.); Stunts, John Stoneham Jr.; Second Unit Director, Jeff Habberstad; Casting, Mali Finn; a Di Bonaventura Pictures production; Dolby; Panavision; Deluxe color; Rated R; 126 minutes; Release date: March 23, 2007.

Mark Wahlberg

## Cast

Bob Lee Swagger  **Mark Wahlberg**
Nick Memphis  **Michael Peña**
Col. Isaac Johnson  **Danny Glover**
Sarah Fenn  **Kate Mara**
Jack Payne  **Elias Koteas**
Alourdes Galindo  **Rhona Mitra**
Louis Dobbler  **Jonathan Walker**
Michael Sandor  **Rade Sherbedgia**
Mr. Rate  **Levon Helm**
Senator Charles F. Meachum  **Ned Beatty**
Russ Turner  **Tate Donovan**
Howard Purnell  **Justin Louis**
Officer Stanley Timmons  **Alan C. Peterson**
Donnie Fenn  **Lane Garrison**
Senior Agent  **Zak Santiago**
Junior Agent  **Michael-Ann Connor**
Underling  **Shawn Reis**
Attorney General Russert  **Brian Markinson**
FBI Director Brandt  **Michael St. John Smith**
Archbishop Desmond Mutumbo  **Dean Monroe McKenzie**
President  **Tom Butler**
Ben Davis  **Adrian Hughes**
Frank Russo  **Darrin Massey**
Dave Simmons  **Mackenzie Gray**
Mrs. Rate  **Rebecca Toolan**
Katy  **Trish Allen**
Diver  **James Wettengl**
and John Tench (Motel Owner); David Bloom (Meachum's Valet); Brad Kelly (Sorenson); David Neale (Spook); Susan Barnett, Ukee Washington, Dagmar Midcap, Darrin Maharaj (TV News Anchors); Anthony McCrae (Jefe); Mike Dopud (Lead Mercenary); Chic Gibson (Mayor of Philadelphia); Danny Hernandez, Jonathan Eusabio (K-9 Cops)

Danny Glover, Elias Koteas, Mark Wahlberg, Rade Sherbedgia, Jonathan Walker

Former military sniper Bob Lee Swagger is engaged by retired colonel Isaac Johnson to help uncover a probable assassination plot, only to have Swagger realize that he has been set up when he ends up accused of the murder of a government official.

Michael Peña, Mark Wahlberg © PARAMOUNT PICTURES

# THE LAST MIMZY

(NEW LINE CINEMA) Producer, Michael Phillips; Executive Producers, Bob Shaye, Justis Greene, Sara Risher; Director, Bob Shaye; Screenplay, Bruce Joel Rubin, Toby Emmerich, based on the short story "All Mimsy Were the Borogroves" by Lewis Padgett; Photography, J. Michael Muro; Designer, Barry Chusid; Costumes, Karen Matthews; Editor, Alan Heim; Music, Howard Shore; Visual Effects, The Orphanage; Visual Effects Supervisor, Eric Durst; Special Effects Supervisor, Alex Burdett; Stunts, Marny Eng; Associate Producer, Jonna Smith; Casting, Margery Simkin; a Michael Phillips production; Dolby; Deluxe color; Rated PG; 90 minutes; Release date: March 23, 2007.

Rhiannon Leigh Wryn

## Cast

Noah Wilder   **Chris O'Neil**
Emma Wilder   **Rhiannon Leigh Wryn**
Jo Wilder   **Joely Richardson**
David Wilder   **Timothy Hutton**
Larry White   **Rainn Wilson**
Naomi Schwartz   **Kathryn Hahn**
Nathanial Boardman   **Michael Clarke Duncan**
Sheila Boardman   **Kirsten Williamson**
Teacher in Meadow   **Irene Snow**
Harry Jones   **Marc Musso**
Girl with Braces   **Nicole Muñoz**
School Guard   **Scott Miller**
Wendy   **Megan McKinnon**
Julie the Babysitter   **Randi Lynne**
Future Scientist   **Tom Heaton**
Future Scientist's Co-Worker   **John Burnside**
Armed Cyborgs   **Samuel Polin, Phillip Brooks**
Technicians   **Daniel Bacon, Carlo Fanella, Paul Jarrett**
Utilities Commissioner   **Jerry Wasserman**
Stu   **Camyra Chai**
Police Captain   **Fred Keating**
Newscaster   **Dagmar Midcap**
Dr. Arnold Rose   **John Shaw**
FBI Task Force Agents   **Patrick Gilmore, Chad Cole**
CPS Officer   **Kaaren de Zilva**
FBI Video Technician   **David Joshi**
Scientists   **Bruce Harwood, Kathleen Duborg, Hiro Kanagawa**
Intel Scientist   **Brian Greene**
Army Officer   **Curtis Caravaggio**
Teenage Cyborgs   **Mackenzie Hamilton, Calum Worthy**
and Elias Calogeros, Caleb Kemble, Joanna Coons, Grace Walker, Evan Leeson, Eliana MacFarlane, Sophia Wik, Amanda Wik, Elora Penner, Sawyer Nicholson, Tamatea Westby (Children in Meadow); Julia Arkos (Kindergarten Teacher)

Timothy Hutton, Chris O'Neil © NEW LINE CINEMA

Chris O'Neil, Timothy Hutton, Rhiannon Leigh Wryn, Joely Richardson

Two children come across a mysterious box containing a rabbit named Mimzy, an emissary from the future who enlists their aide in helping him rescue the future of humanity from pollution and disease.

# PRIDE

Kimberly Elise, Terrence Howard

(LIONSGATE) Produced by Brett Forbes, Patrick Rizzotti, Michael Ohoven, Adam Rosenfelt, Paul Hall; Executive Producers, Terrence Howard, Victoria Frederick, Sam Nazarian, Eberhard Kayser, Malcolm Petal, Kimberly C. Anderson, Michael Paseornek, John Sacchi; Co-Producers, Marc Schaberg, Randy Winograd; Director, Sunu Gonera; Screenplay, Kevin Michael Smith, Michael Gozzard, J. Mills Goodloe, Norman Vance Jr., based on a story by Kevin Michael Smith, Michael Gozzard; Photography, Matthew F. Leonetti; Editor, Billy Fox; Music, Aaron Zigman; Music Supervisor, Jay Faires; Designer, Steve Saklad; Costumes, Paul A. Simmons; Underwater Camera, Pete Romano; Casting, Anya Colloff, Amy McIntyre Britt; a Lionsgate and Element Films presentation of a Cinered, Lionsgate, Element Films and Fortress Features production in association with Paul Hall Productions and LIFT; Dolby; Color; Rated PG; 108 minutes; Release date: March 23, 2007.

Terrence Howard (left) © LIONSGATE

## Cast

Jim Ellis **Terrence Howard**
Elston **Bernie Mac**
Sue Davis **Kimberly Elise**
Bink **Tom Arnold**
Puddin' Head **Brandon Fobbs**
Walt **Alphonso McAuley**
Willie **Regine Nehy**
Hakim **Nate Parker**
Andre **Kevin Phillips**
Jake **Scott Reeves**
Reggie **Evan Ross**
Franklin **Gary Sturgis**
Artrell, Willie's Father **Jesse Moore**
Ophelia, Andre's Mother **Carol Sutton**
Race Official, UOFB **Tony Bently**
Race Official, Mainline **Vance Strickland**
Coach Logan, 1964 **Louis Herthum**
Race Official, PDR **Wayne Ferrara**
Starter, 1964 **George Sanchez**
Ron Lincoln, Employment **Anthony Bean**
City Worker **Jim Ellis III**
and Harold X. Evans (Reverend); Catherine Shreves (TV Reporter); Terence Rosemore (Maintenance Man); Joni L. Marsaw, Courtney Evans, Candice Crump, Shasta Clements (Hot Girls); Ernest Anthony (Bob the Barber)

Desperate for work, Jim Ellis takes a job at a dilapidated recreational center in a poor section of Philadelphia, where he inspires six black teens to take swimming lessons, hoping to turn them into competitive swimmers.

Regine Nehy, Evan Ross, Nate Parker, Terrence Howard, Alphonso McAuley, Brandon Fobbs, Kevni Phillips

# TMNT

Raphael, Leonardo, Michelangelo, Donatello

Casey, Donatello, Michelangelo, Leonardo, April

(WARNER BROS.) Producers, Thomas K. Gray, H. Galen Walker, Paul Wang; Executive Producers, Francis Kao, Peter Laird, Gary Richardson, Frederick U. Fierst; Co-Producer, Felix Ip; Director/Screenplay, Kevin Munroe, based on characters created by Peter Laird, Kevin Eastman; Photography, Steve Lumley; Editor, John Damien Ryan; Music, Klaus Badelt; Music Supervisor, Julianne Jordan; Designer, Simon Murton; Supervising Animator, Kim Ooi; Additional Animation Supervisor, Colin Brady; Lead Character Designer, Jeff Matsuda; Visual Effects Supervisor, Kith Ng; Line Producer, Michael J. Arnold; Casting, Dawn Hershey; an Imagi Animation Studios (U.S./Hong Kong) production; American-Hong Kong; Dolby; Digital; Widescreen; Technicolor; Rated PG; 86 minutes; Release date: March 23, 2007.

## Voice Cast

Casey **Chris Evans**
April O'Neil **Sarah Michelle Gellar**
Splinter **Mako**
Maximillian J. Winters **Patrick Stewart**
Donatello **Mitchell Whitfield**
Leonardo **James Arnold Taylor**
Michelangelo **Mikey Kelley**
Raphael/Nightwatcher **Nolan North**
Narrator **Laurence Fishburne**
and Kevin Smith (Diner Cook); Zhang Ziyi (Karai); John Di Maggio (Colonel Santino); Paula Mattioli (General Serpiente); Kevin Michael Richardson (General Aguila/Additional Voices); Fred Tatasciore (General Gato); Dee Baker, Greg Baldwin, Jeff Bennett, Jim Cummings, Grey DeLisle, Chris Edgerly, Kim Mai Guest, Jennifer Hale, Jess Harnell, Phil LaMarr, Paul Michael Robinson, Tara Strong, Billy West (Additional Voices)

Four sewer-dwelling mutant turtles return to their crime-fighting ways to prevent the destruction of mankind. Earlier live-action films in the series were *Teenage Mutant Ninja Turtles* (New Line, 1990), *Teenage Mutant Ninja Turtles II: The Secret of the Ooze* (New Line, 1991), and *Teenage Mutant Ninja Turtles III* (New Line, 1993).

Raphael, Big Foot

Jersey Devil © WARNER BROS.

# BOY CULTURE

Derek Magyar, Darryl Stephens © TLA RELEASING

(TLA RELEASING) Producers, Stephen Israel, Philip Pierce, Victor Simpkins; Co-Producer, Phil Lobel; Director, Q. Allan Brocka; Screenplay, Philip Pierce, Q. Allan Brocka; Based on the novel by Matthew Rettenmund; Photography, Joshua Hess; Designer, Cecil Gentry; Costumes, Ron Leamon; Editor, Phillip J. Bartell; Music, Ryan Beveridge; Music Supervisor, Bill Coleman; Casting, Linda Phillips Palo, Robert McGee, Jason James; a Boy Culture production; Color; DV-to-HD; Not rated; 88 minutes; Release date: March 23, 2007.

## Cast

X **Derek Magyar**
and Patrick Bauchau (Gregory Talbot); Darryl Stephens (Andrew); Jonathon Trent (Joey); George Jonson (Blondie); Peyton Hinson (Jill); Kyle Santler (Scooter); Emily Brooke Hands (Lucy); Matt Riedy (Frank); Clifford Harrington (Renaldo); Molly Manago (Cheyenne); Demene Hall (Zelma); William Hall, Jr., (Oren); Joël René (Candace); Kibbi Monié (Phyllis); Jesse Archer (Threeway Hottie); Jeffrey Gilbert, David Parker (Wedding Guests); Laprell Nelson (Matthew); Edwin Stone (The Judge); Skip Cohan (Mr. Jowls); Terry Thomas (Chaps); Aaron Holsworth (Daddy's Boy); Michael Cornell (Accountant); Gregory Bickford (Father of Six); Ronald Leamon (The Mummy); Ron Lake (Breath Mints); Shannon Fisher (Gin Martini); Q. Allan Brocka (Bruce Lee); Gerard Parr (The Screamer); Victor Simpkins (Barely Breathing); Chris Barrett, Tye Blue, Eric Douglas, Martin Squires, John Torregiani (Soccer Boys); Erin Kidder, Mikella McIntyre, Cassandra Sanders (Mormon Girls); Chris Bethards (Young Gregory); Joshua Boswell (Young Renaldo); Dylan Shay (Andy); Lucy Shay (Andy's Mom); Joe Barden (John); Brandon Wolfe (Ding); Skyler Leonard (Dong); John M, Brian Bufriend (Hook-Up Guys); Ann Van Alt (X's Mom); George Rickle (X's Dad); Lynnette Boulch (Cashier); Nate Golon, Wes Hurley (Broadway Hot Guys); Hunter Kincaid (Park Cruiser); Martyn Valenzuela (Gym Stud); Adam Wallace (Gym Cruiser); Robert Veliz (Street Cruiser); Robert Lucus (Robber); Pio Frantz (Doorman); Gary Frantz (Bartender); Trevor Scott (Andrew's Third Trick); Rob Call (Muscular Man); Jason Gagnon (Guy with the Biggest Dick); Michael Morroni, Malcolm Smith (Boy Kultur Cruisers); Robert Frazier (Jill's Father); Devielle Johnson (Del, the Groom); Michael Lowrimore (Cute Wedding Guest); Wendy Ashford (Door Girl); Mark Finley (Drag Queen)

Sexually voracious Joey finds himself hopelessly attracted to one of his roommates, X, a hustler, who happens to carry a torch for their other roomie, Andrew, who hasn't quite come to terms with his sexuality.

# FIRST SNOW

(YARI FILM GROUP) Producers, Tom Lassally, Sean Furst, Bob Yari, Bryant Furst, Robin Meisinger; Co-Producers, Chris Miller, Todd Williams, Wolfgang Schamburg; Executive Producers, Dave Gare, Oliver Hengst, Ernst August Schamburg; Director, Mark Fergus; Screenplay, Mark Fergus, Hawk Ostby; Photography, Eric Alan Edwards; Designer, Devorah Herbert; Costumes, Lahly Poore; Music, Cliff Martinez; Editor, Jay Lash Cassidy; Casting, John Papsidera; an El Camino Pictures presentation of a Furst Films/Kustom Entertainment production, a MHF Zweite Academy Film production; American-German; Dolby; Super 35 Widescreen; FotoKem Color; Rated R; 101 minutes; Release date: March 23, 2007.

## Cast

Jimmy Starks **Guy Pearce**
Deirdre **Piper Perabo**
Ed Jacomoi **William Fichtner**
Vacaro **J.K. Simmons**
Vincent McClure **Shea Whigham**
Andy Lopez **Rick Gonzalez**
Maggie **Jackie Burroughs**
Tom Morelane **Adam Scott**
and Portia Dawson (Marci, Waitress); Cherilyn Hayres (Market Clerk); Roy Harrison (Luce Rains); Brian Keith Gamble (Bank Manager); David House (Sammy the Bartender); John Burton, Jr. (Radio DJ); Julie Gawkowski (Receptionist); Gurudarshan Khalsa (Psychic); Steven Quezada (Enrique); Clark Sanchez (Mansonesque Murderer); Dave Mallow (Radio Announcer); Nicholas Ballas (Tavern Owner Pete); Forrest Fyre (Dr. Bates); Callie Anne Morgan (Psychic Woman's Daughter); Jo Ann Soto (Crying Woman); Adriana Cordova (Lopez's Wife); Roy Costley (Sgt VanMeer)

A glib salesman dreads the parole of the one-time friend he helped put behind bars, especially after being told by a fortune teller that he will die after the first snow falls.

Piper Perabo, Guy Pearce © YARI FILM GROUP

# BLADES OF GLORY

Jon Heder, Scott Hamilton, Will Ferrell

Will Arnett, Jenna Fischer, Amy Poehler

(DREAMWORKS) Producers, Ben Stiller, Stuart Cornfeld, John Jacobs; Executive Producer, Marty Ewing; Directors, Will Speck, Josh Gordon; Screenplay, Jeff Cox, Craig Cox, John Altschuler, Dave Krinsky; Story, Craig Cox, Jeff Cox, Busy Philipps; Photography, Stefan Czapsky; Designer, Stephen Lineweaver; Costumes, Julie Weiss; Music, Theodore Shapiro; Music Supervisor, George Drakoulias; Editor, Richard Pearson; Skating Choreographer, Sarah Kawahara; Visual Effects Producer, Randall Starr; Casting, Juel Bestrop, Seth Yanklewitz; Stunts, Doug Coleman, Allen Robinson; a Read Hour/Smart Entertainment production; Dolby; Deluxe color; Rated PG-13; 93 minutes; Release date: March 30, 2007.

## Cast

Chazz Michael Michaels **Will Ferrell**
Jimmy MacElroy **Jon Heder**
Stranz Van Waldenberg **Will Arnett**
Fairchild Van Waldenberg **Amy Poehler**
and Jenna Fischer (Katie Van Waldenberg); William Fichtner (Darren MacElroy); Craig T. Nelson (Coach); Romany Malco (Jesse); Nick Swardson (Hector); Scott Hamilton (Sports Anchor); Andy Richter, Greg Lindsay (Mounties); Rob Corddry (Bryce); Nick Jameson (PA Announcer); Tom Virtue (Floor Manager); Ben Wilson (Fox); William Daniels (Commissioner Ebbers); Zachary Ferren (Young Jimmy); Rémy Girard (Father St. Pierre); Steven Gagnon (Rink Official, World Games); Chris Reed (World Games Paramedic); Luciana Carro (Sam); Nancy Kerrigan (Attractive Official); Ricardo "Smalls" Strickland (Frank the Security Guard); Luke Wilson (Sex Class Counselor); Katherine Towne (Sex Addict); David Pressman (Reporter, Montreal); James Michael Connor (Surly Reporter, Montreal); Craig Gellis (Jail Cell Inmate); Angela Chee (Newswoman); Hans Uder (Usher); Brian Boitano, Dorothy Hamill, Peggy Fleming (Federation Judges); Phil Reeves (Father); Mollie Marie Clinton (Alice); Matt Levin (Matt); Eloise Lynch (Fan); Fiona Gubelmann, Smith Cho (Woodland Fairies); James P. Yorke (Skate Fox); Alysse Alcroft, Taylor Neff, Wendy Wilke (Skate Woodland Fairies); Matt Evers, Keith Joe Dick (Skate Trees); Sunita Param (Reporter); Stephanie Courtney (Reporter at Sign Ups); Lisa-Marie Allen (Middle-Aged Sweater Mom); Elliot Cho (Little Kid); Loretta Fox (Court Stenographer); Kyle Bornheimer (Rink PA Nationals); Jim Lampley (Co-Anchor); Sasha Cohen (Herself); Alison Martin (Judge, Stockholm); Griffin Armstorff (Finnish Skating Prodigy); Grant Thompson (Wallet Mountie); Kelly Gould (Crying Girl); Margaret Roblin (Judge, Montreal); Lisa Paul (Catholic School Girl); Lora Starkman (Girl Who Kisses Chazz); J.D. Cantrell (Future Skater); Kerry Rossall (Fire Extinguisher)

Jon Heder, Will Ferrell © DREAMWORKS

Banned from the men's singles competition for their constant fighting, figure skaters Chazz Michaels and Jimmy MacElroy reluctantly agree to team up as the first male pairs skating team in an effort to restore their reputations and get back on the ice.

## MEET THE ROBINSONS

Uncle Gaston, Grandma Lucille, Cousin Laszlo, Aunt Petunia, Grandpa

(WALT DISNEY PICTURES) Producer, Dorothy McKim; Executive Producers, John Lasseter, William Joyce, Clark Spencer; Director, Stephen Anderson; Screenplay, Jon Bernstein, Michelle Spitz, Don Hall, Nathan Greno, Aurian Redson, Joe Mateo, Stephen Anderson; Based upon the book *A Day with Wilbur Robinson* by William Joyce; Associate Producers, Makul Wigert, David J. Steinberg; Art Director, Robh Ruppel; Co-Art Director, David Goetz; Editor, Ellen Keneshea; Visual Effects Supervisors, Steve Goldberg, Chris Peterson; CG Supervisors, Corey Smith, Marcus Hobbs; Technical Supervisor, Mark Hammel; Layout Supervisor, Scott Beatie; Animation Supervisor, Michael Belzer; Character Design, Joe Moshier; Casting, Jen Rudin Pearson; Dolby; Technicolor; Rated G; 96 minutes; Release date: March 30, 2007.

### Voice Cast

Mildred **Angela Bassett**
Cornelius Robinson **Tom Selleck**
Carl **Harland Williams**
Lucille Krunkelhorn **Laurie Metcalf**
Franny **Nicole Sullivan**
Uncle Art **Adam West**
Doris/CEO/Uncle Spike/Uncle Dimitri/Cousin Laszlo/Uncle Fritz/Aunt Petunia **Ethan Sandler**
Mr. Willerstein **Tom Kenny**
Lewis **Daniel Hansen, Jordan Fry**
Michael "Goob" Yagoobian **Matthew Josten**
Mr. Harrington **John H.H. Ford**
Mrs. Harrington/Receptionist **Dara McGarry**
Coach/Gaston **Don Hall**
Stanley **Paul Butcher**
and Tracey Miller-Zarneke (Lizzy); Wesley Singerman (Wilbur); Jessie Flower (Young Franny); Stephen Jon Anderson (Bowler Hat Guy/Grandpa Bud/Tallulah); Nathan Greno (Lefty); Kellie M. Hoover (Aunt Billie); Aurian Redson (Frankie); Joe Maeo (T-Rex); Joe Whyte (Reporter)

Wilbur, Lewis

Frankie the Frog

Bowler Hat Guy © WALT DISNEY PICTURES

An orphaned whiz kid travels into the future, where he meets an oddball family much like the one he has always longed for.

# THE LOOKOUT

Joseph Gordon-Levitt, Matthew Goode © MIRAMAX FILMS

(MIRAMAX) Producers, Roger Birnbaum, Gary Barber; Executive Producers, Laurie MacDonald, Becki Cross Trujillo, Jonathan Glickman; Director/Screenplay, Scott Frank; Photography, Alar Kivilo; Designer, David Brisbin; Costumes, Abram Waterhouse; Editor, Jill Savitt; Music, James Newton Howard; Associate Producer, Ivan Oyco; Casting, Marcia S. Ross; a Spyglass Entertainment presentation of Lawrence Mark/Parkes-MacDonald/Birnbaum-Barber production; Dolby; Technicolor; Rated R; 102 minutes; Release date: March 30, 2007.

## Cast

Chris Pratt  **Joseph Gordon-Levitt**
Lewis  **Jeff Daniels**
Gary Spargo  **Matthew Goode**
Luvlee Lemons  **Isla Fisher**
Janet  **Carla Gugino**
Robert Pratt  **Bruce McGill**
Barbara Pratt  **Alberta Watson**
Mrs. Lange  **Alex Borstein**
Deputy Ted  **Sergio Di Zio**
Mr. Tuttle  **David Huband**
Kelly  **Laura Vandervoort**
and Greg Dunham (Bone); Morgan Kelly (Marty); Aaron Berg (Cork); Tinsel Korey (Maura); Suzanne Kelly (Nina); Brian E. Roach (Danny); Martin Roach (Loan Officer); Ofield Williams (Reggie); Julie Pederson (Attractive Woman in Bar); Stephen Eric McIntyre (Bartender); Janaya Stephens (Alison Pratt); Marc Devigne (Cameron Pratt); Courtney-Jane White (Cameron's Girlfriend); Thanya Romero (Maid); Paul Christie (Jonathan);Tracy McMahon (Woman Reading at Bar); Gordie Farrell, Toni Reimer (Motorcycle Couple); Ted Felbel (Elderly Man with Walker); Charles Crossin (Department Store Clerk); Chuck Robinson (Farmer on Thresher); Kalyn Bomback (Waitress); John Bluethner (State Trooper); Leslie Bais (Ted's Wife); Harry Nelken (Taxi Driver)

A young man recovering from brain damage following a tragic car accident is enlisted by a former schoolmate to act as a lookout during a robbery at the bank where he works as the night custodian.

# KILLER OF SHEEP

(MILESTONE) Producer/Director/Screenplay/Photography/Editor, Charles Burnett; Black and white; Not rated; 83 minutes; Release date: March 30, 2007. (Note: Although completed in 1973 and festival screened in 1977, this is the official U.S. opening of this film).

## Cast

Stan  **Henry Gayle Sanders**
Stan's Wife  **Kaycee Moore**
Bracy  **Charles Bracy**
Stan's Daughter  **Angela Burnett**
Eugene  **Eugene Cherry**
Stan's Son  **Jack Drummond**

Stan, a slaughterhouse worker, struggles to provide for his family in the Watts neighborhood of Los Angeles.

Kaycee Moore © MILESTONE FILMS

# FIREHOUSE DOG

(20TH CENTURY FOX) Producers, Michael Colleary, Mike Werb; Co-Producer, Michael J. Maschio; Director, Todd Holland; Screenplay, Claire-Dee Lim, Mike Werb, Michael Colleary; Photography, Victor Hammer; Designer, Tamara Deverell; Costumes, Judith R. Gellman; Editor, Scott James Wallace; Music, Jeff Cardoni; Music Supervisor, Patrick Houlihan; Visual Effects Supervisor, Kyle Menzies; Visual Effects, CORE Digital Pictures; Animal Coordinator, Ursula Brauner; Stunts, Shelley Cook; Firefighter Coordinators/Technical Advisers, David I. Smith, Alan Sutton; Associate Producer, Mitch Glick; Casting, Meg Liberman, Cami Patton; a Regency Enterprises presentation of a New Regency production; Dolby; Deluxe color; Rated PG; 111 minutes; Release date: April 4, 2007.

## Cast

| | |
|---|---|
| Shane Fahey | **Josh Hutcherson** |
| Connor Fahey | **Bruce Greenwood** |
| Trey Falcon | **Dash Mihok** |
| Zachary Hayden | **Steven Culp** |
| Joe Musto | **Bill Nunn** |
| Liz Knowles | **Bree Turner** |
| Lionel Bradford | **Scotch Ellis Loring** |
| Pep Clemente | **Mayte Garcia** |
| Terence Kahn | **Teddy Sears** |
| Rex/Dewey | **Arwen, Frodo, Rohan, Stryder** |
| Jasmine "J.J." Presley | **Hannah Lochner** |
| Captain Jessie Presley | **Claudette Mink** |
| Burr Baldwin | **Shane Daly** |
| Corbin Sellars | **Matt Cooke** |
| Felicity Hammer | **Katie Finneran** |
| Oscar | **Brandon Craggs** |
| Josh | **Joseph Zita** |
| Mrs. Renzi | **Kathryn Haggis** |
| Captain Marc Fahey | **Randy Triggs** |
| Animal Control Officer | **Carl Barlow** |
| Dapper Host | **Dan Duran** |
| Perky Co-Host | **Zoe Mugford** |
| City Official | **Eric Weinthal** |
| Lionel's Sons | **Diavion Henningham, Djano Henningham** |
| Parachute Prop Guy | **Jeffrey R. Smith** |
| Neu Hotel Doorman | **Steven Cartwright** |

and Aaron Abrams (Policeman at Bridge); James Arnold (TV Field Reporter); Dan Willmott (Electrician); B.J. McQueen (Tomato Truck Driver); Paul Stephen (Mayor); Ramona Pringle (Picnic Trophy Presenter); Magdalena Alexander (Mayor's Executive Assistant); Joseph Adam, Joanna Bennett (Ceremony Reporters); Sevag Sagherain (Trey's Limo Driver); Dave Grimshaw, Isaac Oton, Sean Lally (Crowd Members); Bob Koherr (Voice of Marc Fahey); Dorly Jean-Louis (TIA Lionel's Wife)

A 12-year-old boy is delighted to find a scruffy-looking dog, unaware that the mutt is a pampered movie star separated from his film crew.

Josh Hutcherson, Bruce Greenwood © 20TH CENTURY FOX

Rex

Rex, Josh Hutcherson

# ARE WE DONE YET?

(COLUMBIA) Producers, Ted Hartley, Ice Cube, Matt Alvarez, Todd Garner; Executive Producers, Heidi Santelli, Aaron Ray, Steve Carr, Derek Dauchy, Neil Machlis; Director, Steve Carr; Screen Story and Screenplay, Hank Nelken; Based on characters created by Steven Gary Banks, Claudia Grazioso; Based on the motion picture *Mr. Blandings Builds His Dream House*, screenplay by Norman Panama, Melvin Frank; Photography, Jack Green; Designer, Nina Ruscio; Costumes, Jori Woodman; Music, Teddy Castellucci; Music Supervisor, Spring Aspers; Editor, Craig P. Herring; Main Titles, Kurtz & Friends; Stunts, Dean Choe; Casting, Lynne Carrow, Susan Brouse; a Revolution Studios presentation of an RKO Pictures production, a Cube Vision production; Dolby; Deluxe color; Rated PG; 92 minutes; Release date: April 4, 2007.

### Cast

Nick Persons  **Ice Cube**
Suzanne Persons  **Nia Long**
Chuck Mitchell Jr.  **John C. McGinley**
Lindsey Persons  **Aleisha Allen**
Kevin Persons  **Philip Daniel Bolden**
Mr. Rooney  **Jonathan Katz**
Mrs. Rooney  **Linda Kash**
and Alexander Kalugin (Russian Contractor); Dan Joffre (Billy Pulu); Pedro Miguel Arce (Georgie Pulu); Tahj Mowry (Danny Pulu); Jacob Vargas (Mike the Plumber); Brenda Prieur (Grandma Pulu); Hayes MacArthur (Jimmy the Bartender); Magic Johnson (Himself); Colin Strange, Gavin Strange, (Persons' Twins); Ellie Mitchell (Tara Mercurio); Chistopher Gauthier (Dancing Man)

Nick Persons moves his family to the suburbs into what he hopes will be his dream house, only to have everything possible go wrong with the structure.

Philip Daniel Bolden, John C. McGinley, Ice Cube © COLUMBIA PICTURES/REVOLUTION STUDIOS

# THE REAPING

Idris Elba, Hilary Swank © WARNER BROS.

(WARNER BROS.) Producers, Joel Silver, Robert Zemeckis, Susan Downey, Herbert W. Gains; Executive Producers, Erik Olsen, Steve Richards, Bruce Berman; Co-Producer, Richard Mirisch; Director, Stephen Hopkins; Screenplay, Carey W. Hayes, Chad Hayes; Story, Brian Rousso; Photography, Peter Levy; Designer, Graham "Grace" Walker; Costumes, Jeffrey Kurland; Editor, Colby Parker Jr.; Music, John Frizzell; Visual Effects Supervisor, Richard Yuricich; Visual Effects, Double Negative, CIS Hollywood, Digiscope, Svengali Effects, Peerless Camera Co.; Stunts, Steven Ritzi; Casting, Lora Kennedy; a Dark Castle Entertainment production, presented in association with Village Roadshow Pictures; Dolby; Panavision; Technicolor; Rated R; 98 minutes; Release date: April 4, 2007.

### Cast

Prof. Katherine Winter  **Hilary Swank**
Doug  **David Morrissey**
Ben  **Idris Elba**
Loren McConnell  **AnnaSophia Robb**
and Stephen Rea (Father Costigan); William Ragsdale (Sheriff Cade); John McConnell (Mayor Brooks); David Jensen (Jim Wakeman); Yvonne Landry (Brynn Wakeman); Samuel Garland (William Wakeman); Myles Cleveland (Kyle Wakeman); Andrea Frankle (Maddie McConnell); Mark Lynch (Brody McConnell); Stuart Greer (Gordon); Lara Grice (Isabelle); Cody Sanders (Hank Small); Burgess Jenkins (David Winter); Sabrina A. Junius (Sarah Winter); Jillian Batherson (Janet); Karen Yum (Nun); Afemo Omilami (Haman); Axel C. Cartagena (Chilean Boy); Javier Ortiz Cortés (Monastery Cop); Iris Martinez (Old Chilean Woman); Axel Anderson (Blind Man); Robert Alonzo, Eddie J. Fernandez (Hazmat Workers); Abraham Henderson, Felipe Febres Rivera, Gregorio Allende, Sixta Rivera Romero (People Speaking in Tongues); Rafael Fuentes Negrón (Padre Bonilla)

Professor Katherine Winter arrives in the Louisiana bayou town of Haven in hopes of finding a rational scientific explanation for the locals who are certain they are experiencing the ten biblical plagues.

# THE HOAX

Richard Gere, Julie Delpy

(MIRAMAX) Producers, Mark Gordon, Leslie Holleran, Joshua D. Maurer, Betsy Beers, Bob Yari; Executive Producers, Anthony Katagas, Gary Levinsohn; Co-Producers, Erin Eggers, Suzanne Patmore Gibbs; Director, Lasse Hallstrom; Screenplay, William Wheeler, based on the book by Clifford Irving; Photography, Oliver Stapleton; Editor, Andrew Mondshein; Music, Carter Burwell; Music Supervisor, Tracy McKnight; Designer, Mark Ricker; Costumes, David Robinson; Casting, Laura Rosenthall, Ali Farrell; a Bob Yari Prods./Mark Gordon Co. presentation of a Hallstrom/Holleran production in association with City Entertainment; Dolby; Color; Rated R; 115 minutes; Release date: April 4, 2007.

## Cast

Clifford Irving **Richard Gere**
Dick Suskind **Alfred Molina**
Andrea Tate **Hope Davis**
Edith Irving **Marcia Gay Harden**
Shelton Fisher **Stanley Tucci**
Nina Van Pallandt **Julie Delpy**
and Eli Wallach (Noah Dietrich); John Carter (Harold McGraw); Christopher Evan Welch (Albert Vanderkamp); Zeljko Ivanek (Ralph Graves); David Aaron Baker (Brad Silber); Peter McRobbie (George Gordon Holmes); John Bedford Lloyd (Frank McCullough); Okwui Okpokwasili (Mailika Vanderkampe); Stuart Margolin (Marty Ackerman); Susan Misner, Jennifer Payne Park (Feral Girls); James Biberi (McGraw-Hill Security Guard); Bob Wiltfong (Sporting Goods Sales Person); Carlton Wilborn (Bahama's Desk Clerk); Myk Watford (Sgt. Daniels); Jeremiah Wiggins (Accountant); Judi Barton (Marion); Stephen Buck (Man with Red Necktie); John Rothman (Puffy Man); Greg Abbey (CBS Reporter); Ed Krane (Interviewer); Sam Kitchin, Don Picard, Tim Gallin (Careful Men); Ted Neustadt (D.A. Newman); Eric Yellin (Man in Blue Jeans); William Fowle (Salesman); Michael Barkann, Ian O'Malley (NBC Reporters); Antonie Knoppers (Frederick Van Pallandt); Jonathan Freeman (Thick Voice); James Riordan (Voice of Senior Nixon Advisor); Marceline Hugot (Talia Merton); Daniel Okrent, R. D. Rosen (Real Publishers); Milton Buras (Howard Hughes); Adam Auslander (Editor at Party); Thomas Mulligan (Bartender); Andrea Bertola (Ballroom Dancer); Marshall Factora (Mailman); Marc Fogel (Painter); Jon Frankel (AP Reporter); Mamie Gummer (Dana); Dennis Karagovalis, Denis McKeown (Reporters); James M. King (Bowling Alley Attendant); Reid Lamberty (ABC Reporter); Aruelio Lima (Cessna Pilot); Elizabeth Marley (Jackie Kennedy); Lisa Marie Palmieri (Socialite); Paul Thornton (Dinner Guest); Kathleen Truitt (Clifford Irving's Book Banquet Date); William Fowle (Car Salesman)

In a desperate effort to resuscitate his dormant career, writer Clifford Irving pretends that he has landed an exclusive deal to write the true story of reclusive billionaire Howard Hughes.

Richard Gere, Marcia Gay Harden

Richard Gere, Alfred Molina, Stanley Tucci © MIRAMAX FILMS

# THE TV SET

Sigourney Weaver

Ioan Gruffudd, Sigourney Weaver

(THINKFILM) Producers, Aaron Ryder, Jake Kasdan; Executive Producers, Lawrence Kasdan, Judd Apatow; Co-Producer, Ron Schmidt; Director/Screenplay, Jake Kasdan; Photography, Uta Briesewitz; Editor, Tara Timpone; Music, Michael Andrews; Music Supervisors, Manish Raval, Tom Wolfe; Designer, Jefferson Sage; Costumes, Debra McGuire; Associate Producers, Carey Dietrich, Paul Pressburger, Howard Tager; Assistant Director, Carey Dietrich; Casting, Amy McIntyre Britt, Anya Colloff; a Wexler Chronicles production; Dolby; Panavision; Technicolor; Rated R; 88 minutes; Release date: April 6, 2007.

## Cast

Mike Klein  **David Duchovny**
Lenny  **Sigourney Weaver**
Richard McCallister  **Ioan Gruffudd**
Alice  **Judy Greer**
and Fran Kranz (Zach Harper); Lindsay Sloane (Laurel Simon); Justine Bateman (Natalie Klein); Lucy Davis (Chloe McCallister); Willie Garson (Brian); M.C. Gainey (Hutch); Wendle Josepher (A.D.); Phil Rosenthal (Exec. #1, Cooper); David Doty (Exec. #2, Rose); Matt Price (Exec. #3, Berg); Simon Helberg (T.J. Goldman); Kaitlin Doubleday (Jesse Filmore); Marcia Moran (Casting Director); Andrea Martin (Becky); Charlotte Salt (Sarah); Vernee Watson-Johnson (Barbara); Molly Bryant (Peggy Wallace); Aidan Mitchell (Simon McCallister); Philip Baker Hall (Vernon Maxwell); Alan Blumenfeld (Dr. Schwartz); Kathryn Joosten (Lois); Stuart Cornfeld (Mixer); Dakota Sky (Jared); Martin Morales (Carlos); Allison Scagliotti (Bethany); Brad Campbell (Coach); Jordan Orr (Robby); Matthew Besser (Market Research Guy); Ilyse Mimoun (Market Researcher); Don Hany (Guy in Mall); Bree Turner (Carla); Amanda Anka (Publicist); Nat Faxon (Reporter); Jonathan Silverman (Himself); Bryan Law (Photographer); R.F. Daley (Guy); Robert Reinis (Chuck Wexler); Seth Green (Slut Wars Host)

Judy Greer, David Duchovny, Willie Garson

Mike Klein finds his idea for a new TV pilot, *The Wexler Chronicles*, being distorted and ruined by executives hoping to appeal to the widest demographic.

David Duchovny © THINKFILM

# GRINDHOUSE

Rose McGowan, Freddie Rodriguez, Marley Shelton, Naveen Andrews

Rose McGowan© DIMENSION FILMS

(DIMENSION) Executive Producers, Bob Weinstein, Harvey Weinstein; Designer, Steve Joyner; Costumes, Nina Proctor; Special Makeup Effects, Gregory Nicotero, Howard Berger; Casting, Mary Vernieu; a Troublemaker Studios production of a Rodriguez/Tarantino double feature; Dolby; Panavision; DV; Technicolor; Rated R; 192 minutes; Release date: April 6, 2007.

## PREVIEWS OF COMING ATTRACTIONS

*Machete*; Director/Screenplay/Photography, Robert Rodriguez;

### Cast

Danny Trejo (Machete); Jeff Fahey (The Boss); Cheech Marin (Padre Benicio Del Toro)

## PLANET TERROR

Producers, Robert Rodriguez, Quentin Tarantino, Elizabeth Avellan; Director/Screenplay/Photography/Music, Robert Rodriguez; Editors, Ethan Maniquis, Robert Rodriguez; Additional Music, Graeme Revell; Special Visual Effects, Troublemaker Digital; Visual Effects Supervisor, Ryan Tudhope; Visual Effects and Animation, The Orphanage; Line Producer, Bill Scott; Associate Producer, Tom Proper; 86 minutes.

### Cast

Cherry Darling  **Rose McGowan**
El Wray  **Freddy Rodriguez**
Dr. William Block  **Josh Brolin**
Dr. Dakota Block  **Marley Shelton**
Sheriff Hague  **Michael Biehn**
J.T.  **Jeff Fahey**
Lt. Muldoon  **Bruce Willis**
Abby  **Naveen Andrews**
Earl McGraw  **Michael Parks**
Tammy  **Stacy Ferguson**
Babysitter Twins  **Electra Avellan, Elise Avellan**
and Leroy Castanon, Katie Knighten, Andrea Lee, Christine Rose (Sickos); Cecilia Conti, Tommy Nix (Paramedics); Jason Douglas (Lewis); Carlos Gallardo (Deputy Carlos); Sammy Harte (Infected Girl); Doran Ingram (Patient); Nicky Katt (Joe); Greg Kelly (Rapist #2); John McLean (Sicko Coach); Julio Oscar Mechoso (Romey); Hung Nguyen (Dr. Crane); Skip Reissig (Skip); Johnny Reno (Sax Survivor); Troy Robinson, Derek Southers (Soldiers); Rebel Rodriguez (Tony Block); Jerili Romeo (Ramona McGraw); Felix Sabates (Dr. Felix); Tom Savini (Deputy Tolo); Quentin Tarantino (The Rapist)

Go-go dancer Cherry Darling and her ex-boyfriend El Wray are among those who team to fight off a horde of flesh-eating zombies, victims of some unorthodox goings-on at a nearby military base.

Bruce Willis

## INTERMISSION TRAILERS

*Werewolf Women of the SS*; Director/Screenplay, Rob Zombie; Photography, Phil Parmet; Music, Tyler Bates;

### Cast

Nicolas Cage (Fu Manchu); Sybil Danning (Gretchen Krupp); Michael Deak (Gun-Wielding Werewolf); Olja Hrustic, Meriah Nelson, Lorielle New (Werewolf Women); Udo Kier (Franz Hess); Test, Vladimir Kozlov (Nazi Boxers); Sheri Moon Zombie (Eva Krupp); Bill Moseley (Dr. Heinrich von Strasser); Tom Towles (Lt. Boorman)

Sydney Tamiia Poitier

*Don't*; Director/Screenplay, Edgar Wright; Music, David Arnold;

### Cast

Will Arnett (Announcer); Matthew Macfadyen (Hatchet Victim); Katie Melua (Brunette with Hatchet Victim); Simon Pegg (Bearded Cannibal); Stuart Wilson (Old Man); Jason Isaacs (Bearded Man); Lucy Punch (Running Blond Woman); Nick Frost (Baby Eater); Kevin Wilson, Nick Wilson (Twins); Rafe Spall (Ghost); Georgina Chapman, Emily Booth, MyAnna Buring (Women)

*Thanksgiving*; Director, Eli Roth; Screenplay, Eli Roth, Jeff Rendell; Photography, Milan Chadima; Music, Nathan Barr;

### Cast

Mark Bakunas (The Deputy); Michael Biehn (Sheriff Hague); Chris Briggs (The Vomiting Cousin); Jeff Fahey (The Well-Dressed Man); Daniel S. Frisch (The Human Turkey); Jay Hernandez (Bobby); Vendula Kristek (The Cheerleader); Jordan Ladd (Judy); Lilia Malkina (The Grandmother); Mike McCarty (The Rioter); Jeff Rendell (The Pilgrim); Eli Roth (Tucker); Karel Vanásek (The Grandfather); Petr Vancura (The Boyfriend); Kevin Wasner (The Turkey Pilgrim); Katherin-Ellen Zabehlicky (The Granddaughter)

## DEATH PROOF

Producers, Elizabeth Avellan, Robert Rodriguez, Erica Steinberg, Quentin Tarantino; Executive Producers, Sandra Condito, Shannon McIntosh; Director/Screenplay/Photography, Quentin Tarantino; Editor, Sally Menke; Main Titles, "The Last Race" music, Jack Nitzsche; Music Supervisor, Mary Ramos; Stunts, Jeff Dashnaw; Associate Producer, Pilar Savone; 87 minutes.

### Cast

Stuntman Mike  **Kurt Russell**
Abernathy  **Rosario Dawson**
Butterfly  **Vanessa Ferlito**
Shanna  **Jordan Ladd**
Pam  **Rose McGowan**
Jungle Julia  **Sydney Tamiia Poitier**
Kim  **Tracie Thoms**
Lee  **Mary Elizabeth Winstead**
Zoe  **Zoe Bell**
Earl McGraw  **Michael Parks**
Dov  **Eli Roth**
Nate  **Omar Doom**
Omar  **Michael Bacall**
and Melissa Arcaro (Venus Envy); Electra Avellan, Elise Avellan (Babysitter Twins); Jamie L. Dunno, Eurlyne Epper (Lanna Frank Friends); Marcy Harriell (Marcy); Nicky Katt (Store Clerk); Jonathan Loughran (Jasper); Marta Mendoza (Punky Bruiser); Tim Murphy (Tim the Bartender); James Parks (Edgar McGraw); Mikhail Sebastian (Hospital Doctor); Monica Staggs (Lanna Frank); Helen Kim (Peg); Tina Rodriguez (Juana); Quentin Tarantino (Warren)

A gang of stunt women find themselves terrorized by a psychotic veteran stunt racer.

Kurt Russell

# DISTURBIA

Aaron Yoo, Shia LaBeouf

(DREAMWORKS) Producers, Joe Medjuck, E. Bennett Walsh, Jackie Marcus; Executive Producers, Ivan Reitman, Tom Pollock; Director, D.J. Caruso; Screenplay, Christopher Landon, Carl Ellsworth; Story, Christopher Landon; Photography, Rogier Stoffers; Designer, Tom Southwell; Costumes, Marie-Sylvie Deveau; Editor, Jim Page; Music, Geoff Zanelli; Music Supervisor, Jennifer Hawks; Visual Effects Supervisor, Mark Freund; Visual Effects, Pacific Title and Art Studio; Stunts, Manny Perry; Associate Producer, Kwame L. Parker; Casting, Deborah Aquila, Tricia Wood; a Paramount release of a DreamWorks presentation in association with Cold Spring Pictures of a Montecito Picture Co. production; Dolby; Deluxe color; Rated PG-13; 104 minutes; Release date: April 13, 2007.

## Cast

Kale Brecht **Shia LaBeouf**
Robert Turner **David Morse**
Ashley Carlson **Sarah Roemer**
Julie Brecht **Carrie-Anne Moss**
Ronnie **Aaron Yoo**
Officer Gutierrez **Jose Pablo Cantillo**
Daniel Brecht **Matt Craven**
Detective Parker **Viola Davis**
Mr. Carlson **Kevin Quinn**
Mrs. Carlson **Elyse Mirto**
Senor Gutierrez **Rene Rivera**
Minnie Tyco **Amanda Walsh**
Judge **Charles Carroll**
and Brandon Caruso, Luciano Rauso, Daniel Caruso (Greenwood Boys); Suzanne Rico, Kent Shocknek (News Anchors); Gillian Shure (Turner's Club Girl); Dominic Daniel (Policeman); Lisa Tobin (Big Wheel Mom); Cindy Lou Adkins (Mrs. Greenwood)

Sentenced to house arrest, teenager Kale Brecht starts spying on his neighbors to pass the time, leading him to suspect that one of them may have committed murder.

Shia LaBeouf

David Morse, Carrie-Anne Moss © DREAMWORKS/COLD SPRING PICTURES

Shia LaBeouf, Sarah Roemer

# LONELY HEARTS

(GOLDWYN) Producers, Holly Wiersma, Boaz Davidson; Executive Producers, John Thompson, Avi Lerner, Danny Dumbort, Trevor Short, Josef Lautenschlager, Andrews Thiesmeyer, Manfred Heid, Gerd Koechlin, Randall Emmet, George Furla; Co-Producers, Kathryn Himoff, Sidney Sherman; Director/Screenplay, Todd Robinson; Photography, Peter Levy; Designer, Jon Gary Steele; Costumes, Jacqueline West; Editor, Kathryn Himoff; Music, Mychael Danna; Music Supervisor, Ashley Miller; Casting, Phyllis Huffmann; a Nu Image/Millennium Films presentation of an Equity Pictures Medienfonds Gmbh production; Dolby; Super 35 Widescreen; Color; Rated R; 107 minutes; Release date: April 13, 2007.

Scott Caan, James Gandolfini, John Travolta

### Cast

Elmer Robinson **John Travolta**
Charles Hildebrandt **James Gandolfini**
Martha Beck **Salma Hayek**
Ray Fernandez **Jared Leto**
Rene Fodie **Laura Dern**
Detective Reilly **Scott Caan**
Janet Long **Alice Krige**
D.A. Hunt **Michael Gaston**
Eastman **Bruce MacVittie**
Eddie Robinson **Dan Byrd**
Detective Tooley **Andrew Wheeler**
Delphine Downing **Dagmara Dominczyk**
Chief MacSwain **John Doman**
Rainelle Downing **Bailee Madison**
Ida **Ellen Travolta**
Officer Chetnick **Jason Gray-Stanford**
Foreman **Sam Travolta**
Young Black Man **James Martin Roberts**
Bank Manager **Kristian Truelsen**
Sara Long **Christa Campbell**
Warden Broady **Marc MacAulay**
and Todd Terry (Thief); Steve Maye (Michigan Cop); Shannon Murphy (Patty Forsythe); Michael Rispoli (Coroner); Nick Loren (Detective January); Jonathan Rau (Uniformed Cop); Karl Anthony (Hotel Clerk); Valerie Grant (Mrs. Clayman); Matt Huffman (Mrs. Clayman's Son); Arian Ash (Marian Duff); Gerald Owens (Postmaster); Petrus Antonius (Landlord); Jeff Farley (Minister); Lauren Leech (Teenage Girl); Allison McKay (Mrs. Paterson); Jack Swanson (Fruit Stand Attendant); Bill Kelley (Rene's Father); Heather Dawn (MacSwain's Secretary); Margaret Travolta (Mineola Dispatcher); Rachel Reynolds (Airplane Passenger); Rachel Specter (Janice); Jimmy Leeward (Pilot); Caroline Ross, Traci Robinson (Prison Matrons); Tom Chapman (Framer); Allen Walls (Featured Dancer)

Salma Hayek

New York detectives Elmer Robinson and Charles Hildebrandt try to catch a psychotic couple luring lonely women to their doom.

Laura Dern © SAMUEL GOLDWYN FILMS

# YEAR OF THE DOG

Thomas McCarthy, Laura Dern

(PARAMOUNT VANTAGE) Producers, Mike White, Ben LeClair, Dede Gardner; Executive Producers, Nan Morales, Brad Pitt; Director/Screenplay, Mike White; Photography, Tim Orr; Designers, Daniel Bradford, Nancy Steiner; Costumes, Stacy M. Horn; Editor, Dody Dorn; Music, Christophe Beck; Visual Effects, Invisible Effects; Visual Effects Supervisor, Dick Edwards; Animal Coordinator/Head Trainer, Ursula Brauner; Casting, Meredith Tucker; a Rip Cord/Plan B production; Dolby; Deluxe color; Rated PG-13; 97 minutes; Release date: April 13, 2007.

## Cast

Peggy **Molly Shannon**
Bret **Laura Dern**
Layla **Regina King**
Pier **Thomas McCarthy**
Newt **Peter Sarsgaard**
Al **John C. Reilly**
Robin **Josh Pais**
Lissie **Amy Schlagel, Zoe Schlagel**
Don **Dale Godboldo**
Holly **Inara George**
Trishelle **Liza Weil**
Pound Employee **Jon Shere**
Al's Girlfriend **Christy Lynn Moore**
Audrey **Audrey Wasilewski**
Brenda **Brenda Canela**
Craig **Craig Cackowski**
and Steve Berg (Steve); Susan Mackin (Susan); Chuck Duffy (Jeff); Sonya Eddy (Nurse); Ursula Brauner (Dog Owner); Giddle Partridge (Blonde Floozie); Benjamin Koesling, Dominik Koesling (Benjy)

When her beloved beagle dies, lonely office worker Peggy goes overboard in her dog obsession, hoping to fill the hole left in her life.

Molly Shannon, Pencil © PARAMOUNT VANTAGE

Molly Shannon, Peter Sarsgaard

John C. Reilly, Molly Shannon

# PERFECT STRANGER

(COLUMBIA) Producer, Elaine Goldsmith-Thomas; Executive Producers, Ron Bozman, Deborah Schindler, Charles Newirth; Director, James Foley; Screenplay, Todd Komarnicki; Story, Jon Bokenkamp; Photography, Anastas Michos; Designer, Bill Groom; Costumes, Renée Ehrlich Kalfus; Music, Antonio Pinto; Music Supervisor, Denise Luiso; Co-Producers, Stephanie Langhoff, Daniel A. Thomas; Casting, Todd Thaler; a Revolution Studios presentation; Dolby; Super 35 Widescreen; Technicolor; Rated R; 109 minutes; Release date: April 13, 2007.

Bruce Willis

### Cast

Rowena Price **Halle Berry**
Harrison Hill **Bruce Willis**
Miles Haley **Giovanni Ribisi**
Narron **Richard Portnow**
Cameron **Gary Dourdan**
Lt. Tejada **Florencia Lozano**
Grace **Nicki Aycox**
Elizabeth Clayton **Kathleen Chalfant**
Senator Sachs **Gordon MacDonald**
Josie **Daniella Van Graas**
Mia Hill **Paula Miranda**
Esmeralda **Patti D'Arbanville**
Gina **Clea Lewis**
Bethany **Tamara Feldman**
Jon Kirshenbaum **Gerry Becker**
Kenneth Phelps **Jared Burke**
Jesse Drake **Jay Wilkison**
Gunnar Hope **Aaron Nauta**
Toni **Jane Bradbury**
Capital Policeman **Jeffrey Bellamy**

Giovanni Ribisi, Halle Berry © COLUMBIA PICTURES

and Charles Thomas (Coroner); Jason Antoon (Bill Patel); Heidi Klum (Herself); Daniel A. Thomas (District Attorney); Jack Mentz (Defense Attorney); Liliane Thomas (Jury Foreman); Todd Komarnicki (CSI Witness); Daniel Cheswick (CSI Guy); James Mazzola (CSI Analyst); Emma Heming (Donna); Kristy Hinze (Carol Whittier); Jay Coyle (Banker); Stephen Eads (Photographer's Assistant); Michael Tolan (Judge); Yvonna Kopacz (Ro's Mother); Jacqueline Cannon (Ro's Mother, Older); Vincent Lamberti (Ro's Father); Maya N. Blake (9-Year-Old Ro); Nadine Jacobson (9-Year-Old Grace); Jonathan Ave, Thomas Sullivan (Reebok Executives); Pat Pritchett Lewis (Human Resources Woman); Gaetano Lisi (Newsstand Vendor); Brandhyze Stanley (Coffee Stand Vendor); Maurice Ballard (Security Guard); Justin Ritson (Man on Elevator); Lauren Potter, Robert L. Haber, Mitch Giannunzio (Clients); John Heinlein (NYPD Computer Tech); Mike O'Brien (Man in Bar); Joe Paparone (Hill's Doorman); James "D-Train" Williams (Singer)

Tracing the emails of her murdered friend to ad exec Harrison Hill, reporter Rowena Price gets a job at his company, in hopes of finding out if he is indeed guilty of the crime.

Bruce Willis, Halle Berry

# FRACTURE

(NEW LINE CINEMA) Producer, Charles Weinstock; Executive Producers, Liz Glotzer, Hawk Koch, Toby Emmerich; Co-Producer, Louise Rosner; Director, Gregory Hoblit; Screenplay, Daniel Pyne, Glenn Gers; Story, Daniel Pyne; Photography, Kramer Morgenthau; Designer, Paul Eads; Costumes, Elisabetta Beraldo; Editor, David Rosenbloom; Music, Mychael Danna, Jeff Danna; Associate Producers, Michael Disco, Samuel J. Brown; Casting, Deborah Aquila, Trisha Wood, Jennifer Smith; a Castle Rock, Charles Weinstock production; Dolby; Super 35 Widescreen; Deluxe color; Rated R; 112 minutes; Release date: April 20, 2007.

Billy Burke © NEW LINE PRODUCTIONS

## Cast

Ted Crawford **Anthony Hopkins**
Willy Beachum **Ryan Gosling**
Joe Lobruto **David Strathairn**
Nikki Gardner **Rosamund Pike**
Jennifer Crawford **Embeth Davidtz**
Lt. Rob Nunally **Billy Burke**
Detective Flores **Cliff Curtis**
Judge Robinson **Fiona Shaw**
Judge Gardner **Bob Gunton**
Norman Foster **Josh Stamberg**
Judge Moran **Xander Berkeley**
Mona **Zoe Kazan**
Resident **Judith Scott**
Ciro **Carlos Cervantes**
Dr. Marion Kang **Petrea Burchard**
Assistant Hotel Manager **Garz Chan**
Gladys **Wendy Cutler**
Lee Gardner **Larry Sullivan**
Peg Gardner **Valerie Dillman**
Uniform Cop **Gonzalo Menendez**
Opera Singer **Vivica Genaux**
and Cooper Thornton (Public Defender); Lyle Kanouse (Messenger); Sandra Prosper (Karla); Monica Garcia (Crawford's Secretary); Joe Spano (Judge Joseph Pincus); Peter Breitmayer (NTSB Guy); Mirron E. Willis (Moran's Bailiff); David Purdham (Burt Wooton); John Littlefield (Cop); Lou Reyes (SWAT Medic); Rainy Kerwin (Wooton Sims Receptionist); R.J. Chambers, Eugene Collier (Bailiffs); Tom Virtue (Attorney Apley); Gunter Simon, Frank Torres (Orderlies); Payton Koch, Cooper Koch, Sophie Hoblit, Caroline Weinstock, Alexander Weinstock (Kids); Michael Khmourov (Russian Man); Julia Emelin (Russian Woman); Yorgo Constantine (Public Defender for the Russians); Alla Korot (Russian Translator); Jeff Enden (Detective); Kaily Smith (Lobruto's Secretary); Retta (Evidence Room Cop)

Rosamund Pike, Ryan Gosling

Anthony Hopkins

Willy Beachum assumes he has been handed an open-and-shut case prosecuting engineer Ted Crawford for shooting his wife, until he realizes that the crafty defendant has carefully plotted the crime in order to establish reasonable doubt.

# IN THE LAND OF WOMEN

(WARNER INDEPENDENT PICTURES) Producers, Steve Golin, David Kanter; Executive Producer, Lawrence Kasdan; Co-Producer, Barbara Kelly; Director/Screenplay, Jon Kasdan; Photography, Paul Cameron; Editor, Carol Littleton; Designer, Sandy Cochrane; Costumes, Trish Keating; Music, Stephen Trask; Casting, Amanda Mackey Johnson, Cathy Sandrich Gelfond, Wendy Weidman; a Castle Rock Entertainment presentation of an Anonymous Content production; Dolby; Panavision; Technicolor; Rated PG-13; 97 minutes; Release date: April 20, 2007.

### Cast

Carter Webb **Adam Brody**
Lucy Hardwicke **Kristen Stewart**
Sarah Hardwicke **Meg Ryan**
Phyllis **Olympia Dukakis**
Paige Hardwicke **Makenzie Vega**
Sofia Buñuel **Elena Anaya**
Nelson Hardwick **Clark Gregg**
Agnes Webb **JoBeth Williams**
and Kelsey Keel, Danielle Savre, Gina Mantegna (Teenage Girls); Rob Reinis (Avi Rosenberg); Dustin Milligan (Eric Watts); Graham Wardle (Gabe Foley); Elise Gatien (Tiffany); Christine Danielle (Tanya); Jeff Cunningham (Howard Portchnik); Tamara Lovegrove, Brittany Starling (Party Girls); Ilyse Mimoun (Nelson's Assistant); Karin Konoval (Dr. Ida Rosen); Ginnifer Goodwin (Janey)

Dumped by his girlfriend, aspiring writer Carter Webb moves to suburban Michigan, where he finds himself involved with housewife Sarah Hardwick and her adolescent daughter.

Meg Ryan, Adam Brody © WARNER INDEPENDENT PICTURES

# STEPHANIE DALEY

Jim Gaffigan, Amber Tamblyn, Melissa Leo © HERE!/REGENT

(REGENT) Producers, Sean Costello, Lynette Howell, Samara Koffler, Jen Roskind; Executive Producers, Tilda Swinton, Doug Dey; Co-Producer, Terry Leonard; Director/Screenplay, Hilary Brougher; Photography, David Morrison; Editor, Keith Reamer; Music, David Mansfield; Music Supervisor, Liz Regan; Designer, Sharon Lomofsky; Costumes, Kurt and Bart; Casting, Nicole Arbusto, Joy Dickson; a RedBone Films/Silverwood Films presentation; Dolby; Deluxe color, HD-to-35mm; Rated R; 92 minutes; Release date: April 20, 2007.

### Cast

Lydie Crane **Tilda Swinton**
Stephanie Daley **Amber Tamblyn**
Paul **Timothy Hutton**
Frank **Denis O'Hare**
Miri **Melissa Leo**
Joe **Jim Gaffigan**
Jane **Deirdre O'Connell**
Rhana **Halley Feiffer**
Mr. Thomas **Neal Huff**
Corey White **Kel O'Neill**
Jack Hutchinson **John Ellison Conlee**
Jeff **Vincent Piazza**
Satin **Caitlin Van Zandt**
Mrs. Werner, Health Teacher **Marceline Hugot**
and Kaiulani Lee (Pastor); Novella Nelson (Dr. Lynn); Susan Ferrara (Reporter); Gene Galusha (Mr. Gilchrist); Susan Kerner (Birth Class Instructor); Trisha LaFache (Karen); Marion McCorry (Mrs. Gilchrist); Michael Nostrand (Intern); Ali Reza (Mr. Scalesi); Adelia Saunders (Rhana's Sister); Constance Wu (Jenn); Harry Zittel (Pratt); Jenny Nay (Teri Thomas); Jullian Cuzzolino (Elizabeth); Dan McCabe (Teenage Boy); Sage Francis (Corey's Friend); David Morrison (Corey's Lawyer); William Malley (Steph's Lawyer)

16-year-old Stephanie Daley is accused of killing her newborn child.

# THE INVISIBLE

Marcia Gay Harden, Justin Chatwin

(HOLLYWOOD PICTURES) Producers, Roger Birnbaum, Gary Barber, Jonathan Glickman, Neal Edelstein, Mike Macari; Executive Producers, William S. Beasley, Peter Possne; Co-Producers, Erin Stam, Rebekah Rudd; Director, David S. Goyer; Screenplay, Mick Davis, Christine Roum; Based upon the novel *Den Osynlige* by Mats Wahl and the Swedish film of the same name; Photography, Gabriel Beristain; Designer, Carlos Barbosa; Costumes, Tish Monaghan; Music, Marco Beltrami; Music Supervisor, Alexandra Patsavas; Editor, Conrad Smart; Visual Effects, Gray Matter Visual Effects; Casting, Juel Bestrop, Seth Yanklewitz; Vancouver Casting, Coreen Mayrs, Heike Brandstatter; a Spyglass Entertainment presentation of a Birnbaum/Barber production; Dolby; Super 35 Widescreen; Technicolor; Rated PG-13; 97 minutes; Release date: April 27, 2007.

## Cast

Nick Powell  **Justin Chatwin**
Annie Newton  **Margarita Levieva**
Diane Powell  **Marcia Gay Harden**
Pete Egan  **Chris Marquette**
Marcus Bohem  **Alex O'Loughlin**
Det. Brian Larson  **Callum Keith Rennie**
Det. Kate Tunney  **Michelle Harrison**
Matty  **Ryan Kennedy**
Dean  **Andrew Francis**
and P. Lynn Johnson (Sharon Egan); Serge Houde (Martin Egan); Desiree Zurowski (Lindy Newton); Mark Houghton (Jack Newton); Alex Ferris (Victor Newton); Tania Saulnier (Suzie); Kevin McNulty (Principal Whitcliff); Laara Sadiq (Ms. Barclay); Aleks Holtz (Football Jock); Cory Monteith (Jimmy); Maggie Ma (Danielle); Sefton Fincham (Sleeping Kid); Ron Selmour (Guillaume); Colby Wilson (Mechanic); Mi-Jung Lee (Newscaster); Jason Diablo (Firefighter); Leanne Adachi (EMT); Chris Shields (CSI Detective); Panou (K-9 Cop); Michael Tales (Young Cop); Christopher Heyerdahl (Dr. Woland); Andrew Coghlan (Trauma Resident)

Justin Chatwin, Margarita Levieva

Callum Keith Rennie, Michelle Harrison © HOLLYWOOD PICTURES

Margarita Levieva, Justin Chatwin

Left for dead, a teen stuck in limbo must solve the mystery behind his killing before he crosses into the beyond.

# NEXT

(PARAMOUNT) Producers, Nicolas Cage, Norm Golightly, Todd Garner, Arne L. Schmidt, Graham King; Executive Producers, Gary Goldman, Jason Koornick, Benjamin Waisbren; Director, Lee Tamahori; Screenplay, Gary Goldman, Jonathan Hensleigh, Paul Bernbaum; Screen Story, Gary Goldman, based on the short story "The Golden Man" by Philip K. Dick; Photography, David Tattersall; Designer, William Sandell; Costumes, Sanja Milkovic Hays; Music, Mark Isham; Editor, Christian Wagner; Special Effects Supervisors, Hans Metz, Clay Pinney; Casting, Denise Chamian; a Revolution Studios and IEG Virtual Studios presentation of a Saturn Films/Broken Road production; Dolby; Deluxe color; Rated PG-13; 96 minutes; Release date: April 27, 2007.

Nicolas Cage, Peter Falk

## Cast

Cris Johnson  **Nicolas Cage**
Callie Ferris  **Julianne Moore**
Liz Cooper  **Jessica Biel**
Mr. Smith  **Thomas Kretschmann**
Cavanaugh  **Tory Kittles**
Security Chief Roybal  **José Zúñiga**
Wisdom  **Jim Beaver**
Jeff Baines  **Jason Butler Harner**
Irv  **Peter Falk**
Kendall  **Michael Trucco**
Mr. Jones  **Enzo Cilenti**
Miss Brown  **Laetitia Danielle**
Mr. Green  **Nicolas Pajon**
Mr. White  **Sergej Trifunovic**
Davis  **Charles Chun**
Showgirl  **Patricia Prata**
Emcee  **Jon Hughes**
Man from Korea  **Jack Ong**
Girl with Necklace  **Alice Kim Cage**
Old Lady in Casino  **Edith Fields**
Blackjack Dealer  **Lorilynn Failor**
Pretty Blonde  **Jessica Barth**
Blonde's Boyfriend  **Logan Christopher**
Drunk Man  **Richard Kay**
Cashier Girl  **Bonita Friedericy**
Gunman  **Danny Downey**
Security Guard  **Michael Runyard**
and Adam Lieberman (Diner Manager); Miranda Frigon (Diner Waitress); Sam Kim, Max Lee (Shadow Techs); Thomas Siyuja Sr. (Shaman); Mavis Jones, Nuce Marshall, Dimitri Watahomigie, Kaynece Watahomigie (Havasupai Children); Paul Rae (Road Crew Foreman); Hinetoa (Dead Girl); Jeff Michael, Lisa Joyner (Themselves); Dean Cudworth (JTTF Sniper Agent); Chris Palermo (SWAT Commander); John Scanlon (Helicopter Pilot)

Jessica Biel, Nicolas Pajon © PARAMOUNT/REVOLUTION STUDIOS

A Vegas magician who has the ability to see a few minutes into the future is enlisted by government agent Callie Ferris in hopes that he can use his special power to stop a terrorist attack on Los Angeles.

Tory Kittles, Julianne Moore

# WAITRESS

Keri Russell, Andy Griffith

(FOX SEARCHLIGHT) Producer, Michael Roiff; Executive Producer, Todd King; Director/Screenplay, Adrienne Shelly; Photography, Matthew Irving; Editor, Annette Davey; Costumes, Ariyela Wald-Cohain; Music, Andrew Hollander; Music Supervisors, Greg Danylyshyn, Gerry Cueller; Designer, Ramsey Avery; Casting, Sunday Boling, Meg Morman; a Night & Day Pictures production; Dolby; Color; Rated PG-13; 107 minutes; Release date: May 2, 2007.

Keri Russell, Nathan Fillion

## Cast

Jenna  **Keri Russell**
Dr. Pomatter  **Nathan Fillion**
Becky  **Cheryl Hines**
Dawn  **Adrienne Shelly**
Cal  **Lew Temple**
Ogie  **Eddie Jemison**
Earl  **Jeremy Sisto**
Old Joe  **Andy Griffith**
Francine Pomatter  **Darby Stanchfield**
Exhausted Mother  **Heidi Sulzman**
Nurse Norma  **Lauri Johnson**
Dr. Lily Mueller  **Sarah Hunley**
Hospital Nurse  **Cindy Drummond**
Minister  **Nathan Dean**
Doctor's Assistant  **Caroline Fogarty**
Pregnant Women  **Christy Taylor, Jennifer Walsh**
Obnoxious Toddler  **Hunter King**
Char  **Donna Leslie**
Ethel  **Nora Paradiso**
Jim  **Danny Allen**
Cake Man  **Andy Ostroy**
and Hailey Parker, Rylee Stefanelli, Bella Stromel (Lulu Newborn); Kira Grace (Lulu at 3 Months); Elaine Levine, Doreen Powell (Women in Pie Contest); Sophie Ostroy (Lulu as Toddler); Eleya Avery-Ault, Evan King, Jesse Schneider, Zoe Schneider, Henry Arthur Smith (Toddlers in Diner); Mackenzie King (Flower Girl)

Cheryl Hines, Keri Russell, Adrienne Shelly

Waitress Jenna's fear that she is trapped in her marriage to her controlling spouse is compounded when she discovers that she is pregnant.

Jeremy Sisto, Keri Russell © 20TH CENTURY FOX

# SPIDER-MAN 3

Bryce Dallas Howard, Topher Grace © COLUMBIA PICTURES

(COLUMBIA) Producers, Laura Ziskin, Avi Arad, Grant Curtis; Executive Producers, Joseph M. Caracciolo, Stan Lee, Kevin Feige; Director, Sam Raimi; Screenplay, Sam Raimi, Ivan Raimi, Alvin Sargent; Screen Story, Sam Raimi, Ivan Raimi; Based on the Marvel Comic Book by Stan Lee and Steve Ditko; Photography, Bill Pope; Designers, Neil Spisak, J. Michael Riva; Costumes, James Acheson; Music, Christopher Young; Original Music Themes, Danny Elfman; Editor, Bob Murawski; Visual Effects Supervisor, Scott Stoydyk; a Marvel Studios/Laura Ziskin production; Dolby; Panavision; Deluxe color; Rated PG-13; 139 minutes; Release date: May 4, 2007.

Kirsten Dunst, Tobey Maguire

## Cast

Spider-Man/Peter Parker  **Tobey Maguire**
Mary Jane Watson  **Kirsten Dunst**
New Goblin/Harry Osborn  **James Franco**
Sandman/Flint Marko  **Thomas Haden Church**
Venom/Eddie Brock  **Topher Grace**
Gwen Stacy  **Bryce Dallas Howard**
May Parker  **Rosemary Harris**
J. Jonah Jameson  **J.K. Simmons**
Captain Stacy  **James Cromwell**
Emma Marko  **Theresa Russell**
Dr. Curt Connors  **Dylan Baker**
Joseph "Robbie" Robertson  **Bill Nunn**
Maitre D'  **Bruce Campbell**
Miss Brant  **Elizabeth Banks**
Hoffman  **Ted Raimi**
Penny Marko  **Perla Haney-Jardine**
Green Goblin/Norman Osborn  **Willem Dafoe**
Ben Parker  **Cliff Robertson**
and Elya Baskin (Mr. Ditkovitch); Mageina Tovah (Ursula); John Paxton (Houseman); Becky Ann Baker (Mrs. Stacy); Stan Lee (Man in Times Square); Michael Papajohn (Dennis Carradine/Carjacker); Joe Manganiello (Flash Thompson); Hal Fishman (Anchorman); Lucy Gordon (Jennifer Dugan); Steve Valentine (Photographer); Tim Maculan (Play Director); Marc Vann (Play Producer); Joe Bays (Jazz Club Manager); Gregg Daniel (Precinct Detective); Rogelio Ramos (Emergency Room Doctor); Timothy Patrick Quill (Crane Operator); Menachem Mendel Boymelgreen, Nasir Stewart, Austin Hendrickson, Taylor Hemhauser (Kids in Times Square); Kathryn Bryding (Woman Outside Theater); Joe Virzi (Police Detective); Bill E. Rogers, Mike Alexander (New Jersey State Policeman); April D. Parker, Edward Padilla, Robert Curtis Brown, Terrell Clayton, Carolyn Neff, Christina Cindrich (Test Site Technicians); Sonya Maddox (ICU Nurse); Andre Blake (Crane Disaster Radio Policeman); Derrick Thomas (Cop at Crane Disaster); Jessi Collins (Mary Jane's Replacement); Michael McLaughlin (Boy at Keys to the City Ceremony); Anne Gartlan (Councilwoman); Emilio Rivera, Keith Woulard (Policemen at Sand Truck); Rey Gallegos (Armored Car Driver); Jim Coope, Dean Edwards, Margaret Laney (Newsstand Patrons); Toni Wynne (Congratulatory Woman at *Daily Bugle*); Aimee Miles (Coffee Shop Waitress); Tanya Sinovec (Jazz Club Waitress); Mark Kubr (Jazz Club Bouncer); Emma Raimi (Girl with Camera); Lorne Raimi, Henry Raimi (Boys at the Final Battle); Samantha Ressler (Girl at the Final Battle); Alan Cohn, Dan Callahan, Ronald King, Carol Chaikin, Daniel Cummings, Vance Hammond (Jazz Club Musicians)

Infected by an alien fungus, Spider-Man finds his darker side overwhelming him just as the city is terrorized by Sandman, an escaped convict transformed into a super villain by a scientific accident, and Venom, a jealous reporter who acquires similar evil powers to Spider-Man. Third in the Columbia series, following *Spider-Man* (2002) and *Spider-Man 2* (2004), with most of the principals returning to their roles.

# LUCKY YOU

Eric Bana, Drew Barrymore

(WARNER BROS.) Producers, Denise Di Novi, Curtis Hanson, Carol Fenelon; Executive Producer, Bruce Berman; Co-Producer, Mari Jo Winlker-Ioffreda; Director, Curtis Hanson; Screenplay, Eric Roth, Curtis Hanson; Story, Eric Roth; Photography, Peter Deming; Designer, Clay A. Griffith; Costumes, Michael Kaplan; Music, Christopher Young; Music Supervisor, CaroL Fenelon; Editors, Craig Kitson, William Kerr; Casting, Mali Finn; a Deuce Three/Di Novi Pictures production, presented in association with Village Roadshow Pictures; Dolby; Panavision; Technicolor; Rated PG-13; 123 minutes; Release date: May 4, 2007.

Charles Martin Smith © WARNER BROS.

## Cast

Huck Cheever  **Eric Bana**
Billie Offer  **Drew Barrymore**
L.C. Cheever  **Robert Duvall**
Suzanne Offer  **Debra Messing**
Ready Eddie  **Horatio Sanz**
Roy Durucher  **Charles Martin Smith**
Lester  **Saverio Guerra**
Michelle Carson  **Jean Smart**
Billie's Admirer  **Joey Kern**
Ginger  **Delaine Yates**
Pawnbroker  **Phyllis Somerville**
Telephone Jack  **Robert Downey, Jr.**
Larita  **Yetta Gottesman**
Bobby Basketball  **Danny Hoch**
Chinese Restaurant Waiter  **Kenny Cau**
Carrie  **Lindsay MacFarland**
Frank Belando  **Bill May**
Sharkey  **Omar Benson Miller**
Room Service Waiter  **Jack Younger**
Roy's Guys  **Tracy Howe, Sonny Surowiec**
Gil Edwards  **Matt Savage**
Gary  **Mykel Shannon Henkins**
Lounge Singer  **Madeleine Peyroux**
Chico Banh  **Kelvin Han Yee**
and Joseph A. Garcia (Poker Player); Alexander Kuznetsov (Alexander Lemke); Hans Howes (Big Buckle Iverson); Bradford English (Tommy the Poker Host); Maya Hazen (Kelly); Daniel Doble (Edwin Daniels); Ed Refuerzo (Filipino Player); Elisabeth Granli (Cocktail Waitress at First Table); Spencer Conner (Cowboy); Sam Farha, Chau Giang, Barry Greenstein, Jason Lester, Ted Forrest, Minh Ly, John Murphy, Erick Lindgren, Daniel Negreanu, Jack Binion, Doyle Brunson, Johnny Chan, Hoyt Corkins, Antonio Esfandiari, Chris "Jesus" Ferguson, Dan Harrington, Phil Hellmuth Jr., Karina Jett, John Juanda, Mike Matusow, Eric Seidel, Mimi Tran, Marsha Waggoner, Robert Williamson III, Cyndy Violette (Themselves); Dara Khy, Joe Witherell, Sheila Hanson, Darunee Doa Hale, Lisa Glossop, Danny Sanchez (Bellagio Dealers); Sam O'Connor (Old Man); Pat Calihan (Man in Cowboy Hat); Tina Schafer (Woman with Straight); Crystal Simanek (Cocktail Waitress); Robby Bostick (Poker Room Host); Olivia Tracey (Isabel); Jimmy Williams, Charlene Sperske, Kyle D. Morris (Dealers); Bill McKinney (Satellite Cashier); Jennifer Harman (Shannon Kincaid); Michael Shannon (Ray Zumbro); Mark Tymchyshyn (Tournament Official); Norris Watsky (Elderly Dealer); Shawn Parr (TV Commentator); Francine Beers (Elderly Player); Laasa Howard (Young Player); Richard Assad (Karim Kasai); Evan Jones (Jason Keyes); John Henningan (Ralph Kaczynski); David Oppenheim (Josh Cohen); Eddie Hill (Washroom Attendant); Ken Davitian, Bob Pepper, Brian Ruppert, Curtis L. Walker (Poker Players)

Professional poker player Huck Cheever hopes to earn $10,000 to buy his way into the World Series poker championships.

# DAY NIGHT DAY NIGHT

(IFC FIRST TAKE) Producers, Julia Loktev, Melanie Judd, Jessica Levin; Director/Screenplay, Julia Loktev; Photography, Benoit Debie; Editors, Michael Taylor, Julia Loktev; Designer, Kelly McGehee; Costumes, Rabiah Troncelliti; Casting, Raphael Laski; a FaceFilm (U.S.)/ZDF (Germany) production in association with Arte (France); American-German-French; Dolby; Color; Not rated; 94 minutes; American release date: May 9, 2007.

Luisa Williams

Luisa Williams (right) © IFC FIRST TAKE

## Cast

She **Luisa Williams**
Commander **Josh P. Weinstein**
Organizers **Gareth Saxe, Nyambi Nyambi**
Bombmaker **Frank Dattolo**
Bombaker's Assistant **Annemarie Lawless**
Driver **Tschi Hun Kim**
Flirt **Richard Morant**
and Jennifer Camilo, Rosemary Apolinaris, Jennifer Restrepo, Julissa Perez (Bathroom Girls)

A young woman is sent by a terrorist organization to Manhattan's Times Square with the intention of detonating the explosives within her backpack.

# GEORGIA RULE

(UNIVERSAL) Producers, James G. Robinson, David Robinson; Executive Producers, Guy McElwaine, Michael Besman, Kevin Reidy; Director, Garry Marshall; Screenplay, Mark Andrus; Photography, Karl Walter Lindenlaub; Designer, Albert Brenner; Costumes, Gary Jones; Music, John Debney; Music Supervisor, Dawn Solér; Casting, Pam Dixon Mickelson; Co-Producer, Bonnie Timmermann; a James G. Robinson presentation of a Morgan Creek production; Dolby; Super 35 Widescreen; Technicolor; Rated R; 113 minutes; Release date: May 11, 2007.

## Cast

Georgia **Jane Fonda**
Rachel **Lindsay Lohan**
Lilly **Felicity Huffman**
and Dermot Mulroney (Dr. Simon Ward); Cary Elwes (Arnold); Garrett Hedlund (Harlan); Hector Elizondo (Izzy); Dylan McLaughlin (Sam); Zachary Gordon (Ethan); Laurie Metcalf (Paula); *Townspeople*: Tereza Stanislav (Violin Teacher); Fred Applegate, Cynthia Ferrer (Townies); Destiney Moore (Waitress); Andreana Betan (Izzy's Niece); Timothy Henning (Liquor Store Owner); Stephanie Caswell (Coffee Shop Waitress); *Simon's Office*: Rance Howard (Dog Bite Man); Alexander Hope (Fern); Shea Curry (Pig Owner Melody); Paul Williams (Mr. Wells); Beth Kennedy (Fat Dog Owner); Sarah Lilly (Pregnant Cat Woman); Scott Marshall (Man Kissing Dog); Zettie M. Ronistal (Violet Seymoure); Cat Stock (Girl with Rabbit); Sandra DeNise (Baby's Mama); Julianne Rose Hall (Ear Biting Baby); *Mormons*: Christine Lakin (Grace Cunningham); Chelsea Swain (June Smith); Mandy Medlin (Mandy); Lauren McLaughlin (Lauren); Michelle Matthews (Michelle); Katherine Helms (Drummer Girl); Anna White (Choir Leader); Jennifer Deminco, Maggie Henry, Nathan Moore, Pat Williams, Adrian Lee Borden, Steve Shane (Choir Students); *July 4th BBQ*: Barbara Marshall (Store Owner); Krista Goodsit (Juggler); Cassie Rowell (Potato Queen); Lily Marshall-Fricker (Lily); Charlotte Marshall-Fricker (Charlotte); Shane Partlow (Cowboy); Sam Marshall (Boy Kicker); Ethan Marshall (Boy with Popsicle); Thomas Henry (Accordion Player)

In an effort to control her rebellious teen daughter, Lilly brings her to Idaho to stay with her demanding grandmother, where all three women hope to come to an understanding of one another.

Felicity Huffman, Jane Fonda © UNIVERSAL PICTURES

# THE WENDELL BAKER STORY

Seymour Cassel, Luke Wilson © THINKFILM

(THINKFILM) Producers, Mark Johnson, David Bushell; Executive Producers, David Bergstein, Tracee Stanley-Newell, Ray Angelic; Directors, Luke Wilson, Andrew Wilson; Screenplay, Luke Wilson; Photography, Steve Mason; Designer, David Bomba; Costumes, Estee Stanley; Editor, Harvey Rosenstock; Music, Aaron Zigman; Music Supervisor, John Bissell; a Mobius Entertainment production in association with MHF Zweite Academy Film production; American-German; Dolby; Deluxe color; Rated PG-13; 102 minutes; Release date: May 18, 2007.

## Cast

Wendell Baker **Luke Wilson**
Neil King **Owen Wilson**
and Kris Kristofferson (L.R. Nasher); Eva Mendes (Doreen); Seymour Cassel (Boyd Fullbright); Harry Dean Stanton (Skip Summers); Eddie Griffin (McTeague); Jacob Vargas (Reyes Morales); Will Ferrell (Dave Bix); Spencer Scott (Grady); Buck Taylor (Bob Draper); Billy Joe Shaver (Rev. Shackleton); Steve Stodghill (Otto Brinker); Gaymond Gestaut (Sony Sr.); Dennis Williams (Leon); Paul Wright (Kaufman); Jo Harvey Allen (Wanda King); Mathew Greer (Eugene); Grant James (Mr. Baird); Azura Skye (May); Angela Alvarado Rosa (Irma); Isis Stephanie Cerda (Flower Girl); Brady Coleman (Freidrich); James Coolidge (Oliver Torres); Grover Coulson (Percy Cates); Juan Garcia III (Prisoner); Bruce Hayes (Office Co-Worker); Miguel Jimenez (Union Cooker); Richard Jones (Dr. Van Horn); Heather Kafka (Marianne); Dennis "Goldie" Lindsey (Inmate); Stephen Moffatt (Resort Waiter); Robert Musgrave (Motorcycle Cop); Glen Powell Jr. (Travis, Paper Boy); Charles Sanders (Infante); Mark Seliger (Cliff Taggert); Stacey Rene Smith (Jogger); Nicole Swahn (Lucy); Joel Trevino (Teo Torres); King Orba (Undercover Agent); John Wells (Frat Boy); John Wirt (Shouting Prison Guard); Mac Davis (Agent Buck); Mike Ritchey (Bus Guard); Lucina Paquet (Mrs. Ogelsby); Randy Stripling (Mr. Montoya); Phyllis Browne (Betty); Dudley Browne (Clark); Brad Arrington (Dr. Crane); Abel Pastor (Older Mexican Man); Matt Hensarling (Gary); Garry Peters (Fed #1); Farco Perella (Investigator); Jesus Tellex (Mexican Father); Ashley Andersen (Capt. Andersen)

Following a prison term, con artist Wendell Baker takes a job at a seedy retirement home, where he gets wind of a diabolical scam tyrannical head nurse Neil King hopes to perpetrate.

# EVEN MONEY

(YARI FILM GROUP) Producers, David Greathouse, Mark Rydell, Danny DeVito, Bob Yari; Executive Producers, Jan Korbelin, Marina Grasic, Thomas Becker, Dennis Brown; Co-Producers, Betsy Danbury, Rita Branch, Johnny Sanchez, Roger Zamudio; Director, Mark Rydell; Screenplay, Robert Tannen; Photography, Robbie Greenberg; Editor, Hughes Winborne; Music, Dave Grusin; Music Supervisor, Richard Glasser; Designer, Rob Pearson; Costumes, Wendy Chuck; Casting, Shari Rhodes; a Bob Yari Prods. presentation of a David Greathouse, Mark Rydell, Apolloproscreen production; Dolby; Deluxe color; Rated R; 113 minutes; Release date: May 18, 2007.

## Cast

Carolyn Carver **Kim Basinger**
Godfrey Snow **Nick Cannon**
Walter **Danny DeVito**
Det. Brunner **Kelsey Grammer**
Tom Carver **Ray Liotta**
Augie **Jay Mohr**
Victor **Tim Roth**
Clyde Snow **Forest Whitaker**
Veronica **Carla Gugino**
and Cassandra Hepburn (Claudia); Grant Sullivan (Murph); Chris Akers (Teammate); Texas Battle (Darius Jackson); Shaunt Benjamin (Det. Jenkins); Amy Boatwright (Debbie, Card Dealer); Rita Branch (Sara Jones); Carson Brown (Nicole Carver); Victoria Chalaya (Bookstore Employee); Ryan Rich, Rose Colasanti, Kyra Lin (Monte Players); Warren Durso (Black,ack Player); Cassandra Eastwood (Sports Enthusiast); Michael Eaves (Play-by-Play Announcer); Jonathan T. Floyd (Michael Black); Michelle Greathouse (Bookstore Employee); James Marsh (Writer in Coffee Shop); Robert Miano (Pit Boss); Robert Peters (John); Jade Ramsey, Nikita Ramsey (Crazy Fans); Mark Rydell (Ivan); Robb Skyler (Blackjack Dealer); Shanelle Workman (Jill); Roger Zamudio (Octavio Juarez)

A disparate group of gamblers, including a failed magician, a blocked writer, and an in-debt handyman, hope to improve their fortunes in Vegas.

Kim Basinger, Danny DeVito © YARI FILM GROUP

# SHREK THE THIRD

Prince Charming

(DREAMWORKS) Producer, Aron Warner; Executive Producers, Andrew Adamson, John H. Williams; Co-Producer, Denise Nolan Cascino; Director, Chris Miller; Co-Director, Raman Hui; Screenplay, Jeffrey Price, Peter S. Seaman, Chris Miller, Aron Warner; Story, Andrew Adamson, based on the book by William Steig; Designer, Guillaume Aretos; Music, Harry Gregson-Williams; Editor, Michael Andrews; Visual Effects Supervisors, Philippe Gluckman, Ken Bielenberg; Head of Character Animation, Tim Cheung; Head of Story, Rejean Bourdages; Head of Layout, Nick Walker; a Paramount release of a DreamWorks Animation SKG presentation of a PDI/DreamWorks production; Dolby; Technicolor; Rated PG; 92 minutes; Release date: May 18, 2007.

## Voice Cast

Shrek **Mike Myers**
Donkey **Eddie Murphy**
Princess Fiona **Cameron Diaz**
Puss in Boots **Antonio Banderas**
QueenLillian **Julie Andrews**
King Harold **John Cleese**
Prince Charming **Rupert Everett**
Merlin **Eric Idle**
Artie **Justin Timberlake**
Evil Queen **Susan Blakeslee**
Doris **Larry King**
Lancelot **John Krasinski**
Captain Hook **Ian McShane**
Mabel **Regis Philbin**
and Amy Poehler (Snow White); Seth Rogen (Ship Captain); Maya Rudolph (Rapunzel); Amy Sedaris (Cinderella); Aron Warner (Wolf); Cody Cameron (Pinocchio/Three Pigs); Christopher Knights (Blind Mice/Heckler/Evil Tree #2/Guard #2); Jasper Johannes Andrews, Zachary James Bernard, Dante James Hauser, Hauser Jordan Alexander Hauser (Ogre Babies); Guillaume Aretos (Raul); Kelly Asbury (Master of Ceremonies/Fiddlesworth);Andrew Birch (Evil Tree #1); Sean Bishop (Drivers Ed Instructor/Hall Monitor/Teacher); Kelly Cooney (Cheerleader/Tiffany/Mother); Walt Dohrn (Van Student/Xavier/Principal Pynchley/Nanny Dwarf/Evil Knight/Singing Villain); Tom Kane (Guard #1); Tom McGrath (Gary); Chris Miller (Puppet Master/Announcer/Mascot/Singing Villain); Latifa Ouaou (Cheerleader/Guinevere/Woman); Alina Phelan (Cheerleader); David P. Smith (Waiter/Evil Dwarf); Mark Valley (Cyclops); Conrad Vernon (Gingerbread Man/Rumplestiltskin/Headless Horseman); Kari Wahlgren (Old Lady); Cheri Oteri (Belle/Actress)

Having turned down the job of ruling Far Far Away, Shrek travels to the land of Worcestershire in hopes of persuading Fiona's half-brother Artie to take the throne. Third entry in the DreamWorks series, following *Shrek* (2001) and *Shrek 2* (2004).

Donkey, Shrek, Puss © DREAMWORKS

Donkey, Shrek, Puss, Fiona

# BROOKLYN RULES

(CITY LIGHTS PICTURES) Producers, Michael Corrente, Marisa Polvino, Richard B. Lewis; Executive Producers, Billy Heinzerling, Steven Bowman, Stewart F. Lane, Bonnie Comley, Rachel Rothman, Gemelli Entertainment, Darren Manelski, Terence Winter, Akiva Goldsman; Co-Producer, Richard Perello; Director, Michael Corrente; Screenplay, Terence Winter; Photography, Richard P. Crudo; Designer, Bob Shaw; Costumes, Juliet Polsca; Editor, Kate Sanford; Music, Benny Rietveld; Music Supervisors, Peter Afterman, Margaret Yen; Visual Effects, Soho VFX; Stunts, Peter Bucossi, Mike Russo; Associate Producers, Julie Bertrand, Chloe O'Connor; Casting, Amanda Mackey, Cathy Sandrich Gelfond, Sig de Miguel, Wendy Weidman; an Eagle Beach Prods., Straight Up Films presentation in association with Southpaw Entertainment and Cataland Films; Dolby; Technicolor; Rated R; 99 minutes; Release date: May 18, 2007.

## Cast

Michael Turner, Jr.   **Freddie Prinze Jr.**
Carmine Mancuso   **Scott Caan**
and Jerry Ferrara (Bobby Canzoneri); Alec Baldwin (Caesar Manganaro); Mena Suvari (Ellen); Monica Keena (Amy); Robert Turano (Mr. Canzoneri); Ursula Abbott (Angela); Paulo Araujo (Young Michael); Marc Alan Austen (Rabbi); P.J. Brown (Earl Webber); Chris Caldovino (Philly Cabrese); Karla Cavalli (Flirty Girl); Bern Cohen (Jeweler Sonnenberg); Tibor Feldman (Prof. Foster); Annie Golden (Dottie, Hamilton House Waitress); Alexa Havins (Brooklyn Girl); John Heinlein (Construction Worker); Rome Kanda (Dealer); Frank Lapetina (Jimmy Bags); Phyllis Kay (Mrs. Canzoneri); Christian Maelen (Gino); Stefanie Marco (Carmine's Bride); Jeffrey M. Marchetti (Shooter); Dan McCabe (Eugene); Lisa Maris (Gino's Girlfriend); Larry Nuñez (Busboy); Brian O'Neill (Priest); John Cenatiempo, Kevin Paul (Bouncers); Anthony Paolucci (Truck Driver); Richard Perello (Pastels Bartender); Alison Raimondi (Girl from Addiction); Ty Thomas Reed (Young Carmine); Staci Rudnitsky (Allison); Daniel Tay (Young Bobby); Kevin Thoms (Todd, Drunk Preppie); Keri Uribe (Rosie); Ed Rubeo (Jeweler #2); James Thompson (Addiction Bouncer); Lin Tucci (Aunt Louise)

Three friends growing up in Brooklyn find their loyalties challenged when one of the boys decides to follow a life of crime, hoping to earn a degree of wealth and respect like that of neighborhood wiseguy Caesar Manganaro.

Freddie Prinze Jr., Jerry Ferrara, Scott Caan © CITY LIGHTS PICTURES

# FAY GRIM

Parker Posey, Jeff Goldblum © MAGNOLIA PICTURES

(MAGNOLIA) Producers, Hal Hartley, Michael S. Ryan, Martin Hagemann, Jason Kliot, Joana Vicente; Executive Producers, Ted Hope, Todd Wagner, Mark Cuban; Director/Screenplay/Music, Hal Hartley; Photography, Sarah Cawley Cabiya; Designer, Richard Sylvarnes; Costumes, Anette Guther, Daniela Selig; Editor, Hal Hartley; Line Producer, Maren Wolk; Casting, Anja Dihrberg, Bernard Karl; an HDNet Films presentation of a Possible Films production in association with This Is That and Zero Fiction with the support of Medienboard Berlin Brandenburg; American-German; Dolby; Color; Sony HD Cam; Not rated; 118 minutes; Release date: May 18, 2007.

## Cast

Fay Grim   **Parker Posey**
Agent Fulbright   **Jeff Goldblum**
and James Urbaniak (Simon Grim); Saffron Burrows (Juliet); Liam Aiken (Ned Grim); Elina Löwensohn (Bebe); Leo Fitzpatrick (Carl Fogg); Chuck Montgomery (Angus James); Thomas Jay Ryan (Henry Fool); DJ Mendel (Father Lang); Megan Gray (Principal); Jasmin Tabatabai (Milla); John Keogh (Prosecutor); Claudia Michelsen (Judge); J.E. Heys (Herzog); Aminata Seck (Woman Visitor at Prison); David Scheller (Convict Husband); Aoibheann O Hara (ER Nurse); Harald Schrott (Andre); Miho Nikaido (Gnoc Deng); Peter Benedict (Raul Picard); Tim Seyfi (Rabbi Todorov); Hubert Mulzer (Minister of Security); Mehdi Nebbou (Islamic Cleric); Suzan Anbeh (Concierge Paris Hotel); Nikolai Kinski (Amin); Robert Seeliger (Agent Hogan); Olga Kolb (Stewardess); Jef Bayonne (French Drug Dealer); Mohamed Makhtoumi (Beaten Man in Paris); René Ifrah (Technician in CIA Van); Sibeli Kekilli (Concierge, First Istanbul Hotel); Erdal Yildiz (Concierge, Second Istanbul Hotel); Adnan Maral (Hassan); Erkan Bektas (Gesham); Anatole Taubman (Jallal); Marko Lakobrija (Jallal s Bodyguard); Karim Cherif (Istanbul Cop in Officer); Ercan Özcelik (Istanbul Detective); Jewgenij Sitochin (Russian Spy); Mark Zak (Saudi Spy); Ian Dickinson (British Spy); Korhan Onur (Istanbul Cop in Street)

A private investigator asks Fay Grim to help recover the manuscripts left behind by her long-absent husband, writer Henry Fool, who had abandoned Fay and her son after committing murder. Sequel to the 1998 film *Henry Fool* with most of the principals returning to their roles.

# PIRATES OF THE CARIBBEAN: AT WORLD'S END

(WALT DISNEY PICTURES) Producer, Jerry Bruckheimer; Executive Producers, Mike Stenson, Chad Oman, Bruce Hendricks, Eric McLeod; Director, Gore Verbinski; Screenplay, Ted Elliott, Terry Rossio; Based on characters created by Ted Elliott, Terry Rossio, Stuart Beattie, Jay Wolpert; Based on Walt Disney's Pirates of the Caribbean; Photography, Darius Wolski; Designer, Rick Heinrichs; Costumes, Penny Rose; Music, Hans Zimmer; Music Supervisor, Bob Badami; Editors, Craig Wood, Stephen Rivkin; Visual Effects Supervisors, John Knoll, Charles Gibson; Casting, Denise Chamian; UK Casting, Priscilla John; Presented in association with Jerry Bruckheimer Films; Distributed by Buena Vista; Dolby; Panavision; Technicolor; Rated PG-13; 168 minutes; Release date: May 25, 2007.

## Cast

Captain Jack Sparrow  **Johnny Depp**
Captain Barbossa  **Geoffrey Rush**
Will Turner  **Orlando Bloom**
Elizabeth Swann  **Keira Knightley**
Admiral Norrington  **Jack Davenport**
Davy Jones  **Bill Nighy**
Governor Weatherby Swann  **Jonathan Pryce**
Pintel  **Lee Arenberg**
Ragetti  **Mackenzie Crook**
Gibbs  **Kevin R. McNally**
and David Bailie (Cotton); Stellan Skarsgård (Bootstrap Bill); Tom Hollander (Lord Cutler Beckett); Naomie Harris (Tia Dalma); Martin Klebba (Marty); David Schofield (Mercer); Lauren Maher (Scarlett); Dermot Keaney (Maccus, Dutchman); Clive Ashborn (Koleniko, Dutchman); Winston Ellis (Palifico, Dutchman); Christopher Adamson (Jimmy Legs, Dutchman); Andy Beckwith (Clanker, Dutchman); Jonathan Linsley (Ogilvey, Dutchman); Chow Yun-Fat (Captain Sao Feng); Keith Richards (Captain Teague); Ghassan Massoud (Captain Ammand); Hakeem Kae-Kazim (Captain Jocard); Dominic Scott Kay (Young Will Turner); Vanessa Branch (Giselle); Reggie Lee (Tai Huang); Marshall Manesh (Sumbhajee); Angus Barnett (Mullroy); Giles New (Murtogg); Takayo Fischer (Mistress Ching); Marcel Iures (Capitaine Chevalle); Sergio Calderon (Captain Vallenueva); James Lancaster (EITC Agent); Toru Tanaka (Tattoo Pirate); Edwin Habacon (Mushroom Ear); Albert Lee (Bathhouse Pirate); Tyler Tuione (Boiler Room Attendant); Larry Leong (Steng); Brendyn Bell (Officer); Greg Ellis (Cabin Boy); Ho-Kwan Tse (Hadras); Peter D. Badalamenti (Penrod); Marc Joseph (Quittance); Chris Symonds, Michael Symonds (Two Head); Humberto Fernández Tristan (Vallenueva's Aide); Omid Djalili (Askay/Pusasn); Lawrence Cummings, Chris M. Allport, Jim Raycroft, Robert Hovencamp, Geoffrey Alch, Ned Wertimer, Samela Beasom, Jessica-Elisabeth, Caesar Peters (Singing Gallows Pirates); Bob Elmore (Executioner); Mark Hildreth (Cryer); Matthew Wolf (Endeavor Officer); J.B. Blanc (Clerk); Rick Mali, Kimo Keoke, David Prak, Henry T. Yamada, Jonathan Limbo, Mick Gallagher, Shin Li Shioung, Quang Huynh, Ronnie Cruz, Thomas Isao Morinaka, Lidet Viravong, Ova Saopeng, Stuart "Phoenix" Wong (Pirates); Christopher S. Capp (Parrot Voice)

Chow Yun-Fat, Johnny Depp

Elizabeth Swann, Will Turner, and Captain Barbossa band together to gather the Nine Lords of the Brethren Court in hopes that they will defeat Lord Beckett and Admiral Norrington, who have joined forces with the vengeful Davy Jones and his Flying Dutchman to loot and destroy all pirate ships on the high seas. Previous entries in the Disney series were *Pirates of the Caribbean: The Curse of the Black Pearl* (2003) and *Pirates of the Caribbean: Dead Man's Chest* (2006), with several of the cast principals repeating their roles.

This film received Oscar nominations for Visual Effects and Makeup.

Geoffrey Rush, Keira Knightley, Johnny Depp

Naomie Harris, Orlando Bloom © DISNEY ENTERPRISES, INC.

# BUG

(LIONSGATE) Producers, Holly Wiersma, Kimberly C. Anderson, Malcolm Petal, Gary Huckabay, Michael Burns, Andreas Schardt; Executive Producers, Malcolm Petal, Kimberly C. Anderson, Michael Ohoven, Jim Seibel; Co-Producer, Bonnie Timmermann; Director, William Friedkin; Screenplay, Tracy Letts, based on his play; Photography, Michael Grady; Editor, Darrin Navarro; Designer, Franco Carbone; Costumes, Peggy Shnitzer; Music, Brian Tyler; Music Supervisor, Jay Faires; Line Producer, Jon Kuyper; Casting, Bonnie Timmerman; a L.I.F.T. production/DMK Mediafilms Intl. production in association with Inferno Distribution LLC; Dolby; Technicolor; Rated R; 101 minutes; Release date: May 25, 2007.

### Cast

Agnes White  **Ashley Judd**
Peter Evans  **Michael Shannon**
Jerry Goss  **Harry Connick, Jr.**
R.C.  **Lynn Collins**
Dr. Sweet  **Brian F. O'Byrne**
Man in Grocery Store  **Neil Bergeron**
Voice of Pizza Harris  **Bob Neill**

A woman tormented by the unsolved disappearance of her son invites an enigmatic young man to share her motel residence, only to succumb to his paranoid insistence that he is infected by an unseen "bug."

Ashley Judd, Michael Shannon, Lynn Collins

Ashley Judd, Michael Shannon

Ashley Judd, Harry Connick Jr.

Brian F. O'Byrne, Michael Shannon © LIONSGATE

# HOLLYWOOD DREAMS

(RAINBOW) Producer, Rosemary Marks; Director/Screenplay/Editor, Henry Jaglom; Photography, Alan Caudillo; Music, Harriet Schock; Set Decorator, Shauna Aronson; Costumes, Selby Van Horne; Line Producer, Allison Wilke; a Rainbow Film Co. production; Color; Rated R; 101 minutes; Release date: May 25, 2007.

## Cast

Margie Chizek **Tanna Frederick**
Robin Mack **Justin Kirk**
Kaz Naiman **Zack Norman**
Caesar DiNatale **David Proval**
Luna **Karen Black**
Aunt Bee **Melissa Leo**
and Jon Robin Baitz (Jonathan Harrington); Sabi Dorr (Sam); Douglas Dunning (McDowell); Alice Evans (Vida); Gerry Katzman (Isaiah); Kim Kolarich (Kiki); Kat Kramer (Tina); Seth McClellan (Shane); Tiarra Mukherjee (Nandita); Keaton Simons (Jimmy); Tania Verafield (Tania); Nadia Witt (Lucy); Seymour Cassel (Rupert); Paz de la Huerta (Wedding Guest); Sally Kirkland (Minister At Wedding); Eric Roberts (Thomas Kurt); F.X. Feeney (Journalist); Kathleen Matson (Photographer); Sabrina Jaglom (Zoe); Simon O. Jaglom (Johnny, Boy on Swing); Mariah Bess (Child Actress); Matthew Pohlson (Jake, Personal Trainer); Richard Schinnow (Leon); Trevor Hale (Butler); Philip Proctor (Theater Director); Henry Jaglom (Voice of Casting Director)

Melissa Leo, Tanna Frederick © RAINBOW FILM COMPANY

Aspiring actress Margie Chizek falls in with a pair of two-bit producers who are trying to pass their straight protégé Robin Mack as gay in hopes of bringing him media attention.

# CRAZY LOVE

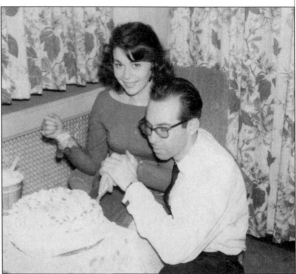

Linda Riss, Burt Pugach

(MAGNOLIA) Producers, Dan Klores, Fisher Stevens; Co-Producers, John Miller-Monzon, David Zieff; Director, Dan Klores; Co-Director, Fisher Stevens; Photography, Wolfgang Held; Editor, David Zieff; Music, Douglas J. Cuomo; a Shoot the Moon production in association with Stevens/Zieff Films; Color/ Black and white; HD; Rated PG-13; 92 minutes; Release date: June 1, 2007. Documentary on how Linda Riss married disbarred lawyer Burt Pugach after he tossed acid in her face, thereby disfiguring and blinding her for life.

## With

Burt Pugach, Linda Riss Pugach, Jimmy Breslin, Rusty Goldberg, Bob Janoff, Rita Kessler, Janet Pomerantz, Margaret Powers, Berry Stainbeck.

Linda Riss, Burt Pugach © MAGNOLIA PICTURES

# KNOCKED UP

(UNIVERSAL) Producers, Judd Apatow, Shauna Robertson, Clayton Townsend; Executive Producers, Seth Rogen, Evan Goldberg; Director/Screenplay, Judd Apatow; Photography, Eric Edwards; Designer, Jefferson Sage; Costumes, Debra McGuire; Music, Loudon Wainwright, Joe Henry; Music Supervisor, Jonathan Karp; Editors, Brent White, Craig Alpert; an Apatow production; Dolby; Technicolor; Rated R; 129 minutes; Release date: June 1, 2007.

Seth Rogen, Harold Ramis

## Cast

Ben Stone **Seth Rogen**
Alison Scott **Katherine Heigl**
Pete **Paul Rudd**
Debbie **Leslie Mann**
Jason **Jason Siegel**
Jay **Jay Baruchel**
Jonah **Jonah Hill**
Martin **Martin Starr**
Jodi **Charlyne Yi**
Charlotte **Iris Apatow**
Sadie **Maude Apatow**
Alison's Mom **Joanna Kerns**
Ben's Dad **Harold Ramis**
Jack **Alan Tudyk**
Jill **Kristen Wiig**
Brent **Bill Hader**
and Ken Jeong (Dr. Kuni); Craig Robinson (Club Doorman); Tim Bagley (Dr. Pellagrino); Loudon Wainwright (Dr. Howard); Stephanie Mnookin (Dr. Howard's Nurse); Adam Scott (Male Nurse); J.P. Manoux (Dr. Angelo); Mo Collins (Doctor); B.J. Novak (Young Doctor); Tami Sagher (Wardrobe Lady); Brianna Lynn Brown, Catherine Reitman, Nick Thune (Alison's Friends); Paul Feig, Ben Meyerson, Wayne Federman (Fantasy Baseball Guys); Melinda Bennett (Dr. Pellagrino's Nurse); Matt McKane (Club Bartender); Steven Brill (Ben's Boss); Ana Mercedes (Maria); Nadine Griffith (Maternity Nurse at Desk); Diane Schaller (Delivery Nurse); Emersen Riley (Jonah's Girlfriend); Stormy Daniels, Nautica Thorn (Lap Dancers); Mary Brill (Real Estate Agent); Lolita Mastrolia (Daughter in Waiting Room); Joseph T. Mastrolia (Father in Waiting Room); Tracy Hartley (Lamaze Instructor); Jeffrey L. Wilson (Record Store Customer); Jessica Alba, Steve Carell, Andy Dick, James Franco, Eva Mendes, Ryan Seacrest, Dax Shepard (Themselves)

Alison Scott is dismayed to learn that she has gotten pregnant by way of a drunken one-night stand with slovenly Ben Stone, whose irresponsible lifestyle makes him a highly unsuitable husband or father.

Katherine Heigl, Seth Rogen © UNIVERSAL STUDIOS

Charlyne Yi, Martin Starr, Jonah Hill, Seth Rogen

Katherine Heigl, Leslie Mann

Maude Apatow, Iris Apatow, Leslie Mann, Paul Rudd

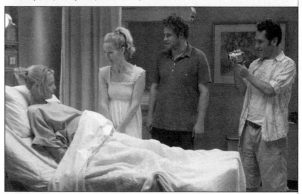
Katherine Heigl, Leslie Mann, Seth Rogen, Paul Rudd

# MR. BROOKS

Demi Moore © MGM

Marg Helgenberger, Kevin Costner, Danielle Panabaker

(MGM) Producers, Jim Wilson, Kevin Costner, Raynold Gideon; Executive Producers, Sam Nazarian, Adam Rosenfelt, Marc Shaberg, Thomas Augsberger; Co-Executive Producer, Malcolm Petal; Director, Bruce A. Evans; Screenplay, Bruce A. Evans, Raynold Gideon; Photography, John Lindley; Designer, Jeffrey Beecroft; Costumes, Judianna Makovsky; Editor, Miklos Wright; Music, Ramin Djawadi; Visual Effects Supervisor, Patrick McClung; Visual Effects, Sway Studios; Stunts, Norman Howell; Associate Producer, Robin Jonas; Casting, Mindy Marin; an Element Films and Relativity Media presentation, in association with Eden Rock Media, of a TIG production; Dolby; Color; Rated R; 120 minutes; Release date: June 1, 2007.

## Cast

Earl Brooks  **Kevin Costner**
Det. Tracy Atwood  **Demi Moore**
Mr. Smith  **Dane Cook**
Marshall  **William Hurt**
Emma Brooks  **Marg Helgenberger**
Hawkins  **Ruben Santiago-Hudson**
Jane Brooks  **Danielle Panabaker**
Nancy Hart  **Aisha Hinds**
Captain Lister  **Lindsay Crouse**
Jesse Vialo  **Jason Lewis**
Sheila  **Reiko Aylesworth**
Thornton Meeks  **Matt Schulze**
and Yasmine Delawari (Sunday); Traci Dinwiddie (Sarah Leaves); Michael Cole (Atwood's Lawyer); Jim Farnum (Master of Ceremonies); Megan Brown, Ross Francis (Dance Couple); Kit Gwin (Det. Carfagno); Marcus Hester (Det. Smolny); Jamie McShane (Crime Lab Technician); Laura Bailey, Jon Paul Burkhart (Flight Attendants); Matthew Posey (AA Leader); Brandon Olive (Summons Server); Rosie Cafarelli (Vaughn); Ben Glass (ER Doctor); Kanin Howell (Pick-Up Driver); Steve Coulter (Roger); Stephen Michael Ayers (Mr. Clifford); Mark Scarboro (Detective); Brad L. Evans (Cop); David Gibbons (Box Plant Manager); Jasa Abreo (On-Plane Flight Attendant); Rommel Sulit (Japanese Client); Phillip DeVona (Police Officer); Van White (Police Officer)

A seemingly respectable citizen tries to curb his homicidal tendencies, while being tempted by his conscience to commit further atrocities.

Dane Cook, Kevin Costner

# OCEAN'S THIRTEEN

Ellen Barkin, Al Pacino

(WARNER BROS.) Producer, Jerry Weintraub; Executive Producers, Susan Ekins, Gregory Jacobs, Frederic W. Brost, Bruce Berman; Director, Steven Soderbergh; Screenplay, Brian Koppelman, David Levien, based on characters created by George Clayton Johnson, Jack Golden Russell; Photography, Peter Andrews; Designer, Philip Messina; Costumes, Louise Frogley; Editor, Stephen Mirrone; Music, David Holmes; Associate Producer, Robin Le Chanu; Casting, Debra Zane; a JW/Section Eight production, presented in association with Village Roadshow Pictures; Dolby; Panavision; Technicolor; Rated PG-13; 122 minutes; Release date: June 8, 2007.

Matt Damon, George Clooney, Brad Pitt © WARNER BROS.

## Cast

Danny Ocean **George Clooney**
Rusty Ryan **Brad Pitt**
Linus Caldwell/Lenny Pepperidge **Matt Damon**
Terry Benedict **Andy Garcia**
Basher Tarr/Fender Roads **Don Cheadle**
Frank Catton **Bernie Mac**
Abigail Sponder **Ellen Barkin**
Willy Bank **Al Pacino**
Virgil Malloy **Casey Affleck**
Turk Malloy **Scott Caan**
Roman Nagel **Eddie Izzard**
Yen/Mr. Weng **Shaobo Qin**
Saul Bloom/Kensington Chubb **Carl Reiner**
Reuben Tishkoff **Elliott Gould**
Livingston Dell **Eddie Jemison**
The V.U.P. **David Paymer**
François Toulour **Vincent Cassel**
Greco Montgomery **Julian Sands**
and Michael Mantell (Dr. Stan); Ray Xifo (Reuben s Butler); Kris Kane (Fired Waitress); Soledad St. Hilaire (Chamber Maid); Olga Sosnovska (Debbie); Noureen DeWulf ( Nuff Said Expo Girl); Jerry Weintraub (Denny Shields); Luis Chávez (Nestor/Nestor s Brother); Ivan Brogger (Shuffle Royale VP); Alex Procopio (Polygrapher); Armen Weitzman (Eugene); Steve Lambert (Roulette Scam Artist); Don McManus (Neil, the Pit Boss); Jon Wellner (Bellman); Mesan Richardson (Hotel Staff); Adrian Neil (Maitre D ); Maggie Rowe (Florist); Adam Lazarre-White (Bank s Junior Executive); Bob Einstein (Agent Caldwell); Michael Miranda (Randall); Oprah Winfrey, Bernie Yuman (Themselves); Angel Oquendo (Ortega, Guard); Wayne Péré (Fireworks Guy); Joe Chrest (Fender Roads  Manager); Tim Conolan, Moira Squier (Agent Caldwell s  Deputies ); Steve Hai (Mr. Weng s Assistant); Michi Yamato (Singing Referee); Bayanbat Davaadalai, Byambajav Ulambayar, Musashimaru, Akebono, Michael S. Meldman (Themselves); Ren Urano (Sumo Referee); Michael Harney (Blackjack Pit Boss); James DuMont (Security Supervisor); Robert Douglas Purcell (Slot Machine Pit Boss); Ashlee Vingle, Andrea Tiede (Cartwheel Girls); Austin Priester (The Real Fender Roads); Margaret Travolta (Bank s Secretary); Jacquie Barnbrook (Slot Machine Winner); Tommy Hinkley (Roulette Dealer); Matt Duggan, Adam Kaiz, Kasey Mahaffy, Nick Puga, Paull Walia (Security Technicians); Scott L. Schwartz (Bruiser); Jorge Luis Abreu (Floor Manager); Diana Donaldson (Benedict s Secretary); Shae Wilson (Ticket Agent)

Danny Ocean and his team of thieves plot to sabotage the opening of egomaniacal Vegas kingpin Willy Bank's lavish new casino as a means of revenge for Bank having cheated their mentor, Reuben Tishkoff, out of a cut of the deal. Third in the WB series, following *Ocean's Eleven* (2001) and *Ocean's Twelve* (2004), with many of the principals repeating their roles.

# SURF'S UP

Lani, Cody Maverick

Chicken Joe, Cody Maverick

**Voice Cast**

Cody Maverick **Shia LaBeouf**
Big Z/Geek **Jeff Bridges**
Lani Aliikai **Zooey Deschanel**
Chicken Joe **Jon Heder**
Reggie **James Woods**
Tank Evans **Diedrich Bader**
Mikey Abromowitz **Mario Cantone**
Kelly **Kelly Slater**
Rob **Rob Machado**
SPEN Announcer **Sal Masekela**
Filmmakers **Ash Brannon, Chris Buck**
Glen Maverick **Brian Posehn**
Edna Maverick **Dana L. Belben**
Arnold **Reed Buck**
Kate **Reese Elowe**
Smudge **Jack P. Ranjo**
Ivan, Glen's Buddy/Others **Matt Taylor**
and Bob Bergen, Jillian Bowen, Johanna Braddy, John Cygan, Courtnee Draper, Bill Farmer, Andy Fischer-Price, Teresa Ganzel, Jess Harnell, Jesse Head, Sherry Lynn, Danny Mann, Mickie McGowan, Alec Medlock, Laraine Newman, Jan Rabson, Meagan Smith, Marisa Theodore, Crawford Wilson, Jacob Zachar (Additional Voices)

A documentary crew follows Rockhopper penguin Cody Maverick as he enters his first pro surfing competition.

This film received an Oscar nomination for Animated Feature.

Cody Maverick, Mikey, Reggie, Tank© COLUMBIA PICTURES/SONY PICTURES

(COLUMBIA) Producer, Christopher Jenkins; Directors, Ash Brannon, Chris Buck; Screenplay, Don Rhymer, Ash Brannon, Chris Buck, Christopher Jenkins; Story, Christopher Jenkins, Christian Darren; Imagery and Animation, Sony Pictures Imageworks Inc.; Designer, Paul Lasaine; Art Director/Character Designer, Sylvain Deboissy; Music, Mychael Danna; Music Supervisor, Liza Richardson; Editor, Ivan Bilancio; Co-Producer, Lydia Bottegoni; Head of Story, Jeff Ranjo; Visual Effects Supervisor, Rob Bredow; Senior Animation Supervisor, David Schaub; Supervising Animators, Renato Dos Anjos, Chris Hurtt, Peter Nash, Chad Stewart; CG Supervisors, Danny Dimian, R. Stirling Duguid, Daniel Kramer, Bert Van Brande; Head of Layout, James Williams; Digital Producer, Chris Juen; Casting, Mary Hidalgo; a Sony Pictures Animation Film; Dolby; Color; Rated PG; minutes; Release date: June 8, 2007.

# FANTASTIC FOUR:
# THE RISE OF THE SILVER SURFER

Michael Chiklis, Julian McMahon

Chris Evans, Ioan Gruffudd, Jessica Alba © 20TH CENTURY FOX

(20TH CENTURY FOX) Produced by Bernd Eichinger, Avi Arad, Ralph Winter; Executive Producers, Stan Lee, Kevin Feige, Chris Columbus, Mark Radcliffe, Michael Barnathan; Co-Producers, Ross Fanger, Lee Cleary; Director, Tim Story; Screenplay, Don Payne, Mark Frost; Story, John Turman, Mark Frost, based on the Marvel Comic Book by Stan Lee, Jack Kirby; Photography, Larry Blanford; Designer, Kirk M. Petruccelli; Costumes, Mary Vogt; Editors, William Hoy, Peter S. Elliot; Music, John Ottman; Special Makeup Effects, Mike Elizalde; Visual Effects Supervisor, Scott Squires; Visual Effects, Weta Digital, Hydraulx, the Orphanage; Special Visual Effects, Giant Killer Robots, Hammerhead Prods.; Creature and Makeup Effects, Spectral Motion; Associate Producers, Allison Calleri, Stewart Bethune; Casting, Christian Kaplan (U.S.), Corren Mayrs, Heike Brandstatter (Canada); a 1492 Pictures/Bernd Eichinger production presented in association with Constantin Film and Marvel Studios; Dolby; Panavision; Deluxe color; Rated PG; 91 minutes; Release date: June 15, 2007.

Silver Surfer

## Cast

Reed Richards (Mr. Fantastic)  **Ioan Gruffudd**
Sue Storm (Invisitble Woman)  **Jessica Alba**
Johnny Storm (Human Torch)  **Chris Evans**
Ben Grimm (The Thing)  **Michael Chiklis**
Victor Von Doom  **Julian McMahon**
Alicia Masters  **Kerry Washington**
General Hager  **Andre Braugher**
Voice of the Silver Surfer  **Laurence Fishburne**
Silver Surfer  **Doug Jones**
Captain Frankie Raye  **Beau Garrett**
Wedding Minister  **Brian Posehn**
Mr. Sherman/Rafke  **Zach Grenier**
Anchorwoman  **Dawn Chubai**
Anchorman  **Chris Gailus**
Baxter Building Doorman  **Kevin McNulty**
Tailor  **Andy Stahl**
Dr. Jeff Wagner  **Kenneth Welsh**
and Debbie Timuss, Moneca Delain, Crystal Lowe (Hot Party Girls); Vanessa Minnillo (Johnny's Wedding Date); Alicia Thorgrimsson (New York Pedestrian); Valerie Tian, Jeanna Haddow, Ali Costigan (New York Teen Girls); Patricia Harras (Fan Four Receptionist); Gonzalo Menendez (Lieutenant); Suzanne Ristic (Airline Woman); Giuliana DePandi (Entertainment Reporter); Lauren Sanchez (Fox News Reporter); Malcolm Boddington (Pub Owner); Cole Landels (Gift Shop Kid); Cameron Cleary (Flower Girl); Stan Lee (Rejected Wedding Guest); Silver Butler (Wedding Planner); Michasha Armstrong (Wedding Security); Hitoshi Ikezaki, Peter Kawasaki (Japanese Fishermen); Fareed Abdelhak (Egyptian Tour Guide)

When their wedding nuptials are interrupted by unexplained meteorological disasters, Sue Storm and Reed Richards summon the other members of the Fantastic Four to stop the Silver Surfer, a metal-based intergalactic traveler intent on destroying the planet. Sequel to the 2005 film *Fantastic Four*, with the principals repeating their roles.

# NANCY DREW

(WARNER BROS.) Producer, Jerry Weintraub; Executive Producers, Susan Ekins, Mark Vahradian, Benjamin Waisbren; Co-Producer, Cherylanne Martin; Director, Andrew Fleming; Screenplay, Andrew Fleming, Tiffany Paulsen; Story, Tiffany Paulsen; Based on characters created by Carolyn Keene; Photography, Alexander Gruszynski; Designer, Tony Fanning; Costumes, Jeffrey Kurland; Music/Music Supervisor, Ralph Sall; Editor, Jeff Freeman; Casting, Pam Dixon; a Jerry Weintraub production, in association with Virtual Studios; Dolby; Panavision; Technicolor; Rated PG; 98 minutes; Release date: June 15, 2007.

Tate Donovan, Emma Roberts

## Cast

Nancy Drew  **Emma Roberts**
Corky Veinshtein  **Josh Flitter**
Ned Nickerson  **Max Thieriot**
Jane Brighton  **Rachael Leigh Cook**
Carson Drew  **Tate Donovan**
Dashiel Zachary Biedermeyer  **Barry Bostwick**
Bess  **Amy Bruckner**
Georgie  **Kay Panabaker**
Dehlia Draycott  **Laura Elena Harring**
Inga Veinshtein  **Daniella Monet**
Trish  **Kelly Vitz**
John Leshing  **Marshall Bell**
Barbara Barbara  **Caroline Aaron**
Landlady  **Pat Carroll**
Principal Fineman  **Phil Abrams**
Costume Lady  **Joanne Baron**
Chief McGinnis  **Cliff Bemis**
Partygoers  **Darnell Dickens, Edgar Borjas**
and Adam Clark (Sgt. Billings); Rich Cooper (Charlie); Vito D'Ambrosio, Thom Williams, Jared Weber (Henchmen); Elyssa Davalos (Twin Palms Manager); David Doty (Father Murphy); Craig Gellis (Thug); Adam Goldberg (Andy, Arrogant Director); Adam Hendershott (Guy at Party); Emmy Laybourne (File Lady); Dana Lee (Louie); Rosemary Morgan, Amanda Maria Lorca, Ahna O'Reilly, Ashley-Nicole Sherman, Shaina Vorspan, Krystle Hernandez ("No" Women); Kaitlyn Van Item Allie Brighton); Robert Merrill ("New Century" Actor); Monica Parker (Hannah); Ryan Raddatz (Assistant Director); Lindsay Sloane (Boutique Clerk); Lucille Soong (Waitress); James Wing Woo (Chinese Priest in Movie); Eddie Jemison (Adoption Clerk); Chris Kattan (Burglar); Bruce Willis (Bruce); Eddie Jemison (Adoption Clerk); Lindsay Sloane (Boutique Clerk)

Max Thieriot, Emma Roberts, Josh Flitter

When amateur sleuth Nancy Drew and her dad move into a mansion once owned by slain movie star Dehlia Draycott, Nancy decides to do some investigating to find out who was responsible for the murder. Previous adaptations of the Carolyn Keene books were *Nancy Drew, Detective* (1938), *Nancy Drew, Reporter* (1939), *Nancy Drew, Trouble Shooter* (1939), and *Nancy Drew and the Hidden Staircase* (1939), all starring Bonita Granville and released by Warner Bros.

Daniella Monet, Kelly Vitz © WARNER BROS.

# A MIGHTY HEART

(PARAMOUNT VANTAGE) Producers, Brad Pitt, Dede Gardner, Andrew Eaton; Co-Producer, Anita Overland; Director, Michael Winterbottom; Screenplay, John Orloff, based on the book *A Mighty Heart: The Brave Life and Death of My Husband, Danny Pearl* by Mariane Pearl; Photography, Marcel Zyskind; Designer, Mark Digby; Costumes, Charlotte Walter; Editor, Peter Christelis; Music, Molly Nyman, Harry Escott;  Makeup and Hair Designer, Marese Langan; Casting, Wendy Brazington; a Plan B Entertainment/Revolution Films production; Dolby; Arri widescreen; Technicolor, HD-to-35mm; Rated R; 103 minutes; Release date: June 22, 2007.

## Cast

Mariane Pearl  **Angelina Jolie**
Danny Pearl  **Dan Futterman**
Captain  **Irrfan Khan**
John Bussey  **Denis O'Hare**
Asra Q. Nomani  **Archie Panjabi**
Randall Bennett  **Will Patton**
Steve LeVine  **Gary Wilmes**
Shabbir  **Mohammed Afzal**
Kaleem Yusuf  **Telal Saeed**
Kashva  **Aliya Khan**
Danny's Taxi Driver  **Mushtaq Ahmed**
Masud the Fixer  **Daud Khan**
Mariane's Taxi Driver  **Arif Khan**
Human Rights Director  **Tipu Taheer**
and Amit Dhawan (Technical Supervisor); Sarah Mone, Bushra Parwani, Zafar Karachiwala, Danish Iqbal, Ali Tejani (Guests); Azfar Ali (Azfar); Amhed Jamal (Khawaja); Perrine Moran (Ruth Pearl); Jeffry Kaplow (Judea Pearl); Ishaque Ahmed (Arif); Alyy Khan (Omar Saeed Sheikh); Adnan Siddiqui (Dost Aliani); Shah Murad Aliani (Farooq); Imran Paracha (Major Major); Imran Patel (Jamal Paracha); Jean-Jacques Scaerou (Philippe Scaerou); Veronique Darleguy (Véronique Laurent); Jillian Armenante (Maureen Platt); Demetri Goritsas (John Skelton); Zach Coffin (Matt MacDowell); Sajid Hasan (Zafir); Farooq Khan (Noor); Mikail Lotia (Hasan); Baba Shaikh (Phone Engineer); Amy Shindler (Michelle Pearl); William Hoyland (John Bauman); Bilal Saeed (Haider); Sean Chapman (U.S. Journalist); Holly Goline (News Producer); Amy Rosenthal (Tamara Pearl); Nour Ayad (Ibrahim the Cook); Lynne Blades (News Reader); Ikram Bhatti (Sheikh Gilani); Fahad Hussein (Farhad Naseem); Taj Khan (Suleiman); Hasan Ali (Cell Phone Worker); Naeem Sogay (Adil); Sujata Humane (Omar s Aunt); Abdul Haq Khan (Omar s Father); Dr. Sayed Masood (Doctor); Imran Hasny (Journalist at Sheraton); Inder Misra (Lawyer); Chad Chenouga (Satchi); Mike Rosen, Jenni Lee, Elizabeth Danheim (Journalists); Tom Spencer (U.S. Phone Journalist); Qasim Iqbal (Hotel Manager); Fabienne Khaldi (Mariane s Mother); Gigi Ledron (Woman in Orange); Aimee Matimbia (French Midwife); Harvesp Chiniwala (Adam Pearl, Baby); Nassim Benbrik (Adam Pearl, Age 4)

Angelina Jolie, Dan Futterman

The true story of journalist Mariane Pearl's five-day ordeal trying to find out her husband's whereabouts after he disappeared on his way to an interview in Karachi, Pakistan.

Archie Panjabi, Irrfan Khan, Angelina Jolie

Denis O'Hare, Gary Wilmes © PARAMOUNT VANTAGE

# EVAN ALMIGHTY

(UNIVERSAL) Producers, Tom Shadyac, Gary Barber, Roger Birnbaum, Neal H. Moritz, Michael Bostick; Executive Producers, Ilona Herzberg, Dave Phillips, Matt Luber; Director, Tom Shadyac; Screenplay, Steve Oedekerk; Story, Steve Oedekerk, Joel Cohen, Alec Sokolow; Based on characters created by Steve Koren, Mark O'Keefe; Photography, Ian Baker; Designer, Linda DeScenna; Costumes, Judy Ruskin, Howell; Music, John Debney; Editor, Scott Hill; a Spyglass Entertainment presentation in association with Relativity Media; a Shady Acres/Barber-Birnbaum/Original Film production; Dolby; Color; Rated PG; 95 minutes; Release date: June 22, 2007.

Steve Carell, Morgan Freeman

## Cast

Evan Baxter **Steve Carell**
God **Morgan Freeman**
Joan Baxter **Lauren Graham**
Dylan Baxter **Johnny Simmons**
Jordan Baxter **Graham Phillips**
Ryan Baxter **Jimmy Bennett**
Congressman Long **John Goodman**
Rita **Wanda Sykes**
Marty **John Michael Higgins**
Eugene **Jonah Hill**
Eve Adams **Molly Shannon**
Congressman Burrows **Harve Presnell**
and P.J. Byrne, Ralph Harris, Arden Myrin (Evan's Staffers); Brian Howe (Builder); Ralph P. Martin (Delivery Guy); Maile Flanagan (Mail Person); Angela Martinez (CNN Reporter); Ed Helms (Ark Reporter, Ed Carson); David Barrera, Jeremiah W. Birkett, Jesse Burch, Rachael Harris, Casey Strand, Wayne Wilderson (Ark Reporters); Dean Norris (Officer Collins); Derick Alexander, Scott Rollins (Capitol Policemen); Madison Mason (Congressman Dodd); Bruce Gray (Congressman Hughes); Paul Collins (Congressman Stamp); Lisa Arch, Judith Benezra, Krista Carpenter, Gerald Downey, Simon Helberg, Dylan Jones, Jay Lay, Suzy Nakamura, Matt Price, Irene Roseen, Larry Sullivan, Audrey Wasilewski, Jon Wellner (Staffers); Channing Chase, Jim Doughan, Shelley Dowdy, Meagen Fay, Pete Gardner, Gregg Goulet, Jan Hoag, Harry S. Murphy, Ruth Williamson (Neighbors); Don Dowe, Shashawnee Hall (Newsroom Camera Operators); Lucia Forte (Court Stenographer); Deborah Carson (Congressional Reporter); Lamont Thompson (Officer M. Gilbert); Larry Dorf (Officer B. McKenzie); Tom Beyer (Newsroom Stage Manager); Topper Shutt (Local Weatherman); Juan M. Fernández, Bridget Ann White (Network Reporters); Roxana Ortega (Reporter in Evan s Office); Brendan Patrick Connor, Charlie Hartsock (Fish n Chips Patrons); William Dennis Hunt, Franklin Dennis Jones, Lillian Lehman, Catherine McGoohan, Phil Reeves, Edmund L. Shaff, Tucker Smallwood, David St. James (Committee Members); Donzella Berry, Brian Carpenter, Thomas Crawford, Gregg Daniel, Bill Debrason, Terry Menefee Gau, Mario Griego, Bonnie Johnson, Ted Johnson, Michael Stanton Kennedy, Frances Mitchell, James Newman, Patrick Pankhurst, Alan Sader, James Shanklin, Robert Shepherd, Rick Warner, Rachel Winfree (Congresspersons); Jon Stewart (Himself)

Recently elected congressman Evan Baxter is visited by God, who tells him he must build an ark in anticipation of the next great flood. Sequel to the 2003 Universal film *Bruce Almighty,* with Steve Carrel and Morgan Freeman repeating their roles.

Johnny Simmons, Graham Phillips © UNIVERSAL STUDIOS

# 1408

(MGM/WEINSTEIN) Producer, Lorenzo di Bonaventura; Executive Producers, Harvey Weinstein, Bob Weinstein, Jake Myers, Richard Saperstein; Director, Mikael Håfström; Screenplay, Matt Greenberg, Scott Alexander, Larry Karaszewski, based on the story by Stephen King; Photography, Benoit Delhomme; Designer, Andrew Laws; Costumes, Natalie Ward; Editor, Peter Boyle; Music, Gabriel Yared; Special Effects Supervisor, Paul Corbould; Visual Effects Supervisors, Sean H. Farrow, Uel Hormann, Matt Hicks, Adam Gascoyne, Stefan Drury, Simon Leech; Visual Effects, the Moving Picture Co., Rainmaker Animation and Visual Effects U.K., Lipsync Post, Senate Visual Effects, Baseblack Visual Effects; Stunts, Paul Herbert; Associate Producers, Kelly Dennis, Antonia Kalmacoff, Jeremy Steckler; Casting, Elaine Grainger; a Dimension Films presentation of a Lorenzo di Bonaventura production; Dolby; Panavision; Technicolor; Rated PG-13; 94 minutes; Release date: June 22, 2007.

John Cusack

## Cast

Mike Enslin **John Cusack**
Gerald Olin **Samuel L. Jackson**
Lily Enslin **Mary McCormack**
Sam Farrell **Tony Shalhoub**
Katie Enslin **Jasmine Jessica Anthony**
Mike's Father **Len Cariou**
Hotel Engineer **Isiah Whitlock, Jr.**
Mr. Innkeeper **Paul Birchard**
Mrs. Innkeeper **Margot Leicester**
Book Store Cashier **Walter Lewis**
Men at Book Signing **Eric Meyers, David Nicholson**
Lady at Book Signing **Holly Hayes**
Young Woman at Book Signing **Alexandra Silber**
Surfer Dude **Johann Urb**
Mailbox Guy **Andrew Lee Potts**
Secretary **Emily Harvey**
Clay the Lawyer **William Armstrong**
Desk Clerk **Kim Thomson**
Assistant Hotel Manager **Drew Powell**
Bellboy Noah **Noah Lee Margetts**
Maitre D' **Gil Cohen-Alloro**
Claw Hammer Maniac **Benny Urquidez**
Factory Owner **Ray Nicholas**
1950s Lady **Tina Maskell**
Kevin O'Malley **Paul Kasey**
and George Cottle, Julian Spencer, Will Willoughby (Mailbox Workers); Angel Oquendo (Taxi Cab Driver); Thomas A. McMahon, Anthony Mazza (Cops); Chris Carey (Fireman); Kevin Dobson (Priest); Lily Grace Alexander (10 Year Old Girl)

John Cusack, Samuel L. Jackson

Author Mike Enslin checks into Manhattan's Dolphin Hotel, determined to debunk the myth that room 1408 is haunted.

John Cusack © MGM/WEINSTEIN CO.

# YOU KILL ME

Ben Kingsley, Téa Leoni

(IFC FILMS) Producers, Al Corley, Burt Rosenblatt, Eugene Musso, Carol Baum, Mike Marcus, Zvi Howard Rosenman; Executive Producers, Tea Leoni, Jonathan Dana; Co-Producer, Kim Olsen; Director, John Dahl; Screenplay, Christopher Markus, Stephen McFeely; Photography, Jeffrey Jur; Designer, John Dondertman, Costumes, Linda Madden; Editor, Scott Chestnut; Music, Marcelo Zarvos; Music Supervisor, John Bissell; Casting, Carol Lewis; a Code Entertainment, Baum, Echo Lake, Rosenman, Bipolar production; Dolby; Super 35 Widescreen; Color, Super 35; Rated R; 92 minutes; Release date: June 22, 2007.

Luke Wilson

## Cast

Frank Falenczyk   **Ben Kingsley**
Laurel Pearson   **Téa Leoni**
Tom   **Luke Wilson**
Edward O'Leary   **Dennis Farina**
Roman Krzeminski   **Philip Baker Hall**
Dave   **Bill Pullman**
Stef Krzeminski **Marcus Thomas**
James Doyle   **Scott Heindl**
Dorris Rainford  **Alison Sealy-Smith**
Walter Fitzgerald  **Aron Tager**
Kathleen Fitzgerald  **Jayne Eastwood**
Stanley   **Aaron Hughes**
Henry   **Devin McCracken**
Emily   **Micheline Marchildon**
Becky   **Katie Messina**
Brenda   **Lorraine James**
Janet   **Joanne Rodriguez**
Nate   **Will Woytowich**
Driver   **Darren Wall**
Sales Clerk   **Tracy McMahon**
and Al Corley (Man in Park); Omar Khari (Juan); David Gillies (Earl); Susan Kelso (Laurel's Mother); Lora Schroeder (Guard); Ruth DeGraves (Rosemary); Sandy Jobin-Bevans (Supervisor Davis)

Ben Kingsley, Bill Pullman

After botching his last job, alcoholic hitman Frank Falenczyk is sent to San Francisco to sober up.

Dennis Farina © IFC FILMS

# SICKO

Michael Moore (left)

(LIONSGATE) Producers, Meghan O'Hara, Michael Moore; Executive Producers, Harvey Weinstein, Bob Weinstein, Kathleen Glynn; Co-Producer, Anne Moore; Director/Screenplay, Michael Moore;Editors, Dan Swietlik, Geoffrey Richman, Chris Seward; Music, Erin O'Hara; Associate Producer, Rehya Young; Line Producer, Jennifer Latham; a Weinstein Co. presentation of a Dog Eat Dog Films production; Dolby; Color; Rated PG-13; 123 minutes; Release date: June 22, 2007. Documentary looking at the inadequacies of America s health care system.

## With

Michael Moore, Tony Benn, Reggie Cervantes, John Graham, William Maher, Linda Peeno.

This film received an Oscar nomination for Documentary Feature.

Michael Moore

Michael Moore (left)

Michael Moore © LIONSGATE

# BROKEN ENGLISH

Parker Posey, Justin Theroux © MAGNOLIA PICTURES

(MAGNOLIA) Producers, Andrew Fierberg, Jason Kliot, Joana Vicente; Executive Producers, Todd Wagner, Mark Cuban; Co-Producer, Keisuke Konishe; Director/Screenplay, Zoe Cassavetes; Photography, John Pirozzi; Editor, Andrew Weisblum; Designer, Happy Massee; Music, Scratch Massive; Casting, Adrienne Stern; an HDNet Films and Magnolia Pictures presentation of a Vox3 Films and Phantom Film Co. Ltd. production in association with Backup Films; Dolby; Color; HD Cam; Rated PG-13; 97 minutes; Release date: June 22, 2007.

## Cast

Nora Wilder **Parker Posey**
Julien **Melvil Poupaud**
Audrey Andrews **Drea de Matteo**
Vivien Wilder-Mann **Gena Rowlands**
Nick Gable **Justin Theroux**
Irving Mann **Peter Bogdanovich**
and Tim Guinee (Mark Andrews); James McCaffrey (Perry); Josh Hamilton (Charlie Ross); Bernadette Lafont (Madame Grenelle); Michael Panes (Glen); Roy Thinnes (Peter Andrews); Philip Pavel (Front Desk Worker); Dana Ivey (Elinor Gregory); William Wise (William Gregory); Caitlin Keats (Jennifer Ross); Russell Steinberg (Carl); Santo Fazio (Bobbi); Michael Kelly (Guy); Jonathan Castro (Little Boy in the Park); John Wernke (Steve); Phyllis Somerville (Psychic); Laurent Pons (French Taxi Driver); Thierry Hancisse (Mr. Larson); Yarol Poupaud (Guillaume); Sebastien Chenut (Sebastien); Karim Gassama (Kareem); Jean-Paul Scarpitta (Jean Paul Clement); Maud Geffray (Waitress)

A lonely hotel events coordinator, fed up with her string of failed relationships, falls in love with a Frenchman, only to find that he must return to Paris.

# LIVE FREE OR DIE HARD

(20TH CENTURY FOX) Producer, Michael Fottrell; Executive Producers, Arnold Rifkin, William Wisher; Co-Producer, Stephen James Eads; Director, Len Wiseman; Screenplay, Mark Bomback; Story, Mark Bomback, David Marconi, based on the article "A Farewell to Arms" by John Carlin and certain original characters by Roderick Thorp; Photography, Simon Duggan; Designer, Patrick Tatopoulos; Costumes, Denise Wingate; Editor, Nicolas de Toth; Music, Marco Beltrami; Made in association with Dune Entertainment, produced in association with Ingenious Film Partners; Dolby; Super 35 Widescreen; Deluxe color; Rated PG-13; Running time: 129 minutes; Release date: June 27, 2007.

## Cast

Det. John McClane **Bruce Willis**
Matt Farrell **Justin Long**
and Timothy Olyphant (Thomas Gabriel); Cliff Curtis (Deputy Director Miguel Bowman); Maggie Q (Mai Lihn); Mary Elizabeth Winstead (Lucy McClane); Kevin Smith (Frederick Kaludis (Warlock)); (Robert Russo); Yorgo Constantine Yancey Arias (Agent Johnson); Andrew Friedman (Casper); Sung Kang (Raj); Matt O'Leary (Clay); Cyril Raffaelli (Rand); Christopher Palermo (Del); Jonathan Sadowski (Trey); Zeljko Ivanek (Molina); Christina Chang (Taylor); Jake McDorman (Jim); Rosemary Knower (Mrs. Kaludis); Gerald Downey (Hoover Agent); Allen Maldonado (Goatee); Jim Cantafio (Deli Owner); Chris Ellis Jr. (Jack Scalvino); Regina McKee Redwing (Nearby Agent); Tony Colitti (Chief Hazmat Agent); Tim de Zarn (Police Sergeant); Kurt David Anderson (Miller); Nadine Ellis (Teller); Ethan Flower (Trader); Nick Jaine (Phone Guy); Tim Russ (Chuck Summer); Joe Gerety (Jack Parry); Edward James Gage (On-Duty PP Operator); David Walrod (Deli Customer); Edoardo Costa (Emerson); John Reha (Slacker Kid); Rick Cramer (MP Rodriguez); Vito Pietanza, Dennis Depew, Howard Tyrone Ferguson (D.C. Cops); John Lacy (EMT); Diana Gettinger (FBI Dispatcher); Melissa Knowles (Freeway Reporter)

Detective John McClane must protect computer hacker Matthew Farrell from being killed by Thomas Gabriel, who has used the unwitting computer nerd as part of a nefarious plot to shut down government operations through technological interference.

Bruce Willis, Justin Long © 20TH CENTURY FOX

# EVENING

Hugh Dancy

Natasha Richardson, Toni Collette

(FOCUS) Producer, Jeffrey Sharp; Executive Producers, Jill Footlick, Michael Hogan, Robert Kessel, Susan Minot, Michael Cunningham; Co-Producers, Luke Parker Bowles, Claire Taylor, Nina Wolarsky; Director, Lajos Koltai; Screenplay, Susan Minot, Michael Cunningham, based on the novel by Susan Minot; Photography, Gyula Pados; Designer, Caroline Hanania; Costumes, Ann Roth, Michelle Matland; Editor, Allyson C. Johnson; Music, Jan A.P. Kaczmarek; Music Supervisor, Linda Cohen; Visual Effects Supervisor, Aaron Weintraub; Choreographer, Chris Michael Peterson; Casting, Billy Hopkins, Suzanne Crowley, Kerry Barden; a Hart Sharp Entertainment production, in association with Twins Financing; Dolby; Panavision; Technicolor; Rated PG-13; 117 minutes; Release date: June 29, 2007.

Patrick Wilson, Claire Danes

## Cast

Ann Grant  **Claire Danes**
Nina Mars  **Toni Collette**
Ann Lord  **Vanessa Redgrave**
Harris Arden  **Patrick Wilson**
Buddy Wittenborn  **Hugh Dancy**
Constance Haverford  **Natasha Richardson**
Lila Wittenborn  **Mamie Gummer**
The Night Nurse  **Eileen Atkins**
Lila Ross  **Meryl Streep**
Mrs. Wittenborn  **Glenn Close**
Luc  **Ebon Moss-Bachrach**
Mr. Wittenborn  **Barry Bostwick**
Ralph Haverford  **David Furr**
Lizzie Tull  **Sarah Viccellio**
Peach Howze  **Cheryl Lynn Bowers**
and Chuck Cooper (Ray); Timothy Kiefer (Karl Ross); Jon Devries (Deaver Ross); David Call (Pip); Robert Walsh (Matt); Kara Doherty (Chloe/Constance, age 6); David Robson (Ethan); Chris Stack (Phil Mars); Margaret Coen (Constance, age 4); Maxine Prescott (Great Aunt Roo); Annie Wardwell (Nina, age 4); Diane Feraco (Irish Maid)

On her death bed, Ann Lord thinks back on how her love for Dr. Harris Arden led to tragedy for her unrequited admirer.

Meryl Streep, Vanessa Redgrave © FOCUS FEATURES

# TRANSFORMERS

Shia LaBeouf © DREAMWORKS/PARAMOUNT

(DREAMWORKS/PARAMOUNT) Producers, Lorenzo di Bonaventura, Tom DeSanto, Don Murphy, Ian Bryce; Executive Producers, Steven Spielberg, Michael Bay, Brian Goldner, Mark Vahradian; Co-Producers, Allegra Clegg, Ken Bates; Director, Michael Bay; Screenplay, Alex Kurtzman, Roberto Orci; Story, Alex Kurtzman, Roberto Orci, John Rogers; Photography, Mitchell Amundsen; Designer, Jeff Mann; Costumes, Deborah L. Scott; Music, Steve Jablonsky; Music Supervisor, Dave Jordan; Editors, Paul Rubell, Glen Scantlebury, Thomas A. Muldoon; Visual Effects Supervisor, Scott Farrar; Visual Effects, Industrial Light & Magic, Digital Domain; Special Effects Supervisor, John Frazier; Animation Supervisor, Scott Benza; Stunts/Associate Producers, Matthew Cohan, Michelle McGonagle; Casting, Janet Hirshenson, Jane Jenkins, Michelle Lewitt; a di Bonaventura Pictures production, presented in association with Hasbro; Released by Paramount Pictures; Dolby; Super 35 Widescreen; Color; Rated PG-13; 140 minutes; Release date: July 2, 2007.

Bonecrusher

## Cast

Sam Witwicky  **Shia LaBeouf**
Mikaela Banes  **Megan Fox**
Captain Lennox  **Josh Duhamel**
USAF Tech Sgt. Epps  **Tyrese Gibson**
Maggie Madsen  **Rachael Taylor**
Glen Whitmann  **Anthony Anderson**
Defense Secretary John Keller  **Jon Voight**
Agent Simmons  **John Turturro**
Tom Banachek  **Michael O'Neill**
Ron Witwicky  **Kevin Dunn**
and Peter Cullen (Voice of Optimus Prime); Julie White (Judy Witwicky); Amaury Nolasco (ACWO Jorge "Fig" Figueroa); Mark Ryan (Voice of Bumblebee); Zack Ward (First Sergeant Donnelly); Bernie Mac (Bobby Bolivia); Darius McCrary (Voice of Jazz); Charles Adler (Voice of Starscream); Lt. Frederic Doss, Charlie Bodin (SOCCENT Op-Centre Techs); Andrew Caldwell, Andrew Altonji (Café Kids); Reno Wilson (Voice of Frenzy); Ashkan Kashanchi (Mahfouz); Rizwan Manji (Akram); Chris Ellis (Admiral Brigham); W. Morgan Sheppard (Captain Witwicky); C.J. Thomason (Sailor); Carlos Moreno, Jr. (Manny); Johnny Sanchez (Clown); John Robinson (Miles); Travis Van Winkle (Trent); Peter Jacobson (Mr. Hosney); Glenn Morshower (SOCCENT Colonel Sharp); Luis Echagarruga, Patrick Mulderrig, Brian Shehan, Michael Trisler (Ranger Team); Joshua Feinman (USAF Staff Sergeant); Steven Ford (Four-Star General); Michael Shamus Wiles (Two-Star General); Craig Barnett (Air Force Major General); Brian Prescott (Keller Aide); Scott Peat (Pentagon Watch Commander); Colleen Porch (Enlisted Aide); Brian Stepanek (Sector Seven Agent); Jamie McBride, Wiley Pickett (FBI Agents); Ronnie Sperling (Lead Scientist); Sean Smith (Scientist); Andy Milder (R&D Team Leader); Brian Reece (Moustache Man); Samantha Smith (Sarah Lennox); Ravi Patel (Telephone Operator); Rick Gomez (Sheriff); Andy Domingues (Deputy); Mike Fisher (Football Coach); Colin Fickes, Tom Lenk, Jamison Yang (Analysts); Esther Scott (Glen's Grandmother); Madison Mason (CNN Reporter); Jeremy Jojola, Jessica Kartalija (News Reporters); J.P. Manoux (Witness); Pete Gardner (Dad); Laurel Garner (Mom in Car); Chip Hormess (Boy in Car); Ray Toth, Dan Ferris (Pilots); Michael Adams, Ron Henry, Benjamin Hoffman, Michael McNabb, Jason T. White (AWACS Controllers); Adam Ratajczak (Control Tower Tech); Maya Klayn, Michelle Pierce, Odette Yustman (Socialites); Bob Stephenson (Xbox Guy); Mason the Mastiff (Himself); Robert Foxworth (Voice of Ratchet); Jess Harnell (Voice of Ironhide/Barricade); Hugo Weaving (Voice of Megatron); Jimmie Wood (Voice of Bonecrusher); Michelle Hower (Fleeing Woman)

The Decepticons, evil robots from outer space, arrive on earth in hopes of finding an all-powerful cube discovered years ago by the ancestor of Sam Witwicky, who joins with the Autobots, a group of shape-shifting robots, to battle their enemy and save the world.

This film received Oscar nominations for Visual Effects, Sound Mixing, and Sound Editing.

# LICENSE TO WED

John Krasinski, Mandy Moore © WARNER BROS.

(WARNER BROS.) Producers, Mike Medavoy, Arnold W. Messer, Nick Osborne, Robert Simonds; Executive Producers, Bradley J. Fischer, David Thwaites, Kim Zubick, Dana Goldberg, Bruce Berman; Co-Producers, Christine Sacani, Louis Phillips, Trevor Engelson; Director, Ken Kwapis; Screenplay, Kim Barker, Tim Rasmussen, Vince Di Meglio; Story, Kim Barker, Wayne Lloyd; Photography, John Bailey; Designer, Gae Buckley; Costumes, Deena Appel; Music, Christophe Beck; Music Supervisor, Spring Aspers; Editor, Kathryn Himoff; Casting, Shani Ginsberg, Jakki Fink; a Robert Simonds/Phoenix Pictures production, presented in association with Village Roadshow; Dolby; Panavision; Technicolor; Rated PG-13; 91 minutes; Release date: July 3, 2007.

### Cast

Reverend Frank **Robin Williams**
Sadie Jones **Mandy Moore**
Ben Murphy **John Krasinski**
Carlisle **Eric Christian Olsen**
and Christine Taylor (Lindsey Jones); Josh Flitter (Choir Boy); DeRay Davis (Joel); Peter Strauss (Mr. Jones); Grace Zabriskie (Grandma Jones); Roxanne Hart (Mrs. Jones); Mindy Kaling (Shelly); Angela Kinsey (Judith the Jewelry Clerk); Rachael Harris (Janine); Brian Baumgartner (Jim); Jess Rosenthal (Jewelry Clerk); Val Almendarez (Jewelry Store Customer); Nicole Randall Johnson (Louise); Tashana Haye (Church Kid Sarah); Sarah Kate Johnson (Church Kid Laurie); Travis Flory (Church Kid Manny); Dominic Swingler, Devin Swingler, Diego Swingler (Joel and Shelly's Kids); Cynthia Ettinger (Macy's Clerk); Gillian Skupa (Macy's Changing Room Lady); Poncho Hodges (Macy's Security Guard); Ruben Garfias (Coach); Kelsey Harper (Carlisle's Girlfriend); David Quinlan (Expectant Father); Irene Karas (Birthing Mom); Derek Green (Doctor); Christine Cannon (Delivery Doctor); Anelia Dyoulgerova (Belly Dancer); Nathan Barrett, Darla Vandenbossche, Sean Tyson, Chiu-Lin Tam, Guy Fauchon (Starbucks Customers); Grant Gershon (St. Augustine's Choir Director); Wanda Sykes (Doctor)

Sadie Jones and Ben Murphy foolishly consent to her family's insistence that their upcoming wedding be performed by Reverend Frank, who forces the young couple to fulfill a "marriage preparation course" before marrying.

# RESCUE DAWN

(MGM) Producers, Elton Brand, Steve Marlton, Harry Knapp; Executive Producers, Elie Samaha, Gerald Green, Nick Raslin, Freddy Braidy; Director/Screenplay, Werner Herzog; Photography, Peter Zietlinger; Art Director, Arin "Aoi" Pinijvararak; Costumes, Annie Dunn; Editor, Joe Bini; Music, Klaus Bartle; Stunts, Chris Carnel; Visual Effects Producer, Chris Woods; Special Effects Supervisor, Adam Horwath; Associate Producers, Adam Rosen, Robyn Klein; Casting, Eyde Belasco; a Gibraltar Entertainment presentation; Dolby; Color; Rated PG-13; 125 minutes; Release date: July 4, 2007.

### Cast

Lt. Dieter Dengler **Christian Bale**
Duane **Steve Zahn**
Gene **Jeremy Davies**
Phisit **Abhijati "Muek" Jusakul**
Procet **Chaiyan "Lek" Chunsuttiwat**
Little Hitler **Teerawat "Ka-Ge" Mulvilai**
Crazy Horse **Yuttana Muenwaja**
Jumbo **Kriangsak Ming-Olo**
Squad Leader **Zach Grenier**
Admiral Berrington **Marshall Bell**
Spook **Toby Huss**
Norman **Pat Healy**
Farkas **Gregory J. Qaiyum**
Jet Pilot **James Oliver**
and Brad Carr (U.S. Navy Pilot); Saichia Wongwiroj (Pathet Lao Guard); François Chau (Province Governor); Somkuan "Kuan" Siroon (Nook the Rock); Chorn Solyda (Walkie Talkie); Craig Gellis (Grunt); Emmanuel O. (Corporal); Richard Manning (Helicopter Pilot); Galen Yuen (Y.C.); Evan Jones (Pilot); Bonnie Z. Hutchinson, Seneca Shahara Brand, Stefany Putnam, Katherine Roberts (Nurses); Andrew Loftus, Colin Crosby (FBI Agents); Chris Tallman (DJ); Chris Butler (Rigger)

The true story of Dieter Dengler, who survived a hellish ordeal in a jungle prison camp after being shot down over Laos in 1965. This story was previously explored by the same director in the 1998 documentary *Little Dieter Needs to Fly.*

Christian Bale © MGM

# HARRY POTTER AND
# THE ORDER OF THE PHOENIX

Imelda Staunton

(WARNER BROS.) Producers, David Heyman, David Barron; Executive Producer, Lionel Wigram; Co-Producer, John Trehy; Director, David Yates; Screenplay, Michael Goldenberg, based on the novel by J.K. Rowling; Photography, Slawomir Idziak; Designer, Stuart Craig; Costumes, Jany Temime; Editor, Mark Day; Music, Nicholas Hooper; Visual Effects Supervisor, Tim Burke; Special Effects Supervisor, John Richardson; Special Visual Effects and Animation, Industrial Light & Magic; Visual Effects, the Moving Picture Co., Framestore-CFC, Rising Sun Picture, Cinesite (Europe), Baseblack, Machine Effects; Creature and Makeup Effects Designer, Nick Dudman; Stunts, Greg Powell; Associate Producer, Tim Lewis; Casting, Fiona Weir; a Heyday Films production; Dolby; J-D-C Widescreen; Technicolor; Rated PG-13; 139 minutes; Release date: July 11, 2007.

Tom Felton, Matthew Lewis, Jamie Waylett, Emma Watson© WARNER BROS.

## Cast

Harry Potter **Daniel Radcliffe**
Ron Weasley **Rupert Grint**
Hermione Granger **Emma Watson**
Bellatrix Lestrange **Helena Bonham Carter**
Rubeus Hagrid **Robbie Coltrane**
Lord Voldemort **Ralph Fiennes**
Albus Dumbledore **Michael Gambon**
Alastor "Mad-Eye" Moody **Brendan Gleeson**
Uncle Vernon Dursley **Richard Griffiths**
Lucius Malfoy **Jason Isaacs**
Sirius Black **Gary Oldman**
Severus Snape **Alan Rickman**
Aunt Petunia Dursley **Fiona Shaw**
Minerva McGonagall **Maggie Smith**
Dolores Umbridge **Imelda Staunton**
Remus Lupin **David Thewlis**
Sybil Trelawney **Emma Thompson**
Argus Filch **David Bradley**
Filius Flitwick **Warwick Davis**
Draco Malfoy **Tom Felton**
Cornelius Fudge **Robert Hardy**
Molly Weasley **Julie Walters**
Arthur Weasley **Mark Williams**
Cho Chang **Katie Leung**
Neville Longbottom **Matthew Lewis**
Luna Lovegood **Evanna Lynch**
and Bonnie Wright (Ginny Weasley); Jason Boyd (Piers); Richard Macklin (Malcolm); Harry Melling (Dudley Dursley); Kathryn Hunter (Mrs. Arabella Figg); Adrian Rawlins (James Potter); Geraldine Somerville (Lily Potter); Robert Pattinson (Cedric Diggory); Miles Jupp (TV Weatherman); Jessica Stevenson (Voice of Mafalda Hopkirk); Natalie Tena (Nymphadora Tonks); George Harris (Kingsley Shacklebolt); Peter Cartwright (Elphias Doge); Bridgette Millar (Emmeline Vance); Timothy Bateson (Kreacher); James Phelps (Fred Weasley); Oliver Phelps (George Weasley); Jamie Wolpert (Newspaper Vendor); Nicholas Blane (Bob); Daisy Haggard (Voice of Lift); Chris Rankin (Percy Weasley); Sian Thomas (Amelia Bones); Jamie Waylett (Vincent Crabbe); Josh Herdman (Gregory Goyle); Ryan Nelson (Slightly Creepy Boy); Devon Murray (Seamus Finnigan); William Welling (Nigel, 2nd Year); Apple Brook (Professor Grubbly-Plank); Alfred Enoch (Dean Thomas); Afshan Azad (Padma Patiil); Shefali Chowdhury (Parvati Patil); Jim McManus (Barman); Nick Shirm (Zacharias Smith); Sam Beazley (Everard); Jon Atterbury (Phineas); Arben Bajraktaraj (Azkaban Death Eater); Richard Leaf (Auror Dawlish); Tony Maudsley (Grawp); Alec Hopkins (Young Severus Snape); Robert Jarvis (Young James Potter); James Walters (Young Sirius Black); Charles Hughes (Young Peter Pettigrew); James Utechin (Young Remus Lupin); Jason Piper, Michael Wildman (Centaurs); Richard Cubison, Peter Best, Tav MacDougall, Richard Trinder (Death Eaters); James Payton (Frank Longbottom)

Rupert Grint, Daniel Radcliffe, Emma Watson

Helena Bonham Carter

Skeptical towards Harry Potter's claims that Lord Voldemort has returned, the Ministry of Magic gives Dolores Umbridge unrestrictive power at Hogwart's, causing Harry to assemble a rebel band called Dumbledore's Army. Fifth in the WB series, following *Harry Potter and the Sorcerer's Stone* (2001), *Harry Potter and the Chamber of Secrets* (2002), *Harry Potter and the Prisoner of Azkaban* (2004), and *Harry Potter and the Goblet of Fire* (2005), with most of the principals returning.

Emma Thompson, Maggie Smith

Mark Williams, Daniel Radcliffe

Gary Oldman, Daniel Radcliffe

# JOSHUA

Vera Farmiga, Sam Rockwell

Jacob Kogan, Vera Farmiga

(FOX SEARCHLIGHT) Producer, Johnathan Dorfman; Executive Producers, Temple Fennell, Dan O'Meara; Co-Producer, George Paaswell; Director, George Ratliff; Screenplay, David Gilbert, George Ratliff; Photography, Benoit Debie; Designer, Rochelle Berliner; Costumes, Astrid Brucker; Editor, Jacob Craycroft; Music, Nico Muhly; Casting, Patricia Dicerto; an ATO Pictures presentation; Dolby; Deluxe color; Rated R; 105 minutes; Release date: July 6, 2007.

## Cast

Brad Cairn  **Sam Rockwell**
Abby Cairn  **Vera Farmiga**
Hazel Cairn  **Celia Weston**
Ned Davidoff  **Dallas Roberts**
Chester Jenkins  **Michael McKean**
Joshua Cairn  **Jacob Kogan**
Stewart Slocum  **Alex Draper**
Betsy Polsheck  **Nancy Giles**
Ms. Danforth  **Linda Larkin**
Pediatrician  **Stephanie Roth Haberle**
Fred Solomon  **Ezra Barnes**
Ruth Solomon  **Jodie Markell**
Henry Abernathy  **Rufus Collins**
Monique Abernathy  **Haviland Morris**
Joe Cairn  **Tom Bloom**
Museum Staffer  **Antonia Stout**
Soccer Dad  **Randy Ryan**
Soccer Teammate  **Evan Seligman**
Singing Boy  **Patrick Henney**
Cabbie  **Gurdeep Singh**
Bike Messener  **Nicholas Guidry**
Homeless Man  **Darrill Rosen**
and Daniel Jenkins (Minister); Erik Solky (Park Patron); Shianne Kolb, Lacey Vill (Lily Cairn)

Brad and Abby Cairn's enigmatic 9-year-old son Joshua's weirdly individualistic behavior increases with the arrival of his baby sister.

Sam Rockwell, Jacob Kogan, Vera Farmiga © FOX SEARCHLIGHT

# TALK TO ME

Chiwetel Ejiofor, Mike Epps © FOCUS FEATURES

Don Cheadle, Chiwetel Ejiofor, Martin Sheen

(FOCUS) Producers, Mark Gordon, Sidney Kimmel, Joe Fries, Josh McLaughlin; Executive Producers, William Horberg, J. Miles Dale, Joey Rappa, Bruce Toll, Don Cheadle; Director, Kasi Lemmons; Screenplay, Michael Genet, Rick Famuyiwa; Story, Michael Genet; Photography, Stephane Fontaine; Designer, Warren Alan Young; Costumes, Gersha Phillips; Editor, Terilyn A. Shropshire; Music, Terence Blanchard; Music Supervisor, Barry Cole; Choreographers, Vicky Lambert, Paul Becker; Casting, Victoria Thomas, Robin D. Cook (Canada); a Mark Gordon Co., Pegasus Films production, presented with Sidney Kimmel Entertainment; Dolby; Super 35 Widescreen; Color; Rated R; 118 minutes; Release date: July 13, 2007.

## Cast

| | |
|---|---|
| Ralph Waldo "Petey" Greene | **Don Cheadle** |
| Dewey Hughes | **Chiwetel Ejiofor** |
| "Nighthawk" Bob Terry | **Cedric the Entertainer** |
| Vernell Watson | **Taraji P. Henson** |
| Milo Hughes | **Mike Epps** |
| E.G. Sonderling | **Martin Sheen** |
| Sunny Jim Kelsey | **Vondie Curtis Hall** |
| Prison Sign-In Guard | **Bruce McFee** |

and Peter MacNeill (Warden Cecil Smithers); Adam Gaudreau (Escorting Guard); J. Miles Dale (Program Director); Sean MacMahon (Ronnie Simmons); Richard Chevolleau (Poochie Braxton); Martin Randez (Hadley); Todd William Schroeder (Guard Captain); Jeff Kassel (Teddy, WOL P.A.); Alison Sealy-Smith (Freda); Warren Alan Young (Bartender); Elle Downs (Peaches); Ngozi Paul (Susan); Malik McCall (Rioter); Herbert L. Rawlings, Jr. (James Brown); Matt Birman (Businessman); Johnie Chase, Eugene Clark, Benz Antoine (Bar Patrons); Vicky Lambert, Mantee Murphy (Backup Singers); Josh McLaughlin (TV News Anchor); Richard Fitzpatrick (Charles Sumner); Damir Andrei (Fred De Cordova); Jim Annan (Tonight Show P.A.); Jim Malmberg (Johnny Carson); Dave Brown (Jail Guard); Robert Tavenor (Engineer)

Don Cheadle, Taraji P. Henson

Cedric the Entertainer

The true story of Petey Greene, a fast-talking street hustler who became a hero to the black community as an outspoken D.C. radio DJ.

# INTERVIEW

Steve Buscemi, Sienna Miller © SONY PICTURES CLASSICS

(SONY CLASSICS) Producers, Bruce Weiss, Gijs van de Westelaken; Executive Producer, Nick Stiliadis; Director, Steve Buscemi; Screenplay, David Schechter, Steve Buscemi, based on the film by Theo Van Gogh and screenplay by Theodor Holman; Photography, Thomas Kist; Editor, Kate Williams; Music, Evan Lurie; Designer, Loren Weeks; Costumes, Vicki Farrell; Casting, Sheila Jaffe; a Cinemavault Releasing presentation of an Ironworks Prods. and Column Pictures production; American-Dutch; Dolby; Color; Sony-HD-cam-to-35mm; Rated R; 84 minutes; Release date: July 13, 2007.

### Cast

Katya **Sienna Miller**
Pierre Peders **Steve Buscemi**
Robert Peders **Michael Buscemi**
Maggie **Tara Elders**
Maitre D' **David Schecter**
Waitress **Molly Griffith**
Woman at Restaurant **Elizabeth Bracco**
Man at Restaurant **James Villemaire**
Fan at Restaurant **Jackson Loo**
Cab Driver **muMs**
and Doc Dougherty (Truck Driver); Donna Hanover (Commentator); Wayne Wilcox (Hunky Actor); Danny Schechter (Political Pundit); Philippe Vonlanthen, Yan Xi (Autograph Seekers); Katja Schuurman (Lady in the Limo); Steve Sands, Craig Grant, JoJo Whilden (Paparazzi); James Franco (Voice of Boyfriend on Phone)

Political journalist Pierre Peders reluctantly agrees to interview seemingly vacuous starlte Katya, only to have their meeting turn increasingly unpredictable as the evening wears on.

# NO END IN SIGHT

(MAGNOLIA) Producers, Charles Ferguson, Jennie Amias, Jessie Vogelson; Executive Producer, Alex Gibney; Director/Screenplay, Charles Ferguson; Photography, Antonio Rossi; Editors, Chad Beck, Cindy Lee; Music, Peter Nashel; Music Supervisor, Tracy McKnight; Iraqi Correspondents, Nir Rosen, Warzer Jaff, Omar S.; Researcher, Christopher Murphy; Associate Producers, Audrey Marrs, E. Mary Walsh; Narrator, Campbell Scott; a Representation Pictures presentation; Color; HD Video; Not rated; 102 minutes; Release date: July 27, 2007. Documentary pointing out the many misjudgments in the Bush administration's invasion of Iraq.

### With

Barbara Bodine, Chris Allbritton, Col. Lawrence Wilkerson, Col. Paul Hughes, Walter Slocombe, Seth Moulton, David Yancey, Gen. Jay Garner, George Packer, Gerald Burke, Hugo Gonzalez, Samantha Power, James Fallows, Linda Bilmes, Maj. Gen. Paul Eaton, Marc Garlasco, Matt Sherman, Nir Rosen, Paul Pillar, Ray Jennings, Richard Armitage, Robert Hutchings, Yaroslav Trofimov, Faisal Al-Zstrabadi, James Bamford, Amazia Baram, Jamal Benomar, Ashton Carter, Ali Fadhil, Omar Fekeiki, Ann Gildroy, Joost Hiltermann, Mahmoud Othman, Robert Perito, Barry Posen, Aida Ussyran.

This film received an Oscar nomination for Documentary Feature.

Paul Bremer, Jay Garner © MAGNOLIA PICTURES

# I NOW PRONOUNCE YOU CHUCK & LARRY

(UNIVERSAL) Producers, Adam Sandler, Jack Giarraputo, Tom Shadyac, Michael Bostick; Executive Producer, Barry Bernardi; Director, Dennis Dugan; Screenplay, Barry Fanaro, Alexander Payne, Jim Taylor; Photography, Dean Semler; Designer, Perry Andelin Blake; Costumes, Ellen Lutter; Music, Rupert Gregson-Williams; Music Supervisors, Michael Dilbeck, Brooks Arthur; Editor, Jeff Gourson; Special Effects Supervisor, Allen L. Hall; Casting, Roger Mussenden; a Happy Madison/Shady Acres production, presented in association with Relativity Media; Dolby; Deluxe color; Rated PG-13; 115 minutes; Release date: July 20, 2007.

## Cast

Chuck Levine  **Adam Sandler**
Larry Valentine  **Kevin James**
Alex McDonough  **Jessica Biel**
Captain Tucker  **Dan Aykroyd**
Duncan  **Ving Rhames**
Clint Fitzer  **Steve Buscemi**
Renaldo Pinera  **Nicholas Turturro**
Steve  **Allen Covert**
Benefits Supervisor  **Rachel Dratch**
Councilman Banks  **Richard Chamberlain**
and Blake Clark (Crazy Homeless Man); Nick Swardson (Kevin McDonough); Mary Pat Gleason (Teresa); Matt Winston (Glen Aldrich); Lance Bass (Band Leader); Dave Matthews (Salesman); Dan Patrick (N.Y. Cop); Rob Corddry (Jim the Protestor); Robert Smigel (Mailman); Richard Kline (Mr. Auerbach); Gary Valentine (Karl Eisendorf); Jonathan Loughran (David Nootzie); Peter Dante (Tony Paroni); J.D. Donaruma (J.D.); Michael Buscemi (Higgy); Cole Morgen (Eric Valentine); Shelby Adamowsky (Tori Valentine); Brad Grunberg (Bernie); John Farley (Criminal Voiceover); Rebecca O'Donohue (Darla); Jessica O'Donohue (Donna); Chandra West (Doctor Honey); Jackie Sandler (Teacher); Judy Sandler (Brooklyn Woman); Sandy Wernick (Jail Guard); Kevin Grady (Bailiff); Dennis Dugan (Cab Driver); Kathleen Doyle (Bernie's Mother); Tila "Tequila" Nguyen, Candace Kita, Jina Song, Jamie Chung, Lean Yada (Hooters Girls); Tyler McKinney (African-American Boy); Delaney Keefe (Pigtailed Girl); Conner Wiles (Jerky Boy); Mark Higgins, David Connare, Tom Silardi, Billy Concha, Darryl Adone, Chris Atwell, Kevin Nolan, Robert Harvey (Firemen); Larry Newman (Officer Newman); Adam Herschman (Mr. Pickles Employee); Michael Westphal, Tracy Bennett (Gay Partygoers); Marc Vann, Bud Mathis, Chuck Church (Protestors); Michael Peter Catanzarite (Doorman); Jennifer Kushner (Lesbian); Lauren Lamonsoff (Cute Girl in Crowd); James Emory (County Clerk); Larry Bullock (Calendar Guy); Tim Wiles (Gay Friend); August "Augie" Johnson, Reagie Clark, Milton Ellis, Anthony Hicks, Ted Perlman (Wedding Singers); Stephen Dress, Taylor Graves (Wedding Musicians); Rob Schneider (Asian Minister)

Worried that he will lose his benefits, widowed firefighter Larry Valentine enters into a faux domestic partnership with another straight fireman, Chuck Levine, an arrangement challenged by the suspicious courts.

Michael Buscemi, Nicholas Turturro, Peter Dante, Kevin James, Jonathan Loughran

Kevin James, Adam Sandler

Jessica Biel © UNIVERSAL STUDIOS

# HAIRSPRAY

Zac Efron, Nikki Blonsky

(NEW LINE CINEMA) Producers, Craig Zadan, Neil Meron; Executive Producers, Bob Shaye, Michael Lynne, Toby Emmerich, Mark Kaufman, Marc Shaiman, Scott Wittman, Adam Shankman, Jennifer Gibgot, Garrett Grant; Co-Producers, Michael Disco, Daryl Freimark, Travis Knox; Director/Choreographer, Adam Shankman; Screenplay, Leslie Dixon, based on the 1988 screenplay by John Waters and the 2002 musical stage play, book by Mark O'Donnell and Thomas Meehan, music by Marc Shaiman, lyrics by Scott Wittman, Marc Shaiman; Photography, Bojan Bazelli; Editor, Michael Tronick; Music, Marc Shaiman; Music Supervisor, Matt Sullivan; Designer, David Gropman; Costumes, Rita Ryack; Visual Effects Supervisors, Lev Kolobov, David M.V. Jones, Mark Freund; Visual Effects, Intelligent Creatures, Riot, Pacific Title; Stunts, Branco Racki; Associate Producers, Anson Downes, Linda Favila; Casting, David Rubin, Richard Hicks; a Zadan/Meron production, in association with Offspring Entertainment, presented in association with Ingenious Film Partners, Dolby; Panavision; Deluxe color; Rated PG; 117 minutes; Release date: July 20, 2007

## Cast

Edna Turnblad **John Travolta**
Velma Von Tussle **Michelle Pfeiffer**
Wilbur Turnblad **Christopher Walken**
Penny Pingleton **Amanda Bynes**
Corny Collins **James Marsden**
Motormouth Maybelle **Queen Latifah**
Amber Von Tussle **Brittany Snow**
Link Larkin **Zac Efron**
Seaweed Stubbs **Elijah Kelley**
Prudy Pingleton **Allison Janney**
Tracy Turnblad **Nikki Blonsky**
Little Inez **Taylor Parks**
Mr. Pinky **Jerry Stiller**
Mr. Spritzer **Paul Dooley**
Cameraman **Darren Frost**
Flasher **John Waters**
Teacher **Joe Parro**
Vicki **Laura Edwards**
Darla **Becca Sweitzer**
Brenda **Cassie Silva**
Noreen **Tiffany Engen**
Doreen **Brooke Leigh Engen**
Shelley **Sarah Jayne Jensen**
Tammy **Hayley Podschun**
Sketch **Nick Braga**
Brad **Curtis Holbrook**
Joey **J.P. Ferreri**
Mikey **Spencer Liff**
Fender **Phillip Spaeth**
and Tabitha Lupien (Becky); Kelly Fletcher (Lou Ann); Jesse Weafer (IQ); Nick Loren (Cop Nick); Brian Hindle, Sheldon Smith, Greg Farkas (Link's Backup Singers); Bruce McFee (Police Chief); Christian Hagen (Male TV Reporter); John Andersen (News Anchorman); Neil Crone (Cop at Protest); George King (Mr. Flak); James Kirchner (Science Geek Teacher); Brendan Wall (Male Cop on TV); Ted Ludzik (Police Sergeant at Protest); Ron Pardo, Geri Hall (*Good Morning Baltimore* Hosts); Seth Howard (Stage Manager); Ricki Lake, Adam Shankman, Marc Shaiman, Scott Wittman (Talent Agents); Anne "Mama" Fletcher (Nurse); Joey Pizzi (Driving Instructor); Zachary Woodlee (Smoking Teacher); C.J. (Janitor); Corey Gorewicz (Bix); Josh Feldman (Jessie); Everett Smith (Paulie); Ariel Reid (Rhonda); Whitney Brown (Hoo Hoo); Jason Dolphin (Tyrone); Anthony "Kanec" Carr (Duane); Christopher Andrew Robinson (Jermaine); Sarah Francis (Janetta); Starr Domingue (Pearl); Shawn Byfield (Little Mo); Shane Simpson (Skillet); Jade Anderson (Stooie); Jayne Eastwood (Miss Wimsey); Anke Rice, Nadine Ellis, Tanee McCall (Dynamites); Gerry Mendicino (Drunk); Nick Settimi (Record Store Owner); Kyle Golemba (Teen); Mary McCandless (Mr. Pinky's Seamstress); Sharron Matthews (Mr. Pinky's Cashier); Jeffrey James (Gawky Kid); Alison Smith, Christine Moore, Emily Andrews, Julianne Jackson, Laura Lawson, Melissa Leifer (Auditionees)

Michelle Pfeiffer © NEW LINE CINEMA

John Travolta, Allison Janney

Jerry Stiller, John Travolta, Nikki Blonsky

Tracy Turnblad realizes her dream of dancing on Baltimore's local *The Corny Collins Show* only to face racism from the network executives, who refuse to allow the program to be integrated. Remake of the 1988 New Line film of the same name.

Amanda Bynes, Elijah Kelley

John Travolta, Queen Latifah

Elijah Kelley, Taylor Parks

# THE SIMPSONS MOVIE

Springfield Citizens (center) Lisa Simpson, Homer Simpson, Bart Simpson, Marge Simpson, Maggie Simpson

Homer Simpson

Bart Simpson

(20TH CENTURY FOX) Producers, James L. Brooks, Matt Groening, Al Jean, Mike Scully, Richard Sakai; Supervising Producer, Richard Raynis; Co-Producer, Jay Kleckner; Animation Co-Producer, Craig Sost; Director, David Silverman; Screenplay, James L. Brooks, Matt Groening, Al Jean, Ian Maxstone-Graham, George Meyer, David Mirkin, Mike Reiss, Mike Scully, Matt Selman, John Swartzwelder, Jon Vitti; Editor, John Carnochan; Music, Hans Zimmer; "The Simpsons Theme," Danny Elfman; Sequence Directors, Mike B. Anderson, Lauren MacMullan, Rich Moore, Steven Dean Moore, Gregg Vanzo; Animation Produced by Film Roman and Rough Draft Feature Animation; Art Director, Dima Malanitchev; Layout Supervisor, Rasoul Azadani; Director of Computer Graphics, Scott Vanzo; Overseas Animation Director, Gary McCarver; Associate Producers, Amanda Moshay, Matt Orefice, Felicia Nalivansky-Caplan; a Gracie Films, Matt Groening production; Dolby; Widescreen; Deluxe color; PG-13; 86 minutes; Release date: July 27, 2007.

## Voice Cast

Dan Castellaneta (Homer Simpson/Itchy/Barney/Grampa/Stage Manager/Krusty the Clown/Mayor Quimby/Mayor's Aide/Multi-Eyed Squirrel/Panicky Man/Sideshow Mel/Mr. Teeny/EPA Official/Kissing Cop/Bear/Boy on Phone/NSA Worker/Officer/Santa's Little Helper/ Squeaky-Voiced Teen); Julie Kavner (Marge Simpson); Nancy Cartwright (Bart Simpson/Maggie Simpson/Ralph/Nelson/Todd Flanders/ TV Daughter/Woman on Phone); Yeardley Smith (Lisa Simpson); Harry Shearer (Scratchy/Mr. Burns/Rev. Lovejoy/Ned Flanders/Lenny/Skull/ President Arnold Schwarzenegger/Kent Brockman/Principal Skinner/ Dr. Hibbert/Smithers/Toll Booth Man/Guard/Otto/Kang); Hank Azaria (Professor Frink/Comic Book Guy/Moe/Chief Wiggum/Lou/Carl/Cletus/ Bumblebee Man/Male EPA Worker/Dome Depot Announcer/Kissing Cop/Carnival Barker/Counter Man/Apu/Drederick Tatum/Sea Captain/ EPA Passenger/Robot/Dr. Nick); Marcia Wallace (Mrs. Krabappel); Tom Hanks, Billie Joe Armstrong, Michael Pritchard, Frank Edwin Wright III (Themselves); Tress MacNeille (Sweet Old Lady/Colin/Mrs. Skinner/ Nelson's Mother/Pig/Cat Lady/Female EPA Worker/G.P.S. Woman/Cookie Kwan/Lindsey Naegle/TV Son/Medicine Woman/Girl on Phone); Pamela Hayden (Milhouse/Rod Flanders);  Joe Mantegna (Fat Tony); Albert Brooks (Russ Cargill); Russi Taylor (Martin); Karl Wiedergott (Man/EPA Driver); Maggie Roswell (Helen Lovejoy); Phil Rosenthal (TV Dad);

Homer Simpson © 20TH CENTURY FOX

After dumping pig waste into an already polluted lake, Homer Simpson causes an environmental nightmare that puts the entire town of Springfield in peril prompting the EPA to place them in quarantine under a giant glass dome. Based on the Fox Channel animated series (1990-present).

Homer Simpson, Bart Simpson

Homer Simpson

Maggie Simpson, Bart Simpson, Lisa Simpson, Marge Simpson, Homer Simpson

# NO RESERVATIONS

Aaron Eckhart, Catherine Zeta-Jones

(WARNER BROS.) Producers, Kerry Heysen, Sergio Aguero; Executive Producers, Susan Cartsonis, Bruce Berman; Co-Producer, Mari Jo Winkler-Ioffreda; Director, Scott Hicks; Screenplay, Carol Fuchs, based on the screenplay *Mostly Martha* by Sandra Nettelbeck; Photography, Stuart Dryburgh; Editor, Pip Karmel; Music, Philip Glass; Music Supervisor, John Bissell; Melissa Toth; Casting, Ronna Kress; a Castle Rock Entertainment presentation in association with Village Roadshow Pictures; Dolby; Super 35 Widescreen; Technicolor; Rated PG; 105 minutes; Release date: July 27, 2007.

## Cast

Kate **Catherine Zeta-Jones**
Nick **Aaron Eckhart**
Zoe **Abigail Breslin**
Therapist **Bob Balaban**
Sean **Brian F. O'Byrne**
Paula **Patricia Clarkson**
Mrs. Peterson **Celia Weston**
and Stephanie Berry (School Principal Ellen Parker); John McMartin (Mr. Peterson); Lily Rabe (Bernadette); Jenny Wade (Leah); Eric Silver (John); Arija Bareikis (Christine); Zöe Kravitz (Charlotte); Matthew Rauch (Ken); Dearbhla Molloy (Anna); Matt Servitto (Doctor); Yevgeniy Dekhtyar (Truffle Dealer); Fulvio Cecere (Fish Vendor Bob); Ako (Vegetable Vendor); Frank Santorelli (Lobster Vendor); A.J. McCloud (Line Cook A.J.); Mario Morales (Line Cook Mario); Monica Trombetta (Liz); Sam Kitchin (Mr. Mathews); Rob Leo Roy (Rare Steak Man); Brian Luna, David Wheir, Joey Cee, Roxanna Hope (Sous Chef Applicants); Katherine Sigismund (Ken s Wife); James Starace (Waiter); Jeanne Omlor (Gigi the Waitress); Noah Petroski, Nicholas Petroski (Sean s Twins); Lorca Simons (Rare Steak Woman); Patrick Zeller (Leah s Husband); Gretchen Wiese (Mrs. Matthews); Ramon Fernandez (Carlos); Angel Rosa, Ignacio Heredero, Albert Martinez (Busboys); Hani Shihada (Chalk Artist); Akira Takayama (Produce Customer); Henry Kwan (Delivery Guy)

After the tragic death of her sister, workaholic New York chef Kate must cope with raising her grieving niece Zoe.

Bob Balaban, Catherine Zeta-Jones

Aaron Eckhart, Abigail Breslin

Patricia Clarkson, Catherine Zeta-Jones © WARNER BROS.

# THE BOURNE ULTIMATUM

(UNIVERSAL) Producers, Frank Marshall, Patrick Crowley, Paul L. Sandberg; Executive Producers, Jeffrey M. Weiner, Henry Morrison, Doug Liman; Director, Paul Greengrass; Screenplay, Tony Gilroy, Scott Z. Burns, George Nolfi; Screen Story, Tony Gilroy, based on the novel by Robert Ludlum; Photography, Oliver Wood; Designer, Peter Wenham; Costumes, Shay Cunliffe; Music, John Powell; Editor, Christopher Rouse; Casting, John Hubbard, Dan Hubbard, Avy Kaufman; Fight Stunt Coordinator, Jeff Imdada; Stunts, Gary Powell, Darrin Prescott, Scott Rogers, Miguel Pedregosa, Evangelos Grecos; a Kennedy/Marshall production, in association with Ludlum Entertainment; Dolby; Super 35 Widescreen; Technicolor; Rated PG-13; Release date: August 3, 2007

Colin Stinton, Paddy Considine

## Cast

Jason Bourne  **Matt Damon**
Nicky Parsons  **Julia Stiles**
Noah Vosen  **David Strathairn**
Ezra Kramer  **Scott Glenn**
Simon Ross  **Paddy Considine**
Paz  **Edgar Ramirez**
Dr. Albert Hirsch  **Albert Finney**
Pam Landy  **Joan Allen**
Tom Cronin  **Tom Gallop**
Wills  **Corey Johnson**
Martin Kreutz  **Daniel Brühl**
Desh  **Joey Ansah**
Neal Daniels  **Colin Stinton**
Jimmy  **Dan Fredenburgh**
Lucy  **Lucy Liemann**
Technicians  **Bryan Reents, Arkie Reece, John Roberson, Russ Huard**
Betancourt  **Mark Bazeley**
Chamberlain  **Sinead O'Keefe**
Agent Hammond  **Chucky Venice**
Agent Kiley  **Scott Adkins**
Russian Policemen  **Branko Tomovic, Laurentiu Possa**
Tactical Team Leader  **Trevor St. John**
Tactical Team Agent  **Albert Jones**
Vosen's Driver  **Jeffrey Lee Gibson**
Morgue Attendant  **Uriel Emil**
NYPD Officers  **Omar Hernández, William H. Burns**
CRI Agent  **Michael Wildman**
Hoody  **Kai Martin**

David Strathairn, Joan Allen, Tom Gallop

Jason Bourne must use his training to outwit and destroy Blackbriar's assassins, who want him dead to ensure he poses no security threat to their operations. Previous series entries from Universal were *The Bourne Identity* (2002) and *The Bourne Supremacy* (2004), with several of the cast principals returning to their roles here.

2007 Academy Award winner for Best Film Editing, Best Sound Mixing, and Best Sound Editing.

Matt Damon © UNIVERSAL STUDIOS

## EL CANTANTE

Jennifer Lopez, Marc Anthony

Marc Anthony

(PICTUREHOUSE) Producers, Julio Caro, Jennifer Lopez, Simon Fields, David Maldonado; Co-Producer, Margo Myers; Director, Leon Ichaso; Screenplay, Leon Ichaso, David Darmstaedter, Todd Anthony Bello; Photography, Claudio Chea; Designer, Sharon Lomofsky; Costumes, Sandra Hernandez; Editor, David Tedeschi; Music, Andres Levin; Music Supervisor, Tracy McKnight; Makeup, Nuria Sitja; Choreographer, Maria Torres; Associate Producer, Nini Mazen; Casting, Ellyn Long Marshall, Maria E. Nelson; a Nuyorican Prods./R-Caro Prods. presentation in association with Union Square Works; Dolby; Deluxe color; Rated R; 116 minutes; Release date: August 3, 2007.

### Cast

Hector Lavoe **Marc Anthony**
Puchi **Jennifer Lopez**
Willie Colón **John Ortiz**
Eddie **Manny Perez**
Ralph Mercado **Vincent Laresca**
Jerry Masucci **Federico Castelluccio**
Johnny Pacheco **Nelson Vasquez**
Sound Engineer **Danny A. Abeckaser**
and Douglas J. Aguirre (Multimedia Producer); Christopher Becerra, Bernard Hernandez (Tito); Denise Blasor (Voiceover Artist); Marcus Collins (Photographer); Anibal De Gracia (Trombonist); Tony Devon (Record Executive); Romi Dias (Priscilla); Glenda Dopazo (Carmen); Michael Caputo, Ivan Cardona, Melissa Otero, Jerry Perez (Salsa Dancers); Brother Douglas (Street Sax Man, 1987); Vaneik Echeverria (Bartender); Jared Everleth (Tito, 4 Years Old); Melissa Gonzalez (Fania All Star Groupie); Hector A. Leguillow (Pianist for Hector's Band, 1968); Deirdre Lorenz (Willie's Girl); Chicko Mendez (Backup Singer); Vianca Mercedes (Cuban Bartender); Jack Mulcahy (Doctor); Andrea Navedo (Puchi's Sister); Antone Pagan (Papo); Jorge Pupo (Trombonist for Lavoe and Colón Bands); Edwin Rivera (Best Friend); Lou Torres (Dayplayer/Piano Player); Richie Viruet (Trjmpet Player)

Marc Anthony, Bernard Hernandez, Jennifer Lopez

Marc Anthony (center) © PICTUREHOUSE

The story of Hector Lavoe, who battled drug addiction while becoming one of the leading names in salsa music.

# UNDERDOG

Underdog, Jim Belushi © WALT DISNEY PICTURES

(WALT DISNEY PICTURES) Producers, Gary Barber, Roger Birnbaum, Jay Polstein, Jonathan Glickman; Executive Producers, Eric Ellenbogen, Bob Higgins, Todd Arnow; Co-Producers, Erin Stam, Rebekah Rudd; Director, Frederik Du Chau; Screenplay, Adam Rifkin, Joe Piscatella, Craig A. Williams; Story, Joe Piscatella, Craig A. Williams, Adam Rifkin; Photography, David Eggby; Designer, Garreth Stover; Costumes, Gary Jones; Editor, Tom Finan; Music, Randy Edelman; Visual Effects Supervisor, Hoyt Yeatman; Visual Effects Producer, Andy Fowler; Visual Effects, Framestore, Cinesite (Europe); Stunts, Bobby Brown; Animal Coordinator, Boone Narr; Casting, Gail Goldberg; a Barber-Birnbaum/Jay Polstein production, in association with Classic Media, presented in association with Spyglass Entertainment; Distributed by Buena Vista Pictures; Dolby; Technicolor; Rated PG; 80 minutes; Release date: August 3, 2007.

## Cast

Dan Unger  **Jim Belushi**
Dr. Simon Barsinister  **Peter Dinklage**
Cad  **Patrick Warburton**
and Alex Neuberger (Jack Unger); Taylor Momsen (Molly); John Slattery (Mayor); Brad Garrett (Voice of Riff Raff); Amy Adams (Voice of Polly); Jason Lee (Voice of Underdog); Samantha Bee (Principal); Timothy Crowe (Police Chief); Larry Vigus (Security Guard); Mario Mariani (Police Officer); Bates Wilder (Cop); Alexander Garde (Small Boy); Christopher Byrnes (Mailman); Joseph Siriani (Newsstand Guy); Sujoy De, Michele Proude (Office Workers); Albert M. Chan (Geek Worker); Jon Pierce (Hot Dog Vendor); Susie Castillo (Diana Floes); Bob Jaffe (Professor); Bruce Serafin (City Worker); Anthony Estrella, Ellen Withrow (School Teachers); Malik McMullen, Lincoln P. Sisson (Bomb Squad Officers); Aaron Dorsey (Little Boy); Walter Covell (Old Man); Kate Lohman (Housewife); Lewis D. Wheeler (Geek with Glasses); John M. Deluca (Newscaster); Frank Ridley (Police Sergeant); Grady Justice (College Guy); Courtney O'Regan (College Girl); Rebekha Aramini (Fox Collar Lady); Richney Fischer (Baseball Dad); Joe Stapleton, Armen Garo (Cat Burglars); Daniel Kirby (News Director); Steve Kidd (Bomb Squad Member); Rena Maliszweski (Mother); Diana Schneider (Police Secretary); Barry Blair (SWAT Captain); Gabriel Field (Lyle); Harry L. Thomas (Police Artist); Amy Tanner (Kissing Girl); Nicole Kopka (Jogger in Park); Adam McCarthy (Capitol City Security #4); Roy Souza, T.J. Paolino, William Alva (Capitol City Cops); Scott Dittman (Hot Dog Contestant); Ezra Buzzington (Referee); Chris Ciulla (Fireman); Jay Leno (Himself); Phil Morris, Michael Massee (Supershep Voices); Cameron A. Clarke (Voice of Little Brown Dog, Supershep); John Di Maggio (Voice of Bulldog, Supershep); Danny Mastrogiorgio (Voice of Crazy Dog); Jess Harnell (Voice of Astronaut); Lonnie Farmer (Passerby); Joseph Bucaro III, Stuart Wilson (Goons), Michael Tyler Henry (Voice of Jack Unger); Tony Moreira (Bomb Squad Officer Farrell)

A genetically enhanced pooch, given the power to fly and communicate with humans, decides to use his unusual capabilities to fight crime and save the world from the diabolical Dr. Simon Barsinister. Based on the cartoon character that appeared on CBS and NBC (1964-70; 1972-73).

Peter Dinklage, Patrick Warburton

Alex Neuberger, Taylor Momsen

# THE TEN

Adam Brody

(THINKFILM) Producers, Jonathan Stern, Ken Marino, David Wain, Paul Rudd, Morris S. Levy; Executive Producers, Danny Fisher, Sam Zietz, Jack Fisher, Michael Almog; Co-Producers, Derrick Tseng, Marcus Lansdell, Max Sinovoi, Michael Califra, Joe Fisher, Michael Bassick; Director, David Wain; Screenplay, Ken Marino, David Wain; Photography, Yaron Orbach; Designer, Mark White; Costumes, Sarah J. Holden; Editor, Eric Kissack; Music, Craig Wedren; Music Supervisor, Tracy McKnight; Animation, Aaron Augenblick; Casting, Beth Bowling, Kim Miscia; a City Lights Pictures presentation in association with Mega Films and Centrifugal Films of a Wain/Marino production; Dolby; Color; Rated R; 99 minutes; Release date: August 3, 2007.

Jessica Alba, Paul Rudd © THINKFILM

## Cast

Jeff Reigert  **Paul Rudd**
Gretchen Reigert  **Famke Janssen**
Kelly LaFonda  **Winona Ryder**
Liz Anne Blazer  **Jessica Alba**
Stephen Montgomery  **Adam Brody**
Gloria Jennings  **Gretchen Mol**
Jesus H. Christ  **Justin Theroux**
Oliver Jennings  **A.D. Miles**
Marc Jacobson  **Oliver Platt**
Dr. Glenn Richie  **Ken Marino**
Duane Rosenblum  **Rob Corddry**
Bernice Jaffe  **Kerri Kenney-Silver**
and Liev Schreiber (Ray Johnson); Joe Lo Truglio (Paul Mardino); Mather Zickel (Louis LaFonda); Michael Ziegfield (Harlan Swallow); Jason Sudeikis (Tony Contiella); Ron Silver (Fielding Barnes); Bobby Canavale (Marty McBride); Kevin Allison (Stanley); Jason Antoon (Salazar "Fred" McBairn); Fernando Baena (Mango Vendor Rodriguez), Matthew Ballard (Defense Attourney Greg Splenda), Siri Baruc (Natalie Freyberg, Party Girl); H. Jon Benjamin (Rhino); Reed Birney (Jim Stansel); Michael Ian Black (Prison Guard Jamberg Saivon); Jonathan Davis (Mexico Narrator); David Fariborz Davoodian (Landlord); Beth Dover (Sheila Contiella); Arlen Escarpeta (Todd Jaffe); Robert Ben Garant, Seth Herzog (Themselves); Edmund Genest (Governor Beaumont Hutchins); Alfredo Gonzalez (Pedicab Driver), Jon Hamm (Skydiving Guide Chris Knarl), Zandy Hartig (Sally/Callie); Nina Hellman (Nurse Nancy Hellman); Todd Holoubek (Cameraman Stuart Blumberg); Alexis Iacono (The Nerd); Thomas Lennon, David Wain (Richie's Friends); Ali Marsh (EB Host George Reardon); Paco Mauri (Alfonso Zavata); Charlie McDermott (Jake Johnson); Michael Mulheren (Big Buster); Novella Nelson (Judge Sophia R. Jackson); Tommy Nelson (Noah Jennings); Heidi Neurauter (Helen Campbell-Holland); Zak Orth (Prosecutor/Tour Guide); Erica Oyama (Bream Benson); Zach Page (Loofie Lavinsky, Smart-Ass Kid); Raisy Pereyra (Dorothy Sheen); Victoria Perez (Rosa Zavata); Andrea Rosen (Polly "Carol" Samuels); Rich Rothbell (Dr. Driscoll); Cedric Sanders (Greg Jaffe); Michael Showalter (Police Lt. Farn Bleern); Scott Sowers (Jury Foreman Barry Noodle); John Tormey (Jerry); Chris Wylde (Kevin Lipworth); Janeane Garofalo (Powerplant Shift Supervisor Beth Soden); Antonio Zavala Kugler (Prison Guard Banderas); Rashida Jones (Hostess Rebecca Fornier); Joe Passaro (Xylophone Player Clovis Handleman); Jerry Grayson (Jnkie Floyd Congril Dillon); John Tormey (Junkie Jerry Park); Philip Levy (Junkie Thomas McKee); Jonathan Stern (Cartoon Voices/Naked Guy); David Dinan (Landlord Izzy Mavis); Andrew Dawson (Principal DiBiaso); Jack Fisher, Seth Herzog, Andy Kaufman, Richard Kessler, Morris S. Levy, Tom McHugh, Phil Michas, Peter Moore, David Ressel, Noam Rosen, Sarge, Eric Tepper, Craig Wedren (Naked Guys)

Each of the Ten Commandments receives a somewhat unorthodox dramatization.

# STARDUST

(PARAMOUNT) Producers, Matthew Vaughn, Lorenzo di Bonaventura, Michael Dreyer, Neil Gaiman; Executive Producers, David Womark, Kris Thykier, Peter Morton, Stephen Marks; Director, Matthew Vaughn; Screenplay, Matthew Vaughn, Jane Goldman, based on the novel by Neil Gaiman, illustrated by Charles Vess; Photography, Ben Davis; Designer, Gavin Bocquet; Costumes, Sammy Sheldon; Editor, Jon Harris; Music, Ilan Eshkeri; Music Supervisor, Liz Gallagher; Digital Visual Effects Supervisor, Mattias Lindahl; Visual Effects Supervisors, Sheila Wickens, Stuart Partridge, Simon Leech, Val Wardlaw, John Lockwood, Steve Street; Special Effects Supervisors, Stuart Brisdon, Nigel Nixon; Digital Visual Effects, Double Negative; Visual Effects, Lipsync Post, Cinesite (Europe), the Senate Visual Effects, Baseblack Visual Effects, Machine, Rushes Post Production; Choreographer, Piers Gielgud; Second Unit Director/Stunts, Simon Crane; Associate Producer, Tarquin Pack; Casting, Lucinda Syson; a Matthew Vaughn/Lorenzo di Bonaventura production, presented in association with MARV Films; Dolby; Panavision; Deluxe color; Rated PG-13; 125 minutes; Release date: August 10, 2007.

## Cast

Yvaine **Claire Danes**
Lamia **Michelle Pfeiffer**
Captain Shakespeare **Robert De Niro**
Tristan Thorn **Charlie Cox**
Victoria **Sienna Miller**
Ferdy the Fence **Ricky Gervais**
Primus **Jason Flemyng**
Secondus **Rupert Everett**
King **Peter O'Toole**
Septimus **Mark Strong**
Una, Witch's Slave **Kate Magowan**
Narrator **Ian McKellen**
Wall Guard **David Kelly**
Ditchwater Sal **Melanie Hill**
Dunstan Thorn **Nathaniel Parker**
Bishop **Struan Rodger**
and Bimbo Hart (Young Scientist); Alastair MacIntosh (Victorian Academic); Ben Barnes (Young Dunstan Thorn); Henry Cavill (Humphrey); Darby Hawker (Grumpy Customer); Frank Ellis (Mr. Monday); Mark Heap (Tertius); David Walliams (Sextus); Julian Rhind-Tutt (Quartus); Adam Buxton (Quintus); Sarah Alexander (Empusa); Joanna Scanlan (Mormo); George Innes (Soothsayer); Jake Curran (Bernard); Grant Burgin (Lackey); Mark Williams (Billy); Olivia Grant (Girl Bernard); Coco Sumner (Yvaine's Sister); Dexter Fletcher (Skinny Pirate); Terry Murphy (Old Pirate); Geoff Bell (Receptionist); Mark Burns (New Bishop); Rab Affleck, Carlos Besse Peres, Chopper, Adam Fogerty, Jordan Lang, Spencer Wilding (Pirates)

Tristan Thorn enters the mythical kingdom of Stormhold, where he tries to protect a falling star that has taken the shape of a beautiful young woman and is being pursued by a wicked witch intent on eating the girl's heart and prolonging her youth.

Robert De Niro, Claire Danes, Charlie Cox

Peter O'Toole

Ricky Gervais, Michelle Pfeiffer © PARAMOUNT PICTURES

## RUSH HOUR 3

Jackie Chan, Chris Tucker © NEW LINE CINEMA

(NEW LINE CINEMA) Producers, Arthur Sarkissian, Roger Birnbaum, Jay Stern, Jonathan Glickman, Andrew Z. Davis; Executive Producer, Toby Emmerich; Co-Producers, James M. Freitag, Leon Dudevoir; Director, Brett Ratner; Screenplay, Jeff Nathanson;Photography, J. Michael Muro; Designer, Edward Verreaux; Costumes, Betsy Heimann; Editors, Don Zimmerman, Dean Zimmerman, Mark Helfrich; Music, Lalo Schifrin; Visual Effects Designer/Supervisor, John Bruno; Special Effects Supervisor, Clayton W. Pinney, Gregoire Delage; Visual Effects, Industrial Light & Magic, CIS Hollywood; Stunts, Conrad E. Palmisano, Eddie Braun; Jackie Chan Stunt Coordinator, Bradley James Allen; Choreographer, Marguerite Derricks; Associate Producers, David A. Gorder, Darryl Jones; Casting, Ronna Kress; a New Line Cinema presentation of an Arthur Sarkissian and Roger Birnbaum production; Dolby; Panavision; Deluxe color; Rated PG-13; 91 minutes; Release date: August 10, 2007.

Hiroyuki Sanada (center)

Roman Polanski

### Cast

Chief Inspector Lee  **Jackie Chan**
Det. James Carter  **Chris Tucker**
Kenji  **Hiroyuki Sanada**
Dragon Lady  **Youki Kudoh**
Varden Reynard  **Max von Sydow**
George  **Yvan Attal**
Genevieve  **Noemie Lenoir**
Soo Yung  **Zhang Jingchu**
Ambassador Han  **Tzi Ma**
Sister Agnes  **Dana Ivey**
Det. Revi  **Roman Polanski**
and Henry Q (Master Yu); Julie Depardieu (George's Wife); Philip Baker Hall (Captain William Diel); Sun Ming Ming (Kung Fu Giant); Mia Tyler (Marsha); Michael Chow (Chinese Foreign Minister); David Niven Jr. (British Foreign Minister); Oanh Nguyen (Mi); Lisa Thornhill (Nurse); M. Kentaro (French Assassin); Andrew Quang (Kung Fu Kid); Ludovic Paris, Richard Dieux, Olivier Schneider (French Cops); Philippe Bergeron (Baccarat Dealer); Daniel Yabut (Croupier); Frank Bruynbroek (Bartender); Lisa Piepergerdes (Falling Woman); Eric Naggar (Front Desk Man); Silvie Laguna (Elevator Woman); Micaelle Mee-Sook (Chinese Waitress); Daniel Decrauze (Singing Guitarist); Ann Christine, Anna Chiu, Heather Mostofizadeh, Jasmine Dustin, Francesca C. Cecil (Dressing Room Girls); David Goldsmith (Clown); Michel Francini (Old Man on Balcony); Hoang Nghi (Eiffel Tower Lookout); Mandy Coulton, Diana Carr, Kayla McGee, Tanja Plecas, Kristin Quinn, Liliya Toneva, Vanessa Tarazona, Rachael Markarian, Laetitia Ray, Toaris Wilson (Gendarmes Dancers); Lisa Baynes, Melissa Cabrera, R.J. Durell, Catherin Ferrino, Loriel Hennington, Jaayda McClanahan, Ann Beth Miller, Victoria Parsons (Follies Dancers)

Officers Lee and Carter head to Paris in an effort to retrieve an important envelope containing key evidence against a secret triad conspiracy. Third entry in the New Line Cinema series, following *Rush Hour* (1998) and *Rush Hour 2* (2001).

# ROCKET SCIENCE

(PICTUREHOUSE) Producers, Effie T. Brown, Sean Welch; Director/Screenplay, Jeffrey Blitz; Photography, Jo Willems; Designer, Rick Butler; Costumes, Ernesto Martinez; Editor, Yana Gorskaya; Music, Eef Barzelay; Music Supervisor, Evyen Klean; Line Producer, Nicole Colombie; Casting, Matthew Lessall; a Duly Noted and B&W Films production, presented with HBO Films; Dolby; Color; Rated 101 minutes; Release date: August 10, 2007.

Vincent Piazza, Reece Daniel Thompson, Aaron Yoo

### Cast

Hal Hefner **Reece Daniel Thompson**
Ginny Ryerson **Anna Kendrick**
Ben Wekselbaum **Nicholas D'Agosto**
Earl Hefner **Vincent Piazza**
Coach Lumbly **Margo Martindale**
Heston **Aaron Yoo**
Lewis Garrles **Josh Kay**
Judge Pete **Stephen Park**
Lewinsky **Maury Ginsberg**
Ram **Utkarsh Ambudkar**
Doyle Hefner **Denis O'Hare**
Juliet Hefner **Lisbeth Bartlett**
Abraham Lincoln **Dionne Audain**
Townsend Prep Debater **Candance Burr Scholz**
English Teacher **Virginia Frank**
Plainsboro Lunch Lady **Marilyn Yoblick**
Honoria **Emily Ginnona**
Stephen Douglas **Dan DeLuca**
Flemming **Michael Kusnir**
Gym Teacher, Coach Cho **John Patrick Barry**
Fern Garrles **Jane Beard**
Lewis's Dad **Herb Merrick**
Junior Philosopher, Lionel **Jonah Hill**
Crystal Hamish-Steinberg **Betsy Hogg**
Phillip **Brandon Thane Wilson**
Plainsboro Debate Team **Zack Arrington, Jaime Chicas, Katrina Hargrave, Erin Loube, Natasha Sattler, Will Shaw, Jeffrey Wei**
Frank Ryerson **David DeBoy**
Hazlet Timer **Andrew Collie**
and Huong Huyuh (Lewinsky's Girlfriend); Katherine Ross Wolfe (Glen Rock Debater); Susan "Tootsie" Duvall (Hazlet Lunch Lady); Elisabeth Noone (Hazlet Coach); Noah Mazaika, Will Parquette (Trophy Presenters); Tara Richter-Smith (Babysitter); Judy Jean Berns (Townsend Prep Receptionist); Jeanette Brox (Townsend Prep Bad Girl); Roland Branford Gomez (Luis); Lee Sellars (New Jersey Debate Official); Joel Marsh Garland (Pizza Server); Dan Cashman (Narrator); Carol A. Florence (Connie Ryerson); Justin Mather (Morristown Debater)

Reece Daniel Thompson

Hal Hefner, whose social skills are severely hampered by a developed stutter, is encouraged by the highly competitive Ginny Ryerson to join the high school debate team.

Anna Kendrick © PICTUREHOUSE

# DELIRIOUS

Steve Buscemi, Michael Pitt © PEACE ARCH RELEASING

(PEACE ARCH RELEASING) Producer, Robert Salerno; Executive Producers, Jimmy de Brabant, Michael Dounaev, Kami Naghdi, Mark Balsam, Gary Howsam, Lewin Webb, Barry Zemel, John Flock, Jennifer Levine; Director/Screenplay, Tom DiCillo; Photography, Frank G. DeMarco; Editor, Paul Zucker; Music, Anton Sanko; Designer, Teresa Mastropiero; a Peace Arch Films/Artina Films production in association with Thema Production; Dolby; Color; Not rated; 107 minutes; Release date: August 15, 2007.

## Cast

| | |
|---|---|
| Les Galantine | **Steve Buscemi** |
| Toby Grace | **Michael Pitt** |
| K'Harma Leeds | **Alison Lohman** |
| Dana | **Gina Gershon** |
| Gabi | **Callie Thorne** |
| Ricco | **Kevin Corrigan** |
| Les' Father | **Tom Aldredge** |
| Jace Hipley | **Richard Short** |

and Doris Belack (Les' Mother); Elvis Costello, Philip Bloch (Themselves); Peter Appel (Feldman); Lynn Cohen (Muffy Morrison); Marcus Collins (Marcus); Greg D'Agostino (Security); Joe D'Onofrio (Vince); Teddy Eck (Dougie); Marshall Factora (Club Patron); Mel Gorham (Tish); Billy Griffith (Hoagie); Amit Gupta (Hotel Guest); Jack Gwaltney (Chuck Sirloin); Amy Hargreaves (Nikki Blake); Corey Hibbert (Orderly); Kristina Klebe (Nurse Kris); Antoinette LaVecchia (Gretchen); Cinqué Lee (Corey); Rodrigo Lopresti (Demo); Carylee McPherson (Publicist); Elizabeth Newman (Red Carpet Celebrity); Sarah Nichols (Robbyn's Make-up Artist); Melissa Rauch (Megan); Tom Stratford (Photographer); Tobias Truvillion (Silky); Nicole Vicius (Robbyn); David Wain (Byron)

Becoming assistant to paparazzi photographer Les Galantine brings aspiring thespian Toby Grace closer to pop star K'Harma Leed and his own degree of success.

# THE 11TH HOUR

(WARNER INDEPDENDENT PICTURES) Producers, Leonardo DiCaprio, Leila Conners Petersen, Chuck Castleberry, Brian Gerber; Executive Producers, Adam Lewis, Pierre Senizergues, Irmelin DiCaprio, Doyle Brunson, Al Decarolis; Directors, Leila Conners Petersen, Nadia Conners; Screenplay, Leonardo DiCaprio, Leila Conners Peterson, Nadia Conners; Photography, Peter Youngblood Hills (16mm), Andrew Rowland (35mm), Brian Knappenberger (interview photography); Editors, Pietro Scalia, Luis Alvarez y Alvarez; Music, Jean Pascal Beintus, Eric Avery; Music Supervisor, Eric Avery; Designer, Nadia Conners; Associate Producer, Stephan McGuire; Narrator, Leonardo DiCaprio; an Appian Way/Greenhorn, Tree Media Group production; Dolby; Color; Rated PG; 95 minutes; Release date: August 17, 2007. Documentary on the unsettling effects of global warming.

## With

Leonardo DiCaprio, Ray Anderson, Kenny Ausubel, Janine Benvus, Tzeporah Berman, Leser Brown, Tim Carmichael, Theo Colborn, Herman Daly, Wade Davis, Peter de Menocal, Brock Dolman, Sylvia Earle, Rick Fedrizzi, Gloria Flora, Omar Freilla, Nathan Gardels, Michel Gelobter, Leo Gerard, Mikhail Gorbachev, Thom Hartmann, Paul Hawken, Stephen Hawking, Richard Heinberg, James Hillman, Jeremy Jackson, Wes Jackson, Tom Linzey, Andy Lipkis, Oren Lyons, Wangari Maathai, Jerry Mander, Bruce Mau, William McDonough, Bill McKibben, Rev. James Parks Morton, Wallace J. Nichols, David Orr, Mathew Petersen, Stuart Pimm, Sandra Postel, Andy Revkin, Stephen Schneider, Paolo Soleri, Paul Stamets, David Suzuki, Joseph Tainter, Betsy Taylor, John Todd, Vijay Vaitheeswaran, Peter Warshall, Sheila Watt-Cloutier, Andy Weil, Diane Wilson, James Woolsey

Leonardo DiCaprio © WARNER INDEPENDENT PICTURES

# THE INVASION

(WARNER BROS.) Producer, Joel Silver; Executive Producers, Roy Lee, Doug Davison, Susan Downey, Steve Richards, Ronald G. Smith, Bruce Berman; Director, Oliver Hirschbiegel; Screenplay, David Kajganich, based on the novel *The Body Snatchers* by Jack Finney; Photography, Rainer Klausmann; Editors, Joel Negron, Hans Funck; Music, John Ottman; Designer, Jack Fisk; Costumes, Jacqueline West; Visual Effects Supervisor, Boyd Shermis; Visual Effects, Hydraulx, Lola VFX, Scanline; Associate Producers, David Gambino, Jessica Alan; Casting, Ronna Kress; a Silver Pictures production in association with Vertigo Entertainment, presented in association with Village Roadshow Pictures; Dolby; Technicolor; Rated PG-13; 99 minutes; Release date: August 17, 2007.

Roger Rees, Nicole Kidman, Daniel Craig © WARNER BROS.

### Cast

Carol Bennell  **Nicole Kidman**
Ben Driscoll  **Daniel Craig**
Tucker Kaufman  **Jeremy Northam**
Oliver  **Jackson Bond**
Dr. Stephen Galeano  **Jeffrey Wright**
Wendy Lenk  **Veronica Cartwright**
Dr. Henryk Belicec  **Josef Sommer**
Ludmilla Belicec  **Celia Weston**
Yorish  **Roger Rees**
Gene  **Eric Benjamin**
Pam  **Susan Floyd**
Carly  **Stephanie Berry**
Belicec's Aide  **Alexis Raben**
Richard Lenk  **Adam LeFevre**
Joan Kaufman  **Joanna Merlin**
and Field Blauvelt (Census Taker); Rhonda Overby (Dina Twain); Reid Sasser (NASA Official); Brandon J. Price (John); Mia Arniece Chambers (Jan); Ava Lenet (Mrs. Cunningham); Michael A. Kelly (Dog Owner); Jeremiah Hake (Andy); Luray Cooper (Cop in Tunnel); Nanna Ingvarsson (Panicked Woman in Tunnel); Jeff Wincott (Transit Cop); Wes Johnson (Newsstand Vendor); Parker Webb (Man in Rags); Cloie Wyatt Taylor (Sobbing Teen); John Colton (Field Reporter); John Leslie Wolfe (Tucker's Colleague); Michael Stone Forrest (Butler); Tim Scanlin (Subway Guy); Tara Garwood (Subway Girl); Genevieve Adell (Sleep-Deprived Screamer); Derren Fuentes (Helpful Cop); Darla Mason Robinson (Crying Woman); Brian Augustus Parnell (Street Cop); Benjamin Bullard (Boy in Train Station); Jean H. Miller (Transition Nurse); Jean B. Schertler (Elderly Lady); James Bouchet (Security Guard); Becky Woodley (Mrs. Robinson)

Jeffrey Wright

D.C. psychiatrist Carol Bennell must fight to save herself and her young son after contaminated spores from space start making emotionless replicas of earthlings once they have fallen asleep and inadvertently succumbed. Previous versions were *Invasion of the Body Snatchers* (Allied Artists, 1956), with Kevin McCarthy; *Invasion of the Body Snatchers* (UA, 1978), with Donald Sutherland; and *Body Snatchers* (WB, 1994), with Meg Tilly.

Daniel Craig, Nicole Kidman

# SUPERBAD

Michael Cera, Jonah Hill

(COLUMBIA) Producers, Judd Apatow, Shauna Robertson; Executive Producers, Seth Rogen, Evan Goldberg; Director, Greg Mottola; Screenplay, Seth Rogen, Evan Goldberg; Photography, Russ Alsobrook; Designer, Chris Spellman; Costumes, Debra McGuire; Music, Lyle Workman; Music Supervisor, Jonathan Karp; Editor, William Kerr; Co-Producer, Dara Weintraub; Casting, Allison Jones; an Apatow Company production; Dolby; Deluxe color; Rated R; 112 minutes; Release date: August 17, 2007.

Michael Cera, Martha MacIsaac © COLUMBIA PICTURES

## Cast

Seth **Jonah Hill**
Evan **Michael Cera**
Fogell ("McLovin") **Christopher Mintz-Plasse**
Officer Slater **Bill Hader**
Officer Michaels **Seth Rogen**
Becca **Martha MacIsaac**
Jules **Emma Stone**
Nicola **Aviva**
Francis the Driver **Joe Lo Truglio**
Mark **Kevin Corrigan**
Homeless Guy **Clement E. Blake**
Liquor Store Cashier **Erica Vittina Phillips**
Liquor Store Clerk **Joseph A. Nuñez**
Greg the Soccer Player **Dave Franco**
Gaby **Marcella Lentz-Pope**
Jesse **Scottie Gerbacia**
Shirley **Laura Seay**
Miroki **Roger Iwami**
Prosthetic Leg Kid **Clint Mabry**
Evan's Mom **Stacy Edwards**
Father with Bat **Mark Rogen**
Good Shopper Cashier **Charlie Hartsock**
Old Lady **Dona Hardy**
Good Shopper Security **Charley Rossman**
Period Blood Girl **Carla Gallo**
Quince Danbury **Ben Best**
Tut Long John Silver **Jody Hill**
Patrick Manchester **Kevin Breznahan**
Benji Austin **David Krumholtz**
Billy Baybridge **Mousa Kraish**
Coffee Fairmount **Nicholas Jasenovec**
James Masselin **Martin Starr**
Wild Bill Cherry **Keith Joseph Loneker**
Kane Cloverdale **Matthew McKane**
Scarlett Brighton **Lauren Miller**
Tiger Greendragon **Peter Salett**
Muffin Selby **Rakefet Abergel**
Mrs. Hayworth **Brooke Dillman**
and Michael Naughton (Gym Teacher); Steve Bannos (Math Teacher); Casey Margolis (Young Seth); Laura Marano (Young Becca); Matthew Bass (Vagtastic Voyager); Aurora Snow, Jenna Haze (Vagtastic Voyage Girls); Ted Haigh (Bartender); Michael Fennessey (Bus Driver); Brian Huskey (Elementary Principal); Clark Duke, Stephen Borrello IV, Naathan Phan (Party Teenagers); Pamella D'Pella (Teacher)

A pair of socially inept teens, about to face an uncertain future apart as they leave high school behind, embark on a night of mishaps as they attempt to buy beer for a party at which they hope at last to score with some girls.

David Krumholtz, Jonah Hill, Kevin Breznahan, Michael Cera

Christopher Mintz-Plasse, Aviva

Jonah Hill, Michael Cera

Michael Cera, Jonah Hill, Christopher Mintz-Plasse

# DEATH AT A FUNERAL

Kris Marshall, Daisy Donovan © MGM

(MGM) Producers, Diana Phillips, Share Stallings, Laurence Malkin, Sidney Kimmel; Executive Producers, William Horberg, Bruce Toll, Andreas Grosch, Philip Elway; Co-Producers, Josh Kesselman, Alex Lewis; Director, Frank Oz; Screenplay, Dean Craig; Photography, Oliver Curtis; Editor, Beverley Mills; Music, Murray Gold; Designer, Michael Howells; Costumes, Natalie Ward; Visual Effects Supervisor, Sue Rowe; Stunts, Gareth Milne; Casting, Gail Stevens; a Sidney Kimmel Entertainment presentation of a Parabolic Pictures (the Netherlands)/Stable Way Entertainment (U.S.) production, in association with VIP Medienfonds 1+2, Target Media (Germany); American-Dutch-German; Dolby; Deluxe color; Rated R; 90 minutes; Release date: August 17, 2007.

## Cast

Daniel **Matthew MacFadyen**
Jane **Keeley Hawes**
Howard **Andy Nyman**
Justin **Ewen Bremner**
Martha **Daisy Donovan**
Simon Smith **Alan Tudyk**
Sandra **Jane Asher**
Troy **Kris Marshall**
Robert **Rupert Graves**
and Peter Egan (Victor); Peter Dinklage (Peter); Peter Vaughan (Uncle Alfie); Thomas Wheatley (Reverend Davis); Brendan O'Hea (Under-taker); Jeremy Booth (Mourner); Angela Curran (Sandra's Friend); Kelly Eastwood (Katie); Gareth Milne (Edward)

Daniel experiences one mishap and uncomfortable revelation after another as family and friends gather for the funeral of his father.

# THE KING OF KONG: A FISTFUL OF QUARTERS

(PICTUREHOUSE) Producer, Ed Cunningham; Director/Photography/Editor, Seth Gordon; Co-Editor, Luis Lopez; Music, Craig Richey; Associate Producers, J. Clay Tweel, Luis Lopez; a Picturehouse presentation of a Launch Pad production; Color; DV; Rated PG-13; 82 minutes; Release date: August 17, 2007. Documentary in which Steve Wiebe challenges Billy Mitchell's position as the undisputed champion of Donkey Kong.

## With

Steve Wiebe, Billy Mitchell, Nicole Wiebe, Steve Sanders, Robert Mruczek, Brian Kuh, Mark Alpiger, Greg Bond, Todd Rogers, Doris Self, Roy Shildt, Mike Thompson, Derek Wiebe, Adam Wood, Steve B. Harris, Craig Glenday, Jillian Wiebe.

Steve Wiebe and Family © PICTUREHOUSE

# RESURRECTING THE CHAMP

Josh Hartnett, Alan Alda

(YARI FILM GROUP) Producers, Mike Medavoy, Bob Yari, Rod Lurie, Marc Frydman; Executive Producers, Arnold W. Messer, Bradley J. Fischer, Louis Phillips, Frederick Zollo; Co-Producers, Murray Ord, Tom Cox, Jordy Randall; Director, Rod Lurie; Screenplay, Michael Bortman, Allison Burnett;Photography, Adam Kane; Designer, Ken Rempel; Costumes, Wendy Partridge; Editor, Sarah Boyd; Music, Larry Groupe; Music Supervisor, Kevin Edelman; Boxing Choreographer, Eric Bryson; Casting, Kathleen Tomasik, Rhonda Fisekci, Candice Elzinga; Dolby; Color; Rated R; 114 minutes; Release date: August 24, 2007.

## Cast

Champ **Samuel L. Jackson**
Erik Kernan **Josh Hartnett**
Joyce Kernan **Kathryn Morris**
Teddy Kernan **Dakota Goyo**
Ralph Metz **Alan Alda**
Polly **Rachel Nichols**
Andrea Flak **Teri Hatcher**
Perlmutter **Kristen Shaw**
Rocky Marciano **Nick Sandow**
Whitley **David Paymer**
Robert Satterfield Jr. **Harry Lennix**
Ike Epstein **Peter Coyote**
and Ryan McDonald (Kenny); Chris Ippolito (Jaws); Jameson Trenholm (Runt); Steve Strachan (Tillman); Eugene Clark (Washburn); Lori Ravensborg (Reporter #1); J. W. Carroll (Roselle); Larry Austin (Crony); Chris Kelly, Sean Olsen (Police Officers); Terrance Morris (Hood); Hannah Stewart (Jenny); Mitchell Frost (Jeremy); Kaya Coleman (Little Girl); Claire Davis (Teacher); Keenan Cheltenham (Teenage Boy); Jesse Lipscombe (McCracken); Troy Amos-Ross (Young Champ); Dave Trimble (Store Manager); John Elway, Jake Plummer, Jake LaMotta (Themselves); Hugh Delaney (Announcer); Stafford Lawrence (Wealthy Man); Suzanne Pringle (Woman with Kenny); Ron Carothers (Champ's Cornerman); Stacey Zurburg (Newsroom Editor); Rod Lurie (Toby Eagleburger); Roxanne Wong (Female in Newsroom); George Green (Elway's Manager); Dennis Belair (1950s Referee); Tom Carey (Office Helper); Pastor Alfred Rampersand (Minister); Glenn Hunter (Young Rocky Marciano); Michael Gleaves (Quarterman); Dale Dye (Voice of The Wow Man, Erik Kernan Sr.); Alex Rynn, Angus McNeilly, Rick Jameson, Matt Mychajliv, Mike Storey (Boxers)

A sports reporter believes he has stumbled upon a story that can prove his value as a journalist when he encounters a one-time middleweight contender who has become a vagrant.

Kathryn Morris, Josh Hartnett

Josh Hartnett, Samuel L. Jackson © YARI FILM GROUP

# THE NANNY DIARIES

Nicholas Reese Art, Scarlett Johansson

(MGM/WEINSTEIN CO.) Producers, Richard N. Gladstein, Dany Wolf; Executive Producers, Harvey Weinstein, Bob Weinstein, Kelly Carmichael; Co-Producer, Gary Binkow; Director/Screenplay, Shari Springer Berman, Robert Pulcini, based on the novel by Emma McLaughlin, Nicola Kraus; Photography, Terry Stacey; Editor, Robert Pulcini; Music, Mark Suozzo; Music Supervisor, Randall Poster; Designer, Mark Ricker; Costumes, Michael Wilkinson; Casting, Ann Goulder; a Weinstein Co. presentation of a Film Colony production; Dolby; Color; Rated PG-13; 105 minutes; Release date: August 24, 2007.

Scarlett Johansson, Laura Linney

## Cast

Annie Braddock  **Scarlett Johansson**
Mrs. X  **Laura Linney**
Lynette  **Alicia Keys**
Harvard Hottie  **Chris Evans**
and Donna Murphy (Judy Braddock); Nicholas Reese Art (Grayer); Judith Roberts (Milicent); Paul Giamatti (Mr. X); Nathan Corddry (Calvin); Julie White (Jane Gould); Julie White John Henry Cox (Dean); Lewis Payton Jr. (Bike Messenger); Sonnie Brown (Human Resources Director); Georgina Chapman (TriBeCa Fashionista); Jodi Michelle Pynn (Screeching Lady); Mike Rad (Dude); Joanna Heimbold (Glamour Mom); Marla Schuaretza (Charity Mom); Phoebe Jonas (Xanax Mom); Allison Sarofim (Eating Disorder Mom); Tina Benko (Shopaholic Mom); Cady Huffman (Divorcing Mom); Kaitlin Hopkins (Bitsy); Reathel Bean (Doorman); Rosa Nino (Maria); Matilda Downey (Polish Nanny); Elle de Amor (Loud Nanny); Sakina Jaffrey (Sima); Alison Wright (Bridget); Pete Heitmann (Guitar Player); Heather Alicia Simms (Murnel); Nina Garbiras (Miss Chicago); Melisa McGregor (Waitress); Rose Gonzalez (South American Nanny); Shalonne Lee (Jamaican Nanny); Ilana Levine (Whiny Mom); Isabel Keating (Paranoid Mom); Patrick Heusinger (Carter); Brendan Griffin (Kenny); Aaron Staton (John); Stephen O'Reilly (Reggie); Charlie Hewson (Jojo); Brande Roderick (Tanya); Nicola Barber (Lizzie); Kevin Kraft, Nicholas Alexiy Moran (Pierrots); James Urbaniak (Educational Consultant); Victoria Boothby (Matriarch); Judith Roberts (Millicent); Eli Harris (Lewis)

Scarlett Johansson, Alicia Keys

Child development major Annie Braddock takes a job playing nanny to the bratty offspring of an unhappy Upper East Side couple.

Scarlett Johansson, Chris Evans © MGM/WEINSTEIN CO.

# THE HOTTEST STATE

Mark Webber, Laura Linney © THINKFILM

Jesse Harris, Catalina Sandino Moreno

(THINKFILM) Producers, Yukie Kito, Alexis Alexanian; Executive Producers, Yasushi Kotani, Taizo Son; Co-Producers, Sheila Jaffe, Jonathan Shoemaker; Director/Screenplay, Ethan Hawke, based on his novel; Photography, Christopher Norr; Designer, Rick Butler; Costumes, Catherine Marie Thomas; Editor, Adriana Pacheco Rincon; Music, Jesse Harris; Music Supervisor, Linda Cohen; Casting, Sheila Jaffe; an Entertainment Farm presentation of a Barracuda Films, Elixir Films, Under the Influence Film production; Dolby; Color; Rated R; 116 minutes; Release date: August 24, 2007.

Mark Webber, Michelle Williams

## Cast

William Harding  **Mark Webber**
Sarah  **Catalina Sandino Moreno**
Vince  **Ethan Hawke**
Jesse  **Laura Linney**
Samantha  **Michelle Williams**
Mrs. Garcia  **Sonia Braga**
Dave Afton  **Jesse Harris**
Harris  **Frank Whaley**
Young Jesse  **Anne Clarke**
Young Vince  **Daniel Ross**
Harris' Mother  **Lynn Cohen**
and Greta Gaines (Faye); Nick McDonnell (Artsy Guy); Alexandra Daddario (Kim); Iraida Polanco (Proprietor); Matt Jade (Head Waiter); Cherami Leigh (Danielle); Elizabeth Marley (Ticket Girl); Lee Miller (Bartender); Glen Powell, Jr. (John Jaegerman); Lara Theodos (Waitress); Josh Zuckerman (Decker)

An aspiring actor and a singing hopeful meet in New York and begin a rocky relationship.

Catalina Sandino Moreno, Mark Webber

# WAR

(LIONSGATE) Producers, Steven Chasman, Christopher Petzel, Jim Thompson; Executive Producers, Mike Elliott, Michael Paseornek, Peter Block, John Sacchi; Co-Producers, Joseph P. Genier, Stephanie Denton; Director, Philip G. Atwell; Screenplay, Lee Anthony Smith, Gregory J. Bradley; Photography, Pierre Morel; Designer, Chris August; Costumes, Cynthia Ann Summers; Editor, Scott Richter; Music, Brian Tyler; Martial Arts Choreographer, Cory Yuen; Stunts, Scott Nicholson; Special Effects Coordinator, Clayton Seheirer; Casting, Maureen Webb, Colleen Rogers; a Lionsgate/Mosaic Media Group production, presented in association with Fierce Entertainment; Dolby; Deluxe color; Rated R; 103 minutes; Release date: August 24, 2007.

Jet Li (center) © LIONSGATE

### Cast

Rogue/Victor Shaw  **Jet Li**
Special Agent Jack Crawford  **Jason Statham**
Li Chang  **John Lone**
Kira Yanagawa  **Devon Aoki**
Benny  **Luis Guzman**
Dr. Sherman  **Saul Rubinek**
Shiro Yanagawa  **Ryo Ishibashi**
Special Agent Goi  **Sung Kang**
Special Agent Wick  **Mathew St. Patrick**
Maria  **Nadine Velazquez**
Jenny Crawford  **Andrea Roth**
Takada  **Kenneth Choi**
Wu Ti  **Mark Cheng**
Temple Garden Warrior  **Kane Kosugi**
Ana Chang  **Kennedy Montano**
Special Agent Tom Lone  **Terry Chen**
Diane Lone  **Steph Song**
Amy Lone  **Annika Foo**
Daniel Crawford  **Nicholas Elia**
Leevie  **Eric Keenleyside**
Det. Gleason  **Paul Jarrett**
Joey Ti  **Johnson Phan**
and Jung Yul Kim (Yuzo); Hiro Kanagawa (Yoshido); Wilken Yam (Wong); Aaron Au (Eddie); Mark Louie (Lau); Jennifer Chung (Zero Teenage Girl); Lucy Lu (Zero Hooker); Randy Lee (Zero Yakuza Making Love); Derek Lowe (Zero Surviving Yanagawa Mobster); John Novak (Capt. Andrews); Don Lew (Yakuza Warrior); Warren Takahachi (Harbor Yanagawa Lt.); Nels Lennarson (Harbor Wu Police Officer); Peter Shinkoda (Harbor Yanagawa Shatei); Meghan Flather (Chinese Call Girl); Thi Tran (Benny's Girl); Mitch Yuen, Brian Ho (Freelancers); Larry Lam (Yanagawa Assassin); Nadia Farès (Jade Agent Kinler); Aaron Pearl (Jade Agent Clark); Timothy Paul Perez (Mexican Interpol Agent); Allan Lysell (Cabin Policeman); Shawn Stewart, Dario Delacio (Mahjong Bouncers); Brett Chan (Wu Ti Buddy); Takashi Kanamori (Card Dealer); Paulina Bui, Angela Fong, Stephanie Poon (Kabuki Dancers)

FBI agent John Crawford hopes to locate an infamous assassin responsible for killing his partner within one of two warring San Francisco gangs.

Jason Statham

# DEDICATION

(WEINSTIEN CO./FIRST LOOK) Producers, David Bromberg, Celine Rattray, Daniela Taplin Lundberg, Galt Niederhoffer; Executive Producers, Justin Theroux, Chip Seelig, Reagan Silber, Luke Weinstock; Co-Producers, Pamela Hirsch, Carina Alves, Jai Stefan; Director, Justin Theroux; Screenplay, David Bromberg; Photography, Steve Kazmierski; Designer, Teresa Mastropierro; Costumes, Heidi Bivens; Editor, Andy Keir; Music, Edward Shearmur; Additional Music, Deerhoof; Music Supervisor, Tracy McKnight; Associate Producer, Jessica Levin; a Plum Pictures presentation in association with Hart/Lunsford Pictures; Dolby; Technicolor; Rated R; 111 minutes; Release date: August 24, 2007.

## Cast

Henry Roth  **Billy Crudup**
Lucy Reilly  **Mandy Moore**
Carol  **Dianne Wiest**
Arthur Planck  **Bob Balaban**
Don Meyers  **Bobby Cannavale**
Allison  **Christine Taylor**
Roger Spade  **Peter Bogdanovich**
and Amy Sedaris (Cassidy's Mom); Catherine Lloy Burns (Mother in Bookstore); John Ellison Canlee (Man at Lucy's); Catherine Kellner (Abusive Mom); Chris Fitzgerald (Robin); Jeremy Shamos (Matthew); Martin Freeman (Jeremy); Tom Wilkinson (Rudy Holt); Charlene Biton (Belle Dancer); Cassidy Hinkle (Cassidy); Chris Misa (Abused Kid); Antonio Parisi (Young Boy); Jicky Schnee (Mandy the Waitress)

Having lost his previous collaborator, temperamental children's author Henry Roth reluctantly agrees to a professional partnership with Lucy Reilly, subjecting her to his abrasive personality in an effort to keep himself from becoming too attached.

Mandy Moore, Martin Freeman © WEINSTEIN CO./FIRST LOOK

# BALLS OF FURY

Christopher Walken © ROGUE PICTURES

(ROGUE PICTURES) Producers, Roger Birnbaum, Gary Barber, Jonathan Glickman, Thomas Lennon; Executive Producers, Ron Schmidt, Derek Evans; Director, Robert Ben Garant; Screenplay, Robert Ben Garant, Thomas Lennon; Photography, Thomas Ackerman; Editor, John Refoua; Music, Randy Edelman; Designer, Jeff Knipp; Costumes, Maryann Bozek; Visual Effects Supervisor, Dennis Berardi; Stunts, Troy Brown; Casting, Julie Ashton-Barson; a Barber/Birnbaum production, presented with Intrepid Pictures and Spyglass Entertainment; Dolby; Panavision; Technicolor; Rated PG-13; 90 minutes; Release date: August 29, 2007.

## Cast

Randy Daytona  **Dan Fogler**
Feng  **Christopher Walken**
and George Lopez (Agent Ernie Rodriguez); Maggie Q (Maggie Wong); James Hong (Master Wong); Terry Crews (Freddy); Robert Patrick (Sgt. Pete Daytona); Diedrich Bader (Gary); Aisha Tyler (Mahogany); Thomas Lennon (Karl Wolfschtagg); Cary-Hiroyuki Tagawa (Mysterious Asian Man); Brett DelBuono (Young Randy, Age 12); Jason Scott Lee (Siu-Foo); Toby Huss (Groundskeeper); Dave Holmes (TV Producer); Heather DeLoach (Teenage Fan); David Koechner (Rick the Birdmaster); Kerri Kenney-Silver (Showgirl); Floyd Vanbuskirk (Old Man); Jenny Robertson (Den Mother); Patton Oswalt (Hammer); Jim Lampley (Sportscaster); Na Shi La (The Dragon); Mather Zickel (Branch Director); Jim Rash (Techie); David Proval (Mob Boss); Philippe Durand (Referee); Masi Oka (Jeff, Bathroom Attendant); Brandon Molale, Guy Stevenson (Male Courtesans); Steve Little (Crazed East German Fan); Cathy Shim (North Korean Attache); Greg Joung Paik (North Korean General); Eugene Choy (Gardener); Matt Sigloch (Commanding Officer); Ede Van Quathem, Marisa Tayui (Geishas); Mark Hyland (Umberto Dinovi); Justin Lopez (Wedge McDonald); Irina Voronina (Coach Schmidt); Darryl Chan (Feng's Bodyguard)

A down-on-his-luck ping-pong player, still trying to recover from his disgrace at the 1988 Olympics, sees his chance for redemption when a government agent asks him to infiltrate a tournament being run by the mysterious Feng, who is clearly up to no good.

# DEATH SENTENCE

Kevin Bacon © 20TH CENTURY FOX

(20TH CENTURY FOX) Producers, Ashok Amritraj, Howard Baldwin, Karen Baldwin; Executive Producers, Andrew Sugerman, Nick Morton, Nick Hamson, Lars Sylvest; Co-Producer, Eric Mitchell; Director, James Wan; Screenplay, Ian Mackenzie Jeffers, based on the novel by Brian Garfield; Photography, John R. Leonetti; Designer, Julie Berghoff; Costumes, Kristin M. Burke; Editor, Michael N. Knue; Music, Charlie Clouser; Music Supervisor, Michelle Silverman; Visual Effects Supervisor, Gregory McMurry; Stunts, Joel Kramer, Steven Ritzi; Casting, Tricia Wood, Jennifer Smith, Deborah Aquila; an Ashok Amritraj/Baldwin Entertainment Group production, presented with Hyde Park Entertainment; Dolby; Super 35 Widescreen; Deluxe color; Rated R; 105 minutes; Release date: August 31, 2007.

## Cast

Nick Hume  **Kevin Bacon**
Billy Darley  **Garrett Hedlund**
Helen Hume  **Kelly Preston**
Lucas Hume  **Jordan Garrett**
Brendan Hume  **Stuart Lafferty**
Det. Jessica Wallis  **Aisha Tyler**
Bones Darley  **John Goodman**
Joe Darley  **Matt O'Leary**
Bodie  **Edi Gathegi**
Heco  **Hector Atreyu Ruiz**
Baggy  **Kanin Howell**
and Dennis Keiffer (Jamie); Freddy Bouciegues (Tommy); Leigh Whannell (Spink); Casey Pieretti (Dog); Rich Ceraulo (Owen); Elizabeth Keener (Amy); Yorgo Constantine (Michael Barring); Juan-Carlos Guzman (Sammy); Judith Roberts (Judge Shaw); Aqeel Hasan (ER Doctor); Kendrick Cross (Armed Guard); Shontelle Thrash (Bank Teller); Michael Burgess, Nick Battiste (Cops); Kristina Sipes (Nurse); Jay Amor (Dock Rat); Desiree Markella (Pointing Cook); Zachary Dylan Smith (Young Brendan)

Devastated when the thug responsible for murdering his son is let off by the courts, Nick Hume decides to carry out his own form of justice, with increasingly tragic results.

# HALLOWEEN

(MGM) Producers, Malek Akkad, Andy Gould, Rob Zombie; Executive Producers, Bob Weinstein, Harvey Weinstein, Matt Stein; Director/Screenplay/Music Supervisor, Rob Zombie, based on the original screenplay by John Carpenter and Debra Hill; Photography, Phil Parmet; Editor, Glenn Garland; Music, Tyler Bates; Original "Halloween" Theme, John Carpenter; Designer, Anthony Tremblay; Costumes, Mary McLeod; Special Makeup Effects, Wayne Toth; Casting, Monika Mikkelsen; a Dimension Films presentation of a Malek Akkad production; Dolby; Super 35 Widescreen; Color; Rated R; 110 minutes; Release date: August 31, 2007.

## Cast

Dr. Samuel Loomis  **Malcolm McDowell**
Deborah Myers  **Sheri Moon Zombie**
Michael Myers  **Tyler Mane**
Laurie Strode  **Scout Taylor-Compton**
Sheriff Lee Brackett  **Brad Dourif**
Annie Brackett  **Danielle Harris**
Judith Myers  **Hanna Hall**
and Bill Moseley (Zach "Z Man" Garrett); Daeg Faerch (Michael, age 10); Kristina Klebe (Lynda); Danny Trejo (Ismael Cruz); William Forsythe (Ronnie White); Ken Foree (Big Joe Grizzly); Udo Kier (Morgan Walker); Clint Howard (Dr. Koplenson); Sid Haig (Chester Chesterfield); Daryl Sabara (Wesley Rhoades) , Daniel Roebuck (Lou Martini); Richard Lynch (Principal Chambers); Dee Wallace (Cynthia Strode); Pat Skipper (Mason Strode); Skyler Gisondo (Tommy Doyal); Jenny Gregg Stewart (Lindsey Wallace); Lew Temple (Noel Kluggs); Tom Towles (Larry Redgrave); Leslie Easterbrook (Patty Frost); Steve Boyles (Stan Payne); Adam Weisman (Steve); Sydnie Pitzer, Myla Pitzer, Stella Altman (Baby Boo); Max Van Ville (Paul); Nick Mennell (Bob Simms); Richmond Arquette (Deputy Charles); Paul Kampf (Officer Lowery); Nikki Taylor Melton, Deven Streeton (Princesses); Sybil Danning (Nurse Wynn); Micky Dolenz (Derek Allen); Mel Fair (Taylor Madison)

Escaping from a maximum security sanitarium, Michael Myers goes on a murderous rampage in his hometown on Halloween night. Remake of the 1978 Compass release, that starred Jamie Lee Curtis and Donald Pleasence.

Tyler Mane, Scout Taylor-Compton © METRO-GOLDWYN-MAYER

# THE NINES

Melissa McCarthy, Elle Fanning © NEWMARKET

(NEWMARKET) Producers, Dan Jinks, Bruce Cohen, Dan Etheridge; Co-Producer, Todd King; Director/Screenplay, John August; Photography, Nancy Schreiber; Editor, Douglas Crise; Music, Alex Wurman; Music Supervisor, Julianne Jordan; Art Director, E. Colleen Saro; Costumes, Molly Elizabeth Grundman; Digital Effects, Look Effects; a Jinks/Cohen Co. production; Color; HD; Rated R; 99 minutes; Release date: August 31, 2007.

## Cast

Gary/Gavin/Gabriel **Ryan Reynolds**
Sarah/Susan/Sierra **Hope Davis**
Margaret/Melissa/Mary **Melissa McCarthy**
Noelle **Elle Fanning**
Themselves **Dahlia Salem, Ben Falcone, John Gatins**
Parole Officer/Agitated Man **David Denman**
Streetwalker **Octavia Spencer**
Piano Player **Andy Fielder**
Delivery Boy **Greg Blaine**
Officer Cooper **Sean Andrews**
Russian Drug Dealer **Nicholas Garren**
Check-in Girl **Malia Herrick**
Christine Walsh **Ellen Treanor**
and Martin Yu, Gregg Nauman (Focus Group Participants); Lorene Scafaria, Jim Rash, Rawson Marshall Thurber, Dan Jinks (Game Night Guests)

Three tales enacted by the same principals: TV actor Gary goes on a drinking binge of despair after his girlfriend leaves him; a high-paid television writer hopes to get a new project launched for his friend Melissa; hoping to find assistance after being stranded by a dead car battery, video designer Gabriel runs into a strange hitchhiker.

# I WANT SOMEONE TO EAT CHEESE WITH

(IFC) Producers, Jeff Garlin, Erin O'Malley, Steve Pink; Executive Producers, Harold Ramis, David Miner, Rob Kolson; Director/Screenplay, Jeff Garlin; Photography, Peter Biagi; Designer, Margaret M. Miles; Editor, Steven Rasch; Music, Rob Kolson; Casting, Marla Garlin; a Sawin' & Puddin' production; Dolby; Color; DV; Not rated; 80 minutes; Release date: September 5, 2007.

## Cast

James Aaron **Jeff Garlin**
Beth **Sarah Silverman**
Stella Lewis **Bonnie Hunt**
Luca **David Pasquesi**
Mrs. Aaron **Mina Kolb**
Dick **Dan Castellaneta**
Herb Hope **Richard Kind**
Charlie **Paul Marursky**
and Rose Adobo (Car Dealership Receptionist); Scott Adsit (Big Galoot); Rebecca Sage Allen (Andrea Hope); Roger Bart (Burl Canasta); Jill Bartlett (Beautiful Woman); Aaron Carter ("Marty"); Steve Dahl (Father); Elle Fanning (Penelope); Gina Gershon ("Mrs. Piletti"); David Hoke (Record Store Clerk); B. Johnson (Glenn); Tim Kazurinsky (Bill Bjango); Amy Kidd (French Woman); Wallace Langham (Claude Cochet); Henriette Mantel (Next Door Neighbor); Rana McAnear (Actress); Larry Neumann, Jr. (Homeless Guy); Jessy Schram (Fake Daughter); Amy Sedaris (Ms. Clark); Joey Slotnick (Larry); Phyllis Smith (Marsha); Michael Stailey (Moviegoer)

A lonely, struggling, overweight actor, who lives with his overbearing mom, believes he has found a long-desired companion when he meets an eccentric ice cream parlor waitress.

Bonnie Hunt, Jeff Garlin © IFC FILMS

# 3:10 TO YUMA

(LIONSGATE) Producer, Cathy Konrad; Executive Producers, Stuart M. Besser, Ryan Kavanaugh, Lynwood Spinks; Director, James Mangold; Screenplay, Halsted Welles, Michael Brandt, Derek Haas, based on the short story by Elmore Leonard; Photography, Phedon Papamichael; Designer, Andrew Menzies; Costumes, Arianne Phillips; Editor, Michael McCusker; Music, Marco Beltrami; Second Unit Director/Stunts, Freddie Hice; Casting, Lisa Beach, Sarah Katzman; a Tree Line Films production; presented in association with Relativity Media; Dolby; Panavision; FotoKem color; Rated R; 120 minutes; Release date: September 7, 2007.

Kevin Durand, Christian Bale, Peter Fonda

Russell Crowe © LIONSGATE

## Cast

Ben Wade **Russell Crowe**
Dan Evans **Christian Bale**
William Evans **Logan Lerman**
Grayson Butterfield **Dallas Roberts**
Charlie Prince **Ben Foster**
Byron McElroy **Peter Fonda**
Emma Nelson **Vinessa Shaw**
Doc Potter **Alan Tudyk**
Marshal Weathers **Luce Rains**
Alice Evans **Gretchen Mol**
Tommy Darden **Johnny Whitworth**
Mark Evans **Benjamin Petry**
Glen Hollander **Lennie Loftin**
Campos **Rio Alexander**
Jackson **Shawn D. Howell**
Jorgensen **Pat Ricotti**
Kinter **Ramon Frank**
Zeke **Luke Wilson**
Sutherland **Brian Duffy**
Tighe **Jason Rodriguez**
Tucker **Kevin Durand**
Crawley **Chris Browning**
Kane **Chad Brummett**
Walter Boles **Forrest Fyre**
Mark Evans **Ben Petry**
Bill Moons **Arron Shiver**
and Deryle Lujan, James Augure (Nez); Sean Hennigan (Marshal Will Doane); Girard Swan (Deputy Harvey Pell); Christopher Berry (Deputy Sam Fuller); David Oliver (Evil Bartender); Jason Henning (Ticket Clerk)

Christian Bale, Gretchen Mol

Desperately in need of money, rancher Dan Evans joins a posse escorting dangerous outlaw Ben Wade to the train that will transport him to prison in Yuma. Remake of the 1957 Columbia film that starred Glenn Ford and Van Heflin.

This film received Oscar nominations for Original Score and Sound Mixing.

Logan Lerman

Ben Foster

Logan Lerman, Christian Bale

# ROMANCE & CIGARETTES

(BOROTURRO) Producers, John Penotti, John Turturro; Executive Producers, Joel Coen, Ethan Coen, Jana Edelbaum, Matthew Rowland, Nick Hill; Director/Screenplay, John Turturro; Photography, Tom Stern; Designer/Costumes, Donna Zakowska; Editor, Ray Hubley; Original Music, Paul Chihara; Music Supervisor, Chris Robertson; Choreographer, Tricia Brook; Additional Choreographers, Margie Gillis ("Delilah" sequence), Moore & Parker ("Red Headed Woman"); Associate Producers, Laurent Lambert, Robin Gold; Casting, Todd Thaler; a United Artists and Joel & Ethan Coen presentation, in association with Icon Entertainment Intl., of a GreeneStreet Films, Janus Films production; Dolby; Panavision; Color; Not rated; 105 minutes; Release date: September 7, 2007.

Kate Winslet © BOROTURRO

## Cast

Nick Murder  **James Gandolfini**
Kitty Murder  **Susan Sarandon**
Tula  **Kate Winslet**
Angelo  **Steve Buscemi**
Cousin Bo  **Christopher Walken**
Fryburg  **Bobby Cannavale**
Baby  **Mandy Moore**
Constance  **Mary-Louise Parker**
Rosebud  **Aida Turturro**
Gracie  **Barbara Sukowa**
Nick's Mother  **Elaine Stritch**
Gene Vincent  **Eddie Izzard**
Frances  **Amy Sedaris**
Police Officer  **P.J. Brown**
Fruitman  **Adam LeFevre**
Medic  **Tonya Pinkins**
and David Thornton (Urologist); Kumar Pullana (Kumar); June Stein (Frances' Mother); Michael McElroy (Ten Commandments Priest); Joseph Longo, Devon McRimmon (Altar Boys); Amedeo Turturro, Ryan Webb, Jacob Lumet-Cannavale (Fryburg Friends); Diego Turturro (Boy on Tricycle); Yianni Digaletos (The Greek); Katherine Turturro (Choir Lady); Cady Huffman, Alexandra Beller, Katherine Borowitz, Tricia Brouk, Mary Bond Davis, LaRita Gaskins, Karen Graham, Kelly Robertson, Daria Hardeman, Lisa Tachick Hooper, Wanda L. Houston, Kate Johnson, Rosalynde LeBlanc, Adele Meyers, Rosetta Mallardi, Emily Molnar, Elizabeth Parkinson, Nourhan Sharif, Valerie Striar, Rebecca Wender, Brian Arch, Félix Blaska, James Borowitz, Joao Caravalho, Alex Escalante, Clarence Figgures, Rudy Heron, Eric Jackson, John Kelly, David Scott Klein, Victorio Korjhan, Gelan Lambert Jr., Laurent Lambert, Raul Merced, Christopher McGovern, Otto Moreira, Christopher Morgan, Vincent Orofino, Joseph Paparone, John Selya, Gus Solomons Jr., John Turturro, Takehiro Ueyama, Dared Wright (Dancers/Singers); Tom Bruno, Scott Friese, Neil Jorgensen, Buddy McKay, Robert Morgan, Robert A. Pennachia, Dave Ryan, Salty, Kendall Washington (Firemen)

James Gandolfini

Susan Sarandon, Christopher Walken

The discovery of her husband's mistress causes a rift in the marriage of working-class couple Nick and Kitty Murder.

# THE HUNTING PARTY

Richard Gere, Terrence Howard © WEINSTEIN CO.

(WEINSTEIN CO.) Producers, Mark Johnson, Scott Kroopf, Bill Block; Executive Producers, Bo Hyde, Martin Schuermann, Adam Merims, Paul Hanson; Director/Screenplay, Richard Shepard, based on the *Esquire* article by Scott K. Anderson; Photography, David Tattersall; Editor, Carole Kravetz-Aykanian; Music, Rolfe Kent; Music Supervisor, Liza Richardson; Designer, Jan Roelfs; Costumes, Beatrix Aruna Pasztor; a Weinstein Co., QED, Intermedia presentation of a Mark Johnson, Intermedia, QED, Cherry Road production; Dolby; Super 35 Widescreen; Technicolor; Rated R; 104 minutes; Release date: September 7, 2007.

### Cast

Simon Hunt **Richard Gere**
Duck **Terrence Howard**
Benjamin Strauss **Jesse Eisenberg**
Mirjana **Diane Kruger**
and Joy Bryant (Duck's Girlfriend); James Brolin (Franklin Harris); Boghdanovic Ljubomir Kerekes (The Fox); Kristina Krepela (Marda); Dylan Baker (Chet, CIA Operative); Mark Ivanir (Boris); Damir Saban (Gert); Snezana Markovic (Una); Goran Kostic (Srdjan); Lejla Hadzimuratovic (Voice of Bosnian Woman); Gordana Vukres (Girl at Awards Ceremony); Sanela Seferagic (Sexy Assistant); Aleksandra Grdic (TriBeCa Loft Girl); Scott Anderson, Harald Doornbos, Philippe Deprez, Eric Rathfelder, Zan Marolt (Journalists); Branko Smiljanic (Nine-Fingered Man); Semir Krivic (Roadhouse Waiter); Nitin Ganatra (Elenath Bharwani); R. Mahalakshmi Devaraj (Miriam); Lucio Slama (Man with Scar); Damir Kukulj (Solitary Man); Kata Ivkovcic (Old Lady Gardening); Srecko Franovic (Young Boy); Sasa Dodik, Amer Isanovic (Bar Patrons); Miraj Grbic, Mladen Vulic (Thugs); Zdravko Kocevar (Sascha); Marinko Prga (Fox's Man with Gun); Luka Peros (Commando #1); Arif Alaibegovic (Old Man with Guitar)

Eager to get his derailed career back on track, news correspondent Simon Hunt convinces seasoned cameraman and callow journalist Duck to journey into Bosnia in hopes of landing an exclusive interview with "The Fox," a despotic leader on the lam who is responsible for the deaths of thousands of Bosnian Muslims.

# FIERCE PEOPLE

(AUTONOMOUS FILMS) Producer, Nick Wechsler; Executive Producers, Keith Addis, Michael Paseornek, Michael Burns, Dirk Wittenborn; Director, Griffin Dunne; Screenplay, Dirk Wittenborn, based on his book; Photography, William Rexer II; Designer, Mark Ricker; Costumes, Monique Prudhomme; Editor, Allyson Johnson; Music, Nick Laird-Clowes; Casting, Amanda Mackey Johnson, Cathy Sandrich Gelfond; an Industry Entertainment/Lions Gate Films production; Dolby; Widescreen; Color; Rated R; 107 minutes; Release date: September 7, 2007.

### Cast

Liz Earl **Diane Lane**
Ogden C. Osborne **Donald Sutherland**
Finn Earl **Anton Yelchin**
Bryce **Chris Evans**
Maya **Kristen Stewart**
Mrs. Langley **Elizabeth Perkins**
Dr. Leffler **Christopher Shyer**
Gates **Blu Mankuma**
and Paz de la Huerta (Jilly); Garry Chalk (McCallum); Ryan McDonald (Ian); Dexter Bell (Marcus Gates); Kaleigh Dey (Paige); Aaron Brooks (Giacomo); Jeff Westmoreland (Whitney); Teach Grant (Dwayne); Chris Shields (Cop); Dirk Wittenborn (Fox Blanchard); Alan Giles (Dignified Old Man); Sibel Thrasher (Creamsicle); Robert Clarke (Herbert the Butler); Eddie Rosales (Iskanani Shaman); Will Lyman (Documentary Narrator); Ben Cotton (Boyfriend); Rekha Sharma (Social Worker); Kimani Ray Smith (Hair Net Man); Ross Viner (Valet)

Young Finn Earl sees a spark of hope in his shaky relationship with his drug addicted mom when they are invited to live at the posh estate of Ogden C. Osborne, with Mrs. Earl serving as a private masseuse.

Diane Lane, Donald Sutherland © AUTONOMOUS FILMS

# SHOOT 'EM UP

Stephen McHattie

(NEW LINE CINEMA) Producers, Susan Montford, Don Murphy, Rick Benattar; Executive Producers, Douglas Curtis, Toby Emmerich, Cale Boyter; Director/Screenplay, Michael Davis; Photography, Peter Pau; Designer, Gary Frutkoff; Costumes, Denise Cronenberg; Editor, Peter Amundson; Music, Paul Haslinger; Music Supervisor, Dana Sano; Visual Effects Supervisor, Edward J. Irastorza; Visual Effects, Mr. X, Inc., HimAnl Prods.; Stunts, Eddie Perez, Jamie Jones; Associate Producer, Jeff Katz; Casting, Deirdre Bowen; a Montford/Murphy production; Dolby; Deluxe color; Rated R; 87 minutes; Release date: September 7, 2007.

Clive Owen, Monica Bellucci

## Cast

Smith **Clive Owen**
Hertz **Paul Giamatti**
Donna Quintano **Monica Bellucci**
Senator Rutledge **Daniel Pilon**
Baby Oliver **Sidney Mende-Gibson, Lucas Mende-Gibson, Kaylyn Yellowlees**
Baby's Mother **Ramona Pringle**
Hammerson **Stephen McHattie**
Lone Man **Greg Bryk**
Hertz's Driver **Julian Richings**
and Tony Munch (Man Who Rides Shotgun); Scott McCord (Killer Shot in Behind); Wiley Pickett (1st Killer); Stephen R. Hart (Club Bouncer); David Ury (Diner Holdup Leader); Mike Rad (Diner Hood with Earring); Andy MacKenzie (Ugly Toenails Hood); Laura De Carteret (Woman in Museum); Ryan Finn (Kid in Museum); Maria Vacratsis (Pawnshop Owner); Suresh John (Motel Manager); Jay Reso (Senator's Guard); Jane McLean (Madam Maddie); Dave Van Zeyl (Diapered Man); Layton Morrison (Dog Handler); Jo-Anne Leach (Woman in Park); Frank Tiefenback (Customer in Alley); David Collins (Museum Guard); Steve Richard (Coffee-Sipping Guard); Harry Karp (Milkshake Slurper); Dean Copkov (Gunman Stabbed in Eye); Michael Edward Rose (Hammerson's Security Guard); Frank Nakashima (Korean Grocer)

Paul Giamatti © NEW LINE CINEMA

Clive Owen

After the child's mother is murdered, Smith finds himself reluctantly taking care of a baby, who is pursued by Hertz and his relentless team of assassins.

# THE BRAVE ONE

(WARNER BROS.) Producers, Joel Silver, Susan Downey; Executive Producers, Herbert W. Gains, Jodie Foster, Dana Goldberg, Bruce Berman; Co-Producer, David Gambino; Director, Neil Jordan; Screenplay, Roderick Taylor, Bruce A. Taylor, Cynthia Mort; Story, Roderick Taylor, Bruce A. Taylor; Photography, Philippe Rousselot; Designer, Kristi Zea; Costumes, Catherine Thomas; Editor, Tony Lawson; Music, Dario Marianelli; Stunts, Steven Ritzi; Associate Producer, Aaron Auch; Casting, Laura Rosenthal; a Silver Pictures production, presented in association with Village Roadshow Pictures; Dolby; Panavision; Technicolor; Rated R; 122 minutes; Release date: September 14, 2007.

Zoë Kravitz, Jodie Foster, Victor Colicchio

## Cast

Erica Bain  **Jodie Foster**
Det. Sean Mercer  **Terrence Howard**
David Kirmani  **Naveen Andrews**
Jackie  **Carmen Ejogo**
Det. Vitale  **Nicky Katt**
Carol  **Mary Steenburgen**
Mortell  **Lenny Venito**
Chloe  **Zöe Kravitz**
Josai  **Ene Oloja**
Lee  **Luis Da Silva, Jr.**
Cash  **Blaze Foster**
Reed  **Rafael Sardina**
Nicole  **Jane Adams**
Murrow  **Gordon MacDonald**
and John Magaro (Ethan); Victor Colicchio (Cutler); Jermel Howard, Dennis White (Thugs on Subway); Julia Garro (Shauna Nelson); James Biberi (Det. Pitney); Brian Delate (Det. O'Connor); Dana Eskelson (Sketch Artist); Angel Sing (Gun Dealer); Yolande Bavan (David's Mother); Ivo Velon (James); Tina Sloan (Stationery Saleswoman); Jaime Tirelli (Pawn Shop Guy); Larry Fessenden (Sandy Combs); An Nguyen (Ida Combs); Brian Tarantina (Gun Store Clerk); Michael Anthony Williams (Subway Dad); Jesus Ruiz (Chief of Detectives); Hope Adams, Joseph Melendez, Ted Neustadt (Press Conference Reporters); Brett Berg (Ethan's Friend); Jeffrey Manko (Emergency Room Doctor); Mick Cunningham (Precinct Cop); Lisa Joyce (CPA Worker); Tom Greer (Desk Cop); David Naizir (Guy Outside Subway Station); Robert Michael McClure (Sound Engineer); Tashya Valdevit (Erica's Nurse); Lai-Si Fernandez (Shauna's Friend); Moisés Acevedo, Dennis Johnson (Reed's Runners); Jack Caruso, Jim Taylor McNickle (Subway Detectives); Rosanne Lucarelli, Leif Riddell, DeShaun Stallworth (Subway Reporters); Michael J. Burg, Creighton James, Clayton Dean Smith, Barbara Gayle, Anna Margaret Hollyman, Lily Mercer (Elevator People); Musto Pelinkovicci (Russian Cab Driver); Dean Meminger (NY1 Reporter); Cheryl Wills (NY1 TV Anchor)

Terrence Howard, Nicky Katt

Naveen Andrews, Jodie Foster © WARNER BROS.

When her fiancé dies following a random assault upon the pair of them, Erica Bain decides to take the law into her own hands, becoming a vigilante set on wiping out New York's criminals.

## ACROSS THE UNIVERSE

(clockwise from top center) Martin Luther McCoy, Dana Fuchs, T.V. Carpio, Ekaterina Sknarina, Evan Rachel Wood, Jim Sturgess, Kiva Dawson, Joe Anderson, Halley Wegryn Gross

(COLUMBIA) Producers, Suzanne Todd, Jennifer Todd, Matthew Gross; Executive Producers, Derek Dauchy, Rudd Simmons, Charles Newirth; Co-Producers, Richard Barratta, Ben Haber; Director, Julie Taymor; Screenplay, Dick Clement, Ian La Frenais; Story, Julie Taymor, Dick Clement, Ian La Frenais; Songs by John Lennon, Paul McCartney, George Harrison, Ringo Starr; Photography, Bruno Delbonnel; Designer, Mark Friedberg; Costumes, Albert Wolsky; Editor, Francoise Bonnot; Music, Elliot Goldenthal; Song Production, T-Bone Burnett, Elliot Goldenthal, Teese Gohl; Music Supervisor, Denise Luiso; Special Effects Supervisor, Steve Kirshoff; Visual Effects Supervisor, Peter Crossman; Visual Effects, Frantic Films, the FX Cartel, Eden FX, HimAnl Prods., Ockham's Razor; Animation, Kyle Cooper; Choreographer, Daniel Ezralow; Stunts, George Aguilar; Casting, Bernard Telsey; a Columbia Pictures, Revolution Studios presentation of a Matthew Gross/Team Todd production; Dolby; Panavision; Deluxe color; Rated PG-13; 131 minutes; Release date: September 14, 2007.

**Cast**

Lucy **Evan Rachel Wood**
Jude **Jim Sturgess**
Max Carrigan **Joe Anderson**
Sadie **Dana Fuchs**
Jo-Jo **Martin Luther McCoy**
Prudence **T.V. Carpio**
Daniel **Spencer Liff**
Molly, Jude's Liverpool Girlfriend **Lisa Hogg**
Cyril **Nicholas Lumley**
Phil **Michael Ryan**
Bum/Pimp/Mad Hippie **Joe Cocker**
Dr. Robert **Bono**
Mr. Kite **Eddie Izzard**
Singing Nurse **Salma Hayek**
and Angela Mounsley (Jude's Mother, Martha); Erin Elliott (Cheer Coach); Robert Clohessy (Jude's Father); Christopher Tierney, Curtis Holbrook, John Jeffrey Martin, Matt Caplan (Dorm Buddies); Timothy R. Boyce, Jr. (Jock); Aisha De Haas, Leah Hocking (Tavern Waitresses); Ellen Hornberger (Lucy's Sister, Julia); Amanda Cole (Emily); Danya Taymor, Sarah Jayne Jensen (High School Girlfriends); Linda Emond (Lucy's Mother); Lynn Cohen (Grandmother Carrigan); Jennifer Van Dyck (Daniel's Mother); Timothy T. Mitchum (Jo-Jo's Brother); Carol Woods (Gospel Singer); Elain Graham (Jo-Jo's Mother); Orfeh, Antonique Smith, Tracy Nicole Chapman, Yassmin Alers, Deidre Goodwin (Hookers); Jacob Pitts, Staceyann Chin (Rap Magazine Employees); Jeanine Serralles (Dani); Leonard Tucker (Katz's Waiter); Daniel Stewart Sherman (Cop at Wharf Warehouse); Harry Lennix (Army Sergeant); Logan Marshall-Green (Paco); James Urbaniak (Sadie's Manager); Kathleen Early (SDR Worker); Ching Valdes-Aran (Luna Park); Daniel Ezralow (Mother Superior); Kiva Dawson, Halley Wegryn Gross (Max's Girls); Luther Creek, Jerzy Gwiazdowski, Arabella Holzbog, Ambrose Martos, Peter Mui, Karine Plantadit, Dan Weltner, Christopher Youngsman (Pranksters); Tracy Westmoreland (Fillmore Manager); Ron Cephas Jones (Black Panther); W.W. Wilson III (Precinct House Sargeant); Luke Cresswell (Tramp Drumming on Bin Lids); Jarlath Conroy (Bartender at Max's Bar); Mandy Gonzales, Destan Owens, Cicily Daniels, Saycon Sengbloh (Sadie's Singers); Sam Kitchin, Chris McGarry (Sergeants on Rooftop); Frank Hopf (Door Officer at Strawberry Records); "Cousin Brucie" Morrow (Himself); Jen Arvay, Joey Chanlin,

Bono

Russ Klein, Eric Michael Kochmer, Elizabeth Newman (Protestors); Andrew Asnes (John); William Atkinson (Sailor); Jason Daniel Audette, Mark A. Bailey, Adrianna Bremont, Marcus Collins, Shawn Luckey, Kel O'Neill, Kristen Silverman (Hippies); Matthew Backer (Guru); Jordan Bass (High School Student/Dancer); Nicole Berger, Sandy Chase, Kathryn Eleni Fraggos, Jeremy Leiner, Tiger Martina, Tim McGarrigal, Melissa Medina, Angel Morales, Matthew Neff, Desmond Richardson (Dancers); Delancey Birzin, Andrew Llera (Princeton Student); Michael Biscardi (5th Ave. Protestor); Adolpho Blaire (Army Recruit); Randy Blair (Mother Face); Gregory Allan Bock (Hippie Protestor #2); Michael Boothroyd, Jordan Spencer, John "J.T." Tully (Dancing Businessmen); Tracey Brennan (College Girl); Brendan Burke (Soldier); Jamal Burke, Laurence Covington, Craig DiFrancia, Jim Ford, Edwin Freeman, Mark Keller, Adam Kerbis, Kent Moran (Football Players); Kevin W. Burns (Telegram Sergeant); Simone Butler (Student Democratic Revolutionary); Kevin Cannon (Professor); Alexis Ann Carra (East Village Denizen); Johnpaul Castrianni (Cavern Loner); Michael Chenevert (Wounded Soldier); Craig Clary (College Student); Courtney Lynne Coleman (High School Student); Rick Collum (Columbia University Student Radical); Evan Crothers (Patient); Cris D'Annunzio (Riot Cop); Mike Dobbins (Student for Democratic Reform); Joe Dolinsky (Hippie Dude); Nick Ellison, Paul Hayes, Barney Taylor, Ben Wilkinson (Cavern Band); Lisa Marie Farago (Bowler); Jack Fitz (Daniel's Uncle); Ramon Flowers (Drag Queen); Angelo Fraboni (Soldier/Dancer/Bowler); Jessica Frank, Kristen Haakerud (Cheerleaders); Kurt Froman (Vietnam Inductee); Samantha Futerman (Prom Dancer); Shane Geraghty (Acrobat); Joey Giambattista (Sadie's Fan); Ryan Lee Gilbert (Student Protestor); Phillip James Griffith (Frat Boy); Abigail Gustafson (Protestor/Flower Child); Jeffrey Hawkins (Soldier/Patient/ Dancer); Chivonne Hill (Detroit Rioter); Bill Irwin (Uncle Teddy); Heather Janneck (Bowling Alley Dancer); Edward Kasche (Underground News Editor); Dominique Kelley (East Village Denizen/Army Recruiter); Mari Koda (Vietnamese Dancer); Conrad Korsch (Upright Bassist); Larry Laboe (Lucy's Ensemble); Perri Lauren (Basketball Teammate); Nicole Lewis (Young Mother); Leo G. Liteman (Roadie); Cynthia Loebe (Diner Waitress); Steve Lord (National Guard Soldier); Cory Mayer (Daniel's Brother); Dolores McDougal (Nurse); Chris McMullin (Security at Filemore East); Keith Moyer, Mark Pricskett (Loft Artist Partygoers); Samantha Musumeci (Daniel's Sister); Bryan Noll (Sadie's Band); Chris Nunez (Department Store Delivery Boy); Kevin Brendan O'Brien (Delicatessen Waiter); John Orion (D.C. Rioter/Hippie at Party); Adesola A. Osakalumi (Black Panther/ Dancer); Justin Osterthaler, Keith Patterson (Princeton Bullies); Richard Kirkman Page (Shipyard Worker); Chris Philip (Columbia College Student); Vitta Quinn (Black-White Painted Mod Girl); Justin Restivo (Merchant Marine); Alexus Robertson (Hippie Guitarist); Thomas Russo (National Guardsman); Luis Salgado (East Village Denizen/Sergeant); Ekaterina Sknarina (Rita); Brian Smyj (Cop); Nikki Snelson, Kevin Alexander Stea (East Village Denizens); Martin Soole (Army Recruit); Frank Stellato (Football Coach); Ronald Sylvers, Kevin Watson (Funeral Attendee); Annie Vanders (Singing Housewife); Noah Weisberg (ACLU Lawyer); Brian M. Wixson (Strawberry Records Hippie); Ira David Wood IV (SDS Revolutionary); Gail Yudain (High School Teacher)

Eddie Izzard © COLUMBIA PICTURES

Englishman Jude ends up in America, where he falls in love with Lucy; their relationship plays out against a backdrop of late 1960s upheaval and change, all set to the music of the Beatles.

This film received an Oscar nomination for Costume Design.

Martin Luther McCoy, Dana Fuchs, Joe Anderson, Jim Sturgess

Salma Hayek (x5)

# IN THE VALLEY OF ELAH

(WARNER INDEPENDENT) Producers, Patrick Wachsberger, Steven Samuels, Darlene Caamano Loquet, Paul Haggis, Laurence Becsey; Executive Producers, Stan Wlodkowski, David Garrett, Erik Feig, James Holt, Emilio Diez Barroso, Bob Hayward; Co-Producers, Dana Maksimovich, Deborah Rennard; Director/Screenplay, Paul Haggis; Story, Mark Boal, Paul Haggis; Photography, Roger Deakins; Designer, Laurence Bennett; Costumes, Lisa Jensen; Editor, Jo Francis; Music, Mark Isham; Stunts, Bobby Burns; Military Consultant, James Dever; Associate Producer, Gregory Gettas; Casting, Sarah Finn, Randi Hiller; a Blackfriar's Bridge production presented in association with Nala Films, Summit Entertainment, Samuels Media; Dolby; Super 35 Widescreen; Technicolor; Rated R; 121 minutes; Release date: September 14, 2007.

## Cast

Hank Deerfield **Tommy Lee Jones**
Det. Emily Sanders **Charlize Theron**
Lt. Kirklander **Jason Patric**
Joan Deerfield **Susan Sarandon**
Sgt. Dan Carnelli **James Franco**
Arnold Bickman **Barry Corbin**
Chief Buchwald **Josh Brolin**
Evie **Frances Fisher**
Cpl. Steve Penning **Wes Chatham**
Spc. Gordon Bonner **Jake McLaughlin**
Mike Deerfield **Jonathan Tucker**
Spc. Ennis Long **Mehcad Brooks**
Det. Nugent **Wayne Duvall**
Pvt. Robert Ortiez **Victor Wolf**
Det. Hodge **Brent Briscoe**
Det. Manny Nunez **Greg Serano**
Lt. Burke **Brent Sexton**
David Sanders **Devin Brochu**
Angie **Zoe Kazan**
Det. Wayne **Glenn Taranto**
Jodie **Jennifer Siebel**
School Janitor **Joseph Bertot**
and Rick Gonzalez (Phone Technician); Loren Haynes (Police Photographer); Babak Tafti (Iraqi Prisoner); Sean Huze (Capt. Jim Osher); Jack Merrill (Medical Examiner); Kathy Lamkin (Chicken Shack Manager); David Doty (Truck Parts Salesman); Pab Schwendimann (Pussy's Bouncer); Josh Meyer (Joseph R. Millard); Ahron Shiver (Cop); Jo Harvey Allen (Jo Anne); Chris Browning (Checker Box Bartender); David House (Morgue Officer); Pierre Barrera (TD's Bartender); Mike Hatfield (Jo Anne's Husband); James Haggis (Soccer Ball Player); Randall Adams (New Recruit); Hans Steckly (Cpl. Steckly)

Retired army Sergeant Hank Deerfield is determined to find out the truth behind his son's mysterious disappearance after returning from the war in Iraq.

This film received an Oscar nomination for Best Actor (Tommy Lee Jones).

Tommy Lee Jones, Wes Chatham

Tommy Lee Jones, Victor Wolf

Charlize Theron, Jason Patric © WARNER INDEPENDENT PICTURES

# KING OF CALIFORNIA

Evan Rachel Wood

Willis Burke II, Gerald Emerick, Angel Oquendo

Michael Douglas, Evan Rachel Wood

(FIRST LOOK) Producers, Alexander Payne, Michael London, Avi Lerner, Randall Emmett; Executive Producers, John Thompson, Trevor Short, Danny Dimbort, Boaz Davidson, George Furla, Elisa Salinas; Co-Producer, George Parra; Director/Screenplay, Mike Cahill; Photography, James Whitaker; Designer, Dan Bishop; Costumes, Ellen Mirojnick, Michael Dennison; Editor, Glenn Garland; Music, David Robbins; Music Supervisor, David Robbins; Makeup, Janeen Schreyer; Casting, Joanna Colbert; a Millennium Films presentation in association with Emmett/Furla Films of an Alexander Payne/Michael London production; American-Mexican; Dolby; Deluxe color; Rated PG-13; 93 minutes; Release date: September 14, 2007.

## Cast

Charlie   **Michael Douglas**
Miranda   **Evan Rachel Wood**
Pepper   **Willis Burks II**
Young Miranda   **Allisyn Ashley Arm**
Joseph   **Greg Davis Jr.**
Sheriff's Deputy   **Gerald Emerick**
McDonald's Customer   **Ashley Greene**
Teacher   **Jeanie Hackett**
Officer Contreras   **Anna Khaja**
Bruce   **Mousa Kraish**
Doug   **Paul Lieber**
Costco Shopper   **Tarri Markell**
Applebee's Manager   **Anne L. Nathan**
and Ho-Kwan Tse, Willis Chung, Victor J. Ho, Max Lee, Branden Weslee Kong (Chinese Refugees); Laura Kachergus (Rita); Kathleen Wilhoite (Kelly); Arthur Santiago (McDonald's Manager); Ian Hopps (Boy); Annie O'Donnell (Greeter); Max Grodénchik (Leonid); Chic Daniel (Older Cop); David J. O Donnell (Fireman); Angel Oquendo (Younger Cop); Will Rothhaar (Security Guard); Wes Sabo (Mike, Estate Security Guard); Jason Aver (Costco Employee); Gary Paul (Cop at Excavation)

Recently released from a mental facility, Charlie once again proves a burden to his beleaguered daughter Miranda when he decides that the long-lost treasure of a 17th-Century Spanish adventurer is hidden near their property.

Michael Douglas © FIRST LOOK PICTURES

# MR. WOODCOCK

(NEW LINE CINEMA) Producers, Bob Cooper, David Dobkin; Executive Producers, Toby Emmerich, Kent Alterman, Karen Lunder, Diana Pokorny; Co-Producer, Brian Inerfeld; Co-Executive Producers, Michele Weiss, Keith Goldberg; Director, Craig Gillespie; Screenplay, Michael Carnes, Josh Gilbert; Photography, Tami Reiker; Editors, Alan Baumgarten, Kevin Tent; Music, Theodore Shapiro; Designer, Alison Sadler; Costumes, Wendy Chuck; Stunts, Gary Jensen, Steve Davison; Casting, Mary Vernieu; a Landscape Entertainment production; Dolby; Super 35 Widescreen; Deluxe color; Rated PG-13; 87 minutes; Release date: September 14, 2007.

## Cast

Jasper Woodcock  **Billy Bob Thornton**
John Farley  **Seann William Scott**
Beverly Farley  **Susan Sarandon**
Maggie Hoffman  **Amy Poehler**
Tracy  **Melissa Sagemiller**
Nedderman  **Ethan Suplee**
Nedderman's Brother  **Jacob Davich**
Young John  **Kyley Baldridge**
Young Nedderman  **Alec George**
Young Watson  **Joseph Michael Sargent**
Hal, Barber #1  **M.C. Gainey**
Barber #2  **Brent Briscoe**
Bookish Guy  **Dave Kuhr**
and Lisa K. Wyatt (Housewife); Kurt Fuller (Councilman Luke Jessop); Michael Santorico (Waiter at Barone's); Corbin Albaugh (Kreamer); Melissa Leo (Sally Jansen); Stephen Monroe Taylor (Oates); Bac DeLorme (A.D.); Jennifer Aspen (Cindy the Realtor); Lyle Kanouse, Van Epperson (Carnies); Zia Harris (Burn Out); Brad Beyer (Jay Elems, Dumb Jock); Michael Mishaw (Lounge Singer); Allisyn Ashley Arm (Scout Girl); Emily Wagner (Cheery Woman); Googy Gress (Earnest Man); Tyra Banks (Herself); David L.M. Mcintyre (Hopeful Man); Jacob Christopher (Young Teenager); Scott Adsit (Cheesy Salesman); Hallie Singleton (Makeup Artist); Scott Stewart (Farley Fan); Pedro Otero, Leonard Concepción (Airplanes); Carissa Koutantzis (Farley Stalker); Brett Smrz (Dunigan); Sam Stefanski, Max Van Ville (Pizza Waiters); Bill Macy (Mr. Woodcock's Dad); Barbara Perry (Old Woman); Martin Charles Warner (Scarduzio); Jack Walsh (Palumbo); Paul Johnson (Announcer); Joshua Feinman (Marine); Kip Martin (Heartland Rocker); Bryant Carroll, Craig Gellis (Tough Guys); Beth Gargan (Manly Woman); Anthony Reynolds (Fireman); Héctor A. García (Hispanic Kid); Lindsay Ballew (Tall Brunette); Sean Dwyer (Paramedic); Ty Rushing (Cop); Dan John Miller (Family Man); Karl Hamann (Trekkie); Tim Frisbie (Older Man); Logan Grove (Birthday Kid); Ralph Lister (Scientist); Archie Hahn III (Gym Teacher); Michael Lodovico (Orderly); Dean A. Parker (Dad); Michael D'Amore (Mr. Wheelchair); Evan Helmuth (Dinosaur/Watson); Josh Shada (Schwartz)

John Farley is horrified to realize that his mother is now dating the gym teacher who made his life a living hell back in school.

Billy Bob Thornton (center)

Susan Sarandon, Seann William Scott

Seann William Scott, Amy Poehler

# PETE SEEGER:
# THE POWER OF SONG

Bob Dylan, Pete Seeger © WEINSTEIN CO.

(WEINSTEIN CO.) Producers, Michael Cohl, William Eigen; Executive Producers, Norman Lear, Toshi Seeger; Line Producers, Nicole Craig, Sarah Cullen; Associate Producers, Lara Bergthold, Kitama Jackson; Director, Jim Brown; Editors, Samuel D. Pollard, Jason Pollard; Dolby; Black and white; Rated PG; 93 minutes; Release date: September 14, 2007. Documentary on legendary singer-composer Pete Seeger.

### With

Pete Seeger, Bob Dylan, Bruce Springsteen, Toshi Seeger, Natalie Maines, Tom Paxton, David Dunaway, Bess Lomax Hawes, Joan Baez, Ronnie Gilbert, Jerry Silverman, Henry Foner, Eric Weissberg, Arlo Guthrie, Peter Yarrow, Mary Travers, Julian Bond, Tom Smothers, Bonnie Raitt, N. Paul Stookey

# THE RAPE OF EUROPA

(MENEMSHA) Producers, Richard Berge, Bonni Cohen, Nicole Newnham; Executive Producer, Bonni Cohen; Co-Producer, Robert M. Edsel; Directors/Screenplay, Richard Berge, Nicole Newnham, Bonni Cohen, based on the book by Lynn H. Nicholas; Photography, Jon Shenk; Editor, Josh Peterson; Music, Marco D'Ambrosio; Narrator, Joan Allen; an Actual Films presentation in association with Agon Arts & Entertainment/Oregon Public Broadcasting of an Actual Films production; Dolby; Color/Black and white; HD; Not rated; 117 minutes; Release date: September 14, 2007. Documentary on Adolph Hitler's attempts to steal the art treasures of Europe during the Nazis' reign of Germany.

© MENEMSHA FILMS

# THE ASSASSINATION OF JESSE JAMES BY THE COWARD ROBERT FORD

(WARNER BROS.) Producers, Brad Pitt, Dede Gardner, Ridley Scott, Jules Daly, David Valdes; Executive Producers, Brad Grey, Tony Scott, Lisa Ellzey, Benjamin Waisbren; Director/Screenplay, Andrew Dominik, based on the novel by Ron Hansen; Photography, Roger Deakins; Art Director, Troy Sizemore; Costumes, Patricia Norris; Editors, Dylan Tichenor, Curtiss Clayton; Music, Nick Cave, Warren Ellis; Special Effects Supervisor, James Paradis; Visual Effects, CIS Hollywood; Stunts, Billy Burton, Brent Woolsey; Associate Producer, Ron Hansen; Casting, Mali Finn; Canadian Casting, Jackie Lind, Deb Green; a Scott Free/Plan B Entertainment production, presented in association with Virtual Studios; Dolby; Super 35 Widescreen; Technicolor; Rated R; 160 minutes; Release date: September 21, 2007.

## Cast

Jesse James  **Brad Pitt**
Robert Ford  **Casey Affleck**
Frank James  **Sam Shepard**
Zee James  **Mary-Louise Parker**
Dick Liddil  **Paul Schneider**
Wood Hite  **Jeremy Renner**
Ed Miller  **Garret Dillahunt**
Dorothy Evans  **Zooey Deschanel**
Henry Craig  **Michael Parks**
Sheriff Timberlake  **Ted Levine**
Charley Ford  **Sam Rockwell**
Martha Bolton  **Alison Elliott**
Governor Crittenden  **James Carville**
Major George Hite  **Tom Aldredge**
Sarah Hite  **Kailin See**
Mary James  **Brooklynn Proulx**
Tim James  **Dustin Bollinger**
Ida  **Lauren Calvert**
and Joel McNichol (Express Messenger); James DeFelice (Baggage Master); J.C. Roberts (Engineer); Darrell Orydzuk (Ukranian Train Passenger); Jonathan Erich Drachenberg (Young Train Passenger); Torben S. Hansen (Danish Train Passenger); Jesse Frechette (Albert Ford); Pat Healy (Wilbur Ford); Joel Duncan (Deputy); Stephanie Wahlstrom (Store Customer); Adam Arlukiewicz (Newsboy); Ian Ferrier (Photographer); Michael Rogers (Onlooker at Jesse's Death); Calvin Bliid (Small Boy at Jesse's Death); Sarah Linda (Bob's Girlfriend); Nick Cave (Bowery Saloon Singer); Matthew Walker (Bowery Saloonkeeper); Michael Copeman (Edward O'Kelly); Laryssa Yanchak (Ella Mae Waterson); Hugh Ross (Narrator)

The true story of how Robert Ford joined Jesse James' band of outlaws, at first hero-worshiping the notorious gunman, only to end up as his executioner.

This film received Oscar nominations for Supporting Actor (Casey Affleck) and Cinematography.

Casey Affleck, Sam Rockwell

Mary-Louise Parker, Brooklynn Proulx, Dustin Bollinger, Brad Pitt

(back row) Garrett Dillahunt, Paul Schneider, Jeremy Renner, Sam Rockwell, Casey Affleck; (seated) Brad Pitt, Sam Shepard © WARNER BROS.

# THE JANE AUSTEN BOOK CLUB

Amy Brenneman, Jimmy Smits

Kevin Zegers © SONY PICTURES CLASSICS

(SONY CLASSICS) Producers, John Calley, Julie Lynn, Diana Napper; Executive Producer, Marshall Rose; Co-Producer, Kelly Thomas; Director/Screenplay, Robin Swicord, based on the novel by Karen Joy Fowler; Photography, John Toon; Designer, Rusty Smith; Costumes, Johnetta Boone; Editor, Maryann Brandon; Music, Aaron Zigman; Music Supervisor, Barklie Griggs; Casting, Deborah Aquila, Tricia Wood, Jennifer Smith; a John Calley/Robin Swicord production in association with Mockingbird Pictures; Dolby; Color; Rated PG-13; 106 minutes; Release date: September 21, 2007.

## Cast

Bernadette  **Kathy Baker**
Jocelyn  **Maria Bello**
Prudie Drummond  **Emily Blunt**
Sylvia Avila  **Amy Brenneman**
Grigg Harris  **Hugh Dancy**
Allegra Avila  **Maggie Grace**
Mama Sky  **Lynn Redgrave**
Daniel Avila  **Jimmy Smits**
Dean Drummond  **Marc Blucas**
Trey  **Kevin Zegers**
Corinne  **Parisa Fitz-Henley**
Dr. Samantha Yep  **Gwedoline Yeo**
Cat  **Nancy Travis**
Pastor  **Ed Brigadier**
Academic Woman  **Catherine Schreiber**
Waiter  **Ned Hosford**
Girl with Dog Collar  **Messy Stench**
Skydive Instructor  **Chris Burkett**
and Stephanie Denise Griffin (Mediator); Myndy Crist (Lynne); Graham Norris (Editor); Kurt Bryant (Rocknasium Instructor); Russ Jones (Parent); Michelle Ewin (Very Young Nurse); Miguel Nájera (Señor Obando)

In an effort to help women get over their troubled relationships, Bernadette launches a book club dedicated to the six novels of Jane Austen.

Kathy Baker, Emily Blunt, Amy Brenneman, Maggie Grace, Maria Bello, Hugh Dancy

# SYDNEY WHITE

Sara Paxton, Amanda Bynes

(UNIVERSAL) Producers, James G. Robinson, Clifford Werber, David Robinson; Executive Producers, Guy McElwaine, Wayne Morris; Director, Joe Nussbaum; Screenplay, Chad Gomez Creasey; Photography, Mark Irwin; Designer, Mark Garner; Costumes, Beverly Safier; Music, Deborah Lurie; Music Supervisor, JoJo Villanueva; Editor, Danny Saphire; Co-Producer, Dara Resnik Creasey; Casting, Pamela Dixon Mickelson; a James G. Robinson presentation of a Morgan Creek production; Dolby; Technicolor; Rated PG-13; 108 minutes; Release date: September 21, 2007.

## Cast

Sydney White **Amanda Bynes**
Rachel Witchburn **Sara Paxton**
Tyler Prince **Matt Long**
Lenny **Jack Carpenter**
Terrence Lubinecki **Jeremy Howard**
Dinky Hotchkiss **Crystal Hunt**
Jeremy **Adam Hendershott**
Gurkin **Danny Strong**
Spanky **Samm Levine**
Christy **Libby Mintz**
Paul White **John Schneider**
and Arnie Pantoja (George); Donté Bonner (Embele); Brian Patrick Clarke (Professor Carleton); Lauren Leech (Katy); Cree Ivey (Young Sydney); Ashley Drane (Alicia); Lisandra Vasquez (Amy); Chris Carberg (Moose); Kierstin Koppel (Goth Girl); Jeff Chase (Big Ron); JoBeth Locklear (Flirty Girl); Tait Moline (Danny the Tranny); Adam Vernier, Carlos Navarro (Football Fans); Nadine Avola ("Pin Me" Sister); David Skyler (Hacker); Phyllis Fludd White (Librarian); Arielle Grace (Student Newscaster); Jennifer Skidmore (Waitress); Pixee Wales (Old Woman); Susie Abromeit (Cheerleader); Brooke Newton (Sorority Girl); Evan Todd (Student); Cornelius John Laws, Brent A. Westwood, Dustin R. Grant, Nathanael P. Morano (Beta Singers)

Fed up with her pretentious sorority sisters, Sydney White takes up housing with seven male social outcasts and rallies them to fight back against the abuse they've encountered.

Matt Long

Donté Bonner, Adam Hendershott, Danny Strong, Jack Carpenter, Amanda Bynes, Jeremy Howard, Arnie Pantoja, Samm Levine

John Schneider, Amanda Bynes © UNIVERSAL STUDIOS

# INTO THE WILD

(PARAMOUNT VANTAGE) Producers, Sean Penn, Art Linson, William Pohlad; Executive Producers, David Blocker, John J. Kelly, Frank Hildebrand; Director/Screenplay, Sean Penn, based on the book by Jon Krakauer; Photography, Eric Gautier; Designer, Derek R. Hill; Costumes, Mary Claire Hannan; Editor, Jay Lash Cassidy; Music, Michael Brook, Kaki King, Eddie Vedder; Music Supervisor, John J. Kelly; Original Songs, Eddie Vedder; Casting, Francine Maisler; a Square One CIH, Linson Film production, presented with River Road Entertainment; Dolby; Super 35 Widescreen; Color; Rated R; 147 minutes; Release date: September 21, 2007.

Brian Dierker, Catherine Keener

## Cast

Christopher McCandless ("Alexander Supertramp")  **Emile Hirsch**
Billie McCandless  **Marcia Gay Harden**
Walt McCandless  **William Hurt**
Carine McCandless  **Jena Malone**
Jan Burres  **Catherine Keener**
Rainey, Marine Coordinator  **Brian Dierker**
Wayne Westerberger  **Vince Vaughn**
Kevin  **Zach Galifianakis**
Tracy Tatro  **Kristen Stewart**
Ron Franz  **Hal Holbrook**
The Bear  **Bart the Bear**
Passerby  **Dan Burch**
The Beast  **Joe Dustin**
Social Worker  **Cheryl Francis Harrington**
Announcer  **John Jabaley**
Mads  **Thure Lindhardt**
Gail Borah  **Robin Mathews**
Sonja  **Signe Egholm Olsen**
Carine, 11 years old  **Haley Ramm**
Chris, 4 years old  **Bryce Walters**
Lee's Ferry Ranger  **Steven Wiig**
Themselves  **Jim Gallien, Leonard Knight**
Graduation Reader  **James O'Neill**
Waitress  **Malinda McCollum**
Building Manager  **Paul Knauls**
Wayne's Crew  **Craig Mutsch, Jim Beidler**
Hutterites  **John Decker, John Hofer, Jerry Hofer, Terry Waldner**
Bar Girl  **Candice Campos**
Man in Phone Booth  **Floyd Wall**
and Jim Davis (Immigration Officer); R.D. Call (Bull); Merritt Wever (Lori); Everett "Insane Wayne" Smith (Insane Cain); Matt Contreras, Denis Sitton (Book Shopper)

Hal Holbrook, Emile Hirsch

Determined to experience the ultimate freedom, recent college grad Chris McCandless leaves behind his comfortable existence and ventures off on a road trip through America, ultimately ending up in the Alaskan wilderness.

This film received Oscar nominations for Supporting Actor (Hal Holbrook) and Film Editing.

Kristen Stewart, Emile Hirsch © PARAMOUNT VANTAGE

# GOOD LUCK CHUCK

(LIONSGATE) Producers, Mike Karz, Barry Katz, Brian Volk-Weiss; Executive Producers, Tracey Edmonds, Russell Hollander, Ogden Gavanski, Michael Paseornek; Co-Producers, Cece Karz, Karen Russell; Director, Mark Helfrich; Screenplay, Josh Stolberg; Photography, Anthony B. Richmond; Designer, Mark Freeborn; Costumes, Trish Keating; Editor, Julia Wong; Music, Aaron Zigman; Music Supervisor, Jay Faires; Associate Producer, Steve Glenn; Casting, Matthew Barry, Nancy Green-Keyes; a Lionsgate and Karz Entertainment production; Dolby; Deluxe color; Rated R; 99 minutes; Release date: September 21, 2007.

**Cast**

Dr. Charlie Logan  **Dane Cook**
Cam Wexler  **Jessica Alba**
Dr. Stu Kaminsky  **Dan Fogler**
Reba  **Ellia English**
Goth Girl  **Sasha Pieterse**
Joe Wexler  **Lonny Ross**
Carol  **Chelan Simmons**
Young Charlie  **Connor Price**
Young Stu  **Troy Gentile**
Birthday Girl  **Mackenzie Mowat**
Jennifer  **Caroline Ford**
Natalie  **Natalie Morris**
and Chang Tseng (Karaoke Singer); Michael Teigen (Wedding D.J.); Chiara Zanni (Bride); Ben Ayres (Groomsman); Carrie Anne Fleming (Dirty Talker); Agam Darshi (Wedding Guest); Crystal Lowe (Cam's Wedding Friend); Steve Glenn (Carol's New Man); Téa Helfrich (Screaming Little Girl); Jasmine Vox (Pleasure); Tava Smiley (Woman in Car); Connor Dunn (Frisbee Kid); Norma Cowley (Frisbee Grandmother); Elizabeth Schnitzker (Ceiling Lover); Michelle Andrew (Red-Haired Lover); Annie Wood (Lara); Eliza Bayne (Wheelbarrow Lover); Ed Welch (Dirty Talker's True Love); Tammy Morris (Contortionist Lover); Camille Atebe (Butch Cop); Jessica Olafson (Kitchen Counter Lover); Susan McLellan (Shower Lover); Zara Taylor (Magazine Lover); Viviana Dal Cengio (Thankful Lover); Cassandra Sawtell (Girl in Penguin Habitat); Ian Farthing (Eleanor's Boyfriend); Charlie Metzger, George Metzger, George Wakeham, Martin Lovick (Singing Quartet); Lindsay Maxwell (McTitty); Aaron Dudley (Not George); Liam James (Boy in Penguin Habitat); Kevin Crofton (Aquaworld Security); June B. Wilde (Desperate Woman); Jodelle Micah Ferland (Lila); Michelle Harrison (Anisha); Steve Bacic (Howard); Georgia Craig (Howard's Wife); Jody Racicot (Ticket Agent); Robert Kelly (Airport Security Guard); Emma Barker (Not Cam); Taayla Markell (Flight Attendant); Heather Doerksen (Woman on Plane)

Dan Cook, Ellia English

Jessica Alba, Dan Fogler, Dane Cook

Lonny Ross © LIONSGATE

A man who has the power to make women find their true love elsewhere after sleeping with him, finds himself in a quandary when he falls for accident-prone Cam, worried that she will leave him after their first time together in bed.

# FEAST OF LOVE

Toby Hemingway

Morgan Freeman, Greg Kinnear, Selma Blair, Stana Katic

(MGM) Producers, Tom Rosenberg, Gary Lucchesi, Richard S. Wright; Executive Producers, David Scott Rubin, Eric Reid, Harley Tannebaum, Lori McCreary, Fisher Stevens, John Penotti; Director, Robert Benton; Screenplay, Allison Burnett, based on the novel by Charles Baxter; Photography, Kramer Morgenthau; Editor, Andrew Mondshein; Music, Stephen Trask; Designer, Missy Stewart; Costumes, Renee Ehrlich Kalfus; Casting, Deborah Aquila, Tricia Wood; a Lakeshore Entertainment production, in association with Greene Street Films, Revelations Entertainment; Dolby; Panavision; Deluxe color; Rated R; 102 minutes; Release date: September 28, 2007.

## Cast

| | |
|---|---|
| Harry Stevenson | **Morgan Freeman** |
| Bradley Smith | **Greg Kinnear** |
| Diana | **Radha Mitchell** |
| David Watson | **Billy Burke** |
| Kathryn | **Selma Blair** |
| Chloe | **Alexa Davalos** |
| Oscar | **Toby Hemingway** |
| Jenny | **Stana Katic** |
| Esther Stevenson | **Jane Alexander** |
| Bat | **Fred Ward** |
| Margaret Vekashi | **Erika Marozsán** |
| Mrs. Maggarolian | **Margo Martindale** |
| Agatha | **Missi Pyle** |
| Janey | **Shannon Lucio** |
| Billy | **Alex Mentzel** |

and Tobias Andersen (Minister); Julie Vhay (Karen Watson); Kate Mulligan (Bartender); David Scott Rubin (Man at Party); Sherilyn Lawson (Nurse); Scott Patrick Green (Young Minister at Funeral); R.J. Belles, Megan Keller (Football Field Lovers).

Greg Kinnear, Radha Mitchell

Distressed when his wife leaves him for a woman and desperate to be in love, Bradley Smith hastily rebounds by starting a relationship with Diana, even though she is still physically involved with someone else.

Morgan Freeman, Jane Alexander © METRO-GOLDWYN-MAYER

# THE GAME PLAN

(WALT DISNEY PICTURES) Producers, Gordon Gray, Mark Ciardi; Executive Producer, Richard Luke Rothschild; Director, Andy Frickman; Screenplay, Nichole Millard, Kathryn Price; Story, Nichole Millard, Kathryn Price, Audrey Wells; Photography, Greg Gardiner; Designer, David J. Bomba; Costumes, Genevieve Tyrrell; Music, Nathan Wang; Music Supervisor, Jennifer Hawks; Casting, Sheila Jaffe; Football Stunts, Mark Ellis; a Mayhem Pictures production; Dolby; Panavision; Technicolor; Rated PG; 110 minutes; Release date: September 28, 2007.

## Cast

| | |
|---|---|
| Joe Kingman | **Dwayne "The Rock" Johnson** |
| Peyton Kelly | **Madison Pettis** |
| Stella Peck | **Kyra Sedgwick** |
| Monique Vasquez | **Roselyn Sanchez** |
| Travis Sanders | **Morris Chestnut** |
| Kyle Cooper | **Hayes MacArthur** |
| Jamal Webber | **Brian White** |
| Clarence Monroe | **Jamal Duff** |
| Karen Kelly | **Paige Turco** |
| Spike | **Tubbs** |
| Coach Mark Maddox | **Gordon Clapp** |
| Tatianna | **Kate Nauta** |
| Samuel Blake, Jr. | **Robert Torti** |
| Larry the Doorman | **Jackie Flynn** |
| Nanny Cindy | **Lauren Storm** |
| Themselves | **Marv Albert, Boomer Esiason, Jim Gray, Stuart O. Scott, Steven Levy** |
| Drake | **Eric Ogbogu** |
| Nichole | **Christine Lakin** |
| Kathryn | **Elizabeth Chambers** |
| Bo the Trainer | **Brian Currie** |
| Dr. Converse | **Fiona Gallagher** |
| ER Doctor | **Jack Eastland** |
| Mrs. Jensen | **Rachel Harker** |

and Ed Berliner (Rebels PR Manager); Armen Garo (Cabbie); Roger T.S. Dillingham, Jr. (Paparazzi); Jay Giannone (Doorman at Club); Tony Renaud (New York Coach); Brianne Crough (Toy Store Ballet Dancer); Kathryn Fiore (Voice of Sara Kelly); Donald L. Banks, Ron Borges, John Clayton, Jay Glazer, John C. McClain, Gary Myers, Chip Namias, Jon Saraceno, Steve Serby, T.J. Simers (Hack Pack); Mike Eruzione, Eddie George, Gavin Maloof, Joe Maloof, Paul Pierce, Wally Szczerbiak, Sebastian Telfair, Jo Jo White (Club Guests); Debbie Connolly (ER Nurse); Lordan Napoli (Toy Store Camille Doll); Yvonne Finnerty (Nanny Yvonne); Kimberly Selby (Barking Crab Waitress); John Duff (Monroe's Brother); Scott Desano (Blake's VP)

Superstar quarterback Joe Kingman's bachelor lifestyle is put to an end by the unexpected appearance of the 8-year-old daughter he never realized he had.

Roselyn Sanchez, Dwayne "The Rock" Johnson

Kyra Sedgwick, Dwayne "The Rock" Johnson, Madison Pettis

Morris Chestnut, Hayes MacArthur, Brian White © DISNEY ENTERPRISES

# THE KINGDOM

Ashraf Barhom, Chris Cooper, Jamie Foxx

(UNIVERSAL) Producers, Michael Mann, Scott Stuber; Executive Producers, Mary Parent, Steven Saeta, Sarah Aubrey, John Cameron, Ryan Kavanaugh; Director, Peter Berg; Screenplay, Matthew Michael Carnahan; Photography, Mauro Fiore; Designer, Tom Duffield; Costumes, Susan Matheson; Music, Danny Elfman; Editors, Kevin Stitt, Colby Parker Jr.; Casting, Amanda Mackey, Cathy Sandrich Gelfond; Stunts, Keith Woulard; a Forward Pass/Stuber-Parent production, presented in association with Relativity Media; Dolby; Technicolor; Rated R; 110 minutes; Release date: September 28, 2007.

Jason Bateman (center) © UNIVERSAL STUDIOS

## Cast

Ronald Fleury **Jamie Foxx**
Grant Sykes **Chris Cooper**
Janet Mayes **Jennifer Garner**
Adam Leavitt **Jason Bateman**
Col. Faris Al Ghazi **Ashraf Barhom**
Sgt. Haytham **Ali Suliman**
Damon Schmidt **Jeremy Piven**
James Grace **Richard Jenkins**
Aaron Jackson **Tim McGraw**
Francis Manner **Kyle Chandler**
Elaine Flowers **Frances Fisher**
Gideon Young **Danny Huston**
Ellis Leach **Kelly Aucoin**
Maricella Canavesio **Anna Deavere Smith**
Miss Ross **Minka Kelly**
Lyla Fleury **Amy Hunter**
Kevin Fleury **T.J. Burnett**
Prince Ahmed Bin Khaled **Omar Berdouni**
Prince Thamer **Raad Rawi**
Gen. Al Abdulmalik **Mahmoud Said**
and Hezi Saddik (Abu Hamza); Uri Gavriel (Izz Al Din); Nick Faltas (Haytham's Father); Ahmed Badran (35-Year-Old Son); Elie Georges El-Khoury (15-Year-Old Grandson); Tom Bresnahan (Rex Burr); Yasmine Hanai (Aunt); Trevor St. John (Earl Ripon); Ashley Scott (Janine Ripon); Sarah Hunley (Maddy Ripon); Brody Tardy (Teddy Manner); Hope Fogle (Mick); Sidney Ortiz (Lulu); Noah Pittenger (Classmate); Damian Foster (Haytham Driver); Kevin Brief (Range Rover Driver); Brian Mahoney (Pitcher); Martin Foxwell (Man at Game); Kavita Parbhakar (Mom at Game); Hrach Titizian, Munthir Salih (Suicide Bombers); Merik Tadros, Sean Donnellan (Reporters); Richard Klein, John Paul Castorena, Antonio Evans, Maryellen Aviano, Markus Flanagan (FBI Agents); Brian Gehl (Stud in Bar); Ali Abboud (Irate Guard); David Brown (Man at Hotel); Firas Salloum (Airport SANG Officer); Anthony Batarse (Inner-Circle); Nabeel Kort, Shant Demirjian (Police Officers); Assad Mohamed (Bomb Site Investigator); Yaser Alamoodi, Haider Almosawi, Saleem Hassan Erakat (Bomb Site Workers); Jasim Tahir (Tank Gunner); Maitham Al-Zubfidy (Main Gate Guard); Alawi Al-Bidery (Machine Gunner); Gino Salvano (Special Forces Officer); Waleed Alsadi (Guard at Café); Mohammed Mohammed, Fouad Al-Hamedany (Internet Teenagers); Ahmed Al-Ibrahim, Yunus Hassan, Charbel Touma, Anthony Salibi (Game Players); Bassam O. Saeed (Al Ghazi Aid); Hasan Chaudhry (Al Ghazi Runner); Nick Hermz (Passport Officer); Eyad Elbitar, Sala Baker (Kidnappers); Kasem Al-Tamimi (Elderly Man); Damian Hajjar, Mario Mercado II (Suweidi Residents); Gaith Al-Jaberi (Al Ghazi's Son)

After a suicide bombing in Saudi Arabia leaves more than 100 Westerners dead, an FBI task force is summoned to track down those responsible.

# THE DARJEELING LIMITED

(FOX SEARCHLIGHT) Producers, Wes Anderson, Scott Rudin, Roman Coppola, Lydia Dean Pilcher; Executive Producer, Steven Rales; Co-Producers, Jeremy Dawson, Alice Bamford, Anadil Hossain; Director, Wes Anderson; Screenplay, Wes Anderson, Roman Coppola, Jason Schwartzman; Photography, Robert Yeoman; Designer, Mark Friedberg; Costumes, Milena Canonero; Editor, Andrew Weisblum; Music Supervisor, Randall Poster; Graphic Artist, Mark Pollard; a Fox Searchlight Pictures, Collage presentation, of an American Empirical Picture production; Dolby; Panavision; Technicolor; Rated R; 91 minutes; Release date: September 29, 2007.

## Cast

Francis Whitman  **Owen Wilson**
Peter Whitman  **Adrien Brody**
Jack Whitman  **Jason Schwartzman**
Rita  **Amara Karan**
Brendan  **Wallace Wolodarsky**
The Chief Steward  **Waris Ahluwalia**
The Father  **Irrfan Khan**
The Mechanic  **Barbet Schroeder**
Alice  **Camilla Rutherford**
The Businessman  **Bill Murray**
Patricia  **Anjelica Huston**
Taxi Driver  **A.P. Singh**
Old Man  **Kumar Pallana**
Waiter  **Dalpat Singh**
German Ladies  **Trudy Matthys, Margot Goedroes**
Electronics Vendor  **Hitesh Sindi**
Shoe Vendor  **Kishen Lal**
Pepper Spray Vendor  **Bhawani Sankar**
Pet Shop Vendor  **Mukhtiar Bhai**
Shoeshine Boy  **Suraj Kumar**
and Kapil Dubey (Boy on Bicycle); Mulchand Dedhia (Engineer); Dinesh Bishnoi (Oldest Boy); Mukesh Bishnoi (Middle Boy); Ramesh Bishnoi (Youngest Boy); Sriharsh Sharma (Boy with Handkerchief); Chanduram Bishnoi (Village Elder); Sajjanji Bishnoi (Doctor); Pukaram Bishnoi (Old Man in Village); Shushila Devi (Mother); Ratan Lal Ji, Mularam Bishnoi, Anand Pathe, Bhawar Lal, Kaana Ram, Rupa Ram, Shava Ram, Bhura Ram, Buramji Ram, Tuka Ram, Bhanwar Singh, Moti Ram, Kishna Ram, Khewal Ram Paliwal, Rajeev Acharya (Villagers); Jai Prakash Sharma (Man on Bus); Badhri Dave (Hindu Priest); Vincetta Easley (Garage Cashier); John Joseph Gallagher (Tow Truck Driver); G.B. Singh (Pilot Captain); Bhavna Narang (Flight Attendant); Sunil Chhabra, Narender Singh Hada (Co-Pilots); Thupten Gyatso (Oberoi); Gurdeep Singh (Chief Steward, Bengal Lancer); Charu Shankar (Stewardess, Bengal Lancer); Natalie Portman (Jack's Ex-Girlfriend)

The estranged Whitman brothers come together for a spiritual journey through India, with the ulterior motive of making contact with their mother, who has cloistered herself inside a Himalayan monastery.

Jason Schwartzman, Amara Karan

Jason Schwartzman, Adrien Brody, Owen Wilson

Waris Ahluwalia, Owen Wilson, Adrien Brody, Jason Schwartzman © 20TH CENTURY FOX

# THE HEARTBREAK KID

(DREAMWORKS/PARAMOUNT) Producers, Ted Field, Bradley Thomas, John Davis; Executive Producers, Marc S. Fischer, Joe Rosenberg, Charles B. Wessler; Co-Producers, Tony Lord, Matthew Weaver; Directors, Peter Farrelly, Bobby Farrelly; Screenplay, Scot Armstrong, Leslie Dixon, Bobby Farrelly, Peter Farrelly, Kevin Barnett; Based on the screenplay by Neil Simon, inspired by the story by Bruce Jay Friedman; Photography, Matthew F. Leonetti; Designer, Sidney J. Bartholomew Jr.; Costumes, Louise Mingebach; Music, Brendan Ryan, Bill Ryan; Editors, Alan Baumgarten, Sam Seig; a Radar Pictures, Davis Entertainment, Conundrum production; Dolby; Super 35 Widescreen; Color; Rated R; 115 minutes; Release date: October 5, 2007.

Ben Stiller, Michelle Monaghan

## Cast

Eddie Cantrow  **Ben Stiller**
Miranda  **Michelle Monaghan**
Doc  **Jerry Stiller**
Lila  **Malin Akerman**
Mac  **Rob Corddry**
Uncle Tito  **Carlos Mencia**
Gayla  **Stephanie Courtney**
Jodi the Bride  **Ali Hillis**
Lila's Mom  **Kathy Lamkin**
Hostess  **Nicol Paone**
Michael  **Joel Bryant**
Martin  **Danny McBride**
Boo  **Scott Wilson**
Beryl  **Polly Holliday**
Tourist Dad  **E.E. Bell**
Tammy  **Lauren Bowles**
10 Year Old Girl at Wedding  **Natalie Carter**
Jodi's Mom  **Leslie Easterbrook**
Buzz  **Roy Jenkins**
Busty Hottub Woman  **Kayla Kleevage**
Twins  **Michael Kromka, Nicholas Kromka**
Tourist Daughter  **Miranda May**
Groomsman  **Brad Newman**
Jodi's Father  **Dean Norris**
Consuela  **Eva Longoria**
River Crossing Father  **Alejandro Patino**
Kid in Batting Cage  **Mishon Ratliff**
and Betsy Rue (Mimi); Lorna Scott (Tourist Mom); Donn Andrew Simmons, Scott Updegrave (Wedding Guests); Amy Sloan (Deborah); Johnny Sneed (Cal); Brian Vowell (Truck Driver); Jerry Sherman (Grandpa Anderson); Gabriel Torres (Cantina Kid); Joel Bryant (Michael the Groom); Kevin Flynn (Flamboyant Man); Gary Riotto (Wedding Coordinator); Mitch Rouse (Bicycle Mugger)

Ben Stiller, Rob Corddry, Lauren Bowles

Eddie Cantrow comes to the dire conclusion that he's made a terrible mistake marrying Lila, a fact compounded by him falling in love with another woman while on his honeymoon. Remake of the 1972 Fox film that starred Charles Grodin, Cybill Shepherd, and Jeannie Berlin.

Ben Stiller, Malin Akerman © DREAMWORKS/PARAMOUNT

# MICHAEL CLAYTON

Tom Wilkinson, George Clooney

Michael O'Keefe, Sydney Pollack

(WARNER BROS.) Producers, Sydney Pollack, Steven Samuels, Jennifer Fox, Kerry Orent; Executive Producers, Steven Soderbergh, George Clooney, James Holt, Anthony Minghella; Director/Screenplay, Tony Gilroy; Photography, Robert Elswit; Designer, Kevin Thompson; Costumes, Sarah Edwards; Editor, John Gilroy; Music, James Newton Howard; Music Supervisor, Brian Ross; Casting, Ellen Chenoweth; a Mirage Enterprises/Section Eight production presented in association with Samuels Media and Castle Rock Entertainment; Dolby; Technicolor; Rated R; 119 minutes; Release date: October 5, 2007.

## Cast

Michael Clayton **George Clooney**
Arthur Edens **Tom Wilkinson**
Karen Crowder **Tilda Swinton**
Marty Bach **Sydney Pollack**
Barry Grissom **Michael O'Keefe**
Don Jefferies **Ken Howard**
Mr. Verne **Robert Prescott**
Detective Dalberto **David Zayas**
Mr. Greer **Denis O'Hare**
Mrs. Greer **Julie White**
Chinese Dealer **Wai Chan**
Players **Alberto Vazquez, Brian Koppelman**
Henry Clayton **Austin Williams**
Ivy **Jennifer Van Dyck**
Gerald **Frank Wood**
Auctioneer **Richard Hecht**
Gabe Zabel **Bill Raymond**
and Sharon Washington (Pam); Amy Hargreaves (Interviewer); Susan Pellegrino (Secretary); Rachel Black (Maude); Matthew Detmer (Todd); John Douglas Thompson (Jail Guard); Merritt Wever (Anna Kaiserson); Brian Poteat (Deposition Lawyer); Christopher Mann (Lt. Elston); Edward Furs (Milwaukee Captain); Katherine Waterston (Third Year); John Gerard Franklin (Correction Officer); Remy Auberjonois (Fifth Year); Pun Bandhu (Fourth Year); Jason Strong (First Year); Paul Oquist (Starter); Terry Serpico (Mr. Iker); Heidi Armbruster (Anna's Sister); Pamela Gray (Cindy Bach); Kevin Hagan (Raymond Clayton); Susan Egbert (Michelle); David Lansbury (Timmy Clayton); Julia Gibson (Stephanie Clayton); Sean Cullen (Det. Gene Clayton); Doug McGrath (Jeff Gaffney); Gregory Dann, Cathy Diane Tomlin (Cops); Sam Gilroy (Copy Kid); Maggie Siff (Attorney #1); Sarah Nichols (Barry's Assistant); Susan McBrien (Jean); Jordan Lage (Partner); Neal Huff, Paul Juhn (Associates); Danielle Skraastad (Voice of Bridget Klein); Tom McCarthy (Voice of Walter); Jonathan Walker (Voice of Del); Cynthia Mace (Voice of Wendy); Michael Countryman (Voice of Evan); Andrew Sherman (Voice of U/North)

Tilda Swinton © WARNER BROS.

Ken Howard, Tilda Swinton, George Clooney

When top litigator Arthur Edens suffers a breakdown while handling a multi-billion dollar lawsuit for a multinational conglomerate, legal fixer Michael Clayton is called in to take care of matters, only to uncover evidence of corporate malfeasance in Edens' case.

2007 Academy Award winner for Best Supporting Actress (Tilda Swinton). This film received additional nominations for Picture, Actor (George Clooney), Supporting Actor (Tom Wilkinson), Director, Original Screenplay, and Original Score.

Austin Williams, George Clooney

Tom Wilkinson, George Clooney

Robert Prescott, Tilda Swinton

# FEEL THE NOISE

Zulay Henao, Omarion Grandberry © TRISTAR PICTURES

(TRISTAR) Producers, Sofia Sondervan, Jennifer Lopez, Simon Fields; Executive Producer, Andrew Lack; Director, Alejandro Chomski; Screenplay, Albert Leon; Photography, Zoran Popovic; Editors, Bill Pankow, Suzy Elmiger, Nico Sarudiansky; Music, Andres Levin; Executive Music Producers, Budd Carr, Nora Felder; Designer, Monica Monserrate; Costumes, Gladyris Silva; Casting, Kim Taylor-Coleman; a Sony BMG Film production, in association with Nuyorican Prods.; Dolby; Color; Rated PG-13; 88 minutes; Release date: October 5, 2007.

## Cast

Rob Vega  **Omarion Grandberry**
C.C.  **Zulay Henao**
Jeffrey Skylar  **James McCaffrey**
Tanya  **Kellita Smith**
Mimi  **Melonie Diaz**
Javi Vega  **Victor Rasuk**
Roberto Vega  **Giancarlo Esposito**
Marivi  **Rosa Arredondo**
Themselves  **Jennifer Lopez, Marc Anthony**
and Lucry (DJ in P.R. Club); Charles Duckworth (Nodde); Carlos Flores (DJ in N.Y. Club); Alexis Garcia (Peter); John A. Garcia (Mr. Chico); Norman Darnell Howell (Notch); Shydel James (DJ Trippe); Jerome I. Jones (Young Rome); Luis Lozada (Vico C.); Cesar A. Lugo (DJ Buda); Joel "Fido" Martinez (Fido); Pras Michel (Electric); Karl W. Morales (Emcee); Raúl Ortiz (Alexis); Meredith Ostrom (Noelia); Rafel Perez-Veve (Mixde); Julio "Voltio" Ramos (Voltio); Cisco Reyes (Pito); Jose Miguel Rocafort (Producer); Rodolfo Rodriguez (New Mayor); Carlos Vega (Guy); Malik Yoba (Mayor)

Fleeing Harlem to escape an inevitable altercation with a local gangster, Rob Vega heads for his estranged dad's Puerto Rico home, where he is introduced to sound of reggaeton, inspiring him and his stepbrother Javi to cut a record.

# THE GOOD NIGHT

(YARI FILM GROUP) Producers, Donna Gigliotti, Bill Johnson; Executive Producers, Jim Seibel, Robert Whitehouse, Oliver Hengst, Ernst-August Schneider; Co-Producer, Nicky Kentish Barnes; Director/Screenplay, Jake Paltrow; Photography, Giles Nuttgens; Designer, Eve Stewart; Costumes, Verity Hawkes; Editor, Rick Lawley; Music, Alec Puro; Associate Producer, Wolfgang Shamburg; Assistant Director, Nick Heckstall-Smith; Casting, Nina Gold; an Inferno Distribution and Tempesta Films presentation of an MHF Zweite Academy Film production in association with Grosvenor Park Media; American-British-German; Dolby; Color; Rated R; 93 minutes; Release date: October 5, 2007.

## Cast

Anna/Melodia  **Penélope Cruz**
Gary  **Martin Freeman**
Dora  **Gwyneth Paltrow**
Paul  **Simon Pegg**
Mel  **Danny DeVito**
Alan Weigert  **Michael Gambon**
and Keith Allen (Norman); Deva Skye Bennett (Ballerina Girl); Steffan Boje (Karl Heinz); Franco Bulaon (Caterer); Sonia Doubell (Shawna); Stephen Graham (Victor); Bruno Lostra, Martino Lazzeri (Italian Slicksters); Meredith MacNeil (Tica); Peter Rnic (Diner); Amber Sealey (Terry); Joyce Springer (Gary's Neighbor)

Gary, a musician facing an uncertain future and an unhappy marriage, finds solace in his dreams, where he becomes obsessed with a mysterious woman who offers herself to him each night.

Penélope Cruz, Simon Pegg © YARI FILM GROUP

# WE OWN THE NIGHT

(COLUMBIA) Producers, Mark Wahlberg, Joaquin Phoenix, Nick Wechsler, Marc Butan; Executive Producers, Todd Wagner, Mark Cuban, Anthony Katagas; Co-Producers, Couper Samuelson, Mike Upton; Director/Screenplay, James Gray; Photography, Joaquin Baca-Asay; Designer, Ford Wheeler; Costumes, Michael Clancy; Music, Wojciech Kilar; Music Supervisor, Dana Sano; Editor, John Axelrad; Casting, Douglas Aibel; a 2929 Productions presentation of a Nick Wechsler production; Dolby; Color; Rated R; 117 minutes; Release date: October 12, 2007.

Mark Wahlberg, Robert Duvall

## Cast

Bobby Green  **Joaquin Phoenix**
Capt. Joseph Grusinsky  **Mark Wahlberg**
Amada Juarez  **Eva Mendes**
Deputy Chief Burt Grusinsky  **Robert Duvall**
Michael Solo  **Antoni Corone**
Marat Buzhayev  **Moni Moshonov**
Pavel Lubyarsky  **Oleg Taktarov**
Vadim Nezhinski  **Alex Veadov**
Jumbo Falsetti  **Danny Hoch**
Capt. Jack Shapiro  **Tony Musante**
Freddie  **Dominic Colon**
Bloodied Patron  **Joseph D'Onofrio**
Kalina Buzhayev  **Elena Solovey**
Sandra Grusinsky  **Maggie Kiley**
Capt. Spiro Giavannis  **Paul Herman**
Russell De Keifer  **Craig Walker**
Claudia  **Claudia Lopez**
Hazel  **Kate Condidorio**
Eli Mirichenko  **Ed Shkolnikov**
Eli and Masha's Children  **Katya Savina, Matthew Djentchouraev**
Nat the Cop  **Scott Nicholson**
Sgt. Provenzano  **Robert Kirk**
Portly Cop  **Al Linea**
and Teddy Coluca, Joseph Coffey (Uniformed Cops); Frank Girardeau (Police Chaplain); Jose E. Soto (Latino Man); Gregory Wilson (Poker Player); Ed Koch (Mayor); Fred Burrell (Commissioner Ruddy); Michael Massimino, Edward Conlon (Hospital Guards); Sharon Wilkins (Nurse); Ross Brodar (Tattooed Man); Francis Toumbakaris (Slavic Youth); Hoon Lee (Emergency Services Driver); Barbara Ann Davison (Neighbor Lady); Irwin Gray (Neighbor); Luigi Scorcia (Luigi); Miriam Cruz (Amada's Mother); Doug Torres (Schneider); Tony Guida (Vitt the Guard); Robert McKay (Riker's Desk Guard); Blaise Corrigan (Uniformed Police Officer); Karl Bury (Random Cop); Coati Mundi (Himself); Joe Forbrich, Robert Pennacchia (Guards); Richard Petrocelli (Tough-Looking Cop); Nik Pjeternikaj (Albanian Drug Lord); Jamal Weathers (Parabolic Engineer)

Mark Wahlberg, Alex Veadov © COLUMBIA PICTURES

Eva Mendes, Joaquin Phoenix

Nightclub entrepreneur Bobby Green finds himself torn between family loyalty and business when his father and brother, both NYC cops, turn to him for assistance in hopes of bringing down a dangerous Russian drug dealer.

# WHY DID I GET MARRIED?

Jill Scott, Denise Boutte, Richard T. Jones

(LIONSGATE) Producers, Tyler Perry, Reuben Cannon; Executive Producer, Michael Paseornek; Co-Producers, Roger M. Bobb, Joseph P. Genier; Director/Screenplay, Tyler Perry, based on his play; Photography, Toyomichi Kurita; Designer, Ina Mayhew; Costumes, Keith G. Lewis; Editor, Maysie Hoy; Music, Aaron Zigman; Music Supervisor, Joel C. High; Casting, Kim Williams; a Tyler Perry Studios/Reuben Cannon Prods./Lionsgate production; Dolby; Arriflex Widescreen; Technicolor; Rated PG-13; 118 minutes; Release date: October 12, 2007.

Janet Jackson, Malik Yoba

## Cast

Terry  **Tyler Perry**
Diane  **Sharon Leal**
Patricia  **Janet Jackson**
Sheila  **Jill Scott**
Gavin  **Malik Yoba**
Mike  **Richard T. Jones**
Marcus  **Michael Jai White**
Sheriff Troy  **Lamman Rucker**
Angela  **Tasha Smith**
Trina  **Denise Boutte**
Pam  **Keesha Sharp**
Keisha  **Kaira Whitehead**
Prof. Stewart  **Sheri Mann Stewart**
Jay  **Brian Bremer**
Walter  **Jamie Moore**
Bartender  **Bart Hansard**
Ticket Attendant  **Randall Sims**
Secretary  **Tina Lee**
Fur Sales Lady  **Desiree Zurowski**
and Darla Vandenbossche (Mountain Woman); Sean Tyson (Mountain Man); Christa Lamos, Dah-uh Morrow, Joniece Abbott-Pratt, Greyson Chadwick (College Students)

Michael Jai White, Tasha Smith

Four couples meet for an annual vacation at a Colorado resort, where they question the pros and cons of their relationships.

Sharon Yeal, Tyler Perry © LIONSGATE

# LARS AND THE REAL GIRL

Bianca, Ryan Gosling, Emily Mortimer, Paul Schneider

Paul Schneider, Emily Mortimer, Ryan Gosling, Bianca

(MGM) Produced by Sidney Kimmel, John Cameron, Sarah Aubrey; Executive Producers, William Horberg, Bruce Toll, Peter Berg; Director, Craig Gillespie; Screenplay, Nancy Oliver; Photography, Adam Kimmel; Editor, Tatiana S. Riegel; Music, David Torn; Designer, Arv Grewal; Costumes, Kirston Mann, Gerri Gillan; Casting, David Rubin, Richard Hicks; a Sidney Kimmel Entertainment, MGM Pictures production; Dolby; Color; Rated PG-13; 106 minutes; Release date: October 12, 2007.

Paul Schneider, Emily Mortimer, Ryan Gosling, Bianca

## Cast

Lars Lindstrom  **Ryan Gosling**
Karin Lindstrom  **Emily Mortimer**
Gus Lindstrom  **Paul Schneider**
Dagmar  **Patricia Clarkson**
Margo  **Kelli Garner**
Mrs. Gruner  **Nancy Beatty**
Reverend Bock  **R.D. Reid**
Mr. Shaw  **Joe Bostick**
Mrs. Schindler  **Liz Gordon**
Mrs. Petersen  **Nicky Guadagni**
Mr. Hofstedtler  **Doug Lennox**
Cindy  **Karen Robinson**
Kurt  **Maxwell McCabe-Lokos**
and Billy Parrott (Erik); Sally Cahill (Deb); Angela Vint (Sandy); Liisa Repo-Martell (Laurel); Boyd Banks (Russell); Darren Hynes (Moose); Victor Gómez (Hector); Tommy Chang (Nelson); Arnold Pinnock (Baxter); Joshua Peace (Jerry); Aurora Browne (Lisa); Alec McClure (Steve); Tannis Burnett (Nurse Amy); Lauren Ash (Holly); Lindsey Connell (Victoria); Aaron Ferguson, Danna Howe, Annabelle Torsein, Tim Blake, Torquil Colbo (Choir Members)

Small town social misfit Lars Lindstrom offers his community a challenge when he introduces a life-sized doll as his girlfriend.

This film received an Oscar nomination for Original Screenplay.

Patricia Clarkson © METRO-GOLDWYN-MAYER

# GONE BABY GONE

John Ashton, Amy Ryan, Ed Harris © MIRAMAX FILMS

(MIRAMAX) Producers, Alan Ladd Jr., Dan Rissner, Sean Bailey; Executive Producer, David Crockett; Co-Producer, Chay Carter; Director, Ben Affleck; Screenplay, Ben Affleck, Aaron Stockard, based on the novel by Dennis Lehane; Photography, John Toll; Designer, Sharon Seymour; Costumes, Alix Friedberg; Editor, William Goldenberg; Music, Harry Gregson-Williams; Associate Producers, Amanda Lamb, Aaron Stockard; Casting, Donna Morong, Nadia Aleyd; a Ladd Co. production; Dolby; Color; Rated R; 115 minutes; Release date: October 19, 2007.

Casey Affleck, Ed Harris, Michelle Monaghan, John Ashton

Morgan Freeman, Casey Affleck, Michelle Monaghan

## Cast

Patrick Kenzie  **Casey Affleck**
Angie Gennaro  **Michelle Monaghan**
Capt. Jack Doyle  **Morgan Freeman**
Remy Bressant  **Ed Harris**
Nick Poole  **John Ashton**
Helene McCready  **Amy Ryan**
Bea McCready  **Amy Madigan**
and Titus Welliver (Lionel McCready); Michael Kenneth Williams (Devin); Edi Gathegi (Cheese); Mark Margolis (Leon Trett); Madeline O'Brien (Amanda McCready); Slaine (Bubba Rogowski); Trudi Goodman (Roberta Trett); Matthew Maher (Corwin Earle); Jill Quigg (Dottie); Sean Malone (Skinny Ray Likanski); Brian Scannell (Lenny); Jay Giannone (Steve Penteroudakis); William Lee (Big Dave); Daniel DeMiller Jr., Kenneth Butler Jr., Stephen Curran, Michael T. Blythe, Bob J. Leary, Mike Pusateri, John McColgam (Fillmore Regulars); Nicholas Donovan, Joseph Thomas-O'Brien (Kids on Bikes); Jimmy LeBlanc (Chris Mullen); Mary Bounphasaysonh (Cheese's Girl); Fanshen Cox (Doyle's Secretary); Kippy Goldfarb (Francine Doyle); Elizabeth Duff (Mrs. Bressant); Cathie Callanan (Mrs. Poole); Cameron Henry (Jimmy Pietro); Bobby Curcuro (Bobby); Kevin Molis (Officer in Procession); Robert Wahlberg (Interrogating Officer); Tom Kemp (Police Captain); Matt Podolske (Officer Riley); Joseph Flaherty (Murphy's Law Bartender); Carla Antonino (Murphy's Law Waitress); Peg Holzemer (Woman at Bar); Chelsea Ladd (Boston Girl); Josh Marchette (Dart Player); Tom McNeeley (Teamster at Bar); Paul Horn, Rena Maliszweski, Suzanne Schemm, Lonnie Farmer, Richard Snee, Dale Place, Gary Tanguay (Newscasters); Ted Reinstein, Celeste Oliva, Patrick Shea, Lewis D. Wheeler, Michele Proude, Tim Estiloz, Karen Eris, John Belche (Field Reporters); Raymond Alongi (West Beckett Police Officer); Joey Vacchio, Eamon M. Brooks, Vincent H. Carolan, Frank G. Sullivan (State Troopers); Karen T. Ahearn (Reunited Police Officer)

Boston detectives Patrick Kenzie and Angie Gennaro find themselves plunged into a moral dilemma when they are hired to find a little girl who has been abducted from her irresponsible single mom.

This film received an Oscar nomination for Supporting Actress (Amy Ryan).

# RENDITION

(NEW LINE CINEMA) Producers, Steve Golin, Marcus Viscidi; Executive Producers, Toby Emmerich, Keith Goldberg, David Kanter, Keith Redman, Michael Sugar, Edward Milstein, Bill Todman Jr., Paul Schwake; Co-Producer, Mark Martin; Director, Gavin Hood; Screenplay, Kelley Sane; Photography, Dion Beebe; Designer, Barry Robison; Costumes, Michael Wilkinson; Editor, Megan Gill; Music, Paul Hepker, Mark Kilian; Visual Effects and Animation, Digital Dimension; Stunts, Cedric Proust; Casting, Francine Maisler, Kate Dowd, Kathleen Driscoll-Mohler; an Anonymous Content production presented in association with Level 1 Entertainment; Dolby; Panavision; Deluxe color; Rated R; 122 minutes; Release date: October 19, 2007.

Jake Gyllenhaal, Igal Naor

### Cast

Douglas Freeman  **Jake Gyllenhaal**
Isabella El-Ibrahimi  **Reese Witherspoon**
Senator Hawkins  **Alan Arkin**
Alan Smith  **Peter Sarsgaard**
Anwar El-Ibrahimi  **Omar Metwally**
Abasi Fawal  **Yigal Naor**
Khalid  **Moa Khouas**
Fatima Fawal  **Zineb Oukach**
Corrine Whitman  **Meryl Streep**
Lee Mayer  **J.K. Simmons**
and Aramis Knight (Jeremy El-Ibrahimi); Rosie Malek-Yonan (Nuru El-Ibrahimi); Laila Mrabti (Lina Fawal); David Fabrizio (William Dixon); Mounir Margoum (Rani); Driss Roukhe (Bahi); Bob Gunton (Lars Whitman); Mrabti Boubker Fahmi (Senior Prison Guard); Nava Ziv (Samia Fawal); Reymond Amsellem (Layla Fawal); Simon Abkarian (Said Abdel Aziz); Wendy Phillips (Samantha); Christian Martin (Senator Lewis' Aide); Hassam Ghancy (Hamadi); Najib Oudghiri (Omar Adnan); Omar Salim (Rashid Salimi); Bunnie Rivera (Corrine's Housekeeper); Noureddine Aberdine (Student Leader); Mohamed El Habib Ahamdane (Hamadi's 2nd in Command); Reguragui Fatima (Khalid's Grandmother); Anne Betancourt (Sharon Lopez); Salaheddine Ben Chegra (Al Jazeera Newscaster); Natalia Zonova (French Tourist); Hassan Hammouch (Hospital Doctor); Thomas Raley, Del Hunter-White (D.C. Security Guards); Skylar Adams, Tim Thomas, Richard Dorton (CIA Agents at D.C. Airport); Abdellah Lamsabhi (Tea House Owner); Lasfar Abdelghani (Hamid, Douglas' Driver); Floella Benjamin (CIA Staffer); Akram Allie, Michael Dube, Pope Jerrod, Anthony Watterson (Cape Town Businessmen); Marisia Moreno (Woman Who Helps Isabella); Tanane Boussif (Prison Soldier); Lofti Hassan (Taxi Driver); El Oualid Mezoaur (Donkey Cart Driver); Craig Johnson, Wade Harlan (Capitol Hill Policemen); Paul Norwood, Steve Tom, Robert Clotworthy (Reception Guests); Muna Otaru (Senate Staffer); Nick Toth (CNN Announcer); David Randolph (Todd Hamilton); Mustapha Louchou (Khalid's Brother); Hadar Ratzon (Safiya)

Zineb Oukach, Mohammad Khouas

Isabella El-Ibrahimi hopes to find out the truth behind her husband's detainment by American authorities on his return trip from Africa, where a suicide bomb has just killed a top CIA officer.

Reese Witherspoon © NEW LINE CINEMA

# RESERVATION ROAD

Joaquin Phoenix, Antoni Corone

Joaquin Phoenix, Elle Fanning, Jennifer Connelly

(FOCUS) Producers, Nick Wechsler, A. Kitman Ho; Executive Producers, Dean M. Leavitt, Gina Resnick; Director, Terry George; Screenplay, John Burnham Schwartz, Terry George, based on the novel by John Burnham Schwartz; Photography, John Lindley; Editor, Naomi Geraghty; Music, Mark Isham; Music Supervisors, Budd Carr, Nora Felder; Designer, Ford Wheeler; Costumes, Catherine George; Casting, Amanda Mackey, Cathy Sandrich Gelfond; a Nick Wechsler/Miracle Pictures production, in association with Volume One Entertainment, presented with Random House Films; Dolby; Technicolor; Rated R; 102 minutes; Release date: October 19, 2007.

## Cast

Ethan Learner **Joaquin Phoenix**
Dwight Arno **Mark Ruffalo**
Grace Learner **Jennifer Connelly**
Ruth Wheldon **Mira Sorvino**
Emma Learner **Elle Fanning**
Lucas Arno **Eddie Alderson**
Josh Learner **Sean Curley**
Sergeant Burke **Antoni Corone**
Steve Cutler **John Slattery**
Minister **John Rothman**
Norris Wheldon **Gary Kohn**
Jimmy McBride **Cordell Clyde Lochin**
Nora Fannelli **Nora Ferrari**
and Samuel Ryan Finn (Cello Player); Susan Powell (Elegant Parent); Kevin Herbst (Driving Trooper); Linda Dano (Grandmother); Geisha Otero (Blanca); Brett Haley (Brett); Sinead Daly (American Girl); Armin Amiri (Rashid); Johnny Tchaikovsky (Jock); Lee Goffin-Bonenfant (Student); Americk Lewis (African-American Student); Danny Johnson (Investigating Trooper); Bill Camp (Desk Trooper); Stephanie Weyman (Cheryl); Raum-Aron (Gerry); Debra Robinson (Parent); Michael Anzalone (Dwight's Neighbor); David Anzuelo (Raul)

Mark Ruffalo, Mira Sorvino

Devastated when his young son is killed by a hit-and-run driver, Ethan Learner seeks legal help, unaware that his lawyer is the man responsible for the accident.

Mark Ruffalo, Joaquin Phoenix © FOCUS FEATURES

# THINGS WE LOST IN THE FIRE

Halle Berry, Benicio Del Toro

(DREAMWORKS/PARAMOUNT) Producers, Sam Mendes, Sam Mercer; Executive Producers, Pippa Harris, Allan Loeb; Co-Producer, Barbara Kelly; Director, Susanne Bier; Screenplay, Allan Loeb; Photography, Tom Stern; Designer, Richard Sherman; Costumes, Karen Matthews; Music, Johan Soderqvist; Themes, Gustavo Santaolalla; Music Supervisor, Susan Jacobs; Editors, Pernille Bech Christensen, Bruce Cannon; Casting, Debra Zane; a DreamWorks presentation of a Neal Street production; Dolby; Panavision; Deluxe color; Rated R; 118 minutes; Release date: October 19, 2007.

## Cast

Audrey Burke **Halle Berry**
Jerry Sunborne **Benicio Del Toro**
Brian Burke **David Duchovny**
Kelly **Alison Lohman**
Neal **Omar Benson Miller**
Howard Glassman **John Carroll Lynch**
Harper Burke **Alexis Llewellyn**
Dory Burke **Micah Berry**
Brenda **Robin Weigert**
Diane **Paula Newsome**
Spring **Sarah Dubrovsky**
Ginnie Burke **Maureen Thomas**
Howard's Wife **Patricia Harras**
Distressed Man **V.J. Foster**
Teresa Haddock **Carolyn Field**
Arnie **James Lafazanos**
and Marlies Dick, Todd Charles Mosher (Police Officers); Liam James (Cousin Dave); Quinn Lord (Cousin Joel); Alejandro Chavarria (Backyard Kid); Ken Tremblett (Brenda's Husband); Hilary Strang (N.A. Meeting Director); Jessica McLeod, Victoria Campbell (Harper's Friends); Gerry Rousseau (John in Alley); Abraham Jedidiah (Mr. Skopes); Adrian Hough, Kendall Cross, Lorena Gale, R. Nelson Brown (N.A. Meeting People); Hakan Coskuner (Alvin the Addict); James R. Baylis (Misunderstood Dealer)

Grieving from the murder of her husband, Audrey Burke takes in her spouse's good friend Jerry Sunborne, a recovering addict who proves instrumental in helping Audrey and her children overcome their loss.

John Carroll Lynch, Benicio Del Toro © DREAMWORKS/PARAMOUNT

Micah Berry, Alexis Llewellyn

# 30 DAYS OF NIGHT

(COLUMBIA) Producers, Sam Raimi, Rob Tapert; Executive Producers, Joe Drake, Nathan Kahane, Mike Richardson, Aubrey Henderson; Co-Producers, Chloe Smith, Ted Adams; Director, David Slade; Screenplay, Steve Niles, Stuart Beattie, Brian Nelson, based on the IDW Publishing comic by Steve Niles, Ben Templesmith; Photography, Jo Willems; Designer, Paul Denham Austerberry; Costumes, Jane Holland; Editor, Art Jones; Music, Brian Reitzell; Special Effects Supervisor, Jason Durey; Special Makeup Effects Coordinator, Gino Acevedo; Visual Effects Supervisor, Charlie McLelland; Stunts, Allan Poppleton; Casting, Mary Vernieu; New Zealand Casting, Liz Mullane; a Ghost House Pictures production, in association with Dark Horse Entertainment; Dolby; Panavision; Color; Rated R; 113 minutes; Release date: October 19, 2007.

Danny Huston

## Cast

Sheriff Eben Oleson  **Josh Hartnett**
Stella Oleson  **Melissa George**
Marlow  **Danny Huston**
The Stranger  **Ben Foster**
Beau Brower  **Mark Boone Junior**
Jake Oleson  **Mark Rendall**
Denise  **Amber Sainsbury**
Deputy Billy Kitka  **Manu Bennett**
Iris  **Megan Franich**
Doug Hertz  **Joel Tobeck**
Lucy Ikos  **Elizabeth Hawthorne**
Carter Davies  **Nathaniel Lees**
Wilson Bulosan  **Craig Hall**
Issac Bulosan  **Chic Littlewood**
John Riis  **Peter Feeney**
Ally Riis  **Min Windle**
Kirsten Toomey  **Camille Keenan**
Peter Toomey  **Jack Walley**
Helen Munson  **Elizabeth McRae**
Tom Melanson  **Joe Dekkers-Reihana**
Paul Jayko  **Scott Taylor**
Gus Lambert  **Grant Tilly**
Malekai Hamm  **Pua Magasiva**
Aaron  **Jared Turner**
and Kelson Henderson (Gabe); John Wraight (Adam Colletta); Dayna Porter (Jeannie Colletta); Kate S. Butler (Michelle Robbins); Patrick Kake (Frank Robbins); Thomas Newman (Larry Robbins); Rachel Maitland-Smith (Gail Robbins); Abbey-May Wakefield (Little Girl Vampire); John Rawls (Zurial); Andrew Stehlin (Arvin); Tim McLachlan (Archibald); Ben Fransham (Heron); Kate Elliott (Dawn); Allan Smith (Khan); Jarrod Martin (Edgar); Sam La Hood (Strigoi); Jacob Tomuri (Seth); Kate O'Rourke (Inika); Melissa Billington (Kali); Aaron Cortesi (Cicero); Matt Gillanders (Daeron)

Ben Foster © COLUMBIA PICTURES

During Barrow, Alaska's month-long stretch of sunlessness, a horde of bloodthirsty vampires invade the town.

Melissa George, Josh Hartnett

# WRISTCUTTERS: A LOVE STORY

Shannyn Sossamon, Shea Whigham © AUTONOMOUS

(AUTONOMOUS) Producers, Adam Sherman, Chris Coen, Tatiana Kelly, Mikal P. Lazarev; Executive Producer, Jonathan Schwartz; Co-Producer, Chapin Wilson; Director/Screenplay, Goran Dukic, based on the novella *Kneller's Happy Campers* by Etgar Keret; Photography, Vanja Cernjul; Designer, Linda Sena; Costumes, Carla Biggert; Editor, Jonathan Alberts; Music, Bobby Johnston; Music Supervisor, Robin Urdang; Visual Effects Supervisor, Chris Dawson; Special Effects Makeup, Sherri Simmons; Line Producer, Charles Berg; Associate Producer, Linda Sena; Casting, Shannon Makhanian; a Halcyon Pictures, Adam Sherman, Crispy Films presentation of a No Matter Pictures production; Dolby; FotoKem color; Rated R; 91 minutes; Release date: October 19, 2007.

## Cast

Zia **Patrick Fugit**
Mikal **Shannyn Sossamon**
Eugene **Shea Whigham**
Desiree **Leslie Bibb**
Nanuk **Mikal P. Lazarev**
Mike **Mark Boone Junior**
Erik **Abraham Benrubi**
and Tom Waits (Kneller); Mary Pat Gleason (Eugene's Mother); Clayne Crawford (Jim); Anthony Azizi (Hassan); Azura Skye (Tanya); Nick Offerman (Max); Sarah Roemer (Rachel); John Hawkes (Yan); Will Arnett (Messiah); Jake Busey (Brian); Cameron Bowen (Big Kostya); Chase Ellison (Little Kostya); Anatol Rezmeritza (Eugene's Father); Adam G. (Native American Gas Station Attendant); Mark Edward Smith (Policeman); Mark Fredrichs (Zia's Father); Aaron Parker Mouser (Max); Zia Harris (Pizza Delivery Guy); Julie Sanford (Zia's Mom); Irwin Keyes, Lonnie Beard (Bartenders); Bridget Powers (Dancer); Amy Seimetz (Nina); Jazzmun (Transvestite); Eddie Steeples (Josh); Bonnie Aarons (Messiah Worshipper); Nils Allen Stewart (Bodyguard); Ava Metz, Troy DeWalt (PICs); Brian David (Way Station Attendant)

In a purgatory for suicides, Zia searches for the girl who caused him to slash his wrists.

# SAW IV

(LIONSGATE) Producers, Gregg Hoffman, Oren Koules, Mark Burg; Executive Producers, Daniel Jason Heffner, James Wan, Leigh Whannell, Stacey Testro, Peter Block, Jason Constantine; Co-Producer, Greg Copeland; Director, Darren Lynn Bousman; Screenplay, Patrick Melton, Marcus Dunstan; Story, Patrick Melton, Marcus Dunstan, Thomas Fenton; Photography, David A. Armstrong; Editors, Kevin Greutert, Brett Sullivan; Music, Charlie Clouser; Designer, David Hackl; Costumes, Alex Kavanagh; Visual Effects Supervisor, Jon Campfens; Casting, Stephanie Gorin; a Twisted Pictures presentation of a Burg/Koules/Hoffman production; Dolby; Deluxe color; Rated R; 92 minutes; Release date: October 26, 2007.

## Cast

Jigsaw/John **Tobin Bell**
Hoffman **Costas Mandylor**
Agent Strahm **Scott Patterson**
Jill **Betsy Russell**
Rigg **Lyriq Bent**
Agent Perez **Athena Karkanis**
and Justin Louis (Art); Simon Reynolds (Lamanna); Donnie Wahlberg (Eric Mathews); Angus Macfadyen (Jeff); Shawnee Smith (Amanda); Bahar Soomekh (Lynn); Dina Meyer (Kerry); Mike Realba (Fisk); Marty Adams (Ivan); Sarain Boylan (Brenda); Billy Otis (Cecil); James Van Patten (Dr. Heffner); David Boyce (Pathologist); Kevin Rushton (Trevor); Julian Richings (Vagrant); Kelly Jones (SWAT Pete); Ingrid Hart (Tracy); Janet Land (Morgan); Ron Lea (Rex); Joanne Boland (Crime Scene Photographer); Zoe Heath (Lab Technician); Bill Vibert (Young Cop); Devon Bostick (Derek); Tony Nappo (Gus); Emmanuelle Vaugier (Addison); Noam Jenkins (Michael); Mike Butters (Paul); J. LaRose (Troy); Oren Koules (The Man); Alison Luther (Young Girl); Kim Roberts (Nurse Deborah); David Webster (Dr. Steve); Sandra Manson (Nurse Patti)

Detective Rigg must track down further torture victims of Jigsaw, in an effort to save their lives or help them meet a more humane demise. Fourth entry in the Lionsgate series, which started in 2004.

Lyriq Bent © LIONSGATE

# BEFORE THE DEVIL
# KNOWS YOU'RE DEAD

Ethan Hawke, Philip Seymour Hoffman © THINKFILM

Ethan Hawke

(THINKFILM) Producers, Michael Cerenzie, Brian Linse, Paul Parmar, William S. Gilmore; Executive Producers, David Bergstein, Jane Barclay, Hannah Leader, Belle Avery, Jeffry Melnick, J.J. Hoffman, Eli Klein, Sam Zaharis; Co-Executive Producers, Guy Pham, Joel Corman; Co-Producers, Jeff G. Waxman, Austin Chick; Director, Sidney Lumet; Screenplay, Kelly Masterson; Photography, Ron Fortunato; Designer, Christopher Nowak; Costumes, Tina Nigro; Editor, Tom Swartwout; Music, Carter Burwell; Casting, Ellen Lewis; a Capitol Films/Funky Buddha Group presentation of a Unity Prods./Linsefilm production; Dolby; Color; Rated R; 116 minutes; Release date: October 26, 2007.

## Cast

Andy **Philip Seymour Hoffman**
Hank **Ethan Hawke**
Gina **Marisa Tomei**
Charles **Albert Finney**
Nanette **Rosemary Harris**
Chris **Aleksa Palladino**
Bobby **Bryan F. O'Byrne**
Martha **Amy Ryan**
Dex **Michael Shannon**
Danielle **Sarah Livingston**
Justin **Blaine Horton**
Katherine **Arija Bareikis**
and Leonard Cimino (William); Lee Wilkof (Jake); Damon Gupton (Doctor); Adrian Martinez (Security Guard); Patrick G. Burns (Priest); Alice Spivak (Receptionist); Natalie Gold (Secretary); Keith Davis (Attendant); Mateo Gómez (Doorman); Myra Lucretia Taylor (Grader); Chris Chalk (Officer); Sakina Jaffrey (Manager); John Knox (Desk Sergeant); James Lally, Jordan Gelber (Agents); Megan Byrne (Nurse); Marcia Jean Kurtz (Hospital Receptionist); Guy A. Fortt (Vendor); Meredith Patterson (Andy's Secretary); Tom Zolandz (Junkie); Paul Butler (Detective); Anita Sklar, Josh Mowery, Diane Bradley, Richard K. Lublin (Mourners); Bob Colletti (Ambulance Driver)

Ethan Hawke, Albert Finney, Marisa Tomei

Two brothers, desperately in need of money, make the dire mistake of participating in a robbery of their parents' jewelry store.

Aleksa Palladino, Michael Shannon, Ethan Hawke

# RAILS & TIES

(WARNER BROS.) Producers, Robert Lorenz, Peer Oppenheimer, Barrett Stuart; Co-Producer, Tim Moore; Director, Alison Eastwood; Screenplay, Micky Levy; Photography, Tom Stern; Designer, James J. Murakami; Costumes, Deborah Hopper; Editor, Gary D. Roach; Music, Kyle Eastwood, Michael Stevens; Casting, Matt Huffman; Dolby; Panavision; Technicolor; Rated PG-13; 101 minutes; Release date: October 26, 2007.

### Cast

Tom Stark **Kevin Bacon**
Megan Stark **Marcia Gay Harden**
Davey Danner **Miles Heizer**
Renee **Marin Hinkle**
Otis Higgs **Eugene Byrd**
Susan Garcia **Laura Cerón**
Judy Neasy **Margo Martindale**
Laura Danner **Bonnie Root**
and Steve Eastin (N.B. Garcia); Kathryn Joosten (Mrs. Brown); Steven M. Porter (Howie Pugh); Jim Cody Williams (Vince the Engineer); Kerri Randles (Rosanna); Stephen Peace (Bartender); Robert Harvey, Michael Otis (Administrators); Ernest Harden Jr., Mike McCaul (Officials); Maya Goldsmith (Sheila); Michael Raynor (Det. Christian Fox); Micky Levy (Det. Ann Crane); John Nielsen (Dr. Offenberger); Dennis Napolitano (Piano Teacher); Mary Beth McDade (News Reporter); Brian Bogulski (Workman #1); Jade Marx (Nurse #1); Nathan Kornelis (Father); Dalton Stumbo (Child)

Suspended from his engineering job, emotionally distant Tom Stark must now face the reality of his wife's fatal illness.

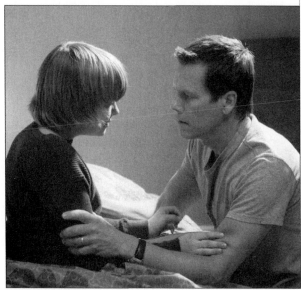

Miles Heizer, Kevin Bacon © WARNER BROS.

# JIMMY CARTER: MAN FROM PLAINS

Jimmy Carter © SONY PICTURES CLASSICS

(SONY CLASSICS) Producers, Jonathan Demme, Neda Armian; Executive Producers, Ron Bozman, Jeff Skoll, Diane Weyermann; Director, Jonathan Demme; Photography, Declan Quinn; Editor, Kate Amend; Music, Djamel Ben Yelles, Alejandro Escovedo; a Participant Prods. presentation of a Clinica Estetico production; Dolby; Color; DCP; Rated PG; 126 minutes; Release date: October 26, 2007. Documentary following the former President as he tours the U.S. to promote his newest book, *Palestine: Peace Not Apartheid.*

### With

Jimmy Carter, Rosalynn Carter, Wolf Blitzer, Alan M. Dershowitz, Terry Gross, Larry King, Jay Leno, Edward Norton, Diane Rehm, Charlie Rose, Tavis Smiley.

# BELLA

(LIONSGATE) Producers, Alejandro Monteverde, Eduardo Verástegui, Leo Severino, Denise Pinkley; Executive Producers, Sean Wolfington, J. Eustace Wolfington, Ana Wolfington, Steve McEveety; Director, Alejandro Monteverde; Screenplay, Alejandro Monteverde, Patrick Million;Photography, Andrew Cadelago; Designer, Richard Lassalle; Costumes, Eden Miller; Editor, Fernando Villena; Music, Stephan Altman; Music Supervisor, Frankie Pike; Casting, Beth Dowling, Kim Miscia; a Metanoia Films presentation in association with the One Media and M Power Worldwide; Dolby; Technicolor; Rated PG-13; 91 minutes; Release date: October 26, 2007.

## Cast

Jose **Eduardo Verástegui**
Nina **Tammy Blanchard**
Manny **Manny Perez**
Mother **Angélica Aragón**
Father **Jaime Tirelli**
Celia **Ali Landry**
Eduardo **Ramon Rodriguez**
and Sophie Nyweide (Bella); Ewa Da Cruz (Veronica); Lukas Behnken (Johannes); Peter Bucossi (Angry Driver); David Castro (David); Michael Chin (Bodega Clerk); Dominic Colon (Pepito); Hudson Cooper (Father on Beach); Tawny Cypress (Frannie); Sara Dawson (Helen); Doug DeBeech (Pieter); Alexa Gerasimovich (Lucinda); Herb Lovelle (Homeless Man); Michael Mosley (Kevin); Wade Mylius (J.J. Janze); Stan Newman (Businessman on Phone); Kola Ogundiran (African Cabbie); Melinda Peinardo (Clinic Nurse); Alfonso Ramírez (Leonardo); Armando Riesco (Francisco); Jamie Schofield (Hostess); James Stanek (Henri); Marilyn Torres (Carla); Teresa Yenque (Amelia)

After his brother fires a waitress for being late, Jose, the restaurant's chef, decides to spend the day with the hapless woman, who has just discovered she is pregnant.

Tammy Blanchard, Eduardo Verástegui © LIONSGATE

# MUSIC WITHIN

Michael Sheen © METRO-GOLDWYN-MAYER

(MGM) Producers, Brett Donowho, Steven Sawalich; Co-Producer, Ron Livingston; Director, Steven Sawalich; Screenplay, Brett McKinney, Mark Andrew Olsen, Kelly Kennemer; Photography, Irek Hartowicz; Designer, Craig Stearns; Costumes, Alexis Scott; Editor, Tim Alverson; Music, James T. Sale; Music Supervisor, Debra Braun; Associate Producer, Frank Vitolo; Casting, Amy McIntyre Britt, Anya Colloff, Corbin Bronson; an Articulus Entertainment and Quorum Entertainment production; Dolby; Deluxe color; Rated R; 93 minutes; Release date: October 26, 2007.

## Cast

Richard Pimentel **Ron Livingston**
Christine **Melissa George**
Art Honeyman **Michael Sheen**
Mike Stoltz **Yul Vazquez**
and Rebecca De Mornay (Richard's Mom); Hector Elizondo (Ben Padrow); Leslie Nielsen (Bill Austin); Ridge Canipe (Young Richard); and Paul Michael (Joe); Clint Jung (Richard's Dad); John Livingston (Mr. Parks); Arlene Ancheta (Chinese Restaurant Owner); Glen Baggerly (D.J.); Alexander Baird (Mr. Parks' Student); Doug Baldwin (Supervisor); Jenni Blong (Shelly); Joel Bryant (Sgt. Taylor); Linda Burden-Williams (Bambi); T.J. Civis (Army Recruiter); Peter Crone (Nikos); Beth Donowho, Chris D. Harder, Brandon Sawalich (Students); Brett Donowho (McMahon); Dale Dye (Capt. Ruzicka); Gary Eubank (Recruiter); Trevi Sawalich, Natiya Guin (Sorority Girls); Benedict Herrman (Emcee); Clint Howard (Clerk); TyZhaun Lewis (Aaron); Shelly Lipkin (VA Doctor); Thaddeus Massey (Customer #1); Shelly Matthews (Caregiver); Betty Moyer (Mrs. Jelt); Daniel Nelson (Birthday Party Boy); David Nelson (Boy at Party); Michael O'Donnell (Franklin); Marion Ross (Grandma); Kevin Sage (PFC Sage); Steven Sawalich (Soldier); Phil Somerville (Vaughn); Cindy Sorenson (Little Person); Gracie Starr (Young Christine); Lauren Stocks (Heather); Janssen Van De Yacht (Toddler Richard); Frank Vitolo (Manager); Nita Whitaker (Hostess)

The true story of how Richard Pimentel's own physical struggles caused him to campaign for the Americans with Disabilities Act in 1990.

# DAN IN REAL LIFE

Steve Carell, Dane Cook © TOUCHSTONE PICTURES

Juliette Binoche, Brittany Robinson, Steve Carell, Norbert Leo Butz

(TOUCHSTONE/FOCUS) Producers, Jon Shestack, Brad Epstein; Executive Producers, Noah Rosen, Darlene Caamaño Loquet, Mari Jo Winkler-Ioffreda; Director, Peter Hedges; Screenplay, Pierce Gardner, Peter Hedges; Photography, Lawrence Sher; Designer, Sarah Knowles; Costumes, Alix Friedberg; Music/Original Songs, Sondre Lerche; Music Supervisor, Dana Sano; Editor, Sarah Flack; Co-Producer, Dianne Dreyer; Casting, Bernard Telsey; a Jon Shestack production; Dolby; Technicolor; Rated PG-13; 98 minutes; Release date: October 26, 2007.

## Cast

Dan Burns  **Steve Carell**
Marie  **Juliette Binoche**
Mitch Burns  **Dane Cook**
Jane Burns  **Alison Pill**
Cara Burns  **Brittany Robertson**
Lilly Burns  **Marlene Lawston**
Nana Burns  **Dianne Wiest**
Poppy Burns  **John Mahoney**
Clay Burns  **Norbert Leo Butz**
Eileen  **Amy Ryan**
Amy  **Jessica Hecht**
and Frank Wood (Howard); Henry Miller (Will); Ella Miller (Rachel); Cameron "C.J." Adams (Elliott Burns); Jessica Lussier (Jessica Burns); Seth D'Antuono (Gus); Margot Janson (Olivia); Willa Cuthrell-Tuttleman (Bella); Emily Blunt (Dr. Ruthie Draper); Felipe Dieppa (Marty Barasco); Matthew Morrison (Policeman); Bernie McInerney (James Lamson); Amy Landecker (Cindy Lamson); Steve Mellor (Bookstore Clerk); Shana Carr (Suzanne Burns); Nicole Morin (Jane, Age 13); Charlotte Davies (Cara, Age 11); Zoe Paulkis (Lilly, Age 4); Lucas Hedges (Dance Partner); Sondre Lerche (Himself); Kato Ådland, Ole Ludvig Krüger, Morten Skage (Wedding Band); Marci Occhino (Wedding Singer)

John Mahoney, Dianne Wiest

Widowed Dan Burns finds himself in an awkward position when he unknowingly falls in love with a woman who turns out to be his brother's new girlfriend.

Steve Carell, Alison Pill

# AMERICAN GANGSTER

Common, Chiwetel Ejiofor

Denzel Washington, Ruby Dee

(UNIVERSAL) Producers, Brian Grazer, Ridley Scott; Executive Producers, Nicholas Pileggi, Steven Zaillian, Branko Lustig, Jim Whitaker, Michael Costigan; Director, Ridley Scott; Screenplay, Steven Zaillian, based on the article "The Return of Superfly" by Marc Jacobson; Photography, Harris Savides; Designer, Arthur Max; Costumes, Janty Yates; Music, Marc Streitenfeld; Editor, Pietro Scalia; Co-Producer, Jonathan Filley; Casting, Avy Kaufman; an Imagine Entertainment presentation in association with Relativity Media, a Brian Grazer production, in association with Scott Free productions; Dolby; Technicolor; Rated R; 157 minutes; Release date: November 2, 2007.

Russell Crowe © UNIVERSAL STUDIOS

## Cast

Frank Lucas  **Denzel Washington**
Det. Richie Roberts  **Russell Crowe**
Huey Lucas  **Chiwetel Ejiofor**
Det. Trupo  **Josh Brolin**
Eva  **Lymari Nadal**
Det. Lou Toback  **Ted Levine**
Nate  **Roger Guenveur Smith**
Det. Freddie Spearman  **John Hawkes**
Moses Jones  **RZA**
Alfonse Abruzzo  **Yul Vazquez**
Jimmy Zee  **Malcolm Goodwin**
Mama Lucas  **Ruby Dee**
Doc  **Ruben Santiago-Hudson**
Laurie Roberts  **Carla Gugino**
Michael Roberts  **Skyler Fortgang**
Javier J. Rivera  **John Ortiz**
Nicky Barnes  **Cuba Gooding, Jr.**
Dominic Cattano  **Armand Assante**
Mrs. Cattano  **Kathleen Garrett**
Charlie Williams  **Joe Morton**
and Richie Coster (Joey Sadano); Bari K. Willerford (Joe Louis); Idris Elba (Tango); Common (Turner Lucas); Warner Miller (Melvin Lucas); Albert Jones (Terrence Lucas); J. Kyle Manzay (Dexter Lucas); Tip Harris (Stevie Lucas); Melissia Hill (Redtop); Quisha Saunders (Darlynn); Kevin Corrigan (Campizi); Robert Funaro (McCann); Jon Polito (Rossi); Tom O'Rourke (Banker); Robert C. Kirk (Police Captain); Tom Stearns (Two-Star General); KaDee Strickland (Richie's Attorney); Jon DeVries (Judge James Racine); Jim R. Coleman (Bailiff); Lee Shepard (Laurie's Attorney); Gavin Grazer (Mike Sobota); Linda Powell (Social Worker); Roxanne Amandez (Paramedic); Norman Reedus (Detective in Morgue); Pierra Francesca (Stewardess); Eddie Rouse (Detective at Party); Mary Ann Urbano (Real Estate Broker); Cedric Sanders, Jason Veasey (Servicemen in Café); Roosevelt Davis (Army Captain); Roger Bart (U.S. Attorney); Eric Silver (White Kid); Mitchell Green (Tango's Bodyguard); Saycon Sengbloh (Tango's Woman); Conor Romero, Daniel Hilt, Daniel Farcher (Tough Teenagers); David Spearman, Maurice Ballard (Civilian Cleaning Staff); Paul Doherty (TV Newscaster

Russell Crowe, Denzel Washington

William Tate (Baptist Minister); George Lee Miles (Frank's Lawyer); Jason Furlani (Bailiff); Chris McKinney (Reporter on TV); Ric Young (Chinese General); David Wayne Britton (Army Colonel); Tommy Guiffre (Medical Examiner); Laurence Lowry (Paramedic); Dan Moran (Army Captain); Marjorie Johnson (Charlene); Larry Mitchell (FBI Agent); Chuck Cooper (Private Doctor); Kevin Geer (Law School Professor); Chance Kelly (MP); Hamilton Clancy (Seller); Sam Freed, Ron Piretti (Judges); Joey Klein (Chemist); Scott Dillin (4th Amigo); Anthony Hamilton (Funk Band Singer); Sarah Hudnut (Assistant Prosecutor); Jeff Greene (Metal Door Worker); Tyson Hall, Kirt Harding, Bryant Pearson (Drug Dealers); Alfredo Luis Santos (Mechanic); William Hudson, Christopher A. Sawyer (Dealers); Dylan Gallagher (Casket Loader); Jehan-Pierre Vassau, Dawn A. Douglas (Narc Officers); Robbie Neigeborn (Cop in Narc Headquarters); Clinton Lowe (Man Arrested in Elevator); Wilhelm Lewis (Head Wedding Photographer); James Hunter, Neville White (Deacons); Lonnie Gaetano (Prison Guard); Jeff Mantel (Officer Walsh); Serena Joan Springle (The Proctor); Nino Del Buono (Announcer); Arthur M. Mercante (Referee); Panama Redd (Policeman); Robert Wiggins (Piano Player); Fab 5 Freddy (Smalls Patron); Jonah Denizard (Store Manager); Steve McAuliff (Mounted Policeman); Clarence Williams III (Bumpy Johnson)

Denzel Washington, Lymari Nadal

The true story of how Jersey cop Richie Roberts set out to bring down powerful Harlem drug lord Frank Lucas.

This film received Oscar nominations for Supporting Actress (Ruby Dee) and Art Direction.

Denzel Washington, Russell Crowe

# BEE MOVIE

Barry B. Benson, Ken

Barry B. Benson, Lou Lo Duca

(DREAMWORKS/PARAMOUNT) Producers, Jerry Seinfeld, Christina Steinberg; Co-Producer, Mark Swift; Directors, Simon J. Smith, Steve Hickner; Screenplay, Jerry Seinfeld, Spike Feresten, Barry Marder, Andy Robin; Additional Screenplay Material, Chuck Martin, Tom Papa; Editor, Nick Fletcher; Music, Rupert Gregson-Williams; Executive Music Producer, Hans Zimmer; Designer, Alex McDowell; Art Director/Character Designer, Christophe Lautrette; Visual Effects Supervisor, Doug Cooper; Head of Story, David Pimentel; Head of Character Animation, Fabio Lignini; Head of Layout, Nol L. Meyer; Associate Producer, Cameron Stevning; Casting, Leslee Feldman; a DreamWorks Animation presentation in association with Columbus 81 Prods.; Dolby; Technicolor; Rated PG; 90 minutes; Release date: November 2, 2007.

## Cast

Barry B. Benson  **Jerry Seinfeld**
Vanessa Bloome  **Renée Zellweger**
Adam Flayman  **Matthew Broderick**
Layton T. Montgomery  **John Goodman**
Ken  **Patrick Warburton**
Mooseblood  **Chris Rock**
Janet Benson  **Kathy Bates**
Martin Benson  **Barry Levinson**
Bee Larry King  **Larry King**
Themselves  **Ray Liotta, Sting**
Judge Bumbleton  **Oprah Winfrey**
Buzzwell  **Larry Miller**
Trudy  **Megan Mullally**
Lou Lo Duca  **Rip Torn**
Bud Ditchwater  **Michael Richards**
Jackson  **Mario Joyner**
Title Narrator/Graduation Announcer  **Jim Cummings**
Splitz/Klauss Vanderhayden  **Tom Papa**
Jock #2  **Andy Robin**
Hector  **David Pimentel**
Andy  **Chuck Martin**
Freddy  **Conrad Vernon**
Buzz/Bob Bumble/Pilot  **David Herman**
Press Person #1  **Carol Leifer**
Uncle Carl  **Jeff Altman**
and Brian Hopkins (Sandy Shrimpkin/TSA Agent); Tress MacNeille (Jeanette Chung/Mother/Cow); Nathan D. Morrissey (Boy Crying/Timmy); Olivia Mattingly (Little Girl); Simon J. Smith (Truck Driver/Chet); Geoff Witcher (Press Person #2/Jock #1); John Di Maggio (Janitor/Bailiff); Barry Marder (Waterbug); Sean Bishop (Ladybug)

Barry B. Benson, Mooseblood © DREAMWORKS

Tired of his routine life inside the hive, ambitious bee Barry B. Benson ventures into the outside world, confronting the human race for the first time.

Adam Flayman, Martin Benson, Janet Benson

Layton T. Montgomery

Ken, Barry B. Benson, Vanessa Bloome

Vanessa Bloome, Barry B. Benson

# MARTIAN CHILD

Bobby Coleman, John Cusack

(NEW LINE CINEMA) Producers, David Kirschner, Corey Sienega, Ed Elbert; Executive Producers, Toby Emmerich, Mark Kaufman, Matt Moore, Mike Drake, David Gerrold; Co-Producers, Seth E. Bass, Jonathan Tolins; Director, Menno Meyjes; Screenplay, Seth E. Bass, Jonathan Tolins, based on the novella *The Martian Child* by David Gerrold; Photography, Robert Yeoman; Designer, Hugo Luczyc-Wyhowski; Costumes, Michael Dennison; Editor, Bruce Green; Music, Aaron Zigman; Associate Producer, Luke Ryan; Casting, Mary Gail Artz; a David Kirschner/Corey Sienega/Ed Elbert production; Dolby; Widescreen; Deluxe Color; Rated PG; 106 minutes; Release date: November 2, 2007.

## Cast

David **John Cusack**
Harlee **Amanda Peet**
Sophie **Sophie Okonedo**
Jeff **Oliver Platt**
Dennis **Bobby Coleman**
Liz **Joan Cusack**
Mimi **Anjelica Huston**
Lefkowitz **Richard Schiff**
and Somewhere (Folmar); Bud (Esther); Taya Calicetto (Andy); David Kaye (Nicholas); Braxton Bonneville (Jonas); Samuel Charles Zak Ludwig (Young David); Samuel Patrick Chu, Ryan Morrissette (Boys at Group Home); Nimet Kanji (Housekeeper); Howard Hesseman (Dr. Berg); Carmen Moore (Miss Margie); Beverley Breuer (Mrs. Tompkins); Jonathan Holmes (Dracoban Director); Andrew McIlroy (Earl of Dracoban); Kimani Ray Smith (Draconian Warrior); Peter Bryant (Policeman at School); David Lewis (Leonard); Edmond Kato Wong (Linus); Joanna Reid (Cashier); Simon Hayama (Baseball Fan); Lauro Chartrand (Tough Cop); Alberto Ghisi (Tough Boy at School); Hrothgar Mathews (Committee Member); Robert Clarke (Observatory Director); Daniel Pepper (Cop, David's House); Angela Besharah (Mary in Photos); Suzy Joachim (Lisa, Jeff's Date at BBQ)

A sci-fi writer adopts a troubled orphan boy who believes he is from another planet.

John Cusack, Anjelica Huston

Bobby Coleman, John Cusack

John Cusack, Sophie Okonedo © NEW LINE CINEMA

# LIONS FOR LAMBS

Andrew Garfield, John Brently Reynolds

Michael Peña, Derek Luke

(MGM) Producers, Robert Redford, Matthew Michael Carnahan, Andrew Hauptman, Tracy Falco; Executive Producer, Daniel Lupi; Director, Robert Redford; Screenplay, Matthew Michael Carnahan; Photography, Philippe Rousselot; Designer, Jan Roelfs; Costumes, Mary Zophres; Editor, Joe Hutshing; Music, Mark Isham; Visual Effects Supervisor, Joseph Grossberg; Associate Producer, William Holderman; Casting, Avy Kaufman; a United Artists presentation of a Wildwood Enterprises, Brat Na Pont Prods., Andell Entertainment production; Dolby; Panavision; Deluxe color; Rated R; 92 minutes; Release date: November 9, 2007.

Meryl Streep, Tom Cruise

## Cast

Professor Stephen Malley **Robert Redford**
Janine Roth **Meryl Streep**
Senator Jasper Irving **Tom Cruise**
Ernest Rodriguez **Michael Peña**
Todd Hayes **Andrew Garfield**
Lt. Col. Falco **Peter Berg**
Howard, ANX Editor **Kevin Dunn**
Lt. Arian Finch **Derek Luke**
and Christopher Carley (Sniper); John Brently Reynolds (Skinny); Paula Rhodes (Summer Hernandez Kowalski, ANX News Reporter); Muna Otaru (Nervous Student); Clay Wilcox (Crew Chief); Sarayu Rao (Senator Irving's Receptionist); Amanda Loncar (Young Assistant); Rick Burns (Senate Employee); Kevin Collins (Ranger); Candace Moon (Fate); Chris Hoffman (Bully Dog); George Back, Kristy Wu, Bo Brown, Josh Zuckerman, Samantha Carro, Christopher Jordan, Angela Stefanelli (Students); Larry Bates, Christopher May, David Pease, Heidi Janson (Soldiers); Louise Linton (Skin Care Consultant); Jennifer Sommerfield, Wynonna Smith (Talk Show Hosts); Babar Peerzada (Afghan Fighter); Wade Harlan, Paul Adams (Helicopter Pilots)

A college professor who saw two of his students enlist to fight in Iraq hopes to convince a current student to take a vested interest in the country's political situation, while Senator Jasper Irving tries to impress upon liberal journalist Janine Roth why the U.S. is fighting overseas.

Robert Redford © METRO-GOLDWYN-MAYER/UA

# FRED CLAUS

(WARNER BROS.) Producers, Joel Silver, David Dobkin, Jessie Nelson; Executive Producer, Paul Hitchcock; Co-Producer, Vince Vaughn; Director, David Dobkin; Screenplay, Dan Fogelman; Story, Jessie Nelson, Dan Fogelman; Photography, Remi Adefarasin; Designer, Allan Cameron; Costumes, Anna Sheppard; Editor, Mark Livolsi; Music, Christophe Beck; Visual Effects Supervisor, Alex Bicknell; Special Effects Supervisor, Neil Corbould; Casting, Lisa Beach, Sarah Katzman; a Silver Pictures production in association with David Dobkin Pictures and Jessie Nelson Prods.; Dolby; Technicolor; Rated PG; 115 minutes; Release date: November 9, 2007.

Paul Giamatti, Vince Vaughn

### Cast

Fred Claus **Vince Vaughn**
Nick (Santa) Claus **Paul Giamatti**
Willie **John Michael Higgins**
Annette Claus **Miranda Richardson**
Wanda **Rachel Weisz**
Mother Claus **Kathy Bates**
Papa Claus **Trevor Peacock**
DJ Donnie **Chris "Ludacris" Bridges**
Charlene **Elizabeth Banks**
Bob Elf **Jeremy Swift**
Linda Elf **Elizabeth Berrington**
Clyde Northcut **Kevin Spacey**
Leon **Rio Hackford**
Samuel "Slam" Gibbons **Bobb'e J. Thompson**
Dr. Goldfarb **Allan Corduner**
Fireman **Christian Hansen**
Young Fred, 6 Yrs. Old **Jordon Hull**
Young Fred, 12 Yrs. Old **Liam James**
Young Nick, 6 Yrs. Old **Theo Stevenson**
and Allison Sparrow (Girl with Plasma TV); Fred Zimmerman (Caroler); Danny McCarthy, Keith Kupferer (Salvation Army Santas); Craig J. Harris (Jermaine Santa); Peter McCabe (Scary Thug); Jonathan Cullen (Guard); Wesley Chu (Bonsai Chef); Claudia Michelle Wallace, Guy Massey (Child Services Agents); Gabriel Pimentel (Head Secret Service Elf); Hassan Chikhaoui, Vitalie Barbara (Secret Service Elves); Morgan Monjauze (Molly Gordon); Caden Niewolnu (Timmy Jackson); Angela Curran (Old Woman Elf); Celia Henebury (Girl Elf); Justin McEwen, Dylan Minnette (Orphanage Kids); Anne White (Midwife); Patrick Zielinski (Cab Driver); William Dick (Group Leader); Frank Stallone, Roger Clinton, Stephen Baldwin (Themselves); Jean-Yves Thual (Mission Control Elf); Burn Gorman, Orlando Seale, Charlie Condou (Elves); Melody Hollis (Timmy Jackson's Sister); Mike Bacarella (Wanda's Neighbor); Bert Matias (Eskimo); Rusty Goffe (Elf/Frosty Bar Man); Peter Bonner (Bonner Elf); Tyler Fagan (Child); Peter McCabe (Scary Thug).

Rachel Weisz, Vince Vaughn

Making an unsavory living in the real world, Santa Claus's younger brother Fred is invited to join his sibling working at the North Pole, where Fred's resentment of Santa's high profile image causes tension.

Vince Vaughn, John Michael Higgins © WARNER BROS.

# MARGOT AT THE WEDDING

(PARAMOUNT VANTAGE) Producer, Scott Rudin; Co-Producer, M. Blair Breard; Director/Screenplay, Noah Baumbach; Photography, Harris Savides; Designer, Anne Ross; Costumes, Ann Roth; Editor, Carol Littleton; Casting, Douglas Aibel; a Scott Rudin production; Dolby; Deluxe color; Rated R; 91 minutes; Release date: November 16, 2007.

## Cast

Margot **Nicole Kidman**
Pauline **Jennifer Jason Leigh**
Malcolm **Jack Black**
Jim **John Turturro**
Dick Koosman **Ciarán Hinds**
Claude **Zane Pais**
Ingrid **Flora Cross**
Maisy Koosman **Halley Feiffer**
Toby **Seth Barrish**
Alan **Matthew Arkin**
Mr. Vogler **Michael Cullen**
Mrs. Vogler **Enid Graham**
Vogler Daughter **Sophie Nyweide**
Vogler Son **Justin Roth**
and Susan Blackwell (Woman on Train); Jonathan Schwartz (Malcolm's Friend); Lisa Emery (Woman with Dog); Michael Medeiros (Karaoke Singer); Ashlie Atkinson (Becky)

Self-absorbed writer Margot agrees to attend the wedding of her sister Pauline to struggling artist Malcolm, all the while making clear her disapproval of the match.

Jennifer Jason Leigh, Jack Black © PARAMOUNT VANTAGE

Nicole Kidman

Nicole Kidman, Zane Pais

Ciarán Hinds, Nicole Kidman

# BEOWULF

(PARAMOUNT) Producers, Steve Starkey, Robert Zemeckis, Jack Rapke; Executive Producers, Martin Shafer, Roger Avary, Neil Gaiman; Co-Producer, Steven Boyd; Director, Robert Zemeckis; Screenplay, Neil Gaiman, Roger Avary; Based on the epic poem; Photography, Robert Presley; Designer, Doug Chiang; Costumes, Gabriella Pescucci; Editor, Jeremiah O'Driscoll; Music, Alan Silvestri; Original Songs, Glen Ballard, Alan Silvestri; Senior Visual Effects Supervisor, Jerome Chen; Executive Visual Effects Producer, Debbie Denise; Senior Visual Effects Producer, Chris Juen; Digital Effects Supervisor, Sean Phillips; Digital Producer, Skye Lyons; Animation Supervisor, Kenn McDonald; Animation and Imagery, Sony Pictures Imageworks; Stunts, Garrett Warren; Casting, Ronna Kress, Nina Gold; a Paramount presentation, in association with Shangri-La Entertainment, of an ImageMovers production; Dolby; Deluxe color; Digital 3-D; Imax 3-D; Rated PG-13; 114 minutes; Release date: November 16, 2007.

## Cast

Beowulf/Golden Man/Dragon  **Ray Winstone**
King Hrothgar  **Anthony Hopkins**
Unferth  **John Malkovich**
Wealthow  **Robin Wright-Penn**
Wiglaf  **Brendan Gleeson**
Grendel  **Crispin Glover**
Ursula  **Alison Lohman**
Grendel's Mother  **Angelina Jolie**
Estrith  **Charlotte Salt**
Wulfgar  **Sebastian Roche**
Olaf  **Chris Coppola**
Gitte  **Sonje Fortag**
Hild  **Sharisse Baker-Bernard**
Cille  **Julene Renee**
Garmund  **Greg Ellis**
Eofor  **Rik Young**
Yrsa  **Leslie Zemeckis**
Aesher  **Woody Schultz**
Hondshew  **Costas Mandylor**
Cain  **Dominic Keating**
Young Cain  **Tyler Steelman**
Musicians  **Paul Baker, John Bilezicjian, Rod D. Harbour, Brice Martin**
Drunken Tane  **Nick Jameson**
Scylding's Watch  **Shay Duffin**
Aethelbeorg  **Jacquie Barnbrook**
Frisian Leader  **Fredrik Hiller**
Beowulf's Scop  **Daniel McGrew**
Beowulf's Jester  **Alan J. Silva**

When the court of King Hrothgar is attacked by the hideous beast Grendel, warrior Beowulf arrives to fight the monster and its equally dangerous mother.

Grendel

Beowulf, Hrothgar

Beowulf, Dragon © PARAMOUNT PICTURES

# MR. MAGORIUM'S WONDER EMPORIUM

(20TH CENTURY FOX) Producers, Richard N. Gladstein, James Garavente; Executive Producers, Joe Drake, Nathan Kahane; Co-Producer, Barbara A. Hall; Director/Screenplay, Zach Helm; Photography, Roman Osin; Editors, Sabrina Plisco, Steven Weisberg; Music, Alexandre Desplat, Aaron Zigman; Designer, Therese DePrez; Costumes, Christopher Hargadon; Visual Effects Supervisor, Raymond Gieringer; Senior Visual Effects Producer, Camille Cellucci; Associate Producer, Jim Miller; Casting, Robin D. Cook, Amanda Mackey Johnson, Cathy Sandrich; a Walden Media and Mandate Pictures presentation of a FilmColony production in association with Gang of Two; Dolby; Panavision; DeLuxe color; Rated G; 94 minutes; Release date: November 16, 2007.

Zach Mills © 20TH CENTURY FOX

## Cast

Mr. Edward Magorium, Avid Shoe-Wearer  **Dustin Hoffman**
Molly Mahoney, the Composer  **Natalie Portman**
Henry Weston, the Mutant  **Jason Bateman**
Eric Applebaum, the Hat Collector  **Zach Mills**
Bellini, the Bookbuilder  **Ted Ludzik**
Jessica, Who Got a Cowboy Hat  **Madalena Brancatella**
Brenda, Who Wants a Mobile  **Paula Boudreau**
Dave Wolf, Who's an Engineer  **Mike Realba**
Kermit the Frog  **Steve Whitmire**
Andy, the Boy Who Likes to Color  **Liam Powley-Webster**
Lora, Who Wants a Fire Engine  **Marcia Bennett**
Jordan, Who Said Hi  **Oliver Madua**
Cassie, the Girl Chased by a Goose  **Samantha Harvey**
Derek, Who Opened the Door  **Jesse Bostick**
Jason, Who's a Little Too Curious  **Isaac Durnford**
Jimmy, Who Captures the Ball  **Daniel J. Gordon**
Ellie Applebaum, the Mom  **Rebecca Northan**
Ari, Who Wants a Book  **Dash Grundy**
Mark, Who Fingerpaints  **Dylan Authors**
Brett, the Yo-Yo Guy  **Aidan Koper**
Angie, Who Was Nearly Hit by a Blimp  **Lin Lin Feng**
Larry, Who Held on for Dear Life  **He Wen**
David, Who Also Held on for Dear Life  **Gan Zhen**
Gia, with a Squid on Her Head  **Quancetia Hamilton**
Eddie, the Dentist  **Matt Baram**
Dr. Dunn, Who Gives People Sedatives  **Jonathan Potts**
Wyatt, Who Sells Hot Dogs  **Matthew Peart**
Tim, the Hot Dog Manager  **David Rendall**
Mrs. Goodman, Who Wants the Store  **Kiele Sanchez**
Tom, the Realtor  **David Collins**
Jack, Who Thinks It's Magic  **Michael Costa-Parke**
Milo, Who's Not Bad  **Milo Gladstein**

Natalie Portman, Jason Bateman

Dustin Hoffman, Natalie Portman

Mr. Magorium, the 243-year-old owner of a magical toy shop, hopes to leave the establishment to his manager and protégé, Molly.

# LOVE IN THE TIME OF CHOLERA

Javier Bardem

(NEW LINE CINEMA) Producer, Scott Steindorff; Executive Producers, Michael Nozik, Dylan Russell, Scott Lastaiti, Danny Greenspun, Robin Greenspun, Andrew Molasky, Chris Law, Michael Roban, Rubria Negrao; Co-Producer, Brantley Dunaway; Director, Mike Newell; Screenplay, Ronald Harwood, based on the novel *El amor en los tiempos del colera* by Gabriel Garcia Marquez; Photography, Affonso Beato; Editor, Mick Audsley; Music, Antonio Pinto; Designer, Wolf Kroeger; Costumes, Marit Allen; Makeup, John E. Jackson; Casting, Susie Figgis; a Stone Village Pictures production, in association with Grosvenor Park Media; Dolby; DeLuxe color; Rated R; 138 minutes; Release date: November 16, 2007.

Unax Ugalde, John Leguizamo © NEW LINE CINEMA

## Cast

Florentino Ariza **Javier Bardem**
Fermina Daza Urbino **Giovanna Mezzogiorno**
Dr. Juvenal Urbino **Benjamin Bratt**
Hildebranda **Catalina Sandino Moreno**
Don Leo **Hector Elizondo**
Lotario Thugut **Liev Schreiber**
Olimpia Zuleta **Ana Claudia Talancón**
Tránsito Ariza **Fernanda Montenegro**
Florentino Ariza (Teen) **Unax Ugalde**
Lorenzo Daza **John Leguizamo**
Digna Pardo **Gina Bernard Forbes**
America Vicuña **Marcela Mar**
Marco Auerilo, 40s **Juan Ángel**
Aurelio's Wife **Liliana Alvarez Gonzalez**
and Catalina Botero (Ofelia Urbino, 40s); Miguel Angel Pazos Galindo (Ofelia's Husband); Maria Cecilia Herrera (Urbino's Sweet Wife); Luis Fernando Hoyos (Urbino Urbino); Carlos Duplat, Francisco Raul Linero (Mourners); Julieth Paola Hoyos Zuñiga (Barefoot Maid); Alicia Borrachero (Escolástica); Gerardo Norberto Arango Echeverri (Priest); Dora Cadavid (Mother Superior); María Eugenia Arboleda (Gala Placidia); Marta Helena Sawades Rodriguez, Lisseth Janeth Figueroa Manzur, Denis Mercado Moreno (Lotario Whores); Beatriz Colombia Ospino (Aging Whore); Jhon Alexander Toro (Ricardo Lighthouse); Julián Díaz (Sweet Seller); Jose Luis Garcia Campos (Porter); Manuel Sarmiento (Belgian Photographer); Rodolfo Enrique Mercado Parra (Benny Centeno); Fernando Cajales (Don Leo's Clerk); Andres Casas (Cholera Boat Man); Rúbria Negrão (Rosalba); Antonio Jose De Lavalle Ospino (Child, 7 Years Old); Oscar Ezequiel Padilla Garcia (Panic Child); Ivan Diaz Pombo (The Sailor); Noëlle Schonwald, Paola Turbay (Attractive Women); Angie Cepeda (Widow Nazaret); Maria Alejandra Fuentes Atencia (Trolley Skinny Girl); Eliris Sierra Gomez (Thin Black Woman); Luis Fernando Gil Caldera (Paper Seller); Andrés Castañedo (Handsome Youth); Nicolas Bolaño Villamil (Baptism Priest); Samuel Aguilar (Marco Aurelio, Newborn); Maria Teresa Mateos Romero (Young Girl); Alejandra Borrero (Doña Blanca); Patricia Castañedo, Laura Garcia Marulanda, Rita Bendek, Rosario Jaramillo (Grand Ladies); Maria Carolina Cuervo (Grand Lady Daughter); Laura Harring (Sara Noriega); Alfonso Wong Mah (Wing Wu Peng); Margálida Castro Rueda (Governess); Ena Ortega de Insignares (Woman with Transito); Marina Chirolla (Old Nurse); Miguel Canal (Boy with Cage); Horacio Tavera (Diego); Salvatore Basile (City Mayor); Adriana Cantor (Andrea Varón); Indhira Serrano (Dr. Barbara Lynch); Nohemi Millan, Isaac Jos Ricardo Aldana (La Boheme Singers); Luis Alberto Moreno Ruiz (Hudson's Driver); Juan Antonio Restom Bitar (Florentino's Clerk); Andrés Parra (Captain Samaritano)

After being rejected by Fermia Daza, Florentino Ariza spends a lifetime of self-imposed loneliness, hoping for the day that she will respond to his unwavering devotion.

# REDACTED

Rob Devaney, Kel O'Neill, Mike Figueroa, Izzy Diaz

Rob Devaney, Yanal Kassay

(MAGNOLIA) Producers, Jennifer Weiss, Simone Urdl, Jason Kliot, Joana Vicente; Executive Producers, Todd Wagner, Mark Cuban; Director/Screenplay, Brian De Palma; Photography, Jonathon Cliff; Editor, Bill Pankow; Designer, Phillip Barker; Costumes, Jamla Aladdin; Special Effects, David Harris; Special Makeup Effects, Adrien Morotan; an HDNet Films presentation of a The Film Farm production; American-Canadian; Dolby; Color; HD; Rated R; 91 minutes; Release date: November 16, 2007.

Patrick Carroll

## Cast

Reno Flake  **Patrick Carroll**
Lawyer McCoy  **Rob Devaney**
Angel Salazar  **Izzy Diaz**
Sgt. Jim Vazques  **Mike Figueroa**
Master Sgt. Sweet  **Ty Jones**
B.B. Rush  **Daniel Stewart Sherman**
Farah  **Zahra Zubaidi**
Arab News Reporter  **Sahar Alloul**
Battalion Commander  **Eric "Happy" Anderson**
Farah's Mother  **Karima Attayeh**
Hadi  **Qazi Freihat**
Embedded Journalist  **Shatha Haddad**
English Newscaster  **Paul Hijazin**
Farah's Father  **Suhail Abdel Hussein**
and Hiyam Abdel Karim (Pregnant Woman); Ohad Knoller (Army Psychiatrist); Shukraya Maran (Young Screaming Woman); Sabrine Munther (Farah's Little Sister); Paul O'Brien (Barton's Father); Adel Odai (Interpreter); Hameed Sahi (Farah's Grandfather); Abigail Savage (Tattooed Kid); Issam Shamary (Pregnant Woman's Brother); Julie Thiery ("Barrage" Narrator); Helen Zamel (Date Girl); Mazen Zoubi (Company Commander); Andrew Cullen, Francois Caillaud, Lara Atalla (Buddies); Dhiaa Kahlil, Yanal Kassay (Soldiers); Nick Seeley (Criminal Investigation Agent #1); Kel O'Neill (Private Gabe Blix)

"Fictional documentary" in which a U.S. soldier in Iraq records the accidental killing of some innocent citizens at an American checkpoint.

Ty Jones © MAGNOLIA PICTURES

# THE MIST

(MGM/WEINSTEIN CO.) Producers, Frank Darabont, Liz Glotzer; Executive Producers, Bob Weinstein, Harvey Weinstein, Richard Saperstein; Co-Producers, Randi Richmond, Anna Garduno, Denise Huth; Director/Screenplay, Frank Darabont, based on the novella by Stephen King; Photography, Rohn Schmidt; Designer, Gregory Melton; Costumes, Giovanna Ottobre-Melton; Editor, Hunter M. Via; Music, Mark Isham; Visual Effects Supervisor, Everett Burrell; Visual Effects, Cafe FX; Special Effects Coordinator, Darrell Pritchett; Creature Effects Makeup, Gregory Nicotero, Howard Berger; Stunts, Steven Ritzi; Casting, Deborah Aquila, Mary Tricia Wood, Jennifer Smith; a Dimension Films presentation of a Darkwoods production; Dolby; Technicolor; Rated R; 127 minutes; Release date: November 21, 2007.

Thomas Jane, Nathan Gamble © METRO-GOLDWYN-MAYER/WEINSTEIN CO.

## Cast

| | |
|---|---|
| David Drayton | **Thomas Jane** |
| Mrs. Carmody | **Marcia Gay Harden** |
| Amanda Dumfries | **Laurie Holden** |
| Brent Norton | **Andre Braugher** |
| Ollie Weeks | **Toby Jones** |
| Jim Grondin | **William Sadler** |
| Dan Miller | **Jeffrey DeMunn** |
| Irene Reppler | **Frances Sternhagen** |
| Sally | **Alexa Davalos** |
| Billy Drayton | **Nathan Gamble** |
| Norm | **Chris Owen** |
| Wayne Jessup | **Sam Witwer** |
| Bud Brown | **Robert C. Treveiler** |
| Myron | **David Jensen** |
| Joe Eagleton | **Jackson Hurst** |
| Tom Smalley | **Greg Brazzel** |
| Donaldson | **Walter Fauntleroy** |
| Man with El Camino | **Sonny Franks** |
| Silas | **Mathew Greer** |

and Louis Herthum (Colonel); Kelly Collins Lintz (Steff Drayton); Susan Watkins (Hattie); Brandon O'Dell (Bobby Eagleton); Juan Pareja (Morales); Ron Clinton Smith (Mr. Mackey); Andy Stahl (Mike Hatlen); Buck Taylor (Ambrose Cornell); Jay Amor, Kevin Beard (Shoppers); Dodie L. Brown (Screaming Woman); Taylor E. Brown (Screaming Child); Derek Cox-Berg, Brian Hunt, Cherami Leigh (Teenagers); Kip Cummings, John F. Daniel, Pamela Houghton (Carmody Followers); Ted Ferguson (Norton Group Member); Travis Fontenot (Hazmat Worker); Amin Joseph (MP); Walt Hollis (Bio Hazard Engineer); Mike Martindale (Sentry); Melissa McBride (Young Mother); Eric Kelly McFarland, Chuck Vail (Military Soldiers); Ritchie Montgomery (Paisley Hat Man); Michaela Morgan (Little Girl); Ginnie Randall, Tiffany Morgan (Women); Steven E. Williams (Mash Group Member); Brian Libby (Biker); Kim Wall (Terrified Woman); Julio Cesar Cedillo (Father); Ron Clinton Smith (Mr. Mackey)

Jeffrey DeMunn, Laurie Holden, Frances Sternhagen, Thomas Jane, Nathan Gamble

A group of townspeople find themselves trapped within a grocery store when a mysterious fog, filled with killer mutants, engulfs the surrounding area.

Thomas Jane, William Sadler, Marcia Gay Harden

# AUGUST RUSH

(WARNER BROS.) Producer, Richard Barton Lewis; Executive Producers, Robert Greenhut, Ralph Kamp, Louise Goodsill, Miky Lee, Lionel Wigram, Richard Burton Lewis; Director, Kirsten Sheridan; Screenplay, Nick Castle, James V. Hart, from a story by Paul Castro, Nick Castle; Photography, John Mathieson; Designer, Michael Shaw; Costumes, Frank L. Fleming; Editor, William Steinkamp; Music, Mark Mancina, Hans Zimmer; Music Supervisors, Anastasia Brown, Julia Michels, Jeffrey Pollack; Song: "Raise it Up" by Jamal Joseph, Charles Mack, Tevin Thomas/performed by Impact; Associate Producer, Gabrielle Jerou; Casting, Melissa Chusid, Amanda Mackey Johnson, Cathy Sandrich; a Southpaw Entertainment production, in association with CJ Entertainment presented with Odyssey Entertainment; Dolby; Super 35 Widescreen; Color; Rated PG; 113 minutes; Release date: November 21, 2007.

Jonathan Rhys Meyers, Freddie Highmore

## Cast

Evan Taylor (August Rush) **Freddie Highmore**
Lyla Novacek **Keri Russell**
Louis Connelly **Jonathan Rhys Meyers**
Richard Jeffries **Terrence Howard**
Maxwell "Wizard" Wallace **Robin Williams**
Thomas Novacek **William Sadler**
The Dean **Marian Seldes**
Arthur **Leon Thomas III**
Reverend James **Mykelti Williamson**
Nick **Aaron Staton**
Marshall **Alex O'Loughlin**
Hope **Jamia Simone Nash**
Professor **Ronald Guttman**
Lizzy **Bonnie McKee**
Mannix **Michael Drayer**
Steve **Jamie O'Keefe**
Jennifer **Becki Newton**
Peter **Tyler McGuckin**
Megan **Megan Gallagher**
Backbeat **Anais Martinez**
Roller Bull **Bilal Bishop**
Feedback **Michael R. Hammonds II**
Joey **Timothy T. Mitchum**
and Henry Caplan (Bill); John Knox (Club Manager); Amy V. Dewhurst (Receptionist); Victor Verhaeghe (Cop); Darrie Lawrence (Old Neighbor); Sean Haberle (Frank); Jamal Joseph (Driver); Robert Aberdeen (Record Executive); Georgia Creighton (Apartment Owner); Joshua Jaymz Doss (Orphanage Kid); Craig Johnson (Orphanage Boy); Dominic Colon (Policeman); Zach Page (Child Guitar Player)

Terrence Howard, Keri Russell

A boy with extraordinary musical gifts hopes to track down his parents, a pair of musicians who separated after conceiving him and are not even aware of his existence.

This film received an Oscar nomination for Original Song ("Raise it Up").

Freddie Highmore © WARNER BROS.

# I'M NOT THERE

Cate Blanchett

(WEINSTEIN CO.) Producers, James D. Stern, John Sloss, John Goldwyn, Christian Vachon; Executive Producers, Hengameh Panahi, Philip Elway, Andrea Grosch, Douglas E. Hansen, Wendy Japhet, Steven Soderbergh, Amy J. Kaufman, John Wells; Co-Producer, Charles Pugliese; Director, Todd Haynes; Screenplay, Todd Haynes, Oren Moverman; Story, Todd Haynes, inspired by the music and many lives of Bob Dylan; Photography, Edward Lachman; Editor, Jay Rabinowitz; Music Supervisors, Randall Poster, Jim Dunbar; Designer, Judy Becker; Costumes, Jon Dunn; Special Effects Supervisor, Louis Craig; Visual Effects Supervisor, Louis Morin; Casting, Laura Rosenthal; an Endgame Entertainment, Killer Films, John Wells and John Goldwyn (U.S.) production, a VIP Medienfonds 4 (Germany) production, in association with Rising Star, in association with Grey Water Park Prods.; American-German; Dolby; Super 35 Widescreen; Color/Black and white; Rated R; 135 minutes; Release date: November 21, 2007.

Christian Bale

Marcus Carl Franklin © WEINSTEIN CO.

## Cast

Jack Rollins/Pastor John  **Christian Bale**
Jude Quinn  **Cate Blanchett**
Woody Guthrie  **Marcus Carl Franklin**
Billy the Kid  **Richard Gere**
Robbie Clark  **Heath Ledger**
Arthur Rimbaud  **Ben Whishaw**
Claire  **Charlotte Gainsbourg**
Allen Ginsberg  **David Cross**
Keenan Jones/Pat Garrett  **Bruce Greenwood**
Alice Fabian  **Julianne Moore**
Narrator  **Kris Kristofferson**
Hobo Joe  **Don Francks**
Hobo Moe  **Roc LaFortune**
Government Agent  **Larry Day**
Carny  **Paul Cagelet**
and Brian R.C. Wilmes (Circus Man); Pierre-Alexandre Fortin (Gorgeous George); Richie Havens (Old Man Arvin); Tyrone Benskin (Mr. Arvin); Kim Roberts (Mrs. Arvin); Eric Newsome (Sixties Narrator); Peter Friedman (Morris Bernstein); David Gow (Variety Show Host); Fanny La Croix (Actress); Kim Gordon (Carla Hendricks); Matthew Harbour, Kyle Switzer (Fans); Terry Haig (Gerry Hamlin); Greg Kramer (Drunk); Gordon Masten (Moonshiner); Bill Croft (Thief); Gabrielle Marcoux (Molly, 6 yrs.); Jessey LaFlamme (Carlie, 3 yrs.); Jennifer Rae Westley (Louise); Pierre LeBlanc, Richard Robitaille (Directors); Tim Post (Newscaster); Ivan Freud, Holly O'Brien (Performers); Danny Blanco (Black Doctor); Susan Glover (Mrs. Peacock); Vito DeFilippo (Mr. Peacock); Andrew Simms (Mr. Snow); Lisa Bronwyn Moore (Mrs. Snow); Jessica Kardos (Nurse); Garth Gilker (Man in Hospital Bed); John Koensgen (Physician); Mark Camacho (Norman); Lorne Brass (Folk Guru); Andrew Shaver (Mikes); Benz Antoine (Bobby Seale/Rabbit Brown); Shaun Balbar (Paparazzi); Joe Cobden (Sonny); Thiéry Dubé (Priest); Kristen Hager (Mona/Polly); Marie-Julie Rivest (Strange Woman); Yolanda Ross (Angela Reeves); Dennis St. John (Captain Henry); Craig Thomas (Huey P. Newton); Max Walker (Boy in Crowd); Michelle Williams (Coco Rivington)

A look at the many personalities and lives of musician Bob Dylan.

# THIS CHRISTMAS

Regina King, Laz Alonso

Idris Elba, Columbus Short

(SCREEN GEMS) Producers, Preston A. Whitmore II, Will Packer; Executive Producers, Ronnie Warner, Paddy Cullen, Mekhi Phifer, Damon Lee, Delroy Lindo; Director/Screenplay, Preston A. Whitmore II;Photography, Alexander Gruszynski; Editor, Paul Seydor; Music Supervisor, Spring Aspers; Designer, Dawn Snyder; Set Decorator, Beau Peterson; Costumes, Francine Jamison-Tanchuk; Casting, Kim Hardin; a Screen Gems presentation of a Rainforest Films production, in association with Facilitator Films; Dolby; Deluxe color; Rated PG-13; 117 minutes; Release date: November 21, 2007.

## Cast

Joseph Black  **Delroy Lindo**
Quentin Whitfield, Jr.  **Idris Elba**
Shirley Ann "Ma'Dere" Whitfield  **Loretta Devine**
Michael "Baby" Whitfield  **Chris Brown**
Devean Brooks  **Keith Robinson**
Malcolm Moore  **Laz Alonso**
Lt. Cpl. Claude Whitfield  **Columbus Short**
Kelli Whitfield  **Sharon Leal**
Mel Whitfield  **Lauren London**
Rosie  **Lupe Ontiveros**
Sandi  **Jessica Stroup**
Gerald  **Mekhi Phifer**
Lisa Moore  **Regina King**
Mo  **David Banner**
Cousin Fred  **Ricky Harris**
Dude  **Ronnie Warner**
and Haskell V. Anderson III (Reverend Caldwell); Ambrosia Kelley (Tori Moore); Javion S. Francis (Keshon Moore); Amy Hunter (Karen); Stacy Meadows (Troy); Brandon Fobbs (Raynard); Mark Craig (Officer #1); Aviva June (Tree Lot Attendant); Nicholas Harvell (Clerk); Brandon T. Jackson (El Rey MC); Shelina Wade (Jazz Songstress); Denetria Champ (Gospel Singer); Garry G. (MP); Mirtha Michelle (Bartender)

Ma'Dere Whitfield invites her family for a long-overdue Christmas reunion, where past secrets and indiscretions are revealed.

Delroy Lindo, Loretta Devine © SCREEN GEMS

Mekhi Phifer, Sharon Leal

# ENCHANTED

(WALT DISNEY PICTURES) Producers, Barry Josephson, Barry Sonnenfeld; Executive Producers, Chris Chase, Sunil Perkash, Ezra Swerdlow; Director, Kevin Lima; Screenplay, Bill Kelly; Photography, Don Burgess; Designer, Stuart Wurtzel; Costumes, Mona May; Music, Alan Menken; Songs, Alan Menken, Stephen Schwartz; Music Supervisor, Dawn Soler; Editors, Stephen A. Rotter, Gregory Perler; Choreographer, John O'Connell; Hand-Drawn Animation Supervisor, James Baxter; Visual Effects Supervisor, Thomas Schelesny; Hag Make-Up Effects, Rick Baker; Visual Effects Producer, Blondell Aidoo; Casting, John Papsidera, Marcia Ross; a Barry Sonnenfeld/Josephson Entertainment production; Dolby; Technicolor; Rated PG; 107 minutes; Release date: November 21, 2007.

Amy Adams © DISNEY ENTERPRISES

**Cast**

Giselle **Amy Adams**
Robert Philip **Patrick Dempsey**
Prince Edward **James Marsden**
Nathaniel **Timothy Spall**
Nancy Tremaine **Idina Menzel**
Morgan Philip **Rachel Covey**
Queen Narissa **Susan Sarandon**
Voice of Pip in Andalasia **Jeff Bennett**
Voice of Pip in New York **Kevin Lima**
Voice of Bluebird/Fawn/Rapunzel **Emma Rose Lima**
Voice of Bunny **Teala Dunn**
Voice of Troll **Fred Tatasciore**
Sunglass Street Vendor **Courtney Williams**
Grumpy **William Huntley**
Angie **Samantha Ivers**
Tess **Elizabeth Mathis**
Derelict Old Man **Edmund Lyndeck**
Phoebe Banks **Tonya Pinkins**
Ethan Banks **Isiah Whitlock, Jr.**
Henry **Tibor Feldman**
Sam **Jodi Benson**
Arty **Matt Servitto**
Sewer Crew Guy **Christopher Maggi**
Clara **Muriel Kuhn**
Bus Driver **Marilyn Sue Perry**
Carl **John Rothman**
Calypso Singer **Marlon Saunders**
Katz Deli Patron **Paul Klementowicz**
May **Michaela Conlin**
Mary Ilene Caselotti **Cathleen Trigg**
and Paige O'Hara (Angela); Danny Mastrogiorgio (Jerry); Julie Andrews (Narrator); Canedy Knowles (Restaurant Patron); Lillian Lifflander (Older Restaurant Patron); Matte Osian (Fire Investigator); Judy Kuhn (Pregnant Woman with Kids); Joseph Siravo (Bartender); Margaret Travolta (Voice of Radio Therapist); Tony Machine (Band Leader); Jon McLaughlin (Ballroom Singer); Helen Stenborg, Anita Keal (Ballroom Ladies); Kater Gordon (Receptionist)

Susan Sarandon

Amy Adams (center)

A wicked queen casts a storybook princess out of their animated kingdom of Andalasia and into the real world of New York City.

This film received three Oscar nominations for Original Song: "Happy Working Song," "So Close," and "That's How You Know."

Patrick Dempsey, Amy Adams

Amy Adams, Jodi Benson

James Marsden, Timothy Spall

# HITMAN

Timothy Olyphant, Olga Kurylenko

Timothy Olyphant

(20TH CENTURY FOX) Producers, Charles Gordon, Askarieh, Pierre-Ange Le Pogam; Executive Producers, Janos Flosser, Vin Diesel; Co-Producer, Daniel Alter; Director, Xavier Gens; Screenplay, Skip Woods, based on the Eidos game *Hitman*; Photography, Laurent Bares; Editors, Carlo Rizzo, Antoine Vareille; Music, Geoff Zanelli; Designer, Jacques Bufnoir; Costumes, Olivier Beriot; Special Effects Supervisor, Philippe Hubin; Makeup and Special Effects Makeup Supervisor, Olivier Afonso; Stunts, Philippe Guegan; Casting, Debbie McWilliams, Bouchra Fakhri, Christian Kaplan; a EuropaCorp–Charles Gordon/Adrian Askarieh production, made in association with Dune Entertainment III; Dolby; Super 35 Widescreen; Deluxe color; Rated R; 93 minutes; Release date: November 21, 2007.

## Cast

Agent 47 **Timothy Olyphant**
and Dougray Scott (Mike Whittier); Olga Kurylenko (Nika Boronina); Robert Knepper (Yuri Marklov); Ulrich Thomsen (Mikhail Belicoff); Henry Ian Cusick (Udre Belicoff); Michael Offei (Jenkins); Christian Erickson (Gen. Kormarov); Eriq Ebouaney (Bwana Ovie); Joe Sheridan (Capt. Gudnayev); James Faulkner (Smith Jamison); Jean-Marc Bellu, Nicky Naude, Abdou Sagna, Ilya Nikitenko, Loïc Molla (Hitmen); Youssef Diawara (Hog-Tied Prisoner); Patrick Ligardes (Another Buyer); Ancuta Radici (The Sad Girl); Peter Hudson (Mr. Price); Cyril Guei (Old SUV Leader); Ivan Yurukov (Russian John); Vladimir Kolev (HRT Guy); Makssim Kolev Genchev (Yuri's Guy #3); Kamen Ivanov (Russian Captain); Stefka Yanorova-Trenfafilova (Belicoff's Wife); Yasmine Meddour (Belicoff's Daughter); Iosis Shamli (SWAT Team Leader #1); Desislava Bakardzhieva, Paul Barrett (Reporters); Viktoria Dimova (Mike's Daughter, 8 yrs); Svezjen Mladenov (Russian Forensic); Byliana Ognyanova Petrinska (Another Officer); Emile Abossolo M'bo (Gen. Ajunwa); Paul Bandey (Director M.C. Ray); Sabine Camille Crossen (June); Dobrin Markov Dosev (Clergyman); Vili Dimitrova (Terrified Maid); Dessislava Zidarova (Belicoff's Whore); Boris Parvanov (Young Agent 47); Velizar Nikolas Binev (The Priest)

Timothy Olyphant

Agent 47, a ruthless hitman working for a mysterious organization called "The Agency," finds himself pursued by Interpol after executing a man he believes to be the Russian head of state.

Timothy Olyphant © 20TH CENTURY FOX

# STARTING OUT IN THE EVENING

(ROADSIDE ATTRACTIONS) Producers, Nancy Israel, Fred Parnes, Andrew Wagner, Gary Winick, Jake Abraham; Executive Producers, Greg Moyer, John Sloss, Douglas Harmon, Allen Myerson; Co-Producer, Mandy Tagger; Director, Andrew Wagner; Screenplay, Fred Parnes, Andrew Wagner, based on the novel by Brian Morton; Photography, Harlan Bosmajian; Designer, Carol Strober; Costumes, Claudia Brown; Editor, Gena Bleier; Music, Adam Gorgoni; Music Supervisor, Linda Cohen; Casting, Cindy Tolan; a Voom HD Pictures presentation of an InDigEnt production; Dolby; Color; HD; Rated PG-13; 110 minutes; Release date: November 23, 2007.

## Cast

Leonard Schiller  **Frank Langella**
Ariel Schiller  **Lili Taylor**
Heather Wolfe  **Lauren Ambrose**
Casey Davis  **Adrian Lester**
Frederick  **Karl Bury**
Victor  **Michael Cumpsty**
Chelsea  **Anitha Gandhi**
Sandra Bennett  **Jessica Hecht**
Cab Driver Ravadip Patel  **Sean T. Krishnan**
Charles  **Jeff McCarthy**
Bartender  **Jerry Walsh**
and Patti Perkins (Dolores); Dennis Parlato, Joie Lee (Authors); Thomas Ryan (Nick); John C. Havens (Jeff the Doorman); Joel West (Waiter); Ali Reza (Doctor)

Leonard Schiller, a once-admired author suffering from writer's block, reluctantly agrees to participate in a series of interviews with a college student who hopes to resurrect Schiller's reputation.

Frank Langella

Frank Langella, Lili Taylor © ROADSIDE ATTRACTIONS

Lauren Ambrose

Frank Langella

# THE SAVAGES

(FOX SEARCHLIGHT) Producers, Ted Hope, Anne Carey, Erica Westheimer; Executive Producers, Alexander Payne, Jim Taylor, Jim Burke, Anthony Bregman, Fred Westheimer; Director/Screenplay, Tamara Jenkins; Photography, Mott Hupfel; Designer, Jane Ann Stewart; Costumes, David Robinson; Editor, Brian A. Kates; Music, Stephen Trask; Casting, Jeanne McCarthy; a This is That production in association with Ad Hominem Enterprises and Cooper's Town Prods. presented in association with Lone Star Film Group; Dolby; Technicolor; HD; Rated R; 113 minutes; Release date: November 28, 2007.

### Cast

Wendy Savage **Laura Linney**
Jon Savage **Philip Seymour Hoffman**
Lenny Savage **Philip Bosco**
Larry **Peter Friedman**
Eduardo **David Zayas**
Jimmy **Gbenga Akinnagbe**
Kasia **Cara Seymour**
Ms. Robinson **Tonye Patano**
Bill Lachman **Guy Boyd**
Nancy Lachman **Debra Monk**
Doris Metzger **Rosemary Murphy**
Burt **Hal Blankenship**
Lizzie **Joan Jaffe**
Real Estate Agent **Laura Palmer**
Mr. Sperry **Salem Ludwig**
Attendant **Sandra Daley**
Matt **Peter Frechette**
Manicurists **Jennifer Lim, Lili Liu**
Nurses **Kristine Nielsen, Cynthia Darlow**
Doctor **Christopher Durham**
Annie **Maddie Corman**
Administrator **Carmen Roman**
Counselor **Nancy Lenehan**
Residents **Michael Higgins, Madeline Lee**
Valley View Nurses **Tijuana Ricks, Tobin Tyler**
Roz **Margo Martindale**
Woman in Parking Lot **Erica Berg**
Howard **Michael Blackson**
Simone **Sidné Anderson**
Woman with Red Pillow **Patti Karr**
and John Bolton (Father in Mall Lot); Zoe Kazan (Student); Lee Sellars (Father); Marianne Weems (Director); Debbi Fuhrman (Physical Therapist); Max Jenkins-Goetz (Boy)

Siblings Jon and Wendy Savage reluctantly join forces when their cantankerous father begins showing signs of senility and requires being placed in a nursing home.

This film received Oscar nominations for Actress (Laura Linney) and Original Screenplay.

Philip Seymour Hoffman, Laura Linney

Laura Linney, Philip Bosco, Philip Seymour Hoffman © FOX SEARCHLIGHT

Laura Linney, Philip Bosco

# AWAKE

Lena Olin © METRO-GOLDWYN-MAYER

Hayden Christensen, Terrence Howard

Hayden Christensen, Jessica Alba

(MGM) Producers, Joana Vicente, Jason Kilot, Bob Weinstein, Fisher Stevens; Executive Producers, Bob Weinstein, Harvey Weinstein, Kelly Carmichael, Tim Williams; Co-Producers, Amy J. Kaufman, Tony Tunnell; Director/Screenplay, Joby Harold; Photography, Russell Carpenter; Editor, Craig McKay; Music, Graeme Revell; Additional Music, Samuel Sim; Music Supervisor, Dan Lieberstein; Designer, Dina Goldman; Costumes, Cynthia Flynt; Casting, Avy Kaufman; a Weinstein Co., Greenestreet Films presentation of a Deutsch/Open City Films, Greenestreet production; Dolby; Super 35 Widescreen; Color; Rated R; 84 minutes; Release date: November 30, 2007.

## Cast

Clay Beresford **Hayden Christensen**
Sam Lockwood **Jessica Alba**
Dr. Jack Harper **Terrence Howard**
Lilith Beresford **Lena Olin**
Dr. Larry Lupin **Christopher McDonald**
Clayton Beresford Sr. **Sam Robards**
Dr. Jonathan Neyer **Arliss Howard**
Dr. Puttnam **Fisher Stevens**
Penny Carver **Georgina Chapman**
Dracula **David Harbour**
Young Clay **Stephen Hinkle**
Financial News Analysts **Denis O'Hare, Ross Klavan**
Brian the Orderly **Charlie Hewson**
Officer Doherty **Court Young**
Dr. Elbogen **Joseph Costa**
Dr. Neyer's Nurse **Poorna Jagannathan**
and Lee Wong (Mr. Waturi) Kae Shimizu (Asian Translator); Steven Rowe (Teacher); Jeffrey Fierson (Head Chef); John C. Havens (Policeman); Richard Thomsen (Minister); Joshua Rollins (Funeral Minister); Brenda Schad (Pregnant Woman); Sam Pitman (Zombie)

A young man, brought into the operating room for a heart transplant, realizes he has not succumbed to the anesthesia and therefore can hear and feel everything happening to him.

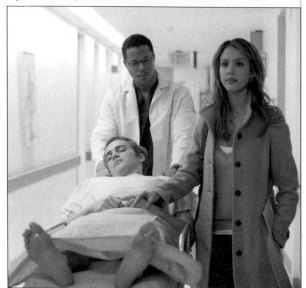

Hayden Christensen, Terrence Howard, Jessica Alba

# JUNO

(FOX SEARCHLIGHT) Producers, Lianne Halfon, John Malkovich, Russell Smith, Mason Novick; Executive Producers, Joe Drake, Nathan Kahane, Daniel Dubiecki; Co-Producers, Jim Miller, Kelli Konop, Brad Van Arragon; Director, Jason Reitman; Screenplay, Diablo Cody; Photography, Eric Steelberg; Designer, Steve Saklad; Costumes, Monique Prudhomme; Editor, Dana E. Glauberman; Music, Mateo Messina; Songs, Kimya Dawson; Music Supervisors, Peter Afterman, Margaret Yen; Casting, Mindy Marin, Kara Lipson; a Mandate Pictures/Mr. Mudd production; Dolby; Deluxe color; Rated PG-13; 96 minutes; Release date: December 5, 2007.

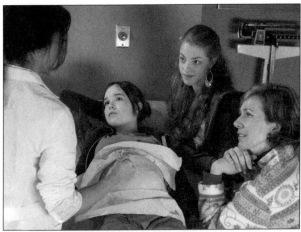

Kaaren de Zilva, Ellen Page, Olivia Thirlby, Allison Janney

Jennifer Garner, Jason Bateman © FOX SEARCHLIGHT

## Cast

Juno MacGuff  **Ellen Page**
Paulie Bleeker  **Michael Cera**
Vanessa Loring  **Jennifer Garner**
Mark Loring  **Jason Bateman**
Bren MacGuff  **Allison Janney**
Mac MacGuff  **J.K. Simmons**
Leah  **Olivia Thirlby**
Gerta Rauss  **Eileen Pedde**
Rollo  **Rainn Wilson**
Steve Rendazo  **Daniel Clark**
Bleeker's Mom  **Darla Vandenbossche**
Vijay  **Aman Johal**
Su-Chin  **Valerie Tian**
Punk Receptionist  **Emily Perkins**
Ultrasound Technician  **Kaaren de Zilva**
Lab Partners  **Steven Christopher Parker, Candice Accola**
Liberty Bell  **Sierra Pitkin**
Chemistry Teacher  **Cut Chemist (Lucas MacFadden)**
Tough Girl  **Eve Harlow**
Nurse  **Kirsten Williamson**
Pretty-to-Goth Girl  **Emily Tennant**
Katrina De Voort  **Ashley Whillans**
Track Announcer  **Jeff Witzke**
Keith  **Colin McSween**
Sex Ed Teacher  **Peggy Logan**
RPG Nerd  **Cameron Bright**
Delivery Room Doctor  **Joy Galmut**
and Wendy Russell, Robyn Ross (Vanessa's Friends); Dallas Hanson, Bryson Russell, Derek Mann, Keith Frost, Grayson Grant, Robin Watts, Tyler Watts, Brandon Barton (Dancing Elk Track Team)

Michael Cera, Ellen Page

Jennifer Garner, Jason Bateman, Ellen Page

Finding out she's pregnant, 16-year-old Juno MacGuff decides to have the baby and give it to a couple seeking an infant to adopt.

2007 Academy Award winner for Best Original Screenplay. This film received additional nominations for Picture, Actress (Ellen Page), and Director.

Allison Janney, Ellen Page, J.K. Simmons

# THE GOLDEN COMPASS

Dakota Blue Richards

(NEW LINE CINEMA) Producers, Deborah Forte, Bill Carraro; Executive Producers, Bob Shaye, Michael Lynne, Toby Emmerich, Mark Ordesky, Ileen Maisel, Andrew Miano, Paul Weitz; Co-Producer, Nikolas Korda; Director/ Screenplay, Chris Weitz, based on the book *Northern Lights* by Philip Pullman; Photography, Henry Braham; Designer, Dennis Gassner; Costumes, Ruth Myers; Editors, Peter Honess, Anne V. Coates, Kevin Tent; Music, Alexandre Desplat; Senior Visual Effects Supervisor, Michael Fink; Visual Effects, Rhythm & Hues, Framestore CFC, Cinesite (Europe), Digital Domain, Rainmaker Animation and Visual Effects U.K., Tippett Studio and Tippett Studio Montreal, Matte World Digital, Digital Backlot, Peerless Camera Co.; Special Effects Supervisor, Trevor Wood; Makeup and Hair Designer, Peter King; Supervising Stunt Coordinator, Vic Armstrong; Casting, Fiona Weir, Lucy Bevan; a Scholastic production/Depth of Field production presented in association with Ingenious Film Partners; Dolby; Panavision; Deluxe color; Rated PG-13; 118 minutes; Release date: December 7, 2007.

## Cast

Mrs. Coulter **Nicole Kidman**
Lyra Belacqua **Dakota Blue Richards**
Lord Asriel **Daniel Craig**
Lee Scoresby **Sam Elliott**
Serafina Pekkala **Eva Green**
and Christopher Lee (First High Councilor); Tom Courtenay (Farder Coram); Derek Jacobi (Magisterial Emissary); Ben Walker (Roger); Simon McBurney (Fra Pavel); Jim Carter (Lord John Faa); Clare Higgins (Ma Costa); Jack Shepherd (Master); Magda Szubanski (Mrs. Lonsdale); Edward De Souza (Second High Councilor); Ian McKellen (Voice of Iorek Byrnison); Ian McShane (Voice of Ragnar Sturlusson); Freddie Highmore (Voice of Pantalaimon); Kathy Bates (Voice of Hester); Kristin Scott Thomas (Voice of Stelmaria); Charlie Rowe (Billy Costa); Steven Loton (Tony Costa); Michael Antoniou (Kerim Costa); Mark Mottram (Jaxer Costa); Jason Watkins (Bolvanger Official); Jody Halse (Bolvanger Orderly); Hattie Morahan (Sister Clara); John Bett (Thorold); John Franklyn-Robbins (Librarian); Jonathan Laury (Younger Fellow); Tommy Luther (Jacob Huismans); James Rawlings (Passing Scholar); Joao de Sousa (Hunt); Habib Nasib Nader (Ragnar); Theo Fraser Steele (Magisterial Officer); Bill Hurst (Police Captain); Elliot Cowan (Commanding Officer); Sam Hoare (Second-in-Command); Paul Antony-Bates (Bolvangar Doctor); Thomas Arnold, David Garrick, Brian Nickels, Gary Kane (Gobblers); Alfred Harmsworth (Gyptian Kid); Charles Evanson, Patrick Cleary, Tarek Khalil, Madrios Ohannessian, Sandra Wolfe (Gyptian Chiefs); Hewson Osbourne, Albert Kendrick, John Cartier, Chris Abbott (Fellows); Alex Terentyev (Tartar Officer); David Forman (Samoyed Kidnapper)

Possessing a valuable golden compass desired by the dictatorial hierarchy of the Magisterium, young Lyra heads for the Arctic Circle to find her uncle, who believes he has uncovered a link to parallel worlds.

2007 Academy Award winner for Best Visual Effects, this film received an additional nomination for Art Direction.

Nicole Kidman, Dakota Blue Richards

Sam Elliott © NEW LINE CINEMA

# GRACE IS GONE

Heidi Phillips, John Cusack, Grace Bednarczyk © WEINSTEIN CO.

(WEINSTEIN CO.) Producers, John Cusack, Grace Loh, Galt Niederhoffer, Daniela Taplin Lundberg, Celine Rattray; Executive Producers, Paul Bernstein, Reagan Silber, Jai Stefan, Todd Traina; Co-Producers, Roberta Burrows, Marilyn Haft, Demetra Diamantopoulos, Jessica Levin, Riva Marker; Director/Screenplay, James C. Strouse; Photography, Jean-Louis Bompoint; Designer, Susan Block; Costumes, Ha Nguyen; Editor, Joe Klotz; Music, Max Richter; Associate Producers, Carina Alves, Doug Dearth, Wes Jones; Casting, Pascal, Tenner, Rudnicke; a Plum Pictures and New Crime Prods. presentation in association with Hart/Lunsford Pictures; Dolby; Color; Rated PG; 92 minutes; Release date: December 7, 2007.

### Cast

Stanley Phillips **John Cusack**
Heidi Phillips **Shélan O'Keefe**
Dawn Phillips **Gracie Bednarczyk**
John Phillips **Alessandro Nivola**
Captain Riggs **Doug Dearth**
Chaplain Johnson **Doug James**
Ear Piercer **Penny Slusher**
and Emily Churchill, Rebecca Spence, Jennifer Tyler, Susan Messing (Women); Zachary Gray (Boy at Pool); Marisa Tomei (Woman at Pool); Dana Lynne Gilhooley (Grace Phillips); Katie Honaker (Voice of Grace Phillips); Mary Kay Place (Woman at Funeral)

Devastated to learn that his wife has been killed while serving in Iraq, Stanley Phillips takes his two young daughters on an impromptu vacation until he can figure how to break the bad news to them.

John Cusack

# THE WALKER

Kristin Scott-Thomas, Lauren Bacall, Woody Harrelson, Lily Tomlin © THINKFILM

(THINKFILM) Producer, Deepak Nayer; Executive Producers, Willi Baer, Steve Christian, James Clayton, Parseghian Planco, Duncan Reid; Director/Screenplay, Paul Schrader; Photography, Chris Seager; Editor, Julian Rodd; Music, Anne Dudley; Designer, James Merifield; Costumes, Nic Ede; Casting, Gilly Poole; a Kintop Pictures, Ingenious Film Partners, Asia Pacific Films, Isle of Man Film presentation; Dolby; Super 35 Widescreen; Deluxe Color; 107 minutes; Release date: December 7, 2007.

Kristin Scott-Thomas, Woody Harrelson

## Cast

Carter Page III **Woody Harrelson**
Lynn Lockner  **Kristin Scott Thomas**
Natalie Van Miter  **Lauren Bacall**
Abigail Delorean  **Lily Tomlin**
Jack Delorean  **Ned Beatty**
Emek Yoglu  **Moritz Bleibtreu**
Senator Larry Lockner  **Willem Dafoe**
and William Hope (Mungo Tenant); Geff Francis (Detective Dixon); Steven Hartley (Robbie Kononsberg); Mary Beth Hurt (Chrissie Morgan); Garrick Hagon (John Krebs); Michael J. Reynolds (Ethan Withal); Allen Lidkey (Andrew Salesperson); Stewart Alexander (Edgar); Andres Williams (Radley); Jason Durran (Officer Green); Marcello Cabezas (Steve); Michael Ahl (Theatregoer); Kelvin Cook (Policeman); Pamela Fischer (Theatre Attendee); Lynn-Jane Foreman (Nosy Neighbor); Simon Hepworth (Eddie); Christian Jones (Male Escort); Anastasia Summers (TV Reporter); Schuster Vance (D.C. Reporter)

Carter Page, an unpaid escort for Washington's elite ladies, finds himself involved in murder when his friend Lynn Lockner's lover ends up stabbed to death.

# I AM LEGEND

(WARNER BROS.) Producers, Akiva Goldsman, James Lassiter, David Heyman, Neal Moritz; Executive Producers, Michael Tadross, Erwin Stoff, Dana Goldberg, Bruce Berman; Co-Producers, Tracy Torme, Jeffrey "J.P." Wetzel; Director, Francis Lawrence; Screenplay, Mark Protosevich, Akiva Goldsman, based on the screenplay by John William and Joyce H. Corrington, based on the novel by Richard Matheson; Photography, Andrew Lesnie; Designer, Naomi Shohan; Costumes, Michael Kaplan; Editor, Wayne Wahrman; Music, James Newton Howard; Visual Effects Supervisor, Janek Sirrs; Visual Effects and Animation, Sony Pictures Imageworks; Visual Effects, CIS-Hollywood; Special Effects Supervisor, Conrad Brink; Creatures Designer, Patrick Tatopoulos; Second Unit Director/Stunts, Vic Armstrong; Casting, Kathleen Chopin; a Weed Road/Overbrook Entertainment production, presented in association with Village Roadshow Pictures; Dolby; Panavision; Technicolor; Rated PG-13; 100 minutes; Release date: December 14, 2007.

Will Smith, Willow Smith, Salli Richardson © WARNER BROS.

## Cast

Robert Neville **Will Smith**
Anna **Alice Braga**
Alpha Male **Dash Mihok**
Ethan **Charlie Tahan**
Zoe **Salli Richardson**
Marley **Willow Smith**
Mike, Military Escort **Darrell Foster**
TV Personality **April Grace**
Alpha Female **Joanna Numata**
Jay, Military Driver **Samuel Glen**
and James McCauley, Marin Ireland, Alexander DiPersia, Abraham Sparrow (Evacuees); Pedro Mojica (Sergeant); Anthony Mazza, Tyree Simpson (Evacuation Cops); Steve Cirbus (Military Police); Calista Hill, Gabriella Hill, Madeline Hill (Little Girl Evacuees); Adhi Sharma (Military Scanning Tech); Blake Lange (Coast Guard Ground Crew); Patrick Fraley (Voice of President); Caitlin McHugh (Special Blond Model); Deborah Collins (Civilian); Mike Patton (Creature Vocals); Abby, Kona (Sam); Katherine Brook, Vince Cupone, Lynná Davis, Anika Ellis, Exo, John Grady, Moses Harris Jr., Kennis Hawkins, Marc Inniss, Eric Jenkins, Reed Kelly, Grasan Kingsberry, Heather Lang, Drew Leary, Asa Liebmann, Deborah Lohse, Jon-Paul Mateo, Ian McLaughlin, Luke Miller, Courtney Munch, Kimberly Shannon Murphy, Okwui Okpokwasili, Erin Owen, Victor Paguia, Paradox Pollack, Will Rawls, William Schultz, Hollie K. Seidel, Hannah Sim, Eric Spear, Mark Steger, Charlie Sutton, David Hamilton Thompson, Anthony Vincent, Greg Wattkis (Infected); Emma Thompson (Doctor)

Alice Braga, Charlie Tahan, Will Smith

Following a horrific plague that wipes out most of the world's population, Robert Neville finds himself the one seemingly healthy human being left in Manhattan, where he is terrorized nightly by a horde of rampaging zombies whom he hopes to cure.

Previous versions of the novel were *The Last Man on Earth* (AIP, 1964), with Vincent Price, and *The Omega Man* (WB, 1971), with Charlton Heston.

Sam, Will Smith

# THE KITE RUNNER

Khalid Abdalla, Ali Danesh Bakhtyari

(DREAMWORKS/PARAMOUNT VANTAGE) Producers, William Horberg, Walter F. Parkes, Rebecca Yeldham, E. Bennett Walsh; Executive Producers, Sidney Kimmel, Laurie MacDonald, Sam Mendes, Jeff Skoll; Co-Executive Producer, Bruce Toll; Director, Marc Forster; Screenplay, David Benioff, based on the novel by Khaled Hosseini; Photography, Roberto Schaefer; Editor, Matt Chesse; Music, Alberto Iglesias; Designer, Carlos Conti; Costumes, Frank Fleming; Kite Master, Basir Beria; Associate Producers, Kwame L. Parker, Leslie McMinn; Casting, Kate Dowd; a DreamWorks Pictures, Sidney Kimmel Entertainment, Participant Prods. presentation of a Sidney Kimmel Entertainment, Parkes/MacDonald production; Dolby; Super 35 Widescreen; Color; Rated PG-13; 128 minutes; Release date: December 14, 2007.

Zekiria Ebrahimi, Homayoun Ershadi

Ahmad Khan, Zekiria Ebrahimi © DREAMWORKS/PARAMOUNT VANTAGE

## Cast

Amir **Khalid Abdalla**
Baba **Homayoun Ershadi**
Young Amir **Zekiria Ebrahimi**
Young Hassan **Ahmad Khan**
Rahim Khan **Shaun Toub**
and Nabi Tanha (Ali); Ali Danesh Bakhtyari (Sohrab); Said Taghmaoui (Farid); Atossa Leoni (Soraya); Abdul Qadir Farookh (General Taher); Maimoona Ghizal (Jamila); Abdul Salam Yusoufzai (Assef); Elham Ehsas (Young Assef); Sayed Jafar Masihullah Gharibzada (Omar); Mir Mahmood Shah Hashimi (Business Man in Baba's Study); Bahram Ehsas (Wali); Tamim Nawabi (Kamal); Mohamad Nabi Attai (Uncle Saifo the Kite Seller); Mohamad Nadir Sarwari (Spice Merchant); Mustafa Haidari (Party Worker); Ahmad Yasar Shir Agha (Birthday Singer); Mohammad Aman Joya (Mahmood); Abdul Azim Wahabzada (Karim); Vsevolod Bardashev (Soviet Union Soldier); Sayed Miran Farhad (Burly Man in Truck); Murina Abudukelimu (Young Wife in Truck); Igor Radchenko (Soviet Union Officer); Larry Brown (Gas Station Customer); L. Peter Callender (Dean of Students); Jesse Robertson (Man at Bar); Josh Chamberlain, Marco Mazariegos, Shaan Price (Pool Players); Qadir Farookh (General Taheri); Peg McKibbin (Flea Market Customer); Chris Verrill (Dr. Starobin); Amar Kureishi (Dr. Amani); Maimoona Ghizal (Jamila Taheri); Mohammad Eshan Aman (Wedding Singer); Yunus Osman (Cemetery Mullah); Mehboob Ali (Pakistan Taxi Driver); Saïd Taghmaoui (Farid); Abdul Salam Yusoufzai (Assef); Mohamad Amin Rahimi (Taliban Stadium Speaker); Aziz Raxidi, Khalil Ahmad Nooryan (Assef Guards); Ali Danish Bakhty Ari (Sohrab); Hammeda Hamraz (Rahim Khan's Neighbor); Ahmad Shah Alam (Man at Mosque); Kaiser Doulat-Beek (Man in the Park); Khaled Hosseini (Doctor in the Park); Habib Zargi (Park Kite Seller); Houshmand Habib (Kite Flyer Kid); Lukas Ferreira (Kite Spooler Kid); Tim Halpin (Soviet Tank Commander)

As the Taliban seizes power in Kabul, Amir, having long ago left Afghanistan for America, returns to his native land in hopes of atoning for betraying the friendship between himself and Hassan when they were boys.
This film received an Oscar nomination for Original Score.

# ALVIN AND THE CHIPMUNKS

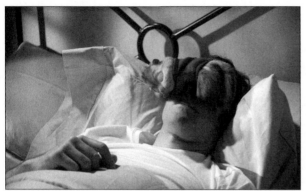

Theodore, Jason Lee

Theodore, Alvin, Simon, Jason Lee

(20TH CENTURY FOX) Producers, Janice Karman, Ross Bagdasarian Jr.; Executive Producers, Karen Rosenfelt, Arnon Milchan, Michele Imperato Stabile, Steve Waterman; Director, Tim Hill; Screenplay, Jon Vitti, Will McRobb, Chris Viscardi; Story, Jon Vitti; Photography, Peter Lyons Collister; Editor, Peter Berger; Music, Christopher Lennertz; Music Supervisor, Julianne Jordan; Designer, Richard Holland; Costumes, Alexandra Welker; Animation Supervisor, Chris Bailey; Special Effects Coordinator, Alan E. Lorimer; Visual Effects Animator, Alberto Abril; Casting, Mindy Marin; a Fox 2000 Pictures and Regency Enterprises presentation of a Bagdasarian Co. production; Dolby; Deluxe color; Rated PG; 91 minutes; Release date: December 14, 2007.

## Cast

Dave Seville **Jason Lee**
Ian Hawk **David Cross**
Claire **Cameron Richardson**
Gail **Jane Lynch**
Voice of Alvin **Justin Long**
and Matthew Gray Gubler (Voice of Simon); Jesse McCartney (Voice of Theodore); Veronica Alicino (Amy); Beth Riesgraf (Mother in Store); Kevin Symons (Ted); Frank Maharajh (Barry); Greg Siebel (Photographer); Oliver Muirhead (Butler); Jayden Lund (Security Guard); Erin Chambers (Press Coordinator); Jillian Barberie (Herself); Chris Classic (DJ); Adam Riancho (Voice of French Doll); Axel Alba (Voice of Spanish Doll); Rosero McCoy (Choreographer); Alexis A. Boyd, Kevin Fisher, Kyndra "Binkie" Reevey, Tucker Barkley, Celestina, Nick Drago, Bryan Gaw, Melanie Lewis, Laura Edwards, Christopher Scott, Marquisa Gardner, Michelle "Jersey" Maniscalco (Dancers); Adriane Lenox (Vet); Dan Tiffany (Engineer); Lorne Green (Director); Allison Karman, Tiara Parker, Kira Verrastro (Interns)

Simon, Alvin, Theodore, David Cross © 20TH CENTURY FOX

Struggling songwriter Dave Seville sees his chance to make it in the recording business at last when he encounters a trio of talking chipmunks. Previous feature based on the characters was the animated film *The Chipmunk Adventure* (Goldwyn, 1987).

Simon, Alvin, Theodore

# CHARLIE WILSON'S WAR

Tom Hanks, Julia Roberts

(UNIVERSAL) Producers, Tom Hanks, Gary Goetzman; Executive Producers, Celia Costas, Ryan Kavanaugh, Jeff Skoll; Co-Producer, Mike Haley; Director, Mike Nichols; Screenplay, Aaron Sorkin; Based on the book by George Crile; Photography, Stephen Goldblatt; Designer, Victor Kempster; Costumes, Albert Wolsky; Music, James Newton Howard; Editors, John Bloom, Antonia Van Drimmelen; Visual Effects Supervisor, Richard Edlund; Casting, Ellen Lewis; a Playtone production, presented in association with Relativity Media and Participant Prods.; Dolby; Super 35 Widescreen; Deluxe color; Rated R; 97 minutes; Release date: December 21, 2007

## Cast

Charlie Wilson **Tom Hanks**
Joanne Herring **Julia Roberts**
Gust Avrakotos **Philip Seymour Hoffman**
Bonnie Bach **Amy Adams**
Doc Long **Ned Beatty**
Jane Liddle **Emily Blunt**
President Zia **Oma Puri**
Zvi **Ken Stott**
Cravely **John Slattery**
Harold Holt **Denis O'Hare**
Crystal Lee **Jud Tylor**
Larry Liddle **Peter Gerety**
Paul Brown **Brian Markinson**
Mike Vickers **Christopher Denham**
Belly Dancer **Tracy Phillips**
Charlie's Angels Receptionist **Wynn Everett**
Marla **Mary Bonner Baker**
Suzanne **Rachel Nichols**
Jailbait **Shiri Appleby**
CIA Award Presenter **Terry Bozeman**
Kelly **Hilary Angelo**
and Cyia Batten (Stacey); Kirby Mitchell (Stoned Guy); Ed Regine (Limo Driver); Daniel Eric Gold (Donnelly); P.J. Byrne (Jim Van Wagenen); Thomas Crawford (Maintenance Man); Joe Roland (McGaffin); Patrika Darbo (Auctioneer); Carly Reeves (Slave Girl); Salaheddine Benchegra (Pakistani Steward); Faran Tahir (Brigadier Rashid); Rizwan Manji (Col. Mahmood); Maurice Sherbanée (Refugee in Wheelchair); Salam Sangi (Refugee Building Wall); Navid Negahban (Refugee Camp Traslator); Mozhan Marno (Refugee Camp Translator); Habib Saba (Afghan Boy); Nadia Miller (Afghan Girl); Michelle Arthur (Refugee Camp Nurse); Shila Vossugh (Refugee Mother); Edward Hunt (Embassy Marine); R.M. Haley (Embassy Official); Michael Spellman (Patrick); Russell Edge (Agent Wells); Joe Sikora, Gabriel Tigerman, Patrick Bentley, Marc Pelina (Chess Players); Ken Stott (Zvi); Ipalé (Egyptian Defense Minister); Mary Bailey (Doc Long's Secretary); Trish Gallaher Glenn (Joanna'e Assistant); Ron Fassler (Mario); Enayat Delawary (Doc Long's Translator); Nancy Linehan Charles (Mrs. Long); Daston Kalili (Mujahideen Translator); Pasha Lynchnikoff, Illia Volok, Alexander Lvovsky (Russian Helicopter Pilots); Sammy Sheik, Moneer Yaqubi, Gabriel Justice (Stingers, Mujahideen); Siyal Mohamad, Quill Roberts (Stinger, Presenters); Jim Jansen, Harry S. Murphy, Spencer Garrett, Kevin Cooney (Congressional Committee)

The true story of how devil-may-care congressman Charlie Wilson hoped to swing a deal to generate covert financial and weapons support for the Afghan Mujahideen to help them defeat the Russians.

This film received an Oscar nomination for Supporting Actor (Philip Seymour Hoffman).

Tom Hanks, Philip Seymour Hoffman, Christopher Denham © UNIVERSAL STUDIOS

# WALK HARD:
# THE DEWEY COX STORY

Jenna Fischer, John C. Reilly

(COLUMBIA) Producers, Judd Apatow, Jake Kasdan, Clayton Townsend; Executive Producer, Lew Morton; Director, Jake Kasdan; Screenplay, Judd Apatow, Jake Kasdan; Photography, Uta Brieswitz; Designer, Jefferson D. Sage; Costumes, Debra McGuire; Music, Michael Andrews; Music Supervisors, Manish Raval, Tom Wolfe; Title song by Marshall Crenshaw, John C. Reilly, Judd Apatow, Jake Kasdan; Editors, Tara Timpone, Steve Welch; Casting, Amy McIntyre Britt, Anya Colloff; a Nominated Films production, in association with Relativity Media; Dolby; Color; Rated R; 96 minutes; Release date: December 21, 2007.

It's a Dewey Cox
**TEENAGER PARTY**

John C. Reilly (center), Matt Besser, Tim Meadows, Chris Parnell © COLUMBIA PICTURES

## Cast

Dewey Cox   **John C. Reilly**
Darlene Madison   **Jenna Fischer**
Pa Cox   **Raymond J. Barry**
Ma Cox   **Margo Martindale**
Edith   **Kristen Wiig**
Nate   **Chip Hormess**
Dewey, Age 8   **Conner Rayburn**
Sam   **Tim Meadows**
Theo   **Chris Parnell**
Dave   **Matt Besser**
Schwartzberg   **David Krumholtz**
Record Producer   **John Michael Higgins**
Stage Manager   **Nat Faxon**
Doctor   **Terrence Beasor**
Old Bluesman   **David "Honeyboy" Edwards**
Harmonica Player   **Gerry Black**
Men at Talent Show   **John Maynard, E.J. Callahan**
MC, Teacher   **Matt Price**
Preacher   **Rance Howard**
Bobby Shad   **Craig Robinson**
and Paul Bates (Nightclub Manager); Oscar Dillon (Audience Guy at Nightclub); Harold Ramis (L'Chaim); Phil Rosenthal (Mazeltov); Martin Starr (Schmendrick); Clement E. Blake (Edith's Father); Jack McBrayer (DJ); Amy Ferguson (Teenager); Paul Feig (Different DJ); Molly Quinn (Teen with Pinups); John Ennis (The Big Bopper); Frankie Muniz (Buddy Holly); Ed Helms (Stage Manager); Jack White (Elvis); Angela Little Mackenzie (Beth Anne); Odette Yustman (Reefer Girl); Scarlett Keegan (Fiddle Player); Steve Bannos (Prison Guard); Willow Geer (Nurse, Rehab); David Doty (Doctor, Rehab); Jack Kehler (Press Conference Reporter); Gerry Bednob (The Maharishi); Paul Rudd (John Lennon); Jack Black (Paul McCartney); Justin Long (George Harrison); Jason Schwartzman (Ringo Starr); Tim Bagley (Press Conference Engineer); Jane Lynch (Gail the Television Reporter); Serria Bishop (African-American Woman, 70's); Debbie Yeh (Asian Woman, 70's); Skyler Gisondo (Dewdrop); Kshitij Pendurkar (Dewey Rahim); Simon Helberg (Dreidel L'Chaim); Jacques Slade (Lil' Nutzzak); Danica Rozelle (Music Video Girl); Lurie Poston, Maggie Mannion (Cox Kids); Stacey Scowley (Pierced Eyebrow Girl); Ajla Hodzic (Pierced Lip Girl); Otis Williams, Ron Tyson, Terry Weeks, Joe Herndon, Bruce Williamson (The Temptations); Lyle Lovett, Cheryl Tiegs, Patrick Duffy, Morgan Fairchild, Cheryl Ladd, Jackson Browne, Jewel, Ghostface Killah, Eddie Vedder (Themselves); Patrick Faucette (Bad Men Bass Player); Ian Roberts (Drug Dealer); Aron Johnson, Jack Saperstein, Taylor Jamison Hubert, Christopher Hurt (Teenage Band); Tyler Nilson (Bert); Deanna Brooks (Hotel Groupie W/Dewey); Michael William Arnold, Chris Blount, Neil Ironfield, Haleigh Ward (Dewey's Children); Jonah Hill (Older Nate)

Mock bio-pic tracing the turbulent and triumphant career of musician Dewey Cox.

## SWEENEY TODD: THE DEMON BARBER OF FLEET STREET

(DREAMWORKS/WARNER BROS.) Producers, Richard D. Zanuck, Walter Parkes, Laurie MacDonald, John Logan; Executive Producer, Patrick McCormick; Co-Producer, Katterli Frauenfelder; Director, Tim Burton; Screenplay, John Logan, based on the musical *Sweeney Todd: The Demon Barber of Fleet Street* by Stephen Sondheim and Hugh Wheeler from an adaptation of *Sweeney Todd* by Christopher Bond; Photography, Darius Wolski; Editor, Chris Lebenzon; Music and Songs, Stephen Sondheim; Designer, Dante Ferretti; Costumes, Colleen Atwood; Visual Effects Supervisor, Chas Jarrett; Associate Producer, Derek Frey; Casting, Susie Figgis; a Parkes/MacDonald production and a Zanuck Co. production; Dolby; Deluxe color; Rated R; Running time: 117 minutes; Release date: December 21, 2007.

Helena Bonham Carter, Edward Sanders

Johnny Depp, Alan Rickman © DREAMWORKS/WARNER BROS.

### Cast

Sweeney Todd (Benjamin Barker)  **Johnny Depp**
Mrs. Lovett  **Helena Bonham Carter**
Judge Turpin  **Alan Rickman**
Beadle Bamford  **Timothy Spall**
Adolfo Pirelli  **Sacha Baron Cohen**
Johanna  **Jayne Wisner**
Anthony Hope  **Jamie Campbell Bower**
Toby  **Edward Sanders**
Beggar Woman  **Laura Michelle Kelly**
Mr. Fogg  **Philip Philmar**
Baby Johanna  **Gracie May, Ava May, Gabriella Freeman**
Policemen  **Jody Halse, Aron Paramor, Lee Whitlock**
Pirelli/Todd Customers  **Nick Haverson, Mandy Holliday**
Elixir Sniffing Customer  **Colin Higgins**
Gasping Man  **John Paton**
Contest Bald Man  **Graham Bohea**
Boy Prisoner  **Daniel Lusardi**
Man in Need of a Shave  **Ian McLarnon**
Shave Customer, Slit Throat  **Phill Woodfine**
Happy Customer  **Toby Hefferman**
Happy Customer's Wife  **Charlotte Child**
Happy Customer's Child  **Kira Woolman**
and Helen Slaymaker, Jess Murphy, Nicholas Hewetson, Adam Roach, Marcus Cunningham (Jolly Friends); David McKail (Minister); Gemma Grey, Sue Maund, Emma Hewitt (Inmates); Buck Holland (Barber Customer); Peter Mountain (Fleet Street Dandy); Harry Taylor (Mr. Lovett); Stephen Ashfield, Jerry Judge, Norman Rees, Jonathan Williams, William Oxborrow, Tom Pearce, Laura Sanchez, Johnson Willis, Jon-Paul Hevey, Liza Sadovy, Jane Fowler, Gaye Brown (Pie Customers)

Johnny Depp

Jamie Campbell Bower, Johnny Depp

Laura Michelle Kelly (center)

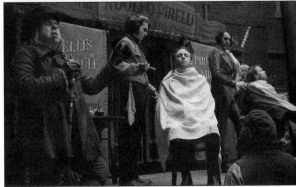

Timothy Spall, Johnny Depp, Mandy Holliday, Sacha Baron Cohen, Nick Haverson

Escaping from prison after being sent away on a trumped-up charge, barber Benjamin Barker returns to London in the guise of Sweeney Todd in order to extract revenge on the judge who ruined his life and stole his family from him.

2007 Academy Award winner for Best Art Direction. This film received additional nominations for Actor (Johnny Depp) and Costume Design.

# NATIONAL TREASURE: BOOK OF SECRETS

Nicolas Cage, Justin Bartha, Jon Voight

(WALT DISNEY PICTURES) Producers, Jerry Bruckheimer, Jon Turteltaub; Executive Producers, Mike Stenson, Chad Oman, Barry Waldman, Charles Segars; Director, Jon Turteltaub; Screenplay, The Wibberlys; Story, Gregory Poirier, The Wibberleys, Ted Elliott, Terry Rossio; Photography, John Schwartzman; Designer, Dominic Watkins; Costumes, Judianna Makovsky; Music, Trevor Rabin; Music Supervisor, Bob Badami; Casting, Ronna Kress; a Jerry Bruckheimer films presentation of a Junction Entertainment production in association with Saturn Films; Distributed by Buena Vista; Dolby; Super 35 Widescreen; Technicolor; Rated PG; 124 minutes; Release date: December 21, 2007

## Cast

| | |
|---|---|
| Ben Gates | **Nicolas Cage** |
| Riley Poole | **Justin Bartha** |
| Abigail Chase | **Diane Kruger** |
| Patrick Gates | **Jon Voight** |
| Emily Appleton | **Helen Mirren** |
| Mitch Wilkinson | **Ed Harris** |
| Sadusky | **Harvey Keitel** |
| The President | **Bruce Greenwood** |
| Connor | **Ty Burrell** |
| Daniel | **Michael Maize** |
| Seth | **Timothy V. Murphy** |
| FBI Agent Spellman | **Alicia Coppola** |
| FBI Agent Hendricks | **Armando Riesco** |
| Dr. Nichols | **Albert Hall** |
| Thomas Gates | **Joel Gretsch** |
| John Wilkes Booth | **Christian Camargo** |
| Michael O'Laughlen | **Brent Briscoe** |
| Charles Gates | **Billy Unger** |
| Agent Craig | **Michael Manuel** |
| Agent Hooper | **Brad Rowe** |
| Lincoln Conspiracy Kid | **Zachary Gordon** |
| Palace Guard Haggis | **Peter Woodward** |
| Control Room Guards | **Olivier Muirhead, Larry Cedar** |
| Agent Hammer | **Troy Winbush** |
| Agent Sledge | **Billy Devlin** |

and William R. Johnson (Agent Stander), Richard Cutting (Agent Tyme), Alicia Leigh Willis (Lady Customer), Rachel Wood (Girl Customer), Lisa Sheldon (Jacqueline), Natalie Dreyfuss (Angry College Girl), Michael Stone Forrest (Press Secretary), David Copeland Goodman (Deputy Press Secretary), Susan Lynskey (Asst. Press Secretary), Patrizia Dizebra (Press Secretary's Secretary), Grant Thompson (Boat Patrolman), Frank Herzog (Frank), Mary Ellen Aviano (Senator's Wife), Jon Abel (Senator), Eric W. Carlson (Air Force General), Randy Travis (Celebrity Music Star), Mary Firestone (FBI Agent Doer), Robert C. Koch (FBI Agent Stayres), Emerson Brooks (FBI Agent Steppes), Tim Talman (FBI Agent Cade), Steve Hibbert (Jonathan Emmett (Palace Guard Sholder), Emily Joyce (Palace Guide), Glenn Beck (Abraham Lincoln), Judy Renihan (Mary Todd Lincoln), Susan Beresford (Mrs. Moutchessington), Demetri Goritsas (Asa Trenchard), Charity Reindorp (Augusta), C.C. Smiff (Major Rathbone), David Ury (Barkeep), Milsey Peter Miles (Beer Truck Driver), Ben Homewood (Taxi Passenger), Mike McCafferty (Snooty Historian), Russ Widdall (Treasure Frantic), Hans G. Struhar (Range Rover Owner), Poetri (Mover), John Travis (Helicopter Pilot Mike)

Bruce Greenwood, Nicolas Cage © WALT DISNEY PICTURES

When newly uncovered pages from John Wilkes Booth's diary implicate his ancestor as a co-conspirator in the Lincoln assassination, Ben Gates sets out to find out the truth behind this shocking revelation. Sequel to the 2004 Disney film *National Treasure*, with the principals repeating their roles.

# P.S. I LOVE YOU

James Marsters, Gerard Butler, Gina Gershon, Lisa Kudrow

Gina Gershon, Hilary Swank

(WARNER BROS.) Producers, Wendy Finerman, Broderick Johnson, Andrew A. Kosove, Molly Smith; Executive Producers, John H. Starke, Lisa Zupan, James Hollond, Donald A. Starr, Daniel J.B. Taylor; Director, Richard LaGravenese; Screenplay, Richard LaGravenese, Steven Rogers; based on the novel by Cecelia Ahern; Photography, Terry Stacey; Designer, Shepherd Frankel; Costumes, Cindy Evans; Editor, David Moritz; Music, John Powell; Music Supervisor, Mary Ramos; Associate Producer, Julie Huntsinger; Casting, Amanda Mackey, Cathy Sandrich Gelfond; an Alcon Entertainment presentation of a Wendy Finerman production, in association with Grosvenor Park Films; Dolby; Color; Rated PG-13; 126 minutes; Release date: December 21, 2007.

## Cast

Holly Kennedy **Hilary Swank**
Gerry Kennedy **Gerard Butler**
Denise Hennessey **Lisa Kudrow**
Sharon McCarthy **Gina Gershon**
John McCarthy **James Marsters**
Patricia Rawley **Kathy Bates**
Daniel Connelly **Harry Connick Jr.**
and Nellie McKay (Ciara); Jeffrey Dean Morgan (William Gallagher); Dean Winters (Tom); Anne Kent (Rose Kennedy); Brian McGrath (Martin Kennedy); Sherie Rene Scott (Barbara); Susan Blackwell (Vicky); Michael Countryman (Ted); Roger Rathburn (Minister); Rita Gardner (Elderly Woman); Gayton Scott (Bridal Shop Tailor); Brian Munn (Patsy); Shepherd Frankel (Guy with Clipboard); Richard Smith (Bouncer); Mike Doyle (Leprechaun); Don Sparks (Mailman); Caris Vujcec (Waitress); Alexandra McGuinness (Local Gal); Aonghus Og McAnally (Bartender); Christopher Whalen, Timo Schnellinger (Men); Danny Calvert, Fred Inkley, Marcus Collins, Richard B. Watson, James Cronin (Gay Men); Matthew Martin, Mark McNutt, Brocton Pierce, Kevin Witt (Bar Patrons)

Hilary Swank, Harry Connick Jr. © WARNER BROS.

Grieving over the death of her husband, Holly Kennedy is surprised to discover that he has arranged to have letters from him arrive for her at different intervals, in an effort to help her overcome her loss.

Jeffrey Dean Morgan

# THE WATER HORSE

Alex Etel

Alex Etel, Crusoe, Priyanka Xi © COLUMBIA PICTURES

(COLUMBIA) Producers, Robert Bernstein, Douglas Rae, Barrie M. Osborne, Charlie Lyons; Executive Producers, Jay Russell, Charles Newirth; Director, Jay Russell; Screenplay, Robert Nelson Jacobs; Based on the book by Dick King-Smith; Photography, Oliver Stapleton; Designer, Tony Burrough; Costumes, John Bloomfield; Music, James Newton Howard; Music Supervisor, Denise Luiso; Song: *"Back Where You Belong (Theme from 'The Water Horse')"* written and performed by Sinéad O'Connor; Editor, Mark Warner; Senior Visual Effects Supervisor, Joe Letteri; Casting, Susie Figgis; New Zealand Casting, Liz Mullane; a Revolution Studios, Walden Media, Beacon Pictures presentation of an Ecosse Films production; American-British; Dolby; Color; Rated PG; 111 minutes; Release date: December 25, 2007.

## Cast

Anne MacMorrow  **Emily Watson**
Angus MacMorrow  **Alex Etel**
Lewis Mowbray  **Ben Chaplin**
Captain Hamilton  **David Morrissey**
Kirstie MacMorrow  **Priyanka Xi**
Sgt. Strunk  **Marshall Napier**
Sgt. Walker  **Joel Tobeck**
Lt. Wormsley  **Erroll Shand**
Older Angus  **Brian Cox**
Jock McGowan  **Bruce Allpress**
and Geraldine Brophy (Gracie); Edward Campbell (Hughie); Nathan Christopher Haase, Megan Katherine (Tourists); Craig Hall (Charlie MacMorrow); Ian Harcourt (Jimmy McGarry); William Johnson (Clyde); Peter Corrigan, Rex Hurst (Jimmy's Buddies); Carl Dixon (Gunner Corbin); Elliot Lawless (Beach Kid); Lorraine McDonald (William's Mother); Edward Newborn (Cpl. Grubbs); Louis Owen Collins (Young Angus); Phil Peleton (Soldier); William Russell (William); Ben Van Lier (Gunner Rapp); Sid, Ralph (Churchill)

Crusoe

Emily Watson, Ben Cooper

In Scotland during World War II, young Angus MacMorrow finds an unusual egg that brings forth a mythical water horse who continues to grow at an alarmingly fast rate.

**GRINDHOUSE**
Above: Rose McGowan, Kurt Russell
© DIMENSION FILMS

**THE KITE RUNNER**
Left: Shaun Toub
© DREAMWORKS/PARAMOUNT VANTAGE

**ACROSS THE UNIVERSE**
Above: Evan Rachel Wood,
Jim Sturgess, T. V. Carpio
© COLUMBIA PICTURES

**MUSIC AND LYRICS**
Right: Drew Barrymore, Hugh Grant
© WARNER BROTHERS

**AMERICAN GANGSTER**
Above: Common, Warner Miller,
Denzel Washington, J. Kyle Manzay,
Chiwetel Ejiofor, Albert Jones
© UNIVERSAL STUDIOS

**HARRY POTTER**
Left: Daniel Radcliffe, Evanna Lynch
© WARNER BROS.

**ATONEMENT**
Above: Keira Knightley
© FOCUS FEATURES

**EASTERN PROMISES**
Right: Viggo Mortensen,
Armin Mueller-Stahl
© FOCUS FEATURES

## I'M NOT THERE
Above: Heath Ledger
© WEINSTEIN CO.

## THE ASSASSINATION OF
## JESSE JAMES BY THE
## COWARD ROBERT FORD
Left: Brad Pitt, Casey Affleck
© WARNER BROS.

## NO COUNTRY
## FOR OLD MEN
Above: Josh Brolin

© MIRAMAX/PARAMOUNT VANTAGE

## BEE MOVIE
Right: Mooseblood, Barry B. Benson

© DREAMWORKS/PARAMOUNT

**SWEENEY TODD**
Above: Jamie Campbell Bower
© DREAMWORKS/WARNER BROS.

**THE GREAT DEBATERS**
Left: Jurnee Smollet,
Denzel Whitaker, Nate Parker
© METRO-GOLDWYN-MAYER

ZODIAC
Above: Robert Downey Jr.,
Jake Gyllenhaal
© PARAMOUNT PICTURES

SUPERBAD
Right: Michael Cera, Jonah Hill
© COLUMBIA PICTURES

**BEOWULF**
Top: Grendel's Mother, Beowulf
© PARAMOUNT PICTURES

**SIMPSONS MOVIE**
Above, right: Marge Simpson, Homer Simpson
© 20TH CENTURY FOX

**ENCHANTED**
Left: Patrick Dempsey, Amy Adams
© DISNEY ENTERPRISES

**INTO THE WILD**
Above: Emile Hirsch
© PARAMOUNT VANTAGE

**I AM LEGEND**
Right: Sam, Will Smith
© WARNER BROS.

## THE BOURNE ULTIMATUM
Left: Matt Damon, Julia Stiles
© UNIVERSAL STUDIOS

## KNOCKED UP
Above, top: Katherine Heigl, Seth Rogen
© UNIVERSAL STUDIOS

## AWAY FROM HER
Above, bottom: Julie Christie, Gordon Pinsent
© LIONSGATE

**3:10 TO YUMA**
Above: Russell Crowe, Christian Bale
© LIONSGATE

**THE DIVING BELL
AND THE BUTTERFLY**
Right: Emmanuelle Seigner
© MIRAMAX FILMS

**GONE BABY GONE**
Above, top: Titus Welliver, Amy Ryan
© MIRAMAX FILMS

**BREACH**
Above, bottom: Ryan Phillippe, Chris Cooper
© UNIVERSAL STUDIOS

**LA VIE EN ROSE**
Left: Marion Cotillard
© PICTUREHOUSE

**SICKO**
Above, top: Michael Moore
© LIONSGATE

**TRANSFORMERS**
Above, bottom: Optimus Prime
© DREAMWORKS/PARAMOUNT

**DISTURBIA**
Right: Shia LaBeouf
© DREAMWORKS

**BRIDGE TO TERABITHIA**
Left: Josh Hutcherson
© WALT DISNEY PICTURES

**300**
Below: Giovanni Cimino,
Lena Headey, Gerard Butler
© WARNER BROS.

**THERE WILL BE BLOOD**
Above: Daniel Day Lewis, Ciaran Hinds
© PARAMOUNT VANTAGE

**HAIRSPRAY**
Right: Christopher Walken, John Travolta
© NEW LINE CINEMA

# THE GREAT DEBATERS

(MGM) Producers, Todd Black, Kate Forte, Oprah Winfrey, Joe Roth; Executive Producers, Bob Weinstein, Harvey Weinstein; Co-Producer, Molly Allen; Director, Denzel Washington; Screenplay, Robert Eisele; Story, Robert Eisele, Jeffrey Porro, based on the article by Tony Scherman; Photography, Philippe Rousselot; Editor, Hughes Winborne; Music, James Newton Howard, Peter Golub; Music Supervisor, G. Marq Roswell; Designer, David J. Bomba; Costumes, Sharen Davis; Casting, Denise Chamian; a Weinstein Co. presentation of a Harpo Films production; Dolby; Panavision; Technicolor; Rated PG-13; 127 minutes; Release date: December 25, 2007.

Jermaine Williams, Denzel Whitaker, Jurnee Smollett, Nate Parker

## Cast

Melvin B. Tolson  **Denzel Washington**
James Farmer Sr.  **Forest Whitaker**
Henry Lowe  **Nate Parker**
Samantha Booke  **Jurnee Smollett**
James Farmer Jr.  **Denzel Whitaker**
Hamilton Burgess  **Jermaine Williams**
Ruth Tolson  **Gina Ravera**
Sheriff Dozier  **John Heard**
Pearl Farmer  **Kimberly Elise**
Helen Farmer  **Devyn Tyler**
Nathaniel Farmer  **Trenton McClain Boyd**
Deputy  **Ritchie Montgomery**
Pig Owner  **Jackson Walker**
Pig Farmer  **Tim Parati**
Dunbar Reed  **Robert X. Golphin**
Harland Osbourne  **Justice Leak**
Harvard Debaters  **Glen Powell Jr., Brad Watkins**
Harvard Dean  **Brian Smiar**
Wilson  **Damien Leake**
Paul Quinn Debaters  **Voltaire Rico Sterling, Stephen Rider**
Paul Quinn Debate Judge  **Gordon Daniels**
Oklahoma City College Debaters  **Donny Boaz, Samuel Elliott Whisnant**
Dr. Jennings  **Bonnie Johnson**
Benita  **Charissa Allen**
Trudell  **Michael Beasley**
Enormous Man  **Gary Mathis**
and George Wilson (Samuel); Fahnlohnee R. Harris (Clementine); Harold X. Evans (William Taylor); J.D. Evermore (Capt. Wainwright); Sharon Jones (Lila); Kelvin Payton (Joseph); Southey Blanton (White Labor Organizer); Michael Mattison, Jeff Braun (White Sharecroppers); Milton R. Gipson (Prairie View Professor); Frank Ridley (Security Guard); Jeremiah Kissel (Radio Announcer at Harvard Debate); Jack Radosta (White Man at Lynching); Marcus Lyle Brown (Howard Debater #1); Alvin Youngblood Hart, Dominique Flemons, Justin Robinson, Rhiannon Giddens (Juke Joint Musicians); Ahmad Powell (Fisk Professor)

Denzel Washington

During the Depression, at all-black Wiley College in Texas, Professor Melvin Tolson chooses four students for a debate team he hopes will eventually compete with Harvard.

Forest Whitaker, Denzel Washington © METRO-GOLDWYN-MAYER

# THE BUCKET LIST

Jack Nicholson

(WARNER BROS.) Producers, Craig Zadan, Neil Meron, Alan Greisman, Rob Reiner; Executive Producers, Jeffrey Stott, Travis Knox, Justin Zackham; Co-Producer, Frank Capra III; Director, Rob Reiner; Screenplay, Justin Zackham; Photography, John Schwartzman; Designer, Bill Brzeski; Costumes, Molly Maginnis; Editor, Robert Leighton; Music, Marc Shaiman; Visual Effects, Ring of Fire, Illusions Arts; Casting, Jane Jenkins, Janet Hirshenson; a Zadan Meron/Reiner Greisman production; Dolby; Technicolor; Rated PG-13; 97 minutes; Release date: December 25, 2007.

## Cast

Edward Cole **Jack Nicholson**
Carter Chambers **Morgan Freeman**
Thomas **Sean Hayes**
Virginia Chambers **Beverly Todd**
Roger Chambers **Alfonso Freeman**
Angelica **Rowena King**
Dr. Hollins **Rob Morrow**
Kai **Annton Berry Jr.**
Shandra **Verda Bridges**
Maya **Destiny Brownridge**
Lee **Brian Copeland**
Instructor **Ian Anthony Dale**
Emily **Jennifer Defrancisco**
Administrator **Angela Gardner**
Mechanic **Noel Guglielmi**
Manny **Jonathan Hernandez**
County Health Director **Hugh B. Holub**
Elizabeth Chambers **Andrea J. Johnson**
Flight Attendant **Dawn Lewis**
Tattoo Artist **Jordan Lund**
Board Chairman **Richard McGonagle**
Richard **Jonathan Mangum**
Nurse Shing **Karen Maruyama**
Attractive Woman #1 **Amber Mead**
and John O'Brien (Executive #1); Serena Reeder (Rachel); Christopher Stapleton (Kyle); Taylor Ann Thompson (Edward's Granddaughter); Alex Trebek (Himself); Roy Vongtama (Doctor #1)

Learning they have terminal cancer, millionaire Edward Cole and his hospital roommate Carter Chambers decide to do all the things they've always wanted to do before their time is up.

Morgan Freeman, Beverly Todd © WARNER BROS.

Jack Nicholson, Morgan Freeman

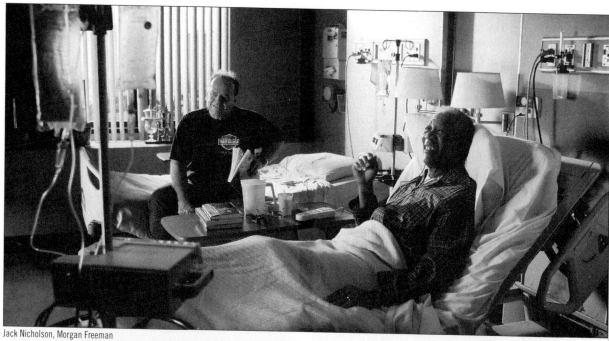

Jack Nicholson, Morgan Freeman

Sean Hayes

Ian Anthony Dale, Jack Nicholson

Rowena King, Morgan Freeman

# THERE WILL BE BLOOD

(PARAMOUNT VANTAGE/MIRAMAX) Producers, Paul Thomas Anderson, Jo Anne Sellar, Daniel Lupi; Executive Producers, Scott Rudin, Eric Schlosser, David Williams; Director/Screenplay, Paul Thomas Anderson; Inspired by the novel *Oil!* by Upton Sinclair; Photography, Robert Elswit; Editor, Dylan Tichenor; Music, Jonny Greenwood; Designer, Jack Fisk; Costumes, Mark Bridges; Stunts, Jeff Habberstad, Myke Schwartz; Casting, Cassandra Kulukundis; a JoAnne Sellar/Ghoulardi Film Co. production; Dolby; Panavision; Deluxe color; Rated R; 158 minutes; Release date: December 26, 2007.

Dillon Freasier, Daniel Day-Lewis

## Cast

Daniel Plainview  **Daniel Day-Lewis**
Eli Sunday/Paul Sunday  **Paul Dano**
Henry Brands  **Kevin J. O'Connor**
Fletcher Hamilton  **Ciarán Hinds**
H.W. Plainview  **Dillon Freasier**
Mary Sunday  **Sydney McCallister**
Abel Sunday  **David Willis**
H.M. Tilford  **David Warshofsky**
William Bandy  **Colton Woodward**
Adult Mary Sunday  **Colleen Foy**
Adult H.W  **Russell Harvard**
Mother Sunday  **Christine Olejniczak**
Ruth Sunday  **Kellie Hill**
H.B. Ailman  **Barry Del Sherman**
Prescott  **Paul F. Tompkins**
Mr. Bankside  **Randall Carver**
Mrs. Bankside  **Coco Leigh**
Al Rose  **James Downey**
Gene Blaize  **Dan Swallow**
Charlie Wrightsman  **Robert Arber**
Geologist  **Bob Bell**
Ben Blaut  **David Williams**
Mrs. Hunter  **Irene G. Hunter**
Elizabeth  **Hope Elizabeth Reeves**
Little Boston Doctor  **John Chitwood**
J.J. Carter  **Tom Doyle**
L.P. Clair  **John Burton**
Bandy  **Hans Howes**
H.W.'s Interpreter  **Robert Hills**
and Martin Stringer, Matthew Braden Stringer, Jacob Stringer, Joseph Mussey (Silver Assay Workers); Harrison Taylor, Stockton Taylor (Baby H.W.); Kevin Breznahan (Signal Hill Man); Jim Meskimen (Signal Hill Married Man); Erica Sullivan (Signal Hill Woman); Joy Rawls, Louise Gregg, Amber Roberts (Eli Followers); John W. Watts, Robert Caroline, Barry Bruce (Oil Workers); Robert Barge (Bartender); Ronald Krut, Huey Rhudy, Steven Barr (Standard Oil Men); Rev. Bob Bock (Priest); Vince Froio, Phil Shelly (Plainview Servants)

Paul Dano, Daniel Day-Lewis © PARAMOUNT VANTAGE

Daniel Day-Lewis

Knowing there is oil to be found in a desolate area of California, prospector Daniel Plainview lays claim to the land, turning it into a booming industrial center while encountering opposition from preacher Eli Sunday.

2007 Academy Award winner for Best Actor (Daniel Day-Lewis) and Best Cinematography. This film received additional nominations for Picture, Director, Adapted Screenplay, Art Direction, Film Editing, and Sound Editing.

Paul Dano

Daniel Day-Lewis, Dillon Freasier

Dillon Freasier, Paul Dano

# DOMESTIC FILMS

## 2007 RELEASES
### JANUARY 1–DECEMBER 31

# CODE NAME: THE CLEANER

(NEW LINE CINEMA) Producers, Jay Stern, Eric C. Rhone, Brett Ratner, Cedric the Entertainer; Executive Producers, Anthony Rhulen, A.J. Dix, William Shively, Lucy Liu, Toby Emmerich, Mark Kaufman, Matt Moore; Co-Producers, John Cheng, Brad Jensen, Robert Merilees; Co-Executive Producer, J. David Brewington Jr.; Director, Les Mayfield; Screenplay, Robert Adetuyi, George Gallo; Photography, David Franco; Designer, Douglas Higgins; Costumes, Jenni Gullet; Editor, Michael Matzdorff; Music, George S. Clinton; Music Supervisor, Kevin Edelman; Casting, Heike Brandstatter, Coreen Mayrs; a RAT Entertainment/a Bird & a Bear/FilmEngine production, presented in association with FilmEngine; DTS Stereo; Technicolor; Rated PG-13; 91 minutes; Release date: January 5, 2007.

## Cast

Cedric the Entertainer (Jake Rodgers); Lucy Liu (Gina); Nicollette Sheridan (Diane); Mark Dacascos (Eric Hauck); Callum Keith Rennie (Shaw); Niecy Nash (Jacuzzi); DeRay Davis (Ronnie); Will Patton (Riley); Kevin McNulty (Dr. Soames); B.J. Davis (Old Timer); Bart Anderson (Charlie); Tom Butler (Crane); Robert Clarke (The Butler); Rick Tae (Mini Bar Attendant); Kurt Max Runte (Dead FBI Agent); David Lewis (Man in Car); Gina Holden (Young Assistant); Kimani Ray Smith (Drug Lord); Dave Hospes, Douglas Chapman, Brad Kelly, Nickolas Baric, Simon Burnett (Agents); Phillip Mitchell, Mike Desabrais (Digital Arts Security Guards); Maxine Miller (Old Lady); Jacqueline Ann Steuart (Hotel Receptionist)

Lucy Liu, Cedric the Entertainer in *Code Name: The Cleaner* © NEW LINE CINEMA

# EVER SINCE THE WORLD ENDED

*Ever Since the World Ended* © CYAN PICTURES

(CYAN PICTURES) Producers, Calum Grant, Joshua Atesh Litle; Executive Producer, Kate Montgomery; Directors, Calum Grant, Joshua Atesh Litle; Screenplay, Calum Grant; Photography, Joshua Atesh Litle; Editors, David Driver, Joshua Atesh Litle; an Epidemic Films production; Color; Widescreen DV; Not rated; 78 minutes; Release date: January 10, 2007.

## Cast

Adam Savage (The Engineer); Mark Routhier (Mad Mark); Angie Thieriot (Mama Eva); Josiah Clark (Josiah, the Woodsman); Jessica Viola (Jessica, a Writer); Dan Plumlee (Dan, a Trapper); Linda Noveroske (Linda); Ronald Chase (Joseph, the Teacher); James Curry (James); Brad Olsen (Santosh, a Traveller); Ed Noisecat (Ed, an Artist); Simon Thieriot, Stewart Fallon (Surfers); Dr. Mary Rutherord (Mary, the Doctor); Aubrey Ankrum (Guy with Hammer); Christine Cannavo (Assistant Engineer); Chris Chambre (Violinist); Rashida Clendening (The Music Teacher); Sally Dana (Sally, House Burning Victim); Chiara Deluca (Student); David Driver (Dave, the Go-to-Guy); Ann Feehan (The Librarian); George Frangides (George, the Curator); Marcus Gorman (Lost Generation Teenager); Matt "TK" Kinney (Matt, North Trip Hiker); Kai Langenberg (Kai, a Fisherman); Stella Lochman (Girl Who Finds Gun); Greg Lucey (Greg, the Stockbroker); Ava Sandripour (Confident Teenager)

# WITH MY BACK TO THE WORLD

(NEW DEAL FILMS) Producer/Director, Mary Lance; Photography, Dyanna Taylor, Mary Lance; Music, Steve Peters; Editors, Mary Lance, Brad Wolfley; Stereo; Color; Not rated; 60 minutes; Release date: January 10, 2007. Documentary on abstract expressionist Agnes Martin.

# GOD GREW TIRED OF US

*God Grew Tired of Us* © NEWMARKET FILMS

(NEWMARKET) Producers, Christopher Quinn, Molly Bradford Pace; Executive Producers, Brad Pitt, Adam Schlesinger, Jack Schneider; Co-Producers, Eric Gilliland, Dermot Mulroney; Director, Christopher Quinn; Photography, Paul Daley; Editor, Geoffrey Richman; Music, Mark McAdam, Mark Nelson, Jamie Staff; Narrator, Nicole Kidman; a Lost Boys of Sudan presentation; Color; HD; Not rated; 86 minutes; Release date: January 12, 2007. Documentary sequel to *Lost Boys of Sudan* (Shadow, 2004), following the lives of three young Sudanese refugees adjusting to life in the United States; with John Bul Dau, Panther Bior, Daniel Abul Pach.

# PRIMEVAL

(HOLLYWOOD PICTURES) Producers, Gavin Polone; Executive Producers, Jamie Tarses, Mitch Engel; Director, Michael Katleman; Screenplay, John Brancato, Michael Ferris; Photography, Edward J. Pei; Designer, Johnny Breedt; Costumes, Diana Cilliers; Editor, Gabriel Wrye; Music, John Frizzell; Visual Effects Supervisor, Paul Linden; Casting, John Papsidera; Distributed by Buena Vista; a Pariah production; Dolby; Panavision; Color; Rated R; 94 minutes; Release date: January 12, 2007.

### Cast

Dominic Purcell (Tim Manfrey); Orlando Jones (Steven Johnson); Brooke Langton (Aviva Masters); Jürgen Prochnow (Jacob Krieg); Gideon Emery (Matthew Collins); Dumisani Mbebe (Harry); Gabriel Malema (Jojo); Linda Mpondo (Gold Tooth); Lehlohonolo Makoko (Beanpole); Eddy Bekombo (Ato); Chris April (Captain); Ernest Ndhlovu (Shaman); Erika Wessels (Dr. Cathy Andrews); Vivian Moodley (Indian UN Officer); Lika van den Bergh (Rachel); Patrick Lyster (Roger Sharpe); Andrew Whaley (Senator Porter); Kevin Otto (UBN Newscaster); Sonia Mbele (Ona); Mathias Tabotmbi (Villager); Kgmotoso Motlosi (Shaman's Son); Thandi Nugbani (Shaman's Wife); Michael Mabizela (Laborer); Thomas Kariuki, Azeez Danmola (Fishermen); Pamphile Nicaye, Emmanuel Nkeshiman, Pierre Calver Nsabimana, Henry Jeane (Burundi Drummers)

# ALONE WITH HER

(IFC FIRST TAKE) Producers, Tom Engelman, Robert Engelman; Director/Screenplay, Eric Nicholas; Photography, Nathan Wilson; Designer, John Mott; Editor, Carl Coughlin; Music, David Russo; Music Supervisor, Peymon Maskan; Casting, Jay Scully, Annie McCarthy; an IFC First Take/The Weinstein Co. production; Color/Black and white; HD; DV; Not rated; 79 minutes; Release date: January 17, 2007.

### Cast

Colin Hanks (Doug), Ana Claudia Talancon (Amy), Jordana Spiro (Jen), Jonathan Trent (Matt), Alex Boling (Barrista), Anthony Armatrading (Cop)

# THE GOODTIMESKID

Sara Diaz in *The GoodTimesKid* © CROOKED TEETH PRODS.

(CROOKED TEETH PRODS.) Producers, Georgina Garcia Riedel, Sara Diaz, Ernesto Garabito; Executive Producers, Richard Abramowitz, Andrew Mencher; Director/Editor, Azazel Jacobs; Screenplay, Gerardo Naranjo, Azazel Jacobs; Photography, Azazel Jacobs, Gerardo Naranjo, Eric Curtis; Designer, Sara Diaz; Music, Mandy Hoffman; Technicolor; Not rated; 73 minutes; Release date: January 17, 2007.

### Cast

Gerardo Naranjo (Rodolfo Cano II); Sara Diaz (Diaz); Azazel Jacobs (Rodolfo Cano); Lucy Dodd (Sidekick); Pat Reynolds (Neighbor); Gill Dennis (Sergeant); Melissa Paull (Ex-Girlfriend); Ivor Pyres, Caro Datum, Toni Oswald, Brian O'Keffe (Birthday Party Guests); Pat DeWitt (Bartender); Rene Navarette, Eddie Navarette, Dick Rude, Anton Schneider, Cali DeWitt (Tough Guys); Robert Rudder (Soldier); Anton Thaqi, Darren Hinton (Enlistees); Marcos Menendez, Danielle Owens, Alessandro Mastrobuono (Soap Opera Actors); Jessica Lynn Sattel (Bus Rider)

# TWO WRENCHING DEPARTURES

Jack Smith in *Two Wrenching Departures*

(INDEPENDENT) Director/Editor, Ken Jacobs; Color; Not rated; 90 minutes; Release date: January 12, 2007. Experimental film, with Jack Smith.

# SACCO AND VANZETTI

(FIRST RUN FEATURES) Producers, Peter Miller, Amy Carey Linton; Executive Producer, Jesse Crawford; Director, Peter Miller; Photography, Stephen McCarthy; Music, John T. Labarbera; Editor, Amy Carey Linton; a Willow Pond Films production; Color/Black and white; Not rated; 81 minutes; Release date: January 21, 2007. Documentary on Italian immigrants Nicola Sacco and Bartolomeo Vanzetti, who were tried for murder in a sensational trial of the 1920s; with the voices of John Turturro (Bartolomeo Vanzetti) and Tony Shalhoub (Nicola Sacco); John Ammerman, William Miller, Anthony Rodriguez, Holly Stevenson (Additional Voices)

Bartolomeo Vanzetti, Nicola Sacco in *Sacco and Vanzetti* ©FIRST RUN FEATURES

# CHINA BLUE

(BULLFROG FILMS) Producer/Director/Photography, Micha X. Peled; Music, Miriam Cutler; Editor, Manuel Tsingaris; an ITVS presentation of a Teddy Bear Films Inc. production; Color; DigiBeta; Not rated; 87 minutes; Release date: January 26, 2007. Documentary on the exploitation of Chinese factory workers.

*China Blue* © BULLFROG FILMS

# FROM OTHER WORLDS

(SHORELINE ENTERTAINMENT) Producers, Linda Moran, Rene Bastian, Diana E. Williams; Director/Screenplay, Barry Strugatz; Photography, Mo Flam; Designer, Charlotte Bourke; Costumes, Antonia Xereas; Editor, Joel Hirsch; Music, Pierre Foldes; Music Supervisor, Mark Wike; Visual Effects Supervisors, Christian D. Bruun, Michael Ventresco; Visual Effects, Quantumfilm, Red Scare; Casting, Jonathan Strauss; a Belladonna Prods. Presentation; Color; Not rated; 88 minutes; Release date: January 26, 2007.

### Cast

Cara Buono (Joanne Schwartzbaum), Isaach De Bankolé (Abraham), David Lansbury (Brian Schwartzbaum), Robert Peters (Steve), Melissa Leo (Miriam), Joel De La Fuente (Alien), Paul Lazar (Larry), Robert Downey Sr. (Baker), Quinn Shephard (Linda Schwartzbaum), Jonah Meyerson (Henry Schwartzbaum), Lori Tan Chinn (Mrs. Kim), Alberto Vazquez (Jerry), Laura Esterman (Psychiatrist), David Smilow (Science Reporter), Tyagi Schwartz (Rosselli), Dennis Albanese (Gambler), Rony Clanton (Frank), Jimmy Gary Jr. (Sam), Gregory Korostishevsky (Small Lab Assistant), Marcia Jean Kurtz (Brian's Mom), Jay Parks (Big Lab Assistant), Ed Wheeler (Guard), Sharon Wilkins (Jill)

# AN UNREASONABLE MAN

Ralph Nader in *An Unreasonable Man* © IFC FILMS

(IFC FIRST TAKE) Producer, Kevin O'Donnell; Executive Producers, Henriette Mantel, Stephen Skrovan; Directors, Henriette Mantel, Stephen Skrovan; Photography, Mark Raker, Leigh Wilson, John Chater, Matt Davis, Steve Elkins, Melissa Donovan, Sandra Chandler; Editors, Alexis Provost, Beth Gallagher; Music, Joe Kraemer; Researchers, Elizabeth Olson, Ellie Knaus; a Two Left Legs production; Color; HD; Not rated; 122 minutes; Release date: January 31, 2007. Documentary on crusading consumer advocate Ralph Nader; with Ralph Nader, Jay Acton, Theresa Amato, Pat Buchanan, Peter Camejo, Scott Carter, Joan Claybrook, John Conyers Jr., Karen Croft, Phil Donahue, James Fallows, Michael Feinstein, Todd Gitlin, Richard Grossman, Greg Kafoury, Jason Kafoury, Carl Mayer, Tarek Milleron, Morton Mintz, Ross Mirkarimi, Jim Musselman, Claire Nader, Laura Nader, Bryce Nelson, James Ridgeway, Harvey Rosenfield, Donald Ross, Rob Weissman, Dr. Sidney Wolfe.

# EAST OF HAVANA

(SONY BMG) Producers, Charlize Theron, Clark Peterson, Meagan Riley-Grant, Juan Carlos Saizarbitoria; Directors /Screenplay, Jauretsi Saizarbitoria, Emilia Menocal; Photography, Christophe Lanzenberg; Editor, Fernando Villena; Music, Paul Heck, Federico Fong; Music Supervisor, Paul Heck; a Denver and Delilah Films Production and Sugar Barons presentation; Color; DV; Not rated; 82 minutes; Release date: February 2, 2007. Documentary on Cuba's hip-hop culture.

## With

Soandres "Soandry" Del Rio Ferrer, Magyori Martinez Veitia, Michel "Mikki Flow" Hermida, Vladimir Abad, Daisy M. Abad, Norma Despaigne, Adrian "El Loco" Espronceda Serpa, Pablo Herrera, Ariel Fernandez Diaz, Carlos "Yimi Konclaze" Rodriguez, Reynor Hernandez Fernandez, Karel Betancocet Benitez, Randy Acosta, Humberto "Papa Humbertico" Cabrera, Denis "Deno" Penalver Medina, Carlos A. Cantero, Alexy "Pelon" Cantero, Axel Tosca.

# PUCCINI FOR BEGINNERS

(STRAND) Producers, Eden Wurmfeld, Gary Winick, Jake Abraham; Executive Producers, John Sloss, Steven Wilson, Jeffrey Roseman, Harvey Rothenberg; Director/Screenplay, Maria Maggenti; Photography, Mauricio Rubinstein; Designer, Aleta Shaffer; Costumes, Antonia Xereas; Editor, Susan Graef; Music, Terry Dame; Music Supervisor, Jim Black; Casting, Todd Thaler; an IFC Prods. presentation of an InDigEnt production in association with Eden Wurmfeld Films; Dolby; Color; HD; Not rated; 82 minutes; Release date: February 2, 2007.

## Cast

Elizabeth Reaser (Allegra); Justin Kirk (Philip); Gretchen Mol (Grace); Jennifer Dundas (Molly); Julianne Nicholson (Samantha); Tina Benko (Nell); Brian Letscher (Jeff); Will Bozarth (Jimmy); Kate Simses (Vivian); Ken Barnett (Scott); Becca Anderson (Waitress); Ashlie Atkinson (Woman on Bench); Jill DeMonstoy (Restaurant Patron); Yoshiro Kono (Sushi Chef); Nick Psinakis (Athletic Guy); Terrence Riordan (Jeff's Buddy); Kenji (Japanese Waiter); Chris LaPanta, Louie Rodriguez (Restaurant Patrons); Bridget Moloney (Actress)

Elizabeth Reaser, Gretchen Mol in *Puccini for Beginners* © STRAND RELEASING

# THE SITUATION

Connie Nielsen in *The Situation* © SHADOW RELEASING

(SHADOW) Producers, Liaquet Ahamed, Michael Sternberg, Neda Armian; Director, Philip Haas; Screenplay, Wendell Steavenson; Photography, Sean Bobbit; Costumes, Anita Yavich, Nezha Dakl; Music, Jeff Beal; Editor, Curtiss Clayton; a Red Wine Pictures production; Dolby; Color; Rated R; 11 minutes; Release date: February 2, 2007.

### Cast

Connie Nielsen (Anna Molyneux); Damian Lewis (Dan Murphy); Mido Hamada (Zaid); John Slattery (Col. Carrick); Tom McCarthy (Maj. Hanks); Mahmoud El Lozy (Duraid); Saïd Amadis (Sheikh Tahsin); Nasser Memarzia (Rafeeq); Omar Berdouni (Bashar); Driss Roukhe (Walid); Peter Eyre (U.S. Embassy Official); Shaun Evans (Wesley); Cobi Mohammed, Mohammed Moutawakil (Iraqi Solders); Mahmoudi M'Barek (Col. Jobouri); Salaheddine Debab, Mehdi Amalou (Bridge Boys); Fatiha Watili (Samira); Cherine Amar (Noor); Hamid Basket (Selim); Zenati Badredine (Drowned Boy's Father); Raqba Amine (Drowned Boy's Uncle); Jaoaud Boughaba (Old Petitioner); Zakaria Attifi, Mohammed Taleb, Adbelhak Lazali, Karam Ghazi (Policemen); Imad Rechiche, Hicham Immounsi (Zaid's Friends); Mohammed Attifi (Taxi Driver); Dan Murphy (Photo Editor); Wendell Steavenson (TV News Reporter); Youssef Brittel (Josef); Khadija Kanouni (Grandmother); Zidani Nabil (Walid's Henchman); Latifa Aboudi, Saida Nhili, Nezha Ait Moumen (Samarra Prostitutes); Sean Gullette (Investigating Officer on Boat); Jamal Laababsi (Butcher); Mehdi Jabori (Soccer Boy); Mehdi Jenani (Severed Hand Boy); Nezha Regragui (Bashar's Mother); Khalid M'Rimi (Translator); Abdelouahab Mouhaddine (Hamid Ali); Jayce Newton (Lt. Walker); Mehdi Wakass, Mounir Benfares (Samarra Kids); Naciri Hamid, Bourhaba (Mujahideens); Ali Hriouech (Kite Boy); Daniel Mulligan ("Journalist Down" U.S. Soldier); Fadila Boussekssou (Al Tawr Old Lady)

# FIRED!

Annabelle Gurwitch in *Fired!* © INTL. FILM CIRCUIT

(INTERNATIONAL FILM CIRCUIT/SHOUT! FACTORY) Producer/Screenplay, Annabelle Gurwitch; Executive Producer, Richard Foos; Directors/Photography/ Editors, Chris Bradley, Kyle Labrache; a Wherespetey?/Intl. Orange production; Color; DV; Not rated; 85 minutes; Release date: February 2, 2007. Documentary in which performers discuss instances when they were fired from an acting gig; with Tim Allen, Andy Borowitz, W. Bruce Cameron, David Cross, Andy Dick, Tate Donovan, Illeana Douglas, Jeff Gralin, Judy Gold, Annabelle Gurwitch, Jeff Kahn, Richard Kind, Anne Meara, Bob Odenkirk, Robert Reich, Jeffrey Ross, Walter Scheib, Harry Shearer, Sarah Silverman, Ben Stein, Fisher Stevens, Paul F. Tompkins, Fred Willard, Roy Zimmerman.

# CONSTELLATION

(FREESTYLE) Producers, Shannon Murphy, Jordan Walker-Pearlman; Executive Producers, Nancy Archuleta, Peter Kleidman, Gabe Neito, Morris Ruskin; Co-Executive Producer, Kristi Gamble; Director/Screenplay, Jordan Walker-Pearlman; Photography, John Njaga Demps; Designer, Liba Daniels; Costumes, Jeanette Guillermo; Editor, Allison Learned Wolfe; Music, Michael Bearden; Music Supervisor, Howie Dorough; a Dawa Movies presentation in association with Starship and Encounter Studios; Panavision; Color; Rated PG-13; 105 minutes; Release date: February 2, 2007.

### Cast

Billy Dee Williams (Helms Boxer), Zoe Saldana (Rosa Boxer), Lesley Ann Warren (Nancy), Hill Harper (Errol Hickman), Melissa De Sousa (Lucy Boxer), Rae Dawn Chong (Jenita), Gabrielle Union (Carmel Boxer), David Clennon (Bear), Clarence Williams III (Forrest Boxer), Ever Carradine (Celeste Korngold), Alec Newman (Kent), Shin Koyamada (Yosito), Daniel Bess (Young Bear), Howie Dorough (Alec, Cab Driver), Adam Nelson (Mathew the Cop), Glenn Plummer (Man #1), Tonea Stewart (Reverend), Jolene Andersen (Woman at Airport), Kathleen Arthur (Young Rosa), David Beier (Army Officer), Molly Beucher (Clerk #2), Omar Burgess (Frustrated Airport Customer), Dakota Carson (Airport Passenger), Erica Monique Coleman (Young Lucy), Joe Cook (Radio DJ), Michael Dean (Anthony Young), Stefan Dickerson (Musician), Ralph Gipson (Airport Employee), Chandler Horkman (Boy), Juliette Jeffers (Clerk), Vatecia L. Little (Funeral Director), Gabe Nieto (Officer Riviera), Morroco Omari (Teacher), Jim Piser (Bartender), Tre Rogers (Young Helms), Anna Rosenbaum (Soldier's Wife #1), Hannah White (Young Celeste)

# RAISING FLAGG

Matthew Arkin, Alan Arkin in *Raising Flagg* © CINEMA LIBRE

(CINEMA LIBRE) Producers, Neal Miller, Nancy Miller; Director, Neal Miller; Screenplay, Neal Miller, Nancy Miller, Dorothy Velasco; Based on the story *Don't You Cry for Me* by John D. Weaver; Photography, Erich Roland; Designer, David Sicotte; Costumes, Ron Leamon; Music, Alan Barcus, Les Hooper; Editors, Paul J. Coyne, Ken Morrisey; Casting, Cathy Henderson, Dori Zuckerman; a Rubicon Film Productions, Ltd. and Oregon Creative, LLC presentation. Dolby; Color; Rated PG-13: 103 minutes; Release date: February 2, 2007.

## Cast

Alan Arkin (Flagg Purdy), Glenne Headly (Ann Marie Purdy), Lauren Holly (Rachel Purdy), Barbara Dana (Ada Purdy), Austin Pendleton (Gus Falk), Richard Kind (Bill Reed), Matthew Arkin (Eldon Purdy), Daniel Quinn (Travis Purdy), Dawn Maxey (Linette Purdy), Robert Robinson (Gus' Lawyer), Jan Hoag (Judge Walker), Clifton James (Ed McIvor), Stephanie Lemelin (Jenny Purdy), Sherilyn Lawson (Paula, Ann Marie's Radio Client), Robert Blanche (Matt Durwood), Raissa Fleming (Grace Durwood), Melisa Kind (Lupe Rodriguez), Anna Stone (Bonnie Salmi), Wrick Jones (John Salmi), Joann Johnson (Gwen Cooper), George Fosgate (Foster Cooper), Heather Lea Garrick (Friend at Courthouse), Janet Penner (Jury Forman #3), Ernie Garrett (Al Smith), Betty Moyer (Cathy Smith), Julian Lamb (Matt Durwood, Jr.), Joshua Thorpe (Doug, Supermarket Punk), Chris Wright (Paul, Supermarket Punk), Lyssa Browne (Tammy Purdy), Jordan Fry (Porter Purdy), Benjamin Lewis (Travis Purdy, Jr.), Abby Lewis (Jamie Porter), Rebecca Nachison (Melinda, Casserole Lady), Vana O'Brien (Edith Purdy), Cheryl Grant (Ann Marie's Friend Andrea), Sylvia Welch (Ann Marie's Friend Sarah), Anne Oxenhandler (Friend at Grange Dance), Lealon Gordon (Gus' Stock Boy Andy)

# BURNING ANNIE

(LIGHTYEAR) Producer, Randy Mack; Executive Producer, David Bernstein; Director, Van Flesher; Screenplay, Randy Mack, Zack Ordynans; Photography, Stephan Schultze; Designers, Kenn Coplan, Jennifer Copp; Music, Dean Harada; Editors, Randy Mack, Chryss Terry, Jeff Orgill; Armak productions; Dolby; Color; Not rated; 95 minutes; Release date: February 7, 2007.

## Cast

Gary Lundy (Max), Sara Downing (Julie), Kim Murphy Zandell (Beth), Brian Klugman (Charles), Jay Paulson (Sam), Rini Bell (Amanda), Todd Duffey (Tommy), Kathleen Perkins (Jen), Jason Risner (Scott), Carrie Freedle (Sara), Jaisey Bates (Amy), Alex Bolano (Young Max), Jeanie Cheek (Judy), Randa Collins (Smokin' Co-Ed), Jim Damron (Building Manager), Teresa Gillmor (Librarian), David Hall (Andy), Regan Kerwin (Donna the Waitress), Randi Lehasky (Stacy), Clint McElroy (Max's Father), Keith Page (Mark), Evan Price (Adolescent Max), Merritt Shaw (Professor), George R. Snider III (Waiter), Amanda Troop (Lisa, Steve's Girl), Angel Zachel (Erica)

# OPERATION HOMECOMING: WRITING THE WARTIME EXPERIENCE

*Operation Homecoming* © THE DOCUMENTARY GROUP

(THE DOCUMENTARY GROUP) Producer/Director, Richard Robbins; Executive Producer, Tom Yellin; Screenplay Stories, Colby Buzzell ("Men in Black"), Edward Parker Gyokeres ("Camp Muckamungus"), Sangjoon Han ("Aftermath"), Ed Hrivnak ("Medavac Missions"), Jack Lewis ("Road Work"), John McCary ("To the Fallen"), Denis Prior ("Distant Thunder"), Michael Strobl ("Taking Chance"), Brian Turner ("Here, Bullet," "What Every Soldier Should Know," Ashbah"); Photography, Jason Ellson; Music, Ben Decter; Editor, Gillian McCarthy; Stereo; HDCAM Color; Not rated; 81 minutes; Release date: February 9, 2007. Documentary on U.S. troops' experiences in Iraq and Afghanistan, based on the soldiers' own writing; with Sharon D. Allen, Colby Buzzell, Richard Currey, Paul Fussell, Edward Parker Gyokeres, Joe Haldeman, Sangjoon Han, Ed Hrivnak, Yusef Komunyakaa, Jack Lewis, John McCary, Tim O'Brien, James Salter, Michael Strobl, Anthony Swofford, Michael Thomas, Brian Turner, Tobias Wolff; and the voices of Beau Bridges, Robert Duvall, Aaron Eckhart, Christopher Gorham, Justin Kirk, John Krasinski, Josh Lucas, Blair Underwood.

# THE LAST SIN EATER

Cadi Forbes, Henry Thomas in *The Last Sin Eater* © FOX FAITH

(FOX FAITH/THE BIGGER PICTURE) Producers, Michael Landon Jr., Brian Bird, Robert Gros; Director/Editor, Michael Landon Jr.; Screenplay, Michael Landon Jr., Brian Bird; Based on the novel by Francine Rivers; Photography, Robert Seaman; Designer, Eric Weiler; Costumes, Nancy Cavallaro; Music, Mark McKenzie; Casting, Victoria Burrows, Scot Boland; a Believe Pictures production; Dolby; Color; Rated PG-13; 117 minutes; Release date: February 9, 2007.

## Cast

Louise Fletcher (Miz Elda), Henry Thomas (Man of God), Liana Liberato (Cadi Forbes), Soren Fulton (Fagan Kai), A.J. Buckley (Angor Forbes), Stewart Finlay-McLennan (Brogan Kai), Peter Wingfield (The Sin Eater), Elizabeth Lackey (Fia Forbes), Thea Rose (Lilybet), Kim Myers (Iona Kai), Gabrielle Fitzpatrick (Bletsung McLeod), Valerie Wildman (Gervase O'Dara), Anne Cullimore Decker (Granny Forbes), Michael Flynn (Laochailand Kai), Molly Jepson (Elen Forbes), Nick Praggastis (Cleet Kai), Parker Hadley (Cullen), Stefania Barr (Glynnis), Dee Macaluso (Eldery Woman's Voice), Don Shanks (Indian Chief), Morgan B. Ackerman (Young Bletsung), Blaze Call (Young Brogan), Christine Elder (Young Miz Elda), Denli McKinney (Young Gervaise), Laron Wilson (Wounded Indian)

# THE BOY WHO CRIED BITCH: THE ADOLESCENT YEARS

(PILGRIMS 7 CORP.) Producer, Saskia Rifkin; Executive Producer/Screenplay, Catherine May Levin; Director, Matthew Levin II; Photography, Daniel Shulman; Designer, Laura Hyman; Music, Róbert Gulya; Casting, Judy Henderson; Color; Not rated; 99 minutes; Release date: February 16, 2007.

## Cast

Adam LaVorgna (Steve), Ronnie Farer (Adelle), Baird Wallace (Mitch), Mark Richard Keith (Jody), Casey Siemaszko (Kenny), Diane Kagan (Grandma), Susan Porro (Ronnie), Chaz Brewer (Dave), Chris Henry Coffey (Rick), Katie Corrado (Stacey), Michael McKenzie (Larry)

# GRAY MATTERS

(YARI FILM GROUP) Producers, Bob Yari, John Hermansen, Jill Footlick, Sue Kramer; Executive Producers, Joey Horvitz, Ted Liebowitz, Alexander Payne, Margaret Riley; Co-Producers, Todd William, Rachel Peters; Director/Screenplay, Sue Kramer; Photography, John S. Bartley; Designers, Linda Del Rosario, Richard Paris; Costumes, Sheila Bingham; Editor, Wendey Stanzler; Music, Andrew Hollender; Choreographer, A.C. Ciulla; Casting, Amanda Mackey, Cathy Sandrich; an El Camino Picture/Yari Film Group presentation in association with Contagious Entertainment of a Bella Films/Archer Entertainment production; Dolby; Color; HD; Rated PG-13; 96 minutes; Release date: February 23, 2007.

## Cast

Heather Graham (Gray), Tom Cavanagh (Sam), Bridget Moynahan (Charlie), Alan Cumming (Gordy), Molly Shannon (Carrie), Sissy Spacek (Dr. Sydney), Rachel Shelley (Julia Barlett), Gloria Gaynor (Herself), Alejandro Abellan (Juan), Don Ackerman (Conrad Spring), Warren Christie (Trevoe Brown), Casey Dubois (Boy in Park), Samantha Ferris (Elaine), Emily Anne Graham (Young Gray), Gillian Hutchison (Hot Dog Girl), Dan Joffre (Las Vegas Minister), Bill Mondy (Mr. Phillips), Timothy Paul Perez (Roberto), Benjamin Ratner (Derek), April Telek (Lana Valentine)

Tom Cavanagh, Heather Graham in *Gray Matters* © YARI FILM GROUP

## URCHIN

(VANGUARD CINEMA) Producers, John Harlacher, David Solomon Rodriguez; Director/Screenplay, John Harlacher; Photography, Luke Leonard; Art Director, Marta Willgoose; Costumes, Sara Dunn; Music, Ronnie Boykins Jr., Robert Edridge-Waks; Editor, Dave Buchwald; a The Enemy, 2 Cities Production; Color; Not rated; 105 minutes; Release date: February 23, 2007.

### Cast

Sebastian Montoya (The Kid), Rick Poli (Goliath), Larry Swansen (The Old Man), Donald Silva (Tom), Gates Leonard (Julia of Scum City), Norm Golden (Dr. Ken), Barbara King (Angela who Knits), Jennifer Boutell (Tom's Wife Dana), Brian King (Meathead), Will Brunson (Sweeny of Scum City), Rudy Costa (Filthy), Jennifer Jurek (Odessa of Scum City), Jesus Martinez (Zed of Scum City), Millicent Martin (Fish Girl of Scum City), Rebecca McBee (Kirby of Scum City), Pili Nathaniel (Mother Mary of Scum City), Yukihiro Nishiyama (Ume of Scum City), Joe Madaffari (Charlie Giglio), Betty Hudson (Sweet Momma Giglio), Xavier O'Connor (Jill the Transsexual Giglio), Mark Abene (The Inside Man), Emmanuel Goldstein (The Outside Man), Kevin G. Shinnick (Mr. O'Mally), Julie Alexandria (Nurse Crab), Rob Pedini (Technical Sam), Natasha Ragsdale (Mildred Giglio), Andrea Ryder (The Bodyguard), Michael Schwartz (The Scoutmaster), Tom X. Chao (Mr. Torney-Punta), Jeremiah Murphy (Two Dollars), Reid Stowe (Himself), Jake Gsell (Janitor's Assistant), Brent Hankins (John or Dave), Davin McLeod (Little Drake), Dave Buchwald (The Mule), Luke Leonard (Video Gustavo), Jack R. Marks (Dock Master), Doug McKrell (Schoolteacher Greg), Krista Leigh Worth (Ken's Wife Elena)

## 65 REVISITED

(PENNEBAKER HEGEDUS) Director/Photography, D.A. Pennbaker; Editor, Walker Lamond; Black and white; Not rated; 65 minutes; Release date: February 27, 2007. Outtakes and additional performances from Pennebaker's 1965 documentary on Bob Dylan, *Don't Look Back*; with Bob Dylan, Joan Baez, Bob Neuwirth, Nico.

## WILD TIGERS I HAVE KNOWN

(IFC FIRST TAKE) Producer/Director/Screenplay/Editor, Cam Archer; Executive Producers, Djuna Bel, Gus Van Sant, Scott Rudin, Jim Hayes, Michele Mulroney, Kieran Mulroney; Photography, Aaron Platt; Music, Nate Archer; Designer, Thecla Niebel; Costumes, Stephanie Volkmar; Casting, Julia Kim; a Cut and Paste Films production; Color; HD; Not rated; 98 minutes; Release date: March 2, 2007.

### Cast

Malcolm Stumpf (Logan), Patrick White (Rodeo), Max Paradise (Joey), Fairuza Balk (Logan's Mom), Kim Dickens (The Counselor), Tom Gilroy (The Principal), Bernadette Wilson (Teacher)

## ROCK BOTTOM

(LOVETT RELEASING) Producers, Jay Corcoran, Colin A. Weil; Executive Producer, Joe Lovett; Director/Photography, Jay Corcoran; Music, Scott Killian; Editor, Kenny Wachtal; a Wringing Hands production; Color; Not rated; 75 minutes; Release date: March 2, 2007. Documentary on the link between the crystal meth epidemic and the rising HIV infection rates.

## FULL OF IT

Ryan Pinkston, Amanda Walsh in *Full of It* © NEW LINE CINEMA

(NEW LINE CINEMA) Producers, Mark Canton, Steve Barnett; Executive Producers, Ryan Kavanaugh, Lynwood Spinks, Toby Emmerich, Matt Moore, Mark Kaufman, JC Spink, Charlie Gogolak; Director, Christian Charles; Screenplay, Jon Lucas, Scott Moore; Story, Yoni Berkovitz, Tony Dreannan, Tom Gammill, Max Pross; Photography, Kramer Morgenthau; Editor, Susan Shipton; Music, John Swihart; Music Supervisor, Dave Hnatiuk; Designer, Kathleen Climie; Costumes, Abram Waterhouse; Casting, Marci Liroff; an Atmosphere Entertainment MM/Mark Canton and Relativity Media production; Dolby; Deluxe color; Rated PG-13; 91 minutes; Release date: March 2, 2007.

### Cast

Ryan Pinkston (Sam Leonard); Kate Mara (Annie Dray); Craig Kilborn (Mike Hanbo); John Carroll Lynch (Mr. Leonard); Cynthia Stevenson (Mrs. Leonard); Amanda Walsh (Vicki Sanders); Derek McGrath (Principal Hayes); Josh Close (Kyle Plunkett); Teri Polo (Mrs. Moran); Carmen Electra (Herself); Matt Gordon (Coach Henderson); Alex House, Nicolas Ouellette (Kyle Sidekicks); Garth Merkeley (Kevin); Sean Hewlett (Spooky Kid); Chas Lawther (Mr. Von Der Ahe); Martin Trudel (Mr. Moran); Benjamin Beauchemin, Kelera Pelletier (Cool Kids); Matthew J. Kok, Devin Stuart (Pimply Faces); Courtney-Jane White (Pottery Girl); Tiffany Swift (Goth Girl); Suzanne Kelly (Pretty Bass Player); Mercedes Leggett, Kevin Williams (Artsy Types); John Bluethner (Referee); Onalee Ames (Cop); Kelsey Koenig (Student #2); Jennifer Luree (Vicki's Friend); Muriel Hogue (Passing Neighbor); Mike Bell, Spencer Duncanson, Rick Skene, Daniel Vassalli (Homecoming Fans); R. Morgan Slade (Nerd Spinning iPod); Dan Matthew, John Larkin, Douglas Zwirz (Band Members)

# THE CATS OF MIRIKITANI

(CORP. FOR PUBLIC BROADCASTING) Producers/Photography, Masa Yoshikawa, Linda Hattendorf; Director, Linda Hattendorf; Editors, Keiko Deguchi, Linda Hattendorf; Music, Joel Goodman; a Lucid Dreaming production in association with Independent Television Service and Center for Asian American Media; Color; DV; Not rated; 74 minutes; Release date: March 2, 2007. Documentary on homeless New York City artist Jimmy Tsutomu Mirikitani.

# BELIEVE IN ME

(IFC) Producers, Caldecott Chubb, John Bard Manulis; Director/Screenplay, Robert Collector; Photography, James L. Carter; Designer, Mark Worthington; Costumes, Aggie Guerard Rodgers; Music, David Torn; Editor, Anthony Redman; a Visionbox Pictures and ChubbCo Film Co. presentation of a Believe in Me production; Color; Rated PG; 131 minutes; Release date: March 9, 2007.

### Cast

Jeffrey Donovan (Clay Driscoll), Samantha Mathis (Jean Driscoll), Bruce Dern (Ellis Brawley), Bob Gunton (Hugh Moreland), Ryil Adamson (Myerson), Pamela Atherton (Ruth Selman), Kristin Brye (Pat Thompson), Mike Carlucci (Voice of Basketball Announcer), Paula Criss (Mrs. Blair), Camilla DeRamus (Mrs. Johnson), Jamie Dickerson (Liz Blair), Sean Dugan (The Heckler), Chris Ellis (Jim Stovall), Brandi Engel (Candy Brown), Chelsea Grear (Melba Johnson), Hailey Grimes (Susan Grove), Kit Gwin (Dorothy Thompson), Doris Hargrave (Miss Rogers), James E. Holloway (Frank Thompson), Jim Holloway (Frank Thompson), Anne Judson-Yager (Ginger Selman), Jodi Kibbe (Dorothy Crossett), Alicia Lagano (Frances Bonner), Anna Christine Lennox (Hannah), Heather Matarazzo (Cindy Butts), Marta McGonagle (Sadie York), Dan Moseley (Sheriff Blessingame), E.J. Nolan (Finals Announcer), Michele Nordin (Helen Burndsides), John Norman (Pastor Ragsdale), Ed Pennybacker (Dr. Coffee), Diane Perella (Mrs. Grove), Dorsey Ray (Preacher Bonner), Robyn Reede (Lucille Shumard), Chloe Russell (Joyce), Charles Sanders (Spainhower), Arron Shiver (Johnny Price), Kerbey Smith (Portia Stovall), Richard Stamm (George Brand), Jennifer Strebeck (Wanda), Kevin Wiggins (Joe Brody)

# MAXED OUT: HARD TIMES, EASY CREDIT, AND THE ERA OF PREDATORY LENDERS

(TRULY INDIE/RED ENVELOPE) Producer/Director/Screenplay, James D. Scurlock; Associate Producers, Alexis Spraic, Lee Thompson; Photography, Jon Aaseng; Editor, Alexis Spraic; a Trueworks production; Dolby; Color; Not rated; 90 minutes; Release date: March 9, 2007. Documentary on the incredible degree of debt accrued by so many Americans; with Chris Barrett, Robin Leach, Luke McCabe, Mark Mumma, Dave Ramsey, Liz Warren.

# THE ULTIMATE GIFT

(FOX FAITH/BIGGER PICTURE) Producers, Rick Eldridge, John Shepherd; Executive Producers, Rick Eldridge, Dave Ross; Co-Executive Producers, Jim Van Eerden, Paul Brooks, Scott Fithian; Director, Michael O. Sajbel; Screenplay, Cheryl McKay, based on the novel by Jim Stovall; Photography, Brian Baugh; Designer, Stephen Storer; Costumes, Jane Anderson; Music, Mark McKenzie; Editor, Scott Chestnut; Casting, Beverly Holloway; a Stanford Financial Group and Life N Media presentation of an Ultimate Gift production in association with Dean River Prods.; Dolby; Color; Rated PG; 114 minutes; Release date: March 9, 2007.

### Cast

Drew Fuller (Jason Stevens); James Garner (Red Stevens); Ali Hillis (Alexia); Abigail Breslin (Emily); Lee Meriwether (Miss Hastings); Brian Dennehy (Gus); Mircea Monroe (Caitlin); Donna Cherry (Sarah Stevens); D. David Morin (Jack Stephens); Rose Bianco (Bella); Mellie Boozer (Party Guest); Robert Cannon (Farmhand); Caleb Chestnut (Voice of Young Jason); Bill Cobbs (Ted Hamilton); Tom Conder (Bum in Park); Brian F. Durkin (Sarah's Boyfriend); Roger W. Durrett (Ruth's Lawyer); Mel Fair (Jack's Lawyer); Dawn Renee Fields (Girl #2 on Bus); Michael Fraguada (The Stranger/Jesus); Daley Fricks, Tracy Fricks, Savannah Leigh Lathan, Justin St. Gelais, Steve St. Gelais (Cancer Patients); Jamie Hall, Tonya Schuffler (Associates); Ray Hammack (Man at Airport); Jeff Joslin (First Class Passenger); Mark Joy (Bill's Lawyer); Victor Lee (Dr. Allen); Catherine McGoohan (Ruth); Tina Murphy (Hampton Receptionist); Peggy Obrien (Nurse); Tim Parati (Tow Truck Driver); Brett Rice (Bill Stevens); Vironica Schreiner, Katie Xie (Entourage); Chad Schuermeyer (Man in Office); Christina Sibley, Brendan Sibley (Girls in Park); David Temple (Ruth's Husband); Pat Yeary (Park Visitor)

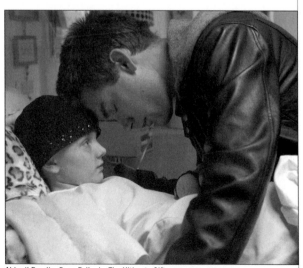

Abigail Breslin, Drew Fuller in *The Ultimate Gift* © 20TH CENTURY-FOX

## ISLANDER

(SLOWHAND) Producers, Thomas Hildreth, Forrest Murray; Director, Ian McCrudden; Screenplay, Ian McCrudden, Thomas Hildreth; Photography, Dan Coplan; Art Director, Mark Gruskin; Costumes, Josie Basford, Nicole Palczynski; Music, Billy Mallery; Editor, Marc Jozefowicz; Casting, Caroline Sinclair, Karen True; a Down East Films presentation; Color; HD; Not rated; 103 minutes; Release date: March 9, 2007.

### Cast

Dick Barron (Maynard), Zack Batchelder (Wyatt), Ron Canada (T. Hardy), Emma Ford (Sara Cole), Philip Baker Hall (Popper), Tom Hildreth (Eben Cole), Amy Jo Johnson (Cheryl Cole), Mark Kiely (Jimmy), James Parks (Pokey), Larry Pine (Old Man Cole), Judy Prescott (Emily Bess), Patricia Randell (Wilma)

## DEAD SILENCE

Ryan Kwanten in *Dead Silence* © UNIVERSAL PICTURES

(UNIVERSAL) Producers, Gregg Hoffman, Oren Koules, Mark Burg; Executive Producer, Peter Oillataguerre; Director, James Wan; Screenplay, Leigh Whannell; Photography, John R. Leonetti; Designer, Julie Berghoff; Costumes, Denise Cronenberg; Editor, Michael N. Knue; Music, Charlie Clouser; Makeup, Leslie A. Sebert; Visual Effect Supervisor, Aaron Weintraub; Visual Effects, Mr. X; Casting, Barbara Fiorentino, Rebecca Mangieri, Wendy Weidman; a Burg/Koules/Hoffman production; Dolby; Technicolor; Rated R; 90 minutes; Release date: March 16, 2007.

### Cast

Ryan Kwanten (Jamie Ashen), Amber Valletta (Ella Ashen), Donnie Wahlberg (Det. Jim Lipton), Michael Fairman (Henry Walker), Joan Heney (Marion Walker), Bob Gunton (Edward Ashen), Laura Regan (Lisa Ashen), Dmitry Chepovetsky (Richard Walker), Judith Roberts (Mary Shaw), Keir Gilchrist (Young Henry), Steven Taylor (Michael Ashen), David Talbot (Priest), Steve Adams (1941 Detective), Shelley Peterson (Lisa's Mom), Austin Majors (Voice of Michael Ashen)

## BEHIND THE MASK: THE RISE OF LESLIE VERNON

(ANCHOR BAY ENTERTAINMENT) Producer/Director, Scott Glosserman; Executive Producers, Al Corley, Andrew Lewis, Eugene Musso, Bart Rosenblatt; Screenplay, Scott Glosserman, David J. Stieve; Photography, Jaron Presant; Designer, Travis Zariwny; Costumes, Raquel L. Jaffe; Music, Gordy Haab; Editor, Sean Presant; Casting, Marisa Ross, Matthew Skrobalak; a Glen Echo Entertainment production in association with Code Entertainment; Dolby; Color; Rated R; 92 minutes; Release date: March 16. 2007.

### Cast

Nathan Baesel (Leslie Vernon); Angela Goethals (Taylor Gentry); Robert Englund (Doc Halloran); Scott Wilson (Eugene); Zelda Rubinstein (Mrs. Collinwood); Bridgett Newton (Jamie); Kate Lang Johnson (Kelly Curtis); Ben Pace (Doug Johnson); Britain Spellings (Todd Best); Hart Turner (Shane); Krissy Carlson (Lauren); Travis Zariwny (Dr. Meuller); Teo Gomez (Stoned Guy); Matt Bolt (Slightly More Stoned Guy); Jenafer Brown (Carrie, Virgin Girl); Kane Hodder (Elm Street Resident); Mia Butler, Morgan Kitzmiller, Hannah Rader (Communion Girls)

## CAFFEINE

(STEAMING HOT COFFEE) Producers, John Cosgrove, Jo Levi DiSante; Executive Producers, David Peters, Terry Dunn Meurer, Laurence Malkin; Co-Producer, Johanna Ray; Director, John Cosgrove; Screenplay, Dean Craig; Photography, Shawn Maurer; Editor, Suzanne Hines; Music, David Kitay; Designer, Edward L. Rubin; Costumes, Oneita Parker; Casting, Johanna Ray; a Cosgrove/Meurer Prods. presentation of a Steaming Hot Coffee production; Dolby; FotoKem color; 89 minutes; Release date: March 16, 2007.

### Cast

Mena Suvari (Vanessa); Marsha Thomason (Rachel); Katherine Heigl (Laura); Andrew Lee Potts (Mike); Mike Vogel (Danny); Breckin Meyer (Dylan); Callum Blue (Charlie); Mark Pellegrino (Tom); Roz Witt (Lucy); Sonya Walger (Gloria); Orlando Seale (Mark); Brian J. Watson (Porn Star); Andrew Abelson (John); Mark Dymond (David); Jules Leyser (Angela); Daz Crawford (Steve); Neil Dickson (Mr. Davies); Mark Dymond (David); Steve Humphreys (Sean); Paula Jane Newman (Annoying Lady); Nikki Collins, Teena Collins (Tarty Girls); Vanessa Peters, Tony Denman, Stephen Heath, Brooke Mason (Customers); Bridget Brno (Naughty Nurse); Hal Oszan (Dude)

# MY BROTHER

(CODEBLACK ENTERTAINMENT) Producers, Gregory Segal, Leslie Ann Fouche, Gingi Rochelle; Executive Producer, Michael Malagiero; Director/Screenplay, Anthony Lover; Photography, John Sawyer; Designer, Evelyn Sakash; Costumes, Roger McKenzie; Casting, Lisa Ganz, Debbie Ganz, Winsome Sinclair; Music, John Califra; Editor, Christian Baker; a Liberty Studios production in association with Angel Baby Entertainment; Dolby; Color; Rated PG-13; 100 minutes; Release date: March 16, 2007.

### Cast

Vanessa Williams (L'Tisha Morton); Nashawan Kearse (Isaiah Morton); Tatum O'Neal (Erica); Fredro Starr (Pharaoh); Christopher Scott (James Morton); Rodney Henry (Young Isaiah); Donovan Jennings (Young James); Masser Metcalf (Fazul); Basil Pologianis (Amir); Brian Delate (Mr. Roland); Dena Tayler (Annie); Ridwan Adhami (Burger King Employee); Eric H. Alexander (Hip-Hop Comic); Mike D. Anderson (Bullie); David Basch (Salvation Army Santa); Anthony Caso (Draper's Security Guard); C. Rayz Walz, Omega Moon, Grafth, Mr. Cheeks (Hip Hop Artists); Bern Cohen (Harvey Mitnick); Kymbali Craig (Angela); Greg D'Agostino (Amusement Park Operator); Len Fero (Louie); Monty C. Floyd (Waiter); Eric Michael Gillett (Administrator); Yaffit Hallely (Bodego Girl); George Hall (Judge Hall); Talent Harris (Joey); Calisse Hawkins (The Wandering Comic); Kerisse Hutchinson (Angela, Sister C); Abdel Jawad (Bodega Owner); Danny Johnson (Rev. Franklin); Big Kap (DJ); John Keegan (Administrator); Brian L. King (Homeless Drunk); Vatecia L. Little (Hooker); Shawn Luckey (Club Patron); Michael Luggio (Mr. Vincent); Areshia McFarlin (Valeria); Johnny Mez (Carnie); Frank Minucci (Lead Limo Driver); Charlie Moss (Mr. Draper); Dante Nero (The Question Comic); Evan Palazzo (Piano Player); Janelle Anne Robinson (Tisha); Steven Rock, Stephen Savona (Administrators); Allysa Sasha (Dancer); Roger Shamas (Rasime); Bershan Shaw (Mrs. Tucker); Franklin Ojeda Smith (Cultural Attache); Brandhyze Stanley (Theresa, Knock Out Girl); Vincent Suarez (Bullie); Attika Torrence (Cigarette Hawker); Kevin Watson (Pink Pimp); Tom Wurl (Draper Manager)

# TORTILLA HEAVEN

Marcelo Tubert in *Tortilla Heaven* © ARCHANGEL RELEASING

(ARCHANGEL RELEASING) Producers, Gilbert Dumontet, Pepe Iturralde, Courtney Mizel, Judy Hecht Dumontet; Executive Producers, Jeffrey Hecht, Mindy Hecht, Larry Mizel, Grupo Chihuahua; Co-Producers, Hiroshi Kubota, Margaret Guerra Rogers, Richard Schwartz, Bau-haus Entertainment, Jon Kuyper, Aladdin Pojhan; Director, Judy Hecht Dumontet; Screenplay, Hecht Dumontet, Julius Robinson; Photography, Chuy Chavez; Editors, Vanick Moradian, Hiroshi Kubota, Rick Fields; Music, Christopher Lennertz; Music Supervisor, Margaret Guerra Rogers; Designers, Anthony Rivero Stabley, Carlos Brown; Costumes, Jennifer Parsons, Carlos Brown; Casting, Pemrick/ Fronk Casting. a Dumontet/Iturralde production; Dolby; Deluxe color; Rated PG-13; 97 minutes; Release date: March 16, 2007.

### Cast

José Zúñiga (Isidor); Miguel Sandoval (Gil Garcia); Olivia Hussey (Petra); George Lopez (Everardo); Marcelo Tubert (Father Pancracio); Irene Bedard (Liberata); Lupe Ontiveros (Adelfa); Alexis Cruz (Marco); Judy Herrera (Dinora); Del Zamora (Ruffino); Laura Salinas, Ana Ortiz, Krissy Matthews (Chicanas); Elaine Miles (Caridad); Elpidia Carrillo (Hermenegilda); Geno Silva (Don Transito); Rick Gutierrez (Bulmaro); Deborah Chavez (Vangie); Scott Cleverdon (Jesus); Jonathan Levit (Dr. Webman); Danny Peck (Maclovio); Courtney Mizel (Jackie); Aaron Talín Webman (Jose)

## AIR GUITAR NATION

Dan Crane in *Air Guitar Nation* © SHADOW DISTRIBUTION

(SHADOW) Producers, Dan Cutforth, Jane Lipsitz, Anna Barber; Executive Producers, Kriston Rucker, Cedric Devitt; Co-Producer, Tim Sullivan; Director, Alexandra Lipsitz; Photography, Tony Sacco; Music, Dan Crane; Editor, Conor O'Neill; a Magical Elves production; Dolby; Color; Rated R; 81 minutes; Release date: March 23, 2007. Documentary on how air guitar became a sensation in the U.S.; with Peter Cilella, Dan Crane, Gordon Hintz, David S. Jung, Zac Murno, Angela Shelton

## THE HILLS HAVE EYES II

(FOX ATOMIC) Producers, Wes Craven, Peter Locke, Marianne Maddalena; Executive Producer, Jonathan Debin; Director, Martin Weisz; Screenplay, Wes Craven, Jonathan Craven; Based on characters created by Wes Craven; Photography, Sam McCurdy; Designer, Keith Wilson; Costumes, Katherine Jane Bryant; Music, Trevor Morris; Editor, Kirk M. Morri; Casting, Mark Bennett; Dolby; Color; Rated R; 89 minutes; Release date: March 23, 2007.

### Cast

Michael McMillian (PFC David "Napoleon" Napoli), Jessica Stroup (PFC Amber Johnson), Daniella Alonso (PFC "Missy" Martinez), Jacob Vargas (PFC "Crank" Medina), Lee Thompson Young (PFC Delmar Reed), Ben Crowley (PFC "Stump" Locke), Eric Edelstein (Cpl. "Spitter" Cole), Flex Alexander (Sgt. Jeffrey "Sarge" Millstone), Michael Bailey Smith (Papa Hades), Archie Kao (Dr. Han), Jay Acovone (Dr. Wilson), Jeff Kober (Col. Lincoln Redding), Philip Pavel (Dr. Paul Foster), David Reynolds (Hansel), Tyrell Kemlo (Stabber), Joseph Beddelem (Insurgent), Jason Oettle (Letch), Reshad Strik (PFC Mickey Elrod), Cécile Breccia (Pregnant Woman), Fatiha Quatil (Afghan Woman), Jeremy Goei (Clyde), Derek Mears (Chameleon), Gáspár Szabó (Sniffer)

## MEMORY

(ALOHA RELEASING) Producers, Jesse Newhouse, Anthony Badalucco, Bennett Davlin; Executive Producers, Robert J. Monroe, Brandon K. Hogan; Director, Bennett Davlin; Screenplay, Bennett Davlin, Anthony Badalucco, Russ Turley; Photography, Peter Benison; Designer, Stephen Geaghan; Costumes, Karen L. Matthews; Music, Anthony Marinelli, Clint Bennett; Casting, Jack Gilardi, Candice Elzinga; an Echo Bridge Entertainment, 3210 Films, Badalucco Productions, Paradox Pictures production; Color; Rated R; 98 minutes; Release date: March 23, 2007.

### Cast

Billy Zane (Taylor Briggs), Tricia Helfer (Stephanie Jacobs), Dennis Hopper (Max Lichtenstein), Ann-Margret (Carol Hargrave), Terry Chen (Dr. Deepra Chang), Deirdre Blades (Alisha Briggs), Scott G. Anderson (Scott McHale), Matt Fentiman (William Terrell), Emily Hirst (Bonnie McHale), Emily Anne Graham (Allison Frost), Alex Ferris (Ricky McHale), Hailey Shand (Lisa Mullens), Alisha Davlin (Young Alisha), Joel McFarlane (Nick Chang), Alexis Llewellyn (Little Girl), Irene Karas (Stella), Dan Pelchat (Spectre), Rekha Sharma (Becka), Jeanette Weinstein (Cheri), Alonso Oyarzun (Night Manager)

## JOURNEY FROM THE FALL

(IMAGIASIAN) Producer, Lam Nguyen; Executive Producers, Alan Vo Ford, Trung Pham, Joseph Faircrest; Director/Screenplay/Editor, Ham Tran; Photography, Guillermo Rosas, Julie Kirkwood; Designers, Tommy TwoSon, Mona Nahm; Costumes, Bao Tranchi; Music, Christopher Wong; an Old Photo Film presentation of a Fire in the Lake production; Dolby; Color; Rated R; 135 minutes; Release date: March 23, 2007.

### Cast

Keiu Chinh (Ba Noi, Grandmother); Long Nguyen (Long); Diem Lien (Mai); Jayvee Mai The Hiep (Thanh); Khanh Doan (Nam); Cat Ly (Phuong); Nguyen Thai Nguyen (Lai); Raul Alba, Javier Ortiz (Bullies); George Bui (Binh); Jose Gutierrez (Bully); Jiruyut Khieosawat (Son); Tere Morris (Miss Patty); Net Ngo (Grandma on Boat); Hieu Nguyen (Trai); Kim Chi Tran Nguyen (Kieu); Lam Nguyen (Khanh); Preston Ti Nguyen (Young Lai); Thomas Thong Nguyen (Old Man in Street); Thuy Nguyen (Granddaughter on Boat); Thuan Phan (Village Woman); Tam Thanh (Tuan); Tanya Wong (Binh's Granddaughter)

# THE HAWK IS DYING

(STRAND) Producers, Jeff Levy-Hinte, Mary Jane Skalski; Executive Producers, Ted Hope, Corbin Day, Jeanne Levy-Hinte; Co-Producer, Joshua Zeman; Director/Screenplay/Music, Julian Goldberger, based on the novel by Harry Crews; Photography, Bobby Bukowski; Editor, Affonso Goncalves; Designer, Judy Becker; Costumes, April Napier; a Big Heart Pictures presentation in association with Exile Prods. of an Antidote Films production in association with This Is That, Next Wednesday; Color; Not rated; 112 minutes; Release date: March 30, 2007.

## Cast

Paul Giamatti (George Gattling), Michelle Williams (Betty), Michael Pitt (Fred), Rusty Schwimmer (Precious), Robert Wisdom (Billy Bob), Ann Wedgeworth (Ma Gattling), Karl Anthony (Dr. Leep), Mark Campbell (Football Player), Katie Dixon (Young Undergrad), Steve DuMouchel (Marvin Hill), John Hostette (Nebbish Professor), Veryl Jones (Ambulance Driver), P.J. Lalka (Little Boy), Bob Lipka (Preacher Roe), Marc Macaulay (Alonzo), Shamrock Shane (Professor), Erica Medina (Little Girl), Ayana Rhoden (Girlfriend), Taylor Simpson (Gray Bony Lady), Matthew Stanton (Peter Sweet).

Michael Pitt, Paul Giamatti in *The Hawk is Dying* © STRAND RELEASING

# BLIND DATING

Chris Pine, Eddie Kaye Thomas in *Blind Dating* © SAMUEL GOLDWYN FILMS

(GOLDWYN) Producers, Costa Theo, Joy Mellins, David Shanks, James Keach; Executive Producers, Jane Seymour, Steven Bickel; Director, James Keach; Screenplay, Christopher Theo; Photography, Julio Macat; Editor, Larry Bock; Music, Heitor Pereira; Music Supervisor, Liz Gallacher; Designer, Eric Weiler; Costumes, Cheri Ingle; Associate Producers, Roger Carey, Costa John Theo; Casting, Lisa Beach, Sarah Katzman, Kate Plantin (U.K.), Cate Praggastis; Dolby; Widescreen; Technicolor; Rated PG-13; 99 minutes; Release date: March 30, 2007.

## Cast

Chris Pine (Danny); Eddie Kaye Thomas (Larry); Anjali Jay (Leeza); Jane Seymour (Dr. Evans); Stephen Tobolowsky (Dr. Perkins); Pooch Hall (Jay); Frank Gerrish (Angelo); Dee Macaluso (Lucia); Amelia Praggastis (Marie); Sendhil Ramamurthy (Arvind); Jennifer Alden (Jasmine); Hudith Benezra (Heidi); Mattie (Bhat's Sister); Skip Carlson (Drunk); Katherine Flynn (Dolores); Sean Hammon, Jake McKenzie (Larry's Friends); Sathya Jesudasson (Mrs. Raja); Ossie Mair (Mr. Bhat); Jayma Mays (Mandy); Katy Mixon (Suzie); Jaysha Patel (Young Jaysha); Austin Rogers (Young Larry); Jodi Russell (Mrs. Van de Meer); Iqbal Theba (Mr. Raja); Zhara Trougi (Aunt); Dhamender Verma (Ravi); Steve Wellington (Young Danny); Ashlyn Yates (Young Marie); John Boccia (Jonnie); Trenton James (French Waiter)

## TEN 'TIL NOON

(SHUT UP & SHOOT PICTURES) Producers, Gavin Franks, Michael Mannheim, Brian Osborne, Michael Creighton Rogers; Director, Scott Storm; Screenplay, Paul Osborne; Photography, Alice Brooks; Designer, Bianca Ferro; Music, Joe Kraemer; Color; Rated R; 80 minutes; Release date: March 30, 2007.

### Cast

Alfonso Freeman (Mr. Jay); Rick D. Wasserman (Larry Taylor); Rayne Guest (Becky Taylor); Jenya Lano (Miss Milch); Thomas Kopache (Mr. Duke); Daniel Hagen (Carter); Dylan Kussman (Rush); Jennifer Hill (Sheba); George Williams (Leo); Daniel Nathan Spector (Walter Cooligan); Jason Hamer (Alan Free); Justin Huen (Ruben); Paul J. Alessi (Nickel); Erin Stutland (Allison); Yvonne Perry (Theater Instructor); Alex McKenzie, Brian Rumsey (Goons); Michael Creighton Rogers, Thom Mattocks (Suited Men); John Girot (Deacon)

## RACE YOU TO THE BOTTOM

Cole Williams, Amber Benson in *Race You to the Bottom* © here!/Regent

(HERE!/REGENT) Producers, Russell Brown, Roni Deitz; Director/Screenplay, Russell Brown; Photography, Marco Fargnoli; Editor, Annette Davey; Music, Ryan Beveridge; Art Director, Doran Meyers; Costumes, Kristen Anacker; Casting, Shannon Makhanian; a Simon Prods. production; Dolby; Color; 72 minutes; Release date: March 30, 2007.

### Cast

Amber Benson (Maggie), Cole Williams (Nathan), Jeremy Lelliott (Nicholas), Justin Zachary (Milo), Danielle Thomas (Carla), Justin Hartley (Milo), Justin Hartley (Joe), Philipp Karner (Eric), Ruben Dario (Angry Man), Kristin Hensley (Angry Woman), Patrick Belton (Tabriz Rug Guy), Al Liner (Marco the Winery Owner), Danny Scheie (Tour Guide), Adam Del Rio (Victor the Waiter), Hannah Evans (Sales Lady), Erin Cahill (Waitress), Kathy Garver (Spa Attendant)

## FIGHTING WORDS

(INDICAN) Producer, Alan Roberts; Executive Producer, Robert Zaytoun; Director/Screenplay, E. Paul Edwards; Photography, Robert Hayes; Designer, Bruce Elric Holthousen; Costumes, Kat Williams; Music, Charles Bernstein; Editors, Alan Roberts, Anthony Bozanich; Casting, David S. Zimmerman, Edmund Gaynes; Color; Rated R; 89 minutes; Release date: April 6, 2007.

### Cast

C. Thomas Howell (David Settles); Jeff Stearns (Jake Thompson); Tara D'Agostino (Marni Elliott); Fred Willard (Longfellow); Fred Williamson (Gabriel); Edward Albert (Marc Neihauser); Michael Parks (Benny the Heckler); Val Lauren (Etch-A-Sketch); Dominic Comperatore (Alan Mitzer); Jen Dede (Lisa); Vanessa Dorman (Shelly Lancaster); Tucker Smallwood (Dr. Franklin); Amir Talai (Ralphie); Joe Restivo (Millhouse); James Parks (Fresno Pete); Jerry Quickley, Rives (Themselves); Justin Urich (Chrome Harley); Judy Ben-Asher (Self Love Sarah); Sabree (Jonetta); Dwight Ewell (Leopold); A. Barrett Worland (Teezer); Marita de Lara (Native American Woman); Andrea Helene (Mousy Woman); Tammy Caplan (Angie); James Dalesandro (Mr. Berto); Marcus A. York (Big Al); Jacob Edwards (Young Jake); Jeanne Festa (Mrs. Thompson); Robert Vernon Eaton (Mr. Thompson); James Tuttle, Scott Khouri (Transvestites); Andrew Kim, Julius Lee (Buddhist Monks); Katie Cooper (Homeless Woman); Emma Ausman, Justin Rubenstein, Kasey Rubenstein, Lizzie White, Margaret White, Mary Catherine White (Kids in Park); Ricardo Berg, Mary Jo Mundy (Little People); Jessica Padilla, Susan Stapczynski, Cory Williams, Rita Aragure (Slam Judges); Chris Saleh (Drummer); Matt Battle (Guitarist)

## JACK SMITH AND THE DESTRUCTION OF ATLANTIS

(SUNDANCE) Producers, Kenneth Wayne Peralta, Mary Jordan; Executive Producers, Richard Prince, Mary Jordan, Ross Morgan, Stephen Kessler, Kenneth Wayne Peralta; Director/Screenplay, Mary Jordan; Photography, Mary Jordan, Jon Fordham; Music, Joel A. Diamond, Robert Aaron, Thurston Moore; Editor, Alex Marquez; a Tongue Press, Monk Media production; Color/Black and white; Not rated; 95 minutes; Release date: April 13, 2007. Documentary on experimental filmmaker Jack Smith; with Agosto Machado, Andrew Sarris, Ari Roussimoff, Billy Name, Ela Troyano, Gary Indiana, George Kuchar, Helen Gee, Henry Hills, Holly Woodlawn, Ira Cohen, Ivan Galietti, Jerry Tartaglia, John Matturri, John Vaccaro, John Waters, John Zorn, Jonas Mekas, Judith Malina, Ken Jacobs, Lawrence Rinder, Mario Montez, Mary Sue Slater, Mary Woronov, Mike Kelley, Nayland Blake, Nick Zedd, Richard Foreman, Robert Heide, Robert Wilson, Ronald Tavel, Sylvere Lotringer, Taylor Mead, Tommy Lanigan-Schmidt, Tony Conrad, Uzi Parnes, William Niederkorn.

## MODERN MAN

(BECKER-SWIBEL PRODS.) Producers/Screenplay, Justin Swibel, Eric Becker; Director/Photography/Editor, Justin Swibel; Designer, Richard Tanis; Dolby; Color; HD; Not rated; 61 minutes; Release date: April 13, 2007.

### Cast

Eric Becker (Modern Man)

## AQUA TEEN HUNGER FORCE COLON MOVIE FILM FOR THEATERS

(FIRST LOOK) Producers, Dave Willis, Matt Maiellaro, Jay Wade Edwards, Ned Hastings; Executive Producers, Mike Lazzo, Keith Crofford; Directors/Screenplay, Matt Maiellaro, Dave Willis; Animation Director, Craig Hartin; Animation, Radical Axis, Big Deal Cartoons, Matthew I. Jenkins Studio; Art Director, Bob Pettitt; Supervising Editor, Jay Wade Edwards; an Adult Swim presentation, in association with First Look Pictures, of a Williams Street production; Dolby; Color; Rated R; 86 minutes; Release date: April 13, 2007.

### Voice Cast

Dana Snyder (Master Shake); Carey Means (Frylock); Dave Willis (Meatwad/Carl/Ignignokt/Video Game Voice); Andy Merrill (Oglethorpe); Mike Schatz (Emory); Matt Maiellaro (Err/Cybernetic Ghost/Satan); C. Martin Croker (Dr. Weird/Steve); Fred Armisen (Time Lincoln); Bruce Campbell (Chicken Bittle); George Lowe (Space Ghost); MC Chris (MC Pee Pants); Chris Kattan (Walter Melon); Neil Peart of Rush (Himself); Isaac Hayes III (Plantation Owner); Tina Fey (Burrito); Jon "Big Jon" Benjamin, Jon Glaser (CIA Agents); Craig Hartin (Rob Goldstein); Matt Harrigan (Linda)

Frylock, Master Shake, Meatwad in *Aqua Teen Hunger Force* © FIRST LOOK

## PATHFINDER

Karl Urban in *Pathfinder* © 20TH CENTURY FOX

(20TH CENTURY FOX) Producers, Mike Medavoy, Arnold W. Messer, Marcus Nispel; Executive Producers, Bradley J. Fischer, Lee Nelson, John M. Jacobsen; Co-Producers, Vincent Oster, Barbara Kelly, Louis Phillips; Director, Marcus Nispel; Screenplay, Laeta Kalogridis, based on a screenplay by Nils Gaup; Photography, Daniel C. Pearl; Designer, Greg Blair; Costumes, Renee April; Editors, Jay Friedkin, Glen Scantlebury; Music, Jonathan Elias; Special Effects Coordinator, Alex Burdett; Visual Effects Supervisor, Randy Goux; Casting, Lynne Carrow, Susan Brouse, Kathleen Tomasik; a Phoenix Pictures production in association with Dune Entertainment and Major Entertainment Partners; American/Canadian; Dolby; Widescreen; Deluxe color, Rated R; 99 minutes; Release date: April 13, 2007.

### Cast

Karl Urban (Ghost); Moon Bloodgood (Starfire); Russell Means (Pathfinder); Clancy Brown (Gunnar); Jay Tavare (Blackwing); Nathaniel Arcand (Wind in Tree); Ralf Moeller (Ulfar); Kevin Loring (Jester); Wayne C. Baker (Indian Father); Michelle Thrush (Indian Mother); Nicole Muñoz (Little Sister); Burkely Duffield (Ghost, 12 Years Old); Ray G. Thunderchild, Duane Howard, Brandon Oakes, Alain Hudon (Elders); Cyler Point (Indian Boy, 7 Years Old); Stefany Mathias (Flashback Mother); John Mann (Viking Doctor); Ken Jones (Ghost Father); Mike Dopud (Tracker/Fork in Road); Woody Jeffreys (Tracker #7); André Todorovic (Villager); Marcel Petit (Tribesman)

## ROCK THE BELLS

GZA in *Rock the Bells* © SEVENTH ART RELEASING

(SEVENTH ART) Producers, Kurt Dalton, Henry Lowenfels, Denis Henry Hennelly, Casey Suchan; Executive Producers, John Murphy, Barry Poltermann, Chang Weisberg, Dan Farah; Directors/Editors, Denis Henry Hennelly, Casey Suchan; Photography, Jeff Bollman, Leif Johnson; Music, J. Force; a Mayfly Films/Civilian Pictures/Guerilla Union presentation of an Open Road Film; Color; DV; Not rated; 113 minutes; Release date: April 13, 2007. Documentary covering the last scheduled concert of the Wu-Tang Clan; with the Wu-Tang Clan, Redman, Dilated Peoples, Chali 2na, DJ NuMark, Sage Francis, MC Supernatural and his son Haj, Eyedea + Abilities, Chang Weisberg, Carla Garcia, Brian Valdez.

## SLOW BURN

(LIONSGATE) Producers, Fisher Stevens, Sidney Kimmel, Bonnie Timmermann, Tim Williams; Executive Producers, John Penotti, Andrew Karsch, Andy Reiner; Co-Producer, Matthew Rowland; Director/Screenplay, Wayne Beach, from a story by Wayne Beach, Anthony Walton; Photography, Wally Pfister; Designer, Tim Galvin; Costumes, Nicoletta Massone; Editor, Kristina Boden; Music, Jeff Rona; Casting, Amanda Harding, Amanda Koblin; a GreeneStreet Films, Sidney Kimmel Entertainment production; Dolby; Color; Rated R; 93 minutes; Release date: April 13, 2007.

### Cast

Ray Liotta (Ford Cole), James Todd Smith/LL Cool J (Luther Pinks), Mekhi Phifer (Isaac Duperde), Bruce McGill (Godfrey), Chiwetel Ejiofor (Ty Trippin), Guy Torry (Chet Torry), Taye Diggs (Jeffrey Sykes), Jolene Blalock (Nora Timmer), Frank Schorpion (Maybank), Donny Falsetti (Delucca), Barbara Alexander (Pratt), Joe Grifasi (Desk Sgt. Drown), Richard Jutras (Leland Neff), Arthur Holden (Felix Lang), Fisher Stevens (Alan Turlock), Robert Reynolds (Police Van Driver), Daniel Hilfer (Kevin), Peter Tambakis (Ellis), Christian Paul (Rupert Greems), Gage Pierre (Crazy Guy)

## REDLINE

Nadja Bjorlin in *Redline* © CHICAGO PICTURES

(CHICAGO PICTURES) Producer/Story, Daniel Sadek; Director, Andy Cheng; Screenplay, Robert Foreman; Photography, Bill Butler; Designer, David L. Snyder; Costumes, Christine Wada; Music, Ian Honeyman, Andrew Raiher; Casting, Joy Todd, Craig Campobasso; Dolby; Color; Not rated; 95 minutes; Release date: April 13, 2007.

### Cast

Nadja Bjorlin (Natasha Martin); Nathan Phillips (Carlo); Angus Macfadyen (Michael); Eddie Griffin (Infamous); Tim Matheson (Jerry Brecken); Jesse Johnson (Jason); Denyce Lawton (Miranda); Neill Skylar (Mary); Barbara Niven (Sally Martin); Marc Crumpton (Trevor); Hal Ozsan (Mike Z); Faleolo Alailima (Diggs); Christopher Backus (Tony Nefuse); Kevin Levrone (Sante); Todd Lowe (Nick); Ben Alexander (Counterfeiter #1); Monica Allgeier (Tina); Jorge Luis Alvarez (Production Assistant #2); Greg Anderson (Club Patron); Jennifer Aspinwall (Massage Girl); Christian Eric Billings (Billionaire); Lance Bruyette (Tom Jansen); Doug Budin (Tommy); Monica Cabral (Hot Girl); Jeff Chase (Gumba #6); Alexandra Cheron (Actress, Model); Colvon Collins (Camera Man); Danica Dias (Tish); Stacey Doss (Cheng's Entourage); Jasmine Dustin (Model); Richard Dyer (Boxer); David Dayan Fisher (The Godfather); Jake Galasso (Henchman); Nicholas Garren (Kickboxer); Michael Hagiwara (Marcus Cheng); Mary Elise Hayden (Liz Athens); Jonathan Hypolite (Red Racing Crew Member); Wyclef Jean (Actor); Charles Kienzle (Race Fan); Amber Lancaster (Hot Girl); Michelle Lenhardt, Ursual Mayes (Flag Girls); Avery Little (Club Goer); Louis Mandylor (Louis); Aalok Mehta (Vikram); Issac Mejia (Mover); Robert Overmyer (Paramedic); Jeran Pascascio (Vikram's Entourage); Joe Sagal (Elvis Announcer); Nina Smidt (Annoucner Girl); Nancy Stelmaszczyk (Actress, Model)

## ALICE NEEL

(ARTHOUSE FILMS) Producers, Rebecca Spence, Ethan Palmer; Director/Screenplay, Andrew Neel; Photography, Andrew Neel, Ethan Palmer, Karl F. Schroder, Hillary Spera; Music, Jonah Rapino; Editor, Luke Meyer; a See Think production; Color; Not rated; 81 minutes; Release date: April 20, 2007. Documentary on artist Alice Neel; with Michel Auder, Phillip Bonosky, Chuck Close, Marlene Dumas, Cristina Lancella, Jeremy Lewison, Juan Martinez, Hartley Neel, Richard Neel, Linda Nochlin, Robert Storr.

# DOWNTOWN: A STREET TALE

(SLOWHAND) Producers, Donald A. Barton, Maria Rita Caso, Helena Cynamon, Joey Dedio, Samuel H. Frankle, T.J. Mancini; Director, Rafal Zielinski; Screenplay, Joey Dedio; Photography, Ken Seng; Costumes, Michael Alsondo; Music, Robert O. Ragland; Editor, Eric Chase; Casting, Heidi Miami Marshall; an Insight Film Studios, Silvio Sardi Communications production; Color; Rated R; 103 minutes; Release date: April 20, 2007.

### Cast

Joey Dedio (Angelo), Genevieve Bujold (Aimee), John Savage (H20), Burt Young (Gus), Lillo Brancato (Lenny), Michael Wright (Rudy), Chad Allen (Hunter), Flora Martínez (Maria), James Ransome (Billy), Domenica Cameron-Scorsese (Cheri), Rachel Vasquez (Ashley), Johnny Sanchez (Tito), Kid Frost (Wilfredo), Chuck Cooper (Sgt. Williams), D. Taylor Loeb (Jolene), Billy Strong (Jeffrey), Sandi Schultz (Jada), Anna Maria Cianciulli (The Mother), Adrian Martinez (Frankie), Kenya Brome (Det. Teesh), Chad Fernandez (Skater), Stu James (Guy #1), Jeremy Richards (Lamont), Marvin W. Schwartz (Bum), Elizabeth Stewart (Victim of Mugging), Mihaela Tudorof (Rachel), Jessica Vash (Office Assistant)

# THE TRIPPER

(COQUETTE PRODS.) Producers, Courteney Cox, David Arquette, Evan Astrowsky, Neil Machlis, Navin Narang; Executive Producers, Jay Cannold, Craig Cannold, Thomas Jane, Steve Niles; Co-Producer, Rick Shephard; Director, David Arquette; Screenplay, David Arquette, Joe Harris; Photography, Bobby Bukowski; Editor, Glenn Garland; Music, Jimmy Haun, Dave Wittman; Additional Music, Fishbone; Music Supervisor, Amanda Scheer Demme; Designer, Linda Burton; Costumes, Van Ramsey; Casting, Johanna Ray; presented in association with RAW Entertainment and Na Vinci Films; Dolby; FotoKem color; Rated R; 97 minutes; Release date: April 20, 2007.

### Cast

Richmond Arquette (Deputy Cooper); Paz de la Huerta (Jade/Summer); Balthazar Getty (Jimmy); Redmond Gleeson (Dylan/Father); Lukas Haas (Ivan); David Arquette (Muff); Courtney Cox Arquette (Cynthia); Stephen Heath (Jack); Brad Hunt (Hank); Thomas Jane (Buzz Hall); Jaime King (Samantha); Jason Mewes (Joey); Chris Nelson(Gus/Reagan); Paul Reubens (Frank Baker); Marsha Thomason (Linda); China Raven Crawford (Paramedic); Alan Draven (Kid); Ben Gardiner (Wilson); Rocky George, DeAndre Gipson, John McKnight, Angelo Moore, John Steward, Curtis L. Storey Jr. (Band); Richard Gross (Cop); Josh Hammond (Tyler); Bert Kinyon (Bert, Lumberjack Foreman); Noah Maschan (Young Gus); Sean O'Brien (Naked Hippie Boy); Rick Overton (Mayor Hal Burton); Waylon Payne (Dean); Richard Reicheg (Newscaster); Elizabeth Ryan (Bull Dyke); Michael Sommers (Patrolman); Kira Syester (Balloon Girl); Nicole Wilder (Naked Hippie Girl); Jud Williford (Protestor #1)

# THE COLLECTOR

(FLOATING STONE PRODS.) Producer/Director/Editor, Olympia Stone; Photography, Daniel Miller, Lloyd Fales, Olympia Stone, Daniel Akiba, Vladimir Minuty; Music, Jason Graves; Color; Not rated; 62 minutes; Release date: April 25, 2007. Documentary on art collector Allan Stone.

# SING NOW OR FOREVER HOLD YOUR PEACE

Mark Feuerstein, Tara Magalski in *Sing Now or Forever Hold Your Peace* © STRAND RELEASING

(STRAND) Producer/Director/Screenplay, Bruce Leddy; Co-Producer, Eliza Steel; Photography, Clyde Smith; Editor, Bill Deronde; Music, Jeff Cardoni; Music Consultant, Sean Altman; Designer, Timothy Whidbee; Costumes, Erika Munro; Casting, Avy Kaufman; a Shut Up and Sing production; Color; 16mm-to-35mm; Not rated; 96 minutes; Release date: April 27, 2007.

### Cast

Molly Shannon (Trish), Mark Feuerstein (Greg), David Harbour (David), Elizabeth Reaser (Julep), David Alan Basche (Steven), Rosemarie DeWitt (Dana), Reg Rogers (Richard), Alexander Chaplin (Ted), Liz Stauber (Michelle), Samrat Chakrabarti (Will), Chris Bowers (Spooner), Camilla Thorsson (Elsa), June Raphael (Tammy), Salvatore Inzerillo (Biker), Joanna Adler (Sheila), Zachary Steel (Zach), Rob Crawford (Sloan), Joshu Biton (The Tree Guy), Isabella Bodnar (Ted's Assistant), Jamie Corvier (Preppy Girl), Lucas Hewitt (Man in Audience), Sarah Lewis (Spanish Speaker), Tara Magalski (Kate), Michael T. Mastrolembo (College Student), Don Sparks (Store Owner), Kevin Weist (The Shutmen Singers)

# KICKIN' IT OLD SKOOL

Miguel A. Nuñez Jr., Jamie Kennedy in *Kickin' It Old Skool* © YARI FILM GROUP

(YARI FILM GROUP) Producers, Philip Glasser, John J. Hermansen, Jamie Kennedy, Bob Yari; Executive Producers, Jeff Cooper, Jeffrey Cooper, Josh H. Etting, Paul C. Rogers, Scott G. Stone, Stuart Stone; Director, Harv Glazer; Screenplay, Trace Slobotkin, Josh Siegal, Dylan Morgan; Photography, Robert M. Stephens; Designer, Tink; Costumes, Maria Livingstone; Editor, Sandy S. Solowitz; Music, Richard Glasser; Choreographer, Adolfo "Shabba-Doo" Quinones; Casting, Roe Baker, Susan Taylor Brouse, Lynne Carrow; a Jizzy Entertainment production in association with Hi-Def Entertainment; Dolby; Color; Rated PG-13; 108 minutes; Release date: April 27, 2007.

## Cast

Jamie Kennedy (Justin Schumacher); Miguel A. Núñez Jr. (Darnell); Maria Menounos (Jennifer); Michael Rosenbaum (Kip); Bobby Lee (Aki); Aris Alvarado (Hector); Debra Jo Rupp (Sylvia Schumacher); Christopher McDonald (Marty Schumacher); Vivica A. Fox (Roxanne); Alexander Calvert (Young Justin); Alan Ruck (Dr. Fry); Jesse "Casper" Brown (Cole); Stuart Stone (DJ Tanner); David Hasselhoff, Emmanuel Lewis (Themselves); Alexia Fast (Young Jennifer); Taylor Beaumont (Young Kip); J.R. Messado (Young Darnell); Anthony Grant (Young Hector); Hanson Ng (Young Aki); Alvin Sanders (School Principal); Burkely Duffield (George Michael Kid); Ryan Schilke (Andrew Ridgeley Kid); Harv Glazer (Chimichanga); Keith Dallas (Security Guard); Regan Oey (Kid in Toy Store); David Allan Pearson (Bank Manager); Michael Miguel Hanus (Gay Dude); Kira Clavell (Yun); Sean Amsing (Falafel Vendor); Frank C. Turner (Crazy Homeless Man); Richard O'Sullivan (Krumping Guy); Shannon Vaisler (Bar Girl); Anna Dillman (Gina); Emily Scorse, Brooklyn Chang (Girls at Dance School); Lakota Huffman (Six-Year-Old Girl); Leah Cairns (Woman at Table); Bill Mondy (TV Bigwig); Terri-Anne Welyki (Bartender); Sevrin Boyd, Adrienne Chan, Sara Fenton, Menina Fortunato, D.J. Goertzen, Jhaymee Hizon, Jheric Hizon, Kelly Koono, Simon "Young" Marlow, Jaayda McClanahan, Meisha Lee, Jennifer Olesiuk, Laurin Padolina, Joanne Pesusich, Luca "Lazylegs" Petuelli, Harj Rai, Kim Sato, Matt Ward, Michael Ward, Jonathan "Havoc" Woods, Reza Zadeh (Dancers)

# ZOO

(THINKFILM) Producers, Peggy Case, Alex Ferris; Executive Producers, Garr Godfrey, Ben Exworthy, Daniel Katz, Mark Urman, Jeff Sackman, Randy Manis; Co-Producer, Megan Griffiths; Director, Robinson Devor; Screenplay, Charles Mudede, Robinson Devor; Photography, Sean Kirby; Designer, Jeanne Cavenaugh; Costumes, Doris Black; Music, Paul Matthew Moore; Editor, Joe Shapiro; a Cook Ding production; Color; Not rated; 80 minutes; Release date: April 27, 2007. Docudrama about people sexually attracted to animals;

## Cast

John Paulsen (Mr. Hands), Richard Carmen (Mr. Hands' Brother), Ken Kreps (Mr. Hand's Father), James Chu (Chinese Businessman), Coyote (Himself), Paul Eenhoorn (Lead Detective), Forest Fousel (Capital Hill Man), Conor Gormally (Mr. Hand's Son), Malayka Gormally (Mr. Hand's Ex-Wife), Tom Gormally (The Polish Man), Brad Harrington (Bremerton Man), Russell Hodgkinson (H), Karl Holzheimer (Photographer), Andrew Scott McIntyre (Military Man), Michael J. Minard (Cop #1)

# THE CONDEMNED

(LIONSGATE) Producer, Joel Simon; Executive Producers, Vince McMahon, Michael Lake, Michael Gruner, George (CQ) Vrabeck, Graham Ludlow, Jed Blaugrund, Peter Block, Jason Constantine, John Sacchi; Co-Producers, John Bonneau, Mara Jacobs, Matt Walden; Director, Scott Wiper; Screenplay, Scott Wiper, Rob Hedden, from a story by Rob Hedden, Andy Hedden, Scott Wiper; Photography, Ross Emery; Editor, Derek G. Brechin; Music Supervisors, Neil Lawi, Jim Johnston; Designer, Graham Walker; Makeup and Hair, Margaret Stevenson; Casting, Tom McSweeney; Presented with WWE Films, of a WWE production, in association with Lionsgate, Colossal Entertainment, New Wave Entertainment; Dolby; Color; Rated R; 113 minutes; Release date: April 27, 2007.

## Cast

Steve Austin (Jack Conrad), Vinnie Jones (Ewan McStarley), Robert Mammone (Ian Breckel), Tory Mussett (Julie), Manu Bennett (Paco), Madeleine West (Sarah), Sam Healy (Bella), Christopher Baker (Eddie), Luke Pegler (Baxter), Rick Hoffman (Goldman), Masa Yamaguchi (Saiga), Emelia Burns (Rio), Dasi Ruz (Rosa), Marcus Johnson (K.C. Mack), Nathan Jones (The Russian), Andy McPhee (Nazi), Rai Fazio (La Bouche), Angie Milliken (Donna Sereno), Sullivan Stapleton (Wilkins), Grant Piro (Moyer), Neil Pigot (Meranto), Jacy Lewis (Assistant), Jared Robinsen (Mike), Andrew Buchanan (Lyle), Brad Haynes (Farland), Martin Challis (Burdick), Annie Jones (Karen), Trent Sullivan (Michael), Joey Massey (Scotty)

# DIGGERS

Ken Marino, Josh Hamilton, Ron Eldard, Paul Rudd in *Diggers* © MAGNOLIA PICTURES

(MAGNOLIA PICTURES) Producers, Jason Kliot, Joana Vicente, Anne Chaisson, Ken Marino; Executive Producers, Mark Cuban, Todd Wagner, David Wain; Co-Producer, Jon Stern; Director, Katherine Dieckmann; Screenplay, Ken Marino; Photography, Michael McDonough; Editors, Malcolm Jamieson, Sabine Hoffman; Music, David Mansfield; Designer, Roshelle Berliner; Costumes, Catherine George; Casting, Cindy Tolan; an HDNet Films production in association with Dirty Rice Pictures; Dolby; Color; HDcam; Not rated; 89 minutes; Release date: April 27, 2007.

## Cast

Paul Rudd (Hunt); Lauren Ambrose (Zoey); Ron Eldard (Jack); Josh Hamilton (Cons); Sarah Paulson (Julie); Ken Marino (Lozo); Maura Tierney (Gina); Beeson Carroll (Hunt's Father); Jack O'Connell (Mr. Wilson); Shannon Barry (Lisa); Andrew Cherry (Anthony Lozo); Alex Pickett (Frankie Lozo, Jr.); Jonny Pickett (Jon Jon Lozo); Caroline Wallis (Donna Lozo); Alison Folland (Beth); Mather Zickel (Alan); John Taylor (A.P.); Michael Potts (South Shell Pot Buyer); Tom Wiggin (Nick the Bartender); Dale Soules (Silly Lilly Waitress); Matthew Glave, Scott Sowers, Chazz Menendez (South Shell Guys); Cindy Smith (South Shell Secretary); Marc Spencer (Radio Announcer Voice); Margie Sutcuoglu (TV Announcer); Charlie Prott (Voice of Call-In Clamdigger)

# SOMETHING TO CHEER ABOUT

(TRULY INDIE/SCREEN MEDIA/LANTERN LANE) Producers, Betsy Blankenbaker, Oscar Robertson; Director/Screenplay, Betsy Blankenbaker; Editor, Steve Marra; a Figaro Films production; Black and white/color; Not rated; 90 minutes; Release date: April 27, 2007. Documentary on the Crispus Attucks Tigers, the first all-black high school basketball team to win the U.S. State Championship; with Hallie Bryant, Ray Crowe, Willie Merriweather, Oscar Robertson.

# THE TREATMENT

(NEW YORKER) Producers, Jonathan Shoemaker, Oren Rudavsky; Director, Oren Rudavsky; Screenplay, Daniel Housman, Oren Rudavsky, based on the novel by Daniel Menaker; Photography, Andrij Parekh; Designer, Edwige Geminel; Costumes, Erika Munro; Editor, Ramon Rivera Moret; Music, John Zorn; Music Supervisor, Jim Black; Casting, Antonia Dauphin, Kathleen Backel; a Shrinkwrap/Center Street production; Dolby; Color, Super16-to-HD; Not rated; 86 minutes; Release date: May 4, 2007.

## Cast

Chris Eigeman (Jake Singer), Famke Janssen (Allegra Marshall), Ian Holm (Dr. Ernesto Morales), Harris Yulin (Dr. Arnold Singer), Stephanie March (Julia), Blair Brown (Miss Callucci), Roger Rees (Leighton Proctor), Stephen Lang (Coach Galgano), Peter Vack (Ted), Griffin Newman (Scott), Josh Barclay Caras (Phil), Matt Stadelmann (Chris), Lindsay Johnson (Walter Cooper), Thomas Bubka (Other Coach), Maddie Corman (Patty McPherson), Stephen Lee Anderson (Bill Daniels), Tyrone Mitchell Henderson (Gerry Leonard), Elizabeth Hubbard (Claire Marshall), Ellen Maguire (School Nurse), Peter Hermann (Steve), Paul Sparks (Andre), Angela Bullock (Walter's Mom), Marceline Hugot (Upstate Nurse), Iraida Polanco (New Maid), Eli Katz (Alex Marshall), Josh Mann (Caterer)

Famke Janssen, Chris Eigeman, Ian Holm in *The Treatment* © NEW YORKER FILMS

# CIVIC DUTY

(FREESTYLE) Producers, Tina Pehme, Kim Roberts, Peter Krause, Andrew Joiner, Andrew Lanter; Executive Producer, Eli Rothman; Co-Producer, Kelly Duncan; Director, Jeff Renfroe; Screenplay, Andrew Joiner; Photography, Dylan MacLeod; Designer, Rick Willoughby; Costumes, Angelina Kekich; Editor, Renfroe; Music, Eli Krantzberg; Music Supervisor, Terry Michael Hudd; Visual Effects Supervisor, Dermot Shane; Casting, Lynne Carrow; a CIA Landslide Pictures presentation in association with Sepia Films and Intandem Films; Dolby; Color; Rated R; 98 minutes; Release date: May 4, 2007.

## Cast

Peter Krause (Terry Allen); Kari Matchett (Marla Allen); Ian Tracey (Lt. Randall Lloyd); Richard Schiff (FBI Agent Tom Hilary); Khaled Abol Naga (Gabe Hassan); Vanessa Tomasino (Bank Teller); Laurie Murdoch (Loan Officer); Michael Roberds (Post Office Clerk); Agam Darshi (Nurse); Mark Brandon (Night Anchor Bret Anderson); Brenda M. Crichlow (Day Anchor Tricia Wise); Val Cole (Morning Anchor Susan Harwood); Mark Docherty (News Reporter Chad Winslow); Michael St. John Smith (Legal Analyst); P. Lynn Johnson (Governor Bradley); Bruno Verdoni (Police Officer); Benita Ha (On Scene News Reporter #2); Allan Duncan (Golf Announcer); Brian Carey, Judy DeAngelis (Radio Announcers); Jessica Wachsman (Computerized Email Voice); Cheryl Uphill (Human Resources Phone Operator); Ed Redman (Sniper)

# THE HIP HOP PROJECT

Christopher "Cannon" Mapp in *The Hip Hop Project* © THINKFILM

(THINKFILM) Producers, Scott K. Rosenberg, Matt Ruskin; Executive Producer, Bruce Willis; Co-Producers, Michelle McElroy, Elsie Choi; Directors, Matt Ruskin, Scott K. Rosenberg; Photography, Ari Issler, Matt Ruskin; Editor, Matt Ruskin; Music, Lord Relic, Third Person, Dr. Holmes, Nas 550; Music Supervisors, Yolanda Ferraloro, Chris "Kharma Kazi" Rolle; Associate Producers, Issler, Melissa Van Allen, Nicole Nelch, Sam Carroll, Janina B. Czerewin, Michelle Clarke; a Pressure Point Films production; Color; Super-16-to-35mm; Not rated; 88 minutes; Release date: May 11, 2007. Documentary on how Chris "Kharma Kazi" Rolle rose from street vagrancy to develop an outreach program to help youngsters pursue their interest in hip-hop music; with Chris "Kharma Kazi" Rolle, Robin "Kheperah" Kearse, Diana "Princess" Lemon, Christopher "Cannon" Mapp, Russell Simmons, Bruce Willis.

# DELTA FARCE

Larry the Cable Guy, Keith David, Bill Engvall, DJ Qualls in *Delta Force* © LIONSGATE

(LIONSGATE) Producers, J.P. Williams, Alan Blomquist; Executive Producers, Emily Wolfe, Tom Ortenberg; Director, C.B. Harding; Screenplay, Bear Aderhold, Thomas F.X. Sullivan; Photography, Tom Priestly; Designer, Cabot McMullen; Costumes, Louise De Teliga; Editor, Mark Conte; Music, James S. Levine; Visual Effects Supervisor, Al Magliochetti; Visual Effects, Eye Candy; Stunts, David Rowden; Associate Producers, Maggie Houlehan, Jennifer Novak; Casting, Lisa Soltau, Deborah George; a Shaler Entertainment/Samwilla production presented with Parallel Entertainment Pictures; Dolby; Color; Rated PG-13; 89 minutes; Release date: May 11, 2007.

## Cast

Larry the Cable Guy (Larry); Bill Engvall (Bill Little); DJ Qualls (Everett Shackleford); Keith David (Sgt. Kilgore); Danny Trejo (Carlos Santana); Marisol Nichols (Maria); Michael Edward Rose (Sgt. Major); Glenn Morshower (General); Christina Moore (Karen); Lorna Scott (Woman at Cowboy Frank's); Parker Goris (Bill's Boy); Michael Papajohn (Bill's Neighbor); Lisa Lampanelli (Connie); Ed O'Ross (Victor); Lance Smith (Sgt. Adams); Bill Doyle (Colonel); McKinley Freeman (Airborne Soldier); Joel McKinnon Miller (Pilot); Chris Spencer (Co-Pilot); Alejandro Patino (Juan); Luis Chávez (Carlos); David DeSantos (Ricardo, Bandito); Toby Holguin, Jimmy Ortega (Banditos); Nicholas Guilak (Luis); Albert Santos (Flaco); Emilio Rivera (Jorge); Shelly Desai (Farmer); Tony Perez (Mayor); Danielle Hartnett (Senorita Magdalena); Carlos Moreno, Jr. (Jaime); Jeff Dunham (Amazing Ken); Rolando Molina (Bartender); Joseph Nunez (Ruben); Esteban Cueto (El Javelina); Tom Rosales (Bandito Guard); Craig Susser (Roger Grabowski); P.J. Walsh (Medic); Matt Riedy (Col. Dalton); Amy Powell (Anchorwoman)

# DUCK

Philip Baker Hall in *Duck* © RIGHT BRAINED RELEASING

(RIGHT BRAINED RELEASING) Producers, Nic Bettauer, Edward L. Plumb; Co-Executive Producer, Domini Hofmann; Director/Screenplay, Nic Bettauer; Photography, Anne Etheridge; Designer, Richard Haase; Costumes, Tilley; Editor, Marcus Taylor; Music, Alan Lazar; Additional Songs, Eels, Leonard Cohen, David Byrne; Lead Duck Trainer, Sue Chipperton, Studio Animal Services; Casting, Bruce H. Newberg; a Nics Pics and 5 Aces presentation; Dolby; Color; Not rated; 96 minutes; Release date: May 11, 2007.

### Cast

Philip Baker Hall (Arthur); Bill Brochtrup (Leopold); Amy Hill (Linh); Noel Guglielmi (JC); French Stewart (Jeffery); Bill Cobbs (Norman); Enrique Almeida, Dan Campbell (Firemen); Tamara Bick, Scott Galbraith (Police); Mary Pat Dowhy, Mark Brady (Animal Control); Annie Burgstede (Nanny); Larry Cedar (Mr. Janney); John Coughlin (Ziggy); Nikki Crawford (Bus Driver); William Rocha, Lou DiMaggio (City Workers); Leah Rowan, Jeremy Lowe, Francesca Adair (Servers); Starletta DuPois (Social Worker); Anne Etue (PET Woman); Loretta Fox (Addict); John Hawkes (Daniel); Gene Hong, Ian Lockhart (City Workers); Gary Kasper (Construction Boss); Nancy Kissam (Dancing Slut); Eric Ladin (Addict); Jill Lover (Hip Designer); Carol Mansell (Frances Chase); Gwendolyn Oliver (Crack Addict); Cedric Pendleton (PET Man); Robert Porter (Angry White Man); Jf Pryor (Begga'); Buckley Sampson (Young Arthur's Wife); Bridgid Sloyan (Party Barfer); Jim Thalman (Young Arthur); Michael Edward Thomas (Stoner); Suzanne Turner (Halloween Mom); Kelvin Yu (Delivery Man)

# THE SALON

(FREESTYLE/THE BIGGER PICTURE) Producers, Mark Brown, Vivica A. Fox, Lita Richardson, Carl Craig; Executive Producer, David Odom; Director/Screenplay, Mark Brown; Based on the play *Beauty Shop* by Shelley Garrett; Photography, Brandon Trost; Designer, Tiffany Zappulla; Costumes, Sarah Trost; Editor, Earl Watson; Casting, Joe Adams; from C4 Pictures, Cush Productions; Color; Rated PG-13; 90 minutes; Release date: May 11, 2007.

### Cast

Vivica A. Fox (Jenny), Darrin Dewitt Henson (Michael), Kym Whitley (Lashaunna), Monica Calhoun (Brenda), Taral Hicks (Trina), Dondre Whitfield (Ricky), De'Angelo Wilson (D.D.), Garrett Morris (Percy), Terrence Howard (Patrick), Brooke Burns (Tami), Sheila Cutchlow (Kandy), Tiffany Adams (Wanda), Mike Brooks (Street Hustler), Tray Chaney (JJ's Homeboy), Antonio D. Charity (Glenn), Dawn Douglas (Brenda's Hair Client), Kara Edwards (Nurse), Donnese Monique (Marketta), Romy J. Park (May-Kym), Dabir Snell (Trey), Jordan Howard (Private Dancer), Greg German.

# SHOWBUSINESS: THE ROAD TO BROADWAY

Natalie Venetia Belcon, John Tartaglia, Stephanie D'Abruzzo in *ShowBusiness: The Road to Broadway* © HERE!/REGENT

(REGENT) Producer/Director, Dori Berinstein; Executive Producers, Stewart Lane, Robin Brown, Mitchell Cannold, Bonnie Lane; Screenplay, Dori Berinstein, Richard Hankin; Photography, Alan Deutsch, Rob VanAlkemade; Editor, Richard Hankin; a Dramatic Forces production; Dolby; Color; Rated PG; 102 minutes; Release date: May 11, 2007. Documentary on the journey to Broadway for the musicals *Avenue Q, Caroline or Change, Taboo,* and *Wicked*; with Harrison Chad, Kristin Chenoweth, Jennifer Cody, Alan Cumming, Raul Esparza, David Finkle, Boy George, Susan Haskins, Tony Kushner, John Lahr, John Lithgow, Robert Lopez, Jeff Marx, Idina Menzel, Euan Morton, Rosie O'Donnell, Tonya Pinkins, Stephen Schwartz, John Tartaglia, Tom Titone, George C. Wolfe.

## CASTING ABOUT

(KINO) Producer, Lewis D. Wheeler; Director, Barry J. Hershey; Photography, Allie Humenuk; Editor, Marc Grossman; a Moving Still Prods. Production; Dolby; Color, DV-to-35mm; 86 minutes; Release date: May 11, 2007. Documentary on the casting process spotlighting several actresses as they compete for three roles in a feature film; with Wendy Elizabeth Abraham, Mädchen Amick, Jeannette Arndt, Solveig August, Nina Bagusat, Kristina Bangert, Silvana Bayer, Emily Behr, Amalie Bizer, Elizabeth Bogush, Tina Bordihn, Hannah Bourne, Jennifer Bradley, Brigid Brannagh, Julia Bremermann, Liz May Brice, Anne-Sophie Briest, Julie Carpineto, Kim Cassidy, Lara Cazalet, Stacey Cervellino, Sarah Charipar, Stephanie Childers, Julia Christina, Diana Cignoni, Darcy Cohler, Jessica Collins, Tiffany Conroy, Mary Kay Cook, Melisande Cook, Honey Crawford, Rosana Crombie, Gesine Cucrowski, Annette Culp, Sandra Darnell, Manao DeMuth, Kelly Dirstine, Melanie Dix, Nora Düding, Heather Dumont, Nicole Eggert, Kerry Elkins, Tania Emery, Jennifer Engstrom, Nicole Ernst, Mareike Fell, Deirdre Fitzmaurice, Molly Flynn, Nina Franoszek, Phoebe Frye, Susanne Gärtner, Jule Gartzke, Johanna Christine Gehlen, Claudia Geisler, Jasmin Great, Sue Gillan, Linda Gillum, Dana Min Goodman, Shana Goodspell, Sharon Göpfert, Eva Habermann, Audrey Hager, Sarah Hankins, Khara Hanlon, Petra Hartung, Lauren Hayward, Darra Herman, Erin Hershey, Michaela Hinnenthal, Elizabeth Hobbs, Deborah Hodges, Alexandra Holden, Lian-Marie Holmes, Holli Hornlien, Susanne Hoss, Simone Huber, Marin Ireland, Sarah Isenberg, Danica Ivancevic, Katie Jeep, Eva Kaminsky, Megan Kellie, Jennifer Kern, Deborah King, Johanna Klante, Anja Kling, Valerie Koch, Naomi Kruass, Lauren Krol, Bettina Kurth, Linda Jae Ladas, Florentine Lahme, Elizabeth Laidloaw, Courtney Lamb, Joy Lamberton, Bettina Lamprecht, Molly Lanzarotta, Gwen Larsen, Laura Latreille, Caroline Lawton, Christina Laarakis, Katrina Lenk, Elin Lundgren, Beate Maes, Julia Malik, Simone Marean, Desirée Matthews, Helen McElwain, Anita McFarlane, Aislín McGuckin, Jameelah McMillan, Coco Medvitz, Kymberly Mellen, Shelley Minto, Juliana Mitchell, Marina Morgan, Michelle Morgan, Sarah Jane Morris, Hemmendy Nelson, Elisabeth Oas, Celeste Oliva, Leigh Oquendo, Clara Perez, Danielle Perry, Jillian Peterson, Eliza Pierson, Katherine Place, Daria Polatin, Carrie Porter, Sabina Riedel, Laura Roges, Nicole Rogers, Katrina Romanoff, Rachel Romanski, Heather Rosbeck, Heidi Saban, Negaar Sagafi, Kria Sakakeeny, Angela Sandritter, Franziska Schlattner, Tracy Schmetterer, Mandy Schneider, Laura Schuhrk, Jenn Schulte, Saskia Schwarz, Laura Schweitzer, Nicole Shalhoub, Lily Shaw, Anna Shemeikka, Krissy Shields, Mika Simmons, Sybil Smith, Patricia Spahn, Kathrin von Steinburg, Julia Stelter, Maria Stevens, Katja Studt, Ann-Cathrin Sudhoff, Clare Swinburne, Isabella Szendzielorz, Mina Tander, Liz Terzo, Elaine Theodore, Patricia Thielemann, Tabea Tiesler, Laura Tonke, Petra Torky, Susite Trayling, Saskia Valencia, Holly Vanasse, Brinley Arden Vickers, Gillian Vigman, Claudia Vogt, Andrea Walker, Anastasia Webb, Sarah Wellington, Alexandra Wescourt, Taylor Wilcox, Jennifer Winters, Amanda Witt, Petra Wright, Dawn Zeek, Krysta Brielle Zeiset, Helen Zellweger.

## DISAPPEARANCES

Kris Kristofferson, Charlie McDermott in *Disappearances* © TRULY INDIE

(TRULY INDIE) Producers, Jay Craven, Hathalee Higgs, J. Todd Harris, Mark Donadio, Miriam Marcus; Executive Producers, Todd Enright, John MacNeil; Director/Screenplay, Jay Craven, based on the novel by Howard Frank Mosher; Photography, Wolfgang Held; Designer, Carl Sprague; Costumes, Jill Kliber; Editor, Beatrice Sisul; Music, Judy Hyman, Jeff Claus; Associate Producers, Lauren Moye, Lisa McWilliams, Bess O'Brien; Line Producer, Stacey Babb; Casting, Helene Rousse; a Frontier Partners and Kingdom County Prods. production in association with Moody Street Pictures; Dolby; Widescreen; Color; Not rated; 118 minutes; Release date: May 11, 2007.

### Cast

Kris Kristofferson (Quebec Bill); Lothaire Bluteau (Carcajou); Gary Farmer (Henry Coville); William Sanderson (Rat Kinneson); Charlie McDermott (Wild Bill Bonhomme); Geneviève Bujold (Cordelia); Luis Guzmán (Brother St. Hilaire); Rusty De Wees (Frog Lamundy); John Griesemer (Brother St. Paul); Munson Hicks (Sheriff); Mark Jenkins, Ken Winter (Henchmen); Tessa Klein (Little Gretchen); Josh Pellerin (Andre LaChance); Heather Rae (Evangeline); Bill Raymond (Compton); William Rough (Bartender); Christy Scott Cashman (Yellow Rose); Steve Small (Origene LaChance)

# THE LAST TIME

(DESTINATION FILMS) Producers, Stavros Merjos, Peter Samuelson, J. Malcolm Petal, Adam Rosenfelt; Executive Producers, Marc Schaberg, Michael Keaton, Brendan Fraser, Sam Nazarian; Co-Producers, Julie Dangel, Jeff Balis, Kimberly C. Anderson; Director/Screenplay, Michael Caleo; Photography, Tim Suhrstedt; Designer, Garreth Stover; Costumes, Shawn-Holly Cookson, Peter Meiselmann; Editors, David Finfer, Thom Noble; Music, Randy Edelman; Music Supervisor, Yolanda Ferraloro; Casting, Anne McCarthy, Jay Scully; an Element Films presentation of an Element Films production in association with Lift Prods. and L.A. Squared; Dolby; Widescreen; Color; Rated R; 96 minutes; Release date: May 18, 2007.

### Cast

Michael Keaton (Ted Riker); Brendan Fraser (Jamie Bashant); Amber Valletta (Belisa); Daniel Stern (John Whitman); Neal McDonough (Hurly); Michael C. Hagerty (Breckenridge); Michael Lerner (Leguzza); Richard Kuhlman (Arthur Crosby); Alexis Cruz (Alvarez); William Ragsdale (Roger); George Anton, Don Lincoln (NY Business Men); Barbara Balentine, Elizabeth Lynch (Office Workers); Allen Boudreaux, Carol Dupuy, Louis Dupuy, Brian Edwards (NY Executives); Felix J. Boyle (Pit Boss); Kristi Chalaire (NY Business Woman); Thomas Crawford (Sales Guru); Lisa Marie Dupree (NY Model); Chuck Halley (NYC Pedestrain with Cell Phone); David Jensen (J.D. Wachowitz); Gus Lynch (Frustrated NY Cabdriver); Caroline McKinley (Madeline); Jon Purvis (Business Associate); Michael Aaron Santos (Brad); Aaron Sauer (Downtown Cabdriver); Billy Slaughter (Intern); Doc Whitney (Sales Exec); Toni Wynne (Coffee Girl)

# I HAVE NEVER FORGOTTEN YOU: THE LIFE & LEGACY OF SIMON WIESENTHAL

Simon Wiesenthal in *I Have Never Forgotten You* © LUMINOUS VELOCITY

(LUMINOUS VELOCITY) Producers/Screenplay, Richard Trank, Marvin Hier; Director, Richard Trank; Photography, Jeff Victor; Music, Lee Holdridge; Editor, Inbal B. Lessner; Narrator, Nicole Kidman; a Moriah Films production; Dolby; Black and white/color; Rated PG-13; 105 minutes; Release date: May 23, 2007. Documentary on Jewish engineer Simon Wiesenthal, who dedicated his life to hunting down Nazis after surviving the Holocaust.

# ORANGE WINTER

Orange Winter © AZ FILMS

(AZ FILMS) Producers, Andrei Zagdansky, Gleb Sinyavsky; Director/Editor, Andrei Zagdansky; Screenplay, Alexander Genis; Photography, Vladimir Guevsky, Igor Ivanov, Pavel Kazantzev; Music, Alexander Goldstein; Narrator, Matthew Gurewitsch; Color/black and white; DigiBeta; Not rated; 72 minutes; Release date: May 23, 2007. Documentary on the Orange Revolution that erupted on the streets of Kiev after the controversial Ukranian presidential election of 2004.

# STEEL CITY

(TRULY INDIE) Producers, Ryan Harper, Rusty Gray, Brian Jun; Executive Producers, Eric Arlt, Mark Covington, Mike Gandy, P.J. Jun; Director/Screenplay/Editor, Brian Jun; Photography, Ryan Samul; Designer, Jack Thomas; Costumes, Meredith J. Murray; Music, Mark Geary; Associate Producers, John Heard, Marisa Johnson, Josh R. Jaggars; Casting, Emily Schweber; a Your Half Pictures production; Color; Super 16; 35mm; Rated R; 96 minutes; Release date: May 25, 2007.

### Cast

John Heard (Carl Lee), Tom Guiry (P.J. Lee), America Ferrera (Amy Barnes), Clayne Crawford (Ben Lee), James McDaniel (Randall Karns), Heather McComb (Lucy Jones), Jamie Anne Brown (Maria Lee), Laurie Metcalf (Marianne Karns), Raymond J. Barry (Uncle Victor Lee), Kristian Best (Michael Karns), Michael Cowan (Carpenter at Fire Job), James DeBello (Danny), Celesta Gentlein (Baby Jenny at 1), Rusty Gray (Marcus), Ricardo Gutierrez (Ralph), James R. Hentrich (Charlie Haskel), Richard Hoffman, Jr. (Carl's Attorney), Amy Holland (Distraught Woman), Ian Ivkovich (Young P.J. Lee), Charlie Keshner (Carl's Jail Officer), Gerald J. Lange, Jr. (Diner Patron), Dennis Lebby (Jimmy), Si Osborne (Det. Brady), James "Bumper" Simpson (Carpenter at Fire Job), George Stumpf (Young Carl), Jani Vorwerk (Young Marianne), Carly Weiss (Jenny at age 2), Robert Wood (Casey)

# FOUR LANE HIGHWAY

(SKY ISLAND FILMS) Producer, Christopher Roberts; Director/Screenplay, Dylan McCormick; Line Producers, Lori Pernal, David L. Oltman; Photography, Randy Drummond; Designer, Cindi Sfinas; Costumes, Bobby Frederick Tilley; Music, Marcelo Zarvos; Editors, Gary Levy, David Klagsbrun; Casting, David Vaccari; an Other Pictures production; Color; Not rated; 104 minutes; Release date: June 1, 2007.

**Cast**

Arthur Aulisi (Brian); Earl Baker (Greg); Jeff Branson (Andy); Dennis Fox (Ed); Dana Goodman (Karen); Greer Goodman (Molly); Zandy Hartig (Stacey); John Hines (Ernie); Garland Hunter (Gallery Owner); Dan Jenkins (Paul); Ayelet Kaznelson (Maya); Wynter Kullman (Caitlin); Katharine Powell, Mary Alexandra Stiefvater, Michie Madison (College Girls); Lesley McBurney (Donna); Dylan McCormick (Eric); Bernie McInerney (Carl); Evan Neumann (Sasha's Guy); Peggy Pope (Waitress); Elizabeth Rodriguez (Sasha); Reg Rogers (Lyle); Ian Root (Phil); Grace Rugen (Libby); Olivia Rugen (Zoe); Fred Weller (Sean)

# I'M REED FISH

Katey Sagal, Jay Baruchel, Alexis Bledel in *I'm Reed Fish* © SCREEN MEDIA

(SCREEN MEDIA/RED ENVELOPE ENTERTAINMENT) Producer, Bader Alwazzan; Executive Producers, Akiva Goldsman, Kerry Foster, Michael Mihalke; Director, Zachkary Adler; Screenplay, Reed Fish; Photography, Doug Chamberlain; Editor, Yuka Reull; Music, Roddy Bottum; Music Supervisor, Toby Record; Designer, Ariana Nakata; Casting, Carol Barlow; a Squared Foot production; Panavision; Deluxe Color; Rated R; 93 minutes; Release date: June 1, 2007.

**Cast**

Jay Baruchel (Reed Fish), Alexis Bledel (Kate Peterson), Schuyler Fisk (Jill Cavanaugh), DJ Qualls (Andrew), A.J. Cook (Theresa), Victor Rasuk (Frank Cortez), Katey Sagal (Maureen), Chris Parnell (Ralph), Shiri Appleby (Kate), Valerie Azlynn (Woman), Jackie Benoit (Imogene Sandstrom), Boti Bliss (Waitress), Blake Clark (Irv Peterson), Tommy Dewey (Rex), Reed Fish (John Penner), Todd Fjelstead (Bartender), Andrew Stubblefield (George Henderson), Rossif Sutherland (Gabe), Jim Cody Williams (Cowboy)

# GRACIE

Carly Schroeder in *Gracie* © PICTUREHOUSE

(PICTUREHOUSE) Producers, Andrew Shue, Lemore Syvan, Elisabeth Shue, Davis Guggenheim; Executive Producers, Dustin Cohn, Tom Fox, Cindy Alston, Mead Welles, Jeff Arnold; Co-Producers, John Shue, Ken Himmelman, Andrew Wiese, Chris Frisina; Director, Davis Guggenheim; Screenplay, Lisa Marie Petersen, Karen Janszen, from a story by Andrew Shue, Ken Himmelman, Davis Guggenheim; Photography, Chris Manley; Designer, Dina Goldman; Costumes, Elizabeth Caitlin Ward; Editor, Elizabeth King; Music, Mark Isham; Music Supervisor, John Houlihan; Soccer Choreographer, Dan Metcalfe; Casting, Laura Rosenthal, Ali Farrell; an Ursa Major Films production in association with Elevation Filmworks; Dolby; Color; Rated PG-13; 92 minutes; Release date: June 1, 2007.

**Cast**

Carly Schroeder (Gracie Bowen), Elisabeth Shue (Lindsay Bowen), Dermot Mulroney (Bryan Bowen), Andrew Shue (Coach Owen Clark), Jesse Lee Soffer (Johnny Bowen), Joshua Caras (Peter), Julia Garro (Jena Walpen), John Doman (Coach Colasanti), Christopher Shand (Kyle Rhodes), Karl Girolamo (Curt), Vasilios "Billy" Mantagas (Craig), Donnie Gray (Donny), Emma Bell (Kate Dorset), Hunter Schroeder (Mike Bowen), Trevor Heins (Daniel Bowen), Madison Arnold (Grandad), John Doman (Coach Colasanti), Karl Schellscheidt (Referee Jay Gavitt), James Biberi (Officer Sal Famulari), Lou Sumrall (Greasy Bouncer), Peter McRobbie (Principal Enright), Chris Heuisler (Rob), Jack Walker (Adam Charles), C.C. Loveheart (Bowsher's Assistant), Leslie Lyles (Chairwoman Connie Bowsher), Tashya Valdevit (Maryellen Connors), Jay Patterson (Boardmember Rice), Brian Simar (Boardmember Fitzpatrick), Robens Jerome (Rodney), Dan Metcalfe (Kingston Coach), Amanda Knox (Columbia Cheerleader), Jesse Lee Soffer (Johnny)

# HOSTEL: PART II

(LIONSGATE) Producers, Mike Fleiss, Eli Roth, Chris Briggs; Executive Producers, Boaz Yakin, Scott Spiegel, Quentin Tarantino; Co-Producers, Daniel Frisch, Philip Waley; Director/Screenplay, Eli Roth, based on his characters; Photography, Milan Chadima; Designer, Robb Wilson King; Costumes, Susanna Puisto; Editor, George Folsey Jr.; Music, Nathan Barr; Visual Effects Supervisors, Avi Das (Barbed Wire FX), Gary E. Beach (Beach VFX-Prague), Vincent Cirelli (Luma Pictures); Special Effects Supervisor, Martin Pryca; Special Makeup Effects Designers, Gregory Nicotero, Howard Berger; Stunts, Pavel Vokoun; Associate Producers, Gabriel A. Roth, Mark Bakunas, Eythor Gudjonnson; Casting, Kelly Martin Wagner; a Next Entertainment/Raw Nerve production; presented with Screen Gems and Quentin Tarantino; Dolby; Widescreen; Deluxe color; Rated R; 94 minutes; Release date: June 8, 2007.

### Cast

Lauren German (Beth); Roger Bart (Stuart); Heather Matarazzo (Lorna); Bijou Phillips (Whitney); Richard Burgi (Todd); Vera Jordanova (Axelle); Jay Hernandez (Paxton); Milan Knazko (Sasha); Stanislav Ianevski (Miroslav); Jordan Ladd (Stephanie); Edwige Fenech (Art Class Professor); Patrik Zigo (Bubblegum Gang Leader); Zuzana Geislerová (Inya); Ivan Furak (Big Guard); Monika Malacova (Mrs. Bathory); Davide Dominici (Riccardo); Petr Vancura (Pavel); Roman Janecka (Roman); Milda Havlas (Desk Clerk Jedi); Liliya Malkina (Make-Up Woman); Susanna Bequer (Italian Translator); Luc Merenda (Italian Detective); Ruggero Deodato (The Italian Cannibal); Philip Waley (Monitor Guard Czelsifan); Rostislav Osicka (Monitor Guard Boxer); Peter Bláha (Drunk Italian); Jiri Barton (Knife Wielding Italian); Nada Vanatkova (Italian Nurse); Jan Nemejovsky (The Doctor); Pierre Peyrichout (Army Man); Riccardo Trombetta (Electrocution Victim); Jiri Hajdyla (Train Waiter); Mirek Cipra (Tub Guard); Mark Taylor (Sir Bruce Bonus); Guilherme Bolliger (Paul Bullen); Chris Hewitt (Drunk British Slob); David Baxa (Hammer Man); Rick James (Nail Man); Mira Nosek (Van Driver); Monika Hladová (Train Waitress); Mollie Andron (Axelle's Next Victim #2); Adam Gazik, Adrian Kotlar, Adriana Godlova, Ales Kotlar, Andrea Varadiova, Dana Matiova, Ervin Varadi, Frantisek Dumka, Frantisek Kotlar, Jakub Surmai, Josef Adamovic, Lucas Cajkovsky, Nikolas Conka, Ondrej Cajkovsky, Petr Conka, Radek Entner, Radek Hrdlicka, Stanislav Conka, Vladimir Churan (Bubble Gum Kids)

Bijou Phillips in *Hostel: Part II* © LIONSGATE

# YOU'RE GONNA MISS ME

Roky Erickson in *You're Gonna Miss Me* © PALM PICTURES

(PALM PICTURES) Producers, Adrienne Gruben, Keven McAlester; Executive Producers, Lauren Hollingsworth, Laura Boyd DeSmeth; Director, Keven McAlester; Photography, Lee Daniel; Color; Not rated; 91 minutes; Release date: June 8, 2007. Documentary on pioneering psychedelic rocker Roger Kynard "Roky" Erickson and his eventual descent into poverty and mental illness; with Evelyn Erickson, Sumner Erickson.

# MIRIAM

(SEVENTH ART RELEASING) Producer/Director, Matt Cimber; Executive Producer, Max Guefen; Screenplay, John Goff, Matt Cimber; Photography, River O'Mahoney Hagg; Editor, Olof Källström; Music, Peter Bernstein; Art Director, Samantha Summers; Costumes, Kathleen Hotmer; Casting, Iris Hampton; from Miriam Prods.; Color; HD; Not rated; 122 minutes; Release date: June 8, 2007.

### Cast

Ariana Savalas (Miriam); Addi Kaplan (Sonja Shafer); Shelly Kurtz (Feliksas); Beata Pozniak (Margritas); Peter J. Lucas (Bijaikis); Dimitri Diatchencko (Alexi); Olga Vilner (Katy); Nina Franoszek (Eleanora); Joshua Arden, Eric Axen (Officers); Benjamin Kobby (Priest); Ashly Dixon (Cate's Best Friend); Eugene Alper (Toyefsky); Markham Reilly (Mrs. Gimpel); Miranda Charney (Girl Exiting with Family); Molly Charney (Little Girl Exiting with Family); Petre Cowan (Vashem); James Elden (Lithuanian); Gadi Erel (Young Pieter); Lynn Fero (Recorder); Scott Frazelle (German Soldier, Beating); Jilon Ghaj (Young German Driver); Katie Lee Harper (Christian, Crying on Street); Lincoln Hoppe (Lead Soldier); Steve Humphreys (S.S. Officer); Danny A. Jacobs (Aron); Stu Levin (Uncle Danilevya); Carrie Maziarz (Upper Class Woman); Stephen Mendel (Pieter Shafer); Dillon Morse (Holocaust Child); Melanie Mullins (Flight Attendant); Joel Nunley (Toyefsky's Assistant); Clint J. Palmer (Mr. Pimple); Elsa Raven (Aunt Levya); Vicki Roberts (Catholic Woman); Irene Roseen (Mrs. Jonikyte); R.J. Schines (Miriam's Brother); Alex Splendore (Simon); Rick Steadman (German Soldier); Natasha Talonz (Churchgoer); DeAnn Trimarchi (Nun); Debra Tylak (Russian Officer); Ryan Van Denburgh (Drugstore Patron); Nadia van de Ven (Lilyana); Gary Weinberg (Vasilenko); Diane Witter (Night Nurse)

# CHALK

Troy Schremmer in *Chalk* © VIRGIL FILMS

(VIRGIL FILMS) Producers, Mike Akel, Angie Alvarez, Graham Davidson; Executive Producers, Michael McAlister, David Gonzales; Director, Mike Akel; Screenplay, Mike Akel, Chris Mass; Photography, Steven Schaefer; Editor, Bob Perkins; Music, Chris Jagich; Associate Producer, Mark Harkrider; a SomeDaySoon production; Color; DV; Not rated; 84 minutes; Release date: June 8, 2007.

## Cast

Troy Schremmer (Mr. Lowrey), Janelle Schremmer (Coach Webb), Shannon Haragan (Mrs. Reddell), Chris Mass (Mr. Stroope), Jeff Guerrero (Mr. G), Jeffrey Travis (Math Teacher)

# GYPSY CARAVAN

(SHADOW DISTRIBUTION) aka *When the Road Bends: Tales of a Gypsy Caravan*; Producer, Jasmine Dellal; Co-Producer, Sara P. Nolan; Executive Producers, San Fu Maltha, Wouter Barendrecht, Michael J. Werner; Director, Jasmine Dellal; Photography, Albert Maysles, Alain de Halleux; Editors, Mary Myers, Jasmine Dellal; a Little Dust production in association with ITVS, Fu Works Filmrights, and Fortissimo Films; Dolby; Color; 16mm; DV; Not rated; 111 minutes; Release date: June 15, 2007. Documentary on the 2001 U.S. "Gypsy Caravan" tour showcasing five bands from four countries; with Fanfare Ciocarlia, Taraf de Haidouks, Antonio El Pipa, Maharaja, Esma Redzepova, Johnny Depp.

# AND THEN CAME LOVE

Kevin Daniels, Vanessa Williams in *And Then Came Love* © FOX MEADOW FILMS

(FOX MEADOW FILMS) Producers, Caytha Jentis, Verne Mattson, Anthony J. Vorhies; Co-Producers, Nancie Ellis, Sashi Balooja, Maggie L. Harrer; Director, Richard Schenkman; Screenplay, Caytha Jentis; Photography, Timothy Naylor; Designer, Mary Frederickson; Costumes, Deborah Medeiros Baker, Editor, Richard LaBrie; Music, Rebecca Lloyd; Casting, James Calleri; Presented in association with ABC Film and Video; Color; HD; Not rated; 90 minutes; Release date: June 15, 2007.

## Cast

Vanessa Williams (Julie), Kevin Daniels (Paul), Michael Boatman (Ted), Jeremy Gumbs (Jake), Eartha Kitt (Mona), Tommy Nelson (Horatio), Stephen Spinella (Stuart), Eileen Alana (Miss Missy), Ben Vereen (Chuck Cooper), Shashi Balooja (Artie), Anna Camp (Kikki), Mike Colter (Yuppie Paul), Peter Conboy (Man on Street), Andrea Darriau (Jittery Woman), Melissa Dye (Linda), Stephanie Garcia (Fashion Editor), Shelly Gibson (Kindergarten Mom), Michael Girts (Office Worker), Rosie Gunther (Carol), Eugene Jones (Paul's Brother), Paula Mandel (Talkative Woman at Bar), Lily Mercer (Francis), Greg Murtha (Man at Book Reading), Sophie Nyweide (Martha), Caryann Villani (Mother), Catrina Villani (Restaurant Patron), Joseph Villani (School Kid), Noah Weisberg (Box Office Attendant)

# BLOOD AND TEARS: THE ARAB-ISRAELI CONFLICT

(THINKFILM) Executive Producers, Brenda Sassoon-Rosmarin, Jeff Helmreich; Director/Screenplay/Editor, Isidore Rosmarin; Resarcher, Elizabeth Levin; Color; Rated PG-13; 73 minutes; Release date: June 15, 2007. Documentary examining the history of the Arab-Israeli conflict; with Akbar Ahmed, Eve Harow, Saeb Erekat, Izzeldin Abuelaish, Benjamin Netanyhau.

# UNBORN IN THE USA: INSIDE THE WAR ON ABORTION

*Unborn in the USA* © FIRST RUN FEATURES

(FIRST RUN FEATURES) Producers, Stephen Fell, Will Thompson; Directors/Screenplay/Editors, Stephen Fell, Will Thompson; Photography, Will Thompson, Stephen Fell, Joseph McKeel; Music, David Worrell; Associate Producer, Lindsey Sheren; a Scuba Rooster production; Color; DV; Not rated; 104 minutes; Release date: June 15, 2007. Documentary on America's pro-life activists.

# COLMA THE MUSICAL

Jake Moreno in *Colma: The Musical* © ROADSIDE ATTRACTIONS

(ROADSIDE ATTRACTIONS) Producers, Paul Kolsanoff, Richard Wong, Angel Vasquez; Director/Photography/Editor, Richard Wong; Screenplay/Music/Lyrics, H.P. Mendoza; Choreographers, Ken Chin, H.P. Mendoza; Casting, H.P. Mendoza, Carol Rosenthal, Fel Phillip Abello; a Greenrocksolid production; Color; MiniDV-to-DigiBeta; Not rated; 113 minutes; Release date: June 22, 2007.

## Cast

Jake Moreno (Billy), H.P. Mendoza (Rodel), L.A. Renigen (Maribel), Sigrid Sutter (Tara), Brian Raffi (Julio), Gigi Guizado (Kattia), Larry Soriano (Rodel's Father), Kat Kneisel (Joanne), Paul Kolsanoff (Kevin), Allison Torneros (Amanda), Jim Wierzba (Hulk Hogan), David Scott Keller (Michael), Paula Baldin (Young Girl), Tristan Ott (Hipster Guy)

# IN BETWEEN DAYS

Jiseon Kim in *In Between Days* © KINO

(KINO) Producer, Bradley Rust Gray; Co-Producer, Jennifer Weiss; Director/Editor, So Yong Kim; Screenplay, So Yong Kim, Bradley Rust Gray; Photography, Sarah Levy; American-Canadian-South Korean; Dolby; Color; 16mm-to-DV; Not rated; 82 minutes; Release date: June 27, 2007.

## Cast

Jiseon Kim (Aimie), Taegu Andy Kang (Tran), Bokja Kim (Mom), Nathan Rodriguez (Peter)

# OVER THE GW

(SEVENTH ART) Producers, Nick Gaglia, Theresa Gaglia; Line Producer, George Gallagher; Director/Screenplay/Photography/Editor, Nick Gaglia; Color; DV; Not rated; 75 minutes; Release date: June 27, 2007.

## Cast

George Gallagher (Tony), Kether Donohue (Sofia Serra), Albert Insinnia (Dr. Hiller), Nicholas Serra (Dad), Minnie Kraskowsky (Grandma), G.R. Johnson (Mr. Morris), Justin Swain (James), Steve Stanulis (Guy), Julia Moriarty (Mom), Jessika Graff (Jeanie), Michael Mathis (Joe), Juliana Huestis (Darla), Megan Ribera (Jennifer), Carrie Keranen (Dawn), Nick Gaglia (Joe Joe), Tory Andrews (Barry), Torey Marks (Ana), Juliana Kiara (Lindsay), Anna Farrell (Marie), Sarah-Ann Rodgers (Mrs. Hiller), John Aidan (Bobby), Amelia Buckley (Nadine), Adam Rosenblatt (Radam), Grant Udoff (Jase), Jeff Silverman (Tom), Lisa Fernandez (Lisa), Salvatore Cancassi (Skeet), Gordon King (Fabian), Chima Chikazunga (Sharif), Howard Parke (Detective), Robert Youngren (Tom's Dad), Anthony Paska (Dylan), Jess Fulena (Susan), Tanya Washington (Madeline), Dan Falcone (Josh), Marissa Wein (Marge), Jenn McNulty (Patricia), Eva Gaglia (Sister), Bob Socci (Man in Pew)

## DR. BRONNER'S MAGIC SOAPBOX

Emanuel Bronner in *Dr. Bronner's Magic Soapbox* © BALCONY RELEASING

(BALCONY RELEASING) Producers, Sara Lamm, Zachary Mortensen, Cheri Anderson; Executive Producer, Matt Aselton; Director, Sara Lamm; Photography, Andrew Nagata, Sara Lamm; Editor, Kay Finch; Music, Pierre de Gaillande; a Reckon So presentation of a Reckon So, Ghost Robot production; Color, DV; Not rated; 88 minutes; Release date: June 29, 2007. Documentary on the curious life of German soap maker Emanuel Bronner.

## NICE BOMBS

(SEVENTH ART) Producers, Kristie Alshaibi, Ben Berkowitz, Ben Redgrave; Executive Producers, Studs Terkel, William Haddad, Justin Moyer; Director /Photography, Usama Alshaibi; Editors, Amy Cargill, Michael Palmerio, Usama Alshaibi; Music, Naeif Rafeh, Issa Boulos; an Artvamp/Benzfilm Group production; Color; HD; Not rated; 76 minutes; Release date: July 11, 2007. Documentary on Iraq at the onset of the American occupation; with Usama Alshaibi, Kristie Alshaibi, Hameed Alshaibi, Tareef Alshaibi.

Hameed Alshaibi in *Nice Bombs* © SEVENTH ART RELEASING

## CAPTIVITY

Elisha Cuthbert in *Captivity* © LIONSGATE

(LIONSGATE) Producers, Mark Damon, Sergei Konov, Gary Mehman, Leonid Minkovski; Executive Producer, Valery Chumak; Director, Roland Joffe; Screenplay, Larry Cohen, Joseph Tura, based on a story by Larry Cohen; Photography, Daniel J. Pearl; Editor, Richard Nord; Music, Marco Beltrami; Music Supervisors, Frankie Pine, Allison Wright Clark; Designer, Addis Gadzhiev; Associate Producers, Marius Vilunas, Alla Kharebova; Casting, Dianne Crittenden, Karen Rea; a Lionsgate and After Dark Films presentation of a Foresight Unlimited (U.S.) production in association with Ramco (Russia); American-Russian; Dolby; Deluxe color; Rated R; 85 minutes; Release date: June 13, 2007.

### Cast

Elisha Cuthbert (Jennifer Tree); Daniel Gillies (Gary Dexter); Pruitt Taylor Vince (Ben Dexter); Michael Harney (Det. Bettinger); Laz Alonso (Det. Ray Di Santos); Maggie Damon (Det. Susan Luden); Chrysta Olson (Mary D'Abro); Carl Paoli, Trent Broin (Victims); Elijah Runcorn (Young Ben); Remy Thorne (Young Gary)

# EL INMIGRANTE

(INDICAN) Producers, John Sheedy, David Eckenrode, John Eckenrode; Executive Producer, Rick Carlson; Directors, John Sheedy, David Eckenrode, John Eckenrode; Photography, John Sheedy, David Eckenrode; Designer, John Eckenrode; Editors, David Eckenrode, John Eckenrode; Music, Matthew Valverde; a 6512 Prods./Ouzel Motion Pictures/Impala Roja production; American-Mexican; 2005; Color; DV; Not rated; 90 minutes; Release date: July 13, 2007. Documentary on illegal Mexican aliens, focusing on the killing of Eusebio de Haro Espinosa.

# IN SEARCH OF MOZART

(DIRECT CINEMA) Producer/Director/Screenplay/Photography, Phil Grabsky; Editor, Phil Reynolds; Associate Producer, Nicky Thomas; Narrator, Juliet Stevenson; a Seventh Art Prods. Production; Color; Not rated; 128 minutes; Release date: July 20, 2007. Documentary on Wolfgang Amadeus Mozart; with Renée Fleming, Lang Lang, Louis Langrée; voices of Debbie Arnold, John Davies; Sam West (Wolfgang Mozart), Sean Barrett (Leopold Mozart), Frank Adams-Brown (Mozart as a Child).

# WALKING TO WERNER

(LINAS FILMS) Producer, Dayna Hanson; Director/Editor, Linas Phillips; Photography, Linas Phillips, Benjamin Kasulke; Music, Justin Hubbard; a Linas Films production; Color; DV cam; Not rated; 94 minutes; Release date: July 20, 2007. Documentary in which Linas Phillips films his journey from Seattle to Los Angeles to meet his hero, filmmaker Werner Herzog; with Linas Phillips, Werner Herzog, Dayna Hanson, Benjamin Kasulke.

Linas Phillips in *Walking to Werner* © LINAS FILMS

# DAVID & LAYLA

David Moscow, Shiva Rose in *David & Layla* © JEFF LIPSKY

(JEFF LIPSKY) Producer/Director/Screenplay, Jay Jonroy, inspired by a true story; Co-Producers, Aimee Schoof, Richard Horowitz, Gill Holland; Photography, Harlan Bosmajian; Editor, Egon Kirincic; Music, Richard Horowitz, John Lissauer; Designer, Peter Yesair; Costumes, Zulema Griffin; Casting, Adrienne Stern; a NewRoz Films presentation of a Films Intl. and Intrinsic Value Films production; American-Iraqi; Dolby; Color; Not rated; 105 minutes; Release date: July 20, 2007.

**Cast**

David Moscow (David Fine); Shiva Rose (Layla); Callie Thorne (Abby); Peter Van Wagner (Mel Fine); Polly Adams (Judith Fine); Will Janowitz (Woody Fine); Ed Chemaly (Uncle Ali "Al"); Anna George (Zina); Alexander Blaise (Francois); Tibor Feldman (Rabbi Rabinovich); Ken Kliban (Dr. Jacobson); Albert Macklin (Dr. Susswein); Hany Kamal (Imam); Joseph Kamal (Howar); Anahid (Aunt Aftaw Khan); Randy Cherkas (Ken); Ali Farahnakian (Dr. Ahmad); C.S. Lee (Yun); Jason Catalano (Waiter at Newroz Restaurant); Angel Sing (Mr. Wong); Izzy Ruiz (Solo); Brian Gersh (Farhad "Fred"); Alex Hoffman (Newroz); Dorit Elena (Belly Dancer); Azziza Abdullah, Sam Davoodi, Alwand Jaff, Nassim Khavaran, Khaled Uthman (Kurdish Wedding Dancers); Harry Askenazi, John Molinelli (Uniformed Cops); Stephen Cauaretta, John Daly (Fishermen); Philip Galinsky (Bra Salesman); Courtney Grant, Robert S. Goldstein, Andrea Meyer, Michelle Lynn Morris, Lela White (Jewish Wedding Dancers); Lisa Marie Palmieri (Jealous Wife); Michael Postiglione, Richard Wisneski, Emil Zarbailov (Gang Members); Esfandiar Pourmand (Def Player); Linda Powell (Officer); Thomas Russo, David Primack (Jr. Rabbis); David Ruby (Vasectomy Patient); Fruzan Seifi (Club Band Leader); Vlada Tomova (Wedding Band Leader); Florence Wack (Muslim Prayer)

# THE DEVIL CAME ON HORSEBACK

Brian Steidle in *The Devil Came on Horseback* © IFC

(IFC) Producers, Ricki Stern, Annie Sundberg, Gretchen Wallace, Jane Wells, Ira Lechner, Eileen Haag, Cristina Ljungberg; Directors, Annie Sundberg, Ricki Stern; Photography, Jerry Risius, Phil Cox, Tim Hetherington, William Rexer II, Annie Sundberg, John Keith Wasson; Editor, Joey Grossfield; Music, Paul Brill; Associate Producers, Seth Keal, Jed Alpert, Ted Greenberg; a Break Thru Films production in association with Global Grassroots and Three Generations; Dolby; Color; DV; Not rated; 88 minutes; Release date: July 25, 2007. Documentary in which Marine Captain Brian Steidle witnesses the genocide in Darfur firsthand; with Brian Steidle, Gretchen Wallace, Nicholas Kristof, John Prendergast, Luis Moreno Ocampo, Sen. Barack Obama, Elie Wiesel.

# ARCTIC TALE

(PARAMOUNT VANTAGE) Producers, Adam Leipzig, Keenan Smart; Executive Producers, Kevin McCarey, John Bard Manulis; Co-Producer, Chris Miller; Directors, Adam Ravetch, Sarah Robertson; Screenplay, Linda Wolverton, Moses Richards, Kristin Gore; Photography, Adam Ravetch; Editor, Beth Spiegel; Music, Jody Talbot; Music Supervisor, Frankie Pine; Narrator, Queen Latifah; a Paramount Vantage presentation of a National Geographic production in association with Visionbox Films; Dolby; Color; Rated G; 96 minutes; Release date: July 25, 2007. Documentary on the wildlife of the frozen north; with Katrina Agate, Zain Ali, Preston Bailey, Kwesi Boakye, Michael Huang, Sierra Marcoux, Dante Pastula, Peyton Pearson, Isabella Peschardt, Christina Robinson, Lili Sepe, Ke'ala Valencia (Kids in End Credits).

*Arctic Tale* © PARAMOUNT VANTAGE

# I KNOW WHO KILLED ME

Brian Geraghty, Lindsay Lohan in *I Know Who Killed Me* © TRISTAR

(SONY PICTURES ENTERTAINMENT/TRISTAR) Producer, Frank Mancuso Jr.; Executive Producers, Tom Gores, Johnny O. Lopez; Co-Producers, David Grace, Aaron Mazzolini; Director, Chris Sivertson; Screenplay, Jeffrey Hammond; Photography, John R. Leonetti; Editor, Lawrence Jordan; Music, Joel McNeely; Designer, Jerry Fleming; Costumes, Rachel Sage Kunin; Casting, Dino Ladki; a TriStar Pictures presentation of a 360 Pictures production; Dolby Deluxe color; HD-to-35mm; Rated R; 108 minutes; Release date: July 27, 2007.

**Cast**

Lindsay Lohan (Aubrey Fleming/Dakota Moss); Julia Ormond (Susan Fleming); Neal McDonough (Daniel Fleming); Brian Geraghty (Jerrod Pointer); Garcelle Beauvais-Nilon (Agent Julie Bascombe); Spencer Garrett (Agent Phil Lazarus); Gregory Itzin (Dr. Greg Jameson); Art Bell (Himself); Eddie Steeples (Saeed the Prosthetic Tech); Bonnie Aarons (Fat Teena); Kenya Moore (Jazmin); Thomas Tofel (Douglas Norquist); Rodney Rowland (Kenny Scaife); David Figlioli (Lanny Rierden); Jessica Lee Rose (Marcia); Megan Henning (Anya); Michael Adler (Dr. Alex Dupree); Amy Fuehrer, Stacy Daniel (Reporters); Michael Esparza (Gilberto); Jane Galloway (Nurse Irma Beck); Cornelia Guest (Dr. Hannah Sommerly); Jason Wilburn, Jesse Hlubik (FBI Agents); David A. Kimball (Surgeon); Theo Kypri (The Blue Man); Paula Marshall (Marnie Toland); Brian McNamara (Fred Toland); Jennifer O'Kain (Mrs. Post); Michael Papajohn (Jacob K./Joseph K.); Colleen Porch (Vicky Redfeather); Donovan Scott (Sheriff Leon Cardero); Marc Senter (Pete the Biology Student); Will Shaffer (Painted Football Fan); Dan Walters (Dennis Macbreen); David Weisenberg (Anesthesiologist)

# TRANSFORMATION: THE LIFE AND LEGACY OF WERNER ERHARD

(SCREEN MEDIA VENTURES) Producer/Director/Screenplay/Editor, Robyn Symon; Executive Producer, Walter Maksym; Photography, Horacio Marquínez; Music, John Martyn; a Symon Productions, Inc. and Eagle Island Films production; NTSC Color; Not rated; 62 minutes; Release date: July 27, 2007. Documentary on EST creator Werner Erhard; with Werner Erhard, Warren Bennis, Don Lattin, Randy McNamara, Laurel Scheaf, Art Schreiber, Jane Self.

## WHO'S YOUR CADDY?

(MGM) Producers, Tracey E. Edmonds, Christopher Eberts, Arnold Rifkin, Kia Jam; Executive Producers, Bob Weinstein, Harvey Weinstein, Shakim Compere, Ross M. Dinerstein, Queen Latifah, Marvin Peart, Chris Roberts, Bobby Schwartz; Co-Producer, John Duffy; Co-Executive Producers, Damon Lee, Michael McQuarn; Director, Don Michael Paul; Screenplay, Don Michael Paul, Bradley Allenstein, Robert Henny; Photography, Thomas Callaway; Editor, Vanick Moradian; Music, Jon Lee; Music Supervisor, Michael McQuarn; Designer, Paul Jackson; Costumes, Jayme Bohn; Associate Producers, Nicole Haeussermann, Sheila Kerrigan; Casting, Jeff Gerrard; an Our Stories Film and Dimension Films presentation of a Rifkin-Eberts/Kia Jam production in association with Eleven Eleven Films; Dolby; FotoKem color; Rated PG-13; 92 minutes; Release date: July 27, 2007.

### Cast

Antwan "Big Boi" Andre Patton (C-Note); Jeffrey Jones (Cummings); Tamala Jones (Shannon Williams); Sherri Shepherd (Lady G); Faizon Love (Big Large); Finesse Mitchell (Dread); Garrett Morris (The Reverend); Tony Cox (Big Willie Johnson); Cam Gigandet (Mick); Chase Tatum (Kidd Clean); Jenifer Lewis (C-Note's Mom); Susan Ward (Mrs. Cummings); Mick Partridge (Valet); Jim Piddock (Harrington); Samantha Lemole (Secretary); Todd Sherry (Realtor); Robert Curtis Brown (Frosty); Andy Milonakis (Wilson); Lil' Wayne (Himself); Bruce Bruce (Golf Ball Eddie); James Avery (Caddy Mack); Jimmy Waitman (Speedo Man); Chris Howell (Distinguished Gentleman); Bill Sloan (Mayor); Terry Crews (Tank), Rodrick Mosley (Bouncer); Dana Michael Woods (Lil' Rod); Kim Morgan Greene (Brownie Woman); Kristopher Bailey (Konkrete Legend); Corey Andrews, Nathaniel "Supa Nate" Elder, James "Lil Brotha" Patton (Konkrete Members); Matias Magrini (Matias); Theresa King (Polo Player); Jesper Parnevik (Himself); Ron Clinton Smith (Police Captain); Michael Burgess (Carolina Cop); Bob Johnson (Exclusive Club Member); Ross King (Famous Golf Announcer); Lester "Mighty Rasta" Speight (Hardcore Inmate); David Britt (Toupee'd Husband); Michael Cavanaugh (John Marshall); Robert Henny (Harry Beanbag)

## LAURA SMILES

(EMERGING PICTURES) Producers, Ted Hartley, Ric Arthur; Executive Producers, Joe Di Maio, Paul Speaker, Michael Klein, Robert Cain; Director/Screenplay, Jason Ruscio; Photography, Sion Michel; Editor, Scott Martin; Music, John Davis; Designer, Bryce Holtshousen; Costumes, Azalia Snail; a Ted Hartley/RKO Pictures presentation of an RKO Pictures production; Dolby; Color; DV/HD; Not rated; 98 minutes; Release date: July 27, 2007.

### Cast

Petra Wright (Laura), Kip Pardue (Chris), Jonathan Silverman (Paul), Mark Derwin (Mark), Ted Hartley (Therapist), Stephen Sowan (Billy), Scott Chernoff (Emperor), Jack Fitz (Accident Witness)

## THE CAMDEN 28

(FIRST RUN FEATURES) Producer/Director/Screenplay, Anthony Giacchino; Photography, David Dougherty; Editor, Brandon Park; Music, Michael Giacchino; an ECC Media production; Color/Black and white; DV; Not rated; 83 minutes; Release date: July 27, 2007. Documentary on the 1971 break-in at a draft board in Camden, NJ, by 28 members of the Catholic Left protesting the Vietnam War; with Michael Doyle, John Swinglish, Bob Hardy, Michael Giocondo, Joan Reilly, Howard Zinn, many others.

## PUNK'S NOT DEAD

Drunk Tank Girls in *Punk's Not Dead* © VISION FILMS

(VISION FILMS) Producers, Susan Dynner, Todd Traina; Executive Producers, Markus Kaeppeli, Panos Nicolaou; Co-Producer, Patrick Nelson Barnes; Director, Susan Dynner; Photography, Susan Dynner, Markus Kaeppeli, Emma Pantall; Editor, Patrick Nelson Barnes; an Aberration Films and Red Rover Films production; Color/Black and white; Multiformat-to-Digital-Beta; Not rated; 105 minutes; Release date: July 27, 2007. Documentary looking at the punk music scene from 1977 to the present; with The Addicts, Alkaline Trio, Anti-Flag, Angelic Upstarts, The Anti-Nowhere League, The Ataris, Bad Religion, Bang Sugar Bang, Jello Biafra, Black Flag, The Briefs, The Business, Buzzcocks, The Casualties, Channel 3, The Circle Jerks, Cock Sparrrer, The Damned, Dead Kennedys, DEK, DI, The Diffs, DOA, The Exploited, Funeral Dress, GBH, The God Awfuls, Good Charlotte, Green Day, Billy Idol, The (International) Noise Conspiracy, Iron Cross, L7, MC5, Minor Threat, My Chemical Romance, Naked Agression, Narcoleptic Youth, NOFX, The Offspring, Pennywise, Peter & the Test Tube Babies, Pogo Atak, The Ramones, Rancid, Henry Rollins, Scream, Sex Pistols, Sham 69, T.V. Smith, Social Distortion, Stiff Little Fingers, Story of the Year, The Subhumans, Sum 41, Texas Terri, Thrice, Total Chaos, TSOL, The U.K. Subs, The Used, Vice Squad, The Voids, X, Youth Brigade, 999, Craig Aaronson, Lorraine Ali, Alternative Tentacles, BYO Records, Mitch Cramer, Jim Guerinot, Barry Jones, Kevin Lyman, Legs McNeil, Chris Morris, Kelly Osbourne, Alan Parker, Jennie Smith, Rob Schwartz, Stormy Sheppard, Stryker, Steve Van Doren.

## THE LIST

(MOUNTAIN TOP RELEASING) Producers, Gary Wheeler, Kevin Downes; Executive Producer, Robert Whitlow; Director, Gary Wheeler; Screenplay, Gary Wheeler, Robert Whitlow, Michelle Hoppe, Johnston H. Moore; Photography, Tom Priestley Jr.; Designer, John D. Kretschmer; Costumes, Jeanie Baker; Music, James Covell; Editor, Jonathan Olive; Casting, Mark Fincannon; from Level Path productions; Color; Rated PG; 105 minutes; Release date: August 3, 2007.

### Cast

Malcolm McDowell (Desmond Larochette), Chuck Carrington (Renny Jacobsen), Hilarie Burton (Jo Johnston), Will Patton (Harriston), Pat Hingle (Gus Eicholtz), Mary Beth Peil (Daisy Stokes), Elizabeth Omilami (Mama A), Afemo Omilami (AL Jenkins), R. Keith Harris (Bart Maxwell), Steve Ayres (Robert Roget), Richard Fullerton (Jerrod Weiss), Richard K. Olsen (Michael Flournoy), Nicholas Pryor (Harold Smithfield), Frank Hoyt Taylor (Amos Candler), Tim Ware (Thomas Layne), Joe Inscoe (Jefferson McClintock), Geoff Ludlow (Handsome FBI Agent), Clay Broaddus (FBI Agent), Danny Vinson (Tow Truck Driver), Jimmy Hager (Gullah Storyteller), Bonnie Johnson (Bonnie), Korey Scott Pollard (Frank), Cassandra Stark (Woman in Restaurant), Ken West (The Judge)

## HOT ROD

(PARAMOUNT) Producers, Lorne Michaels, John Goldwyn; Executive Producers, Will Ferrell, Jimmy Miller, Jill Messick; Co-Producer, Louise Rosner; Director, Akiva Schaffer; Screenplay, Pam Brady; Photography, Andrew Dunn; Editor, Malcolm Campbell; Music, Trevor Rabin; Music Supervisor, Steven Baker; Designer, Stephen Altman; Costumes, Patricia Monaghan; Casting, Allison Jones; a Michaels/Goldwyn production; Dolby; Color; Rated PG-13; 83 minutes; Release date: August 3, 2007.

### Cast

Andy Samberg (Rod Kimble); Isla Fisher (Denise); Jorma Taccone (Kevin Powell); Bill Hader (Dave); Danny McBride (Rico); Ian McShane (Frank Powell); Sissy Spacek (Marie Powell); Will Arnett (Jonathan); Chris Parnell (Barry Pasternak); Chester Tam (Richardson); Mark Acheson (Homeless Dude); Brittany Tiplady (Maggie); Ken Kirzinger (Trailer Guy); Britt Irvin (Cathy); Alana Husband (Waitress); Andrew Moxham (Sullivan); Terri O'Neill (Angry Mom); Alvin Sanders (Furious Boss); Chris Eastman, Paulo Ribeiro (EMTs); Carly McKillip (High School Girl); Donavon Stinson (Heckler); John B. Destry (Projectionist); Doug Abrahams (Police Officer); Frank C. Turner (Fisherman); Henry Michaels (Boy Stealing Wheelchair); Gillian Barber, Sammy Fattedad, William S. Taylor (Riot Singers); Mi-Jung Lee (Newswoman); Carrie Ruscheinsky (Hippie Girl); Charlie Hope, Mathew Gallagher, Victoria Campbell (Autograph Kids); Titan Toyish, Alain Moschulski ("Gown"); Jesse Haddock, Ometa Gittens (Crowd Members); Aaron Au (Taco); Brett Chan (Grilled Cheese); John Burnside (Scrooge)

## IF I DIDN'T CARE

(ARTISTIC LICENSE FILMS) Producers, Benjamin Cummings, Orson Cummings; Executive Producer, Kathy Lieb; Co-Producer, Gigi Causey; Directors/Screenplay, Benjamin Cummings, Orson Cummings; Photography, Brian Pryzpek; Designer, Lucio Seixas; Costumes, Nina Schelich; Editor, Geoffrey Richman; Music, Michael Tremante; Music Supervisor, Gary Calamar; Casting, Adrienne Stern; a Sweetooth production; Dolby; Color; Not rated; 75 minutes; Release date: August 3, 2007.

### Cast

Bill Sage (Davis Meyers), Roy Scheider (Linus), Susan Misner (Hadley Templeton), Noelle Beck (Janice Meyers), Ronald Guttman (Ayad), Alex Kilgore (Hamster), Mirelly Taylor (Maria), Brian McQuillan (Officer Hoyle), Ben Cummings (Cop), Piras Sebastian (Crime Scene Photographer), Phyllis Somerville (Daisy), Casey Van Maanen (Lab Technician)

## BRATZ

(LIONSGATE) Producers, Avi Arad, Steven Paul, Isaac Larian; Executive Producer, Benedict Carver; Co-Producer, Kyla Kraman; Director, Sean McNamara; Screenplay, Susan Estelle Jansen; Story, Adam De La Pena, David Eilenberg; Photography, Christian Sebaldt; Designer, Rusty Smith; Costumes, Bernadene Morgan; Editor, Jeff W. Canavan; Music, John Coda; Original Songs, Ron Fair, Stephanie Ridel, Nick Scapa; Visual Effects Supervisor, Avi Das; Visual Effects, Barbed Wire FX, Edgeworx; Line Producer, Eric M. Breiman; Casting, Joey Paul Jensen; a Crystal Sky Pictures production in association with Arad Prods.; Dolby; FotoKem color; Rated PG; 110 minutes; Release date: August 3, 2007.

### Cast

Nathalia Ramos (Yasmin); Janel Parrish (Jade); Logan Browning (Sasha); Skyler Shaye (Cloe); Chelsea Staub (Meredith Dimly); Anneliese van der Pol (Avery); Malese Jow (Quinn); Ian Nelson (Dylan); Stephen Lunsford (Cameron); Lainie Kazan (Bubbie); Jon Voight (Principal Berkman); William May (Manny); Emily Everhard (Cherish Dimly); Chet Hanks (Dexter); Carl Rux (Mr. Whitman/DJ Wax); Kim Morgan Greene (Katie, Chloe's Mom); Sasha Cohen (Bethany); Andrea Edwards (Goalie); Constance Hsu (Julie, Jade's Mom); Tami-Adrian George (Allison, Sasha's Mom); Kadeem Hardison (Sasha's Dad); Sean Patrick McNamara (Tom McShavie); Lee Reherman (Vice Principal Sludge); Daniel Booko (Jock); Zach Cumer (Science Nerd); Jerad Anderson, Jordan Benedict (Football Jocks); Scot Nery (Juggling Boy); Brando Murphy (Loner Boy); Sarah Hernandez (Greenie Girl); DJ Rick Adams (Less Boreman); Jackie Kreisler (Pretzel Person); Damian Daly (Gamer Geek Clique Leader); Kelly Crean (Mrs. Funk); Steven Anthony Lawrence (Plunger Man); Michael Stellman (Magician); Nira DeLuna (50 States Girl); Susie Singer Carter (Barbara Baxter Dimly); Paula Froelich (Herself); Haley Busch (Confession Girl); Emma Raimi (Little Girl)

# DADDY DAY CAMP

Cuba Gooding Jr., Joshua McLerran in *Daddy Day Camp* © TRISTAR PICTURES

(SONY PICTURES ENTERTAINMENT) Producers, William Sherak, Jason Shuman; Executive Producers, John Davis, Matt Berenson, Derek Dauchy, Richard Hull, Chris Emerson, Nancy Kirhoffer, Jefferson Richard; Co-Producers, Rhiannon Meier, Adam F. Goldberg; Director, Fred Savage; Screenplay, Geoff Rodkey, J. David Stern, David N. Weiss; Story, Geoff Rodkey, Joel Cohen, Alec Sokolow; Photography, Geno Salvatori; Designer, Eric Weiler; Costumes, Carolyn Leone; Editor, Michael Aller; Music, Jim Dooley; Music Supervisors, Manish Raval, Tom Wolfe; Casting, Lindsey Hayes Kroeger, David H. Rapaport; a TriStar Pictures and Revolution Studios presentation of a Davis Entertainment Co. and Blue Star Entertainment production; Dolby; Technicolor; Rated PG; 89 minutes; Release date: August 8, 2007.

## Cast

Cuba Gooding Jr. (Charlie Hinton), Lochlyn Munro (Lance Warner), Richard Gant (Col. Buck Hinton), Tamala Jones (Kim Hinton), Paul Rae (Phil Ryerson), Joshua McLerran (Dale), Spencir Bridges (Ben Hinton), Brian Doyle-Murray (Uncle Morty), Dallin Boyce (Max Ryerson), Telise Galanis (Juliette), Taggart Hurtubise (Carl), Molly Jepson (Becca), Tad D'Agostino (Robert), Tyger Rawlings (Billy West), Talon G. Ackerman (Jack), Zachary Allen (Mullethead), Sean Patrick Flaherty (Bobby J), Richard J. Clifford (Thumson), Frank Gerrish (Plumber), Paul Kiernan (Bill), JJ Neward (Syl), Christy Summerhays (Margo), Kate Fischer (Clique Girl), Jorji Diaz Fadel (Innocent Child), Dimitrius Deslis (Mr. West), Ginger Williams (Mrs. Rugul), Janice Power (Mrs. Mayhoffer), Jennifer Lyon (Mrs. Simmons), Bart Johnson (Phil Jacobs), Melinda Ratner (Mary Sullivan), Robin De Santis (Camp Counselor #1), Carson McKinney (Hiker)

# DESCENT

(CITY LIGHTS PICTURES) Producers, Morris S. Levy, Rosario Dawson, Talia Lugacy; Executive Producers, Danny Fisher, Jack Fisher, Joe Fisher, Gary S. Gumowitz, Michael Almog, Michael Califra, Michael Bassick, Jess Mogul; Co-Producers, Jeff Mazzola, John Scaccia, Marcus Lansdell; Co-Executive Producer, Phil Michas; Director, Talia Lugacy; Screenplay, Brian Priest, Talia Lugacy; Photography, Christopher LaVasseur, Jonathan Furmanski; Designer, Tristam Steinberg; Costumes, Amy Ritchings; Editor, Frank Reynolds; Music, Alex Moulton; Music Supervisor, Stephanie Diaz-Matos; Associate Producer, Isabel Celeste; Casting, Adrienne Stern; a presentation in association with Mega Films of a Trybe Films production; Dolby; Color; Rated R; 100 minutes; Release date: August 10, 2007.

## Cast

Rosario Dawson (Maya); Chad Faust (Jared); Marcus Patrick (Adrian); Christopher DeBlasio (Frat Brother); Sergia Louise Anderson (Christie); Chuck Ardezzone, Robert Haley, Brian M. Wixson (Gruff Men); Scott Bailey (Alex); Tomm Bauer, Aran Bertetto, Melaena Cadiz, Tim Curcio (Students); Peter Bongiorno (Coach); Jon Budinoff (Friendly Guy); Kevin Cannon (Gruff Hood); Anthony Chiochi (Anthony); Isabel Dawson (Bartender); Jacqueline Duprey (Celeste); Tate Ellington (George); Vanessa Ferlito (Latina Girl); Abigail Forman (Ashleigh); Connor Fux (Steve); Alexie Gilmore (Seline); Spencer Grammer (Stephanie); Tommy Guiffre (Danny); Wilson Jermaine Heredia (Diego); Charlie Hewson (Usher); Aisleagh Jackson (Volunteer Girl); Colombe Jacobsen-Derstine (Nadia); Suzy Kaye (Cafeteria Girl); Dennis Leeflang (Club Goer); Brooke Sunny Moriber, Jasmine Lobe (Dorm Girls); Adam Mucci (Football Guy); James O'Toole (Craig); Marshal Pailet (Sammy); Rosalie Perez (Rosalie); Cosmo Pfeil (Brock); Scott Porter (Brooks); Ashleigh Prather (Mandy); Paul Sado (Josh); Christen Satchelle (College Kid); Jonathan Neil Schneider (Archeology Professor); Jennifer Sciole (Mary); Steve Sirkis (Frat Boy); George Spielvogel III (Mathew); Aaron Staton (Campus Guy); James A. Stephens (Prof. Byron); Lynne Marie Stetson (Pneumonia Girl); Phoebe Strole (Innocent Girl); Francie Swift (Clair); Johnathan Tchaikovsky (Tyler); Tracie Thoms (Denise); Alysha Umphress (Andrea); Lee Van Bradley (Harlan); Dana Varon (Rebecca); Nicole Vicius (Melanie); Matthew J. Walters (Tim); Chris Wylde (Chris)

# HANNAH TAKES THE STAIRS

(IFC FIRST TAKE) Producers, Anish Savjani, Joe Swanberg; Director/Screenplay/Photography/Editor, Joe Swanberg; Music, Kevin Bewersdorf; a Film Science production; Color; HD Video; Not rated; 83 minutes; Release date: August 22, 2007.

## Cast

Greta Gerwig (Hannah), Kent Osborne (Matt), Andrew Bujalski (Paul), Ry Russo-Young (Rocco), Mark Duplass (Mike), Todd Rohal (Brian Duges), Tipper Newton (Minnie), Kris Williams (Gaby), Ivan Albertson (Stephen), Kevin Bewersdorf (Guy Who Lays Down), Mathan Adloff (Friend at Party)

# ILLEGAL TENDER

(UNIVERSAL) Producer, John Singleton; Executive Producers, Dwight Williams, Preston L. Holmes; Director/Screenplay, Franc. Reyes; Photography, Frank Byers; Designer, Keith Brian Burns; Costumes, Rahimah Yoba; Music, Heitor Pereira; Editor, Tony Ciccone; Casting, Sig De Miguel; a New Deal Entertainment production; Dolby; FotoKem color; Rated R; 107 minutes; Release date: August 24, 2007.

### Cast

Rick Gonzalez (Wilson DeLeon, Jr.); Wanda De Jesus (Millie DeLeon); Dania Ramirez (Ana); Antonio Oritz (Randy); Teo Calderon (Choco); Jessica Pimentel (Young Millie DeLeon); Manny Perez (Wilson DeLeon, Sr.); Julie Carmen (Nilsa); Michael Philip Del Rio (Lugo); Samuel Molina (Older Man); Rick Sepulveda (Joey); D.C. Benny (Ceasar); Mercedes Mercado, Carmen Perez (Latina Killers); Zulay Henao (Mora); Jessica Pimentel (Young Millie); Angelic Zambrana (Young Jessenia); Ronald Escobar (Javier's Man #1); Gary Perez (Javier Cordero); Sherionne Lanier (Ana's Friend); Joaquin T. Archuleta (Ana's Dad); Benny Nieves (Ralph); Selenis Leyva (Wanda); Atanacio Hernandez (Connecticut Hitman); Stracy Diaz (Connecticut Hitwoman); Miguel Ángel Suárez (Soloman); Delilah Cotto (Jessenia); Tego Calderon (Choco); Sanya Merced, Jessica Reyes (Escorts); Virginia Romero (Crazy Latina); Mario D'Leon (Long Island Hitman); Elliot Santiago (Hitman); Angel DeCastro (Taxi Driver)

# EYE OF THE DOLPHIN

(MONTEREY MEDIA) Producers, Susan Johnson, Michael D. Sellers; Executive Producers, Pamela Vlastas, Tre Lovell, Stephen Hayes, Peter Graham, Doug Jewell, Donald A. Barton, Robert Kecskemet, Amy Summer, Peer Oppenheimer; Co-Producer, Jacob Moser; Co-Executive Producers, John Remark, James Via, Robert Fredriks, Anthony Milan; Director, Michael D. Sellers; Screenplay, Wendell Morris, Michael D. Sellers; Photography, Guy Livneh; Designer, Freddie Naff; Costumes, Leslie Yarmo; Editor, Brent Schoenfeld; Music, Alan Derian; Casting, Matthew Lessall; a Moviebank production in association with 120 dB Films, MB Partners, and Goldmill Prods.; Dolby; Color; Rated PG-13; 102 minutes; Release date: August 24, 2007.

### Cast

Carly Schroeder (Alyssa), Adrian Dunbar (Dr. James Hawk), George Harris (Daniel), Katharine Ross (Lucy), Jane Lynch (Glinton), Christine Adams (Tamika), Rudy Levarity (Coakley), Joey Jam (Decker), Vivica Watkins (Cornelia), Christopher Herrod (Shelby), Andrea Bowen (Candace), Wendy Braun (Suzanne Harrison), Escher Holloway (Trevor), Robert Keskemety (Tourist at Bar), Alexa Motley (Dumb Tourist), Kelly Vitz (Michelle)

# RIGHT AT YOUR DOOR

Mary McCormack in *Right at Your Door* © ROADSIDE ATTRACTIONS

(ROADSIDE) Producers, Palmer West, Jonah Smith; Co-Producers, Jesse Johnston, Stephanie Lewis; Director/Screenplay, Chris Gorak; Photography, Tom Richmond; Editor, Jeffrey M. Werner; Music, Tomandandy; Designer, Ramsey Avery; Costumes, Rebecca Bentjen; VFX Supervisor, Joe Bauer; Special Effects Supervisor, Pete Novitch; Line Producer, Julie M. Anderson; Casting, Emily Schweber, Jennifer Levy; a Thousand Words presentation; Dolby; FotoKem color, Super-16-to-35mm; Rated R; 96 minutes; Release date: August 24, 2007.

### Cast

Mary McCormack (Lexi); Rory Cochrane (Brad); Tony Perez (Alvaro); Scotty Noyd Jr. (Timmy); Jon Huertas (Rick); Max Kasch (Cpl. Marshall); Will McCormack (Jason); Emeka Nnadi, Marisol Ramirez (Synthetic Soldiers); Hector Luis Bustamante (Store Owner); Alejandra Flores (Terrified Woman on Street); Christopher Rocha (Hurried Man); Soledad St. Hilaire (Hardware Woman); Nigel Gibbs (Another Officer); Jenny O'Hara (Lexi's Mother); Jessica Freitas (Gail); Nina Barry (Kathy Reynolds); Ed Francis Martin (Juan Martinez); David Richards (Neil Simmons); Kimberly Scott (Voice of City Official)

# KAMP KATRINA

(CARNIVALESQUE FILMS) Producers, Deborah Smith, Dale Smith, Ashley Sabin; Directors, Ashley Sabin, David Redmon; Photography/Editors, Tim Messler, Ashley Sabin, David Redmon; Music, Eric Taxier; Color; DV; Not rated; 73 minutes; Release date: August 24, 2007. Documentary on the mini-communities created by the New Orleans survivors of Hurricane Katrina.

# SEPTEMBER DAWN

(SLOW HAND RELEASING/BLACK DIAMOND PICTURES) Producers, Scott Duthie, Christopher Cain, Kevin Matossian; Executive Producers, Michael Feinberg, Patrick Imeson, Wendy Hill-Tout; Director, Christopher Cain; Screenplay, Carole Whang Schutter, Christopher Cain; Photography, Juan Ruiz-Anchia; Designer, Rick Roberts; Costumes, Carol Case; Editor, Jack Hofstra; Music, William Ross; Stunts, Tom Glass; Casting, Lynn Kressel; a Black Diamond Pictures presentation of a September Dawn (U.S.)/Voice Pictures (Canada) production; American-Canadian; Dolby; FotoKem color; Rated R; 110 minutes; Release date: August 24, 2007.

### Cast

Jon Voight (Jacob Samuelson); Trent Ford (Jonathan Samuelson); Tamara Hope (Emily Hudson); Jon Gries (John D. Lee); Taylor Handley (Micah Samuelson); Huntley Ritter (Robert Humphries); Krisinda Cain (Young Woman); Shaun Johnston (Capt. Fancher); Lolita Davidovich (Nancy Dunlap); Dean Cain (Joseph Smith); Terence Stamp (Brigham Young); Carter Burns (Boy); Tom Carey (Mormon Fighter); Peter Skagen, Geoff Erwin (Guards); Hal Kerbes (Highbee); Daniel Libman (Rev. Hudson); Chad Jobert (Soldier); Sean Anthony Olsen (Mormon Rifleman); Pete Seadon (Father); Barbara Gates Wilson (Martha Hudson); Stacey Zurburg (Another Woman)

# CLOSING ESCROW

(MAGNOLIA) Producer, Kristen Cox; Executive Producers, Armen Kaprelian, Randall P. Dark; Director/Screenplay/Editor, Armen Kaprelian, Kent Llewellyn; Photography, Scott Billups; Set Decorator, Josh Rose; Visual Effects Supervisor, Billups; an Awkward Silence production in association with HD Vision Studios and 16X9 Prods.; Color; HD; Rated PG; 93 minutes; Release date: August 24, 2007.

### Cast

April Barnett (Tamika), Rob Brownstein (Allen), Colleen Crabtree (Mary), Andrew Friedman (Tom), Wendi McLendon-Covey (Hillary), Kirstin Pierce (Kelly), Ryan Smith (Richard), Bruce Thomas (Peter), Patty Wortham (Dawn), Cedric Yarbrough (Bobby), Jillian Boyd (Mindy Watts, Listing Agent #5), Gabe Estrada (Restaurant Manager), Brian Habicht (Ernie), Samantha Holt (Julie), Leah Price (Real Estate Agent)

# SKID ROW

(SCREEN MEDIA FILMS) Producers, Pras, Teryn Fogel, Rob A. Wisdom; Directors, Ross Clarke, Niva Dorell, Marshall Tyler; Photography, Andrew Brinkman; Music, Craig Eastman, Klaus Badelt; Editor, Brendan Cusack; an Experience Experience (e2), Skid Row production; Color; Rated R; 80 minutes; Release date: August 24, 2007. Documentary on a section of Los Angeles in which some 11,000 homeless dwell.

# QUIET CITY

(600 WEST PRODS.) Producers, Ben Stambler, Brendan McFadden; Director/Editor, Aaron Katz; Screenplay, Aaron Katz, Erin Fisher, Cris Lankenau; Photography, Andrew Reed; Music, Keegan DeWitt; Color; Not rated; 78 minutes; Release date: August 29, 2007.

### Cast

Erin Fisher (Jamie), Cris Lankenau (Charlie), Sarah Hellman (Robin), Joe Swanberg (Adam), Tucker Stone (Kyle), Liz Bender (Liz), Karrie Crouse (Karrie), Keegan DeWitt (Keegan), Daryl Huhn (Daryl), Michael Tully (Michael), C. Mason Wells (Chris)

# SELF-MEDICATED

Monty Lapica in *Self-Medicated* © THINKFILM

(THINKFILM) Producers, Tommy Bell, Monty Lapica; Director/Screenplay, Monty Lapica; Photography, Denis Maloney; Editor, Timothy Kendall; Music, Anthony Marinelli; Designer, Nicholas Ralbovsky; Costumes, Shawn-Holly Cookson; Line Producers, Michael Feifer, Michael Silberman; Casting, Lindsay Chag; Color; Not rated; 108 minutes; Release date: August 31, 2007.

### Cast

Diane Venora (Louise Eriksen); Monty Lapica (Andrew Eriksen); Greg Germann (Keith); Kristina Anapau (Nicole); Matthew Carey (Aaron); Michael Bowen (Dan Jones); Shane Stuart (Seth Calenes); Richard Weisner (Mikey); William Stanford Davis (Gabe); Kelly Kruger (Tori); Karim Prince (Steve); Glenndon Chatman (John); Noah Segan (Trevor); Marcus Toji (Mike); Michael Mantell (Dr. Reinholtz); Faleolo Alailima (Kawa); Melli Barksdale (Ward Patient); Ray Benson (Andrew's Father); Anna Chudoba (Nurse in Hawaii); Staci Cross (Jessica); Randy Crowder (Teacher); Josh Drennen, Travis Stanberry (Paintball Victims); Danica Stewart, Nicole Garza (Casino Girls); Cathy Lind Hayes (Brightway Nurse); Terence Bernie Hines (Security Guard); Chris Leone, Courtney Vine (Brightway Patients); Zach Moyes (Aaron's Brother); Jennifer Parsons (Mrs. Fehringer); Jason Reynolds (Student); Nathan Sabatka (Young Andrew); Enrique Sapene (Jesse Perez)

# 10 QUESTIONS FOR THE DALAI LAMA

(MONTEREY MEDIA) Executive Producers, Rick Ray, Sharon Ray; Director/Screenplay/Editor, Rick Ray; Photography, Rick Ray, Elana Ben Amir; Music, Peter Kater; a Rick Ray Films production; Color; Not rated; 85 minutes; Release date: August 31, 2007. Documentary in which filmmaker Rick Ray prepares for an audience with the Dalai Lama.

# LADRÓN QUE ROBA A LADRÓN

Gabriel Soto, Miguel Varoni in *Ladrón Que Roba a Ladrón* © LIONSGATE

(LIONSGATE) Producers, Roni Menendez, James McNamara, Benjamin Odell; Co-Producer, Meta Valentic; Director/Editor, Joe Menendez; Screenplay, Jose Angel Henrickson; Photography, Adam Silver; Designer, Christopher Tandon; Costumes, Elaine Montalvo; Music, Andres Levin; a Panamax Films production in association with Narrow Bridge Films; Dolby; Technicolor; Rated PG-13; 99 minutes; Release date: August 31, 2007.

### Cast

Fernando Colunga (Alejandro Toledo); Miguel Varoni (Emilio Lopez); Julie Gonzalo (Gloria); Oscar Torre (Miguelito); Gabriel Soto (Anival Cano); Ivonne Montero (Rafaela); Saúl Lisazo (Moctesuma "Mocte" Valdez); Ruben Garfias (Rafa); JoJo Henrickson (Julio Miranda); Sonya Smith (Veronica Valdez); Richard Azurdia (Primitvo); Jon Molerio (Booth Guard); Eduardo Antonio Garcia (Sergio, Mocte's Bodyguard); Rick Majera, J. Teddy Garces (Building Guards); Lidia Pires (Blanca); Roberto Medina (Chava); Silvia Curiel (Maria); Art Bonilla (Coyote); Elan Garfias (Claudito); James Charles Leary (Building Manager); Manolo Travieso (Dr. Antonio Panaco); Ross Gibby (Detective); James M. McNamara (Father O'Malley); Jossra Jinaro (Reporter); Pedro Pano, Minerva García (Testimonials); Iglesias Estefania, Chase McKenna (Hot Babes); Jonathon Downs, C-Sharp (Upscale Party Guests); Robert Arevalo (Mayor's Bodyguard); George Boyd (Catarino); Tim Camarillo (Valet); Galo Make Canote (Protestor); Rico Devereaux (Businessman); Roberto Flores (Pelocine); Nickolas Ray Hernandez (Striking Worker); Rob Macie (Immigrant); Joe Menendez (Cameraman)

# FRESHMAN ORIENTATION

Mike Erwin, Sam Huntington in *Freshman Orientation* © HERE!/REGENT

(HERE!/REGENT ENTERTAINMENT) aka *Home of Phobia*; Producers, Adam Rosenfelt, Dan Halsted, Judd Payne, Matthew Rhodes, Malcolm Petal; Executive Producers, Robert Greenblatt, David Janollari, Sam Nazarian; Co-Producers, Marc Schaberg, Randy Winograd; Director/Screenplay, Ryan Shiraki; Photography, Amelia Vincent; Designer, Frank Zito III; Costumes, Liz Staub; Editor, David Codron; Music, Tomandandy; Music Supervisor, Suzanne Coffman; Casting, Roger Mussenden, Elizabeth Torres; an Element Films presentation of a Greenblatt-Janollari Studios/Persistent Entertainment production in association with LIFT Prods.; Dolby; Color; Rated R; 92 minutes; Release date: August 31, 2007.

### Cast

Sam Huntington (Clay Adams), Marla Sokoloff (Marjorie), Mike Erwin (Matt), Heather Matarazzo (Jessica), Kaitlin Doubleday (Amanda), Bryce Johnson (Tazwell), Jud Tylor (Serena), Rachel Dratch (Very Drunk Chick), John Goodman (Rodney), Dicky Barrett (Homophobic Cop), Jonathan Watts Bell (Bad Dancer), Palma Botterell (Alan), Skylar Duhe (Bessie Friend), Antonio Echeverria (Party Guy), Meagen Fay (Mrs. Paul), Shannon Floyd (Hippie Chick), Loren Kinsella (Really Drunk Chick), Rachel Klein (Midwestern Girl), Murphy Martin (Fraternity Member), Mark McLachlan (Cullen), Jeffrey Muller (Sherman Jessop), Michael Osborne (Artsy Dude), Mary Payne (Fern), Michael Salinas (Brennan), Ashley Sherman (Bessie)

# MUSICIAN

(SHERIFFMOVIE) Producers, Jason Davis, Daniel Kraus; Director/Photography/Editor, Daniel Kraus; Music, Ken Vandermark; Color; DV; Not rated; 60 minutes; Release date: September 5, 2007. Documentary on Chicago musician Ken Vandermark, who specializes in atonal improvisational jazz.

# THE BROTHERS SOLOMON

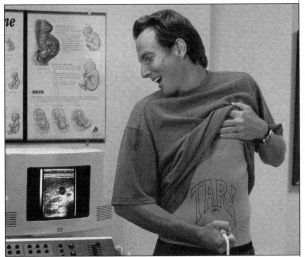

Will Arnett in *The Brothers Solomon* © TRISTAR PICTURES

(SONY PICTURES ENTERTAINMENT) Producers, Tom Werner, Matt Berenson; Executive Producers, Caryn Mandabach, Paddy Cullen; Co-Producer, Gail Laskowski; Director, Bob Odenkirk; Screenplay, Will Forte; Photography, Tim Suhrstedt; Editor, Tracey Wadmore-Smith; Music, John Swihart; Music Supervisors, G. Marq Roswell, Adam Swart; Designer, John Paino; Costumes, Melina Root; Visual Effects Supervisor, Raymond McIntyre Jr.; Associate Producer, Michael Shear; Casting, Lisa Beach, Sarah Katzman; a TriStar Pictures, Revolution Studios presentation of a Carsey-Werner Films production; Dolby; Deluxe color; Rated R; 93 minutes; Release date: September 7, 2007.

## Cast

Will Arnett (John Solomon); Will Forte (Dean Solomon); Chi McBride (James); Kristen Wiig (Janine); Malin Akerman (Tara); Lee Majors (Ed Solomon); Michael Ormsby (Young John); Bob Odenkirk (Jim Treacher); Sam Lloyd (Dr. Spencer); Charles Chun (Dr. Wong); Ryun Yu (Dr. Wang); Bill Hader (Recumbent Biker); Jenna Fischer (Michelle); Susanne Wright (Erica); Derek Waters (Video Store Clerk); Chandler Hill (Ron); Ashley Johnson (Patricia); Brooke Bloom (Grocery Shopper); Anna Becker (Grocery Checker); Brian Scolaro (Medical Delivery Guy); Anita Maria Taylor (Video Store Customer); Nicole Randall Johnson (Birthing Instructor); Michael Naughton (Dad #1); Steven Pierce (Husband #2); Todd Farr (Ken); Barbara Perry (Old Woman); Casey Rose Wilson (Fertility Clinic Worker); Bruce Green (Sleazy Guy); Hyla Matthews (Jenny's Mom); Aly Carpenter (Jenny); Eric Hoffman (Cop); Jason Pardo (New Dad); John Colton (Older Gentleman); Fatma Dabo (Tribal Woman); Rob McKittrick (Man in the Street); Ginger Williams (Lady with Buggy); Jesse Warren (Brad); Andrew Friedman (Nervous Dad); Mark Anthony Williams, Raymond T. Williams (Janine's Co-Workers); Ryan Wynott (Young Dean)

# GREAT WORLD OF SOUND

(MAGNOLIA) Producers, Melissa Palmer, David Gordon Green, Richard Wright, Craig Zobel; Executive Producers, Daniela Taplin Lundberg, Matt Chapman, Mike Chapman; Co-Producer, Sophia Lin; Director, Craig Zobel; Screenplay, George Smith, Craig Zobel; Photography, Adam Stone; Designer, Richard Wright; Costumes, Elizabeth Steinfels; Editors, Tim Streeto, Jane Rizzo; Music, David Wingo; Associate Producers, Steven Holtzman, Adam Paroo; Casting, Susan Shopmaker Casting, Erica Palgon; Additional casting, Corrigan & Johnston Casting, Tonya Shuffler; a GWS Media presentation in association with Plum Pictures; Color; HD; Rated R; 106 minutes; Release date: September 14, 2007.

## Cast

Pat Healy (Martin); Kene Holliday (Clarence); Robert Longstreet (Layton); Rebecca Mader (Pam); John Baker (Shank); Tricia Paoluccio (Gloria); Michael Harding (Fred); Barlow Jacobs (Henry); Carver Johns (Walter); Mark Scarboro (Bill); Frances Green, Justin St. Gelais, Renee St. Gelais (Restaurant Patrons); James Green (Bartender); Libertad Green (Waitress); Scott Reynolds (Salesman); Collette Wolfe (Airline Employee)

Kene Holliday, Pat Healy in *Great World of Sound* © MAGNOLIA PICTURES

# IRA AND ABBY

Jennifer Westfeldt, Chris Messina in *Ira and Abby* © MAGNOLIA PICTURES

(MAGNOLIA) Producer, Brad Zions; Executive Producers, Jennifer Westfeldt, Ilana Levine, Jorge M. Perez; Co-Producer, Declan Baldwin; Director, Robert Cary; Screenplay, Jennifer Westfeldt; Photography, Harlan Bosmajian; Editor, Phillip J. Bartell; Music, Marcelo Zarvos; Designer, Ray Kluga; Costumes, Doug Hall; Associate Producer, Stu Pollard; Casting, Bernie Telsey, David Vaccari; a Breakout Pictures production, in association with Team Todd; Color; HD; Not rated; 100 minutes; Release date: September 14, 2007.

**Cast**

Chris Messina (Ira Black), Jennifer Westfeldt (Abby Willoughby), Frances Conroy (Lynne Willoughby), Fred Willard (Michael Willoughby), Judith Light (Arlene Black), Robert Klein (Seymour Black), Maddie Corman (Lea), Jason Alexander (Dr. Morris Saperstein), Mary Louise Burke (Janice), Donna Murphy (Dr. Goldman), Hayden Adams (Kissing Subway Guy), Robert Bagnell (Jimmy), Ken Barnett (Bobby), Brad Bellamy (Henry), Matthew Del Negro (Seth), Jon Hamm (Ronnie), Darrell Hammond (Dr. Rosenblum), Peter Hirsch (Dr. Goldberg), Ilana Levine (Aurora Finklestein), David Margulies (Dr. Friedman), Michael McGrath (Tony), Modi (Marvin), Chris Parnell (Dr. Silverberg), Kali Rocha (Tracey), Ramon Rodriguez (Subway Robber), Asa Somers (Gus), Kevin Sussman (Lenny), Ronald Sylvers (Subway Passenger), Nathalie Twaddle (Caterwaiter), Amy Wilson (Patient)

# DARKON

(SEETHINK/OVIE) Producers, Ethan Palmer, Tom Davis, Christopher Kikis, Thoma Kikis, Nicholas Levis, Cherise Wolas, Alan Zelenetz; Directors, Andrew Neel, Luke Meyer; Photography, Karl Schroder, Hillary Spera; Editor, Brad Turner; Music, Jonah Rapino; an Ovie Entertainment presentation of a SeeThink, Ovie Entertainment production; Color; DV; 93 minutes; Release date: September 14, 2007. Documentary on Baltimoreans who participate in a role-playing game called Darkon; with Skip Lipman (Bannor), Daniel McArthur (Trivius), Rebecca Thurmond (Nemesis), Kenyon Wells (Keldar).

# TOOTS

(MENEMSHA) Producers, Alicia Sams, Whitney Dow, Kristi Jacobson; Executive Producers, James P. MacGilvray, Alan Mattone; Director, Kristi Jacobson; Photography, Daniel B. Gold; Editors, Lewis Erskine, Penelope Falk; Music, Mark Suozzo; a Catalyst Films production; Color/black and white; Not rated; 85 minutes; Release date: September 14, 2007. Documentary on flamboyant restaurateur Bernard "Toots" Shor; with Maury Allen, Dave Anderson, Yogi Berra, David Brown, Bill Buchbinder, John Clancy, Perian Conerly, Walter Cronkite, Peter Duchin, Whitey Ford, Bill Fugazy, Pat Futcher, Bill Gallo, Joe Garagiola, Frank Gifford, Pete Hamill, Kerry Jacobson, Harry Lavin, Larry Merchant, Liz Murray, LeRoy Neiman, Nick Pileggi, Charle Reilly, Gianni Russo, Dick Sherman, Bert Randolph Sugar, Gay Talese, Mike Wallace, Sidney Zion.

# ANGELS IN THE DUST

(CINEMA LIBRE STUDIOS) Producers, Louise Hogarth, James Egan, Rosalie Pelser; Executive Producer, Diane Weyermann; Director/Screenplay, Louise Hogarth; Photography, May Rigler; Music, Joseph Julián González, Simphiwe Dana; Editor, Melina Briana Epler; a Participant Productions, Dream Out Loud Production; South African; Dolby; Color; HD; Not rated; 95 minutes; American release date: September 14, 2007. Documentary on how Marion Cloete and her family established the rural village and school of Boikarabelo in South Africa; with Marion Cloete.

# MOVING MCALLISTER

(FIRST INDEPENDENT PICTURES) Producers, Jason Faller, Ben Gourley, Kynan Griffin; Executive Producers, T.R. Gourley, Maclain Nelson; Director, Andrew Black; Screenplay, Ben Gourley; Photography, Doug Chamberlain; Designer, Anne Black; Costumes, Brittney Leavitt; Editors, Masahiro Hirakubo, Chantelle Squires; Music, Didier Lean Rachou; Music Supervisor, Debra A. Baum; Casting, Linda Phillips-Palo; a Camera 40 production, presented in association with Revel Entertainment; Dolby; Widescreen; Color; Rated PG-13; 89 minutes; Release date: September 14, 2007.

**Cast**

Ben Gourley (Rick Robinson), Mila Kunis (Michelle McAllister), Jon Heder (Orlick "Orlie" Prescott Hope), Rutger Hauer (Maxwell McAllister), Hubbel Palmer (Carl), Billy Drago (The Lady), Peter Jason (Mr. Robinson), Cathrine Grace (Mrs. Robinson), Patrika Darbo (Debbie), William Mapother (Bob), Zach Ward (Earl), Mark Cantor (Business Traveler), Tomek Debowski (Himself), Tennay Evans (Thompson), Allyson Everitt (Waitress), Mary Pat Gleason (Margerie), Whit Hertford (Fastfood Cashier), Geoffrey Lewis (Crazy Old Martin), Ashley Munns (Sexy Cow Girl), Maclain Nelson (Beau Diddly), Mark Noakes (Astronaut), Lucila Solá (Petals), Joe Unger (Lanky)

# THE LAST WINTER

James LeGros in *The Last Winter* © IFC FIRST TAKE

(IFC FIRST TAKE) Producers, Larry Fessenden, Jeffrey Levy-Hinte; Executive Producers, Jeanne Levy-Church, Sigurjon Sighvatsson; Co-Producer, Kristen Kusama; Director, Larry Fessenden; Screenplay, Larry Fessenden, Robert Leaver; Photography, G. Magni Agustsson; Designer, Halfdan Larus Pedersen; Costumes, Helga Stefansdottir; Editor, Larry Fessenden; Music, Jeff Grace; Ambient Score, Anton Sanko; VFX Supervisor, Glenn McQuaid; Special Makeup FX, Stefan Jorgen Agustsson; Casting, Laura Rosenthal; an Antidote Films production in association with Zik Zak Filmworks; American-Icelandic; Dolby; Widescreen; Color; Not rated; 107 minutes; Release date: September 19, 2007.

## Cast

Ron Perlman (Ed Pollack), James Le Gros (James Hoffman), Connie Britton (Abby Sellers), Zachary Gilford (Maxwell McKinder), Kevin Corrigan (Motor), Jamie Harrold (Elliot Jenkins), Pato Hoffmann (Lee Means), Joanne Shenandoah (Dawn Russell), Larry Fessenden (Charles Foster), Halfdan Theodorsson (Gary)

# MY NAME IS ALAN, AND I PAINT PICTURES

Alan Russell-Cowan in *My Name is Alan, and I Paint Pictures* © RAW MEDIA NETWORK

(RAW MEDIA NETWORK) Producer, Colleen Ryan; Executive Producers, Christine Fulton, Zev Greenfield; Director/Screenplay, Johnny Boston; Photography, Jarred Alterman, Thomas Scarlett, Parker Gowan, Alex Wolfe, Brian McArdle; Editor, Todd Drezner; Dolby; Color; Not rated; 86 minutes; Release date: September 19, 2007. Documentary on paranoid schizophrenic street artist Alan Russell-Cowan; with Alan Russell-Cowan, Monika Russell-Cowan, Richard Russell-Cowan, Raymond Bell, Bill Coffeill, Tats Cru, Bizz DeCrenza, David Dvorak, Randy Hannah, Dr. Stephen Hirsch, Nancy Hoffman, Shedrick Jackson, Oliver Kamm, John Kasper, Tristan Koch, Daniel Kunitz, Arnold Lehman, John Maizels, Elizabeth Marks, Shawn McLean, Don Morris, Jessica Oliver, Darryl Pierre, Clem Richardson, Maggie Robbins, Alex Rumula, Jeff Serota, Robert Storr, Francisca Surrez, Dominic Trepel, Pamela Willoughby.

# SEA OF DREAMS

(SUCCESS FILMS) Producers, Jose Bojorquez, Nickolay Todorov; Executive Producers, Pedro DeKeratry, Robert Katz; Director, Jose Bojorquez; Screenplay, Jose Bojorquez, David Howard; Photography, Christopher Chomyn; Editor, Tia Nolan; Music, Luis Bacalov; Music Supervisor, David Franco; Designer, Gloria Carrasco; Costumes, Sergio Ruiz; Casting, Emily Schweber; a Success Films production in association with Robert Katz Entertainment; Mexican-American; Dolby; Color; Rated PG; 99 minutes; Release date: September 21, 2007.

## Cast

Johnathon Schaech (Marcelo), Sendi Bar (Grecia), Angélica Maria (Rina), Nicholas Gonzalez (Sebastian), Seymour Cassel (Tomaso), Sonia Braga (Nurka), Julio Bekhor (Luis), Gastón Melo (Priest), Tina Romero (Raquel), Pablo Santos (Benjamin), Daniela Schmidt (Isabella), Jessica Valdes (Grecia as a Teenager), Priscilla Aispura (Isabella as a Teenager), Cosme Alberto (Sebastian as a Teenager), Pedro de Velasco (Luis as a Teenager), Eva Frajko (Paloma), Jose Antonio Gaona (Benjamin's Friend), Juan Rios (Cristobal)

## ADRIFT IN MANHATTAN

Heather Graham, Victor Rasuk in *Adrift in Manhattan* © SCREEN MEDIA FILMS

(SCREEN MEDIA FILMS) Producers, Steven J. Brown, Joshua Blum, Ian Jessel; Executive Producers, Dave Scoggin, J.A. Bremont, G. Michael Harris, Jijo Reed, Ben Cohen, Bobby Yoshizumi, Amy Hobby; Director, Alfredo de Villa; Screenplay, Nat Moss, Alfredo de Villa; Photography, John Foster; Designer, Charlotte Bourke; Costumes, Julia Mitchelle Santiago; Editor, John Coniglio; Music, Michael A. Levine; Casting, Adrienne Stern; a Cineglobe and Noble Group presentation of a Washington Square production; Dolby; Color; HD; Rated R; 91 minutes; Release date: September 21, 2007.

### Cast

Heather Graham (Rose Phipps), William Baldwin (Mark Phipps), Dominic Chianese (Tommaso Pensara), Victor Rasuk (Simon Colon), Erika Michels (Claire Phipps), Marlene Forte (Marta Colon), Elizabeth Peña (Isabel Parades), Jesse Green (Man at Poetry Reading), Nicole Kohnen (Karen), Nicole Leach (Melanie), Karen Olivo (Ana), Keren Love Perilman (Jen), Richard Petrocelli (Mr. Sneider), Frank Picarazzi (Subway Musician), James P. Stephens (Waiter), Marti Vendetti (Clinic Receptionist), Nani Walker (Girl on Subway)

## RANDY AND THE MOB

Ray McKinnon in *Randy and the Mob* © CAPRICORN PICTURES

(CAPRICORN PICTURES) Producers, Lisa Blount, Walton Goggins, David Koplan; Executive Producers, Benjy Griffith, Phil Walden; Co-Producer, D. Scott Lumpkin; Director/Screenplay, Ray McKinnon; Photography, Jonathan Sela; Editor, Jim Makiej; Music, John Swihart; Designer, Chris Jones; Costumes, April Napier; Casting, Shay Griffin, Emily Schweber; a Ginny Mule production, in association with Timbergrove Entertainment; Color; Rated PG; 91 minutes; Release date: September 21, 2007.

### Cast

Ray McKinnon (Randy Pearson/Cecil Pearson), Walton Goggins (Tino Armani), Lisa Blount (Charlotte Pearson), Tim DeKay (Bill), Bill Nunn (Wardlowe Gone), Brent Briscoe (Griff Postell), Paul Ben-Victor (Franco), Sam Frihart (Four), Burt Reynolds (Elmore Culpepper)

## CHARLIE

(CHIQUI PRODUCTION) Producers, Salvatore Interlandi, Adam McClelland, Erik S. Weigel; Executive Producer, Wil Röttgen; Director/Screenplay, Salvatore Interlandi; Photography, Daniel Sharnoff; Designer, Jason Noto; Costumes, Cynthia Mitchell; Editors, Salvatore Interlandi, Adam McClelland; a WinSome production; Dolby; Color; HD; Not rated; 88 minutes; Release date: September 26, 2007.

### Cast

D.J. Mendel (Charlie); Tim Donovan, Jr. (Tommy); Denise Greber (Anna); Maria Buttazzoni (Maria); Melaena Cadiz (Shannon); Gabriela Crocco (Gabriela); Robert Cucuzza (Eugene); Ewa Da Cruz (Emma); Britt Genelin (Cheryl); Iva Gocheva (Belle); Kourtney Rutherford (Alyssa); Mark Breese, Ned Martin, Greg DeLiso (Bar Fight Patrons)

# BANISHED

(ITN PRODS.) Producers, Omid Shabkhiz, Blaney Lamont; Executive Producers, Hamid Shabkhiz, Mandana Shabkhiz; Director/Photography/Editor, Omid Shabkhiz; Screenplay, Omid Shabkhiz, Peter Banifaz; Color; Not rated; 72 minutes; Release date: September 26, 2007.

### Cast

Marco Arras (Sorbo); C.J. Baker (Mel); Peter Banifaz (Theodore Strietzman); AmirAli Barani (Ohar Odette); Arman Behrad (Man with Briefcase); Brian Behrad (Chris); Deborah Behrad (Victim); Jennifer Chan (Mr. Tanaka's Girlfriend); Robert Costanzo (Sal); Koji Fueta (Japanese Mob Guy); Liron Gerti (Kelly Vespa); Sam Hale (Johnny Gunz); Shervin Kamali (Cladio); Farzad Khorshidian (Man in Trunk); Michelle Kolb (Deborah Taylor); Payman Mahdavian, Pouyan Niknejad (Hitmen); D.W. Miller (Norm); Mohammadreza Mozeni, Farzin Saberi (House Victims); Nariman Norouz (Charlie Vespa); Mark Ofuji (Mr. Tanaka); David Scott (Bartender); Omid Shabkhiz (Michael Genova); Michael Vitiello (Italian Mob Guy)

# TRADE

(LIONSGATE) Producers, Roland Emmerich, Rosilyn Heller; Executive Producers, Asok Amritraj, Robert Leger, Tom Ortenberg, Michael Wimer, Nick Hamson, Peter Landesman, Lars Sylvest; Co-Producers, Amanda DiGiulio, Jakob Claussen, Thomas Woebke, Ossie von Richtofen; Director, Marco Kreuzpainter; Screenplay, Jose Rivera, based on the article "The Girls Next Door" by Peter Landesman; Story, Peter Landesman, Jose Rivera; Photography, Daniel Gottschalk; Designer, Bernt Capra; Costumes, Carol Oditz; Editor, Hansjorg Weissbrich; Music, Jacobo Lieberman, Leonardo Heiblum; Music Supervisor, Lynn Fainchtein; Casting, Aleta Chapelle (U.S.), Carla Hool (Mexico); a Centropolis Entertainment and VIP Medienfond 4 production; Dolby; Deluxe color; Rated R; 119 minutes; Release date: September 28, 2007.

### Cast

Kevin Kline (Ray Sheridan), Cesar Ramos (Jorge), Alicja Bachleda-Curus (Veronica), Paulina Gaitan (Adriana), Kathleen Gati (Irina Silayeva), Marco Perez (Manuelo), Linda Emond (Patty Sheridan), Zack Ward (Alex Green), Kate del Castillo (Laura), Tim Reid (Det. Hank Smith), Pavel Lychnikoff (Vadim Youchenko), Anthony Crivello (Det. Henderson), Evan Adrian (Student), Howard Alonzo (Delivery Guy), Richard Barela (Detainee), Aimee-Lynn Chadwick (School Girl), Bo Greigh (1st Deputy), Dale Malley (Hotel Owner), Barbara Mayfield (Waitress in the Diner), Paul McGowen (Firefighter), Leland Pascual (Thai Boy), Marco Pérez (Manuelo), Matt Sanford (Cyber Café Manager), William Sterchi (Gary), Matthew Timmons (Border Policeman)

# OUTSOURCED

Josh Hamilton in *Outsourced* © LANTERN LANE ENTERTAINMENT

(LANTERN LANE ENTERTAINMENT) Producer, Tom Gorai; Executive Producers, David Skinner, George Wing; Co-Producer, Gwen Bialic; Director, John Jeffcoat; Screenplay, George Wing, John Jeffcoat; Photography, Teodoro Maniaci; Editor, Brian Berdan; Music, B.C. Smith; Music Supervisors, John Jeffcoat, Tom Gorai; Designer, Fali Unwala; Costumes, Heidi Bivens, Veera Kapur; Casting, Ellen Chenoweth, Kathleen Chopin; a ShadowCatcher Entertainment, Tom Gorai production; Dolby; Color; HDCam-to-35mm; Rated PG-13; 102 minutes; Release date: September 28, 2007.

### Cast

Josh Hamilton (Todd Anderson), Ayesha Dharker (Asha), Larry Pine (Bob), Asif Basra (Purohit N. Virajnarianan), Matt Smith (Dave), Arjun Mathur (Gaurav)

# ITTY BITTY TITTY COMMITTEE

(POWER UP FILMS) Producers, Andrea Sperling, Lisa Thrasher; Executive Producer, Stacy Codikow; Director, Jamie Babbit; Screenplay, Tina Mabry, Abigail Shafran; Photography, Christine A. Maier; Editor, Jane Abramowitz; Music, Radio Sloan; Designer, Nina Alexander; Costumes, Melissa Meister; an Andrea Sperling production, in association with Lisa Thrasher; Color; HD-to-35mm; Not rated; 86 minutes; Release date: September 28, 2007.

### Cast

Melonie Diaz (Anna), Nicole Vicius (Sadie), Daniela Sea (Calvin), Carly Pope (Shuli), Lauren Mollica (Aggie), Deak Evgenikos (Meat), Guinevere Turner (Reporter), Melanie Mayron (Courtney), Jenny Shimizu (Laurel), Lauren Mollica (Aggie), Leslie Grossman (Maude), Jimmi Simpson (Chris), Ana Mercedes (Kate)

# THE PRICE OF SUGAR

(MITROPOULOS FILMS) Producers, Bill Haney, Eric Grunebaum; Executive Producer, Tim Disney; Director, Bill Haney; Screenplay, Bill Haney, Peter Rhodes; Photography, Jerry Risius, Eric Cochran; Editor, Peter Rhodes; Music, Claudio Ragazzi; Color; DV; Not rated; 90 minutes; Release date: September 28, 2007. Documentary on the efforts of Father Christopher Hartley's efforts to better the lot of Haitian workers in the Dominican Republic; with Christopher Hartley; Narrator, Paul Newman.

# LAKE OF FIRE

*Lake of Fire* ©THINKFILM

(THINKFILM) Producer/Director/Photography, Tony Kaye; Executive Producers, Tony Kaye, Yan Lin Kaye; Co-Executive Producers, Steve Golin, David Kanter, Lenny Bekerman; Editor, Peter Goddard; Music, Anne Dudley; an Above the Sea production; Black and white; 35mm; HDCAM; Not rated; 152 minutes; Release date: October 3, 2007. Documentary on the ever-controversial abortion debate; with Alan Dershowitz, Noam Chomsky, Nat Hentoff, Dallas Blanchard, Norma McCorvey, Peter Singer, Randall Terry, Frederick Clarkson, Bill Baird, Frances Kissling, Michael Griffin, Paul Hill.

# JACK KETCHAM'S
# THE GIRL NEXT DOOR

(MODERNCINÉ) Producers, Andrew van den Houten, William M. Miller; Co-Producer, Robert Tonino; Director, Gregory Wilson; Screenplay, Daniel Farrands, Philip Nutman, based on the book by Jack Ketcham; Photography, William M. Miller; Designer, Krista Gall; Costumes, Michael Bevins; Music, Ryan Shore; Editor, M.J. Fiore; Casting, Cindi Rush; Color; Rated R; 91 minutes; Release date: October 3, 2007.

## Cast

Bluthe Auffarth (Meg Loughlin), Daniel Manche (David Moran), Blanche Baker (Ruth Chandler), Graham Patrick Martin (Willie Chandler, Jr.), Benjamin Ross Kaplan (Donny Chandler), Austin Williams (Ralphie "Woofer" Chandler), William Atherton (Adult David), Kevin Chamberlin (Officer Jennings), Dean Faulkenberry (Kenny), Gabrielle Howarth (Cheryl Robinson), Spenser Leigh (Denise Crocker), Grant Show (Mr. Moran), Catherine Mary Stewart (Mrs. Moran), Peter Stickles (EMT), Madeline Taylor (Susan Loughlin), Michael Zegen (Eddie)

# KURT COBAIN: ABOUT A SON

*Kurt Cobain: About a Son* © BALCONY RELEASING

(BALCONY) Producers, Shirley Moyers, Noah Khoshbin, Chris Green; Executive Producer, Ravi Anne; Co-Producer, Michael Azerrad; Director, A.J. Schnack; Photography, Wyatt Troll; Editor, A.J. Schnack; Original Music, Steve Fisk, Benjamin Gibbard; a Sidetrack Films presentation of a Bonfire Films of America production; Color; Not rated; 97 minutes; Release date: October 3, 2007. Documentary on late rocker Kurt Cobain, featuring narration by Cobain from tapes he recorded a year before his suicide in 1994.

# THE SEEKER:
# THE DARK IS RISING

(20TH CENTURY FOX) Producer, Marc Platt; Executive Producers, Ron Schmidt, Adam Siegel, Jared LeBoff; Director, David L. Cunningham; Screenplay, John Hodge, based on the novel *The Dark is Rising* by Susan Cooper; Photography, Joel Ransom; Editors, Geoffrey Rowland, Eric A. Sears; Music, Christophe Beck; Music Supervisor, Patrick Houlihan; Designer, David Lee; Costumes, Vinilla Burnham; Visual Effects Supervisor/Second Unit Director, James E. Price; Visual Effects, Rising Sun Pictures, Digital Domain, Hydraulx, Riot, Mr. X; Makeup Effects Supervisor, Gary Tunnicliffe; Stunts, Troy Brown; Casting, Cathy Sandrich, Amanda Mackey (U.S.), Jina Jay (U.K.); a Marc Platt production presented with Walden Media; Dolby; Color; Rated PG; 99 minutes; Release date: October 5, 2007.

## Cast

Alexander Ludwig (Will Stanton); Christopher Eccleston (The Rider); Frances Conroy (Miss Greythorne); Ian McShane (Merriman Lyon); Wendy Crewson (Mary Stanton); John Benjamin Hickey (John Stanton); Gregory Smith (Max Stanton); James Cosmo (Dawson); Jim Piddock (Old George); Drew Tyler Bell (James Stanton); Amelia Warner (Maggie Barnes); Edmund Entin (Robin Stanton); Gary Entin (Paul Stanton); Emma Lockhart (Gwen Stanton); Jordan J. Dale (Stephen Stanton); Samantha Lawson (Saleswoman); Geoff Bell, Gary J. Tunnicliffe (Security Guards); Maria Miroiu (Rider's Mother); Sylvester Morand (Vicar); Mark Donovan (Fight Promoter); Stephen Evans (Trickster)

# FOR THE BIBLE TELLS ME SO

The Reitan Family in *For the Bible Tells Me So* © FIRST RUN FEATURES

(FIRST RUN FEATURES) Producer, Daniel Karslake; Executive Producers, Michael Huffington, Bruce Bastian, Robin Voss, Robert Greenbaum, Keith Lewis; Co-Producers, Nancy Kennedy, Helen Mendoza; Director, Daniel Karslake; Photography, Kevin Bond, Leonard Chamblee, Tyrone Edwards, Tom Fahey, Mark Falstad, Bob Gunter, Guy Hernandez, Greg Hoerdemann, Brian Knappenberger, Bruce Liffiton, Jared Manders, Jim Mathers, Kat Patterson, Dave Roberson, Mike Simon, Rob Van Pragg, Brad Waigt, Ian Young; Editor, Nancy Kennedy; Music, Scott Anderson, Mark Suozzo; Music Supervisor, Susan Jacobs; Animation, Powerhouse Animation Studios; Supervising Animator, Jason Williams; a VisionQuest Prods. and the Atticus Group production; Color; Not rated; 101 minutes; Release date: October 5, 2007. Documentary on Christianity's stance on homosexuality, with Gene Robinson, Imogene Robinson, Victor Robinson, Isabella "Boo" McDaniel, Brenda Poteat, David Poteat, Tonia Poteat, Randi Reitan, Phil Reitan, Jake Reitan, Britta Reitan, Jane Gephardt, Dick Gephardt, Chrissy Gephardt, Mary Lou Wallner.

# A MAN NAMED PEARL

(TENTMAKERS ENTERTAINMENT) Producer, Scott Galloway; Executive Producer, Cecil Stokes; Directors, Scott Galloway, Brent Pierson; Photography, J. Steven Anderson; Music, Fred Story; Editor, Greg Grzeszczak; Color; Not rated; 78 minutes; Release date: October 5, 2007. Documentary on self-taught topiary artist Pearl Fryar.

# DESERT BAYOU

(CINEMA LIBRE) Producers, Alex LeMay, Jimmy Finkl, Mike Russell, Marybeth Mazzone; Executive Producers, Alex LeMay, Jimmy Finkl; Co-Producer, Sarah Radcliffe; Director, Alex LeMay; Screenplay, Thomas G. Lemmer, from a story by Michael Reynolds; Photography, Andrew Dryer, Peter Biagi; Editors, Martin Nelson, Mike Russell; Music, Geno Lenardo; Narrator, Art Hoyle; a Taproot Prods. Production; Color; DV; Not rated; 90 minutes; Release date: October 5, 2007. Documentary on 600 black citizens of New Orleans who were relocated to Salt Lake City following the devastation of Hurricane Katrina; with Master P, Tamu Smith, Curtis Pleasant, Shmuley Boteach, Beverly Wright, Karyn Dudley, Rocky Anderson.

# MY KID COULD PAINT THAT

(SONY CLASSICS) Producer, Amir Bar-Lev; Executive Producers, John Battsek, Andrew Ruhemann; Co-Producer, Stephen Dunn; Director, Amir Bar-Lev; Photography, Matt Boyd, Nelson Hume, Bill Turnley; Editors, John Walter, Michael Levine; Music, Rondo Brothers; an A&E Independent Films presentation in association with BBC of an Axis Films and Passion Films production; Color; Sony HDCAM; Rated PG-13; 82 minutes; Release date: October 5, 2007. Documentary on how young Marla Olmstead displayed a remarkable talent for abstract painting by the time she was four years old; with Mark Olmstead, Laura Olmstead, Marla Olmstead, Zane Olmstead, Anthony Brunelli, Stuart Simpson, Michael Kimmelman, Elizabeth Cohen.

Marla Olmstead in *My Kid Could Paint That* © SONY PICTURES CLASSICS

# BROKEN

Heather Graham, Jeremy Sisto in *Broken* © TRULY INDIE

(TRULY INDIE) Producers, Brian R. Etting, Jerry Wayne; Director, Alan White; Screenplay, Drew Pillsbury; Story, Jeff Lister, Drew Pillsbury; Photography, Neil Shapiro; Designer, Charisse Cardenas; Costumes, Louise de Teliga; Music, Jeehun Hwang; Songs, The Brian Jonestown Massacre; Editor, Jay Nelson; Casting, Victoria Burrows, Scot Boland; a Walk on the Beach production; Color; Rated R; 97 minutes; Release date: October 5, 2007.

### Cast

Heather Graham (Hope), Jeremy Sisto (Will), Randall Batinkoff (Cliff), Jake Busey (Vince), Michael A. Goorjian (Thomas), Linda Hamilton (Karen), Tess Harper (Clare), Bianca Lawson (Mia), Mark Sheppard (Malcolm), Valerie Azlynn (Jessica), James Brandon (Alex), Scarlett Chorvat (Girl), Chad Cunningham (David), Kevin Daniels (Franklin), Joe Hursley (Rob), Martin Kelly (Ethan), Marc Lynn (Allen), Billy Marti (Drug Dealer), Navid Negahban (Keith), Adam Nelson (Neal), Peter Pasco (Nick), Jessica Stroup (Sara), Arthur Williams, Jr. (The Cook)

# STRANGE CULTURE

(L5 PRODS.) Producers, Lise Swenson, Steven Beer, Lynn Hershman Leeson; Executive Producers, Melina Jampolis, Jessie Fuller; Co-Producers, Loren Smith, Barbara Tomber; Director/Screenplay/Editor, Lynn Hershman Leeson; Photography, Hiro Narita; Music, The Residents; Designer, Ben Leon; Casting, Jennifer Dean; Color; HD; Not rated; 75 minutes; Release date: October 5, 2007. Semi-documentary on how college professor Steve Kurtz was accused of bioterrorism by the government.

### Cast

Steve Kurtz (Himself); Thomas Jay Ryan (Steve Kurtz); Tilda Swinton (Hope Kurtz); Peter Coyote (Robert Ferrell); Josh Kornbluth (Phil/Lynn Hershman Leeson); Shoresh Alaudini (Loren); Cassie Powell (Lise); Larissa Clayton (Char); Jakob Bokulich, Marcie Prohofsky, Richard Wenzel (FBI Agents); Beatriz da Costa; Dr. Susan Leeson; Keith Olbermann; Lucia Sommer; Nato Thompson; Paul Vanouse.

# FINISHING THE GAME: THE SEARCH FOR A NEW BRUCE LEE

Roger Fan in *Finishing the Game* © IFC FIRST TAKE

(IFC FIRST TAKE) Producers, Julie Asato, Salvador Gatdula, Justin Lin; Executive Producers, Joan Huang, Jeff Gou; Co-Producers, Candi Guterres, Evan Leong; Director, Justin Lin; Screenplay, Josh Diamond, Justin Lin; Photography, Tom Clancey; Designer, Candi Guterres; Costumes, Annie Yun; Editor, Greg Louie; Music, Brian Tyler; Music Supervisor, Ernesto M. Foronda; Stunts, Don Tai Theerathada; Casting, Brad Gilmore; a Trailing Johnson Prods. production in association with Cherry Sky Films; Dolby; FotoKem color; Not rated; 88 minutes; Release date: October 5, 2007.

### Cast

Roger Fan (Breeze Loo); Sung Kang (Colgate Kim); James Franco (Rob Force); McCaleb Burnett (Trarrick Tyler); Jim Patrick (Frisco Sniper); Mousa Kraish (Raja Moore); Dustin Nguyen (Troy Poon); M.C. Hammer (Agent); Ron Jeremy (Porn Director); Monique Curnen (Saraghina Rivas); Cassidy Freeman (Jackie); Jake Sandvig (Ronny Kirschenbaum); Alden Ray (Elden); Jimmy Dean Carlson (Gaffer); Breon Ansley (Oliver); James Issac Barry (Ricky); Vail Bloom (Cassie); Lyrics Born (J.M.); Wilmer Calderon (Cesar); Melina Chiaverini (Marilyn Monroe); Nickolas Ray Hernandez (Paquero); Nathan Jung (Nazi Fu Manchu); Vu Dao, Ruffy Landayan, Stephen Oyoung, Daniel Zhao (Bruce Lee Wannabes); Meredith Scott Lynn (Eloise Gazdag); Betty Murphy (Mrs. Garrison); Leonardo Nam (Eli); Bernardo Pena (Remy Nguyen); Joanne Sims (Shirley); Michael Swan (Larry); George Takei (Man in Black); Aiko Tanaka (Nunchuck Girl); Brian Tee (MacChang); Dennis P. Thomas (Denise); Jason J. Tobin (Toby Jackson); Kathy Uyen (Kimberly); Tony Young Jr. (Father); Christina Blevins, Melissa Farrow, Simone Lotter, Michelle Mastrorio (Eloise's Entourage); Georgette Brotherson (*A Raisin in the Sun* Actress); Sonja Fisher (Suburban Housewife); Lyndsey Gayer (Angry Protestor); Jsplif, Kevnish, Prohgress (Chinese Delivery Boys)

# SKID MARKS

(DIVERSA FILMS) Producers, Thomas A. Seitz, Chuck Colclasure; Executive Producer, John Weinstein; Director, Karl Kozak; Screenplay, Karl Kozak, Don J. Rearden, Kraig Wenman; Photography, Scott Peck; Designer, Mark Helmuth; Costumes, Shawnelle Cherry; Music, Larry Groupé; Editors, Joe Richardson, Jeff Murphy; Casting, Stephen Snyder; a Skid Marks production; Dolby; Eastmancolor; Not rated; 93 minutes; Release date: October 5, 2007.

### Cast

Tyler Poelle (Rich); Mikey Post (Louis "One Foot" Jones); Scott Dittman (Karal, aka The Human Stain); Les Jennings (T-Bone); Kathy Uyen (Lai Mei); Tim Piper (Bob "The Brain"); David Schultz (Neil); Dianna Agron (Megan); Chuck Kelley (Sarge); Lars Roman (Captain Limison); Joel Roman (No-Legs); Peter Buitenhek (Patient in Bed); Joe Caldwell (Murder Ball Guy); Eva Derrek (Stripper); Emily Freeman (Roller Girl); Matthew Funk (DEA Agent); Johnny Giordano (Toga Frat Guy); Paul Grace (Cop); Ron E. Harris (DMB Instructor); Jeri Holst (Sherry Limison); Erica Dian Jones, Alexis Zibolis (Nurses); Stephen Katz (Fry Cook); Monique La Barr (Jacques' Girlfriend); Akira Lane (Exotic Dancer); Charlotte Marie (Waitress); Kelicea Meadows (Sinderella); Wrenna Monet (Bikini Co-Ed); Sam Nainoa (Half-Naked Patient); J.R. Nutt (Leonard); Tye Rainford (Limison's Girlfriend); Stacy Paul Rugely (70s Pimp); Michael Q. Schmidt (The Very Indignant Jogger); Combiz Shams (Frat Toga Boy); Gubbi Sigurdsson (Patient in Wheelchair); Billy Snow (Paramedic #1); Stevan Turk (Hospital Security Guard); Ken Wells (Other Frat Toga Guy); Andy White (Roger's Friend #1); Matthew Wolf (Jacques); Don Worley (Proctologist)

# GOLDA'S BALCONY

(SEVENTH ART RELEASING) Producer, Tony Cacciotti; Executive Producer, David Steiner; Director, Jeremy Kagan; Screenplay, William Gibson, based on his play; Photography, Jacek Laskus; Editor, David Kashevaroff; Music, Yuval Ron; an East-West Ventures production; Color; DV; Not rated; 90 minutes; Release date: October 10, 2007.

### Cast

Valerie Harper (Golda Meir)

# HOUSE

(THE BIGGER PICTURE) Producers, Joe Goodman, Bobby Neutz, Michael Webber, Ralph Winter; Executive Producers, Wojtek Frykowski, Marek Sledziewski; Director, Robby Henson; Screenplay, Rob Green, based on the novel by Ted Dekker and Frank Peretti; Photography, Marcin Koszalka; Costumes, Violetta Jezewska; Music, David E. Russo; Editor, Andrea Bottiglerio; a Namesake Entertainment, More Entertainment production; Color; Not rated; 101 minutes; Release date: October 10, 2007.

### Cast

Allana Bale (Susan); J.P. Davis (Randy); Jeffrey de Graft-Johnson (Deputy); Pawel Delag (Police Officer); Heidi Dippold (Stephanie); Leslie Easterbrook (Betty); Julie Ann Emery (Leslie); Mark Fierer (Randy's Father); Holly McClure, Joe Goodman (EMS); Andrew Gorzen (Leslie's Uncle); Michael Madsen (Officer Lawdale); Bill Moseley (Stewart); Bobby Neutz (Sheriff); Albert Pietrzak (Young Randy); Reynaldo Rosales (Jack); Weonika Rosati (Officer's Wife); Florentyna Synowiecka (Melissa); Lew Temple (Pete)

# THE FINAL SEASON

(YARI FILM GROUP) Producers, Michael Wasserman, Steven Schott, Tony Wilson, D. Parker Widemire Jr., Herschel Weingrod; Executive Producers, Sean Astin, Carl Borack; Director, David Mickey Evans; Screenplay, Art D'Alessandro, James Grayford; Photography, Daniel Styoloff; Designer, Chester Kaczenski; Costumes, Lynn Brannelly-Newman; Editor, Harry Keramidas; Music, Nathan Wang; Special Effects Coordinator, Ken Gorrell; Stunts, Jim Wilkey; Line Producer, Kenneth Burke; Associate Producers, Terry Trimpe, Vaughan Halyard; Casting, Rosemary Welden; a Final Partners presentation of a Carl Borack/TMRC production, in association with Fobia Films; Dolby; Color; Rated PG; 113 minutes; Release date: October 12, 2007.

### Cast

Sean Astin (Kent Stock); Powers Boothe (Coach Jim Van Scoyoc); Rachael Leigh Cook (Polly Hudson); James Gammon (Jacob Akers); Larry Miller (Roger Dempsey); Marshall Bell (Harvey Makepeace); Tom Arnold (Burt Akers); Michael Angarano (Mitch Akers); Angela Paton (Anne Akers); Matthew W. Allen (Umpire); Mackenzie Astin (Chip Dolan); Holly Bonelli (Jen Maples); Parisse Boothe (Jean Marie); Jill Brockhohn, Jimmy Brockhohn (Students); Dayton Callie (Mr. Stewart); Brett Claywell (Patrick Iverson); Michael Cornelison (Father Schultz); David Davis, Brooke Lemke (Fans); Eddie Driscoll (Larry Johnson); James Gammon (Jared Akers); Kim Grimaldi (Mrs. Stewart); Joe Heath (Painted F, Letter T); Jesse Henecke (Principal Halberstrom); Lucinda Jenney (Sheryl Van Scoyoc); Nick Livingston (Kevin Stewart); Roscoe Myrick (Sammy); Angela Paton (Ann Akers); Lindsey Pena (Tabby); Alexander Roos (Steve Myers); Danielle Savre (Cindy Iverson); James Serpento (Sam Rydell); Ed Vos (Sheriff); Mark Yuhasz (Young Farmer)

# NAKED BOYS SINGING

(STRAND) Producer, Kirkland Tibbels; Executive Producers, Kermit Johns, G. Sterling Zinsmeyer; Directors, Robert Schrock, Troy Christian; Original Author, Robert Schrock; Music and Lyrics, Stephen Bates, Shelley Markham, David Pevsner, Rayme Sciaroni, Binyumen Schaechter, Perry Hart, Jim Morgan, Trance Thompson, Mark Winkler, Marie Caine, Mark Savage, Bruce Villanch, Robert Shrock; Editors, Troy Christian, Jerry Evans; Casting, Peter Matyas; a Funny Boys Films production; Dolby; Color; HD; Not rated; 95 minutes; Release date: October 12, 2007.

**Cast**

Andrew Blake Ames (Jack's Song), Jason Currie (Entertainer), Jaymes Hodges (Nothin' but the Radio On), Joseph Keane (Perky Porn Star), Anthony Manough (Muscle Addiction), Joe Souza (Bliss of a Bris/Announcer), Kevin Alexander Stea (Naked Maid), Phong Truong (Window to the Soul), Salvatore Vassallo (Conductor), Vincent Zamora (Window to Window)

# KING CORN

(BALCONY) Producer/Director, Aaron Woolf; Executive Producer, Sally Jo Fifer; Co-Producers, Curt Ellis, Ian Cheney; Screenplay, Aaron Woolf, Ian Cheney, Curt Ellis, Jeffrey K. Miller; Photography, Sam Cullman, Aaron Woolf, Ian Cheney; Editor, Jeffrey K. Miller; Music, the WoWz; a Mosaic Films production, in association with ITVS; Color; DV-to-35mm; Not rated; 90 minutes; Release date: October 12. 2007. Documentary in which Ian Cheney and Curt Ellis investigate the corn industry; with Ian Cheney, Curt Ellis, Stephen Macko, Chuck Pyatt, Ricardo Salvador, Dawn Cheney, Rich Johnson, Al Marth, Michael Pollan, Scott McGregor, Bob Bledsoe, Sue and Dean Jarrett, Allen Trenkele, Loren Cordain, Audrae Erickson, Fray Mendez, Farida Khan, Sabita Moktan, Earl Butz.

Ian Cheney, Curtis Ellis in *King Corn* © BALCONY RELEASING

# CANVAS

Joe Pantoliano, Devon Gearhart, Marcia Gay Harden in *Canvas* © SCREEN MEDIA FILMS

(SCREEN MEDIA) Producers, Sharon Lane, Adam Hammel, Lucy Hammel, Joe Pantoliano, Bill Erfuth; Executive Producer, Alan Rolnick; Co-Producer, Eddie Mordujovich; Co-Executive Producers, Bruce Beresford, George Hickenlooper; Director/Screenplay, Joseph Greco; Photography, Rob Sweeney; Designer, Bill Cimino; Costumes, Nancy Jarzynko; Editor, Nina Kawasaki; Music, Joel Goodman; Associate Producer, Caroline O'Brien; Casting, Ed Arenas; a Rebellion Pictures presentation in association with LMG Pictures; Dolby; Color; Rated PG-13; 100 minutes; Release date: October 12, 2007.

**Cast**

Joe Pantoliano (John Marino); Marcia Gay Harden (Mary Marino); Devon Gearhart (Chris Marino); Sophia Bairley (Dawn); Marcus Johns (Sam); Antony Del Rio (Gregg); Brandon Agan (Basketball Player); Nicholas Alexander, Danny Rawley (Students); Irene B. Colletti (Donna); Bill Erfurth (Officer Savage); Matthew T. Gitkin (Boat Salesman); Paul Las (Hector Villarosa); Emma Lockhart (Tiffeny); Owen Miller (Police Officer #2); Sandra Milliner (Loud Woman); Griffin Miner (Young Chris); Casey Travers (Mick); Tim Ware (Principal)

# FAT GIRLS

(HERE!/REGENT) Producers, Ash Christian, Kim Fishman; Executive Producers, Michele Levy, Howard P. Cohen, Anita Collen, Phil Collen, Friley Davidson, Chris De Camp; Director/Screenplay, Ash Christian; Photography, Vincent Wrenn; Editor, Karl Kimbrough; Music, Chris Gubisch; Designer, Lynne Moon; a Cranium Entertainment production in association with Hear No Evil Films; Color; Video; Rated R; 88 minutes; Release date: October 12, 2007.

## Cast

Ash Christian (Rodney Miller); Ashley Fink (Sabrina Thomas); Jonathan Caouette (Seymour Cox); Robin de Jesus (Rudy); Deborah Theaker (Judy); Ellen Albertini Dow (Mildred); Justin Bruening (Bobby); Alexa Havins (Tina); Evan Miller (Ted); Joe Flaten (Joey); Charles Baker (Roller Rink Attendant); Geoffrey Betts (Birthday Saloon Worker); DeAnne Bonneau (Carol); Ouida White, Trich Zaitoon, Allyn Carrell, Donna Sue Nickason (Church Women); Abby Cohen (Nursing Home Volunteer); Alyssa Joy Cook (Ted's Little Sister); Drew Cook (High School Student); Richard D. Curtin (Preacher); Jennifer Jane Emerson (Muff); Juli Erickson (Grandma); Jessica Haney, Kalisa Wade (Student Council Sluts); Scott Jacqmein (Hot Blonde Frat Ho); Grant James (Grandpa); Carrie Lasly (Sunday School Teacher); Jeremy Lasly (Child, Sunday School Class); Linda Leonard (Mary); Selene Luna (Little Woman); Taylor Madison (Student); Kevin Milligan, Morgane Wood (Drunk Teens); Irvin Mosley, Jr. (Old Man); Linda J. Park (Katie Chin); John Phelan (Coach Saunders); Richard Porter (Stoner); Alexis Posey, Nicholas Posey (Birthday Party/Reunion/Sunday School Class); Gianna Redeemer (Rudy's Family Member); Michelle Renee (Rudy's Mother); Jesse Romero (Young Rodney); Becky Jane Romine (School Counselor); Andres Alfonso Ruzo, Toim Zembrod (Hicks); Dustin Sautter (Waiter); Mitchell Self (Dad); Anita Thomas (Pat); Tom Young (Bobby Sr.)

Ash Christian, Ashley Fink in *Fat Girls* © HERE!/REGENT

# BERKELEY

Henry Winkler, Nick Roth in *Berkeley* © JUNG R RESTLESS

(JUNG R RESTLESS) Producers, Bobby Roth, Jeffrey White; Executive Producers, Lon Bender, Cosmas Paul Bolger Jr.; Director/Screenplay, Bobby Roth; Photography, Steve Burns; Designer, Henry G. Sanders; Costumes, Naila Aladdin Sanders; Music, Christopher Franke; Editors, Carsten Becker, Emily Wallin; Casting, Stacey Rosen; a Jeffrey White production; Color; Rated R; 88 minutes; Release date: October 12, 2007.

## Cast

Nick Roth (Ben); Laura Jordan (Sadie); Henry Winkler (Sy); Sarah Carter (Alice); Tom Morello (Blue); Jake Newton (Henry); Sebastian Tillinger (Mishkin); Wade Allain-Marcus (Buddy); Bonnie Bedelia (Hawkins); Sarah Bibb (Susie); Ruby Roth (Pearl); Thomas Gibson (Thomas the Valet); Reed Diamond (Ralph); Henry G. Sanders (Gadsen); Tracey Walter (Draft Board Doctor); Amelia Mulkey (Swedish Backpacker); Riki Lindhome (Fighting Girl); Rob Nilsson (Coach); Todd Felix (Young Democrat); Marissa Tait (Eve); Nelson Franklin (Frat Prez); Skyler Shaye (Blonde at Library); Corey Haddon (Jesus); Georgia X. Lifsher (Adeline House Girl); Tiffany Paralta (Pretty Hippie Girl); Kate Lang Johnson (Prom Queen); Thomas Schmid (Dean Craft); Irv Kershner (Statistics Professor); Dave Jacobs (Marijuana Cultivator); Alana Boatwright (Registrator); Julie Gribble (Kent State Girl); Pamela Norris, Curt Holley, Yrneh Brown (Black Panthers); Sarah Allan, Emily Kosloski, Robert Mamman, Jim Patneaude, Michael J. Silver (Mimes); Judy Dixon (Nurse); Mark Elias (Scared Student); Andrew Hunt (Draft Inductee); Lanre Idewu (Aggressive Black Panther); Peter Coyote (Narrator)

# PASSAGE TO ZARAHEMLA

(HEIMERDINGER ENTERTAINMENT) Producers, Chris Heimerdinger, Brian Brough; Director, Chris Heimerdinger; Photography, Travis Cline; Designer, Gary Sivertsen; Costumes, Shari Phman; Music, Sam Cardon; Editor, John Lyde; a Candlelight Media Group production; Color; Rated PG-13; 107 minutes; Release date: October 15, 2007.

### Cast

Summer Naomi (Kerra McConnell), Moronai Kanekoa (Kiddoni), Brian Kary (Brock McConnell), D.K. Walker (Clacker), Sila Agavale (Kush), Jose Bacio (Adder), Bryce Chamberlain (Grandpa Lee), Chris Heimerdinger (Chris McConnell), Spencer King (Lobo), Jenny Latimer (Natasha), Seth Packard (Spree), Alex Petrovitch (Hitch), William Rubio (Prince)

# TRIGGER MAN

(KINO) Producer, Peter Phok; Executive Producer, Larry Fessenden; Director/Screenplay/Photography/Editor, Ti West; Music, Jeff Grace; Visual Effects Supervisor, Glenn McQuaid; Associate producers, T.J. Healy II, Chris Tigani; a Glass Eye Pix presentation in association with ECR Productions; Stereo; Color; DV; Not rated; 80 minutes; Release date: October 17, 2007.

### Cast

Reggie Cunningham (Reggie), Ray Sullivan (Ray), Sean Reid (Sean), Larry Fessenden (Henchman), Heather Robb (Jogger), James Felix McKenney (Shooter), Daniel Mazikowski (Photographer), Seth Abrams (Seth)

*Trigger Man* © KINO

# THE COMEBACKS

(20TH CENTURY FOX) Producers, Peter Abrams, Andrew Panay, Robert L. Levy; Executive Producer, Adam F. Goldberg; Co-Producers, Laura Greenlee, Kevin Sabbe, Michael Schreiber; Director, Tom Brady; Screenplay, Ed Yeager, Joey Gutierrez, from a story by John Aboud, Michael Colton, Adam J. Epstein, Andrew Jacobson; Photography, Anthony B. Richmond; Editor, Alan Edward Bell; Music, Christopher Lennertz; Designer, Marc Fisichella; Costumes, Salvador Perez; a Fox Atomic presentation of a Tapestry Films production; Dolby; Deluxe color; Rated PG-13; 84 minutes; Release date: October 19, 2007.

### Cast

David Koechner (Coach Lambeau Fields); Carl Weathers (Freddie Wiseman); Melora Hardin (Barb Fields); Matthew Lawrence (Lance Truman); Brooke Nevin (Michelle Fields); Nick Searcy (Mr. Truman); George Back (Buddy Boy); Noureen DeWulf (Jizminder Featherfoot); Jesse Garcia (Jorge Juanson); Jackie Long (Trotter); Robert Ri'chard (Aseel Tare); Martin Spanjers (Randy Randinger); Jermaine Williams (IPod); Finesse Mitchell (Titans Coach); Will Arnett (Mailman); Dax Shepard (Sheriff); Bradley Cooper (Cowboy); Jon Gries (Barber); Andy Dick (Toilet Bowl Referee); Eric Christian Olsen (Foreign Exchange Student); Frank Caliendo (Chip Imitation); Stacy Keibler (All-American Mom); Drew Lachey (All-American Dad); Jason Sklar, Randy Skarl (Superfans); Kerri Kenney-Silver (Sports Judge); Jullian Grace (Maria Sharapova Look-Alike); Dennis Rodman (Warden); Bill Buckner, Eric Dickerson, Michael Irvin, Chris Rose, John Salley, Lawrence Taylor (Themselves); Shannon Woodward (Emily); Brittany Buckner (Kelly); Lindsay Gareth (Brittany); Emma Heming (Megan); Kai Donovan Brady (Young Lance); Adam Apodaca (Maddonald); David Blue (LaCrosse Partgoer); Kevin Patrick Burke (Zidane Look-Alike); Ren Casey (Cubs Fan); John W. Clark (Venus Williams Look-Alike); Ken Medlock (Pitching Coach); Don Milligan (Referee #2); Holmes Osborne (Man in Suit); Chase Penny (Troy); Casey Sander (Clint); Jason Widener (Vince); Akima "Rick" Castaneda (Jizminder's Father); Jim Cody Williams (Salamander); Maurice LaMarche (Announcer); Jerry Sherman (Rookie); Leigh Morgan, Rico Devereaux (Reporters); Rodney Saulsberry (Voice of God); Daniel Abikasis, Ryan Adams, Russell Thomas (Football Players); Akima (Chief Featherfoot); Tony Alameda (Tattooed Convict); Evena Alexander (Hot Tub Girl); Trevont Armond (Titan Fan); David Black (Cameraman); Dre Bowie (Titan Football Player); Jennifer Brasuell, Kristine May (Cheerleaders); Alex E. Burns (Limousine Driver); Monica Cabral (Soccer Girl); Dorothy Camak (Prom Date); D.T. Carney (Team Unbeatable); Allie Cohen (Titan Cheerlader); Ryan O'Neil DeSouza (Cuban Refugee); Aidan Gonzales, Andrew Gonzales (Baby Lance); Tony Gonzalez (Choreographer); Derek Graf (Turbo); Timo Malaika Howard (ACL's Wife); Trae Ireland (Minnesota Viking Player); Lu Johnson (Chet, Down Marker Ref); Matt Leonard (Scary Lineman); Chauntal Lewis (Freddy's Girl); Debra Ling (Hottie); Eric Mandia (Comebacks Football Player); Jerrod Montgomery (Cubs Center Fielder); Chris Moss (Football Dancer and Cheerleader); Bruce Nicholson (Armed Guard #1); Tarah Paige (Heidi, Cheerleader); Paige Peterson (Trotter's Girl); Jean-Michel Richaud (Voice of Scary Lineman); Jeff Sanders (Player #1 in Shower); Marty Eli Schwartz (Taser Cop); Marquita Scott (Titan Cheerleader); Robb Sykler (Marv Albert); Joshua Gates Weisberg (Toilet Bowl Fan); Tony Wilde (Autistic Kid)

# SARAH LANDON AND THE PARANORMAL HOUR

(FREESTYLE) Producers, Fred Comrie, John Comrie, Lisa Comrie; Executive Producer, Mark Borde; Director, Lisa Comrie; Screenplay, John Comrie, Lisa Comrie, from a story by John Comrie; Photography, Andrew Kuepper; Designer, Kurt Braun; Editor, Andrew Cohen; Music, Joseph Conlan; a Sunset Creek production, in association with White Night Prods.; Dolby; Technicolor; Rated PG; 81 minutes; Release date: October 19, 2007.

## Cast

Rissa Walters (Sarah Landon); Dan Comrie (Matt Baker); Brian Comrie (David Baker); Kurt Braun (Hank); Triston Coleman (Young David); Rick Comrie (Johnny Woods); Alessandra Daniele (Young Sarah); Nicole Des Coteaux (Mary Ann Baker); Patricia Dimeo (Vera Waters); Sylvia Enrique (Frida); Joe Momma Ernst, Ronda Ernst (House Shoppers); Michael A. Evans (Lee Baker); Geof Gibson (Phil); Kevin Guild (Mechanic); Rusty Hanes (Ben Woods); Jane Harris (Thelma Shaw); Butch Hillman (Chester Miles); Laura Hiltz (Mrs. Van Camp); Dakota Jade (Young Megan); Dave Lindley (Ron); Kendell Lindley (Justin Van Camp); Olivia Novrit (Yolanda Lopez); Wendy Perkins (Sarah's Mother); Jack Pine-Rusk (Young Matt); Michael Silva (Carlos)

# BLACK WHITE + GRAY: A PORTRAIT OF SAM WAGSTAFF AND ROBERT MAPPLETHORPE

(ARTHOUSE FILMS) Producer/Director/Screenplay, James Crump; Executive Producers, Stanley Buchthal, David Koh, Maja Hoffmann; Photography, Christopher Felver, Harry Geller, Paul Lundahl, Eric Koziol; Editors, Dave Giles, William Davis; Music, J. Ralph; Narrator, Joan Juliet Buck; an LM Media GmbH, Arthouse Films production; American-German; Black and white/color; Not rated; 77 minutes; Release date: October 19, 2007. Documentary on the professional and personal relationship between two major figures in the world of photography, curator Sam Wagstaff and photographer Robert Mapplethorpe; with Sam Wagstaff, Patti Smith, Dominick Dunne, Dick Cavett, Eugenia Parry, Pierre Apraxine, Philippe Garner, Timothy Greenfield-Sanders, Jean-Jacques Naudet, John Szarkowski, Ingrid Sischy, Ralph Gibson, Jeffrey Fraenkel, Richard Tuttle, Clark Worswick, Raymond Foye, Agnes Martin.

Robert Mapplethorpe, Sam Wagstaff in *Black White + Gray* © ARTHOUSE FILMS

# MEETING RESISTANCE

*Meeting Resistance* © NINE LIVES

(NINE LIVES DOCUMENTARY PRODS.) Producer, Daniel J. Chalfen; Executive Producers, Dal La Magna, Molly Bingham, Steve Connors; Directors, Steve Connors, Molly Bingham; Photography, Steve Connors; Editor, David Emanuele; Co-Editor, Joel Plotch; Music, Richard Horowitz; a Nine Lives Documentary production; Color; DV; Not rated; 84 minutes; Release date: October 19, 2007. Documentary profiling eight Iraqi resistance fighters.

# THE BEACH PARTY AT THE THRESHOLD OF HELL: THE HISTORY OF NEW AMERICA, PART 1

(NATIONAL LAMPOON) Producer, Jamie Bullock; Co-Producer, Ryan Turi; Directors, Kevin Wheatley, Jonny Gillette; Screenplay, Kevin Wheatley; Photography/Editor, Cameron Pearce; Music, Russ Howard III; Music Supervisor, Dane Morton; Designer, Scott Wheatley; Makeup, Emily Kravitz; Special Effects Supervisors, Scott Wheatley, Michael Deweeze; Visual Effects Supervisor, Pearce; Animation, Project 450, Kevin Wheatley; Associate Producers, Scott Addison Clay, Nick Bodkins; Casting, Kevin Wheatley; a Threshold Prods., Slugmonkey Alliance Films presentation; Color/black and white; Widescreen; DV; Rated R; 102 minutes; Release date: October 19, 2007.

## Cast

Kevin Wheatley (Tex Kennedy), Bill English (Benjamin Remington), Chandler Parker (Yul the Robot), Jonathan Davidson (Javier Castro), Ted Schneider (Marcellus St. Joan), Jamie Bullock (Cannibal Sue), Alex Reznik (Yorick), Paul Whitty (Quincy the Robot), Stewart Carrico (Zach/Thorn), Lea Coco (Vincent "Jackie" Remington), Daniel Baldwin (Clark Remington), Jane Seymour (President Lauren Coffey), Tony Hale (Remington Biographer), Richard Riehle (Narrator/Paranormal Historian), Morgan Carson (Ginsberg), Scott Addison Clay (Blowgun Child), Katherine Cunningham-Eves (Veronica), Henry Dittman (Sue Biographer), Katherine Flynn (Allison), Callam Ingram (TV Son), Claire Lautier (TV Mom), Gerald Mack (Mercenary), J.P. Manoux (TV Dad), Alcorn Minor (Xavier), Jim Ryan (Henry Edison), Ryan Turi (Richie), Henry Vick (The Grashtowner), Andrew W. Walker (Franklin)

## THE TEN COMMANDMENTS

Moses in *The Ten Commandments* © PROMENADE PICTURES

(PROMENADE PICTURES) Producers, John Stronach, Cindy Bond; Executive Producers, Frank Yablans, Trevor Yaxley, Ron Booth, Karen Glasser, John McAdams, Brad Cummings, Eric Chan, Chua Woo; Directors, Bill Boyce, John Stronach; Screenplay, Ed Naha; Lead Animator, Peter Monga; Lead Compositor, Mark Bowen; Music, Reg Powell; Designer, Henoch Kloosterboer; a Promenade, Ten Chimneys Entertainment (U.S.) presentation of a Huhu Studios (New Zealand)/iVL Animation (Singapore) production; American-New Zealand-Singaporean; Dolby; Widescreen; Color; Rated PG; 88 minutes; Release date: October 19, 2007. VOICE

### Cast

Christian Slater (Moses), Alfred Molina (Ramses), Elliott Gould (God), Ben Kingsley (Narrator), Christopher Gaze (Aaron), Kathleen Barr (Miriam), Lee Tockar (Dathan), Matt Hill (Joshua), Jane Mortifee (Zipporah), Nico Ghisi (Ramses' Son), Colin Murdock (Elderly Slave), Kitanou St. Germain (Princess)

## LOCAL COLOR

(NU IMAGE FILMS) Producers, David Permut, Mark Sennet, Julie Lott Gallo, James W. Evangelatos; Executive Producers, Charlie Arneson, Allen Clauss, John Papadakis, Katherine Angelos Cusenza, Richard Lott, Diana Lott, Tom Adams, Denise Evangelatos Adams; Co-Producers, Robert L. Brown, Evan Hoyt Wasserstrom, Steven A. Longi, Shannon Bae, Bruce Dunn; Director/Screenplay, George Gallo; Photography, Michael Negrin; Editor, Malcolm Campbell; Music, Chris Boardman; Designer, Robert Ziembicki; Costumes, Emily Draper; Casting, Lynn Kressel; an Alla Prima Prods., Permut Presentations presentation of a James W. Evangelatos, Julie Lott Gallo production; Dolby; Widescreen; Color; Rated R; 107 minutes; Release date: October 19, 2007.

### Cast

Armin Mueller-Stahl (Nicoli Seroff), Trevor Morgan (John Talia, Jr.), Ray Liotta (John Talia, Sr.), Samantha Mathis (Carla), Ron Perlman (Curtis Sunday), Diana Scarwid (Edith Talia), Julie Lott (Sandra Sunday), Charles Durning (Yammi), Tom Adams (Grey Artist), Taso Papadakis (Mechanized Artist), David Sosna (Mr. Ross), Nancy Casemore (Mrs. Huntington-Quail), David Sheftell (Girly Voiced Kid), Tim Velasquez (No Good Teenager)

## MOONDANCE ALEXANDER

(MOTION PICTURE CORP. OF AMERICA) Producers, Michael Damian, Janeen Damian, Laurette Bourassa, Doug Steeden; Director, Michael Damian; Screenplay, Michael Damian, Janeen Damian; Photography, Julien Eudes; Designer, Myron Hyrak; Costumes, Carol Chase; Music, Mark Thomas; Editors, Bridget Dumford, Avril Beukes; Casting, Rhoda Fisekci; a Riviera Films production in association with Orchard Park Productions and Jordan Films Inc.; Dolby; Color; Not rated; 93 minutes; Release date: Oct. 19, 2007.

### Cast

Kay Panabaker (Moondance), Don Johnson (Dante), Lori Loughlin (Gelsey), James Best (McClancy), Sasha Cohen (Fiona Hughes), Whitney Sloan (Megan Montgomery), Joe Norman Shaw (Ben Wilson), Mimi Gianopoulos (Bella), Josh Wilson (Aedan Tomney), Landon Liboiron (Freddie), Greg Lawson (Miles), Julia Maxwell (Rachel), Brian Gromoff (Judge Tyler), Jemma Blackwell (Judge Harvey), Kirk Heuser (Announcer), Tom Carey (Tom Wyman), Tanya Dixon (Shannon McGinnis), Chanel Sponchia (Sara), Heather Seagrave (Aubry), Joyce Doolittle (Rose), Joe Cipriano (Himself)

## MR. UNTOUCHABLE

Thelma Gant, Nicky Barnes in *Mr. Untouchable* © MAGNOLIA PICTURES

(MAGNOLIA) Producers, Mary-Jane Robinson, Alex Gibney, Jason Kliot, Joana Vicente; Executive Producers, Todd Wagner, Mark Cuban; Director, Marc Levin; Photography, Henry Adebonojo; Editor, Emir Lewis; Music, Hi-Tek; Music Supervisor, John McCullough; Archive Researcher, Will Albright; Associate Producers, Will Albright, Emir Lewis; Supervising Producer, Daphne Pinkerson; an HDNet presentation, in association with Damon Dash Enterprises and Blowback Prods.; Color/Black and white; HD Video; Not rated; 92 minutes; Release date: October 26, 2007. Documentary on '70s Harlem gangster and drug kingpin Nicky Barnes; with Nicky Barnes, Thelma Gant, Joseph "Jazz" Hayden, Jackie Hayden, Leon "Scrap" Batts, Carole Hawkins, Frank James, David Breitbart, Don Ferrarone, Louie Diaz, Bobby Nieves, Robert Geronimo, Robert Fiske Jr., Tom Sear, Benito Romano, Louie Jones, Fred Ferretti.

# SLIPSTREAM

Christian Slater, Anthony Hopkins in *Slipstream* © STRAND RELEASING

(STRAND) Producers, Stella Arroyave, Robert Katz; Executive Producer, Betsy Danbury; Director/Screenplay/Music, Anthony Hopkins; Photography, Dante Spinotti; Designer, Ismael Cardenas; Costumes, Julie Weiss; Editor, Michael R. Miller; Visual Effects Supervisor, Payam Shohadai; a Slipstream LLC production; Dolby; Panavision; Black and white/Deluxe color; Rated R; 97 minutes; Release date: October 26, 2007.

## Cast

Anthony Hopkins (Bonhoeffer); Stella Arroyave (Gina); Christian Slater (Ray/Matt Dobbs/Patrolman #2); John Turturro (Harvey Brickman); Michael Clarke Duncan (Mort/Phil Henderson/Patrolman); Camryn Manheim (Barbara); Jeffrey Tambor (Geek/Jeffrey/Dr. Geekman); S. Epatha Merkerson (Bonnie); Fionnula Flanagan (Bette Lustig); Michael Lerner (Big Mikey); Christopher Lawford (Lars); Lisa Pepper (Tracy/Nurse); Gavin Grazer (Gavin/Ambulance Driver); Aaron Tucker (Chauffeur/Aaron); Lana Antonva (Lily); Kevin McCarthy (Himself); Lindsay Barth (Shelly's Sister); Dean Bitter (News Reporter); Gene Borkan (Mel); Donna G. Earley (Wardrobe Girl); Carlos Yul Love, Charlie Edwards (Helpful Motorists); Jennifer Franklin (Shelly); Monica Garcia (Monica/Shocked Motorist); Saginaw Grant (Eddie); John Littlefield (Shooter/Burt, 1st AD); William Lucking (Det. Buzz Larabee); Jennifer Mann (Joanie/Jennifer); Charlene Masuda (Dolly Parton Lookalike); Ana Matallana (Woman in Café, Limo, and Diner); Ken Millen (Dr. Cohen); Ana Maria Montero (Anchorwoman); Richard Putnam (Camera Assistant/Helpful Motorist #1); Riccardo Spinotti (Second AD/Paramedic); Jana Thompson (Marcia); Scott Treger (Scott/Hitchhiker); Luciane Tucker (Other Woman in Café, Limo, and Diner)

# BLACK IRISH

(ANYWHERE ROAD/PALISADES) Producers, Brad Gann, J. Todd Harris, Kelly Crean, Mark Donadio, Jeffrey Orenstein; Executive Producers, Marc Toberoff, Miriam Marcus, Barry Levy; Co-Executive Producers, Gal Lipkin, Jon Freis; Director/Screenplay, Brad Gann; Photography, Michael Fimognari; Designer, Sharon Lomofsky; Costumes, Virginia Johnson; Editor, Andrea Bottigliero; Music, John Frizzell; Music Supervisor, Brian Ross; Associate Producers, Laray Mayfield, Frederick Johntz, Sayda Foell; Casting, Laray Mayfield; a Falcon Film Funding presentation of an IPW/Creanspeak Entertainment production in association with Purple Princess Prods. and Moody Street Pictures; Dolby; Technicolor; Rated R; 94 minutes; Release date: October 26, 2007.

## Cast

Brendan Gleeson (Desmond McKay); Michael Angarano (Cole McKay); Tom Guiry (Terry McKay); Emily Van Camp (Kathleen McKay); Melissa Leo (Margaret); Michael Rispoli (Joey); Finn Curtin (Coach); Francis Capra (Anthony); Ken Arpino (Valet); Wilson Better (Graves); Mark S. Cartier (Mr. Quint); Peter Darrigo, Joseph Zamparelli (Track Buddies); Steen Paul Davis, Shawn Doherty, Dave Matt (Valets); Bonnie Dennison (Donna O'Leary); William Ellis (Busboy/Student); John Fiore (Orsini); Steve Flynn (Stolen Car Victim); Joanna Herrington (Mrs. O'Leary); David Ian, Tom Kemp (Priests); Caryn Andrea Lindsey (Pregnant Girly #1); Andrea Lyman (Nurse); Joe McEachem (Cop); Kate Murphy (Restaurant Patron); Kevin O'Donnell (Fired Busboy); Carmel O'Reilly (Sister Agatha); Danielle Perry (Sister Mary Elise); Patrick Pitu (Boy on Bus); Frank T. Wells (Father Magruder); Bates Wilder (Officer Cowen); Scott Winters (Doctor); Peter Ziobro (Bus Stop Patron)

Melissa Leo, Brendan Gleeson, Emily Van Camp, Michael Angarano, Tom Guiry in *Black Irish* © ANYWHERE ROAD

# A BROKEN SOLE

(PRISM PLAYHOUSE) Producers, Susan Charlotte, Stan Cohen; Co-Producers, Rosemarie Salvatore, Lou Salvatore, Sylvia Steiner, David S. Steiner, Marguerite Jossel; Director, Antony Marsellis; Screenplay, Susan Charlotte, from her play; Photography, Dan Karlok, Ken H. Keller; Editors, Robert Reitano, William Kelly, David Ray; a Shoemaker/Broken Sole production; Color; DV; Not rated; 101 minutes; Release date: November 2, 2007.

**Cast**

Danny Aiello (The Shoemaker), Margaret Colin (Nan), Judith Light (Hilary), Bob Dishy (Cabbie), Laila Robins (Passenger), John Shea (Bob), Rebekkah Ross (Louise's Voice)

# CONFESSIONS OF A SUPERHERO

(ARTS ALLIANCE AMERICA/RED ENVELOPE ENTERTAINMENT) Producers, Jamie Patricof, Charlie Gruet, Matt Ogens; Co-Producer, Mark Meyers; Director, Matt Ogens; Photography, Charlie Gruet; Editors, Rick Lobo, Mick LeGrande, Jason Djang, Michael Victor; Music, Greg Kuehn; Associate Producers, Shawn Bennett, Jordan Ehrlich, Elizabeth McIntyre, Zev Suissa, Spencer Parker; a Hunting Lane Films, Smokeshow Films, Ogens production, in association with HKM, TradeMark Films; Color, HD; 24p Mini-DV-to-HD, Super 8-to-HD; Rated R; 93 minutes; Release date: November 2, 2007. Documentary on four wannabes who dress as superheroes on Hollywood Boulevard, in hopes of being discovered; with: Christopher Lloyd Dennis, Joe McQueen, Jennifer Gehrt, Maximus "Batman" Allen, Leron Gubler, Johnny Grant, Stan Lee, Margot Kidder.

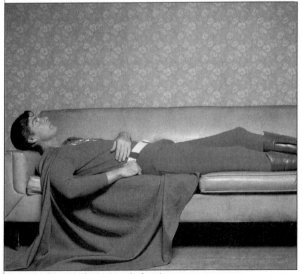

Christopher Dennis in *Confessions of a Superhero* © ARTS ALLIANCE AMERICA

# DARFUR NOW

(WARNER INDEPENDENT PICTURES) Producers, Cathy Shulman, Don Cheadle, Mark Jonathan Harris; Executive Producers, Jeff Skoll, Diane Weyermann, Omar Amanat, Matt Palmieri, Gary Greenebaum, Dean Schramm; Co-Producer, Lenore Zerman; Director/Screenplay, Theodore Braun; Photography, Kirsten Johnson; Editors, Edgar Burcken, Leonard Feinstein; Music, Graeme Revell; a Crescendo, Mandalay Independent Pictures production, presented with Participant Prods.; Dolby; Color; HD; Rated PG; 99 minutes; Release date: November 2, 2007. Documentary on the ongoing genocide in Africa; with Don Cheadle, George Clooney, Adam Sterling, Hejewa Adam, Luis Moreno-Ocampo, Pablo Recalde, Ahmed Mahammed Abaka, Hawa Abaker, Kalatumh Adam, Xabier Aguirre, Sam Brownback, Hillary Rodham Clinton, Essa Faal, Vanessa Haas, Nimeri Issa, Asha Abdal Khaleeq, Béatrice Le Fraper du Hellen, John McCain, Jason Miller, Abdalmahmood Abdalhaleem, Abedowale Omofade, John Prendergast, Pablo Recalde, Hawa Saleman, Arnold Schwarzenegger, Musa Shari, Dana Sterling, Wayne Sterling, James Sweeney, Jennifer Trone.

*Darfur Now* © WARNER INDEPENDENT PICTURES

# QUANTUM HOOPS

(GREEN FOREST FILMS) Producer/Director/Screenplay/Photography/Editor, Rick Greenwald; Music, Brian Arbuckle; Associate Producer, Lauren Langford; Narrator, David Duchovny; Color/Black and white; HD; Not rated; 84 minutes; Release date: November 2, 2007. Documentary on California Institute of Technology's basketball team; with Roy Dow, Jordan Carlson, Chris Yu, Ben Sexon, Robert Grubbs.

# NOTE BY NOTE:
# THE MAKING OF STEINWAY L1037

(ARGOT PICTURES) Producer/Director, Ben Niles; Photography, Ben Wolf, Ben Niles, Luke Geissbuhler; Editors, Purcell Carson, Geoff O'Brien; a Plow production; Color; HD; Not rated; 81 minutes; Release date: November 7, 2007. Documentary on the journey of a Steinway grand piano from an Alaskan lumber yard to the concert hall; with Hank Jones, Lang Lang, Pierre-Laurent Aimard, Kenny Barron, Bill Charlap, Harry Connick Jr., Helene Grimaud, Marcus Roberts.

# P2

(SUMMIT ENTERTAINMENT) Producers, Alexandre Aja, Gregory Levasseur, Patrick Wachsberger, Erik Feig; Executive Producers, Bob Hayward, David Garrett, Alix Taylor; Co-Producers, Daniel Jason Heffner, Greg Copeland, Jean Song; Director, Franck Khalfoun; Screenplay, Franck Khalfoun, Alexandre Aja, Gregory Levasseur; Photography, Maxime Alexandre; Designer, Oleg Savytski; Costumes, Ruth Secord; Editor, Patrick McMahon; Music, Tomandandy; Music Supervisor, Buck Damon; Visual Effects Supervisor, Jamison Scott Goei; Casting, Mark Bennett; an Aja/Levasseur production; Dolby; Deluxe color; Rated R; 98 minutes; Release date: November 9, 2007.

### Cast

Wes Bentley (Thomas), Rachel Nichols (Angela Bridges), Miranda Edwards (Jody), Jamie Jones (Newsman), Grace Lynn Kung (Elevator Gal), Paul Sun-Hyung Lee (Man in Elevator), Stephanie Moore (Lorraine), Simon Reynolds (Bob Harper), Philip Williams (Cop #1)

# THE INSURGENTS

(VAGRANT FILMS/SLAMDANCE MEDIA GROUP) Producers, Greg Segal, John Gallagher, Elana Pianko, Stan Erdreich, Mike Parness; Director/Screenplay, Scott Dacko; Photography, Learan Kahanov; Editor, Bob Reitano; Music, Ben Butler, Mario Grigorov; Designer, John El Manahi; Costumes, Dara Ettinger; Casting, Adrienne Stern; a Revel Films production, in association with Angel Baby Entertainment and Full Glass Films in conjunction with Allumination FilmWorks; Color; Widescreen; HD; Not rated; 83 minutes; Release date: November 9, 2007.

### Cast

John Shea (Robert); Henry Simmons (Marcus); Juliette Marquis (Hana); Michael Mosley (James); Mary Stuart Masterson (Director); Scott Dacko (Skeptic); Chris Sorensen, Jesse Steaccato (Yuppies); Anne Hardick (Anne with an E); Justin Daniel Elliot (Bartender)

# HOLLY

Thuy Nguyen, Ron Livingston in *Holly* © SLOWHAND CINEMA

(SLOWHAND CINEMA) Producers, Nava Lavin, Guy Jacobson, Adi Ezroni, Guy Moshe; Executive Producer, Amit Kort; Director, Guy Moshe; Screenplay, Guy Jacobson, Guy Moshe, from a story by Guy Jacobson; Photography, Yaron Orbach; Editor, Isabela Monteiro de Castro; Music, Ton-that Tiet; Designer, Gabriel Higgins; Costumes, Rotem Noyfeld; Associate Producers, Jenni Trang Le, Daniel Kedem, Svet Batten; a Priority Films, Max Entertainment presentation of a Priority Films production; American-French-Israeli-Cambodian; Dolby; Widescreen; Color; Rated R; 114 minutes; Release date: November 9, 2007.

### Cast

Ron Livingston (Patrick); Virginie Ledoyen (Marie); Chris Penn (Freddie); Udo Kier (Klaus); Thuy Nguyen (Holly); Sahajak Boonthanakit (Tommy); Kosal Dang (Kiri); Sorn Tola, Chit Socheata, Lina, Srey Cham (Girls); Mudha Dann (Police Officer); Kun Daravann (Police Lieutenant); Sethy Dy (Park); Adi Ezroni (Emma); Hugh Kirk (Backpacker #1); Trungta Kostichimongkol (Ma); Teerawat Mulvilai (Ohn); Net Ngo (Café Owner); Tor Nhim (Boat Crew Member); David Ohm (Kid); Montakan Ransibrahmanakul (Mama San); Keo Ratha (Captain); Kem Sereyvuth (Gas Vendor); Keo Seriemony (Dacil); Tharinee Songkiatthana (Barbara); Pen Sopheap (Gang Leader); Hun Sophy (Thom); Hy Sorim (Doctor); Pornpatchaya Supannarat (Lan); Osnat Tamir (Sharon); Sou Viseth, Bun Tana, Chhor Van (Brokers); Chaiyaporn Torphorn (Vibal); Kowit Wattanakul (Vietnamese Official)

# WAR DANCE

(THINKFILM) Producer, Albie Hecht; Executive Producers, Susan MacLaury, Mark Urman, Daniel Katz; Co-Producers, Josie Swantek, Kari Kim; Directors, Sean Fine, Andrea Nix Fine; Photography, Sean Fine; Editor, Jeff Consiglio; Music, Asche & Spencer; Music Supervisor, George Acogny; Associate Producer, Andrew Herwitz; a Shine Global presentation of a Fine Films production; HD24P Panasonic Varicam; Color; Rated PG-13; 105 minutes; Release date: November 9, 2007. Documentary on how several students at Uganda's Patongo Primary School were given a chance to compete in a nationwide music contest.

# THE LIFE OF REILLY

Charles Nelson Reilly in *The Life of Reilly* © CIVILIAN PICTURES

(CIVILIAN PICTURES) Producers, Bob Fagan, Wrye Martin, Carrie Heckman, Peter McDonnell, John Lyons Murphy; Executive Producers, David Dahlman, Steve Farr; Directors, Frank Anderson, Barry Poltermann; Screenplay, Charles Nelson Reilly, Paul Linke; Photography, Tony Balderrama; Editor, Barry Poltermann; Music, Frank Anderson; Designer, Sean Carson; a L'Orange Films production in association with Civilian Pictures; Color; Not rated; 84 minutes; Release date: November 9, 2007. Documentary on actor-director Charles Nelson Reilly and his one-man show about his career and life; with Charles Nelson Reilly.

# STEAL A PENCIL FOR ME

Ina Soep, Jack Polak in *Steal a Pencil for Me* © SEVENTH ART RELEASING

(SEVENTH ART) Producers, Michele Ohayon, Theo Van de Sande; Executive Producer, Ted Sarandos; Director/Screenplay, Michele Ohayon; Photography, Theo Van de Sande; Editor, Kate Amend; Music, Joseph Julian Gonzalez; a Diamond Lane Films production; Color; Not rated; 97 minutes; Release date: November 9, 2007. Documentary on Holocaust survivor Jack Polak, who spent time in a concentration camp in which both his wife and his mistress were also prisoners; with Jack Polak, Ina Soep; and the voices of Ellen Ten Damme (Ina), Jeroen Krabbé (Jack).

# CHOKING MAN

(INTL. FILM CIRCUIT) Producers, Joshua Zeman, Zachary Mortensen, Steve Barron; Director/Screenplay, Steve Barron; Photography, Antoine Vivas Denisov; Editors, Jon Griggs, Todd Holmes; Music, Nico Muhly; Designer, Ethan Tobman; Costumes, Rebecca Hofherr; Casting, Maria Nelson, Ellyn Marshall; a Riley Films presentation of a Ghost Robot production; Dolby; Color; Not rated; 84 minutes; Release date: November 9, 2007.

### Cast

Octavio Gómez (Jorge), Eugenia Yuan (Amy), Aaron Paul (Jerry), Mandy Patinkin (Rick), Kate Buddeke (Terri), Mando Alvarado (Chef), Paolo Andino (Choking Man), Oliver Barron (Construction Worker), Philippe Brenninkmeyer (Germanic Man), Marika Daciuk (Rick's Wife), Rupak Ginn (Din), Al Roffe (Cook)

# I'LL BELIEVE YOU

(STAND UP FILMS/FREESTYLE) Producer, Ted Sullivan; Executive Producers, Leo Redgate, Kevin Sullivan; Co-Producers, Laura Corrin, Michael Mitri, Jayson Wahlstrom; Director, Paul Francis Sullivan; Screenplay, Paul Francis Sullivan, Sean McPharlin, Ted Sullivan; Photography, John Mans; Editors, Jon Griggs, Greg Lee, Ted Sullivan; Music, J.J. McGeehan; Designer, Michael Shindler; Associate Producers, Carrie Specht, Joshua Pollack; Casting, Laura Corrin; a Boy in the Drain production; Color; Rated PG; 81 minutes; Release date: November 9, 2007.

### Cast

David Alan Basche (Dale Sweeney); Patrick Warburton (Dr. Seth Douglas); Cece Pleasants (Paige Zinke); Patrick Gallo (Officer Nick Senna); Fred Willard (Mr. Fratus); Chris Elliott (Eugene the Gator Guy); Doc Dougherty (Agent Cheswick); Siobhan Fallon Hogan (Larry Jean); Thomas Gibson (Kyle Sweeney); Ed Helms (Leon); Chris MacKenzie (Agent Bancini); Mo Rocca (Dr. Francis H. Flenderman, Ph.D.); Susie Felber (Rhonda from Melbourne Beach); Ritch Duncan (Craig the Engineer); Susannah Keagle (Sandee); Lisa Zambetti (Stephanie); Nanna Sigurdardottir (Corrine Sweeney); Eric Fellon (Surfer Asleep on Bench); Brody Stevens (Eldon Endicott, the Hoagie Guy); Jean Newell (Marie the Waitress); Ted Chasky (Ned from Palm Bay); Carol Halliburton (Kyle's Maid); Charles Lemon (Jimmy); Lisa Vioni (Woman with Baby); Sascha Saballett (Bill, the Delivery Guy); Kayla Etri (Student Who Figures it Out); Bill Williams (Police Officer Bill); Paul Francis Sullivan (Dr. Mortimer); P.J. Marino (Jeff the Paramedic); Jonathan Corbett (Doug the Paramedic); Sean McPharlin (Orderly); Ted Sullivan (Orderly with Cigarette); James Oakes (The Rescuer); Dan Cronin (Tardy Visitor); Livia Scott (Tourist); Michael Bernard, Josh Comers, Chris DeLuca, Lynn Harris, Eric Kirchberger, Rob Paravonina, Becky Poole, Bob Powers, Chris Regan (Caller Voices); Grant Calof (Crank Caller); Craig Chamberlin (Restaurant Diner); Christian Finnegan (Calle Stew from Viera); Lucille Gallo (LuLu at Slacker's Grill); Amy Larimer (Caller with 87 Haunted Cats); Amanda Melson (Fanny, the Vampire Lover); Ben Sharples (Ned Firewall)

# ELECTRIC APRICOT

(NATIONAL LAMPOON) aka *National Lampoon Presents Electric Apricot: Quest for Festeroo*; Producer, Jason McHugh; Executive Producer/Photography, Matthew J. Powers; Director/Screenplay/Music, Les Claypool; Editors, Les Claypool, Agent Ogden; a National Lampoon presentation, with Bay Area Independent Theaters, of a National Lampoon production; Color; DV; Rated R; 91 minutes; Release date: November 9, 2007.

### Cast

Les Claypool (Lapland Micolovich, "Lapdog"); Adam Gates (Steve "Aiwass" Trouzdale); Bryan Kehoe (Steve "Gordo" Gordon); Jonathan Korty (Herschel Tambor Brilstein); Jason McHugh ("Smilin'" Don Kleinfeld); Kyle McCulloch (Drew Shackleford); Brian Kite (Dr. Brian "Bucky" Lefkowitz); Dian Bachar (Stacey "Skip" Holmes); Seth Green (Jonah, "The Taper"); Matt Stone (Taper Guy); Bob Weir, Mike Gordon (Themselves); Arj Barker (The Cube); Oz Fritz (Oz George); Fred Heim (Officer McFlounce); Sirena Irwin (The Photographer); Lawrence Brooke (Narrator); Brian Kite (Dr. Brian "Bucky" Lefkowitz); Gabby LaLa (Mei Pang); Sam Maccarone (Billy Bob the Bartender); Slawek Michalak (Hydro Salesman); Matthew J. Powers (Davis Mindelhof); Jason Thompson (Jake the Band Tech); Derek Walls (Duck the Band Tech)

# MR. BLUE SKY

(BLUE CACTUS PICTURES) Producer, Karuna Eberl; Executive Producers, Tom Paddy Lee, Gigi Grillot; Director, Sarah Gurfield; Screenplay, Tom Paddy Lee; Photography, Jim Timperman; Designer, Meg Pinsonneault; Costumes, Breanna Price; Music, Mark Petrie; Editor, Timothy M. Snell; Casting, Ricki Maslar; Color; Not rated; 93 minutes; Release date: November 9, 2007.

### Cast

Chaney Kley (Greg Adams); Richard Karn (John Adams); Mary Kate Schellhardt (Bonnie Tailor); Nancy Rita Wolfe (Pam Little); Ken Rosier (Clayton Hounsou); Dax Ravina (Kevin); Zachary Sauers (Young Greg); Kaitlyn Lee Cruz (Young Bonnie); Lauren Potter (Young Andra Little); Haley Ramm (Jessica Green); Katelyn Reed (Corey); Brent Borrelli (Joey); Jessica Barth (Sherry); Rachael Gillam (Amanda); Celia Xavier (Superintendent Barrillos); Lou Mulford (Joyce Adams); Max Shippee (Mr. Harrison); Laura Voss (Yoga Instructor); Rosemarie Lee (Grandmother); James Runcon, Ronnie Steadman (Joggers)

# THE SENSATION OF SIGHT

David Strathairn, Daniel Gillies in *The Sensation of Sight* © EITHER/OR FILMS

(either/or films) Producers, Mark S. Constance, David Strathairn, Madeline Ryan, Darren Moorman; Executive Producer, Buzz McLaughlin; Director/Screenplay, Aaron J. Wiederspahn; Photography, Christophe Lanzenberg; Designer, Shawn Carroll; Costumes, Daphne Javitch; Editor, Mario Ontal; Casting, Michele Ortlip; Color; Not rated; 134 minutes; Release date: November 9, 2007.

### Cast

David Strathairn (Finn), Ian Somerhalder (Drifter), Daniel Gillies (Dylan), Jane Adams (Alice), Ann Cusack (Deanna), Joseph Mazzello (Tripp), Elizabeth Waterston (Daisy), Scott Wilson (Tucker), Lisa Bostnar (Police Officer), Ellen Colton (Neighbor), John Griesemer (Principal), Joanna Herrington (Teacher), Cassidy Hinkle (Ruthie), Adam LeFevre (Alice's Boss), Tony Swingle (Josh), David Szehi (Bartender)

# CHRISTMAS IN WONDERLAND

Chris Kattan, Carmen Electra in *Christmas in Wonderland* © YARI FILM GROUP

(YARI FILM GROUP) Producers, Kirk Shaw, Laurette Bourassa, Doug Steeden; Executive Producers, Bob Yari, Alexander Tabrizi, Henry Boger; Director, James Orr; Screenplay, Wanda Birdsong Shope, James Orr, Jim Cruickshank; Photography, DC Manwiller; Designer, Craig Lathrop; Costumes, Mary Hyde Kerr; Music, Terry Frewer; Editor, Jana Fritsch; Casting, Roe Baker; an Insight Film Studios production; Dolby; Color; Rated PG; 96 minutes; Release date: November 9, 2007.

## Cast

Matthew Knight (Brian Saunders); Chris Kattan (Leonard Cardoza); Cameron Bright (Danny Saunders); Preston Lacy (Sheldon Cardoza); Amy Schlagel, Zoe Schlagel (Mary Saunders); Carmen Electra (Ginger Peachum); Matthew Walker (Santa); Tim Curry (McLoosh); Patrick Swayze (Wayne Saunders); Marty Antonini (Elliot Block); Rick Ash (Bartender); Suzanna Bastien (Clerk); Matt Bellefleur (Walter Crump); Morgan Brayton, Karen Johnson-Diamond (Casiers); Courtney Brin (Ticket Counter Agent); Rachel Hayward (Judy Saunders); Mark Holik (Husband); Maureen Jones (Lingerie Girl); Michelle Molineaux (Spa Attendant); Duncan Ollerenshaw (Guy in Lingerie Store); MacKenzie Porter (Shane); Paul Punyi (Priest); Sean Tyson (Randolph); Donovan Workun (Smith); Melanie Yeats (Luane)

# WHAT WOULD JESUS BUY?

(WARRIOR POETS RELEASING) Producers, Peter Hutchison, Stacey Offman, Morgan Spurlock; Executive Producers, Marshall Cordell, Kathrin Werner, Felix Werner, Jedd Wider, Todd Wider; Co-Producer, Jeremy Chilnick; Director/Screenplay, Rob VanAlkemade; Photography, Alan Deutsch, Daniel Marracino, Martin Palafox, Alex Stikich, Rob VanAlkemade; Editors, Gavin Coleman, Stela Georgieva, Rob VanAlkemade; Music, William Moses; Music Supervisor, Dondi Bastone; Associate Producer, Andie Grace; a Morgan Spurlock presentation of a Warrior Poets production, in association with Werner Film; Dolby; Color; HD; Rated PG; 90 minutes; Release date: November 16, 2007. Documentary on the commercialization of Christmas, focusing on Rev. Bill Talen and the Church of Stop Shopping.

# SMILEY FACE

(FIRST LOOK PICTURES) Producers, Henry Winterstern, Kevin Turen, Steve Golin, Alix Madigan-Yorkin, Gregg Araki; Executive Producers, Jorg Westerkamp, Thomas Becker, Stuart Burkin, H. Jason Beck; Co-Producer, Hans C. Ritter; Director/Editor, Gregg Araki; Screenplay, Dylan Haggerty; Photography, Shawn Kim; Music, David Kitay; Music Supervisor, Tracy McKnight; Designer, John Larena; Costumes, Monika Mikkelsen; Produced in association with Anonymous Content and Desperate Pictures; Dolby; Color; Rated R; 84 minutes; Release date: November 16, 2007.

## Cast

Anna Faris (Jane); Danny Masterson (Steve the Roommate); Adam Brody (Steve the Dealer); Jane Lynch (Casting Director); John Krasinski (Brevin Ericson); Marion Ross (Shirley); Michael Hitchcock (Laundry Room Man); John Cho (Mikey); Danny Trejo (Albert); Roscoe Lee Browne, Scott "Carrot Top" Thompson (Themselves); Ben Falcone (Agent); Brian Posehn (Bus Driver); Rick Hoffman (Angry Face); Matthew J. Evans (Bobby); Davenia McFadden (Bus Passenger); Joey Coco Diaz (Security Guard); Jim Rash (Casting Assistant); Jayma Mays (Actress in Waiting Room); Kai Cofer (Man with Weird Beard), Michael Shamus Wiles (Officer Jones); Robert Michael Morris (Man Walking Dog); Richard Riehle (Mr. Spencer); Natasha Williams (Motorcycle Rider); Chad Mountain (Marijuana Jesus); Dave Allen, James Mathis III (Hippies); Dylan Haggerty (Ferris Wheel Attendant); William Zabka (Prison Guard); Sam Nainoa (Mattress Delivery Guy #1)

Anna Faris in *Smiley Face* © FIRST LOOK PICTURES

# WHO IS NORMAN LLOYD?

Norman Lloyd in *Who is Norman Lloyd?* © JOURNEYMEN FILMS

(JOURNEYMEN FILMS) Producers, Joseph Scarpinito, Michael Badalucco; Director, Matthew Sussman; Photography, Arthur S. Africano; Editor, Ray Hubley; Associate Producer, Mindy Farabee; Color/Black and white; Not rated; 83 minutes; Release date: November 23, 2007. Documentary on veteran actor Norman Lloyd; with Norman Lloyd, Peggy Lloyd, Ray Bradbury, Roy Christopher, Cameron Diaz, Tom Fontana, Samuel Goldwyn Jr., Arthur Hiller, Patricia Hitchcock, Karl Malden, John Martello, Elliott Reid.

# EVERYTHING'S COOL

(CITY LIGHTS) Producers, Daniel B. Gold, Judith Helfand, Chris Pilaro, Adam Wolfensohn; Directors, Daniel B. Gold, Judith Helfand; Photography, Daniel B. Gold; Editors, Toby Shimin, Jacob Steingroot; Music, Stephen Thomas Cavit; Music Supervisor, Beth Urdang; Associate Producers, Jennifer Eggleston, Sara Porto Nolan, Anna Hurley; Color; HD; Not rated; 100 minutes; Release date: November 23, 2007. Documentary on global warming, with Bill McKibben, Ross Gelbspan, Dr. Heidi Cullen, Michael Shellenberger, Ted Nordhaus, Rick Piltz, Bish Neuhauser, Sheila Watt-Cloutier.

# HE WAS A QUIET MAN

(QUIET MAN PRODS.) Producer, Mike Leahy; Executive Producers, Jason Hallock, Frank Cappello; Director/Screenplay, Frank Cappello; Photography, Brandon Trost; Art Director, Michael Barton; Costumes, Sarah Trost; Editor, Kirk Morri; Casting, Don Phillips, Jason Mundy; Color; Not rated; 95 minutes; Release date: November 23, 2007.

## Cast

Christian Slater (Bob Maconel); Elisha Cuthbert (Venessa Parks); William H. Macy (Gene Shelby); Jamison Jones (Scott Harper); K.C. Ramsey (Jackson); Sascha Knopf (Paula); David Wells (Ralf Coleman); Christina Lawson (Nancy Felt); Bill Rothbard (Phil); John Gulager (Maurice Gregory); Greg Baker (Copy Boy); Stanley C. Hall (Paul); Livia Treviño (Shelby's Secretary); Jim Tyndall (Henry); Frankie Lou Thorn (Jessica Light); Michael DeLuise (Det. Sorenson); Sewell Whitney (Derrick Miles); Lisa Arianna (Assistant); Randolph Mantooth (Dr. Willis); Tina D'Marco (Nurse); Brian Lohmann (Maitre D'); Paul D. Roberts (Waiter); Maggie Wagner (Phil's Wife); Nicole Hawkyard, Cyndi Marinangel, Michelle Tolan (Neighbors); Courtney Moorehead (Woman in Red); Jason Trost (Disgusted Audience Member); Maggie Wagner (Phil's Wife)

William H. Macy, Christian Slater © QUIET MAN PRODUCTIONS

# BADLAND

(COPEX DISTRIBUTION) Producers, Olimpia Lucente, Jorg G. Neumann; Executive Producers, Claudia Dummer-Manasse, Joseph Bitonti, Gordon Guiry, Michel Shane, Anthony Romano; Director/Screenplay/Editor, Francesco Lucente; Photography, Carlo Varini; Music, Ludek Drizhal; Designer, John Bitonti; Stunts, Jodi Stecyk; Casting, Joy Todd, Craig Campobasso; Dolby; Technicolor; Rated R; 160 minutes; Release date: November 30, 2007.

## Cast

Jamie Draven (Jerry); Grace Fulton (Celina); Vinessa Shaw (Nora); Chandra West (Oli); Joe Morton (Max); Tom Carey (Louie); Patrick Richards (Alex); Jake Church (Stevie); Louie Campbell (Ray); Jenae Adam, Luc Adam, Amy Cook, Ryan Cook, Giulia Varini, Serena Varini (Kids at Playground); Larry Austin (Motel Owner); Harvey Bourassa, Albert Hurd, Audrey Kyllo, Charles Reach, John Trowbridge, Bob Wilson (Café Customers); Dennis Corrie (Fire Captain Baker); Brian Gromoff (Rancher); Chris Ippolito (Kid at Garage); Sean Anthony Olsen, Stirling Karlsen (Sheriff's Deputies); Daniel Libman (Television News Reporter); Darren Lumsden (Police K-9 Officer); Pete Seadon (Sheriff Thomas Pellegrino); Chris Manyluk, Keith White (Patrol Officers)

# OSWALD'S GHOST

*Oswald's Ghost* © SEVENTH ART RELEASING

(SEVENTH ART RELEASING) Producer/Director/Screenplay, Robert Stone; Photography, Howard Shack; Editors, Robert Stone, Don Kleszky; Music, Gary Lionelli; an American Experience presentation, in association with the BBC, of a Robert Stone production; American-British; Color/Black and white; Not rated; 83 minutes; Release date: November 30, 2007. Documentary on the enduring impact of the November 1963 assassination of President John F. Kennedy; with Norman Mailer, Gary Hart, Dan Rather, Mark Lane, Edward Jay Epstein, Tom Hayden, Josiah Thompson, Todd Gitlin, Hugh Aynesworth.

# PROTAGONIST

(IFC) Producers, Jessica Yu, Elise Pearlstein, Susan West; Executive Producers, Greg Carr, Noble Smith; Director/Screenplay/Editor, Jessica Yu; Photography, Russell Harper, Karl Hahn; Music, Jeff Beal; Puppet Designer, Janie Geiser; Casting, Linda Montagne; a Diorama Films production in association with the Carr Foundation; Dolby; Color; HD; Rated R; 90 minutes; Release date: November 30, 2007. Documentary in which four diversely dysfunctional men act out in extreme ways before working towards overcoming their problems; with Hans Joachim-Klein, Mark Pierpont, Joe Loya, Mark Salzman.

# THE SASQUATCH GANG

(SCREEN MEDIA FILMS) formerly *The Sasquatch Dumpling Gang*; Producers, Jeremy Coon, Adam Kassen, Mark Kassen, Randy Holleschau, Kevin Spacey, Dana Brunetti; Co-Producer, Craig Anderson; Director/Screenplay, Tim Skousen; Photography, Munn Powell; Designer, Cory Lorenzen; Costumes, Kim Wingard; Editors, Jeremy Coon, Tim Skousen; Music, John Swihart; Music Supervisor, Tracy Lynch-Sanchez; Stunts, Steve Buckley; Associate Producers, Sarah Serata, Danny Wright; Casting, Jeffery Passero; a Jeremy Coon and Trigger Street production in association with Trigger Street Independent and Crazy Dreams Entertainment; Dolby; Panavision; Deluxe color; Rated PG-13; 86 minutes; Release date: November 30, 2007.

## Cast

Jeremy Sumpter (Gavin Gore); Justin Long (Zerk Wilder); Carl Weathers (Dr. Artimus Snodgrass); Addie Land (Sophie Suchowski); Hubbel Palmer (Hobie Plumber); Joey Kern (Shirts); Rob Pinkston (Maynard Keyes); Michael Mitchell (Shane Bagwell); Jon Gries (Officer Ed Chillcut); Veanne Cox (Lenora Gore); Ray Santiago (Crone); Stephen Tobolowsky (Ernie Dalrymple); Jeff D'Agostino (Dagan); Don Burns (Dentist); Lindsay Chestler, Sydney Chestler, Aleeza McKarem, Abby McKinney, Anberlin McVey, Sarah Christine Pletcher (Classmates); Lorinda Christene (Onlooker); Brenna Haukedahl (Girl in Amusement Park); Carter Haukedahl (Boy in Amusement Park); Nurmi Husa (Angry Neighbor); Val Landrum (Blondeen); Daniel Nelson, David Nelson, Elijah Nelson (Boys in Woods); Eric Newsome (Shirt's Dad); Katie O'Grady (Candice); Lance Rich (Melvin); Margaret Santoro (Vanessa); Hayley Skousen (Roxie); Todd Skousen (Frankie); Lauren Stocks (Shirt's Mom); Nico Varela (Boy in Classroom)

Justin Long in *The Sasquatch Gang* © SCREEN MEDIA FILMS

# SEX AND BREAKFAST

(FIRST LOOK) Producers, Michael Brandman, Chip Diggins, Andrew Adelson; Executive Producers, Steven Molasky, Steven Brandman; Co-Producer, Joanna Miles; Director/Screenplay, Miles Brandman; Photography, Mark Schwartzbard; Designer, David Chapman; Costumes, Elaine Montalvo; Editor, Dana Shockley; Music Supervisor, Danny Exum; Associate Producer, Straw Weisman; Casting, Mary Vernieu; a Brandman Prods. presentation of a CinemaLab production; Color; HD; Rated R; 81 minutes; Release date: November 30, 2007.

### Cast

Macaulay Culkin (James), Kuno Becker (Ellis), Eliza Dushku (Renee), Alexis Dziena (Heather), Joanna Miles (Dr. Wellbridge), Eric Lively (Charlie), Jaime Ray Newman (Betty), Tracie Thoms (Tenant), Anita Gnan (Mickey), Robert Carradine (Angry Driver), John Pleshette (Older Man in Elevator), Maree Cheatham (Older Woman in Elevator), Vincent Jerosa (Brian), Margaret Travolta (Gale), Kory Hutchinson (Athletic Man in Diner), Nikki Kemp (Athletic Woman in Diner)

# TONY 'N' TINA'S WEDDING

(EMERGING PICTURES) Producers, Roger Paradiso, Michael Tadros, Tony Travis, Mark Lipsky; Co-Producers, Justin Morrit, Glen Trotliner, Pat McCorkle; Director/Screenplay, Roger Paradiso, based on a play by Artificial Intelligence; Photography, Giselle Chamma; Designer, Patricia Woodbridge; Costumes, Richard Owings; Editor, Jennifer Davidoff Cook; Music Producer, Joey Carbone; Executive Music Producer, Tony Travis; Choreographer, Lisa Shriver; Associate Producers, Michael Tadross Jr., Terry Ladin; Casting, Pat McCorkle; a Greenwich Street production in association with Drewmark Prods.; Dolby; Color; Rated R; 108 minutes; Release date: November 30, 2007.

### Cast

Joey McIntyre (Tony), Mila Kunis (Tina), Priscilla Lopez (Mrs. Vitale), John Fiore (Mr. Nunzio), Krista Allen (Maddy), Kim Director (Connie), Richard Portnow (Vinnie Black), Daisy Eagan (Donna Marsala), Dean Edwards (Father Mark), Guillermo Diaz (Raphael), Matthew Saldivar (Barry), Adrian Grenier (Michael), Mary Testa (Sister Clare), Donnie Keshawarz (Donnie Dulce), Tony Travis (Zeppo the Bartender), Sebastian Stan (Johnny), Jon Bernthal (Dominic), Mariann Tepedino (Mariann), Lenny Venito (Sal), Richard Robichaux (Joey Vitale), Vanessa Paradis (Marina Galino), Letty Serra (Grandma Nunzio), Miari Peterson (Celeste), Lou Martini, Jr. (Swinger), George Papas (Altar Boy), S. Michael Bellomo (Cop), John Capo (Mikey Black), Anthony Colangelo (Young Joey), Paul Heyman (Gino), Haley Joel (The Blonde), Richard Mamary (The Limo Driver), Lisa Miller (Patty), Megan O'Leary (Waitress), Joanna Parson (Band Member), Nick Raynes (Mickey), Laura Jean Salerno (Babydoll), Matthew Salvatore (Young Tony), Michael Straka (Stickey)

# MAMA'S BOY

Diane Keaton, Jon Heder in *Mama's Boy* © WARNER BROS.

(WARNER BROS.) Producer, Heidi Santelli; Executive Producers, Ravi Mehta, Steve Carr, Mark Gill; Director, Tim Hamilton; Screenplay, Hank Nelken; Photography, Jonathan Brown; Designer, Jon Gary Steele; Costumes, Shay Cunliffe; Editor, Amy E. Duddleston; Music, Mark Mothersbaugh; Casting, Jeanne McCarthy; a Carr/Santelli production; Dolby; Technicolor; Rated PG-13; 92 minutes; Release date: November 30, 2007.

### Cast

Diane Keaton (Jan Mannus), Jon Heder (Jeffrey Mannus), Jeff Daniels (Mert Rosenbloom), Anna Faris (Nora Flannigan), Eli Wallach (Seymour Warburton), Dorian Missick (Mitch), Sarah Chalke (Maya), Mary Kay Place (Barbara), Marcos Akiaten (Shaman), Luke Barnett (Cool Guy Skater), Dennis Cockrum (Bus Driver), Rhys Coiro (Trip), Jessie Graff (Wrestler), Simon Helberg (Rathkon), Laura Kightlinger (Mert's Secretary), Jeremy Kramer (Frito's Executive), Jenny Ladner (Alison), Dinker Mehta (Pizza Delivery Man), Evan Peters (Keith), Tyler Shea Sohooli (Skyler)

# UNDOING

(INDICAN) Producers, Karin Chien, Sung Kang, George Huey, Eric Yu-jin Kim, Catherine Park; Executive Producers, Phil Lam, Bilifield Cheng, Geoffrey Tse Twei Chen; Director/Screenplay, Chris Chan Lee; Photography, John DeFazio; Designer, Lissette Schettini; Costumes, Barbara Anderson; Editors, Greg Louie, Howard Leder; Music, Ceiri Torjussen; a co-production of A Space Between, Group Hug Productions, and EK Films; Color; HD; Not rated; 90 minutes; American release date: November 30, 2007.

### Cast

Sung Kang (Samel Kim); Kelly Hu (Vera); Tom Bower (Don Osa); Russell Wong (Leon); Jose Zuniga (Randall); Leonardo Nam (Joon); Mary Mara (Kasawa); Julie Ling (Linda, Joon's Sister); Bobby Lee (Kenny); Kenneth Choi (Danny); Ron Yuan, DC Wolfe (Danny's Goons); David Connolly (Phil); Jennifer Tung (Jane); Rain Chung (Mr. Shin); Michael Li, Jen Sung Outerbridge (Gunmen)

# BILLY THE KID

(ELEPHANT EYE FILMS) Producers, Jennifer Venditti, Chiemi Karasawa; Executive Producers, Barnet Liberman, Bob Alexander; Director, Jennifer Venditti; Photography, Donald Cumming, Paris Kain; Music, Christian Zucconi, Guy Blakeslee; Editors, Michael Levine, Enat Sidi; Associate Producers, Jordan Mattos, Danielle DiGiacomo; an Eight Films and Isotope Films presentation, in association with IndiePix; Color; HD; Not rated; 85 minutes; Release date: December 5, 2007. Documentary recording the day-to-day life of Billy Price, a 15-year-old Maine high schooler, prone to outbursts of violence; with Billy Price, Penny Baker, Heather Pelletier.

# MAN IN THE CHAIR

Michael Angarano, Christopher Plummer in *Man in the Chair* © OUTSIDER PICTURES

(OUTSIDER) Producers, Michael Schroeder, Randy Turrow, Sarah Schroeder; Executive Producer, Peter Samuelson; Director/Screenplay, Michael Schroeder; Photography, Dana Gonzales; Designer, Carol Strober; Costumes, Tricia Gray; Editor, Terry Cafaro; Music, Laura Karpman; Makeup, Adam Brandy; Associate Producer, Michael P. Angarano; Casting, Ed Mitchell; an Elbow Grease Pictures production; Dolby; Panavision; Deluxe color; Rated PG-13; 109 minutes; Release date: December 7, 2007.

**Cast**

Christopher Plummer (Flash Madden), Michael Angarano (Cameron Kincaid), M. Emmet Walsh (Mickey Hopkins), Robert Wagner (Taylor Moss), Joshua Boyd (Murphy White), Mimi Kennedy (Mom), Mitch Pileggi (Floyd), Tracey Walter (Mr. Klein), Taber Schroeder (Brett Raven), Jodi Ashworth (Orson Welles), John Rezig (Young Flash), George Murdock (Richard), Margaret Blye (Mildred Bahr), James O'Connell (Big John), Ellen Geer (Mrs. Erskine), Allan Rich (Speed), Julia Vera (Montana), Rob Reinis (Teacher), Carlene Moore (Woman), Ed Marques (Man), Pete Antico (Murray), Steven Christopher Parker (Projectionist), Brad Grunberg (Video Store Manager), David McDivtt (Camera Crew), Jesus Mayorga (Kid), Kevin Benton (Security Guard), Declan Joyce (Officer Rowe), Robert Harvey (Butch), Sonia Enriquez (Swimmer), Arne Starr (Gregg Toland)

# THE AMATEURS

(NEWMARKET) aka *The Moguls*; Producer, Aaron Ryder; Executive Producers, Malcolm Ritchie, Jill Tandy, Michael Kuhn; Co-Producer, Laura Greenlee; Director/Screenplay, Michael Traeger; Photography, Denis Maloney; Designer, Bob Ziembicki; Costumes, Ernesto Martinez; Editor, Raul Davalos; Music, Nic. tenBroek; Music Supervisor, Larry Marks; Line Producer, Laura Greenlee; Associate Producer, Colleen Woodcock; Supervising Producer, Mark Wolfe; Casting, Nancy Nayor-Battino; a Qwerty Films presentation of an N1 European Film Produktions/Raygun production; Dolby; CFI color; Rated R; 100 minutes; Release date: December 7, 2007.

**Cast**

Jeff Bridges (Andy Sargentee), Ted Danson (Moose), William Fichtner (Otis), Patrick Fugit (Emmett), Tim Blake Nelson (Barney), Joe Pantoliano (Some Idiot), Glenne Headly (Helen Tatelbaum), Lauren Graham (Peggy), Jeanne Tripplehorn (Thelma), Isaiah Washington (Homer), Valerie Perrine (V), Eileen Brennan (Mrs. Cherkiss), John Hawkes (Moe), Brad Henke (Ron), Steven Weber (Howard), Alex Linz (Billy), Judy Greer (Ellie), Troy Brenna (Ernest), Tom Bower (Floyd), Dawn Didawick (Clara), Jayne Taini (Mrs. Morelli), Fiona Hunter (Veronica), Brad Garrett (Wally), Elden Henson (Salesman), Aldo Bigante (Jack), Eliot Cates (Reverend), Norm O'Neill (Clara's Mom)

# DIRTY LAUNDRY

(CODEBLACK ENTERTAINMENT) Executive Producers, Nathan Hale Williams, McCrary Anthony, Adrienne Lopez, Maurice Jamal, Gabrielle Glore, Maria Weaver Watson, Yolonda Baker Marshall; Director/Screenplay, Maurice Jamal; Photography, Rory King; Editor, Gene Graham; Designer, Norval Johnson; Casting, La Rivers, Joe Lorenzo, Richard Pelzer; a Mojam Entertainment, Inhale Entertainment, Crystal McCrary Anthony presentation; Stereo; Color/Black and white; DV; Not rated; 100 minutes; Release date: December 7, 2007.

**Cast**

Rockmond Dunbar (Patrick/Sheldon), Loretta Devine (Evelyn), Jenifer Lewis (Aunt Lettuce), Terri J. Vaughn (Jackie), Sommore (Abby), Maurice Jamal (Eugene), Aaron Grady Shaw (Gabriel), Joey Costello (Ryan), Alec Mapa (Daniel), Veronica Webb (Susan), Bobby Jones (Pastor James), Marcus Patrick (Rene), Gregy Alan Williams (Percy), Leigh Taylor-Young (Mrs. James), Nathan Hale (Peanut), Phillip Bloch (Hot Dog Vendor), Chelsea Botts (Girl #1), Michael Ciesla (Waiter), Nikita Collier (Snow Cone Girl), Clay Drinko (Bradley), Markelle Gay (Young Eguene), Bradley Griffith (Office Assistant #1), Denitra Isler (Norma Jean), Nicole Jackson (Cookie), Wendell James (Church Member), Brandin Jenkins (Dre Dre), Nadji Jeter (Boy #1), La Rivers (Tanya Elise), Kate Secor (Liz), Eric Watson (Clarine), Austin Whittaker (Young Patrick/Sheldon)

# 'TIS AUTUMN:
# THE SEARCH FOR JACKIE PARIS

(OUTSIDER PICTURES) Director/Screenplay, Raymond De Felitta; Photography, Jeremy Saulnier, Chad Davidson, Eli Heitin, Ruben O'Malley, David Zellerford; Editor, John Wayland; Producer, David Zellerford; a Hangover Lounge presentation; Color; DV/16mm/Super-8: Not rated; 101 minutes; Release date: December 7, 2007. Documentary on how acclaimed bebop jazz singer Jackie Paris later fell into relative obscurity; with Jackie Paris, Jeanie Paris, Anne Marie Moss, Joan Paris, Stacy Paris, Michael Paris, Norman Bogner, Joe Franklin, Billy Vera, J.D. Ehrhard, Howard Rumsey, Will Friedwald, Harlan Ellison, Ruth Price, Gene Davis, Dr. Billy Taylor, Mark Murphy, Ira Gitler, Terry Gibbs, James Moody, Teddy Charles, Phil Schaap, Ray Passman, George Wein; and Peter Bogdanovich, Frank Whaley, Nick Tosches (Readings).

# NOËLLE

(GENER8XION ENTERTAINMENT) Producers, David Wall, Kerry Wall, Sean Patrick Brennan, Lenny Manzo; Executive Producers, David Wall, Kerry Wall, John Brennan, Sean Patrick Brennan, Denise DeFelice Hopkins, the American Bible Society, Bob Cotton, Fred T. Fox III, J. Carr Bettis, Venley Starr, Yale Farar; Director/Screenplay, David Wall; Photography/Editor, Beecher Cotton; Music, Andrew Ingkavet; Art Director, Sean Patrick Brennan; a Volo Films production; Dolby; FotoKem color; Rated PG; 90 minutes; Release date: December 7, 2007.

### Cast

David Wall (Father Jonathan Keene); Kerry Wall (Marjorie Worthington); Sean Patrick Brennan (Father Simeon Joyce); Jean Bates (Eleanor Worthington); Curt Dewitz (Seth Harrod); Daffyd Rees (Dermott); Brennan Wall (Noëlle); David Hickey (Thomas Shepley); Ciaran O'Reilly (Finn Shepley); Kevin McElroy (Jewel King); J. Scott Henderson (Swift King); Michael Sweet (Speed King); Luiz Baille (Ari Viloso); Bill Gleeson (Bill); Sandra Casey (Lydie Viloso); Kenny McGilvray (Kenny); Joe Cromarty (Joe); Ed Etsten (Rock); Norma Monbouquette (Jane); Jack Kerig (Eugene); Stephen Russell (Bob); Seamus Healy (Mike); Pat O'Brien (Pat); June Douglas-White (Nancy); Jan Anderson (Norma); Phelim Meehan (Phelim); Jennemae Mahan (Amanda); Denise King (Joan); Jack Wall (Tuxedo Love Boy); Liam Wall (Christmas Play Narrator); Dr. Hub Mathewson (Doctor); Tom Summers (Man on Ladder); Lenny Manzo (Bus Driver); Renee Ramirez, Cecilia Briggi, Sammy Bazarewsky (Library Kids); Grace Cangiano (Grace Keene); Nicolo Gulla, Aiden Keene, Christian Keene (Child Shepherds); Genny Paige, Addie-Eileen Paige, Erin Mahoney (Wise Children); George Cagiano (Joseph Child); Paula Ramirez (Mary Child); Gabrielle Trappe (Pretty Girl at Party); Kristine Pregot (Hospital Receptionist)

# THE PERFECT HOLIDAY

(YARI FILM GROUP) Producers, Mike Elliott, Joseph P. Genier, Marvin Peart, Shakim Compere, Queen Latifah, Leifur B. Dagfinnsson; Executive Producer, BTB; Co-Producers, Lance Rivera, Rodney Shealey; Director, Lance Rivera; Screenplay, Lance Rivera, Marc Calixte, Nat Mauldin, Jeff Stein; Story, Lance Rivera, Marc Calixte; Photography, Teodoro Maniaci; Designer, Anne Stuhler; Costumes, Misa Hylton-Brim; Editor, Paul Trejo; Music, Christopher Lennertz; Music Supervisor, Paul Di Franco; Associate Producers, Otis Best, Stevie "Black" Lockett; Casting, Leah Daniels-Butler; a Capital Arts Entertainment production presented with Destination Films, in association with Flavor Unit Films and Truenorth; Dolby; Color; Rated PG; 96 minutes; Release date: December 12, 2007.

### Cast

Morris Chestnut (Benjamin Armstrong); Gabrielle Union (Nancy); Queen Latifah (Mrs. Christmas); Terrence Howard (Bah Humbug); Malik Hammond (John-John); Charlie Murphy (J-Jizzy); Khail Bryant (Emily); Faizon Love (Jamal); Katt Williams (Delicious); Jeremy Gumbs (Mikey); Jill Marie Jones (Robin); Rachel True (Brenda); Pedro Kim (Clerk); David Anzuelo (Maintenance Man); Frank Bonsangue (Police Sergeant); John Bryant (Rottweiler); Paul Woodburn (Driver); Modi (Father in Line); Amber Joy Williams (5-Year-Old in Line); Ira Hawkins (Judge); Conor Carroll, Reymond Wittman (Kids on Jamal's Lap); Brian Gilbert (Kid with List); Victoria Pannell (Sassy Little Girl on Street); Christopher Burns (Man in Crowd); Lisa Datz (Melody); Dylan Hartigan (Nerdy Kid on Lap); Mary L. Narango (Receptionist); Sandra "Pepa" Denton (V-Jay); Susan Barrett (Woman in Crowd); Mike Elliott (Mr. Sing-a-long); Evelyn Taucher (Old Lady); Didi Gruenwald (Annabella); Maria Ford (Herself)

# NANKING

(THINKFILM) Producers, Ted Leonsis, Bill Guttentag, Michael Jacobs; Co-Producer, Violet Du Feng; Directors/Story, Bill Guttentag, Dan Sturman; Screenplay, Bill Guttentag, Dan Sturman, Elisabeth Bentley; Photography, Buddy Squires; Editors, Hibah Frisina, Charlton McMillan, Michael Schweitzer; Music, Philip Marshall; Associate Producers, Elizabeth Bentley, Jo Ann Jacobs; Line Producers, Dylan Nelson, Katie Strand, Karen Lin; HBO Documentary Films, Purple Mountain Productions; Dolby; Color/Black and white; Rated R; 90 minutes; Release date: December 12, 2007. Documentary on the slaughter of more than 200,000 Chinese during the 1937–38 Japanese occupation of Nanking, with Hugo Armstrong (John Magee), Rosalind Chao (Chang Yu Zheng), Stephen Dorff (Lewis Smythe), John Getz (George Fitch), Woody Harrelson (Bob Wilson), Mariel Hemingway (Minnie Vautrin), Michelle Krusiec (Yang Shu Ling), Leah Liang (Banner Girl), Chris Mulkey (Mills McCallum), Jürgen Prochnow (John Rabe), Sonny Saito (Higashi Sakai), Graham Silbey (Miner Searle Bates), Mark Valley (Stage Manager), Robert Wu (Li Pu).

# LOOK

(VITAGRAPH) Producers, Brad Wyman, Barry Schuler; Executive Producers, Donald Kushner, Richard Bishop; Director/Screenplay, Adam Rifkin; Photography, Ron Forsythe; Editor, Martin Apelbaum; Music, BT; Music Supervisor, 3 AM; Costumes, Erica Fyrie; Visual Effects Supervisor, Scott Billups; Associate Producer, Daniel Weisinger; Line Producer, Alwyn Hight Kushner; Casting, Deanna Brigidi; a Schuler/Wyman production; Color/Black and white; HD Video; Not rated; 102 minutes; Release date: December 14, 2007.

## Cast

Jamie McShane (Berry Krebbs), Spencer Redford (Sherri Van Haften), Hayes MacArthur (Tony Gilbert), Nichelle Hines (Lydia), Ben Weber (Marty), Chris Williams (George Higgins), Jennifer Fontaine (Louise), Giuseppe Andrews (Willie), Miles Dougal (Carl), Rhys Coiro (Ace), Sebastian Feldman (Ron), Adam Bitterman (Cop #1), Michael Cooke (Mr. Van Haften), Troy DeWalt (Racist Lawyer), Jackie Geary (Paige), Tom Hodges (Stuart), Haley Hudson (Amanda), Bailee Madison (Megan), Shane McAvoy (Tyler Winters), Tracey McCall (Grace), Fred Ochs (High School Principal), Karani Ravenscroft (Attorney), Paul Schackman (Ben), Rachel Vacca (Naomi), Dori Valleroy (Mrs. Van Haften), John Landis (Himself)

# THE SINGING REVOLUTION

*The Singing Revolution* © ABRAMORAMA

(ABRAMORAMA) Producers, Maureen Castle Tusty, James Tusty, Bestor Cram, Artur Talvik, Piret Tibbo-Hudgins, Thor Halvorssen; Executive Producers, Steve Jurvetson, Karla Jurvetson; Director/Screenplay, James Tusty, Maureen Castle Tusty, Mike Majoros; Photography, Miguelangel Aponte Rios, Jeremy Leach, Christopher Szwedo; Editor, Mike Majoros; Music, John Kusiak; Narrator, Linda Hunt; a Mountain View Prods. (U.S.) production in association with Allfilm (Estonia)/Northern Light Prods. (U.S.); Color; DV; Not rated; 94 minutes; Release date: December 14, 2007. Documentary on how Estonia maintained its tradition of choral singing at the 1969 Laulupidu music festival, defying Soviet occupation.

# ARRANGED

(FILM MOVEMENT) Producers/Directors, Diane Crespo, Stefan C. Schaefer; Executive Producers, Andrew Lund, Yuta Silverman; Screenplay, Stefan C. Schaefer; story by Stefan C. Schaefer, Yuta Silverman; Photography, Dan Hersey; Editor, Erin Greenwell; Music, Sohrab Habibion, Michael Hampton; Designer, Keren Kohenostumes, Beth Kelleher; a Cicala Filmworks production; Color; HD; Not rated; 93 minutes; Release date: December 14, 2007.

## Cast

Zoe Lister Jones (Rochel); Francis Benhamou (Nasira); John Rothman (Matan); Mimi Lieber (Sheli); Laith Nakli (Abdul-Halim); Marcia Jean Kurtz (Principal Jacoby); Doris Belack (Elona); Trevor Braun (Avi); Daniel London (Elliot); Arian Moayed (Ahmed); Peggy Gormley (Miriam); Jake Robards (Matt); Alysia Reiner (Leah); David Castro (Eddie); Peter Appel (Yitzak Bello); James Arden (Party Pot Smoker); Alison Becker (Beth Calloway); Sanjit De Silva (Jamil); Lissette Espaillat (Maria); Laura Esterman (Judit); Emma Lesser (Eva); Jason Liebman (Gideon); Sarah Lord (Naomi); Larry Mills (Lazar Ben Fischel); Bridget Moloney (Teacher #1); Remy K. Selma (Abu Jamil); Nicole Shalhoub, Alia Catherine Tarraf (Women); Gina Shmuckler (Amina); Gary Shteyngart (Lionya Abramovich); Max Shulman (Seth)

# A WALK INTO THE SEA: DANNY WILLIAMS AND THE WARHOL FACTORY

(ARTHOUSE FILMS) Producers, Tamra Raven, Doug Block; Executive Producer, Sasha Robinson; Co-Producer, Kelly DeVine; Director, Esther B. Robinson; Photography, Adam Cohen; Editors, Shannon Kennedy, James K. Lyons; Music, T. Griffin; a Thatgrl Films, in association with Chicken & Egg Pictures production; Color/Black and white; DigiBeta projection; Not rated; 77 minutes; Release date: December 14, 2007. Documentary on filmmaker Danny Williams, who disappeared mysteriously after making an impression at Andy Warhol's Factory; with Brigid Berlin, Gerard Malanga, Paul Morrissey, John Cale, Callie Angell, Albert Maysles, Nat Finkelstein, Julia Robinson, Nadia Williams.

Danny Williams in *A Walk into the Sea* © ARTHOUSE FILMS

# FLAKES

(IFC FIRST TAKE) Producers, Mark Ross, Gary Winick, Jake Abraham, Karey Kirkpatrick; Director, Michael Lehmann; Screenplay, Chris Poche, Karey Kirkpatrick; Photography, Nancy Schreiber; Editor, Nicholas C. Smith; Music, Jason Derlatka, Jon Ehrlich; Art Director, Matthew Munn; Costumes, Jill Newell; an InDigEnt production; Color; HD Video; Not rated; 84 minutes; Release date: December 19, 2007.

Aaron Stanford, Christopher Lloyd in *Flakes* © IFC FIRST TAKE

## Cast

Aaron Stanford (Neal Downs); Zooey Deschanel (Pussy Katz); Kier O'Donnell (Stuart); Ryan Donowho (Skinny Larry); Frank Wood (Bruce); Izabella Miko (Strawberry); Christopher Lloyd (Willie); Christopher C. Brown (Construction Worker); Robb Conner (Winston); Gary Desroche (Lawyer); Anthony Michael Frederick (Process Serving Deputy); Anthony Gangi (Waiter); Jaime San Andres (Bartender); Tanner James (Laundromat Guy Removing Pants); Mark Krasnoff (Enrique); Ann Mahoney (Astrid); John McConnell (Ashton Hale); Sean Patterson (Arbitrator); Danielle Rees (Gigi); Allison Robin, Glenn Robin, Henry Robin (Hossier Family); Gary Michael Smith (Lawyer); Sarah E. Spencer (News Reporter); Marco St. John (Tre Zeringue); Rusty Tennant (Midwestern Tourist); Blaine Cade, Shannon Hubbell (Customers); Kennedy Morgan, Michaels Morgan, Pepper Morgan, Taylor Drew Morgan, Wayne Douglas Morgan (Protestors)

# STEEP

*Steep* © SONY PICTURES CLASSICS

(SONY PICTURES CLASSICS) Producers, Jordan Kronick, Gabrielle Tenenbaum; Executive Producers, Tom Yellin, Mark Obenhaus, J. Stuart Horsfall; Co-Producer /Second Unit Director, William A. Kerig; Director/ Screenplay, Mark Obenhaus; Photography, Erich Roland; Editor, Peter R. Livingston Jr.; Music, Anton Sanko; Associate Producer, Caitlin Costin; Narrator, Peter Krause; a Documentary Group presentation, in association with High Ground Prods.; Dolby; Color/Black and white; Rated PG; 92 minutes; Release date: December 21, 2007. Documentary following a group of "extreme" skiers as they risk their lives for their sport; with Doug Coombs, Stefano De Benedetti, Shane McConkey, Chris Davenport, Eric Pehota, Ingrid Backstrom, Anselme Baud, Bill Briggs, Andrew McLean, Seth Morrison, Glen Plake.

# BLONDE AMBITION

(FIRST LOOK INTL.) Producers, Joe Simpson, Justin Berfield, Lati Grobman, David E. Ornston, Jeff Rice, Richard Salvatore, Mercy Santos; Director, Scott Marshall; Screenplay, John Cohen, Matthew Flanagan, David McHugh, Jessica O'Toole, Amy Rardin; Photography, Mark Irwin; Designer, Bob Ziembicki; Costumes, Sara Markowitz; Editor, Tara Timpone; Casting, Brinkley A. Maginnis; a Millennium Films, Papa Joe Films production; Color; Rated PG-13;93 minutes; Release date: December 21, 2007.

## Cast

Jessica Simpson (Katie), Luke Wilson (Ben), Rachael Leigh Cook (Haley), Andy Dick (Frankie), Larry Miller (Richard Connelly), Willie Nelson (Pap Paw), Penelope Ann Miller (Sandra Connelly), Drew Fuller (Billy), Piper Mackenzie Harris (Amber Perry), Karen McClain (Betty), Ritchie Montgomery (Mr. Carruthers), Sarah Ann Schultz (Samantha), Niki Spiridakos (Aphrodite), Evie Thompson (Young Katie), Julian Tizian (Young Billy), Preston Vanderslice (Kyle), Paul Vogt (Floyd)

# AVPR:
# ALIEN VS. PREDATOR – REQUIEM

Victoria Bidewell, Alien in *AVPR: Alien vs. Predator—Requiem*

(20TH CENTURY FOX) Producers, John Davis, David Giler, Walter Hill; Executive Producers, Paul Deason, Robbie Brenner; Directors, The Brothers Strause; Screenplay, Shane Salerno, based on the "Alien" characters created by Dan O'Bannon, Ron Shusett and the "Predator" characters created by Jim Thomas, John Thomas; Photography, Daniel C. Pearl; Editor, Dan Zimmerman; Music, Brian Tyler; Designer, Andrew Neskoromny; Costumes, Angus Strathie; Creature Effects Designers/Creators, Alec Gillis, Tom Woodruff Jr.; Original "Alien" Creatures Designer, H.R. Giger; Casting, Mindy Marin (U.S.), Coreen Mayrs, Heike Brandstatter (Canada); a John Davis/Brandywine production in association with Dune Entertainment; Dolby; Deluxe color; Rated R; 94 minutes; Release date: December 25, 2007.

## Cast

Steven Pasquale (Dallas); Reiko Aylesworth (Kelly); John Ortiz (Morales); Johnny Lewis (Ricky); Ariel Gade (Molly); Kristen Hager (Jesse); Sam Trammell (Tim); Robert Joy (Col. Stevens); David Paetkau (Dale); Tom Woodruff Jr. (Alien); Ian Whyte (Predator); Chelah Horsdal (Darcy); Meshach Peters (Curtis); Matt Ward (Mark); Michal Suchának (Nick); David Hornsby (Drew); Chris William Martin (Deputy Ray); James Chutter (Deputy Joe); Phil Uhler, Kevin Haaland (Deputies); Gina Holden (Carrie); Kurt Max Runte (Buddy); Liam James (Sam); Tim Henry (Dr. Lennon); Tom McBeath (Karl); Ty Olsson (Nathan); Anthony Harrison (Ritchie); Lloyd Berry (Homeless Harry); Rekha Sharma (Nurse Helen); Catherine Lough Haggquist (Tina); Victoria Bidewell (Pregnant Sue); Dalias Blake (Lt. Wood); Tim Perez (Mr. Thomas); Rainbow Sun Francks (Earl); Juan Riedinger (Scotty); Val Cole (Broadcaster); Andrew Hegge (Tank Driver); Ryan Robbins (Truck Driver); Curtis Caravaggio (Special Forces Commander); Françoise Yip (Ms. Y); John Wardlow (Homeless Guy); Nesta Chapman (Homeless Lady); Glen Brkich (National Guard); Jay-Lyn Green, Ilu Wexu (Pregnant Women); Adrian Hough (ER Resident Doc); Karen van Blankenstein (ER Doctor #2)

# HONEYDRIPPER

(EMERGING PICTURES) Producer, Maggie Renzi; Director/Screenplay/Editor, John Sayles; Photography, Dick Pope; Music, Mason Daring; Music Supervisor, Tim Bernett; Designer, Toby Corbett; Costumes, Hope Hanafin; Makeup, Diane Maurno; Associate Producers, Ira Deutchmann, Susan Kirr, Mark Wynns; Casting, John Hubbard; a Honeydripper Films production; Dolby; Color; Rated PG-13; 122 minutes; Release date: December 28, 2007.

## Cast

Danny Glover (Tyrone Purvis); Lisa Gay Hamilton (Delilah); Yaya DaCosta (China Doll); Charles S. Dutton (Maceo); Vondie Curtis-Hall (Slick); Gary Clark Jr. (Sonny Blake); Mable John (Bertha Mae); Stacy Keach (Sheriff Pugh); Nagee Clay (Scratch); Absalom Adams (Lonnie); Arthur Lee Williams (Metalmouth Sims); Ruben Santiago-Hudson (Stokely); Davenia McFadden (Nadine); Daryl Edwards (Shack Thomas); Mary Steenburgen (Amanda Winship); Sean Patrick Thomas (Dex); Eric L. Abrams (Ham); Kel Mitchell (Junebug); Keb' Mo' (Possum); Tom Wright (Cool Breeze); Donnie L. Betts (Mr. Simmons); John Sayles (Zeke); Larry Coker (Driver); Brian D. Williams (Luther); Santana Shelton (Opal); Danny Vinson (Judge Gatlin); Brent Jennings (Ned); Steve Holmes, Ledyard Williamson (Deputies); Albert Hall (Reverend Cutlip); Ronald McCall (King); Eddie Mallard III (Nat); Eddie Shaw (Time Trenier); Eric Housh (Clerk); Stephan Hundley (Young Henry); James Crittenden (Old Man Toussaint); Mitch Harbeson (Army Jeep Driver)

Hoping to book a local guitar player to help bring business to his failing roadhouse, Tyrone Purvis instead ends up with itinerant bluesman Sonny Blake, who displays his own special flair for the instrument.

Danny Glover, Lisa Gay Hamilton in *Honeydripper*

# FOREIGN FILMS

**A**

## 2007 RELEASES
### JANUARY 1–DECEMBER 31

# HAPPILY N'EVER AFTER

The Wizard © LIONSGATE

(LIONSGATE) Producer, John H. Williams; Executive Producer, Rainer Soehnlein; Co-Producer, J. Chad Hammes; Co-Executive Producers, Dr. Carl Woebcken, Ralph Kamp, Louise Goodsill; Director, Paul J. Bolger; Screenplay, Rob Moreland; Photography, David Dulac; Designer, Deane Taylor; CGI Supervisor, Fabrice Delapierre; Animation Director, Dino Athanassiou; Additional Animation, Nitrogen Studios Canada, the Lab Sydney, Mr. X, Bardel Entertainment, Elliott Animation, Quadriga FX; Casting, Ruth Lambert; Presented in association with Vanguard Films, Odyssey Entertainment, BAF Berlin Animation Film, BFC Berliner Film Co. of a BAF Berlin Animation Film, BFC Berliner Film Co. Vanguard Animation production; German-American; Dolby; Color; Rated PG; 87 minutes; American release date: January 5, 2007.

## Voice Cast

Ella **Sarah Michelle Gellar**
Rick **Freddie Prinze, Jr.**
Mambo **Andy Dick**
Munk **Wallace Shawn**
Prince Humperdink **Patrick Warburton**
The Wizard **George Carlin**
Frieda **Sigourney Weaver**
and John Di Maggio (Dwarf #1/Dwarf #2/Giant); Lisa Kaplan (Fairy Godmother); Jill Talley (Stepsister #2/Witch #2/Baby's Mother); Tom Kenny (Amigo #3/Dwarf #3/Messenger/Wolf #2); Tress MacNeille (Witch #1); Michael McShane (Rumplestiltskin); Rob Paulsen (Amigo #2); Jon Polito (Wolf #1); Phil Proctor (Amigo #1); Kath Soucie (Stepsister #1/Baby/Red Riding Hood); Lee Arenberg, John Cygan, Jennifer Darling, Debi Derryberry, Patti Deutsch, Shae D'Lyn, Andrew Dolan, Bill Farmer, Jack Fletcher, Roger Jackson, Sherry Lynn, Mickie McGowan, Laraine Newman, Jan Rabson, Kevin Michael Richardson, James Kevin Ward, April Winchell (Additional Voices)

When the Wizard takes a break, the wicked Frieda takes control of Fairy Tale Land, hoping to make all the famous storybook characters miserably unhappy.

# COMEDY OF POWER

(KOCH LORBER) aka *L'ivresse du Pouvoir*; Producer, Patrick Godeau; Executive Producer, Francoise Galfre; Co-Producer, Alfred Hurmer; Director, Claude Chabrol; Screenplay, Odile Barski, Claude Chabrol; Photography, Eduardo Serra; Designer, Francoise Benoit-Fresco; Costumes, Mic Cheminal; Editor, Monique Fardoulis; Music, Matthieu Chabrol; Casting, Cecile Maistre; a Patrick Godeau presentation of an Aliceleo, France 2 Cinema, Ajoz Films, Integral Film production, with participation of Filmforderungsanstalt (FFA), Canal Plus, CineCinema; French-German, 2006; Dolby; Color; Not rated; 110 minutes; American release date: January 5, 2007.

## Cast

Jeanne Charmant-Killman **Isabelle Huppert**
Michel Humeau **François Berléand**
Jacques Sibaud **Patrick Bruel**
Philippe Charmant-Killman **Robin Renucci**
Erika **Maryline Canto**
Félix **Thomas Chabrol**
and Jean-François Balmer (Boldi); Pierre Vernier (President Martino, Jacques Boudet Descarts); Philippe Duclos (Jean-Baptiste Holéo); Jean-Christophe Bouvet (Me Parlebas); Roger Dumas (Rene Lange); Yves Verhoeven (Benoît); John Arnold, Michel Scourneau (Jaguar Men); Jacques Bounaich (Prison Guard); Benoît Charpentier (Economics Journalist); Laurence Colussi (Secretary);Raphaël Neal, Dominique Daguier (Strangers); Stéphane Debac (Cop); Pierre-François Dumeniaud (Leblanc); Raphaëlle Farman (Opera Singer); Pierre-Henri Gibert (Financier); Michèle Goddet (Nicole Humeau); Cyril Guei (African Diplomat); Sophie Guiter (Evelyne); Jean-Marie Juan (Marco); Aïcha Kossoko (Nurse Jeanne); Nathalie Kousnetzoff (Michèle); Hubert Saint-Macary (Prison Director); Guy Perrot (Physician)

Examining magistrate Jeanne Charmant-Killman sets out to prove that wealthy Michel Humeau is involved in illegal business dealings.

Isabelle Huppert © KOCH LORBER FILMS

## THE ITALIAN

(SONY CLASSICS) aka *Italianetz*; Producer, Andrei Zertsalov; Executive Producer, Olga Agrefenina; Director, Andrei Kravchuk; Screenplay, Andrei Romanov; Photography, Alexander Burov; Art Director, Vladimir Diatlenko, Andrei Rudiev; Costumes, Marina Nikolayeva, Natalia Baranova; Editor, Tamara Lipartiya; Music, Alexander Knieffel; a Lenfilm Studios production, with the support Russian Ministry of Culture; Russian, 2005; Rated PG-13; 99 minutes; American release date: January 19, 2007.

### Cast

Vanya Solntsev  **Kolya Spiridonov**
Madam  **Maria Kuznetsova**
Grisha  **Nikolai Reutov**
Kolyan  **Denis Moiseenko**
Sery  **Sasha Sirotkin**
Timokha  **Andrei Yelizarov**
Bloke  **Vladimir Shipov**
Natasha  **Polina Vorobieva**
Irka  **Olga Shuvalova**
and Dima Zemlyanko (Anton), Yuri Itskov (Headmaster), Dariya Lesnikova (Mukhin's Mother), Rudolf Kuld (Guard)

Six-year-old Vanya must choose between being adopted by a foreign family or finding the mother who abandoned him.

Kolya Spiridonov

Olga Shuvalova, Andrei Yelizarov, unknown, Denis Moiseenko, Kolya Spiridonov (back to camera) © SONY PICTURES CLASSICS

## BLOOD AND CHOCOLATE

Olivier Martinez, Hugh Dancy © MGM

(MGM) Producers, Hawk Koch, Richard Wright, Wolfgang Esenwein, Tom Rosenberg, Gary Lucchesi; Executive Producers, Robert Bernacchi, Ehren Kruger; Co-Producers, Peter Rogers, Gudrun Anja Stadelmann, Andrei Boncea; Director, Katja von Garnier; Screenplay, Ehren Kruger, Christopher Landon; Based on the novel by Annette Curtis Klause; Photography, Brendan Galvin; Designer, Kevin Phipps; Costumes, Marco Scotti; Music, Johnny Klimek, Reinhold Heil; Editors, Martin Walsh, Emma E. Hickox; Visual Effects Supervisor, Rob Duncan; a Berrick Filmproduktion production in association with Lakeshore Entertainment; British-German-Romanian-American; Dolby; Super 35 Widescreen; Deluxe color; Rated PG-13; 98 minutes; American release date: January 26, 2007.

### Cast

Vivian  **Agnes Bruckner**
Gabriel  **Olivier Martinez**
Aiden  **Hugh Dancy**
Astrid  **Katja Riemann**
Rafe  **Bryan Dick**
Ulf  **Chris Geere**
Gregor  **Tom Harper**
and John Kerr (Finn); Jack Wilson (Willem); Vitalie Ursu (Constani); Bogdan Voda (Albu); Kata Dobó (Beatrice); Rodica Mandache (Mrs. Bellagra); Helga Racz (Young Vivian); Lia Bugnar (Young Vivian's Mother); Mihai Calin (Vivian's Sister); David Finti (Vivian's Brother); Anatole Taubman (Bartender); Pete Lee-Wilson (Krall); Maria Dinulescu (Sexy Redhead); Raluca Aprodu, Simona Cuciurianu (Girlfriends); Alexandru Barba (Little Boy); Romeo Raicu (Truck Driver); Iulian Pana (Club Bouncer); Tudor Istodor (Desk Man); Mihai Dinvale (Maitre D'); Florin Busuioc (Jail Guard); Jasmin Tabatabai (Nightclub Singer); Silviu Sanda, Cristian Anca, Razvan Gorcinski, Dan Mihai Leompescu, Cristi Dimitriu (Band); Samela A. Beasom, Susan Judy, Christen Herman, Daniel J. Plaster (Choir)

Having fallen in love with Aiden, werewolf Vivian hopes to resist her violent tendencies and give herself to the human, much to the displeasure of her wolfpack.

# HANNIBAL RISING

(MGM/WEINSTEIN) Producers, Dino De Laurentiis, Martha De Laurentiis, Tarak Ben Ammar; Executive Producers, James Clayton, Duncan Reid; Co-Producers, Chris Curling, Philip Roberton, Petr Moravec; Director, Peter Webber; Screenplay, Thomas Harris, based on his book; Photography, Ben Davis; Designer, Allan Starski; Costumes, Anna Sheppard; Music, Ilan Eshkeri, Shigeru Umbeay Ashi; Editors, Pietro Scalia, Valerio Bonelli; Casting, Leo Davis; a Dino De Laurentiis production in association with Quinta Communications and Ingenious Film Partners; British-Czech Republic-French-Italian; Dolby; Super 35 Widescreen; Color; Rated R; 121 minutes; Release date: February 9, 2007.

Gong Li

## Cast

Hannibal Lecter **Gaspard Ulliel**
Lady Murasaki **Gong Li**
Grutas **Rhys Ifans**
Kolnas **Kevin McKidd**
Inspector Popil **Dominic West**
Dortlich **Richard Brake**
Milko **Stephen Walters**
Grentz **Ivan Marevich**

and Aaran Thomas (Hannibal, 8 years); Helena Lia Tachovska (Mischa); Richard Leaf (Father Lecter); Michele Wade (Nanny); Martin Hub (Lothar); Ingeborga Dapkunaite (Mother Lecter); Joerg Stadler (Berndt); Timothy Walker (S.S. Major); Goran Kostic (Pot Watcher); Radek Bruna (Radio Operator); Ota Filip (Lecter Cook); Vaclav Pacal (German Sergeant); Seon Rogers (Tank Commander); Jaroslav Psenicka, Pavel Kratky, Petr Hnetkvosky (Tank Crewmen); Toby Alexander, Ladislav Hampl (Monitors); Joe Sheridan (Headmaster); Dominique Bettenfeld (Chef); Jos Houben (Serge); Nancy Bishop (Marielle); Zdenek Dvoracek, Miroslav Mavratil (Butcher Brothers); Charles Maquignon (Paul the Butcher); Vladimir Kulhavy (Vegetable Dealer); Denis Menochet (Chief of Police); Jan Nemejovsky (Mortician); Václav Chalupa (Mortician's Assistant); Martin Hancock (Polygraph Operator); Thomás Palaty (Popil's Assistant); Matthew Blood-Smyth, Michal Havelka (Policemen); Jaroslav Vizner (Onlooker); Hugh Ross (Professor Dumas); Elsa Mollien, Linda Svobodova (Students); Paul Ritter (Prisoner Louis); Robert Russell (Prison Doctor); Ivo Novák, Dalibor Pavelka (Russian Soldiers); Todd Kramer (Desk Officer); John Early (Drunken Man); Dmitrij Matus (Dorlich's Desk Sergeant); Brian Caspe (Sneaky Officer); Vitezslav Bouchner (Headwaiter); Beata Ben Ammar (Madame Kolnas); Robbie Kay (Kolnas's Son); Vanesa Novakova (Kolnas's Daughter); Marek Vasut (Captain); Milos Kulhavy (Tattooed Thug); Pavel Bezdek (Dieter); Veronika Bellová (First Woman Captive); Marko Igonda (Mueller); Lana Likic (Maid); Petra Lustigova (Eva); Jiri Subrt (Hercule)

Gaspard Ulliel (standing)

A look back on how Hannibal Lecter developed his violent, cannibalistic tendencies. Previous films featuring the character of Lecter were *Manhunter* (DEG, 1986), *The Silence of the Lambs* (Orion, 1991), *Hannibal* (MGM, 2001), and *Red Dragon* (Universal, 2002).

Gaspard Ulliel © WEINSTEIN CO./MGM

# CLOSE TO HOME

(IFC FIRST TAKE) aka *Karov la Bayit*; Producers, Marek Rozenbaum, Itai Tamir; Director/Screenplay, Vidi (Vardit) Bilu, Dalia Hager; Photography, Yaron Scharf; Editor, Joelle Alexis; Music, Yontan Bar Giora; Designer, Avi Fahima; Costumes, Li Alembik; a Transfax Film Prod. production; Israeli; Dolby SR; Color, HD-to-35mm; 98 minutes; American release date: February 16, 2007.

**Cast**

Smadar  **Smadar Sayar**
Mirit  **Naama Shendar**
and Irit Suki, Katia Zimbris, Ami Weinburg, Danny Geva, Anna Stephan, Ilanit Ben Yaakov, Sharon Reginiano, Jana Ettinger, Shlomo Vishinsky, Tsafit Shpan, Shiran Fresco, Lee Michael, Lotan Sapir

Two teenage girls form a friendship while assigned to military duty in Jerusalem.

Naama Schendar

Smadar Sayar, Naama Schendat © IFC FILMS

# AVENUE MONTAIGNE

(THINKFILM) aka *Fauteuils d'orchestre* (*Orchestra Seats*); Producer, Christine Gozlan; Director, Daniele Thompson; Screenplay, Daniele Thompson, Christopher Thompson; Photography, Jean-Marc Fabre; Designer, Michele Abbe; Costumes, Catherine Leterrier; Music, Nicola Piovani; Editor, Sylvie Landra; Casting, Stephane Foenkinos; an Alain Sarde presentation of a Thelma Films, StudioCanal, TF1 Films, Radis Film production with the participation of Canal Plus, CineCinema and with the support of the Region Ile de France; French, 2006; Dolby; Super 35 Widescreen; Color; Rated PG-13; 105 minutes; American release date: February 16, 2007.

Cécile De France

## Cast

Jessica **Cécile De France**
Catherine Versen **Valérie Lemercier**
Jean-François Lefort **Albert Dupontel**
Valerntine Lefort **Laura Morante**
Jacques Grumberg **Claude Brasseur**
Frédéric Grumberg **Christopher Thompson**
Claudie **Dani**
Valérie **Annelise Hesme**
Marcel **François Rollin**
Brian Sobinski **Sydney Pollack**
Daniel Bercoff **Daniel Benoin**
Magali Garrel **Françoise Lépine**
Pascal **Guillaume Gallienne**
Grégoire Bergonhe **Christian Hecq**
Margot **Julia Molkhou**
Madame Roux **Suzanne Flon**
Félix **Michel Vuillermoz**
Serge **Laurent Mouton**
Themselves **Werner, Simon de Pury**
Marc Rioufol **Claude Mercier**
"La Dame-Pipi" **Michèle Brousse**
Elle-même **Ève Ruggieri**
Makeup Artist **Susana Poveda**
Japanese Journalist **Kaori Tsuji**
Translator **Franck Amiack**
Taxi Chauffeurs **Ahcène Nini, Mikis Cerleix**
and Caroline Morin (Dresser); Laurent Petitgirad (Orchestra Chef); Thierry Métaireau (Manager); Sabrina Ouazani (Rachida); Serge Bento (Faithful Man); Brigitte Defrance (Faithful Woman); Daniel Delfosse (Window Washer); Yannick Dyvrande (Plazza Bar Waiter); Martine Erhel (Catherine's Mother); Eric Moreau (Stagehand); Frantz Morel (Receptionist); Antoine Nembrini (Engineer); Sigolène Vinion (Ungaro Saleswoman)

Cécile De France, Christopher Thompson

Sydney Pollack © THINKFILM

A naïve young woman takes a waitressing job at a Parisian café near a theatre, a concert hall, and an auction house, becoming involved with the lives of people from each of the venues.

# STARTER FOR 10

Alice Eve, Dominic Cooper

(PICTUREHOUSE) Producers, Tom Hanks, Gary Goetzman, Pippa Harris; Executive Producers, Sam Mendes, Steven Shareshian, Nathalie Marciano, Michelle Chydzik Sowa; Co-Producer, Mary Richards; Director, Tom Vaughan; Screenplay, David Nicholls, based on his novel; Photography, Ashley Rowe; Music, Blake Neely; Music Supervisors, Deva Anderson, Delphine Robertson; Editors, Jon Harris, Heather Persons; Designer, Sarah Greenwood; Costumes, Charlotte Morris; Casting, Nina Gold; an HBO Presentation (U.S.), in association with BBC Films (U.K.) of a Playtone Picture (U.S.) production, in association with Neal Street Prods. (U.K.); British-American; Dolby; Color; Rated PG-13; 96 minutes; Release date: February 23, 2007.

James McAvoy, Rebecca Hall

## Cast

Brian Jackson   **James McAvoy**
Alice Harbinson   **Alice Eve**
Rebecca Epstein   **Rebecca Hall**
Julie Jackson   **Catherine Tate**
Spencer   **Dominic Cooper**
Patrick Watts   **Benedict Cumberbatch**
Tone   **James Corden**
Bamber Gascoigne   **Mark Gatiss**
Michael Harbinson   **Charles Dance**
Rose Harbinson   **Lindsay Duncan**
Young Brian   **Joseph Friend**
Martin Jackson   **James Gaddas**
Bamber Gascoigne   **Mark Gatiss**
University Challenge Competitors   **Robert Cawsey, Rasmus Hardiker**
Dr. Morrison   **Guy Henry**
Josh   **Simon Woods**
and Sule Rimi (Marcus); Joe Van Moyland (Hippy at the Party); Rebecca Hall (Rebecca Epstein); Elaine Tan (Lucy Chang); Ian Bonar (Colin); Reuben Henry Biggs (Anthony Salmon); Ben Willbond (University Challenge Coordinator); Su Elliott (Cleaning Lady); Gerard Monaco (Waiter); John Hensaw (Des); Bethan Bevan (Cordelia Sykes); Raj Ghatak (Nigel De Havilland); Tom Allen (Tristram Neville); Kenneth Hadley (Television Director); Nicholas Gleaves (Speaker for Nuclear Disarmament)

Hoping to fit in and prove his skills at university, Brian Jackson joins the school's University Challenge team, where he falls in love with teammate Alice Harbinson.

Lindsay Duncan, Charles Dance © PICTUREHOUSE

# AMAZING GRACE

(ROADSIDE ATTRACTIONS/GOLDWYN FILMS) Producers, Edward Pressman, Terrence Malick, Patricia Heaton, David Hunt, Ken Wales; Executive Producers, Jeanney Kim, James Clayton, Duncan Reid; Co-Producer, Mark Cooper; Director, Michael Apted; Screenplay, Steven Knight; Photography, Remi Adefarasin; Designer, Charles Wood; Costumes, Jenny Beavan; Editor, Rick Shaine; Music, David Arnold; Music Supervisor, Lindsay Fellows; Casting, Nina Gold; a Samuel Goldwyn Films, Roadside Attractions, Bristol Bay Prods. presentation, in association with Ingenious Film Partners 2, of a Sunflower production; British; Dolby; Color; Rated PG; 116 minutes; American release date: February 23, 2007.

Ioan Gruffudd, Romola Garai

### Cast

William Wilberforce **Ioan Gruffudd**
Barbara Spooner **Romola Garai**
William Pitt **Benedict Cumberbatch**
John Newton **Albert Finney**
Lord Charles Fox **Michael Gambon**
Thomas Clarkson **Rufus Sewell**
Oloudagh Equiano **Youssou N'Dour**
Lord Tarleton **Ciarán Hinds**
Duke of Clarence **Toby Jones**
Henry Thornton **Nicholas Farrell**
and Sylvestra Le Touzel (Marianne Thornton); Jeremy Swift (Richard the Butler); Stephen Campbell Moore (James Stephen); Bill Paterson (Lord Dundas); Nicholas Day (William Dolben); Richard Bailey, Robert Roy Collins, Peter Halpin (Clerks); Alex Blake (Heckler); Sean Bloc, Jazz Dhiman, Aaron Sweeney, Nick Thomas-Webster, Andrew Whipp (Members of Parliament); Martin Nigel Davey (The Boat Servant); Georgie Glen (Hannah Moore); Derek Hagen (Parliament Messenger); David Hunt (Lord Camden); Tom Knight (Physician); Richard Ridings (Speaker, Parliament); Alwyn Scott, Adam Woodroffe (Parliamentary Clerks); Angie Wallis (Marjorie)

Youssou N'Dour

The true story of William Wilberforce, a member of the House of Commons, who fought passionately to abolish slavery in 18th-century England.

Ioan Gruffudd

Albert Finney, Ioan Gruffudd © GOLDWYN FILMS

# EXTERMINATING ANGELS

Margaret Zenou, Frédéric van den Driessche © IFC FIRST TAKE

(IFC FIRST TAKE) aka *Les anges exterminateurs*; Produced by Jean-Claude Brisseau, Milena Poylo, Gilles Sacuto; Director/Screenplay, Jean-Claude Brisseau; Photography, Wildred Sempe; Editor/Designer/Costumes, Maria Luisa Garcia; Music, Jean Musy; Associate Producer, Lise Bellynck; a La Sorciere Rouge and TS Prods. presentation of a La Sorciere Rouge, TS Prods. production, with participation of CNC, CineCinema in association with Sofica Soficinema 2; French; Dolby; Color; Not rated; 102 minutes; American release date: March 7, 2007.

## Cast

François  **Frédéric van den Driessche**
Charlotte  **Maroussia Dubreuil**
Julie  **Lise Bellynck**
Stéphanie  **Marie Allan**
Apparition #1/Rebecca  **Raphaele Godin**
Apparition #2  **Margaret Zenou**
François' Woman  **Sophie Bonnet**
Grandmother  **Jeanne Cellard**
Virginie  **Virginie Legeay**
Olivia  **Estelle Galarme**
Agnès  **Marine Danaux**
Céline  **Apolline Louis**
and François Négret (Stéphanie's Friend), Christophe Maillard (The Producer), Françoise Bonnet (Neighbor), Olivier Perot (Policeman)

Filmmaker François embarks into dangerous territory when he decides to audition actresses to find out why the forbidden can induce pleasure in some women.

# THE HOST

Song Kang-ho, Ko A-sung

(MAGNOLIA) aka *Guimul*; Producer, Choi Yong-bae; Executive Producers, Choi Yong-bae, Kim Woo-taek, Jeong Tae-sung; Co-Producer, Jo Neung-yeon; Director/Story, Bong Joon-ho; Screenplay, Bong Joon-ho, Ha Jun-weon, Baek Cheol-hyeon; Photography, Kim Hyeong-gu; Designer, Ryu Seong-heui; Costumes, Jo Sang-gyeong; Editor, Kim Sun-min; Music, Lee Byeong-woo; Visual Effects: Animation, The Orphanage (San Francisco); Visual Effects Supervisor, Kevin Rafferty; Special Creature Effects, Jang Heui-cheol; a Chungeorahm Film, Showbox/Mediaplex (South Korea)/Happinet Corp. (Japan) presentation, in association with participation of OCN, Knowledge & Creation Ventures Co., IBK Capital Corp., Cineclick Asia, Cowell, BiNext Capital, IMM Investment Corp., SBS, M-Venture Investment, Tube Pictures Co., Sego Entertainment Co., CJ Venture Investment, Boston Investment Co., of a Chungeorahm Film production; South Korean-Japanese, 2006; Dolby; Color; 118 minutes; American release date: March 9, 2007.

## Cast

Gang-Du Park  **Song Kang-ho**
Hie-bong Park  **Byeon Hie-bong**
Nam-il Park  **Park Hae-il**
and Nam-Joo Park (Bae Du-na), Ko A-sung, Lee Dong-ho, Lee Jae-eung, Yun Je-mun, Kim Roi-ha, Park No-shik, Yim Pil-sung, Scott Wilson

A gigantic mutant tadpole, created by the careless dumping of formaldehyde, rises from the Han River to cause destruction in Seoul.

Ko A-sung © MAGNOLIA PICTURES

# BEYOND THE GATES

Hugh Dancy

John Hurt

(IFC FILMS) aka *Shooting Dogs*; Producers, David Belton, Pippa Cross, Jens Meurer; Executive Producers, David M. Thompson, Paul Trijbits, Ruth Caleb, Karsten Stoter, Richard Alwyn; Director, Michael Caton-Jones; Screenplay, David Wolstencroft; Story, Richard Alwyn, David Belton; Photography, Ivan Strasburg; Designer, Bertram Strauss; Costumes, Dinah Collin; Editor, Christian Lonk; Music, Dario Marianelli; Casting, Karen Lindsay-Stewart, Hope Azeda; a BBC Films and U.K. Film Council presentation in association with Invicta Capital and Filmstiftung NRW of a CrossDay/Egoli Tossell production in association with BBC Films; British-German; Dolby; Super 35 Widescreen; Cinepostproduktion Geyer color; Rated R; 115 minutes; American release date: March 9, 2007.

## Cast

Father Christopher  **John Hurt**
Joe Connor  **Hugh Dancy**
Captain Charles Delon  **Dominique Horwitz**
Sibomana  **Louis Mahoney**
Rachel  **Nicola Walker**
Roland  **Steve Toussaint**
Francois  **David Gyasi**
Edda  **Susan Nalwoga**
Julius  **Victor Power**
Mark  **Jack Pierce**
Boniface  **Musa Kasonka, Jr.**
Pierre  **Kizito Ssentamu Kayiira**
Marie  **Clare-Hope Ashitey**

British school teacher Joe Connor arrives in Kingali to teach at the Ecole Officielle, a secondary school that has become a makeshift shelter for both Tutsis and Hutus at the height of the Rwandan genocide.

Hugh Dancy © IFC FILMS

# THE WIND THAT SHAKES THE BARLEY

(IFC) Producer, Rebecca O'Brien; Executive Producers, Ulrich Felsberg, Andrew Lowe, Nigel Thomas, Paul Trijbits; Co-Producer, Redmond Morris; Director, Ken Loach; Screenplay, Paul Laverty; Photography, Barry Ackroyd; Designer, Fergus Clegg; Costumes, Eimer Ni Mhaoldomhnaigh; Editor, Jonathan Morris; Music, George Fenton; Casting, Oonagh Kearney; a Sixteen Films, Matador Pictures, Regent Capital, UK Film Council, Irish Film Board, Filmstiftung Nordrhein-Westfalen, Element Films, BIM Distribuzione, EMC Produktion, Tornasol Films, Diaphana Distribution, Pathe Distribution, Cineart, TV3 Ireland, Film Coopi production; Irish-British-Italian-German-Spanish, 2006; Dolby; Deluxe color; Not rated; 126 minutes; American release date: March 16, 2007.

Cillian Murphy

## Cast

Damien O'Donovan **Cillian Murphy**
Teddy O'Donovan **Pádraic Delaney**
Dan **Liam Cunningham**
Sinead **Orla Fitzgerald**
Peggy **Mary Riordan**
Bernadette **Mary Murphy**
Micheail **Laurence Barry**
and **Damien Kennedy** (Finbar); **Frank Bourke** (Leo); **Myles Horgan** (Rory); **Martin Lucey** (Congo); **Aidan O'Hare** (Steady Boy); **Shane Casey** (Kevin); **John Crean** (Chris); **Mairtin de Cogain** (Sean); **Keith Dunphy** (Terence); **Kieran Hegarty** (Francis); **Gerard Kearney** (Donacha); **Shane Nott** (Ned); **Kevin O'Brien** (Tim); Gary McCarthy, Tim O'Mahon, Graham Browne, Owen Buckley, Aidan Fitzpatrick, Vince Hannington, Denis Kelleher, Colin McClery, Finbar O'Mahon, John Quinlan (Volunteers); Peggy Lynch (Singer at Wake); Noel O'Donovan (Station Guard); Peter O'Mahoney (Stoker); Barry Bourke (Policeman); Frank O'Sullivan, Diarmuid Ó'Dálaigh (Men in Pub); Corina Gough (Woman in Search); Roger Allam (Sir John Hamilton); Sabrina Barry (Julia); William Ruane (Johnny Gogan); Danny Riordan, Peg Crowley (Elderly Couple); Fiona Lawton (Lily); Kieran Aherne (Sweeney); Clare Dineen (Mrs. Rafferty); Sean McGinley (Father Denis); Thomas Ohealaithe (Boy on Bike); Nora Lynch (Mother of Sick Child); Denis Conway (Priest); Barry Looney, Connie O'Connail, Aine O'Connor, Francis O'Connor, Peadr O'Riada (Ceilidh Band); Neil Brand (Newsreel Piano Accompanist); Tom Charnock (Sergeant at Cottage); Alan Ready (Sergeant at Station); Mark Wakeling (Lieutenant); Antony Byrne (The Interrogator); Marcy Anthony, Bill Armstrong, Christopher Bown, Mark Bryce, Alex Dee, Jonny Holmes, Allan Huntley, Bill Hurst, Daniel Kington, Jamie Lomas, Anthony Martin, Owen McQuade, Richard Oldham, Colin Parry, Scott Peden, Bernie Sweeney, Derek Taylor, Neil Alan Taylor, Gregor Wood (British Soldiers); Fergus Burke (Theatre Attendant)

Liam Cunningham

Intending to leave behind his Irish village to take work in a London hospital, Dr. Damien O'Donovan instead joins the Irish Republican Army after witnessing the senseless death of an innocent citizen at the hands of the British troops.

Pádraic Delaney, Aidan O'Hare, Cillian Murphy © IFC FILMS

# COLOR ME KUBRICK

(MAGNOLIA) aka *Colour Me Kubrick: A True ... ish Story*; Producers, Brian Cook, Michael Fitzgerald; Executive Producers, Luc Besson, Pierre-Ange Le Pogam, Steve Christian, Donald A. Starr, Daniel J.B. Taylor, Colin Leventhal; Co-Producer, Penelope Glass; Director, Brian Cook; Screenplay, Anthony Frewin; Photography, Howard Atherton; Designer, Crispian Sallis; Costumes, Vicki Russell; Editor, Alan Strachan; Music, Bryan Adams; Casting, Gail Stevens; a Colour Me K. (U.K.)/EuropaCorp (France) production, in association with Isle of Man Film, First Choice Films, with participation of Canal Plus, TPS Star; British-French, 2005; Dolby; Color; Not rated; 86 minutes; American release date: March 23, 2007.

John Malkovich

### Cast

Alan Conway  **John Malkovich**
Lee Pratt  **Jim Davidson**
Jasper  **Richard E. Grant**
Rupert Rodnight  **Luke Mably**
Hud  **Marc Warren**
Norman  **Terence Rigby**
Melvyn  **James Dreyfus**
Cyril  **Peter Bowles**
Dr. Stukeley  **Ayesha Dharker**
Robert  **Robert Powell**
Mordecai  **Henry Goodman**
Adibe  **Maynard Eziashi**
Freddie  **Leslie Phillips**
Madam  **Honor Blackman**
Frank Rich  **William Hootkins**
and Marisa Berenson (Alex Witchell); Lynda Baron (Mrs. Vitali); Ken Russell (The Man in a Nightgown); Peter Sallis (The Second Patient); Jack Ryan (Steve); Tom Allen (Charles); Scott Baker (Waiter); Nick Barber (Denzil); Angus Barnett (Ace); Linda Bassett (Trolley Lady); Jonathan Benson (Aristocratic Guest); Paul Burnham (Hex Mortimer); Paul Chowdhry (Club Announcer); Kammy Darweish, Teresa Churcher, Bindu De Stoppani (TV Journalists); Enzo Cilenti (Waldegrave); Toby Cook (Young Guy); Phil Cornwell (Police Duty Sgt.); Oliver Cotton (PC Metcalf); Jamie Davis (Duane); Bryan Dick (Sean); Gabriel Diggs (DJ in Nightclub); Shaun Dingwall (Maître D'); Panikos Efthimiou (Andros); James Faulkner (Oliver); Lance Forbes (Ned Bridges); Rebecca Font (Maureen); Nitin Ganatra (Deepak); Sam Gordon (Police Officer #1); Burn Gorman (Willie); Spencer Hawken (Man at Bar); Head-On (Exterminating Angels); Nolan Hemmings (Butch Roberts); John Leyton (Lord Charles Benson); Ruth Negga (Lolita); Shaun Parkes (Mental Patient #2); Sam Redford (Toby); Audrey Tom (Valerie); Jeremy Turner-Welch (David); Mark Umbers (Piers); Joe Van Moyland (Spencer); Al Weaver (Darren); Mark Webb (Policeman)

John Malkovich

The true story of how conman Alan Conway schemed to get himself perks and attention from the gullible public by passing himself off as reclusive filmmaker Stanley Kubrick.

Jim Davidson, John Malkovich © MAGNOLIA PICTURES

## THE PAGE TURNER

Déborah François, Pascal Greggory

Antoine Martynciow, Catherine Frot

(TARTAN) aka *La Tourneuse de pages*; Producer, Michel Saint-Jean; Executive Producer, Tom Dercourt; Director, Denis Dercourt; Screenplay, Denis Dercourt, Jacques Sotty; Photography, Jerome Peyrebrune; Editor, Francois Gedigier; Music, Jacques Lemonnier; Art Director/Costumes, Antoine Platteau; Casting, Brigitte Moidon; a Diaphana Films presentation of a Diaphana Films production, in association with France 3 Cinema, Les Films a Un Dollar production, with participation of Canal Plus, CineCinema; French; Dolby; Color; Not rated; 85 minutes; American release date: March 23, 2007.

### Cast

Ariane Fouchécourt  **Catherine Frot**
Mélanie Prouvost  **Déborah François**
Jean Fouchécourt  **Pascal Greggory**
Virginie  **Clotilde Mollet**
Laurent  **Xavier de Guillebon**
Madame Prouvost  **Christine Citti**
Monsieur Prouvost  **Jacques Bonnaffé**
Tristan Fouchécourt  **Antoine Martynciow**
Mélanie as a Child  **Julie Richalet**
Jackie Onfray  **Martine Chevallier**
Werker  **André Marcon**
Radio Presenter  **Arièle Butuax**
Monique  **Michèle Ernou**
Physician  **François Guillaume**
Clothing Saleswoman  **Julie Primot**
Nurse  **Danièle Renaud**

Catherine Frot, Déborah François

Déborah François, Catherine Frot © TARTAN USA

In order to take revenge on a man who, years earlier, had caused her to fail a piano audition and ruin her career plans, a young woman insinuates herself into his household.

# AFTER THE WEDDING

(IFC) aka *Efter brylluppet*; Producer, Sisse Graum Jorgensen; Executive Producers, Peter Aalbaek Jensen, Peter Garde; Co-Producer, Gillian Berrie; Director, Susanne Bier; Screenplay, Anders Thomas Jensen; Story, Susanne Bier, Anders Thomas Jensen; Photography, Morten Soborg; Editors, Pernille Bech, Morten Hojbjerg; Music, Johan Soderqvist; Art Director, Soren Skjaer; Costumes, Manon Rasmussen; a Zentropa Entertainments16 production, in association with After the Wedding/Sigma Films, with participation of DR, Sveriges Television, Invicta Capital; Danish; Dolby; Color; Rated R; 115 minutes; American release date: March 30, 2007.

Mads Mikkelsen

### Cast

Jacob **Mads Mikkelsen**
Jørgen **Rolf Lassgård**
Helene **Sidse Babett Knudsen**
Anna **Stine Fischer Christensen**
Christian **Christian Tafdrup**
Martin **Frederik Gullits Ernst**
Morten **Kristian Gulltis Ernst**
Annette **Ida Dwinger**
Grandmother **Mona Malm**
Mille **Neel Rønholt**
and Anne Fletting (Secretary); Henrik Larsen (Chauffeur); Niels Anders Thorn (Priest); Henning Jensen (Man at Birthday); Thomas Voss (Young Waiter); Troels Il Munk (Head Waiter); Julie R. Ølgaard (Hotel Girl); Claus Flygare, Jonathan Spang (Wedding Chauffeurs); Meenal Patel (Mrs. Shaw); Neeral Mulchandani (Pramod, 8 years old); Rita Angela, Marie-Louise Coninck (Older Women); Vallabh Gada, Hitesh Kotak (Suits); Suhita Thatte (Indisk Kvinde).

Sidse Babett Knudsen, Mads Mikkelsen

While in Denmark to secure some money for his Indian orphanage, Jacob ends up at a wedding where he becomes certain that he and the bride have met earlier.

© IFC FILMS

Mads Mikkelsen

# BLACK BOOK

Carice van Houten, Michiel Huisman

(SONY CLASSICS) aka *Zwartboek*; Producers, San Fu Maltha, Jens Meurer, Teun Hilte, Jos van der Linden, Frans van Gestel, Jeroen Beker; Executive Producers, Andreas Grosch, Andrea Schmid, Marcus Schoefer, Henning Molfenter, Carl Woebcken, Jamie Carmichael, Graham Begg, Sarah Giles; Co-Producers, Adrian Politowski, Jeremy Burdek, Nadia Khamlichi, Marc Noyons, Justine Paauw; Director, Paul Verhoeven; Screenplay, Gerard Soeteman, Paul Verhoeven; Story, Gerard Soeteman; Photography, Karl Walter Lindenlaub; Designer, Wilbert van Dorp; Costumes, Yan Tax; Editors, Job ter Burg, James Herbert; Music, Anne Dudley; Make-Up, Winnie Gallis, Dick Naastepad; Special Effects, Harry Wiessenhaan; Associate Producer, Jindra Markus; Casting, Hans Kemna, Job Gosschalk (Netherlands), Risa Kes (Germany); Stunts, Willem de Beukelaer; a Fu Works presentation, in association with Egoli Tossell Film, Clockwork Pictures, Studio Babelsberg, Motion Picture Investment Group, Motel Films, Hector, ContentFilm Intl., of a VIP Medienfonds 4 production, in association with AVRO; Dutch-German-British-Belgian, 2006; Dolby; Super 35 Widescreen; Color; Rated R; 144 minutes; American release date: April 4, 2007.

## Cast

Rachel Stein/Ellis de Vries  **Carice van Houten**
Ludwig Muentze  **Sebastian Koch**
Hans Akkermans  **Thom Hoffman**
Ronnie  **Halina Reijn**
Günther Franken  **Waldemar Kobus**
Gerben Kuipers  **Derek de Lint**
General Käutner  **Christian Berkel**
Wim Smaal  **Dolf de Vries**
Van Gein  **Peter Blok**
Rob Maalderink  **Michiel Huisman**
Tim Kuipers  **Ronald Armbrust**
Kess  **Frank Lammers**
Joop  **Matthias Schoenaerts**
Theo  **Johnny de Mol**
Maarten  **Xander Straat**
Mrs. Smaal  **Diana Dobbelman**
Anny  **Rixt Leddy**
Linda  **Lidewij Mahler**
Herman  **Pieter Tiddens**
Cas  **Gijs Naber**
Siem  **Dirk Zeelenberg**
David  **Michiel de Jong**
Driver Müntze  **Jobst Schibbe**
Joseph  **Boris Saran**
Mr. Stein  **Jack Vecht**
Mrs. Stein  **Jacqueline Blom**
Brother Max  **Seth Kamphuijs**
Skipper Willi  **Herman Boerman**
Farmer  **Reinier Bulder**
Mr. Tjepkema  **Bert Luppes**
and Marissa Van Eyle (Mrs. Tjepkema); Heleen Mineur (Stientje Tjepkema); Bas van der Horst (Jantje Tjepkema); Foeke Kolff, Merel van Houts, Charlotte Rinnooy Kan, Maaike Kempeneers (Tjepkema Children); Janni Goslinga (Lady in Fur Coat); Wimie Wilhelm (Female Prison Guard); Theo Maassen (Prison Guard with Baret); Tjebbo Gerritsma (Prison Guard with Accordion); Timothy Deenihan (Canadian Colonel); Nolan Hemmings (Captain of British Intelligence); Garrick Hagon (British General); Ronald de Bruin, Menno Van Beekum (Dutch SDs in Train); Marcel Musters (Henk); Hugo Metsers (Shock Trooper); Rian Gerttisen, Susan Visser (Drunken Women in Prison); Maiko Kemper (Siegfried); Carsten Sasse (German Sentry); Liza de Weerd (Receptionist); Willem de Wolf (Property Man); Oded Menashe (Husband of Rachel); Roni Yedid (Rachel's Daughter); Tomer Agami (Rachel's Son); Gabriela Lewis (Tour Guide)

Rachel Rosenthal-Stein looks back on how she survived during World War II while working for the resistance, which led to her unexpectedly falling in love with a Gestapo chief.

Waldemar Kobus, Halina Reijn © SONY PICTURES CLASSICS

# PRIVATE FEARS
# IN PUBLIC PLACES

André Dussolier, Sabine Azéma

Isabelle Carré, Lambert Wilson © IFC FILMS

(IFC) aka *Coeurs*; Producer, Bruno Pesery; Executive Producer, Julie Salvador; Director, Alain Resnais; Screenplay, Alain Resnais, Jean-Michel Ribes, Alan Ayckbourn, from Alan Ayckbourn's play *Private Fears in Public Places*; Photography, Eric Gautier; Editor, Herve de Luze; Music, Mark Snow; Designers, Jacques Saulnier, Jean-Michel Ducourty, Solange Zeitoun; Costumes, Jackie Budin; a Soudaine Compagnie, Arena Films, France 2 Cinema (France)/BIM Films (Italy) co-production, in association with Banque Populaire Images 6; French-Italian; Dolby; Panavision; Color; Not rated; 123 minutes; American release date: April 13, 2007.

## Cast

Nicole  **Laura Morante**
Dan  **Lambert Wilson**
Lionel  **Pierre Arditi**
Gaëlle  **Isabelle Carré**
Thierry  **André Dussollier**
Charlotte  **Sabine Azéma**
Arthur's Voice  **Claude Rich**
TV Speaker  **Francoise Gillard**
TV Host  **Anne Kessler**
Poet  **Roger Mollien**
Art Critic  **Florence Muller**
Architect  **Michel Vuillermoz**

The lives of several unfulfilled, middle-class Parisians intersect by chance.

# WHOLE NEW THING

(PICTURE THIS!) Producers, Camelia Frieberg, Kelly Bray; Executive Producer, Camelia Frieberg; Director, Amnon Buchbinder; Screenplay, Amnon Buchbinder, Daniel McIvor; Photography, Christopher Ball; Designer, Bill Fleming; Costumes, Lin Chapman; Music, David Buchbinder; Editor, Angela Baker; a Palpable Prods. and Acuity Pictures production; Canadian, 2005; Dolby; Color; Not rated; 92 minutes; American release date: April 6, 2007.

## Cast

Aaron Webber (Emerson); Robert Joy (Rog); Rebecca Jenkins (Kaya); Daniel MacIvor (Don Grant); Kathryn MacLellan (Ms. McPherson); Drew O'Hara (Todd); Ryan Hartigan (Jeff); Geordie Brown (Buddy); Callum Keith Rennie (Denny); Jackie Torrens (Claire); Lisa Lelliott (Massage Guest); Leah Fassett (Laura); Samantha Spencer (Debra); Rebecca Regan (Teri); Marguerite McNeil (Don's Mother); Hugh Thompson (Claude); Linda Busby (Mrs. Colley); Brian Heighton (Office Man); Dylan Aucoin, Alexandra Ashley, Caleb Buchbinder, Stephanie Champan, P.J. Crosby, Leah Cunningham, Toni Grossett, Bruce Murphy, Branden O'Brien, Colin Rogers, Mitchell Taylor (School Kids); Terry Coolen, Darcy Lindzon (Washroom Men); Dennis Brown, Pauline Kaill, Veronique MacKenzie-Bourne (Teachers); Susan Bone, Peter M. Davison, Armand J. Grenier, Don Himmelman, Sally Lawrence, Rob Moir, Grace McKnight, Paul Newton (Potuck Guests).

Daniel MacIvor, Aaron Webber

Aaron Webber © PICTURE THIS!

# HOT FUZZ

(ROGUE) Producers, Nira Park, Tim Bevan, Eric Fellner; Executive Producer, Natascha Wharton; Director, Edgar Wright; Screenplay, Edgar Wright, Simon Pegg; Photography, Jess Hall; Designer, Marcus Rowland; Costumes, Annie Hardinge; Editor, Chris Dickens; Music, David Arnold; Visual Effects Supervisor, Richard Briscoe; Casting, Nina Gold; a Universal Pictures presentation in association with StudioCanal of a Working Title production in association with Big Talk Prods.; British; Dolby; Super 35 Widescreen; Color; Rated R; 120 minutes; American release date: April 20, 2007.

### Cast

Sgt. Nicholas Angel **Simon Pegg**
PC Danny Butterman **Nick Frost**
Inspector Frank Butterman **Jim Broadbent**
DS Andy Andy Wainwright **Paddy Considine**
Simon Skinner **Timothy Dalton**
Joyce Cooper **Billie Whitelaw**
Tom Weaver **Edward Woodward**
DS Andy Cartwright **Rafe Spall**
PC Doris Thatcher **Olivia Colman**
Rev. Philip Shooter **Paul Freeman**
Met Sergeant **Martin Freeman**
Met Chief Inspector **Bill Nighy**
Met Police Inspector **Steve Coogan**
Sergeant Turner **Bill Bailey**
Mary Porter **Julia Deakin**
James Reaper **Kenneth Cranham**
Annette Roper **Patricia Franklin**
Leslie Tiller **Anne Reid**
Dr. Robin Hatcher **Stuart Wilson**
Roy Porter **Peter Wright**
Sgt. Tony Fisher **Kevin Eldon**
PC Bob Walker **Karl Johnson**
and Robert Popper ("Not" Janine); Joe Cornish (Bob); Chris Waitt (Dave); Eric Mason (Bernard Cooper); Tom Strode Walton, Troy Woollan, Rory Lowings (Underage Drinkers); Trevor Nichols (Greg Prosser); Elizabeth Elvin (Sheree Prosser); Lorraine Hilton (Amanda Paver); Kevin Wilson, Nicholas Wilson (Butcher Brothers); Sampson (Saxon); Graham Low (The Living Statue); Adam Buxton (Tim Messenger); Stephen Merchant (Peter Ian Staker); Elvis (The Swan); Tim Barlow (Mr. Teacher); Ben McKay (Peter Cocker); Rory McCann (Michael Armstrong); Alice Lowe (Tina); Ron Cook (George Merchant); David Threlfall (Martin Blower); Lucy Punch (Eve Draper); David Bradley (Arthur Webley); Colin Michael Carmichael (Heston Services Clerk); Maria Charles (Mrs. Reaper); Alexander King (Aaron A. Aaronson); Cate Blanchett (Jeanine); Peter Jackson (Santa); Garth Jennings (Crack Addict); Edgar Wright (Shelf Stacker)

Incorruptible, by-the-book police officer Nicholas Angel is exiled to a seemingly sleepy West Country village where he teams up with local cop Danny Butterman to find out why select citizens are being gruesomely murdered.

Nick Frost, Simon Pegg

Nick Frost, Simon Pegg

Simon Pegg, Nick Frost © ROGUE PICTURES

# THE VALET

(SONY CLASSICS) aka *La Doublure*; Producer, Patrice Ledoux; Director/Screenplay, Francis Veber; Photography, Robert Fraisse; Designer, Dominique Andre; Costumes, Jacqueline Bouchard; Editor, Georges Klotz; Music, Alexandre Desplat; Casting, Francoise Menidrey; a Gaumont presentation, in association with Columbia Pictures Films Prod. France, of a Gaumont, EFVE Films, TF1 Films Prod., Kairos Films production, with the participation of Artemis, Canal Plus, CineCinema; French; Dolby; Technovision; Color; Rated PG-13; 85 minutes; American release date: April 20, 2007.

Karl Lagerfeld, Alice Taglioni

## Cast

François Pignon   **Gad Elmaleh**
Elena Simonsen   **Alice Taglioni**
Pierre Levasseur   **Daniel Auteuil**
Christine Levasseur   **Kristin Scott Thomas**
Master Foix   **Richard Berry**
Émilie   **Virginie Ledoyen**
Richard   **Dany Boon**
André Pignon   **Michel Jonasz**
Physician   **Michel Aumont**
Paul   **Laurent Gamelon**
Pascal Bouliveau   **Patrick Mille**
Louise Pignon   **Michèle Garcia**
Berman   **Philippe Magnan**
Hervé   **Jean-Yves Chilot**
Marie   **Irina Nionva**
and Philippe Beglia (Hotel Manager), Noémie Lenoir (Karine), Sandra Moreno (Levasseur's Secretary), Jean-Pol Brissart (Mauricet), Philippe Brigaud (Monsieur Hervé), Alexandre Brik (Ken, the Makeup Artist), Thierry Humbert (Paparazzi), Paulette Frantz (Richard's Mother), Thierry Nenez (Perrache), Karl Lagerfeld (Himself)

Michèle Garcia, Michel Aumont

When an incriminating photo reveals Pierre Levasseur arguing with his mistress Elena Simonsen, his attorney tracks down a passerby in the shot, with the intention of having him move in with Elena and pass him off as her real lover.

Daniel Auteuil, Kristin Scott Thomas

Gad Elmaleh, Dany Boon © SONY PICTURES CLASSICS

## JINDABYNE

Tatea Reilly

(SONY CLASSICS) Producer, Catherine Jarman; Executive Producers, Philippa Bateman, Garry Charny; Director, Ray Lawrence; Screenplay, Beatrix Christian, based on the short story "So Much Water So Close to Home" by Raymond Carver; Photography, David Williamson; Designer/Costumes, Margot Wilson; Editor, Karl Sodersten; Music, Paul Kelly, Dan Luncombe; Casting, Susie Maizels; an April Films presentation with Film Finance Corp. Australia and Babcock & Brown in association with Redchair Films; Australian; Dolby; Panavision; Color; Rated R; 123 minutes; American release date: April 27, 2007.

Leah Purcell, Deborra-Lee Furness

### Cast

Claire  **Laura Linney**
Stewart Kane  **Gabriel Byrne**
Jude  **Deborra-Lee Furness**
Carl  **John Howard**
Carmel  **Leah Purcell**
Rocco  **Stelios Yiakmis**
Billy "The Kid"  **Simon Stone**
Tom  **Sean Rees-Wemyss**
Caylin-Calandria  **Eva Lazzaro**
Vanessa  **Betty Lucas**
Gregory  **Chris Haywood**
Susan  **Tatea Reilly**
Caylin, Calandria's Mother  **Maya Daniels**
and Max Cullen (Terry); Alice Garner (Elissa); Ted Bowers (Ted); Bob Baines, Mala Ghedia (Doctors); Victoria Allen (Girl at Garage); Dean Freeman (Younger Park Ranger); Rod Mason (Elder Park Ranger); Fay Butcher (Coral); Glenda Linscott (Detective); Stephen Barker (Top Cop); Mary Kostakidis (Newsreader); Jie Pittman, Amanda Bond, Braydn Pittman (Susan's Cousins); P.J. Williams, David Evans (Laborers); Kevin Smith (Susan's Father); Pamela Young (Susan's Mother); Bronwyn Penrith, Barbara Stacy, Sylvia Scott (Aunties); Ursula Yovich (Alice, Susan's Sister); Gordon Jenkinson (Butcher); Maureen Green (Alma); Binowee Bayles (Mother); Charles "Bud" Tingwell (Minister); Biwali Bayles (Son)

Gabriel Byrne, Stelios Yiakmis, John Howard, Simon Stone

Gas station owner Stewart Kane and his friends face a moral dilemma when they discover the corpse of a young woman during their fishing trip.

Laura Linney © SONY PICTURES CLASSICS

# SNOW CAKE

Sigourney Weaver, Alan Rickman

Sigourney Weaver

(IFC FIRST TAKE) Producers, Gina Carter, Jessica Daniel, Andrew Eaton, Niv Fichman; Executive Producers, Robert Jones, Michael Winterbottom, David M. Thompson, Henry Normal, Steve Coogan; Co-Producer, Sheena Macdonald; Director, Marc Evans; Screenplay, Angela Pell; Photography, Steve Cosens; Designer, Matthew Davies; Costumes, Debra Hanson; Editor, Marguerite Arnold; Music, Broken Social Scene; Associate Producers, Larry Weinstein, Barbara Willis Sweete; Casting, John Buchan; a U.K. Film Council/Telefilm Canada presentation, in association with Baby Cow Prods., TVA Films, BBC2 Films, the Movie Network, Chum Television and Movie Central, of a Revolution Films (U.K.)/Rhombus Media (Canada) production, with participation of Astral Media, Canadian Television Fund; British-Canadian; Dolby; Color; Not rated; 111 minutes; American release date: April 27, 2007.

Carrie-Anne Moss, Alan Rickman

## Cast

Alex Hughes **Alan Rickman**
Linda Freeman **Sigourney Weaver**
Maggie **Carrie-Anne Moss**
Dirk Freeman **David Fox**
Ellen Freeman **Jayne Eastwood**
Vivienne **Emily Hampshire**
Clyde **James Allodi**
and Janet van de Graaf (Meryl), Julie Stewart (Florence), Selina Cadell (Diane Wooton), Callum Keith Rennie (John Neil), John Bayliss (Priest), Jackie Laidlaw (Louise), Susan Coyne (Deborah, a Neighbor), Robert Smith Jones (Dick, a Neighbor), Jackie Brown (Waitress), Johnny Goltz (Rookie Cop), Mark McKinney (Neighbor), Nia Roberts (Janet, the Vet), Dov Tiefenbach (Jack, the Optician), Scott Wickware (Senior Cop)

Alan Rickman, Sigourney Weaver © IFC FIRST TAKE

Following an automobile accident in which his passenger was killed, Alex Hughes contacts the girl's high-functioning autistic mom to break the bad news.

# PARIS, JE T'AIME

(FIRST LOOK) Producers, Claudie Ossard, Emmanuel Benbihy; Executive Producer, Rafi Chaudry; Co-Producers, Burkhard Von Schenk, Stefan Piech, Matthias Batthyany; Co-Executive Producers, Chris Bolzli, Gilles Caussade, Sam Englebardt, Ara Katz, Chad Troutwine, Frank Moss, Maria Kopf; Based on an original idea by Tristan Carne; Supervising Editors, Simon Jacquet, Frederic Auburtin; Music, Pierre Adenot; Designers, Bettina Von Den Steinen; Transitional Segment Directors, Frederic Auburtin, Emmanuel Benbihy; Associate Producer, Henri Jacob; Casting, Nathalie Cheron; a Victoires Intl. and Pirol Film Prods. presentation of a Victoires Intl. (France)/Pirol Film Prods. (Liechtenstein)/Filmazure (Switzerland) co-production with participation of Canal Plus; French-Lichtensteinian-Swiss; Dolby; Color; Rated R; 120 minutes; American release date: May 4, 2007.

Steve Buscemi in Tuileries © FIRST LOOK FEATURES

## MONTMARTRE

Director/Screenplay, Bruno Podalydes; Photography, Matthieu Poirot Delpech; Editor, Anne Klotz

### Cast

Young Woman **Florence Muller**
Doctor **Hervé Pierre**
Driver **Bruno Podalydès**

## QUAIS DE SEINE

Director, Gurinder Chadha; Screenplay, Paul Mayeda Berges, Gurinder Chadha; Photography, David Quesemand; Editor, Simon Jacquet

### Cast

Zarka **Leila Bekhti**
François **Cyril Descours**
Arnaud **Julien Beramis**
Manu **Thomas Dumerchez**
Black Girls **Daniely Francisque, Audrey Fricot**
Zarka's Grandfather **Salah Teskouk**

## LE MARAIS

Director/Screenplay, Gus Van Sant; Photography, Pascal Rabaud

### Cast

Marianne **Marianne Faithfull**
Elie **Elias McConnell**
Gaspard **Gaspard Ulliel**
Printer **Christian Bramsen**

## TUILERIES

Directors/Screenplay, Joel and Ethan Coen; Photography, Bruno Delbonnel

### Cast

The Tourist **Steve Buscemi**
Julie **Julie Bataille**
Axel **Axel Kiener**
Child in the Metro **Gulliver Hecq**
Mother in the Metro **Frankie Pain**

## LOIN DU 16ÈME

Directors/Screenplay, Walter Salles and Daniela Thomas; Photography, Eric Gautier

### Cast

Ana **Catalina Sandino Moreno**
Bourgeoise Mother **Marina Moncade**

## PORTE DE CHOISY

Director/Screenplay, Christopher Doyle, in collaboration with Gabrielle Keng, Kathy Li; Photography, Kathy Li; Editor, Simon Jacquet

### Cast

Monsieur Henny **Barbet Schroeder**
Madame Li **Li Xin**
Buddhist **Aurélien Blain-King**
Old Chinese Woman **Xing Xing Cheng**
Chinese Woman with Makeup **Hélène Patarot**

## BASTILLE
Director/Screenplay, Isabelle Coixet; Photography, Jean-Claude Larrieu; Editor, Simon Jacquet

### Cast

The Husband **Sergio Castellitto**
The Wife **Miranda Richardson**
The Mistress **Leonor Watling**
The Doctor **Javier Cámara**
Young Woman with Red Coat **Emilie Ohana**

## PLACE DES VICTOIRES
Director/Screenplay, Nobuhiro Suwa; Photography, Pascal Marti; Editor, Hisako Suwa

### Cast

Suzanne **Juliette Binoche**
The Cowboy **Willem Dafoe**
The Father **Hippolyte Girardot**
Justin **Martin Combes**
Isis **Roxane Pelicer**

## TOUR EIFFEL
Director/Screenplay, Sylvain Chomet; Photography, Eric Guichard; Special effects, Pieter Van Houtte, Raf Schoenmaker

### Cast

Little Jean-Claude **Dylan Gomong**
Male Mime **Paul Putner**
Female Mime **Yolande Moreau**
and Emmanuel Layotte (Café Waiter); Madeleine Malroux, Simone Malroux (Women in Café)

## PARC MONCEAU
Director/Screenplay, Alfonso Cuaron; Photography, Michael Seresin; Editor, Alex Rodríguez

### Cast

Vincent **Nick Nolte**
Claire **Ludivine Sagnier**
Sara **Sara Martins**

Li Xin, Barbet Schroeder in Porte De Choisy

## QUARTIER DES ENFANTS ROUGES
Director/Screenplay, Olivier Assayas; Photography, Eric Gautier; Editor, Luc Barnier

### Cast

Liz **Maggie Gyllenhaal**
Ken **Lionel Dray**
Joana **Joana Preiss**

## PLACE DES FÊTES
Director/Screenplay, Olivier Schmitz; Photography, Michel Amatheiu; Editor, Isabel Meier

### Cast

Hassan **Seydou Boro**
Sophie **Aïssa Maïga**

## PIGALLE
Director/Screenplay, Richard LaGravanese; Photography, Gérard Sterin; Editor, Simon Jacquet

### Cast

Bob Leander **Bob Hoskins**
Fanny Forestier **Fanny Ardant**

## QUARTIER DE LA MADELEINE
Director/Screenplay, Vincenzo Natali; Photography, Tetsuo Nagata

### Cast

The Tourist **Elijah Wood**
The Vampire **Olga Kurylenko**
Vampire's Victim **Wes Craven**

## PÊRE-LACHAISE
Director/Screenplay, Wes Craven; Photography, Maxime Alexandre; Editor, Stan Collet

### Cast

Frances **Emily Mortimer**
William **Rufus Sewell**
Oscar Wilde **Alexander Payne**

Rufus Sewell, Emily Mortimer in Pêre-Lochaise

## FAUBOURG SAINT-DENIS
Director/Screenplay, Tom Tykwer; Photography, Frank Griebe; Editor, Mathilda Bonnefoy

### Cast

Francine **Natalie Portman**
Thomas **Melchior Beslon**

Gena Rowlands in Quartier Latin

## QUARTIER LATIN
Directors, Gerard Depardieu, Frederic Auburtin; Screenplay, Gena Rowlands; Photography, Pierre Aïm; Editor, Simon Jacquet

### Cast

Ben **Ben Gazzara**
Gena **Gena Rowlands**
Café Owner **Gérard Depardieu**

## 14TH ARRONDISSEMENT
Director/Screenplay, Alexander Payne; Photography, Denis Lenoir; Editor, Simon Jacquet

### Cast

Carol **Margo Martindale**

18 brief tales taking place in Paris, as seen by 18 different filmmakers.

Margo Martindale in 14th Arrondissement

# AWAY FROM HER

Julie Christie, Gordon Pinsent

(LIONSGATE) Executive Producers, Atom Egoyan, Doug Mankoff; Co-Producer, Victoria Hirst; Producers, Daniel Iron, Simone Urdl, Jennifer Weiss; Director/Screenplay, Sarah Polley; Based on the short story "The Bear Came Over the Mountain" by Alice Munro; Photography, Luc Montpellier; Designer, Kathleen Climie; Costumes, Debra Hanson; Music, Jonathan Goldsmith; Editor, David Wharnsby; Casting, John Buchan; a Film Farm and Foundry Films production in association with Capri Releasing, HanWay Films, and Echo Lake Productions, produced with the participation of Telefilm Canada, CTF, TMN/SE/HGF, OMDC; Canadian; Dolby; Technicolor; Rated PG-13; 110 minutes; American release date: May 4, 2007.

### Cast

Fiona  **Julie Christie**
Grant  **Gordon Pinsent**
Marian  **Olympia Dukakis**
Aubrey  **Michael Murphy**
Kristy  **Kristen Thomson**
Madeleine Montpellier  **Wendy Crewson**
Dr. Fischer  **Alberta Watson**
Young Fiona  **Stacey LaBerge**
Veronica  **Deanna Dezmari**
Phoebe Hart  **Clare Coulter**
William Hart  **Thomas Hauff**
Nurse Betty  **Grace Lynn Kung**
Theresa  **Lili Francks**
Liam  **Andrew Moodie**
Mrs. Albright  **Judy Sinclair**
Michael  **Tom Harvye**
Eliza  **Carolyn Hetherington**
Singing Nurse  **Melanie Merkosky**
Mrs. Jenkins  **Jessica Booker**
Rebecca Albright  **Janet van de Graaf**
and Vanessa Vaughan (Stella), Catherine Fitch (Receptionist), Ron Hewat (Frank), Jason Knight (Young Grant), Nina Dobrev (Monica)

Grant tries courageously to accept his wife Fiona's gradual loss of memory and awareness when she is diagnosed with Alzheimer's disease and institutionalized, where she bonds with a fellow patient.

This film received Oscar nominations for Best Actress (Julie Christie) and Adapted Screenplay.

Gordon Pinsent, Kristen Thomson

Gordon Pinsent, Olympia Dukakis © LIONSGATE

# BRAND UPON THE BRAIN

Sullivan Brown

(THE FILM COMPANY/VITAGRAPH) Producers, Amy E. Jacobson, Gregg Lachow; Executive Producers, Jody Shapiro, Philip Wohlstetter, A.J. Epstein; Director, Guy Maddin; Screenplay, Guy Maddin, George Toles; Photography, Benjamin Kasulke; Editor, John Gurdebeke; Music, Jason Staczek; Designer, Tania Kupczak; Costumes, Nina Moser; Associate Producer, Brian Grant; Casting, Joy Fairfield; Canadian-American; Super 8-to-HDCAM; Black and white; Not rated; 95 minutes; American release date: May 9, 2007.

## Cast

Grown-up Guy Maddin  **Erik Steffen Maahs**
Mother  **Gretchen Krich**
Young Guy Maddin  **Sullivan Brown**
Sis  **Maya Lawson**
Chance Hale/Wendy Hale  **Katherine E. Scharhon**
Father  **Todd Jefferson Moore**
Savage Tom  **Andrew Loviska**
Neddie  **Kellan Larson**
Young Mother  **Cathleen O'Malley**
Old Father  **Clayton Corzatte**
Old Mother  **Susan Corzatte**
Murderous Sister  **Annette Toutonghi**
Oarsmen  **David Lobo, Eric Lobo**
Adopting Couple  **Sarah Harlett, Dan Tierney**
Narrator  **Isabella Rossellini**
Baby Mother  **Clara Grace Svenson**

Returning to his childhood home on Black Notch Island to paint a lighthouse, Guy Maddin's arrival brings back a flood of memories. This film played with an accompanying live orchestra.

Gretchen Krich © THE FILM COMPANY/VITAGRAPH

# 28 WEEKS LATER

(FOX ATOMIC) Executive Producers, Danny Boyle, Alex Garland; Producers, Enrique Lopez Lavigne, Andrew Macdonald, Allon Reich; Co-Producer, Bernard Bellew; Director, Juan Carlos Fresnadillo; Screenplay, Rowan Joffe, Juan Carlos Fresnadillo, Enrique Lopez Lavigne, Jesus Olmo; Photography, Enrique Chediak; Editor, Chris Gill; Music, John Murphy; Designer, Mark Tildesley; Costumes, Jane Petrie; Special Makeup Effects, Dave Bonneywell, Anthony Parker; Visual Effects Supervisor, Sean Mathiesen; Digital Visual Effects, Rising Sun Pictures, Animal Logic, LipSync Post, Rainmaker Animation & Visual Effects U.K., the Mill, the Senate Visual Effects, Rushes, Chocolate Lab., FrameStore CFC, Prime Focus; Casting, Shaheen Baig; a Fox Atomic (U.S.)/DNA Films (U.K.) presentation, in association with U.K. Film Council, of a Figment Films (U.K.)/Sogecine, Koan Films (Spain) production, in association with Dune Entertainment; British-Spanish-American; Dolby; Super 35 Widescreen; Deluxe color; Rated R; 99 minutes; American release date: May 11, 2007.

Rose Byrne, Jeremy Renner, Mackintosh Muggleton, Imogen Poots

## Cast

Don Harris **Robert Carlyle**
Maj. Scarlet **Rose Byrne**
Sgt. Doyle **Jeremy Renner**
Flynn **Harold Perrineau**
Alice Harris **Catherine McCormack**
Andy Harris **Mackintosh Muggleton**
Tammy Harris **Imogen Poots**
Gen. Stone **Idris Elba**
Karen **Emily Beecham**
Jacob **Shahid Ahmed**
Sally **Amanda Walker**
Geoff **Garfield Morgan**
Boy in Cottage **Bean El-Balawi**
DLR Soldier **Meghan Popiel**
Military Officer **Stewart Alexander**
Senior Medical Officer **Philip Bulcock**
Rooftop Soldier **Tristan Tait**
Medical Officer **William Meredith**
Bunker Soldier **Matt Reeves**
Bunker Major **Thomas Garvey**
Medical Center Lobby Soldier **Tom Bodell**
Carpark Soldier **Andrew Byron**
and Sarah Finigan, Roderic Culver, Maeve Ryan, Ed Coleman, Karen Meagher, Amanda Lawrence, Simon Delaney, Drew Rhys-Williams (Carpark Civilians); Raymond Waring (Sam); Kish Sharma (Depot Man); Jane Thorne (Depot Woman)

Left for dead by her guilt-ridden husband, Alice Harris, who seems to be immune from the infection being spread throughout England by a plague of zombies, becomes a possible hope for finding a vaccine. Sequel to the 2003 film *28 Days Later*.

Robert Carlyle © 20TH CENTURY FOX

# ONCE

Hugh Walsh, Alaistair Foley, Gerry Hendrick, Glen Hansard, Markéta Irglová

Glen Hansard

(FOX SEARCHLIGHT) Producer, Martina Niland; Executive Producer, David Collins; Director/Screenplay, John Carney; Photography, Tim Fleming; Editor, Paul Mullen; Music, Glen Hansard, Markéta Irglová; Song "Falling Slowly" by Glen Hansard, Markéta Irglová; Designer, Tamara Conboy; a Summit Entertainment release of a Samson Films production in association with the Irish Film Board and RTE; Irish; Color; Rated R; 86 minutes; American release date: May 16, 2007.

## Cast

Guy **Glen Hansard**
Girl **Markéta Irglová**
Bassist Dude **Alaistair Foley**
Singers at Party **Catherine Hansard, Pete Short, Fergus O'Farrell**
Baby **Kate Haugh**
Husband **Senan Haugh**
Heroin Addict **Darren Healy**
Lead Guitarist **Gerry Hendrick**
Guy's Dad **Bill Hodnett**
Girl's Mother **Danuse Ktrestova**
Drunk **Pat McGrath**
Bank Manager **Sean Miller**
Eamon **Geoff Minogue**
Men watching TV **Wiltold Owski, Krzysztos Tiotka, Tomek Glowacki, Attila Kouvacs**
and Marcella Plunkett (Ex-Girlfriend), Praghosa (Hari Krishna), Hugh Walsh (Timmy Drummer), Mal Whyte (Bill), Niall Cleary (Bob), Bob Hban, Bernard Gibsenen, Paul Clarke (Shop Assistants), Martina Akindojctimi, Ruslan Mannanu, Francis Usanga, Prince Tylot Khumaho, Joe Adebe (People on Stoop), Maire Walsh (Woman on Bus), Dave Cleary (Host at Party), Keith Byrne (Guy in Piano Shop)

Markéta Irglová, Glen Hansard

A part-time street musician sees his chance for fame and possible romance when a Czech immigrant with aspirations to write songs helps him put together a recording session.

2007 Academy Award winner for Best Original Song ("Falling Slowly").

Markéta Irglová, Glen Hansard © 20TH CENTURY FOX

# PRIVATE PROPERTY

Isabelle Huppert, Yannick Renier, Jérèmie Renier © NEW YORKER FILMS

(NEW YORKER) aka *Nue propriété*; Producer, Joseph Rouschop; Co-Producers, Martine de Clermont Tonnerre, Donato Rotunno; Executive Co-Producer, Arlette Zylberberg; Director, Joachim Lafosse; Screenplay, Joachim Lafosse, Francois Pirot; Photography, Hichame Alaouie; Designers, Ana Falgueres, Sabine Riche, Regine Constant; Costumes, Nathalie Du Roscoat; Editor, Sophie Vercruysse; a Tarantula (Belgium/Luxembourg)/Mact Prods. (France)/RTBF (Belgium) co-production, with the participation of Region Wallonne (Wallimage), Fonds de soutien a la production audiovisuelle du Grand-Duche de Luxembourg, Canal Plus, and Cinecinema, in association with Soficas, Cofinova 2, Sogecinema 2; Belgian-Luxembourgian-French; Dolby; Color; Not rated; 92 minutes; American release date: May 18, 2007.

## Cast

Pascale  **Isabelle Huppert**
Thierry  **Jérémie Renier**
François  **Yannick Renier**
Jan  **Kris Cuppens**
Anne  **Raphaëlle Lubansu**
Luc  **Patrick Descamps**
Dirk  **Dirk Tuypens**
Gerda  **Sabine Riche**
Jan's Friends  **Philippe Constant, Catherine Salée**
Karine  **Delphine Bibet**

Tensions erupt between divorcee Pascale and her two spoiled sons when she decides to sell the comfortable house bought by her ex-husband in order to open a bed and breakfast instead.

# THE BOSS OF IT ALL

(IFC FIRST TAKE) aka *Direktøren for det hele*; Producers, Meta Louise Foldager, Vibeke Windelov, Signe Jensen; Executive Producers, Lene Borglum, Peter Albaek; Director/Screenplay, Lars von Trier; Photography, Automavision; Editor, Molly M. Stensgaard; Costumes, Manon Rasmussen; a Zentropa Entertainments 21 (Denmark)/Memfis Film Intl. (Sweden)/Slot Machine (France)/Lucky Red (Italy) production, in association with Pain Unlimited, Trollhattan Film, Liberator2, Zik Zak Filmworks, Orione Cinematografica, with participation of DR, Film I Väst, Sveriges Television, Canal Plus; Danish-Swedish-French-Italian, 2006; Dolby; Color, 16mm-to-35mm; Not rated; 98 minutes; American release date: May 23, 2007.

## Cast

Kristoffer/Svend E  **Jens Albinus**
Ravn  **Peter Gantzler**
Finnur  **Fridrik Thor Fridriksson**
Tolk, Interpreter  **Benedikt Erlingsson**
Lise  **Iben Hjejle**
Nalle  **Henrik Prip**
Heidi A.  **Mia Lyhne**
Gorm  **Casper Christensen**
Mette  **Louise Mieritz**
Spencer  **Jean-Marc Barr**
Kisser  **Sofie Gråbøl**
Jokumsen  **Anders Hove**
Narrator  **Lars von Trier**

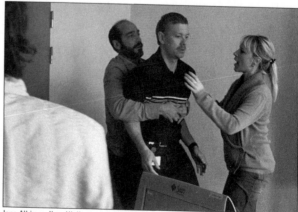

Jens Albinus, Iben Hjejle © IFC FIRST TAKE

Ravn hopes to sell his company to temperamental Icelander Finnur, only to realize that he will only do business with the non-existent phantom boss that Ravn has invented.

# GOLDEN DOOR

Charlotte Gainsborough

(MIRAMAX) aka *Nuovomondo*; Producers, Alexandre Mallet-Guy, Fabrizio Mosca, Emanuele Crialese; Executive Producers, Bernard Bouix, Tommaso Calevi; Director/Screenplay, Emanuele Crialese; Photography, Agnes Godard; Designer, Carlos Conti; Costumes, Mariano Tufano; Editor, Maryline Monthieux; Music, Antonio Castrignano; a Memento Films Production (France)/Titti Films, Respiro (Italy)/ARTE France Cinema production, in collaboration with Rai Cinema and with the participation of Canal Plus; Italian-German-French; Dolby; Super 35 Widescreen; Color; Rated PG-13; 117 minutes; American release date: May 25, 2007.

Vincenzo Amato

Charlotte Gainsborough, Vincenzo Amato, Filippo Pucillo, Aurora Quattrocchi, Francesco Casisa

## Cast

Lucy Reed  **Charlotte Gainsbourg**
Salvatore Mancuso  **Vincenzo Amato**
Donna Fortunata  **Aurora Quattrocchi**
Angelo Mancuso  **Francesco Casisa**
Pietro Mancuso  **Filippo Pucillo**
Rita D'Agonstini  **Federica de Cola**
Rosa Napolitano  **Isabella Ragonese**
Don Luigi  **Vincent Schiavelli**
Mangiapane  **Massimo Laguardia**
Don Ercole  **Filippo Luna**
Del Fiore  **Andrea Prodan**
Dr. Zampino  **Ernesto Mahieux**

Aurora Quattrocchi, Vincenzo Amato © MIRAMAX FILMS

Salvatore Mancuso and his two young sons, along with two women promised as brides, leave their impoverished life in Italy to establish themselves in America.

# ANGEL-A

(SONY CLASSICS) Producer/Director/Screenplay, Luc Besson; Photography, Thierry Arbogast; Designer, Jacques Bufnoir; Costumes, Martine Rapin; Editor, Frederic Thoraval; Music, Anja Garbarek; Special Effects, Pierre Buffin; Casting, Swan Pham; a EuropaCorp, TF1 Films, Apipoulai production with participation of Canal Plus in association with Sofica EuropaCorp.; French, 2005; Dolby; Super 35 Widescreen; Black and white; Rated R; 90 minutes; American release date: May 25, 2007.

### Cast

Andre **Jamel Debbouze**
Angela **Rie Rasmussen**
Franck **Gilbert Melki**
Pedro **Serge Riaboukine**
Head Criminal **Akim Chir**
U.S. Secretary **Olivier Claverie**
St. Lazare Woman **Solange Milhaud**
Dernier Client **Franck Olivier Bonnet**
Police Commissioner **Michel Chesneau**
and Loïc Pora, Jérôme Guesdon (Criminals); Michel Bellot (U.S. Orderly); Laurent Jumeaucourt (Le Dragueur); Grigori Manoukov (Roumain Waiter); Alain Zef (Sommelier); Jean-Marco Montalto (Receptionist); Francko Eric Balliet dit Parigo (Bodyguard); Jil Milan, Tonio Descanvelle (Angela's Clients); Venus Boone (Mother); M Thaler (Father Todd)

Facing death if he does not pay a debt, Andre attempts to jump off a bridge but instead ends up saving the life of a beautiful, would-be suicide.

Jamel Debbouze, Rie Rasmussen © SONY PICTURES CLASSICS

# PAPRIKA

Dr. Chiba, Tokita © SONY PICTURES CLASSICS

(SONY CLASSICS) Producers, Maruta Jungo, Takiyama Masao; Executive Producers, Jungo Maruta, Masao Takiyama; Director, Satoshi Kon; Screenplay, Seishi Minakimi, Satoshi Kon, based on a novel by Yasutaga Tsutsui; Photography, Michiya Kato; Editor, Seyama Takeshi; Music, Susumu Hirasawa; Art Director, Nobutaka Ike; Character Designer/Animation Director, Masashi Ando; a Madhouse, Sony Pictures Entertainment (Japan) production; Japanese, 2006; Dolby; Color; Rated R; 91 minutes; American release date: May 25, 2007.

### Voice Cast

Paprika/Dr. Astuko Chiba **Megumi Hayashibara**
Sei-jiroh Inui **Toru Emori**
Tora-taroh Shima **Katsunosuke Hori**
Kohsaku Tokita **Toru Furuya**
Detective Toshimi Kogawa **Akio Ohtsuka**
Morio Osanai **Kouichi Yamadera**
Guy **Hideyuki Tanaka**
A Doll **Satomi Kohrogi**

Dr. Atsuko Chiba's invention for recording dreams falls into the wrong hands.

Shima

# DAY WATCH

(FOX SEARCHLIGHT) aka *Dnevnoy Dozor*; Producers, Konstantin Ernst, Anatoly Maximov; Director, Timur Bekmambetov; Screenplay, Sergei Lukyanenko, Aleksandr Talal, Timur Bekmambetov, based on a novel by Sergei Lukyanenko; Photography, Sergei Trofimov; Designers, Valery Viktorov, Mukhtar Mirzakeev, Nikolai Ryabtsev; Costumes, Varya Avdyushko; Editor, Dmitri Kiselev; Music, Yuri Potyeyenko; Special Effects, Pavel Perepyolkin; Visual Effects, Nick Damico; Visual Effects Supervisor, Aleksandr Gorokhov; a First Channel Kino, Film Co. Tabbak, Baselevs Prod. Production; Russian, 2006 Dolby; Super 35 Widescreen; Color; Rated R; 139 minutes; American release date: June 1, 2007.

## Cast

Anton   **Konstantin Khabensky**
Svetlana   **Mariya Poroshina**
Geser   **Vladimir Menshov**
Olga   **Galina Tyunina**
Zavulon   **Viktor Vrezhbitsky**
Alisa   **Zhanna Friske**
Yegor   **Dima Martynov**
Kostya   **Aleksei Chadov**
Kostya's Father   **Valeri Zolotukhin**
Zoar   **Nurzhuman Ikhtymbayev**
Semyon   **Aleksei Maklakov**
Bear   **Aleksandr Samojlenko**
and Gosha Kutsenko (Ignat); Irina Yakovleva (Galina Rogova); Yegor Dronov (Tolik); Nikolai Olyalin (Inquisitor); Rimma Markova (Witch Darya); Anna Slyu (Tiger Cub, Tigryonok); Igor Lifanov (Parrot, Popugay); Sergei Trofimov (Zavulon's Secretary); Mariya Mironova (Yegor's Mother); Anna Dubrovskaya (The Vampiress); Sergei Ovchinnikov, Anton Stepanenko (Themselves)

Dima Martynov, Zhanna Friske

Anton, a member of Moscow's Night Watch, is dismayed to discover that his 12-year-old son has joined the Dark forces. Sequel to *Night Watch* (Fox Searchlight, 2006).

Mariya Poroshina

Konstantin Khabensky © 20TH CENTURY FOX

# BELLE TOUJOURS

Bulle Ogier, Michel Piccoli

(NEW YORKER) Producers, Miguel Caldhile, Serge Lalou; Director/Screenplay, Manoel de Oliveira; Photography, Sabine Lancelin; Editor, Valerie Loiseleux; Designer, Christian Magis; Costumes, Milena Canonero; a Filbox Produc- coes/Les Film d'Ici coproduction; Portuguese-French, 2006; Dolby; Color; Not rated; 72 minutes; American release date: June 8, 2007.

## Cast

Henri Husson **Michel Piccoli**
Séverine Serizy **Bulle Ogier**
Barman **Ricardo Trêpa**
Young Prostitute **Leonor Baldaque**
Old Prostitute **Julia Buisel**
Musical Director **Lawrence Foster**

Séverine Serizy tries her best to avoid a confrontation with Henri Husson, who threatens to reveal the secret about her to which only he is privy. Follow-up to *Belle du Jour* (1967; US: Allied Artists, 1968), with Piccoli repeating his role.

Michel Piccoli, Ricardo Trêpa

Bulle Ogier

Michel Piccoli © NEW YORKER FILMS

# LA VIE EN ROSE

Marion Cotillard © PICTUREHOUSE

(PICTUREHOUSE) aka *La Môme*; Producer, Alain Goldman; Co-Producer, Timothy Burrill; Director, Olivier Dahan; Screenplay, Olivier Dahan, Isabelle Sobelman; Photography, Tetsuo Nagata; Designer, Olivier Raoux; Costumes, Marit Allen; Editor, Richard Marizy; Music, Christopher Gunning; Musical Director, Edouard Dubois; Makeup, Didier Lavergne; Additional Makeup, Loulia Sheppard; Associate Producer, Catherine Morisse; Casting, Olivier Carbone; a Legende presentation of a Legende, TF1 Films Prods./Songbird Pictures (U.K.)/Okko Prods. (Czech Rep.) production; French-British-Czech; Dolby; Super 35 Widescreen; Color; Rated PG-13; 140 minutes; American release date: June 8, 2007.

## Cast

Edith Piaf  **Marion Cotillard**
Anetta  **Clotilde Courau**
Louis Gassion  **Jean-Paul Rouve**
Mômone  **Sylvie Testud**
Louis Barrier  **Pascal Greggory**
Marcel Cerdan  **Jean-Pierre Martins**
Titine  **Emmanuelle Seigner**
Louis Leplée  **Gerard Départieu**
and Catherine Allégret (Louise); Caroline Silhol (Marlene Dietrich); Alban Casterman (Charles Aznavour); Marc Barbé (Raymond Asso); Manon Chevallier (Edith, age 5); Pauline Burlet (Edith, age 8); Marc Gannot (Marc Bonel); Caroline Raynaud (Ginou); Marie-Armelle Deguy (Marguerite Monno); Valérie Moreau (Jeanne); Jean-Paul Muel (Bruno Coquatrix); André Penvern (Jacques Canetti); Mario Hacquard (Charles Dumont); Aubert Fenoy (Michel Emer); Félix Belleau (Robert Juel); Ashley Wanninger (Leplée's Assistant); Nathalie Dorval (Mireille); Chantal Bronner (Josette); Cylia Malki (Philipo); Nathalie Dahan (Yvonne); Laurent Olmedo (Jacques Pills); Harry Hadden-Paton (Doug Davis); Laurent Schilling (Claude); Dominique Bettenfeld (Albert); Édith Le Merdy (Simone Margantin); Josette Ménard (Mamy); Emy Lévy, Laura Stainkrycer, Lucie Brezovska, Vera Havelková (Brothel Girls); Jan Kuzelka (Brothel Customer); Dominique Paturel (Lucien Roupp); Nicholas Pritchard (Jameson); William Armstrong (Clifford Fisher); Martin Sochor, Frederika Smetana, Lenka Kourilova (O'Dett Audience Members); Pierre Derenne (P'tit Louis); Jan Filipensky (Fire Eater); Laura Menini (Circus Dancer); Oldrich Hurych (Clown); Mathias Honoré (M. Loyal); Diana Stewart (American Woman); Jean-Jacques Desplanque (Tony Zale); Alain Figlarz (Boxing Trainer); Robert Paturel (Boxing Ring Corner Man); Olivier Curveiller (Inspector Guillaume); Sébastien Tavel (Interviewer); Agathe Bodin (Suzanne); Nicole Dubois (Seamstress); Martin Janis (Jean Mermoz); Eric Franquelin (Etienne); Marc Chapiteau (Mitty Goldin); Maureen Demidof (Marcelle); Philippe Bricard (Man in Lannes); Olivier Raoux (Waiter); Nathalie Cox (Pin-Up); Pierre Peyrichout (Journalist); Helena Gabrielva (Drunk Woman); Jaroslav Vizner (New Year's Eve Man); Sophie Knittl, Hélène Genet (Bar Customers); Farida Amrouche (Aïcha); Lilian Cebrian (Palm Reader); Nioclas Simon (Journalist by the Church); Pascal Mottier (Boy); Thierry Guilbault (Ostende Doctor); Garrick Hagon (American Doctor); Ginou Richer (Neighbor); Vladimir Javorský (Street Spectator); Denis Menochet (Journalist in Orly); David Jahn (A Soldier); Sylvie Guichenuy (A Woman in the Street); Fabien Duval (Policeman); Maya Barsony (Girl at the Bar Counter); Paulina Nemcova (American Journalist); Rodolphe Saulnier (Barman); Fedele Papalia (Diner Waiter); Zdena Herfortova (Woman, Etoile Café); Pier Luigi Colombetti (Brasserie Owner); Olivier Carbone (Transvestite); Elliot Dahan, Isaac Dahan (Children); Laurence Gormezano (Brasserie Waitress); Jil Aigrot (Singing Voice of Adult Piaf); Cassandre Berger (Singing Voice of child Piaf); Christophe Kourotchkine (Civilian Policeman); Christophe Odent (Dr. Bernay); Robert Nebrenský (Doctor in Dreux); Jaromír Janecek (Show Manager in Dreux); Christopher Gunning, Richard Hein (Orchestra Conductors)

Sylvie Testud, Marion Cotillard

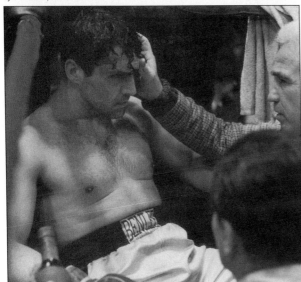

Jean Pierre-Martins

Gerard Dépardieu, Marion Cotillard

Jean-Paul Rouve, Pauline Burlet

A look at the turbulent personal and professional life of French singer Edith Piaf.

2007 Academy Award winner for Best Actress (Marion Cotillard) and Best Makeup. This film received an additional nomination for costume design.

# FIDO

Carrie-Anne Moss, Billy Connolly © LIONSGATE

(LIONSGATE) Producers, Blake Corbet, Mary Anne Waterhouse; Executive Producers, Peter Block, Jason Constantine, Patrick Cassavetti, Shelley Gillen, Daniel Iron; Co-Producers, Trent Carlson, Kevin Eastwood, Heidi Levitt; Director, Andrew Currie; Screenplay, Robert Chomiak, Andrew Currie, Dennis Heaton, from an original story by Dennis Heaton; Photography, Jan Kiesser; Designer, Rob Gray; Costumes, Mary E. McLeod; Editor, Roger Mattiussi; Music, Don Macdonald; Music Supervisor, Sarah Webster; Prosthetic Makeup FX, Todd Masters; VFX supervisor, James Tichenor; Casting, Heidi Levitt, Lynne Carrow; a TVA Films presentation of an Anagram Pictures production in association with Telefilm Canada; Canadian; Dolby; Super 35 Widescreen; Color; Rated R; 91 minutes; American release date: June 15, 2007.

## Cast

Helen Robinson **Carrie-Anne Moss**
Fido **Billy Connolly**
Bill Robinson **Dylan Baker**
and K'Sun Ray (Timmy Robinson); Henry Czerny (Mr. Bottoms); Tim Blake Nelson (Mr. Theopolis); Sonja Bennett (Tammy), Jennifer Clement (Dee Dee Bottoms), Rob LaBelle (Frank Murphy), Aaron Brown (Roy Fraser), Brandon Olds (Stan Fraser), Alexia Fast (Cindy Bottoms), Doug Abrahams (Commanding Officer), Geoff Adams (Public Service Officer), Mike Azevedo (Henderson Zombie), Raymond E. Bailey (Floyd), Mary Black (Mrs. Henderson), Clint Carlton (Returns Room Customer), Lauro Chartrand (Bezerk Zombie), Harold Courchene (Zombie Grandpa), Liam Crocker (Zombie Paperboy), Bernard Cuffling (Mr. Henderson), Andrew Hedge (Human Worker), Michael Irwin (Human Milkman), Carl-James Kalbfleisch (Child Zombie), David Kaye (Narrator), Raphael Kepinski (Collar Light Zombie), John B. Lowe (Priest), Tiffany Lyndall-Knight (Miss Mills), Barbara Moss (Helen's Mom), Michael P. Northey (Joe Petersen), Lauren Oleksewich (TV Girl), Andy Parkin (Dr. Hrothgar Geiger), Rick Pearce (Poacher Driver), Lynn Pendleton (1940s Mother), Taylor Petri (Little Girl), Glen Power (Zombie Milkman), Glenn Richards (Vicious Zombie), Jacob Rupp (Returns Room Clerk), Chad Sayn (Poacher), Adam Scorgie (Miss Mills's Boyfriend), Jan Skorzewski (Eating Zombie), Gary Slater (Father Zombie), Kevin Tyell (Zombie's Victim)

In a world where zombies have been domesticated, lonely outcast Timmy Robinson makes friends with Fido, the living-dead helper his mother has hired to keep up appearances with the neighbors.

# EAGLE VS. SHARK

(MIRAMAX) Producers, Ainsley Gardiner, Cliff Curtis; Executive Producer, Emanuel Michael; Director/Screenplay, Taika Waititi; Story, Loren Horsley, Taika Waititi; Photography, Adam Clark; Designer, Joe Bleakley; Costumes, Amanda Neale; Editor, Jono Woodford-Robinson; Music, the Phoenix Foundation; an Icon production; a Whenua Films presentation in association with the NZ Film Commission and Unison Films; New Zealand; Dolby; Whenua color; Rated R; 94 minutes; American release date: June 15, 2007.

## Cast

Lily **Loren Horsley**
Jarrod **Jemaine Clement**
Jonah **Brian Sergent**
Nancy **Rachel House**
Doug Davis **Craig Hall**
Damon **Joel Tobeck**
and Taika Cohen (Gordon); Aaron Cortesi (Duncan); Dave Fane (Eric Elisi); Rachel Forman (Kissing Girl); Adam Gardiner (Tony); Cori Gonzales-Macuer (Mark); Taneka Heke (Jarrod's Mum); Morag Hills (Vinny); Cohen Holloway (Mason); Anna Horsley (Meaty Love Girl); Gentiane Lupi (Tracy); Chelsie Preston-Crayford (Jenny); Tyrell Samia (Skateboarding Boy); Madeleine Sami (Burger Girl Customer); Bernard Stewart (Zane); Dylan Taylor (Meaty Love Boy); Joel Tobeck (Damien); Matt Wheelan (Kissing Boy); Kura Sanderson, Riley Brophy, Rosie Graham, Justin Wu (Kids)

A meeting at a costume party leads to quick sex for socially awkward Jarrod and Lily, who then struggle to build a relationship.

Jemaine Clement, Loren Horsley © MIRAMAX FILMS

# LADY CHATTERLEY

Jean-Louis Coullo'ch, Marina Hands © KINO

(KINO) Producer, Gilles Sandoz; Director, Pascale Ferran; Screenplay, Roger Bohbot, Pascale Ferran, Pierre Trividic, based on the novel *John Thomas and Lady Jane* by D.H. Lawrence; Photography, Julien Hirsch; Editors, Mathilde Muyard, Yann Dedet; Music, Beatrice Thiriet; Art Director, Alan Leonis; Costumes, Marie-Claude Albert; Sound (Dolby), Jean-Pierre Laforce; a Maia Films, Arte France Cinema, Les Films du Lendemain (France)/Saga Films (Belgium) production; French-Belgian, 2006; Dolby; Color; Not rated; 168 minutes; American release date: June 29, 2007.

## Cast

Lady Constance Chatterley  **Marina Hands**
Oliver Parkin  **Jean-Louis Coullo'ch**
Clifford Chatterley  **Hippolyte Girardot**
Mrs. Bolton  **Hélène Alexandridis**
Hilda  **Hélène Fillieres**
Constance's Father  **Bernard Verley**
Tommy Dukes  **Sava Lolov**
Harry Winterslo  **Jean-Baptiste Montagut**
Marshall  **Michel Vincent**
Kate  **Christelle Hes**
Field, the Chauffeur  **Joël Vandael**
Doctor  **Jacques De Bock**
Emma Flint  **Ninon Brétécher**
Haberdasher  **Anne Benoît**
Duncan Forbes  **Jean-Baptiste de Laubier**
Haberdahser Client  **Nathalie Eno**
Arthur  **Jean-Michel Vovk**
Miner  **William Atkinson**

In this adaptation of the second version of D.H. Lawrence's controversial novel, Lady Constance Chatterley forsakes her paralyzed, older husband Clifford to act on her desires for gamekeeper Oliver Parkin.

Jean-Louis Coullo'ch, Marina Hands

Jean-Louis Coullo'ch

# BLACK SHEEP

Peter Feeney

Oliver Driver

(IFC FIRST TAKE) Producer, Philippa Campbell; Director/Screenplay, Jonathan King; Photography, Richard Bluck; Designer, Kim Sinclair; Costumes, Pauline Bowkett; Editor, Chris Plummer; Music, Victoria Kelly; Creature Effects, WETA Workshop; Effects Designer/Supervisor, Richard Taylor; Stunts, Augie Davis; Casting, Liz Mullane; a Hoyts Distribution (in New Zealand)/IFC and Weinstein Co. (in U.S.) release of a New Zealand Film Commission presentation of a Live Stock Films production, in association with Escapade Pictures, Singlet Films; New Zealand; Dolby; Super 35 Widescreen; Color; Not rated; 86 minutes; American release date: June 22, 2007

## Cast

Henry Oldfield **Nathan Meister**
Experience **Danielle Mason**
Angus Oldfield **Peter Feeney**
Tucker **Tammy Davis**
Mrs. Mac **Glenis Levestam**
Dr. Rush **Tandi Wright**
Grant **Oliver Driver**
Oliver Oldfield **Matthew Chamberlain**
Young Henry **Nick Fenton**
Young Tucker **Sam Clarke**
Young Angus **Eli Kent**
Taxi Driver **Nick Blake**
Muldoon **Richard Chapman**
Winston **Louis Sutherland**
Brash **Ian Harcourt**
Prebble **James Ashcroft**
Mike **Mick Rose**
Were Sheep **Kevin McTurk**
Investor **Richard Whiteside**

Angus' genetic experimentation accidentally unleashes a herd of blood-thirsty sheep to terrorize the New Zealand countryside.

Danielle Mason, Nathan Meister © IFC FIRST TAKE

# VITUS

(SONY CLASSICS) Producers, Christian Davi, Christof Neracher, Fredi M. Murer; Director, Fredi M. Murer; Screenplay, Peter Luisi, Fredi M. Murer, Lukas B. Suter; Photography, Pio Corradi; Set Designer, Susanne Jauch; Costumes, Sabine Murer; Editor, Myriam Flury; Music, Mario Beretta; an FFM, Hugofilm presentation of a Vitusfilm production; Swiss, 2006; Dolby; Color; Rated PG; 120 minutes; American release date: June 29, 2007.

## Cast

Vitus von Holzen, age 12 **Teo Gheorghiu**
Vitus, age 6 **Fabrizio Borsani**
Helen von Holzen **Julika Jenkins**
Leo von Holzen **Urs Jucker**
Grandfather **Bruno Ganz**
Luisa **Eleni Haupt**
Isabel, age 12 **Kristina Lykowa**
Isabel, age 19 **Tamara Scarpellini**
Hoffman Junior **Daniel Rohr**
Hoffman Senior **Norbert Schwientek**
Gina Fois **Heidy Forster**
Conservatorium Director **Daniel Fueter**
Kindergarten Teacher **Livia S. Reinhard**
and Thomas Mathys (Doctor), Ursula Reiter (Neurologist), Stefan Witschi (Landlord), Stefan Schertenleib (Jens), Frank Demenga (Dr. Knaak)

Tired of being treated different from other kids, a 12-year-old piano prodigy pretends that a fall has caused him to lose his talent.

Julika Jenkins, Urs Jucker

Julika Jenkins, Fabrizio Borsani

Bruno Ganz, Teo Gheorghiu © SONY PICTURES CLASSICS

Daniel Rohr, Tamara Scarpellini, Heidy Forster, Bruno Ganz, Eleni Haupt

# ONE TO ANOTHER

Jean-Christophe Bouvet, Arthur Dupont

Arthur Dupont, Lizzie Brocheré

Guillaume Baché, Arthur Dupont

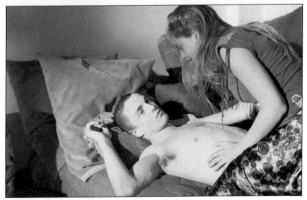

Guillaume Gouix, Lizzie Brocheré © STRAND RELEASING

(STRAND) aka *Chacun sa nuit*; Producers, Karina Grandjean, Pascal Arnold, Jean-Marc Barr; Directors, Pascal Arnold, Jean-Marc Barr; Screenplay, Pascal Arnold; Photography, Jean-Marc Barr; Designer, Serge Borgel; Costumes, Mimi Lempicka, Antigone Chilling; Editor, Chantal Hymans; Music, Irina Decermic; a La Fabrique de Films, Toloda production, in co-production with Zentropa Entertainment, Liberator Prods., with the participation of Canal Plus; French-Danish, 2006; Dolby; Color; DV-to-35mm; Not rated; 98 minutes; American release date: June 29, 2007.

## Cast

Lucie **Lizzie Brocheré**
Pierre **Arthur Dupont**
Nicolas **Guillaume Baché**
Sébastien **Pierre Perrier**
Baptiste **Nicolas Nollet**
Agnès **Valérie Mairesse**
Paul **Karl E. Landler**
Damien **Matthieu Boujenah**
Vincent Sylvaire **Jean-Christophe Bouvet**
Lieutenant **Pierre Beziers**
and Antoine Coesens (M. Saunier), Guillaume Gouix (Romain the Skinhead), Claude Lecat (Mme Saunier), Stéphane Dauch (Psychiatrist), Marion Donon (Julie), Fabrice Michel (Serge), Rémi Laugier (Crematorium Employee)

When the sexually aggressive Pierre ends up murdered, his devoted sister Lucie tries to find out who among their clique might be responsible.

# INTRODUCING THE DWIGHTS

(WARNER INDEPENDENT) aka *Clubland*; Producer, Rosemary Blight; Executive Producers, Scott Garvie, Ben Grant, Cass O'Connor, Tristan Whalley, Antonio Zeccola; Director, Cherie Nowlan; Screenplay, Keith Thompson; Photography, Mark Wareham; Designer, Nell Hanson; Costumes, Emily Seresin; Editor, Scott Gray; Music, Martin Armiger; Casting, Niki Barrett; a Film Finance Corp. Australia presentation of an RB Films production in association with Goal Post Film, Shaftesbury Films, New South Wales Film & TV Office, Sunday Night Movies, and Palace Films; Australian; Dolby; Color; Rated R; 109 minutes; American release date: July 4, 2007.

Brenda Blethyn, Philip Quast, Richard Wilson

## Cast

Jean **Brenda Blethyn**
Tim **Khan Chittenden**
Jill **Emma Booth**
John **Frankie J. Holden**
Lana **Rebecca Gibney**
Ronnie Stubbs **Philip Quast**
Shane **Russell Dykstra**
Kelly **Katie Wall**
Mark **Richard Wilson**
Tori **Tracie Sammut**
Brett **Justin Martin**
Colin **David Webb**
Sharon **Susan Kennedy**
Terry the Baker **Peter Callan**
and Paul Barry, Brendan Clearkin, Bob Marcs (The Nest Managers); Yessilia Liawijaya, Lynette Barrow, Gigi Connelly (Canteen Girls); Sheirdan Farr, Korrin Reardon, Haylee McGuire, Belinda Astridge (Showgirls); Phillip Rutter (Pokie Man); Darren Carr (Ted the Ventriloquist); Ronnie Ronalde (Whistler); Hannah Garbo, Patric Kuo (Students); Ray Nowlan, June Nowlan, Kylie Stibbard, Linda Frazer (Jill's Relatives); Louis Stibbard (Louis); Brandan Montana (Magician); Christine Davies (Magician's Assistant); Roger Fong (Shane's Boyfriend); Sky Tse, Antony Ponner (Hapless Men); Vernon Hayman (Wheelchair Man); Ellen Bailey (Bridesmaid); Kim Constable, Mark Lord, Noel Taylor, Rod Crundwell, Brenton Dehn, Malcolm Quine, Peter Cross (Wedding Reception Band)

Brenda Blethyn, Frankie J. Holden

A divorced, middle-aged entertainer, whose career has never blossomed as she had hoped, still presses on with her second-string engagements, barely noticing that her two grown sons are coping with problems of their own.

Emma Booth, Khan Chittenden © WARNER INDEPENDENT

# MY BEST FRIEND

Dany Boon, Daniel Auteuil

Daniel Auteuil

Dany Boon, Daniel Auteuil

(IFC) aka *Mon meilleur ami*; Producers, Olivier Delbosc, Marc Missonnier; Director, Patrice Leconte; Screenplay, Jérôme Tonnerre, Patrice Leconte; Story, Olivier Dazat; Photography, Jean-Marie Dreujou; Designer, Ivan Maussion; Costumes, Annie Perier Bertaux; Editor, Joëlle Hache; Music, Xavier Demerliac; Casting, Gérard Moulevrier; a Fidelite Films/TF1 Films Prod./Lucky Red production in association with Wild Bunch; French, 2006; Dolby; Widescreen; Color; Rated PG-13; 95 minutes; American release date: July 13, 2007.

## Cast

François Coste **Daniel Auteuil**
Bruno Bouley **Dany Boon**
Catherine **Julie Gayet**
Louise Coste **Julie Durand**
Étienne Delamotte **Henri Garcin**
M. Bouley **Jacques Mathou**
Mme Bouley **Marie Pillet**
Julia **Élizabeth Bourgine**
Letellier **Jacques Spiesser**
Marianne **Audrey Marnay**
and Anne Le Ny, Pierre Aussedat (At Screening of *Réponses à tout*), Philippe Du Janerand (Luc Lebinet), Fabienne Chaudat (Mme Lebinet), Marie Mergey (The Widow), Andrée Damant (Breton Passenger), Etienne Draber (Speaker), Jean-Pierre Foucault (Himself), Marine Laporte (Britney), Titouan Laporte (Léonardo)

In order to win a bet from his business colleague, François Coste, a coldhearted antiques dealer with seemingly no social life, has ten days to prove he actually has someone he can call a "best friend."

Daniel Auteuil, Julie Gayet © IFC FILMS

# CASHBACK

(MAGNOLIA) Producers, Lene Bausager, Sean Ellis; Executive Producer, Daphne Guinness; Director/Screenplay, Sean Ellis; Photography, Angus Hudson; Editors, Scott Thomas, Carlos Domeque; Music, Guy Farley; Designer, Morgan Kennedy; Costumes, Vicki Russell; Line Producer, Marshall Leviten; Associate Producer, Winnie Lee; a Left Turn Films presentation in association with Daphne Guinness of a Bausager/Ellis production; British; Dolby; Panavision; Color; Rated R; 102 minutes; Release date: July 20, 2007.

### Cast

Ben Willis  **Sean Biggerstaff**
Sharon Pintey  **Emilia Fox**
Sean Higgins  **Shaun Evans**
Suzy  **Michelle Ryan**
Jenkins  **Stuart Goodwin**
Barry Brickman  **Michael Dixon**
Matt Stephens  **Michael Lambourne**
Brian  **Marc Pickering**
and Nick Hancock (Rory), Frank Hesketh (Young Ben), Irene Bagach (Beautiful Girl), Howard Ward (Referee), Daphne Guinness (Anna Shapiro), Samantha Bloom (Mrs. Booth), Keeley Hazell (Naked Girl), Janine-May Tinsley (Natalie), Emilia Fenton (Tanya Green), Gayle Dudley (Natalie's Mum), Cherie Nichole (Shampoo Girl #2), Just Ardalana-Raikes (Time Traveller), Martin Ballantyne (Strip Club Patron), Honey Carmichael (Gothic Girl), Herika Fernanda (Gallery Visitor), Marysia Kay (Girl in Gallery)

Having trouble sleeping after breaking up with his girlfriend, Ben Willis takes a night job at a supermarket, where his artistic imagination runs wild.

Emilia Fox, Sean Biggerstaff

Irene Bagach

Emilia Fox

Shaun Evans, Sean Biggerstaff, Stuart Goodwin, Michael Dixon © MAGNOLIA PICTURES

# GOYA'S GHOSTS

(GOLDWYN/IDP) Producer, Saul Zaentz; Executive Producer, Paul Zaentz; Co-Producers, Denise O'Dell, Mark Albela; Director, Milos Forman; Screenplay, Milos Forman, Jean-Claude Carrière; Photography, Javier Aguirresarobe; Designer, Patrizia von Brandenstein; Costumes, Yvonne Blake; Editor, Adam Boome; Music, Varhan Bauer; Casting, Michelle Guish, Camilla-Valentine Isola; a Xuxa Production/Saul Zaentz production in association with Kanzaman Films, with the participation of Antena 3; Spanish-American; Dolby; Technicolororlor; Rated R; 117 minutes; American release date: July 20, 2007.

## Cast

Brother Lorenzo **Javier Bardem**
Inés/Alicia **Natalie Portman**
Francisco Goya **Stellan Skarsgård**
King Carlos IV **Randy Quaid**
Tomás Bilbatúa **José Luis Gómez**
Father Gregorio **Michael Lonsdale**
Queen Mary Luisa **Blanca Portillo**
Maria Isabel Bilbatúa **Mabel Rivera**
Napoleon Bonaparte **Craig Stevenson**
and José Alias (Coachman); Wael Al Moubayed (Deaf Interpreter to Goya); Simón Andreu (Asylum Director); Frank Baker, David Calder (Monks of the Inquisition); Carlos Bardem (French Officer); Antonio Bellido (Judge); Manolo Caro, Balbino Acosta (Familiars); Genoveva Casanova (Cortesana); Mercedes Castro (Doña Julia); Manuel de Blas, Victor Israel, Ramón Langa, Andrés Lima, Enrique Martínez (Monks); Eusebio Lázaro (Frame Maker); Emilio Linder (Man at the Church); Helena Lorentzen (Aristocrat on Balcony); Cayetano Martínez de Irujo (Wellington); Tamar Novas (Apprentice); Toni Rodriguez (Asylum Man); Benito Sagredo (Guard); Jack Taylor (Chamberlain); Aurélia Thiérrée (Henrietta); Fernando Tielve (Álvaro Bilbatúa); Unax Ugalde (Ángel Bibatúa); Julian Wadham (Joseph Bonaparte)

In late 18th Century Spain, one of Francisco Goya's models falls victim to the Inquisition.

Natalie Portman

Stellan Skarsgård

Randy Quaid

Javier Bardem © SAMUEL GOLDWYN FILMS

# SUNSHINE

Cliff Curtis

Michelle Yeoh

## Cast

Robert Capa  **Cillian Murphy**
Mace  **Chris Evans**
Cassie  **Rose Byrne**
Corazon  **Michelle Yeoh**
Capt. Kaneda  **Hiroyuki Sanada**
Dr. Searle  **Cliff Curtis**
Harvey  **Troy Garity**
Trey  **Benedict Wong**
Capt. Pinbacker  **Mark Strong**
Voice of Icarus  **Chipo Chung**
Capa's Sister  **Paloma Baeza**
Capa's Nephew  **Archie Macdonald**
Capa's Niece  **Sylvie Macdonald**

A team of scientists hopes to reignite the sun and save the planet from freezing to death.

Chris Evans, Hiroyuki Sinada, Cliff Curtis, Michelle Yeoh, Benedict Wong, Rose Byrne, Cillian Murphy

(FOX SEARCHLIGHT) Producer, Andrew Macdonald; Co-Producer, Bernard Bellew; Director, Danny Boyle; Screenplay, Alex Garland; Photography, Alwin Kuchler; Designer, Mark Tildesley; Costumes, Suttirat Anne Larlarb; Editor, Chris Gill; Music, John Murphy, Underworld; Makeup Designer, Mark Coulier; Visual Effects Supervisor, Tom Wood; Special Effects Supervisor, Richard Conway; Stunts, Julian Spencer; Casting, Donna Isaacson, Gail Stevens; a Fox Searchlight Pictures (U.S.)/DNA Films (U.K.) presentation, in association with U.K. Film Council, Ingenious Film Partners, of a DNA Films production, in association with Dune Entertainment, Major Studio Partners; British-American; Dolby; Hawk Scope/Super 35 Widescreen; Deluxe color; Rated R; 107 minutes; American release date: July 20, 2007.

Cillian Murphy © FOX SEARCHLIGHT

# THIS IS ENGLAND

Andrew Ellis, Andrew Shim, Kieran Hardcastle, Joe Gilgun, Jack O'Connell

(IFC FIRST TAKE) Producer, Mark Herbert; Executive Producers, Tessa Ross, Peter Carlton, Paul Trijbits, Kate Ogborn, Will Clarke, Hugo Heppell; Director/Screenplay, Shane Meadows; Photography, Danny Cohen; Designer, Mark Leese; Costumes, Jo Thompson; Editor, Chris Wyatt; Music, Ludovico Einaudi; Music Supervisor, John Boughtwood; a Warp Films production in association with Big Arty Prods. and Ingenious Film Partners for Film4, the UK Film Council, EM Media, Screen Yorkshire; British; Dolby; Color; 16mm-to-35mm; Not rated; 101 minutes; American release date: July 27, 2007.

Thomas Turgosse

## Cast

Shaun **Thomas Turgosse**
Combo **Stephen Graham**
Cynth **Jo Hartley**
Milky **Andrew Shim**
Lol **Vicky McClure**
Woody **Joe Gilgun**
Gadget **Andrew Ellis**
Meggy **Perry Benson**
Banjo **George Newton**
Lenny **Frank Harper**
Pukey Nicholls **Jack O'Connell**
Mr. Sandhu **Kriss Dosanjh**
Kes **Kieran Hardcastle**
Kelly **Chanel Cresswell**
Pob **Sophie Ellerby**
Shoe Shop Assistant **Hannah Walters**
Mr. Dudley **Dave Laws**
Bully **Michael Socha**
Teachers **Ian Smith, Dave Blant**
Teasing Kids **Matthew Blamires, James Burrows**
and Harpal Hayer, Terry Haywood, Nimesh Jani (Football Kids); Rosamund Hanson (Smell, aka Michelle)

Chanel Cresswell, Thomas Turgosse, Vicky McClure, Daniele Watson

After standing up to a gang of skinheads, 12-year-old Sean wins the respect of their leader and is inducted into the group.

Stephen Graham © IFC FIRST TAKE

# MOLIÈRE

(SONY CLASSICS) Producers, Olivier Delbosc, Marc Missonnier; Executive Producer, Christine de Jekel; Director, Laurent Tirard; Screenplay, Laurent Tirard, Grégoire Vigneron; Photography, Gilles Henry; Designer, Françoise Dupertuis; Costumes, Pierre-Jean Larroque, Pui Laï Huam, Gilles Bodu-Lemoine; Editor, Valerie Deseine; Music, Frédéric Talgorn; Hair Stylist, Jean-Pierre Berroyer; Casting, Stéphane Foenkinos; a Fidelite presentation of a Fidelite Films, France 2 Cinema, France 3 Cinema production, in association with Wild Bunch, with the participation of Canal Plus; French; Dolby; Panavision; Color; Rated 120 minutes; American release date: July 27, 2007.

Ludivine Sagnier, Romain Duris

## Cast

Jean-Baptiste Poquelin **Romain Duris**
M. Jourdain **Fabrice Luchini**
Elmire Jourdain **Laura Morante**
Dorante **Edouard Baer**
Célimène **Ludivine Sagnier**
Henriette Jourdain **Fanny Valette**
Louison Jourdain (Child) **Mélanie Dos Santos**
Valère **Gonzague Requillart**
Thomas **Gilian Petrovski**
Madeleine Béjart **Sophie-Charlotte Husson**
Dance Master **Arié Elmaleh**
Painting Instructor **Eric Berger**
Catherine de Brie **Anne Suarez**
Marquise du Parc **Annelise Hesme**
Gros-René **Luc Tremblais**
Monsieur **Nicolas Vaude**
Bonnefoy **Philippe Du Janerand**
Toinette **Isabelle Caubère**
Cyrano **Pierre Laplace**
Jean Poquelin **Wilfred Benaïche**
Louis Béjart **François Civil**
Pinel **Jean-Michel Lahmi**
Geneviève **Marie Gili-Pierre**
Dorante Solicitor **Francis Van Litsenborgh**
Huissier Delbosc **Yves Robin**
Huissier Missonnier **François Toumarkine**
Laquais Jourdain **Nicolas Guilllot**
and David Capelle, Frédéric Longbois (Jourdain Servants); Florence d'Azémar (Célimène's Servant); Stéphane Foenkinos (Célimène's Valet); Antoine Blanquefort (Marquis); Caroline Gillain (Louison Jourdan, 21 years); Daphné de Quatre Barbes (Dorine); Ivan Cori (Young Actor); Clio Baran (Young Actress); Jean-Claude Jay (Charles Dufresne); Julien Etienne (Precieux)

Fabrice Luchini, Romain Duris, Laura Morante

Millionaire Jourdain springs Jean-Baptiste Poquelin from debtors' prison so that the playwright can write a farce that will help his "benefactor" win widowed Célimène.

Romain Duris © SONY PICTURES CLASSICS

# BECOMING JANE

Anne Hathaway, James McAvoy

In a turn of events not unlike those in some of her subsequent novels, aspiring writer Jane Austen rebukes the idea of marrying for wealth, instead losing her heart to a penniless trainee lawyer, Tom Lefroy.

James McAvoy, Anne Hathaway

(MIRAMAX) Producers, Graham Broadbent, Robert Bernstein, Douglas Rae; Executive Producers, Nicole Finnan, Jeff Abberley, Julia Blackman, Tim Haslam; Co-Producers, James Flynn, Morgan O'Sullivan, James Saynor; Director, Julian Jarrold; Screenplay, Sarah Williams, Kevin Hood; Photography, Eigil Bryld; Editor, Emma E. Hickox; Music, Adrian Johnston; Designer, Eve Stewart; Costumes, Eimer Ni Mhaoldomhnaigh; Makeup and Hair Designer, Veronica Brebner; Casting, Gail Stevens, Gillian Reynolds; a Miramax Films, HanWay Films, U.K. Film Council, Irish Film Board presentation, in association with 2Entertain and BBC Films, of an Ecosse Films production, in association with Blueprint Pictures, Scion Films, Octagon Films; British-American; Dolby; Widescreen; Deluxe color; Rated PG; 120 minutes; American release date: August 3, 2007.

## Cast

Jane Austen **Anne Hathaway**
Tom Lefroy **James McAvoy**
Mrs. Austen **Julie Walters**
Rev. Austen **James Cromwell**
Lady Gresham **Maggie Smith**
Henry Austen **Joe Anderson**
Eliza De Feuillide **Lucy Cohu**
Mr. Wisley **Laurence Fox**
Judge Langlois **Ian Richardson**
Cassandra Austen **Anna Maxwell Martin**
John Warren **Leo Bill**
Lucy Lefroy **Jessica Ashworth**
Mr. Lefroy **Michael James Ford**
Robert Fowle **Tom Vaughan-Lawlor**
Mrs. Radcliffe **Helen McCrory**
and Guy Carleton, Russell Smith (Coachmen); Philip Culhane (George Austen); Louise Marie Kerr (Admirer); Sophie Vavassuer (Jane Lefroy); Gina Costigan (Caroline); Chris McHallem (Mr. Curtis); Don Dogarty (Michael Patric); Tara Nixon O'Neill (Wine Whore); Tom Maguire (Miscreant); Lynda Lee (Soprano)

James McAvoy

Anne Hathaway, Jessica Ashworth, Lucy Cohu © MIRAMAX FILMS

# BLAME IT ON FIDEL!

(KOCH LORBER) aka *La Faute à Fidel!*; Producer, Sylvie Pialat; Executive Producer, Mathieu Bompoint; Co-Producer (Italy), Fabio Conversi; Director/ Screenplay, Julie Gavras, based on the novel *Tutta Colpa di Fidel* by Domitilla Calamai; Script Collaborators, Arnaud Cathrine, Jacques Fieschi, Olivier Dazat; Photography, Nathalie Durand; Editor, Pauline Dairou; Music, Armand Amar; Designer, Laurent Deroo; Costumes, Annie Thiellement; Casting, Coralie Amedeo; a Gaumont presentation of a Gaumont, Les Films du Worso, B Movie, France 3 cinema co-production; French-Italian; Dolby; Widescreen; Color; Not rated; 98 minutes; American release date: August 3, 2007.

## Cast

Anna de la Mesa **Nina Kervel-Bey**
Marie de la Mesa **Julie Depardieu**
Fernando de la Mesa **Stefano Accorsi**
François de la Mesa **Benjamin Feuillet**
Bonne Maman **Martine Chevallier**
Bon Papa **Olivier Perrier**
Isabelle **Marie Kremer**
and Gabrielle Vallières (Cécile), Marie-Noelle Bordeaux (Filomena), Raphaël Personnaz (Mathieu), Mar Sodupe (Marga), Christiana Markou (Panayota), Thi Thy Tien N'Guyen (Maï-Lahn), Raphaëlle Molinier (Pilar), Carole Franck (Sister Geneviève), Marie Llano (Mother Anne-Marie), Marie Payen (Mother Hen), Lucienne Hamon (Suzanne), Francisco López Ballo (Emilio), Francisco Pizarro Saenz de Urtury (Pierre)

Impressionable 9-year-old Anna tries to grasp the political situation when her wealthy parents smuggle her father's sister and niece out of Spain, only to find themselves influenced by her strong Communist beliefs.

Julie Depardieu, Benjamin Feuillet, Stefano Accorsi © KOCH LORBER

# DANS PARIS (INSIDE PARIS)

Guy Marchard, Louis Garrel

Romain Duris © IFC

(IFC FIRST TAKE) Producer, Paulo Branco; Director/Screenplay, Christophe Honoré; Photography, Jean-Louis Vialard; Editor, Chantal Hymans; Music, Alex Beaupain; Designer, Samuel Deshors; Costumes, Pierre Canitrot; Casting, Richard Rousseau; a Gemini Films production; French, 2006; Dolby: Color; Not rated; 92 minutes; American release date: August 8, 2007.

## Cast

Paul **Romain Duris**
Jonathan **Louis Garrel**
Mirko **Guy Marchand**
Anna **Joana Preiss**
Alice **Alice Butaud**
The Mother **Marie-France Pisier**
and Helena Noguerra (The Girl on the Scooter), Judith El Zein (Girl Who Thinks It's Raining), Annabelle Hettmann (The Girl in the Window), Mathieu Funck-Brentano (The Boy with a Cigarette), Lou Rambert Preiss (Loup)

After breaking up with his girlfriend, Paul moves in with his irresponsible brother Jonathan and their father, and proceeds to plunge deeper and deeper into despair.

# 2 DAYS IN PARIS

Julie Delpy, Adam Goldberg, Adan Jodorowsky

(GOLDWYN) Producers, Julie Delpy, Christophe Mazodier, Thierry Potok; Executive Producer, Charles Paviot; Co-Producers, Werner Wiersing, Ulf Israel; Director/Screenplay/Music, Julie Delpy; Photography, Lubomir Bakchev; Art Director, Barbara Marc; Costumes, Stephan Rollot; Editor, Julie Delpy, Etienne Boussac, Jeffrey M. Werner; Associate Producer, Hubert Toint; Casting, Fabienne Bichet; a Polaris Film Prod. & Finance, Tempete Sous Un Crane Prod. (France)/3L Filmproduktion (Germany) production, in association with Back Up Media; French-German; Color; DV-to-35mm; Rated R; 94 minutes; American release date: August 10, 2007.

Adam Goldberg, Julie Delpy

## Cast

Jack **Adam Goldberg**
Marion **Julie Delpy**
Lukas **Daniel Brühl**
Anna **Marie Pillet**
Jeannot **Albert Delpy**
Rose **Alexia Landeau**
Mathieu **Adan Jodorowsky**
Manu **Alex Nahon**
Robbed Woman **Charlotte Maury-Sentier**
Vanessa **Vanessa Seward**
Gaël **Thibault De Lussy**
First Taxi Driver **Chick Ortea**
Tax Driver with Dog **Patrick Chupin**
Arab Taxi Driver **Antar Boudache**
Racist Taxi Driver **Ludovic Berthillot**
Music-Loving Taxi Driver **Hubert Toint**
Sandra **Sandra Berrebi**
Edouard **Arnaud Beunaiche**
Micha Sisinsky **Claude Harold**
and Benjamin Baroche (Doctor); Jean-Baptiste Puech, Clément Rouault (Firemen); Nanou Benhamou (Fast-Food Employee); Emma Piesse (Emma)

Julie Delpy, Marie Pillet

Tension erupts in Jack and Marion's relationship when they decide to visit her parents in Paris on their way back to New York.

Julie Delpy, Adam Goldberg, Albert Delpy © SAMUEL GOLDWYN FILMS

## MANDA BALA (SEND A BULLET)

© CITY LIGHTS PICTURES

(CITY LIGHTS PICTURES) Producers, Jason Kohn, Jared Ian Goldman, Joey Frank; Executive Producers, Julio De Pietro, Mario Kohn; Director, Jason Kohn; Photography, Heloisa Passos; Editors, Andy Grieve, Doug Abel, Jenny Golden; a Kilo Films presentation; Brazilian-American; Widescreen; Casablanca color; Not rated; 85 minutes; American release date: August 17, 2007. Documentary looking into the corruption and violence in modern Brazil, with special emphasis on an amphibian breeder, a plastic surgeon, and a professional kidnapper.

### With

Jader Barbalho, Claudio Fonteles, Helbio Dias, Juarez Avelar, Paulo Lamarao, Mario Lucio Avelar

## MR. BEAN'S HOLIDAY

(UNIVERSAL) Producers, Peter Bennett-Jones, Tim Bevan, Eric Fellner; Executive Producers, Richard Curtis, Simon McBurney; Director, Steve Bendelack; Screenplay, Hamish McColl, Robin Driscoll; Story, Simon McBurney; Original Character Creators, Rowan Atkinson, Richard Curtis; Co-Producers, Caroline Hewitt, Debra Hayward, Liza Chasin; Photography, Baz Irvine; Designer, Michael Carlin; Costumes, Pierre-Yves Gayraud; Music, Howard Goodall; Music Supervisor, Nick Angel; Editor, Tony Cranstoun; Casting, Nina Gold, Juliette Menager; a Working Title production in association with Tiger Aspect Pictures, presented in association with StudioCanal; British; Dolby; Color; Rated G; 90 minutes; American release date: August 24, 2007.

### Cast

Mr. Bean **Rowan Atkinson**
Sabine **Emma De Caunes**
and Karel Roden (Emil); Max Baldry (Stepan); Willem Dafoe (Carson Clay); Jean Rochefort (Maitre D'); Steve Pemberton (Vicar); Lily Atkinson (Lily at the Stereo); Preston Nyman (Boy with Train); Sharlit Deyzac (Buffet Attendant); Francois Touch (Busker Accordion); Arsaen Mosca, Stephane Debac (Traffic Controllers); Philippe Spall (French Journalist); Pascal Jounier (Tipsy Man); Emmanuelle Cosso (Hairdresser); Francis Coffinet (Undertaker); Catherine Hosmalin (Ticket Inspector); Zakie Delem (Woman on Bench); Anthony Morabito (Man in Toilet); Buskers: Adilson Montiero (Percussion), Michel Estrade (Trumpet), Stefan Mellino (Guitar), Francois Chanut (Double Bass), Fabien Arnaud (Banjo), Evelyne Guyon (Saxophone), Adrien Rodrigue (Violin), Francois Roche (Trombone), Bams Betga-Tchouni (Singer), Louis Gomis (DJ); Gilles Gaston Dreyfus (Station Master); Julie Fournier (Emil's Wife); Flamina Cinque (Hotel Maid); Urbain Cancelier (Bus Driver); Dimitri Radochevitch (Chicken Farmer); Luc Antoine Salmon (Man on Mobilette)

Mr. Bean causes havoc on the continent when he wins a train trip to the French Riviera.

Rowan Atkinson, Max Baldry © UNIVERSAL STUDIOS

## THE BUBBLE

(STRAND) aka *Ha-Buah*; Producers, Gal Uchovsky, Ronen Ben Tal, Amir Feingold; Executive Producers, Moshye Edry, Leon Edry, David Silber, Micky Rabinovich; Director, Eytan Fox; Screenplay, Gal Uchovsky, Eytan Fox; Photography, Yaron Scharf; Editors, Yosef Grunfeld, Yaniv Raiz; Music, Ivri Lider; Designer, Oren Dar; Costumes, Ido Dolev; Casting, Yael Aviv; an Uchovsky Fox production in association with Metro Communications, Ronen Ben Tal Prods., Fiengold Prods., United King Films, Hot and Keshet; Israeli, 2006; Dolby; Color; Not rated; 117 minutes; American release date: September 7, 2007.

### Cast

Noam **Ohad Knoller**
Ashraf **Yousef "Joe" Sweid**
Lulu **Daniella Wircer**
Yelli **Alon Freidmann**
Shaul **Zion Baruch**
Golan **Zohar Liba**
Sharon **Oded Leopold**
Rana **Ruba Blal**
Jihad **Shredy Jabarin**
Orna **Yael Zafrir**
Ella **Noa Barkai**
Chiki **Kotam Ishay**
Dalfi **Eliana Bekiyer**
Dana **Avital Barak**
and Lior Ashkenazi, Yossi Marshak (Actors in *Bent*); Housin Yassin (Ashraf's Father); Eva Khoury (Ashraf's Mother); Meirav Shefer (Noam's Mother); Ben Kitsony (Young Noam); Abed Darwhish (Young Ashraf); Zineb Darwhish (Young Rana); Anat Hadid (Young Ashraf's Mother); Ychie Darwish (Young Ashraf's Father); Nehaia Gmal (Ashraf's Neighbor); Alon Hamawi (Officer at Checkpoint); Nadav Nates (Soldier at Checkpoint); Dorin Munier (Pregnant Woman); Dani Segev (Doctor at Checkpoint); Amir Sevi (Journalist); Mira Awad (Samira); Amos Fraidlin, Gur Piepskovits, Anna Michael Landsman (Café Interviewees); Ayelet Margalit (Mrs. Tip); Miki Avital ("Third Ear" Salesman); Dikla Sachs, Gal Eylon (Britney Customers); Irit Passy (Pop Idol Customer); Keren Menachem (Soap Store Clerk); Nira Rabinowich (Friendly Customer); Orly Tobaly, Shira Rosenfeld (Soap Store Customers); Lilach Shalom (Clerk at "Time Out"); Omer Solomon, Oren Berger (Soldiers in Jeep); Nader "Steve" Natur, Tawfik Taia (Jihad's Friends); Chanit Shamir (Yelli's Mother); Moshe Rosen (Yelli's Father); Stav Meron (Yelli's Brother); Yaron Milgrom (Juggler); Dana Modan, Guy Pines, Ivri Lider, Miki Bouganim (Themselves)

Noam, a young Israeli soldier who shares a flat in Tel Aviv with another gay man and a straight woman, hopes to accommodate a Palestinian on whom he has developed a crush when the latter shows up at his door, looking for a place to stay after losing his ID card.

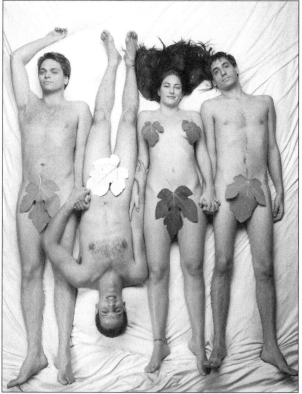

Ohad Knoller, Yousef "Joe" Sweid, Daniella Wircer, Alon Freidmann

Yousef "Joe" Sweid, Daniella Wircer, Alon Freidmann, Ohad Knoller

# DECEMBER BOYS

(WARNER INDEPENDENT) Producer, Richard Becker; Co-Producer, Jay Sanders; Executive Producers, Jonathan Shteinmen, Hal Gaba; Director, Rod Hardy; Screenplay, Marc Rosenberg, based on the novel by Michael Noonan; Photography, Dave Connell; Designer, Les Binns; Costumes, Marriott Kerr; Editor, Dany Cooper; Music, Carlo Giacco; a Film Finance Corp., South Australian Film Commission, Becker Entertainment, Village Roadshow Pictures presentation of a Richard Becker production, in association with MB2 Film, Media; Australian; Dolby; Super 35 Widescreen; Color; Rated PG-13; 103 minutes; American release date: September 14, 2007.

Lee Cormie, Christian Byers, James Fraser, Daniel Radcliffe

### Cast

Maps **Daniel Radcliffe**
Misty **Lee Cormie**
Spark **Christian Byers**
Spit **James Fraser**
Lucy **Teresa Palmer**
Teresa **Victoria Hill**
Fearless **Sullivan Stapleton**
Bandy McAnsh **Jack Thompson**
Mrs. McAnsh **Kris McQuade**
Father Scully **Frank Gallacher**
Narrator/Adult Misty **Max Cullen**
Shellback **Ralph Cotterill**
Watson **Paul Blackwell**
Reverend Mother **Judi Farr**
Sister Beatrice **Carmel Johnson**
Sister Edna **Carole-Anne Fooks**
and Rory Walker (Father); Suzie Wilks (Mother); Michael Norman (Adult Spark); Mike Welton (Adult Spit); Kobe Donaldson (Willie); Julian Jones (Older Boy); Andy McPhee (Foreman); Laura Weston (Curvy Blonde); Kasey Willson, Susie Struth, Anna Westley (Cartwheeling Nuns)

Four boys are sent from an Outback orphanage for an idyllic "holiday" by the sea, where they hope someone will want to adopt them.

Christian Byers, Daniel Radcliffe, Lee Cormie © WARNER INDEPENDENT PICTURES

Teresa Palmer, Daniel Radcliffe

# EASTERN PROMISES

(FOCUS) Producers, Paul Webster, Robert Lantos; Executive Producers, Stephen Garrett, David M. Thompson, Jeff Abberley, Julia Blackman; Co-Producer, Tracey Seaward; Director, David Cronenberg; Screenplay, Steve Knight; Photography, Peter Suschitzky; Designer, Carol Spier; Costumes, Denise Cronenberg; Editor, Ronald Sanders; Music, Howard Shore; Casting, Deirdre Bowen, Nina Gold; a Kudos Pictures/Serendipity Point Films production in association with Scion Films, in association with Astral Media, Coros Entertainment, and Telefilm Canada, presented in association with BBC Films; British-Canadian; Dolby; Deluxe color; Rated R; 100 minutes; American release date: September 14, 2007.

Viggo Mortensen, Naomi Watts © FOCUS FEATURES

### Cast

Nikolai **Viggo Mortensen**
Anna **Naomi Watts**
Kirill **Vincent Cassel**
Semyon **Armin Mueller-Stahl**
Helen **Sinéad Cusack**
Azim **Mina E. Mina**
Stepan **Jerzy Skolimowski**
Yuri **Donald Sumpter**
Ekrem **Josef Altin**
Soyka **Aleksandar Mikic**
Tatiana **Sarah-Jeanne Labrosse**
Chemist **Badi Uzzaman**
Nurse **Dona Croll**
Dr. Aziz **Raza Jaffrey**
Maria **Shannon-Fleur Roux**
Senior Officer **Rhodri Wyn Miles**
Kirilenko **Tereza Srbova**
Valery **Michael Sarne**
Customer **Lalita Ahmed**
Tatiana's Voice **Tatiana Maslany**
Violin Girl **Lillibet Langley**
Azim's Wife **Mia Soteriou**
Head Waiter **Radoslaw Kaim**
Pimp **Elisa Lasowski, Cristina Catalina, Alice Henley**
Prostitutes **Faton Gerbeshi**
Chechens **David Papava, Tamer Hassan**
Junior Waiter **Gergo Danka**
and Boris Isarov, Yuri Klimov (Russian Bosses); Andrzej Borkowski (The Gypsy); Olegar Fedoro (Tattooist)

Mina E. Mina, Vincent Cassel, Viggo Mortensen

The diary of a girl who has died in childbirth ends up with hospital midwife Anna, who doesn't realize she holds an explosive piece of incriminating evidence against members of the Russian mafia.

This film received an Oscar nomination for Best Actor (Viggo Mortensen).

Viggo Mortensen, Armin Mueller-Stahl

# SILK

(PICTUREHOUSE) Producers, Niv Fichman, Nadine Luque, Domenico Procacci, Sonoko Sakai; Executive Producers, Tom Yoda, Yasushi Shiina, Akira Ishii, Camela Galano, Jonathan Debin, Patrice Theroux, Alessandro Baricco; Director, François Girard; Screenplay, François Girard, Michael Golding, based on the novel by Alessandro Baricco; Photography, Alain Dostie; Editor, Pia Di Ciaula; Music, Ryuichi Sakamoto; Designers, Francois Seguin, Emita Frigato (Italy), Fumio Ogawa (Japan); Costumes, Carlo Poggioli, Kazuko Kurosawa; Casting, Susie Figgis; presented in association with Alliance Atlantis (Canada)/Asmik Ace Entertainment (Japan)/Medusa Film (Italy) of a Rhombus Media (Canada)/Fandango (Italy)/Bee Vine Pictures (Japan) production, in association with Productions Soie, Vice Versa Films, with the participation of IFF/CINV, Telefilm Canada, T.Y. Limited, the Works Media Group; Canadian-Japanese-Italian; Dolby; Super 35 Widescreen; Deluxe color; Rated R; 109 minutes; American release date: September 14, 2007.

Michael Pitt, Keira Knightley

## Cast

Hervé Joncour **Michael Pitt**
Hélène Joncour **Keira Knightley**
Hara Jubei **Kôji Yakusho**
Baldabiou **Alfred Molina**
Madame Blanche **Miki Nakatani**
Ludovic **Mark Rendall**
The Girl **Sei Ashina**
Mayor Joncour **Kenneth Welsh**
Umon **Jun Kunimura**
Trader **Callum Keith Rennie**
Priest **Carlo Cecchi**
Verdun **Toni Bertorelli**
Café Verdun Men **Tony Vogel, Luca De Bei**
Mme. Joncour **Martha Burns**
Clerk **Michael Golding**
Béatrice Berbek **Chiara Stampone**
M. Chabert **Marc Fiorini**
M. Loiseau **Leslie Csuth**
and Toru Tezuka (Japanese Guide); Hiroya Morita, Hiroshi Oguchi, Michio Akahane (Japanese Elders); Akini Ando (Ronin); Kanata Hongô (Japanese Boy); Dimitri Carella, Dominick Carella (2-Year-Old Ludovic); Naoko Watanabe (Japanese Girl); Honjo Hidetaro (Shamisen Player); Nana Nagao, Saki Aoi (Geishas); Yuya Takagawa, Taro Suwa (Japanese Traders); Katy Saunders, Maddalena Maggi (Brothel Hostesses); Miki Nakatani (Madame Blanche); Max Malatesta (Customs Officer); Joel Adams (4-Year-Old Ludovic); Edward Licht (Diplomat); Domenico Procacci (Ambassador); Nicola Tovaglione (10-Year-Old Ludovic); Francesco Carnelutti (Doctor); Makoto Inamiya, Makoto Matsubara, Yuki Kawanishi, Hidenori Shimizu, Hiroki Takano (Japanese Traders, Elders)

Alfred Molina, Michael Pitt © PICTUREHOUSE

After marrying a beautiful young schoolteacher, Hervé Joncour heads off on a long journey that leads him to Japan, where he hopes to find uninfected silkworm eggs.

# RESIDENT EVIL: EXTINCTION

Milla Jovovich

(SONY PICTURES ENTERTAINMENT) Producers, Bernd Eichinger, Samuel Hadida, Robert Kulzer, Jeremy Bolt, Paul W.S. Anderson; Executive Producers, Martin Moszkowicz, Victoria Hadida, Kelly Van Horn; Director, Russell Mulcahy; Screenplay, Paul W.S. Anderson, based on the Capcom video game *Resident Evil*; Photography, David Johnson; Designer, Eugenio Caballero; Costumes, Joseph Porro; Editor, Niven Howie; Music, Charlie Clouser; Visual Effects Supervisors, Dennis Berardi, Evan Jacobs; Creature Designer/Supervisor, Patrick Tatopoulos; Casting, Victoria Burrows, Scot Boland; a Screen Gems/Davis Films/Constantin Film (U.K.) presentation of a Constantin Film (U.K.)/Davis Films/Impact Pictures (Canada) production; British-Canadian; Dolby; Super 35 Widescreen; Deluxe color; Rated R; 94 minutes; American release date: September 21, 2007.

## Cast

Alice **Milla Jovovich**
Carlos Olivera **Oded Fehr**
Claire Redfield **Ali Larter**
Dr. Isaacs **Iain Glen**
Betty **Ashanti**
Mikey **Christopher Egan**
K-Mart **Spencer Locke**
and Matthew Marsden (Slater); Linden Ashby (Chase); Jason O'Mara (Albert Wesker); Mike Epps (L.J.), Joe Hursley (Otto); John Eric Bentley (Umbrella Tech); James Tumminia (Lab Tech); Kirk B.R. Woller (Scientist); Rick Cramer (Ice Hockey, Corridor Guard); Madeline Carroll (White Queen); Peter O'Meara (British Envoy); William Abadie (French Envoy); Ramón Franco (Runty); Shane Woodson (Piggy); Valorie Hubbard (Ma); Geoff Meed (Pock Mark); Rusty Joiner (Eddie); Brian Steele (Rancid, Tyrant); Connor McCoy (Small Boy); Gary A. Hecker (Tyrant Voice); Gary Hudson (Umbrella Captain)

Having developed a super form of telekinesis, Alice is sought by the Umbrella Corp. for diabolic means, while battling the hordes of zombies roaming the mostly decimated landscape.

Sequel to *Resident Evil* (Screen Gems, 2002) and *Resident Evil: Apocalypse* (2004), with Jovovich repeating her role and Fehr returning from the second installment.

Ashanti

Ali Larter, Oded Fehr, Milla Jovovich © SCREEN GEMS

# LUST, CAUTION

Lee-Hom Wang, Yuen Johnson, Ying-hsien Kao

Lee-Hom Wang (center)

(FOCUS) aka *Se, Jie*; Producers, Bill Kong, Ang Lee, James Schamus; Executive Producers, Ren Zhonglun, Darren Shaw; Co-Producers, Doris Tse, David Lee; Director, Ang Lee; Screenplay, Wang Hui-ling, James Schamus, based on the short story by Eileen Chang; Photography, Rodrigo Prieto; Editor, Tim Squyres; Music, Alexandre Desplat; Designer/Costumes, Pan Lai; Casting, Rosanna Ng; a Haishang Films presentation, in association with Focus Features, River Road Entertainment, Sil-Metropole Organisation, Shanghai Film Group Corp.; Hong Kong-American-Chinese; Dolby; Deluxe color; Rated NC-17; 157 minutes; American release date: September 28, 2007.

### Cast

Mr. Yee **Tony Leung Chiu Wai**
Wang Jiazhi **Wei Tang**
Mrs. Yee **Joan Chen**
Kuang Yu Min **Lee-Hom Wang**
Old Wu **Chung Hua Tou**
Lai Shu Jin **Chih-ying Chu**
Huang Lei **Ying-hsien Kao**
Liang Jun Sheng **Yue-Lin Ko**
Auyang Ling Wen **Johnson Yuen**
Tsao **Kar Lok Chin**
Ma Tai Tai **Su Yan**
Hsiao Tai Tai **Caifei He**
Wang's Aunt **Ruhui Song**
Jewelry Shop Manager **Anupam Kher**
Leung Tai Tai **Liu Jie**
Liao Tai Tai **Hui-Ling Wang**
and Akiko Takeshita (Japanese Tavern Boss); Hayato Fujiki (Japanese Colonel Sato); Yu Lai Cheng (HKU Theater Audience); Li Dou (Old Man at Bookstore); Yuji Kojima (Japanese Commander Taicho);

Wei Tang, Tony Leung Chiu Wai

During the Japanese occupation of Shanghai, a resistance group recruits young Wang Jiazhi to insinuate herself into the confidence of traitorous businessman Yee in hopes that she will be able to assassinate him, only to have Wang fall unexpectedly in love with him.

Joan Chen, Wei Tang, Tony Leung Chiu Wai © FOCUS FEATURE

# CONTROL

Sam Riley

Sam Riley, Alexandra Maria Lara

(WEINSTEIN CO.) Producers, Orian Williams, Anton Corbijn, Todd Eckert; Executive Producers, Iain Canning, Akira Ishii, Korda Marshall, Lizzie Francke; Co-Producers, Peter Heslop, Deborah Curtis, Tony Wilson; Director, Anton Corbijn; Screenplay, Matt Greenhalgh, based on the book *Touching From the Distance* by Deborah Curtis; Photography, Martin Ruhe; Designer, Chris Richmond; Editor, Andrew Hulme; Music, New Order; a Becker Intl. (Australia) presentation of a Northsee Ltd (U.K.) production, in association with EM Media (U.K.)/IFF, CINV, 3 Dogs and a Pony (Japan)/Warner Music (U.K.); British-Australian-Japanese; Dolby; Black and white; Rated R; 121 minutes; American release date: October 10, 2007.

Toby Kebbell, Sam Riley, James Anthony Pearson, Joe Anderson, Harry Treadway, Craig Parkinson

## Cast

Ian Curtis  **Sam Riley**
Debbie Curtis  **Samantha Morton**
Tony Wilson  **Craig Parkinson**
Annik Honoré  **Alexandra Maria Lara**
Peter Hook  **Joe Anderson**
Bernard Summer  **James Anthony Pearson**
Rob Gretton  **Toby Kebbell**
Stephen Morris  **Harry Treadway**
Terry Mason  **Andrew Sheridan**
Twinny  **Robert Shelly**
Nick Jackson  **Matthew McNulty**
Martin Hannett  **Ben Naylor**
Public GP  **Herbert Grönemeyer**
Tramp  **Nigel Harris**
Corrine Lewis  **Nicola Harrison**
Earnest Richards  **Tim Plester**

Sam Riley, Samantha Morton © WEINSTEIN CO.

The true story of the troubled life of Ian Curtis, lead singer for the British punk band Joy Division.

# SLEUTH

(SONY CLASSICS) Producers, Jude Law, Simon Halfon, Tom Sternberg, Marion Pilowsky, Kenneth Branagh, Simon Moseley; Co-Producer, Ben Jackson; Director, Kenneth Branagh; Screenplay, Harold Pinter, based on the play by Anthony Shaffer; Photography, Haris Zambarloukos; Editor, Neil Farrell; Music, Patrick Doyle; Designer, Tim Harvey; Costumes, Alexandra Byrne; Makeup/Hair/Prosthetics Designer, Eileen Kastner-Delago; Visual Effects Supervisor, Richard Higham; a Riff Raff (U.S.)/Timnick Films (U.K.) production, presented with Castle Rock Entertainment; British-American; Dolby; Panavision; Deluxe color; Rated R; 88 minutes; American release date: October 12, 2007.

Jude Law

## Cast

Andrew Wyke    **Michael Caine**
Milo Tindle    **Jude Law**
Man on TV    **Harold Pinter**

Confronted by his wife's lover, well-to-do mystery author Andrew Wyke exacts his revenge by persuading the younger man to commit a fake robbery.

Remake of the 1972 20th Century Fox release of the same name that starred Laurence Olivier and Michael Caine.

Michael Caine, Jude Law

Michael Caine

Michael Caine, Jude Law © SONY PICTURES CLASSICS

# ELIZABETH: THE GOLDEN AGE

Abbie Cornish, Cate Blanchett, Christian Brassington

(UNIVERSAL) Producers, Tim Bevan, Eric Fellner, Jonathan Cavendish; Executive Producers, Debra Hayward, Liza Chasin, Michael Hirst; Co-Producer, Mary Richards; Director, Shekhar Kapur; Screenplay, William Nicholson, Michael Hirst; Photography, Remi Adefarasin; Designer, Guy Hendrix Dyas; Costumes, Alexandra Byrne; Editor, Jill Bilcock; Music, Craig Armstrong, Ar Rahman; Music Supervisor, Nick Angel; Visual Effects Supervisor, Richard Stammers; Makeup and Hair Designer, Jenny Shircore; Cate Blanchett's Makeup and Hair, Morag Ross; Stunts, Greg Powell; Casting, Fiona Weir; a Working Title production presented in association with StudioCanal with MP Zeta; British-French; Dolby; Super 35 Widescreen; Deluxe color; Rated PG-13; 114 minutes; American release date: October 12, 2007.

Clive Owen © UNIVERSAL STUDIOS

## Cast

Queen Elizabeth I  **Cate Blanchett**
Sir Francis Walsingham  **Geoffrey Rush**
Sir Walter Raleigh  **Clive Owen**
Robert Reston  **Rhys Ifans**
King Philip II of Spain  **Jordi Molla**
Bess Throckmorton  **Abbie Cornish**
Mary Stuart  **Samantha Morton**
Sir Amyas Paulet  **Tom Hollander**
Spanish Archbishop  **Antony Carrick**
Dr. John Dee  **David Threlfall**
Thomas Babington  **Eddie Redmayne**
Lord Howard  **John Shrapnel**
Sir Christopher Hatton  **Laurence Fox**
Calley  **Adrian Scarborough**
Francis Throckmorton  **Steven Robertson**
Infanta  **Aimee King**
Annette  **Susan Lynch**
Laundry Woman  **Elise McCave**
Margaret  **Penelope McGhie**
Savage  **Stuart McLoughlin**
Palace Doorkeeper  **Robert Styles**
Don Guerau De Spes  **William Houston**
Court Ladies  and **Coral Beed, Rosalind Halstead**
Manteo  **Steven Loton**
Wanchese  **Martin Baron**
and David Armand (Walsingham's Agent); Jeremy Barker (Ramsey); George and Innes (Burton); Adam Godley (William Walsingham); Kirstin Coulter Smith (Mary Walsingham); Kelly Hunter (Ursula Walsingham); Christian Brassington (Archduke Charles); Robert Cambrinus (Count Georg von Helfenstein); Sam Spruell (Torturer); Tim Preece (Old Throckmorton); Vidal Sancho (Spanish Minister); Benjamin May (Dance Master); David Sterne (Cellarman); Kate Fleetwood (Woman with Baby); Glenn Doherty (Royal Servant); Chris Brailsford (Dean of Peterborough); Dave Legeno (Executioner); Antony Carrick (Spanish Archbishop); David Robb (Admiral Sir William Winter); Alex Giannini, Joe Ferrera (Spanish Officers); Jonathan Bailey, Alexander Barnes, Charles Bruce, Jeremy Cracknell, Benedict Green, Adam Smith, Simon Stratton, Crispin Swayne (Courtiers); Kitty Fox, Kate Lindesay, Katherine Templar (Mary Stuart's Ladies-in-Waiting); Hayley Burroughs, Kirsty McKay, Lucia Ruck Keene, Lucienne Venisse-Back (Queen Elizabeth's Ladies-in-Waiting)

Queen Elizabeth I faces the threat of Catholic traitors under the influence of her cousin Mary Stuart and the possibility of war with Spain. Sequel to the 1998 Gramercy film *Elizabeth,* with Blanchett and Rush repeating their roles.

A 2007 Academy Award winner for Best Costume Design, this film received an additional nomination for Best Actress (Cate Blanchett).

# O JERUSALEM

Ian Holm, Tovah Feldshuh © GOLDWYN FILMS

(GOLDWYN) Producers, Andre Djaoui, Elie Chouraqui, Jean-Charles Levy, Jean Frydman, Andy Grosch; Executive Producer, David Korda; Co-Producers, David Korda, Jeff Geoffray, Walter Josten, Jeff Konvitz, Mark Damon, Marcus Schofer; Director, Elie Chouraqui; Screenplay, Elie Chouraqui, Didier Lepecheur, based on the novel by Dominique Lapierre, Larry Collins; Photography, Giovanni Fiore Coltellacci; Set Designer, Giantito Burchiellaro; Costumes, Mimi Lempicka; Editor, Jacques Witta; Music, Stephen Endelman; Associate Producers, Caroline Dhainaut-Nollet, Anouk Nora, Laure-Anne Rossignol, Patrick Irwin, Nicolas Manuel; a Les Films De L'Instant, France 2 Cinema (France)/Cinegram (Greece)/Films 18 (U.K.)/Titania Produczioni (Italy)/GG Israel Studios (Israel) co-production, in association with Forecast Pictures (France)/VIP Medienfonds 3, VIP Medienfonds 4 (Germany)/Rising Star, Blue Rider (U.S.)/Box Film (U.K.), with the participation of Canal Plus; French-Greek-British-Italian-Israeli-German-American; Dolby; Color; Rated R; 100 minutes; American release date: October 17, 2007.

### Cast

Bobby Goldman **J.J. Field**
Saïd Chahine **Saïd Taghmaoui**
Roni **Daniel Lundh**
Jacob **Mel Raido**
David Levin **Patrick Bruel**
Hadassah **Maria Papas**
Abdel Khader **Peter Polycarpou**
and Ian Holm (Ben Gurion); Tovah Feldshuh (Golda Meir); Tom Conti (Sir Cunningham); Cécile Cassel (Jane), Mhairi Steenbock (Cathy), Shirel (Yaël), Anatol Yusef (Major Tell); Jamie Harding (Amin Chahine), Robert Atiko (Jamil Mordam), Daniel Ben Zenou (Daoud), John Howarth (Husseini), Dominic Jephcott (Major Stevens), Daniel Kischinovsky (Sergei), Ryan Kruger (Jewish Extremist), Derek Lawson (Mechanic), Matthew Marsh (Sir Gordon), Gordon Newell (Harry), Christopher Simon (Malmond Pasha), Jonathan Uziel (Post Manager), René Zagger (Golan)

The friendship between two Jews and an Arab Muslim is tested during the birth of Israel.

# DARKBLUEALMOSTBLACK

(STRAND) aka *Azuloscurocasinegro*; Executive Producer, Jose Antonio Felez; Director/Screenplay, Daniel Sanchez Arevalo; Photography, Juan Carlos Gomez; Editor, Nacho Ruiz Capillas; Music, Pascal Gaigne; Art Director, Federico Garcia Cambero; a Tesela P.C. production with the participation of TVE, Canal Plus; Spanish; Dolby; Widescreen; Color; Not rated; 105 minutes; American release date: October 19, 2007.

### Cast

Jorge **Quim Gutiérrez**
Paul **Marta Etura**
Israel **Raúl Arévalo**
Antonio **Antonio de la Torre**
Andrés **Héctor Colomé**
Natalia **Eva Pallarés**
Fernando **Manuel Morón**
Ana **Ana Wagener**
Roberto **Roberto Enríquez**
and Natalia Mateo (Official); Alba Gárate (Alba); Marta Aledo (Bank Employee); Carmen Arévalo (Master of Ceremonies); Joaquin Notario, Esther Ortega, Fernando Lage, Alex O'Dogherty (Staff); Daniel Muriel (Gonzalo); Julián Villagrán (Emilio); Teresa Soria Ruano (Intern); Francisco Javier Mendo Flores (Prisoner); Mila Kusmina (Boy's Mother); Belén Chanes (Prison Official); Nacho Sandoval (Intern with Broom); María Gómez Macua (Bebé)

Jorge is forced to put his own life and career on hold when his father suffers a debilitating stroke, while his friend Israel begins to question his sexuality after finding out a secret about his own dad.

Quim Gutiérrez, Raúl Arévalo © STRAND RELEASING

# SOUTHLAND TALES

Jon Lovitz, Cheri Oteri

(GOLDWYN/DESTINATION) Produced by Sean McKittrick, Bo Hyde, Kendall Morgan, Matthew Rhodes; Executive Producers, Bill Johnson, Jim Seibel, Oliver Hengst, Katarina K. Hyde, Judd Payne, Tedd Hamm; Director/Screenplay, Richard Kelly; Photography, Steven Poster; Designer, Alexander Hammond; Costumes, April Ferry; Editor, Sam Bauer; Music, Moby; Special Effects Supervisor, Thomas Tannenberger; Casting, Venus Kanani, Mary Vernieu; a Universal Pictures and Cherry Road Films presentation of a Cherry Road Films/Darko Entertainment and MHF Zweite Academy Film production in association with Inferno Distribution and Eden Roc Productions with Persistent Entertainment; German-American-French; Dolby; Panavision; Color; Rated R; 144 minutes; American release date: November 14, 2007.

Sarah Michelle Gellar, Dwayne Johnson © GOLDWYN/DESTINATION

## Cast

Boxer Santaros/Jericho Kane **Dwayne Johnson**
Roland Taverner/Ronald Taverner **Seann William Scott**
Krysta Kapowski/Krysta Now **Sarah Michelle Gellar**
Dr. Soberin Exx **Curtis Armstrong**
Bergie Taverner **Robert Benz**
Bing Zinneman **Todd Berger**
Brandt Huntington **Joe Campana**
Jimmy Hermosa **Aaron Dillar**
Cyndi Pinziki **Nora Dunn**
Starla Von Luft **Michele Durrett**
Shane Laverne **Jaret Gardiner**
General Teena MacArthur **Janeane Garofalo**
Dr. Inga Von Westphalen **Beth Grant**
Dion Warner/Dion Element **Wood Harris**
Dr. Linda Lao **Jinah Kim**
Walter Mung **Christopher Lambert**
Vaughn Smallhouse **John Larroquette**
Serpentine **Bai Ling**
Deena Storm **Gianna Luchini**
Bart Bookman **Jon Lovitz**
Sheena Gee **Abbey McBride**
Madeline Frost Santaros **Mandy Moore**
Kenny Chan **Mike Nielsen**
Senator Bobby Frost **Holmes Osborne**
Zora Charmichaels **Cheri Oteri**
Veronica Mung/Dream **Amy Poehler**
Martin Kefauver **Lou Taylor Pucci**
Nana Mae Frost **Miranda Richardson**
Shoshana Cox **Jill Ritchie**
Seamus Storm **Kevin Robertson**
Dr. Katarina Kuntzler **Zelda Rubinstein**
Fortunio Balducci **Will Sasso**
Baron Von Westphalen **Wallace Shawn**
Hideo Takehashi **Sab Shimono**
Simon Theory **Kevin Smith**
Dennis Voogler **Phil Sternberg**
Private Pilot Abilene **Justin Timberlake**
Teri Riley **Lisa K. Wyatt**
Themselves **Carlos Amezcua, Rebekah Del Rio, Lisa Feinstein**
UPU 4 Officers **Chris Ciulla, Shannon Holmes**
Reporter **Shari Dunn**
Soldier Falcon **Jon Falcone**
Megazepplin Waitress **Katherine Kendall**

Following a nuclear attack, a group of disparate characters face a fascistic American government.

# THE DIVING BELL AND THE BUTTERFLY

(MIRAMAX) aka *Le Scaphandre et le papillon*; Producers, Kathleen Kennedy, Jon Kilik; Executive Producers, Pierre Grunstein, Jim Lemley; Director, Julian Schnabel; Screenplay, Ronald Harwood, based on the book *Le Scaphandre et le papillon* by Jean-Dominique Bauby; Photography, Janusz Kaminski; Set Designers, Michel Eric, Laurent Ott; Costumes, Olivier Beriot; Editor, Juliette Welfing; Music, Paul Cantelon; Music Supervisor, Julian Schnabel; Visual Effects Supervisors, Malika Mazaurie, Yann Blondel; Visual Effects, Eclair; Associate Producer, Leonard Glowinski; a Pathe Renn Production presentation, in co-production with France 3 Cinema, with the support of La Region Nord, with the participation of Canal Plus and Cinecinema, in association with Banque Populaire Images 7, in association with the Kennedy/Marshall Co. and Jon Kilik; French; Dolby; Color; Rated PG-13; 114 minutes; American release date: November 30, 2007.

Marie-Josée Croze

## Cast

Jean-Dominique Bauby **Mathieu Amalric**
Céline Desmoulin **Emmanuelle Seigner**
Henriette Durand **Marie-Josée Croze**
Claude **Anne Consigny**
Dr. Lepage **Patrick Chesnais**
Roussin **Niels Arestrup**
Marie Lopez **Olatz López Garmendia**
Father Lucien **Jean-Pierre Cassel**
Joséphine **Marina Hands**
Papinou **Max Von Sydow**
Laurent **Isaach De Bankolé**
Empress Eugénie **Emma de Caunes**
Dr. Mercier **Jean-Philippe Écoffey**
and Gérard Watkins (Doctor Cocheton); Nicolas Le Riche (Nijinsky); François Delaive (Male Nurse); Anne Alvaro (Betty); Françoise Lebrun (Mme Bauby); Zinedine Soualem (Joubert); Agathe de La Fontaine (Inès); Franck Victor (Paul); Laure de Clermont (Diane); Théo Sampaio (Théophile); Fiorella Campanella (Céleste); Talina Boyaci (Hortense); Georges Roche (Fourneau); Yves-Marie Coppin (Fisherman); Virginie Delmotte (Nurse); Daniel Lapostolle, Philippe Roux (Staff); François Filloux (Male Night Nurse); Elvis Polanski (Jean-Do, Child); Cedric Brelet von Sydow (Young Papinou); Sara Séguéla (Lourdes, Paraplegic); Vasile Negru (Violinist); Marie Meyer, Ilze Bajare, Anna Chyzh (Models); Antoine Bréant (Assistant to Jean-Baptiste Mondino); Azzeinde Alaïa, Michael Wincott, Jean-Baptiste Mondino, Lenny Kravitz, Farida Khelfa (Themselves)

Mathieu Amalric, Emmanuelle Seigner

Left immobilized following a stroke, Jean-Dominique Bauby finds freedom through his memory and imagination.

This film received Oscar nominations for Director, Adapted Screenplay, Cinematography, and Film Editing.

Max von Sydow, Mathieu Amalric © MIRAMAX FILMS

# ATONEMENT

Keira Knightley, Saoirse Ronan © FOCUS FEATURES

James McAvoy, Keira Knightley

(FOCUS) Producers, Tim Bevan, Eric Fellner, Paul Webster; Executive Producers, Richard Eyre, Robert Fox, Ian McEwan, Debra Hayward, Liza Chasin; Co-Producer, Jane Frazer; Director, Joe Wright; Screenplay, Christopher Hampton, based on the novel by Ian McEwan; Photography, Seamus McGarvey; Designer, Sarah Greenwood; Costumes, Jacqueline Durran; Editor, Paul Tothill; Music, Dario Marianelli; Makeup/Hair Designer, Ivana Primorac; Special Effects Supervisor, Mark Holt; Visual Effects Supervisor, John Moffatt; Casting, Jina Jay; a Universal Pictures presentation, in association with StudioCanal and Relativity Media, of a Working Title production; British-American-French; Dolby; Deluxe color; Rated R; 130 minutes; American release date: December 7, 2007.

## Cast

| | |
|---|---|
| Robbie Turner | **James McAvoy** |
| Cecilia Tallis | **Keira Knightley** |
| Briony, age 18 | **Romola Garai** |
| Briony, age 13 | **Saoirse Ronan** |
| Older Briony | **Vanessa Redgrave** |
| Grace Turner | **Brenda Blethyn** |
| Lola Quincey | **Juno Temple** |
| Leon Tallis | **Patrick Kennedy** |
| Paul Marshall | **Benedict Cumberbatch** |
| Emily Tallis | **Harriet Walter** |
| Fiona MacGuire | **Michelle Duncan** |
| Sister Drummond | **Gina McKee** |
| Tommy Nettle | **Daniel Mays** |
| Danny Hardman | **Alfie Allen** |
| Pierrot Quincey | **Felix von Simson** |
| Jackson Quincey | **Charlie von Simson** |
| Luc Cornet | **Jérémie Renier** |
| Pierrot, age 14 | **Jack Harcourt** |
| Jackson, age 14 | **Ben Harcourt** |
| Frank Mace | **Nonso Anozie** |
| Police Inspector | **Peter Wight** |
| Singing Housemaid | **Ailidh Mackay** |
| Betty | **Julia West** |
| Police Constable | **Leander Deeny** |
| Police Sergeant | **Peter O'Connor** |
| Frenchman #1 | **Michel Vuillermoz** |

and Jamie Beamish, Nick Bagnall, Neil Maskell, Billy Seymour (Soldiers in Bray Bar); Charlie Banks, Madeline Crowe, Scarlett Dalton, Olivia Grant, Katy Lawrence, Jade Moulla, Georgia Oakley, Alice Orr-Ewing, Catherine Phips, Bryony Reiss, Sarah Shaul, Anna Singleton, Emily Thomson (Probationary Nurses); Mark Holgate, Matthew Forest (Soldiers at Hospital Entrance); Vivienne Gibbs (Staff Nurse); Paul Harper (Soldier with Ukelele); Ryan Kiggell (Registrar); Anthony Minghella (Interviewer); John Normington (Vicar); Jay Quinn (Soldier Who Looks Like Robbie); Kelly Scott (Hospital Administration Assistant); Richard Stacey (Injured Sergeant); Tilly Vosburgh (Mother of Evacuees); Ben Webb (Evacuee Child #3)

James McAvoy

Saoirse Ronan

Keira Knightley

Romola Garai, Keira Knightley, James McAvoy

Misinterpreting the passion between her sister Cecilia and Robbie Turner, the family groundskeeper, 13-year-old Briony Tallis inadvertently tears the two lovers apart with her accusations.

2007 Academy Award winner for Best Original Score, this film receieved additional nominations for Best Picture, Supporting Actress (Saoirse Ronan), Adapted Screenplay, Cinematography, Art Direction, and Costume Design.

# THE BAND'S VISIT

Rinat Matatov, Shlomi Avraham, Saleh Bakri

(SONY CLASSICS) aka *Bikur Ha-tizmoret*; Producers, Eilon Ratzkovsky, Ehud Bleiberg, Yossi Uzrad, Koby Gal-Raday, Guy Jacoel; Co-Producers, Sophie Dulac, Michel Zana; Director/Screenplay, Eran Kolirin; Photography, Shai Goldman; Editor, Arik Lahav Leibovitz; Music, Habib Shehadeh Hanna; Designer, Eitan Levi; Costumes, Doron Ashkenazi; Line Producer, Tami Kushnir; Casting, Orit Azoulay; a July August Prods. (Israel)/Bleiberg Entertainment (USA)/Sophie Dulac Prods. (France) production; Israeli-American-French; Dolby; Color; Rated PG-13; 86 minutes; American release date: December 7, 2007.

Imad Jabarin, Itzik Konfino © SONY PICTURES CLASSICS

## Cast

Papi **Shlomi Avraham**
Lieutenant Colonel Tawfiq Zacharya **Sasson Gabai**
Dina **Ronit Elkabetz**
Haled **Saleh Bakri**
Simon **Khalifa Natour**
Major General Camal Abdel Azim **Imad Jabarin**
Iman **Tarak Kopty**
Fauzi **Hisham Khoury**
Makram **Francois Kheel**
Saleh **Eyad Sheety**
Itzik **Rubi Moscovich**
Iris **Hilla Surjon Fischer**
Avrum **Uri Gabriel**
Lea **Ahuva Keren**
Yula **Rinat Matatov**

The Alexandria Ceremonial Police Band find themselves stranded in an Israeli town in the middle of the desert.

Rubi Moscovich, Ronit Elkabetz, Shlomi Avraham

Sasson Gabai, Saleh Bakri, Khalifa Natour, Imad Jabarin, Eyad Sheety

# REVOLVER

(GOLDWYN) Producers, Luc Besson, Virginie Silla; Executive Producer, Steve Christian; Co-Producer, Pierre Spengler; Director/Screenplay, Guy Ritchie; Adapted by Luc Besson; Photography, Tim Maurice Jones; Designer, Eve Stewart; Costumes, Verity Hawkes; Editors, James Herbert, Ian Differ, Romesh Aluwihare; Music, Nathaniel Mechaly; Line Producer, Steve Clark-Hall; Stunts, Paul Herbert; Casting, Mindy Marin, Gail Stevens; a Luc Besson presentation of a EuropaCorp production in co-production with Revolver Pictures Ltd. in association with Toff Guy Films and Isle of Man Film with the participation of Canal+ and of TPS Star; French-British, 2005; Dolby; Technovision; Color; Rated R; 115 minutes; American release date: December 7, 2007.

### Cast

Jake Green  **Jason Statham**
Dorothy Macha  **Ray Liotta**
Zach  **Vincent Pastore**
Avi  **Andre Benjamin**
French Paul  **Terrence Maynard**
Billy  **Andrew Howard**
Sorter  **Mark Strong**
Lily Walker  **Francesca Annis**
Doreen  **Anjela Lauren Smith**
Rachel  **Elana Binysh**
Ivan, Billy's Bodyguard  **Faruk Pruti**
Teddy, Billy's Bodyguard  **Shend**
Al  **Bill Moody**
Joe  **Stephen Walters**
Benny  **Vincent Riotta**
Lord John  **Tom Wu**
Eddie A  **Ian Puleston-Davies**
Eddie B  **Jimmy Flint**
Eddie C  **Brian Hibbard**
Fat Dan  **Bruce Wang**
Wong  **Tony Tang**
Lou  **George Sweeney**
Slim Biggins  **Martin Herdman**
Patrick  **Tony Denham**
Rade  **Serge Soric**
and Trevor Stuart (Mr. Horowitz), Togo Igawa (Fred), Gary Tang (Tim), Evie Garratt (Old Lady), Abbi Bashir (North African Man), Benjamin Feitelson (Doug Finny), Ricky Grover (Hamish), Louis Dempsey (Macha's Pit Boss Slick), Mario Woszcycki (Macha's Elevator Man), Mem Ferda (Macha's Goon), Eddy Lemar (Macha's Doorman), Kamay Lau (Waitress), Jeffrey Rudom (Fat Man), Mercedes Grower (Billy's Wife), Hon Ping Tang (Lord John's Man), Brendon Burns (Electrician), Joerg Stadler (Prisoner)

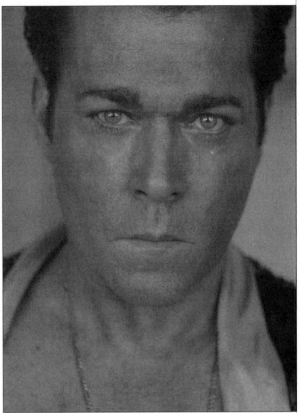

Ray Liotta

Andre Benjamin © SAMUEL GOLDWYN FILMS

Released from prison, Jake Green gets his revenge on Dorothy Macha at the casino tables, only to have the angered hood order a hit on him.

# GOODBYE BAFANA

Joseph Fiennes, Diane Kruger © PARAMOUNT VANTAGE

(PARAMOUNT VANTAGE) Producers, Jean-Luc van Damme, Ilann Girard, Andro Steinborn; Executive Producers, Kami Nagdhi, Michael Dounaev, Jimmy De Brabant, Kwesi Dickson; Co-Producers, David Wicht, Stephen Margolis, Roberto Cipullo, Gherardo Pagliel; Director, Bille August; Screenplay, Greg Latter, Bille August, based on the book by Bob Graham, James Gregory; Photography, Robert Fraisse; Editor, Herve Schneid; Music, Dario Marianelli; Original Songs, Manqobba, Johnny Clegg; Designer, Tom Hannam; a Banana Films (Belgium)/Arsam Intl. (France)/X Filme Creative Poole (Germany) production, in co-production with Fonema (Italy)/Future Films (U.K.)/Marmont Film Prod. (Belgium)/Film Afrika (South Africa); Belgian-French-German-South African; Dolby; Super 35 Widescreen; Color; Not rated; 118 minutes; American release date: December 14, 2007.

## Cast

James Gregory **Joseph Fiennes**
Nelson Mandela **Dennis Haysbert**
Gloria Gregory **Diane Kruger**
Winnie Mandela **Faith Ndukwana**
Zindzi Mandela **Terry Pheto**
Walter Sisulu **Leslie Mongezi**
Raymond Mhlaba **Zingi Mtuzula**
Brett Gregory **Shiloh Henderson**
Maj Pieter Jordaan **William Houston**
Ahmed Kathrada **Mehboob Bawa**
Brigadier Kemp **Adrian Galley**
and Warrick Grier (Vann Niekerk), Sizwe Msutu (Cyril Ramaphosa), Matthew Roberts (National Secuirty Agent), Eduan van Jaarsveldt (Sgt. Chris Brits)

Bigoted James Gregory's eyes are opened to the dangers of apartheid after he is named warden and put in charge of political prisoner Nelson Mandela.

# YOUTH WITHOUT YOUTH

(SONY CLASSICS) Producer/Director/Screenplay, Francis Ford Coppola; Based on the novella by Mircea Eliade; Executive Producers, Anahid Nazarian, Fred Roos; Photography, Mihai Malaimare Jr.; Editor, Walter Murch; Music, Osvaldo Golijov; Designer, Calin Papura; Costumes, Gloria Papura; Associate Producer, Masa Tsuyuki; Casting, Florin Kevorkian; an American Zoetrope presentation of an SRG Atelier (Romania)/Pricel (France)/BIM Distribuzione (Italy) production; Romanian-French-Italian-American; Dolby; Widescreen; Color/Black and white; HD-to-35mm; Rated R; 124 minutes; American release date: December 14, 2007.

## Cast

Dominic Matei **Tim Roth**
Laura/Veronica/Rupini **Alexandra Maria Lara**
Professor Stanciulescu **Bruno Ganz**
Dr. Josef Rudolf **Andre M. Hennicke**
Woman in Room 6 **Alexandra Pirici**
Prof. Giuseppe Tucci **Marcel Iures**
Pandit **Adrian Pintea**
Dr. Gavrila **Florin Piersic Jr.**
Dr. Chirila **Zoltan Butuc**
Anetta **Adriana Titieni**
Davidoglu **Mircea Albulescu**
Professor **Dan Astileanu**
Grenzschutz **Cristian Balint**
Dr. Neculache **Theodor Danetti**
Gertrude **Roxana Guttman**
Agent **Matt Damon**
Bartender **Dragos Bucur**
Taxi Driver **Andrei Gheorghe**
Cook **Dorina Lazar**
Teller **Rodica Lazar**
and Anamaria Marinca (Hotel Receptionist), Hodorog Anton Mihail (Doru, the Guard), Mihai Niculescu (Vaian), Gelu Nitu (Policeman), Mirela Oprisor (Craita), Alexandru Repan (Dr. Chavannes), Dan Sandulescu (Nicodim), Andi Vasluianu (Intern)

After being hit by lightning, elderly linguist Dominic Matei begins growing younger, giving him a second chance at life.

Tim Roth © SONY PICTURES CLASSICS

# PERSEPOLIS

Guardians with Marjane

(SONY CLASSICS) Producers, Marc-Antoine Robert, Xavier Rigault; Directors/Screenplay, Marjane Satrapi, Vincent Paronnaud; Based on the graphic novels by Marjane Satrapi; Editor/Digital Compositing, Stephane Roche; Music, Olivier Bernet; Designer, Marisa Musy; Animation Coordinator, Christian Desmares; Animation Production Manager, Olivier Bizet; Layout Artist, Jing Wang; Animation Assistant, Thierry Peres; Animation Studio, Perseprod; Animation, Je Suis Bien Content, Pumpkin 3D; Animators, Marc Jousset, Pascal Cheve, Louis Viali; Associate Producer, Kathleen Kennedy; a Marc-Antoine Robert and Xavier Rigault presentation of a 2.4.7 Films, France 3 Cinema, the Kennedy/Marshall Co., Franche Connection Animations, Diaphana Distribution production in partnership with Celluloid Dreams, Sony Pictures Classics, Sofica EuropaCorp, and Soficinema in collaboration with CNC; French-American; Dolby; Black and white/Color; Rated PG-13; 95 minutes; American release date: December 25, 2007.

Mother, Marjane

Grandmother, Marjane

### Voice Cast

Marjane as a teenager and adult **Chiara Mastroianni**
Tadji **Catherine Deneuve**
Marjane's Grandmother **Danielle Darrieux**
Ebi **Simon Abkarian**
Marjane (child) **Gabrielle Lopes**
Uncle Anouche **Francois Jerosme**

Young Marjane, growing up in Teheran, experiences firsthand the radical changes in her country brought on by the Islamic Revolution.

This film received an Oscar nomination for Animated Feature.

Revolutionary, Marjane © SONY PICTURES CLASSICS

# THE ORPHANAGE

Belén Rueda

(PICTUREHOUSE) aka *El Orfanato*; Producers, Mar Targarona, Joaquin Padro, Alvaro Augustin; Executive Producer, Guillermo del Toro; Director, Juan Antonio Bayona; Screenplay, Sergio G. Sanchez; Photography, Oscar Faura; Art Director, Josep Rosell; Costumes, Maria Reyes; Editor, Elena Ruiz; Music, Fernando Velazquez; Visual Effects, DDT; Makeup, Lola Lopez; a Guillermo del Toro presentation of a Rodar y Rodar, Telecinco Cinema production, in collaboration with Warner Bros. Spain, in collaboration with Telecinco, Wild Bunch, Asturias Paraiso Natural, Televisio de Catalunya; Mexican-Spanish; Dolby; Super 35 Widescreen; Color; Rated R; 100 minutes; American release date: December 28, 2007.

Geraldine Chaplin

## Cast

Laura **Belén Rueda**
Carlos **Fernando Cayo**
Simón **Roger Princep**
Pilar **Mabel Rivera**
Benigna **Montserrat Carulla**
Enrique **Andrés Gertrúdix**
Balaban **Edgar Vivar**
Aurora **Geraldine Chaplin**
Tómas **Óscar Casas**
Young Laura **Mireia Renau**
Rita **Georgina Avellaneda**
Martín **Carla Godillo Alicia**
Alicia **Carmen López**
Guillermo **Óscar Lara**
and Enric Arquimbau (Group Therapist), Blanca Martinez (Woman in Group Therapy), Carol Suárez (Young Benigna), Isbale Friera (Antonia Nurse), Fernando Marrot (Doctor), Jordi Cardus (Blind Kid), Pedro Morales (Father #2)

Returning to the orphanage where she was raised in hopes of turning it into a home for disabled children, Laura finds herself and her family confronting unsettling demons from her past, leading to the mysterious disappearance of her son.

© PICTUREHOUSE

# FOREIGN FILMS B

## 2007 RELEASES
JANUARY 1–DECEMBER 31

FOREIGN FIGHTERS

# I LOVE YOU

(DOORS ART FOUNDATION) aka *Volim Te*; Producer, Mario Oreskovic; Director/Screenplay, Dalibor Matanic; Photography, Branko Linta; Designer, Zeljka Buric; Costumes, Ana Savic Gecan; Editor, Tomislav Pavlic; Music, Jura Ferina, Pavle Miholjevic; a Hrvatska Radiotelevizija (Croatian Radiotelevision) production; Croatian, 2005; Color; Not rated; 83 minutes; American release date: January 3, 2007.

## Cast

Kresimir Mikic (Kreso), Ivana Roscic (Konobarica), Ivana Krizmanic (Ana), Bohan Navojec (Zac), Angelo Jurkas (Robi), Zrinka Cvitesic (Squash Girl), Natasa Janjic (Natasa), Leon Lucev (Mario), Ana Stunic (Escort), Bozidar Oreskovic (Kresin Father), Biserka Ipsa (Kresina Mother).

# THR3E

(BIGGER PICTURE/FOX FAITH) Producers, Joe Goodman, Bobby Neutz, Ralph Winter; Executive Producers, Marek Sledziewski, Wotjek Frychowski, Max Ryan, Jerry Rose; Co-Producers, Michael Webber, Kelly Neutz; Director, Robby Henson; Screenplay, Alan McElroy, based on the book by Ted Dekker; Photography, Sebastian Milaszewski; Designer, Wojciech Zogala; Costumes, Kaja Srodka; Editor, Anuree De Silva; Music, David Bergeaud; Casting, Karen Meisels; a Namesake Entertainment production in association with Total Living Network and Movieroom Prods.; Polish-American; Dolby; Color; Rated PG-13; 105 minutes; Release date: January 5, 2007.

## Cast

Marc Blucas (Kevin Parson); Laura Jordan (Samantha Shear); Justine Waddell (Jennifer Peters); Max Ryan (Milton); Sherman Augustus (Det. Bill); Priscilla Barnes (Belinda Parson); Tom Bower (Eugene Parson); Jeffrey Lee Hollis (Bobby Parson); Bill Moseley (Slater); Philip Dunbar (Dr. Francis); Kevin Downes (Henry); Jack Ryan (Tall Mean Boy); Kai Schoenhals (Hot Dog Vendor); Bruno Jasienski (Young Kevin); Allana Bale (Young Samantha); Holly McClure (News Anchor); Darylin Goodman (News Anchor); Carol Pence (TV Reporter); Lin Ciangio (Receptionist); Adam Malecki (Roy Peters); Josh Skjold (Det. Tom); Jerry Rose, Alfred Richard Kyle, Andrew Gorzen (Policemen); Joe Goodman (Reporter); Troy T.G. Boleyn (John, Examiner/Forensics); Chris Hook, Nik Goldman (Forensics); Ernest Ivanda (Punk #1); Zbigniew Modej (Bus Driver); Marek Sledziewski (Bouncer); Marta Gierszanin (Cindy).

# TEARS OF THE BLACK TIGER

(MAGNOLIA) aka *Fah talai jone*; Executive Producers, Pracha Maleenont, Brian L. Marcar, Adirek Wattaleela; Producer, Nonzee Nimibutr; Director/Screenplay, Wisit Sasanatieng; Photography, Nattawut Kittikhun; Designer, Ek lemchuen; Costumes, Chaiwichit Somboon; Editor, Dusanee Puinongpho; Music, Amornbhong Methakunavudh; Casting, Pasiree Panya; Thailand, 2000; Dolby; Color; Not rated; 113 minutes; American release date: January 12, 2007.

## Cast

Chartchai Ngamsan (Seua Dum, "Black Tiger"), Stella Malucchi (Rumpoey), Supakorn Kitsuwon (Mahasuan), Arawat Ruangvuth (Police Capt. Kumjorn), Sombati Medhanee (Fai), Pairoj Jaisingha (Phya Prasit), Naiyana Shiwanun (Rumploey's Maid), Kanchit Kwanpracha (Kamnan Dua, Dum's Father), Chamloen Sridang (Sgt. Yam).

# ABDUCTION:
# THE MEGUMI YOKOTA STORY

Megumi Yokota in *Abduction: The Megumi Yokota Story* © SAGEWOOD CINEMA VENTURES

(SAGEWOOD CINEMA VENTURES) Producers, Chris Sheridan, Patty Kim; Executive Producer, Jane Campion; Directors/Screenplay, Chris Sheridan, Patty Kim; Photography/Editor, Chris Sheridan; Music, Shoji Kameda; a Safari Media production in association with the BBC; British-American; Color; DV; Not rated; 85 minutes; Release date: January 12, 2007. Documentary on the mysterious 1977 disappearance of 13-year-old Megumi Yokota; with Teruaki Masumoto, Sakie Yokota, Shigeru Yokota.

# VERDICT ON AUSCHWITZ

(FIRST RUN FEATURES) Producer, Gerhard Hehrleine; Directors, Rolf Bickel, Dietrich Wagner; Photography, Armin Alker, Dominjk Schunk; Editor, Sigrid Rienäcker; German, 1993; Color/B&W; Not rated; 180 minutes. American release date: January 12, 2007. Documentary on the Frankfurt Auschwitz trials of 1963–65.

## DAM STREET

(GLOBAL FILM INITIATIVE) aka *Hong yan*; Producer, Fang Li; Co-Producer, Sylvain Bursztejn; Director, Li Yu; Screenplay, Li Yu, Fang Li; Story, Fang Li, Li Yu; Photography, Wang Wei; Editor, Karl Riedl; Music, Liu Sijun; Art Director, Cai Weidong; Costumes, Li Xuan; a Laurel Films production, in association with Rosem Films (France), with participation of Fonds Sud Cinema; French-Chinese, 2005; Dolby; Color; Not rated; 90 minutes; American release date: January 17, 2007.

**Cast**

Liu Yi (Yun), Huang Xingrao (Xiao-yong), Li Kechun, Wang Yizhu, Liu Rui.

## REGULAR LOVERS

Clotilde Mesme, Louis Garrel in *Regular Lovers* © ZEITGEIST FILMS

(ZEITGEIST) aka *Les Amants réguliers*; Producer, Gilles Sandoz; Director, Philippe Garrel; Screenplay, Philippe Garrel, Marc Cholodenko, Arlette Langmann; Photography, William Lubtchanski; Sets, Nikos Meletopoulos, Mathieu Menut; Costumes, Justine Pearce, Cécile Berges; Editor, Mathilde Muyard; Music, Jean-Claude Vannier; a Maia Films production, in association with Arte France; French, 2005; Dolby; B&W; Not rated; 175 minutes; American release date: January 19, 2007.

**Cast**

Louis Garrel (François Dervieux), Clotilde Hesme (Lilie), Julien Lucas, Mathieu Genet, Marc Barbe.

## SCREAMERS

Serj in *Screamers* © MAYA RELEASING

(MAYA RELEASING) Producers, Nick de Grunwald, Tim Swain, Peter McAlevey, Carla Garapedian; Director, Carla Garapedian; Photography, Charles Rose; Editor, Bill Yahraus; Music, Jeff Atmajian; Music Supervisor, Liz Gallacher; a BBC Television and the Raffy Manoukian Charity presentation of a MG2 Prods. production in association with Isis Prods. U.K.; British Color; HD; Rated R; 91 minutes; American release date: January 26, 2007. Documentary in which heavy metal band System of a Down draw attention to the Armenian genocide of 1915; with Serj Tankian, Daron Malakian, Shavo Odadjian, John Dolmayan, Samantha Power, Stepan Haytayan, Maritza Ohanesian, Peter Galbraith, Salih Booker, Sibel Edmonds, Dennis Hastert.

## FUNNY MONEY

(THINKFILM) Producers, Herb Nanas, Brad Siegel, Leslie Greif; Executive Producers, Jeff Franklin, Philip von Alvensleben, Harry Basil, Ray Cooney; Co-Producers, Pat McCorkle, Peter Perrotta; Director, Leslie Greif; Screenplay, Harry Basil, Leslie Greif, based on the play by Ray Cooney; Photography, Bill Butler; Designer, Stephen Lineweaver; Costumes, Donna Zakowska; Editors, Stephen Adrianson, Stephen Lovejoy, Terry Kelley; Music, Andrea Morricone; Music Supervisor, Bill Ewart; Animation, Trick Digital; Casting, Pat McCorkle; a FWE Picture Co. production in association with Tobebo Filmproduktion GmbH & Co. KG; German-American-Romanian; Dolby; FotoKem color; Rated R; 97 minutes; American release date: January 26, 2007.

**Cast**

Chevy Chase (Henry), Penelope Ann Miller (Carol Perkins), Armand Assante (Genero), Robert Loggia (Feldman), Christopher McDonald (Vic), Alex Meneses (Gina), Guy Torry (Angel), Kevin Sussman (Denis Slater), Rebecca Wisocky (MM. Virginia), Marty Belafsky (Stan Martin), Marco Assante (Bartender), Harry Basil (Retarded Party Guest), Zoltan Butuc (Mr. Big), Matt De Matt (Business Man), Sorin Misiriantu (Vlad), Joanne Rubino (Susan), Henry Fleming Wood (Party Guest).

# IN THE PIT

*In the Pit* © KINO INTL.

(KINO) Producer, Juan Carlos Rulfo; Executive Producer, Eugenia Montiel; Director/Photography, Juan Carlos Rulfo; Editor, Valentina Leduc; Music, Leo Heiblum; a La Media Luna Producciones production; Mexican, 2006; New Art Lab color, DV; Not rated; 84 minutes; American release date: February 2, 2007. Documentary on the dangers faced by Mexican workmen while building the second level of Mexico City's Periférico Freeway; with Shorty, El Grande, Juan Diaz "El Guapo" Calvario, Jose Galcada, Vincenio Martinez, Chompiros, Natividad Sanchez Montes, Tomas Jose Leon, Salvador Castelo, Nabar.

## TAZZA: THE HIGH ROLLERS

(CJ ENTERTAINMENT) aka *Tajja*; Producers, Cha Seung-jae, Kim Mi-heui; Executive Producers, Kim Ju-song, Choi Wan; Co-Producer, Kim Se-hwan; Director/Screenplay, Choi Dong-hoon, based on the comic book by Heo Yeong-man, Kim Se-yeong; Photography, Choi Yeong-hwan; Editor, Shin Min-gyeong; Music, Jang Yeong-gyu; Designer, Yang Hong-sam; Costumes, Jo Sang-gyeong; Action Director, Jeon Mun-shik; Special Visual Effects, Zuzak Visual Effects Studio; a CJ Entertainment, IM Pictures presentation of a Sidus FNH, Charm Films production; South Korean, 2006; Dolby; Widescreen; Color; Not rated; 139 minutes; American release date: February 2, 2007.

### Cast

Cho Seung-woo (Go-ni), Baek Yun-shik (Pyung Gyung-jang), Kim Hye-su (Madam Jung), Yu Hae-jin, Kim Yun-seok, Lee Su-gyeong, Kim Jeong-ran, Kim Gyeong-ik, Ju Jin-mo, Kim Sang-ho, Kim Eung-su, Baek Do-bin, Seo Dong-su, Gweon Tae-weon, Jo Sang-geon.

# THE DECOMPOSITION OF THE SOUL

(CENTRE DE L'AUDIOVISUAL À BRUXELLES) aka *La Décomposition de l'âme*; Directors, Massimo Iannetta, Nina Toussaint; Photography, René Fromont; Editor, Sandrine Deegen; an Image Crétion, Lichtfilm production; Belgian-German, 2002; Color; Not rated; 82 minutes; American release date: February 7, 2007. Documentary on how the East German police treat prisoners; with Sigrid Paul, Hartmut Richter.

# BLACK FRIDAY

(ADLABS) Producer, Arindam Mitra; Director/Screenplay, Anurag Kashyap, based on the book by Hussain Zaidi; Photography, Nataraja Suubramanian; Designer, Wasiq Khan; Costumes, Fabeha; Editor, Aarti Bajaj; a Mid Day Multimedia Limited production; Indian, 2004; Color; Not rated; 143 minutes; American release date: February 9, 2007.

### Cast

Kay Kay Menon (Rakesh Maria), Pavan Malhotra (Tiger Memon), Aditya Srivastava (Badshah Khan), Dibyendu Bhattacharya (Yeda Yakub), Kishore Kadam (Dangle), Gajraj Rao (Dawood Phanse), Zakir Hussain (Nand Kumar Chougale).

# NOTES ON MARIE MENKEN

Marie Menken in *Notes on Marie Menken* © FIRST RUN/ICARUS

(FIRST RUN/ICARUS) Producer/Director, Martina Kudlacek; Photography, Wolfgang Lehner, Joerg Th. Burger, Kudlacek; Editor, Henry Hills; Music, John Zorn; a Mina Film production, supported by B.K.A. Kunst, Wien Kultur; Austrian-American; Dolby; Color/B&W, 16mm/DV-to-35mm; Not rated; 102 minutes; American release date: February 9, 2007. Documentary on experimental filmmaker Marie Menken; with Joseph J. Menkevich, Jonas Mekas, Alfred Leslie, Gerard Malanga, Billy Name, Kenneth Anger, Peter Kubelka, Mary Woronov.

# GRBAVICA

Mirjana Karanovic, Luna Mijovic in *Grbavica* © STRAND RELEASING

(STRAND) Producers, Barbara Albert, Damir Ibrahimovic, Bruno Wagner; Co-Producers, Boris Michalski, Damir Rihtaric; Director/Screenplay, Jasmila Zbanic; Photography, Christine A. Maier; Art Director, Kemal Hrustanovic; Costumes, Lejla Hodzic; Editor, Niki Mossbock; Music, Enes Zlatar; a Coop99 (Austria)/Deblokada (Bosnia-Herzegovina)/Noir film (Germany)/Jadran (Croatia) co-production in cooperation with ZDF, ARTE; Austrian-Bosnian/Herzegovinan-German-Croatian; Dolby; Color; Not rated; 91 minutes; American release date: February 14, 2007.

## Cast

Mirjana Karanovic (Esma), Luna Mijovic (Sara), Leon Lucev (Pelda), Kenan Catic (Samir), Jasna Ornela Berry (Sabina), Dejan Acimovic (Cenga), Bogdan Diklic (Saran), Emir Hadzihafizbegovic (Puska), Ermin Bravo (Prof. Muha), Semka Sokolovic-Bertok (Pelda's Mother), Maike Höhne (Jabolka), Jasna Zalica (Plema), Nada Djurevska (Aunt Safija), Minka Muftic (Vasvija), Dunja Pasic (Mila), Sedina Muhibic (Maja), Sabina Turulja (Zehra), Vanesa Glodo (Dzemila), Sanja Buric (Mirha), Hasija Boric (Fadila).

# BAMAKO

(NEW YORKER) Producers, Abderrahmane Sissako, Denis Freyd; Director/Screenplay, Abderrahmane Sissako; Photography, Jacques Besse; Designer, Mahamadou Kouyaté; Costumes, Maji-da Abdi; Editor, Nadia Ben Rachid; an Archipel 33, Chinguitty Films, Mali Images, Arte France Direction de la Fiction, François Sauvagnargues, Chargé de Programme, Arnaud Louvet production in association with Louverture Films; Malian-American-French, 2006; Dolby; Color; Not rated; 115 minutes; American release date: February 14, 2007.

## Cast

Aïssa Maïga (Melé); Tiécoura Traoré (Chaka); Hélène Diarra (Saramba); Habib Dembélé (Falaï); Djénéba Koné (Chaka's Sister); Hamadoun Kassogué (Journalist); Hamèye Mahalmadane (Presiding Judge); Aïssata Tall Sall, William Bourdon (Plaintiff's Counsel); Roland Rappaport, Mamadou Konaté, Mamadou Savadogo (Defense Counsel); Magma Gabriel Konaté (Public Prosecutor); Zegué Bamba, Aminata Traoré, Madou Keita, Georges Keita, Assa Badiallo Souko, Samba Diakité (Witnesses); Danny Glover, Elia Suleiman, Dramane Bassaro, Jean-Henri Roger, Zeka Laplaine, Ferdinand Batsimba (The Cowboys).

# ANTIBODIES

(SLOWHAND) aka *Antikörper*; Producers, Theo Baltz, Boris Schonfelder; Co-Producers, Rainer Kolmel, Christian Alvart; Director/Screenplay, Christian Alvart; Photography, Hagen Bogdanski; Designer, Christian M. Goldbeck; Costumes, Silke Sommer; Editor, Philipp Stahl; Music, Michl Britsch; Visual Effects Supervisors, Dominik Trimborn, Katja Muller; Casting, Sabine Frielinghaus; a Kinowelt Filmverleih release (in Germany) of a Kinowelt Filmproduktion presentation of a Medienkontor production; German, 2005; Dolby; Widescreen; Color; Not rated; 127 minutes; American release date: February 16, 2007.

## Cast

Wotan Wilke Möhring (Michael Martens), Andre Hennicke (Gabriel Engel), Heinz Hoenig (Seiler), Ulrike Krumbiegel (Rosa Martens), Hauke Diekamp (Christian Diekamp), Jürgen Schornagel (Sucharzewski), Norman Reedus (Schmitz), Christian von Aster (Wagner), Waltraud Witte (Mrs. Hering), Konstantin Graudus (Wosniak), Gudrun Ritter (Mrs. Sucharzewski), Laura Alberta Szalski (Sarah Martens), Klaus Zmorek (Bosowski), Domenico D'Ambrosio (Technician), Holger Franke (Karl Prebisch), Jockel Tschiersch (Gabhart), Hans Diehl (Priest), Bruno Grass (Frank Flieder), Natascha Paulick (Maria Flieder), Frank Kusche (Attendant Schmidtzen), Elisa Schrey (Anna, Crying Girl), Edie Samland (Esther Gabhart), Stefanie Fuchs (Moni), Isabel Bongard (Lucia Flieder), Marie Lindner (Tamara Gabhart), Dietmar Horst Hedram (Junkie), Laila Mohmand (Prostitute), Martin Umbach (Psychiatrist), Holger Reibiger (Attendant), Nina Proll (Lucy), Nadeshda Brennicke (Nightclub Singer), Coco Brown (Michelle), Lydia Kavungu (Joy), Rainer Laupichler (Kneiff), Milton Welsh (Fricke).

# THE WAYWARD CLOUD

(INDEPENDENT) aka *Tian bian yi duo yun*; Producer, Bruno Pésery; Director/ Screenplay, Ming-liang Tsai; Photography, Pen-jung Liao; Designer, Kam-tim Yip; Costumes, Huey Mei Sun; Editor, Sheng-Chang Chen; an Arena Films, Homegreen Films, Wild Bunch, Arte France Cinéma production; French-Tai; Dolby; Color; Not rated; 112 minutes; American release date: February 22, 2007.

## Cast

Kang-sheng Lee (Hsiao-Kang); Shiang-chyi Chen (Shiang-chyi); Yi-Ching Lu (Mother); Kuei-Mei Yang, Sumomo Yozakura (Taiwanese Porn Actors).

# THE ABANDONED

(LIONSGATE) Producers, Julio Fernandez, Carlos Fernandez; Co-Producer, Kwesi Dickson; Director, Nacho Cerda; Screenplay, Nacho Cerda, Karim Hussani, Richard Stanley; Photography, Xavi Gimenez; Designer, Balter Gallart; Costumes, Sandra Klincheva; Editor, Jorge Macaya; Music, Alfons Conde; Special Makeup Effects, Creature Effects; Digital Visual Effects, Infinia; Casting, Steve Daly, Luci Lenox; presented in association with After Dark Films of a Filmax Entertainment (Spain) presentation of a Castelao (Spain) production in co-production with Future Films (U.K.) and Radiovision (Bulgaria); Spanish-British-Bulgarian, 2006; Dolby; Super 35 Widescreen; Color; Rated R; 99 minutes; American release date: February 23, 2007.

## Cast

Anastasia Hille (Marie Jones), Karel Roden (Nicolai), Valentin Ganev (Andrei Misharin/Kilya Kaidavosky), Carlos Reig-Plaza (Anatoliy), Paraskeva Djukelova (Marie's Mother), Kalin Arsov (Bearded Russian Patriarch, 1966), Svetlana Smoleva (Bearded Patriarch's Wife, 1966), Anna Panayotova (Bearded Patriarch's Daughter, 1966), Jordanka Angelova (Blind Woman, Present Day), Valentin Goshev (Patriarch, Present Day), Jasmina Marinova (Patriarch's Wife), Monica Baunova (Emily), Marta Yaneva (Natalya).

# THE TASTE OF TEA

(VIZ PICTURES) aka *Cha no aji*; Producers, Kazuto Takida, Kazutoshi Wadakura; Director/Screenplay/Editor, Katsuhito Ishii; Photography, Kosuke Matushima; Designer, Yuji Tsuzuki; Costumes, Ikuko Utsunomiya; Music, Tempo Little; a Grasshoppa production; Japanese; Dolby; Color; Not rated; 143 minutes; American release date: February 23, 2007.

## Cast

Maya Banno (Sachiko Haruno), Takahiro Sato (Hajime Haruno), Tadanobu Asano (Ayano Haruno), Satomi Texuka (Yoshiko Haruno), Tatsuya Gashuin (Akira Todoroki), Tomoko Nakajima (Akira Terako), Ikki Todoroki (Himself), Tomokazu Miura (Nobuo Haruno), Anna Tsuchiya (Aoi Suzuishi).

# GLASTONBURY

(THINKFILM) Producer, Robert Richards; Executive Producers, Jane Hawley, Dave Henderson, Tracey Scoffield, Jeremy Thomas; Co-Producer, Ann Faggetter; Director/Photography, Julien Temple; Editors, Niven Howie, Tobias Zaldua; a BBC Films, HanWay Films, and Emap Performance presentation of a Newhouse Nitrate production; British, 2006; Color; Various-formats-to-35mm; Not rated; 138 minutes; American release date: February 23, 2007. Documentary on Britain's long-running Glastonbury rock festival; with David Bowie, T. Rex, Radiohead, REM, Coldplay, Oasis, Pulp, Blur, Chemical Brothers, Joe Strummer, Primal Scream, Fatboy Slim, Rolf Harris, Ray Davies, Alabama 3, Nick Cave, Massive Attack, Tinariwen, Faithless, Bjork, Dr. John, Orbital, Prodigy, Melanie, Richie Havens, New Order, David Gray, Babyshambles, Skatallites, Stereo MCs, Velvet Underground, Scissor Sisters, Alice Coltrane.

# INTO GREAT SILENCE

(ZEITGEIST) aka *Die Grosse Stille*; Producers, Philip Groening, Michael Weber, Andres Pfaffli, Elda Guidinetti; Co-Producer, Frank Evers; Executive Producers, Joerg Schulze, Philip Groening; Director/Screenplay/Photography/Editor, Philip Groening; a Bavaria Film Intl. presentation of a Philip Groening Film (Germany)/Ventura Films (Switzerland)/Bavaria Film, Cine Plus (Germany) production, in cooperation with ARTE/ZDF, Bayerischer Rundfunk, TSI Televisione Svizzera, with the support of Filmstiftung NRW, FFA, Filmbuero NRW; German-Swiss, 2005; Dolby; Color; HD; Super-8-to-35mm; Not rated; 160 minutes; American release date: February 28, 2007. Documentary on the Grand Prior of the Carthusian Order, a monastery in the French Alps.

# BORDER POST

(DOORS ARTS FOUNDATION) aka *Karaula*; Producers, Ademir Kenovic, Danijel Hocevar, Vladimir Anastasov, Boris T. Matic, Zoran Cvijanovic, Milko Josifov, Mike Downey, Sam Taylor; Director, Rajko Grlic; Screenplay, Ante Tomic, Rajko Grlic, based on Ante Tomic's short story; Photography, Slobodan Trninic; Designers, Goran Jaksimovic, Kemal Hrustanovic, Kiril Spaseski; Costumes, Sabina Buzdon; Editor, Andrija Zafranovic; Music, Sanja Ilic; a Refresh Prods. (Sarajevo)/Vertigo, Emotionfilm (Ljubljana)/Sektor Film (Skopje)/Propeler Film, NP7, Croatian Radio TV (Zagreb)/Yodi Movie Craftsman (Belgrade)/Film and Music Entertainment (London) co-production; Bosnian-Slovenian-Macedonian-Croatian-Serbian-British; Dolby; Color; Not rated; 94 minutes; American release date: March 7, 2007.

## Cast

Toni Gojanovic (Siriscevic), Sergej Trifunovic (Ljuba Paunovic), Emir Hadzihafizbegovic (Porucnik Safet Pasic), Verica Nedeska-Trajkova (Mirjana), Bogdan Diklic (Pukovnik Rade Orhideja), Miodrag Fisekovic (Gvozdenovic), Franjo Dijak (Budiscak), Petre Arsovski (Ilievski), Tadej Troha (Lanisnik), Zoran Ljutkov (Milco), Igor Bencina (Vladika), Selim Sendzul (Mica), Almedin Leleta (Hasan), Hrvoje Keckes (Milijenko), Ilina Corevska (Konobarica), Petar Mircevski (Milovanovic).

# A JOURNEY OF DMITRY SHOSTAKOVICH

Dmitry Shostakovich in *A Journey of Dmitry Shostakovich* © HOROVOD

(HOROVOD) Producer, Oksana Dvornichenko; Director/Screenplay, Oksana Dvornichenko; Photography, July Olshvang; Editors, Alexander Sokin, Vladimir Samorodov; Russian-American; Black and white/color; Not rated; 75 minutes; American release date: March 14, 2007. Documentary on Russian composer Dmitry Shostakovich, using selections from his diaries and letters; with George Watts, Helga Landauer (voices).

# ADAM'S APPLES

Ulrich Thomsen in *Adam's Apples* © OUTSIDER PICTURES

(OUTSIDER PICTURES) aka *Adams aebler*; Producers, Tivi Magnusson, Mie Andreasen; Director/Screenplay, Anders Thomas Jensen; Photography, Sebastian Blenkov; Editor, Anders Viladsen; Music, Jeppe Kaas; Art Director, Mia Stensgaard; Costumes, Jane Whittaker; a Nordisk Film release of an M&M Prods. production, in association with DR TV, Filmfyn; Danish, 2005; Dolby; Widescreen; Color; Not rated; 93 minutes; American release date: March 16, 2007.

## Cast

Ulrich Thomsen (Adam Pedersen), Mads Mikkelsen (Ivan), Nicolas Bro (Gunnar), Paprika Steen (Sarah Svendsen), Ali Kazim (Khalid), Ole Thestrup (Dr. Kolberg), Nikolaj Lie Kaas (Holger), Gyrd Løfqvist (Poul Nordkap), Lars Ranthe (Esben), Peter Reichardt (Nalle), Tomas Villum Jensen (Arne), Peter Lambert (Jørgen).

# NOMAD: THE WARRIOR

(WEINSTEIN CO.) aka *Kochevnik*; Producers, Pavel Douvidzon, Ram Bergman, Rustam Ibragimbekov; Executive Producers, Milos Forman, Sergey Azimov, Serik Zhybandykov; Directors, Sergei Bodrov, Ivan Passer; Screenplay, Rustam Ibragimbekov; Photography, Dan Laustsen, Ueli Steiger; Designer, Miljen "Kreka" Kljakovic; Costumes, Marit Allen, Michael O'Conner; a Kazakhfilm (Kazakhstan)/Wild Bunch (France) production in association with Irbus, True Stores Prods.; Kazakhstani-French, 2005; Dolby; Widescreen; Color; Rated R; 112 minutes; American release date: March 16, 2007.

## Cast

Kuno Becker (Mansur), Jay Hernandez (Erali), Jason Scott Lee (Oraz), Doskhan Zholzhaksynov (Galdan Ceren, the Jungar Sultan), Ayana Yesmagambetova (Gaukhar), Mark Dacascos (Sharish), Erik Zholzhaksynov (Barak), Dilnaz Akhmadieva (Hocha), Azis Beyshinaliev (Ragbat).

# BLESSED BY FIRE

(KOCH LORBER) aka *Illuminados por el fuego*; Producer, Carlos Ruta; Director, Tristan Bauer; Screenplay, Edgardo Esteban, Gustavo Romero Borri, Tristan Bauer, Miguel Bonasso, based on the book by Edgardo Esteban and Romero Borri; Photography, Javier Julia; Art Director, Graciela Fraguglia; Music, Federico Bonasso, Leon Gieco; Editor, Alejandro Brodersohn; a Universidad Nacional de General San Martin production in association with Canal Plus, INCAA; Argentine-Spanish, 2005; Dolby; B&W/color; Not rated; 100 minutes; American release date: March 21, 2007.

## Cast

Gastón Pauls (Esteban Leguizamón), Pablo Ribba (Vargas), Cesar Albarracin (Juan), Jose Luis Alfonso, Hugo Carrizo, Virginia Innocenti, Juan Leyrado, Arturo Bonin, Miguel Angel Ramos.

Gastón Pauls in *Blessed by Fire* © KOCH LORBER

# OFFSIDE

(SONY CLASSICS) Producer/Director/Editor, Jafar Panahi; Screenplay, Jafar Panahi, Shadmehr Rastin; Photography, Mahmoud Kalari; Art Director, Iraj Raminfar; Iranian, 2006; Dolby; Color; Rated PG; 93 minutes; American release date: March 23, 2007.

## Cast

Sima Mobarak-Shahi (First Girl), Shayesteh Irani (Smoking Girl), Ayda Sadeqi (Soccer Girl), Golnaz Farmani (Girl with Tchador), Mahnaz Zabihi (Female Soldier), Nazanin Sediq-zadeh (Young Girl), Safdar Samandar (Soldier from Azerbaijan), Mohammad Kheir-abadi (Soldier from Mashad), Masoud Kheymeh-kabood (Soldier from Tehran), Mohsen Tabandeh (Ticket Seller).

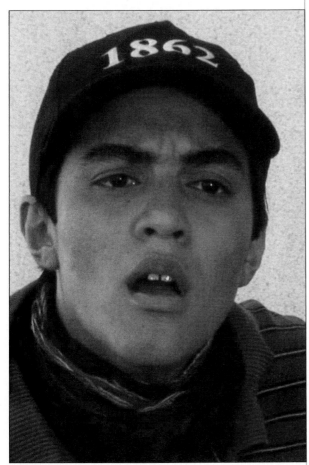

Shayesteh Irani in *Offside* © SONY PICTURES CLASSICS

# THE PRISONER OR: HOW I PLANNED TO KILL TONY BLAIR

Yunis Abbas in *The Prisoner, or How I Killed Tony Blair* © TRULY INDIE

(TRULY INDIE/RED ENVELOPE) Producer, Petra Epperlein; Directors, Petra Epperlein, Michael Tucker; Photography/Editor, Michael Tucker; a Pepper and Bones production; German-American; Color; Rated PG-13; 72 minutes; American release date: March 23, 2007. Documentary on how journalist Yunis Khatayer Abbas ended up an Abu Ghraib prisoner because authorities believed he was trying to assassinate Prime Minister Tony Blair.

# U-CARMEN

(KOCH LORBER) Producers, Mark Dornford-May, Ross Garland; Screenplay, Mark Dornford-May, Andiswa Kedama, Pauline Malefane, based on the opera libretto by Ludovic Halévy, Henri Meilhac; Photography, Giulio Biccari; Desginer, Craig Smith; Costumes, Jessica Dornford-May; Music, Georges Bizet; Editor, Ronelle Loots; a Spier Films production; South African, 2005; Dolby; Color; Not rated; 122 minutes; American release date: March 28, 2007.

## Cast

Pauline Malefane (Carmen), Andile Tshoni (Jongikhaya), Lungelwa Blou (Nomakhaya), Zorro Sidloyi (Lulamile Nkomo), Andries Mbali (Bra Nkomo), Zamile Gantana (Captain Gantana), Andiswa Kedama (Amanda), Ruby Mthethwa (Pinki), Ross Garland (Policeman).

# SUMMER IN BERLIN

(D STREET RELEASING) aka *Sommer vorm Balkon*; Producers, Stefan Arndt, Peter Rommel; Executive Producer, Jutta Frech; Director, Andreas Dresen; Screenplay, Wolfgang Kohlhaase; Photography, Andreas Höfer; Designers, Susanne Hopf, Natalja Meier; Music, Pascal Comelade; Editor, Jörg Hauschild; a Peter Rommel Productions, X-Filme Creative Pool production; German, 2005; Dolby; Color; Not rated; 107 minutes; American release date: March 30, 2007.

### Cast

Inka Friedrich (Katrin Engel), Nadja Uhl (Nike), Andreas Schmidt (Ronald), Stephanie Schönfeld (Tina), Vincent Redetzki (Max), Christel Peters (Helene), Kurt Radeke (Oskar), Hannes Stelzer (Mr. Neumann), Barbara Bachmann (Helene's Daughter), Traute Hoess (Agency Chief), Hans-Ulrich Laux (Trucker), Maximilian Moritz (Rico), Lil Oggesen (Charly), Fritz Roth (Chef Pupperfirma), Veit Schubert (Pharmacist).

# LOS MUERTOS

(FACETS MULTIMEDIA) Producers, Micaela Buye, Ilse Hughan, Marianne Slot; Executive Producers, Florencia Enghel, Vanessa Ragone; Director/Screenplay/ Designer, Lisandro Alonso; Photography, Cobi Migliora; Music, Flor Maleva; Editors, Lisandro Alonso, Ezequiel Borovinsky; a Ventura Film, Fortune Silms, Slot Machine, Arte France Cinema production; Argentine-French-Dutch-Swiss, 2004; Dolby; Color/B&W; Not rated; 78 minutes; American release date: April 6, 2007.

### Cast

Argentino Vargas (Vargas), Francisco Dornez, Yolanda Galarza, Victor Varela, Francisco Salazar, Hilda Chamorro, Ángel Vera, Javier Lenciza, Raúl Fagundez.

Argentina Vargos in *Los Muertos* © FACETS MULTIMEDIA

# PING PONG

(VIZ PICTURES) Producers, Shinji Ogawa, Sanae Suzuki, Fumihiko Inoue; Executive Producer, Yasushi Shiina; Director, Sori; Screenplay, Kankuro Judo, based on the comic by Taiyou Matsumoto; Photography, Akira Sakou; Designer, Kouichi Kanekatsu; Music Supervisor, Hiroshi Futami; Editor, Souichi Ueno; an Asmik Ace Entertainment production, in association with Shogakukan, Tokyo Broadcasting System, BS-1, Imagica, and Nippon Shuppan Hanbai; Japanese, 2002; Dolby; Color; Not rated; 114 minutes; American release date: April 6, 2007.

### Cast

Yosuke Kubozuka (Peco), Arata (Smile), Sam Lee (China), Shidou Nakamura (Dragon), Koji Ohkura (Akuma), Naoto Takenaka (Butterfly Joe), Mari Natsuki (Obaba).

# DARATT

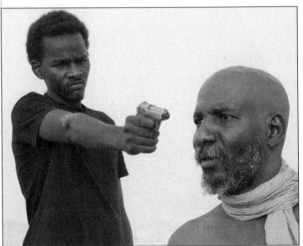

Ali Bacha Barkai, Youssouf Djaoro in *Daratt* © ARTMATTAN

(ARTMATTAN) aka *Dry Season*; Producers, Abderrahmane Sissako, Mahamat-Saleh Haroun; Executive Producer, Franck-Nicolas Chelle; Director/Screenplay, Mahamat-Saleh Haroun; Photography, Abraham Haile Biru; Music, Wasis Diop; Editor, Marie-Hélène Dozo; a Chinguitty Films/Goi-Goi Prods. co-production in association with Entre Chien et Loup, Illuminations Films for New Crowned Hope; French-Belgian-Chadian-Austrian, 2006; Color; Not rated; 96 minutes; American release date: April 6, 2007.

### Cast

Ali Bacha Barkai (Atim), Youssouf Djaoro (Nassara), Aziza Hisseine (Aicha), Djibril Ibrahim (Moussa), Khayar Oumar Defallah (Gumar Abatcha), Fatime Hadje (Moussa's Aunt), Abderamane Abakar (Soldier).

# THE COP, THE CRIMINAL AND THE CLOWN

Roy Dupuis, Lucie Laurier in *The Cop, The Criminal and The Clown* © LONELY SEAL

(LONELY SEAL) aka *C'est pas moi, c'est l'autre*; Producers, Chuck Smiley, Paul Painter; Executive Producer, Jean Zaloum; Director, Alain Zaloum; Screenplay, Luis Furtado; Photography, Éric Moynier; Costumes, Nicole Pelletier; Music, Dave Gale, Andy Bush; Editors, Richard Comeau, Jean-Pierre Cereghetti; a Screen People, Istar, Accolade Films co-production; Canadian-French, 2004; Color; Not rated; 90 minutes; American release date: April 6, 2007.

## Cast

Roy Dupuis (Vincent Papineau/Claude Laurin); Anémone (Carlotta Luciani); Michel Muller (Marius); Lucie Laurier (Lucie); Alan Shearman (Green); Luck Mervil (Dieudonné); Benoît Briére (Michel Van Der Loo); Ghyslain Tremblay (Faithful Suicide); Raymond Cloutier (Lévesque); Carolien Néron (Laurence); Annie Dufresne (Claude's Blonde); Emmanuel Auger (Fabien); Roc LaFortune (Joe); Louis-Georges Girard (Concierge); Tobie Pelletier (Thief on Skateboard); Jean Frenette (Asselin); Jean-Guy Bouchard (Bob); Tony Robinow (Blackboard Buyer); Joseph Antaki (Djamel); Fayolle Jean (Rock, the Dealer); Khanh Hua (Kim); Matthew Smiley (Fabio, the Pimp); Garry S. Mailloux, Jasson Finney (Receivers).

# RED ROAD

(TARTAN FILMS) Producer, Carrie Comerford; Executive Producers, Gillian Berrie, Sisse Graum Joergensen; Director/Screenplay, Andrea Arnold, based on characters developed by Lone Scherfig, Anders Thomas Jensen; Photography, Robbie Ryan; Editor, Nicolas Chaudeurge; Designer, Helen Scott; Costumes, Carole K. Millar; Casting, Kahleen Crawford; a UK Film Council, Scottish Screen, Glasgow Film Office, BBC Films in association with Zoma Films, Verve Pictures presentation of a Sigma Films (U.K.)/ Zentropa Entertainments5 (Denmark) production; British-Danish, 2006; Dolby; Color; HD-to-35mm; Not rated; 113 minutes; American release date: April 13, 2007.

## Cast

Kate Dickie (Jackie), Tony Curran (Clyde), Martin Compston (Stevie), Natalie Press (April), Andrew Armour (Alfred), John Comerford (Man with Dog), Paul Higgins (Avery).

# EVERYTHING'S GONE GREEN

Paolo Costanzo, Steph Song in *Everything's Gone Green* © THINKFILM

(THINKFILM) Producers, Elizabeth Yake, Henrik Meyer, Chris Nanos; Executive Producers, Michael Baker, Dan Lyon, Scott Mackenzie, Morris Ruskin; Director, Paul Fox; Screenplay, Douglas Coupland; Photography, David Frazee; Designer, Peter Andringa; Costumes, Sheila White; Editor, Gareth C. Scales; Casting, Robin C. Cook, Corinne Clark, Jennifer Page; a Radke Films production, in association with True West Films; Canadian; Dolby; Color; Rated R; 95 minutes; Release date: April 13, 2007.

## Cast

Paolo Costanzo (Ryan), Steph Song (Ming), JR Bourne (Bryce), Aidan Devine (Alan), Susan Hogan (Ryan's Mom), Tom Butler (Ryan's Dad), Peter Kelamis (Kevin), Gordon Michael Woolvett (Spike), Katharine Isabelle (Heather), Chiu-Lin Tam (Granny), Camyar Chai (Surjinder), Tara Wilson (Marcia), Jennifer Kitchen (Linda), Alexus Dumont (Wendy), Don Thompson (Mr. Connor), Chang Tseng (Mr. Ho), Mark Gibbon (Rory), Melanie Blackwell (Winners Receptionist), Kit Koon (Ms. Hamada), Steven Cree Molison (Biker), Terry Weaver (Fired Winners Employee).

# THE GLAMOROUS LIFE OF SACHIKO HANAI

Emi Kuroda in *The Glamorous Life of Sachiko Hanai* © PALM PICTURES

(PALM PICTURES) aka *Hatsujô kateikyôshi: sensei no aijiru*; Producers, Kinugawa Nakahito, Morita Kazuto, Masuko Kyoichi; Executive Producer, Asakura Daisuke; Director, Mitsuru Meike; Screenplay, Takao Nakano; Photography, Hiroshi Ito; Designer, Meike; Music, Taro Hishioka; Editor, Naokki Kaneko; Japanese, 2003; Dolby; Color; Not rated; 90 minutes; American release date: April 13, 2007.

## Cast

Yukijiro Hotaru (Toshio), Takeshi Ito (Kim), Emi Kuroda (Sachiko), Shinji Kubo (President George W. Bush).

# DREAMING LHASA

(FIRST RUN FEATURES) Producer, Ritu Sarin; Executive Producers, Jeremy Thomas, Richard Gere, Raj Singh; Directors, Ritu Sarin, Tenzing Sonam; Screenplay, Tenzing Sonam; Photography, Ranjan Palit; Editor, Paul Dosaj; Music, Andy Spence; Designer, Rachna Rastogi; Casting, Dorjee, Dawa Narongsha; a White Crane Films presentation in association with Jeremy Thomas; British-Indian, 2005; Dolby; Prasad Film Labs color; Not rated; 90 minutes; American release date: April 13, 2007.

## Cast

Tenzin Chokyi Gyatso (Karma), Jampa Kalsang (Dhondup), Tenzin Jigme (Jigme), Phuntsok Namgyal Dhumkhang, Tsering Topgyal Phurpatsang.

# VOICE OF A MURDERER

(CJ ENTERTAINMENT) aka *Geu nom moksori*; Producer, Eugene Lee; Executive Producer, Kim Ju-seong; Director/Screenplay, Park Jin-pyo; Photography, Kim Woo-hyeong; Editor, Kim Mi-ju; Music, Lee Byeong-woo; Art Director, Lee In-ok; Costumes, Shin Seung-heui; South Korean; a Zip Cinema production; South Korean; Dolby; Widescreen; Color; Not rated; 122 minutes; American release date: April 13, 2007.

## Cast

Seol Gyeong-gu (Han Kyung-bae), Kim Nam-ju (Oh Ji-sun), Gang Dong-weon, Kim Yeong-cheol, Song Yeong-chang, Go Su-heui, Kim Gwang-gyu, Im Jong-yun, Na Mun-heui, Yun Je-mun, Choi Jeong-yun.

# SYNDROMES AND A CENTURY

Sakda Kaewbuadee, Arkanae Cherkam in *Syndromes and a Century* © STRAND RELEASING

(STRAND) aka *Sang sattawat*; Producer, Apichatpong Weerasethakul; Executive Producers, Keith Griffiths, Simon Field, Eric Chan, Tiffany Chan; Director/Screenplay, Apichatpong Weerasethakul; Photography, Sayombhu Mukdeeprom; Designer, Akekarat Homlaor; Costumes, Virasinee Tipkomol, Askorn Sirikul; Editor, Lee Chatametikool; Music, Kantee Anantagant; a New Crowned Hope (Austria) in association with Fortissimo Films, Backup Films, in co-production with Anna Sanders Films (France), Tifa (Thailand) presentation of a Kick the Machine production (Thailand), with the participation of the Fonds Sud Cinema, Ministry of Culture and Communication, CNC, Ministry of Foreign Affairs; Thai-Austrian-French; Dolby; Color; 104 minutes; American release date: April 18, 2007.

## Cast

Nantarat Sawaddikul (Dr. Tei), Jaruchai Iamaram (Dr. Nohng), Sophon Pukanok (Noom), Arkanae Cherkam (Ple), Sakda Kaewbuadee (Sakda), Nu Nimsombon (Toa).

# TIE XI QU: WEST OF TRACKS

(AD VITAM DISTRIBUTION) Producers, Bing Wang, Zhu Zhu; Director/Photography, Bing Wang; Editors, Bing Wang, Adam Kerby; a Wang Bing Film Workshop production; Chinese; Color; Not rated; Three parts: *Rust* (240 minutes); *Remnants* (176 minutes); *Rails* (105 minutes); American release date: April 18, 2007. Documentary on the decaying conditions of the industrial Tie Xi district in Shenyan, in Northern China.

# GOODBYE, MOMO

(ARTMATTAN) aka *A dios momo*; Producers, Raul Pochintesta; Executive Producers, Sergio Aguero, Carlos Ricagni; Director/Screenplay, Leonardo Ricagni; Photography, Pablo Vera; Editor, Marcela Saenz; Music, Emilio Kauderer; Designer, Jose Pedro Giordano; a Fabrication Films, Mojo Films presentation; Uruguay; Color; DV; Not rated; 108 minutes; American release date: April 20, 2007.

### Cast

Mathias Acuna (Little Obdulio), Jorge Esmoris, Marco Da Costa, Washington "Canario" Luna, Marcel Keoroglian, Carmen Abella.

# TRIAD ELECTION

(TARTAN USA) aka *Hak se wui yi wo wai gwai*; Producers, Dennis Law, Johnnie To; Executive Producers, Charles Heung, Dennis Law; Director, Johnnie To; Screenplay, Yau Nai-hoi, Yip Tin-shing, Cheng Siu-keung; Editors, Law Wing-cheong, Jeff Cheung; Music, Robert Ellis-Geiger; Art Director, Tony Yu; a One Hundred Years of Film, Milkyway Image presentation of a Milkyway Image production; Hong Kong, 2006; Dolby; Widescreen; Color/B&W; Not rated; 92 minutes; American release date: April 25, 2007.

### Cast

Simon Yam (Lam Lok), Louis Koo (Jimmy Lee), Wong Tin-lam (Uncle Teng), Yao Yung (Xi), Lam Suet (Big Head), Nick Cheung (Jet), Lam Ka-tung (Kun), Mok Sing-lun (Kwok), Cheung Siu-Fai (Mr. So), Mark Cheng (Bo), Tam Ping-Man (Uncle Cocky), Pauline Pan (Janice), Andy On (Lik), Albert Cheung (Mr. Shu), Jonathan Lee (Denny Lam).

Simon Yam (center) in *Triad Election* © TARTAN USA

# POISON FRIENDS

Dominique Blanc, Malik Zidi in *Poison Friends* © STRAND RELEASING

(STRAND) aka *Les Amitiés maléfiques*; Producers, Manni Mortazavi, Yorrick Le Saux, David Mathieu-Mahias; Director, Emmanuel Bourdieu; Screenplay, Emmanuel Bourdieu, Marcia Romano; Photography, Yorick Le Saux; Editor, Benoit Quinon; Music, Gregoire Hetzel; Designer, Nicolas de Boiscuille; a 4A4 Prods. presentation and production, with participation of CNC; French; Dolby; Widescreen; Color; Not rated; 103 minutes; American release date: April 27, 2007.

### Cast

Malik Zidi (Eloi Duhaut), Natacha Régnier (Marguerite), Alexandre Steiger (Alexandre Pariente), Thibault Vinçon (André Morney), Thomas Blanchard (Edouard Franchon), Jacques Bonnaffé (Prof. Mortier), Dominique Blanc (Florence Duhaut), Francoise Girard, Botum Dupuis.

# WIND CHILL

(TRISTAR) Producers, Peter Czernin, Graham Broadbent; Executive Producers, George Clooney, Ben Cosgrove, Steven Soderbergh; Co-Producer, Peter Lhotka; Director, Gregory Jacobs; Screenplay, Joe Gangemi, Steven Katz; Photography, Dan Laustsen; Designer, Howard Cummings; Costumes, Trish Keating; Editor, Lee Percy; Music, Clint Mansell; Visual Effects Supervisor, Jon Cowley; Visual Effects, Technical Creative Services Vancouver; Casting, Amanda Mackey, Cathy Sandrich Gelfond; a TriStar Pictures presentation of a Blueprint Pictures (U.K.)/Section Eight (U.S.) production; British-American; Dolby; Panavision; Deluxe color; Rated R; 91 minutes; American release date: April 27, 2007.

### Cast

Emily Blunt (Girl), Ashton Holmes (Guy), Martin Donovan (Highway Patrolman), Ned Bellamy (Snowplow Driver), Ian Wallace (Priest), Donny Lucas (Stranger), Chelan Simmons (Blonde Girl), Darren Moore (Clerk), Linden Banks (Proctor), Caz Darko (Teenage Boy), Heath Horejda (Teenage Boy)

## THE SHORT LIFE OF JOSE ANTONIO GUTIERREZ

(ATOPIA) aka *Das Kurze Leben des José Antonio Gutierrez*; Executive Producer, Gerd Haag; Co-Producers, Peter Spoerri, Heidi Specogna; Director/Screenplay, Heidi Specogna; Photography, Rainer Hoffmann; Editor, Ursula Hof; a TAG/TRAUM and PS Film presentation in association with ZDF; German-Swiss, 2006; Color; DV-to-35mm; 90 minutes; American release date: April 27, 2007. Documentary on the first U.S. soldier killed in the 2003 Iraqi invasion; with Patrick Atkinson, Fabian Giron, Veronica Morales, Engracia Gutierrez, Wendy Perlera, Nora Mosquera, David Gonzales, Marc Montez, Miguel Perez.

## MISSING VICTOR PELLERIN

(ATOPIA) aka *Rechercher Victor Pellerin*; Executive Producer, Douglas Bensadoun; Director/Screenplay/Photography/Editor, Sophie Deraspe; Music, Julien Roy; Les Films Siamois; Canadian, 2006; Dolby; Color; Not rated; 102 minutes; American release date: May 2, 2007. Documentary on how promising artist Victor Pellerin destroyed his work and disappeared from Montreal in the early 1990s.

## L'ICEBERG

Philippe Martz, Fiona Gordon in *L'Iceberg* © FIRST RUN FEATURES

(FIRST RUN FEATURES) Producers, Dominique Abel, Fiona Gordon; Directors/Screenplay, Dominique Abel, Fiona Gordon, Bruno Romy; Photography, Sebastian Koeppel; Editor, Sandrine Deegen; Music, Jacques Luley; Art Director, Laura Couderc; a Courage mon Amour Films/RTBF/FAG Prod. production; Belgian, 2005; Dolby; Color; Not rated; 84 minutes; American release date: May 4, 2007.

### Cast

Fiona Gordon (Fiona), Dominique Abel (Julien), Philippe Martz (René the Sailor), Lucy Tulugarjuk (Nattikuttuk), Thérèse Fichet (Fernande), Georges Jorge (Achille), Louis Lecouvreur (Léon), Bruno Romy (Georges), Lola Hélie (Lola), Ophelie Rousseau (The Girl), Robin Goupil (The Son).

## I DON'T WANT TO SLEEP ALONE

Lee Kang-Sheng, Norman Atun in *I Don't Want to Sleep Alone* © STRAND RELEASING

(STRAND) aka *Hei yan quan*; Producers, Bruno Pesery, Vincent Wang; Executive Producers, Simon Field, Keith Griffiths, Wouter Barendrecht, Michael J. Werner; Director/Screenplay, Tsai Ming-Liang; Photography, Liao Pen-Jung; Editor, Chen Sheng-Chang; Designers, Lee Tian-Jue, Gan Siong-King; Costumes, Sun Hui-May; a Soudaine Compagnie (France)/Homegreen Films (Taiwan)/New Crowned Hope Festival Vienna 2006 (Austria) production, with the participation of the Government Information Office of the Republic of China, Centre National del la Cinematographie, with the support of EMI Music Taiwan, Dama Orchestra Malaysia; Malaysian-Thai-Austrian; Dolby; Color; Not rated; 117 minutes; American release date: May 9, 2007.

### Cast

Lee Kang-Sheng (Hsiao-kang), Chen Shiang-Chyi (Chyi), Norman Atun (Rawang), Pearlly Chua (Lady Boss).

## ALLEGRO

(INTERNATIONAL FILM CIRCUIT) Producer, Tine Grew Pfeiffer; Director, Christoffer Boe; Screenplay, Christoffer Boe, Mikael Wulff; Photography, Manuel Alberto Claro; Editor, Peter Brandt; Music, Thomas Knak; Designer, Nikolaj Danielsen; Costumes, Gab Humnicki; Animation/Visual Effects Designer, Martin D. Thurah; an Alphaville Pictures Copenhagen production, with participation of Danish Film Institute, DR TV Danish Broadcasting Corp., SF Film, Nordisk Film & Television Fund; Danish, 2005; Dolby; Color/B&W; Super-16/DV-to-35mm; Not rated; 90 minutes; American release date: May 9, 2007.

### Cast

Ulrich Thomsen (Zeeterstrøm), Helena Christensen (Andrea), Henning Moritzen (Tom), Svetoslav Korolev (Young Zetterstrøm), Niels Skousen (The Cook), Nicolas Bro (Terence Sander), Ellen Millingsø (Clara), Per Fly (Spectator), Benedikte Hansen (Piano Teacher), Jon Lange (Morten), Nikolaj Lie Kaas (Alex in the Zone), Knud Romer Jørgensen (Man in Shorts).

## PROVOKED: A TRUE STORY

Naveen Andrews, Aishwarya Rai in *Provoked: A True Story* © EROS

(EROS) Producer, Sunanda Murali Manohar; Executive Producers, J. Murali Manohar, Firuzi Khan; Director, Jag Mundhra; Screenplay, Carl Austin, Rahila Gupta, based on the book *Circle of Light* by Rahila Gupta, Kiranjit Ahluwalia; Photography, Madhu Ambat; Editors, Mundhra, Sanjeev Mirajkar; Music, A.R. Rahman; Designer, Peter Joyce; Costumes, Sarah Tapscott; Casting, Patricia Rose; an Eros Intl. release of a Media One Global Entertainment presentation, in association with Motion Picture Partners Intl. and British Media Fund Intl.; Indian-British; Dolby; Widescreen; Color; Not rated; 111 minutes; American release date: May 11, 2007.

### Cast

Aishwarya Rai (Kiranjit Ahluwalia), Miranda Richardson (Veronica Scott), Naveen Andrews (Deepak Ahluwalia), Rebecca Pidgeon (Miriam), Nandita Das (Radha Dalal), Robbie Coltrane (Lord Edward Foster), Steve McFadden (DS Ron Meyers), Raji James (Anil Gupta), Nicholas Irons (PC James O'Connell), Deborah Moore (Jackie), Lorraine Bruce (Doreen), Ray Panthaki (Ravi), Leena Dhingra (Sheela), Julie T. Wallace, Maxine Finch (Lula), Claire Louise Amias (Young Nurse), Wendy Albiston (Guard Miller), Karen David (Asha), Guy Siner (Prosecutor), John Alford (Chris Jones-Legal Aid Solicitor), Ashwani Chopra (News Vendor), Judith Jacob (Guard Tyler), Steve McFadden (DS Ron Meyers), Marsha Rice (Mrs. Byron), Julie T. Wallace (Gladys).

## SIX DAYS

(SEVENTH ART RELEASING) Producers, Ina Iceman, Ark Bernstein, Luc Martin-Gusset; Director, Ilan Ziv; Screenplay, Stephen Phizicky; Photography, Andrei Chabot; Editors, Alfonso Peccia, Benjamin Duffield; Music, Vincent Stora; Narrator, John Tarzwell; an Instinct Films production in association with Pro-ductions Point due Jour and Alma Films, in co-production with ARTE France, Society Radio Canada and Channel 10-Israel; Israeli-Canadian-French; Color/B&W, DV; Not rated; 107 minutes; American release date: May 18, 2007. Documentary on the Six-Day War of 1967 between Israel and Egypt.

## ROLLING LIKE A STONE

(AUTO IMAGES) Producers, Magnus Gertten, Stefan Berg, Nilla Dahl; Directors, Magnus Gertten, Stefan Berg; Photography, Stefan Berg; Editor, Jesper Osmund; Music, Metro Jets (Magnus Borjeson and David Birde); released by the Swedish Film Institute; Swedish; Color; Not rated; 65 minutes; American release date: May 18, 2007. Documentary in which Swedish rock bands reflect on their fleeting meeting with the Rolling Stones in 1965.

## SEVERANCE

Judit Viktor, Danny Dyer, Juli Drajkóin in *Severance* © MAGNOLIA

(MAGNOLIA) Producer, Jason Newmark; Executive Producers, Michael Kuhn, Steve Christian, Malcolm Ritchie, Jill Tandy; Co-Producer, Alexandra Arlango; Director, Christopher Smith; Screenplay, James Moran, Christopher Smith; Story, James Moran; Photography, Ed Wild; Editor, Stuart Gazzard; Music, Christian Henson; Designer, John Frankish; Costumes, Stephen Noble; Visual Effects Supervisors, Phil Attfield, Simon Frame; Special Make-up Effects, Millennium F/X; Casting, William Davies, Gail Stevens; a Qwerty Films, U.K. Film Council presentation, in association with Isle of Man Film, of an N1 European Film Produktions (Germany)/Dan Films (U.K.) production; German-British; Dolby; Color; Not rated; 95 minutes; American release date: May 18, 2007.

### Cast

Danny Dyer (Steve); Laura Harris (Maggie); Tim McInnerny (Richard); Toby Stephens (Harris); Claudie Blakley (Jill); Andy Nyman (Gordon); Babou Ceesay (Billy); David Gilliam (George); Matthew Baker (Nose-feratu); Juli Drajkó (Olga); Judit Viktor (Nadia); Sándor Boros (Coach Driver); Levente Törköly (Lodge Killer); János Oláh (Flamethrower Killer); Attila Ferencz (Head-squish Killer); Bela Kasi (Headbutt Killer); Roalnd Kollárszky (Knife-in-Butt Killer); Péter Katona (Stone Thrower Killer); Levente Lezsák (Landmine Killer); Nick Greenall (Big Gun Killer); Steve Dawson (Guard #1 in Harris' Story); John Frankish (Dr. John "Victor" Frankish in Jill's Story); Johnnnie Schinas (Long-Haired Girl in Richard's Dream); Leon MacPherson, Arnold Zarom (Corporate Video Palisade Workers); Laura Bushell, John Cole, Murray Golding, Jamie Higgins, Nerys Martin, Stephanie Ratcliff, Cindi Svensson (Corporte Video Office Blondes).

## FLANDERS

Adélaïde Leroux, Inge Decaesteker in *Flanders* © IFC FILMS

(IFC) aka *Flandres*; Producers, Jean Brehat, Rachid Bouchareb; Executive Producer, Muriel Merlin; Director/Screenplay, Bruno Dumont; Photography, Yves Cape; Editor, Guy Lecorne; Costumes, Cedric Grenapin, Alexandra Charles; Line Producers, Michele Grimaud, Abdellaziz Ben Mlouka (Tunisia); Casting, Claude Debonnet; a 3b Prods. Production with Arte France Cinema, CRRAV Nord-Pays de Calais, Le Fresnoy; French; Dolby; Color; Not rated; 91 minutes; American release date: May 18, 2007.

### Cast

Adélaïde Leroux (Barbe), Samuel Boidin (Demester), Henri Cretel (Blondel), Jean-Marie Bruveart (Briche), David Poulain (Leclercq), Patrice Venant (Mordac), David Legay (Lieutenant), Inge Decaesteker (France).

## MEMORIES OF TOMORROW

(ELEVEN ARTS) aka *Ashita no kioku*; Producers, Sunao Sakagami, Tatsuo Kawamura; Executive Producer, Ken Watanabe; Director, Yukihiko Tsutsumi; Screenplay, Hakaru Sunamoto, Uiko Miura, based on the novel by Hiroshi Ogiwara; Photography, Satoru Karasawa; Editor, Nobuyuki Ito; Music, Michiru Oshima; Designer, Hajime Oikawa; a Toei Co. production; Japanese; Dolby; Color/B&W; Not rated; 122 minutes; American release date: May 18, 2007.

### Cast

Ken Watanabe (Masayuki Saeki), Kanako Higuchi (Emiko Saeki), Kenji Sakaguchi (Naoya Ito), Kazue Fukiishi (Rie Saeki), Asami Mizukawa (Keiko Ikuno), Noritake Kinashi (Shigeyuki Kizaki), Mitsuhiro Oikawa (Takehiro Yoshida), Eriko Watanabe (Kimiko Hamamo), Teruyuki Kagawa (Atsushi Kawamura), Hideji Otaki (Usaburou Sugawara).

## 9 STAR HOTEL

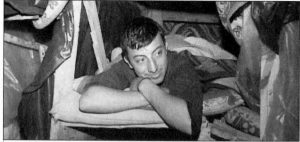

*9 Star Hotel* © KOCH LORBER

(KOCH LORBER) aka *Malon 9 Kohavim*; Producers, Edna Kowarsky, Elinor Kowarsky; Director/Photography, Ido Haar; Editors, Ido Haar, Era Lapid; an Eden production; Israeli; Color; DigiBeta; Not rated; 78 minutes; American release date: May 23, 2007. Documentary about illegal Palestinian construction workers building an Israeli city within the Occupied Territories.

## RADIANT CITY

The Moss Family in *Radiant City* © ODEON FILMS

(ODEON FILMS) Producers, Shirley Vercruysse, Bonnie Thompson; Executive Producer, Graydon McRea; Directors/Screenplay, Gary Burns, Jim Brown; Photography, Patrick McLaughlin; Editor, Jonathan Baltrusaitus; Music, Joey Santiago; Designer, John Sherrington; a National Film Board of Canada presentation (in Canada) of an NFB production, in co-production with Burns Film; Canadian; Color; Not rated; 86 minutes; American release date: May 25, 2007. Documentary on North America's suburban sprawl since World War II; with Kyle Grant, Amanda Guenther, Daniel Jeffery, Mikeala Jeffery, Jane McFarlane, Curt McKinistry, Hong Cheng, Bob Legare, Chantal Perron, Karen Planden.

## MAGIC MIRROR

(NEW YORKER) aka *Espelho Mágico*; Producer, Miguel Cadilhe; Director/Screenplay, Manoel de Oliveira, based on a novel by Agustina Bessa-Luis; Photography, Renato Berta; Editor, Valerie Loiseleux; Designer, Monica Baldaque; Costumes, Arlete Campos; A Filbox Producoes production; Portuguese, 2005; Dolby; Color; Not rated; 137 minutes; American release date: May 25, 2007.

### Cast

Ricardo Trépa (Jose Luciano), Leonor Silveira (Alfreda), Luís Miguel Cintra (Filipe Quinta), Michel Piccoli (Prof. Heschel), Marisa Paredes (Nun), Leonor Baldaque (Vincenta/Abril), Glória de Matos (Nurse Hilda), Isabel Ruth (Celsa Adelaide), Adelaide Teixeira (Queta), Diogo Dória (Comissary), José Wallenstein (Américo), Maestro Atalaya (Prof. Oboé), Padre João Marques (Priest Feliciano).

## AMU

Konkona Sensharma, Ankur Khanna in *Amu* © EMERGING PICTURES

(EMERGING PICTURES) Producers, Shonali Bose, Aidan Hill, Atiya Bose; Director/Screenplay, Shonali Bose; Photography, Lourdes Ambrose; Editor, Bob Brooks; Music, Nandlal Nayak; a Jonai production; Indian, 2005; 102 minutes; American release date: May 25, 2007.

### Cast

Konkona Sensharma (Kaju "Amu"), Brinda Karat (Keya), Ankur Khanna (Kabir), Chaiti Ghosh (Tuki), Aparna Roy (Grandmother), Yashpal Sharma (Gobind), Ashish Ghosh (Uncle), Ruma Ghosh (Aunt), Loveleen Mishra (Leelavati), Brajesh Mishra (Chachaji), Bharat Kapoor (Arun Sehgal), Lushin Dubey (Meera Sehgal), Rajendra Gupta (KK), Ganeve Rajkotia (Shanno Kaur), Kuljit Singh (Gurbachan Singh), Ekta Sood (Amu), Harshit Sood (Arjun), Mohini Mathur (Durga), Kirandeep Sharma (Shanti Kumar).

## TEN CANOES

Jamie Gulpilil in *Ten Canoes* © PALM PICTURES

(PALM PICTURES) Producers, Rolf de Heer, Julie Ryan; Executive Producers, Sue Murray, Domenico Procacci, Bryce Menzies; Director/Screenplay, Rolf de Heer; in consultation with the people of Ramingining; Co-Director, Peter Djigirr; Photography, Ian Jones; Editor, Tania Nehme; Music, Steven Wilinydjanu Maliburr, Rupert Gaykamangu, Kelvin Dangawarra Gaykamangu, Roy Gaykamangu, Richard Birrinbirrin, Peter Minygululu, Billy Black, John Nudumul, Mark Muruwirri; Art Director, Beverley Freeman; a Palace Films release of a Film Finance Corp. Australia presentation of a Fandango Australia, Vertigo production, in association with South Australian Film Corp., Adelaide Film Festival, SBS Independent; Australian, 2006; Dolby; Widescreen; Atlab color/B&W; Super 35 Widescreen; 91 minutes; American release date: June 1, 2007.

### Cast

Crusoe Kurddal (Ridjimiraril); Jamie Gulpilil (Dayindi/Yeeralparil); Richard Birrinbirrin (Birrinbirrin); Peter Minygululu (Minygululu); Frances Djulibing (Nowalingu); Sonia Djarrabalminym (Banalandju); Cassandra Malangarri Baker (Munandjarra); Philip Gudthaykudthay (The Sorcerer); David Gulpilil Ridjimiraril Dalaithngu (The Storyteller)

## WHAT THE SNOW BRINGS

(ELEVEN ARTS) aka *Yuki ni negau koto*; Producer, Masako Tanabe; Executive Producers, Naoki Kai, Masaaki Wakasugi; Director, Kichitaro Negishi; Screenplay, Masato Kato, based on the novel by Sho Narumi; Photography, Hiroshi Machida; Designer, Fumio Ogawa; Music, Gorou Ito; Editor, Akimasa Kawashima; an Artist Film, Be-Wild production; Japanese; Color; Not rated; 112 minutes; American release date: June 1, 2007.

### Cast

Yusuke Iseya (Manabu Yazaki), Koichi Sato (Takeo Yazaki), Kyôko Koizumi (Haruko Tanaka), Kazue Fukiishi (Makie Shudo), Tesuya Deguchi (Yuhara), Denden (Tamotsu Fujimaki), Teruyuki Kagawa (Ogasawara), Mitsuko Kusabue (Shizuko Yazaki), Ryuta Okamoto (Tominaga), Kippei Shiina (Kurokawa), Masahiko Tsugawa (Ozeki), Hiroshi Yamamoto (Tetsuo Kato), Tsutomu Yamazaki (Tanba).

## 12:08 EAST OF BUCHAREST

(TARTAN) aka *A fost sau n-a fost?*; Producer/Director/Screenplay, Corneliu Porumboiu; Executive Producer, Daniel Burlac; Photography, Marius Panduru; Editor, Roxana Szel; Music, Rotaria; Designer, Daniel Raduta; a 42 Km Film production; Romanian; Dolby; Color; Not rated; 89 minutes; American release date: June 6, 2007.

**Cast**

Mircea Andreescu (Emanoil Piscoci), Teodor Corban (Virgil Jderescu), Ion Sapdaru (Tiberiu Manescu), Mirela Cioaba (Doamna Manescu), Cristina Ciofu (Vali), Constantin Dita (Tibi), Luminita Gheorghiu (Doamna Jderescu), Lucian Iftime (Lica).

## GHOST TRAIN

(ADV FILMS) aka *Otoshimono*; Director, Takeshi Furusawa; Screenplay, Takeshi Furusawa, Erika Tanaka; Japanese, 2006; Color; Not rated; 92 minutes; American release date: June 6, 2007.

**Cast**

Erika Sawajiri, Chinatsu Wakatsuki, Shun Oguri, Aya Sugimoto, Itsuji Itao, Miyoko Asada.

## THE LAST HANGMAN

(IFC) aka *Pierrepoint*; Producer, Christine Langan; Executive Producers, Andy Harries, Rebecca Eaton, Jeff Pope, Paul Tribjits; Director, Adrian Shergold; Screenplay, Jeff Pope, Bob Mills; Photography, Danny Cohen; Editor, Tania Reddin; Music, Martin Phipps; Designer, Candida Otton; Art Director, Andrea Coathupe; Costumes, Mary Jane Reyner; a U.K. Film Council and Capitol Films presentation of a Granada production, in association with Masterpiece Theater; British; Dolby; Color; HD-to-35mm; 94 minutes; American release date: June 8, 2007.

**Cast**

Timothy Spall (Albert Pierrepoint), Juliet Stevenson (Annie Pierrepoint), Cavan Clerkin (George Cooper), Eddie Marsan (James "Tish" Corbitt), Christopher Fulford (Sykes), James Corden (Kirky), Joyia Fitch (Elizabeth Volkenrath), Clive Francis (Monty), Claire Keelan (Jessie), Ben McKay (Timothy Evans), Tobias Menzies (Lt. Llewelyn), Michael Norton (Josef Kramer), Paul Ready (Anthony David Farrow), Peter Ryder (Protester), Sheyla Shehovich (Irma Grese), Mary Stockley (Ruth Ellis), Tim Woodward (Governor of Holloway).

## NORIKO'S DINNER TABLE

(TIDEPOINT PICTURES) aka *Noriko no Shokutaku*; Producer, Takeshi Suzuki; Executive Producer, Yutaka Morohashi; Director/Screenplay, Sion Sono, based on his novel; Director/Screenplay, Sion Sono; Photography, Souhei Tanigawa; Editor, Junichi Ito; Music, Tomoki Hasegawa; Art Director, Toru Fujita; a Mother Ark Co. production; Japanese; Color; DV-to-35mm; Not rated; 153 minutes; American release date: June 13, 2007.

**Cast**

Kazue Fukiishi (Noriko Shimabara), Tsugumi (Kumiko), Ken Mitsuishi (Tetsuzo Shimabara), Yuriko Yoshitaka (Yuka Shimbara), Shirô Namiki (Ikeda), Sanae Miyata (Taeko Shimabara).

## LIGHTS IN THE DUSK

Janne Hyytiäinen, Maria Järvenhelmi in *Lights in the Dust* © STRAND RELEASING

(STRAND) aka *Laitakaupungin Valot*; Producer/Director/Screenplay/Editor, Aki Kaurismaki; Photography, Timo Salminen; Designer, Markku Patila; Costumes, Outi Harjupatana; a Sputnik Oy production, in association with YLE TV-1, Pandora Film in co-production with ZDF/Arte, Pyramid Prods., BIM Distribuzione, C More Entertainment, with support from the Finnish Film Foundation; Finnish; Dolby; Color; Not rated; 77 minutes; American release date: June 13, 2007.

**Cast**

Janne Hyytiäinen (Koistinen); Ilkka Koivula (Lindholm); Maria Järvenhelmi (Mirja); Maria Heiskanen (Aila); Sergei Doudko, Andrei Gennadiev, Artruas Pozdniakovas (Russians).

# MACBETH

Sam Worthington, Victoria Hill in *Macbeth* © TRULY INDIE

(TRULY INDIE/UNION STATION MEDIA) Producer, Marin Fabinyi; Executive Producers, Michael Gudinski, Gary Hamilton, Greg Sitch, Antonio Zeccola; Co-Executive Producers, Michael Whyke, Terrence Yason, Peter Phelan; Co-Producers, Geoffrey Wright, Victoria Hill, Jenni Tosi; Director, Geoffrey Wright; Screenplay, Geoffrey Wright, Victoria Hill, adapted from the play by William Shakespeare; Photography, Will Gibson; Designer, David McKay; Costumes, Jane Johnston; Editor, Jane Usher; Music, John Clifford White; Casting, Marianne Jade, Louise Mitchell; a Film Finance Corp. Australia presentation, in association with Film Victoria, Arclight Films, and Paradigm Hyde Films, of a Mushroom Pictures production; Australian; Dolby; Color; HD-to-35mm; Not rated; 109 minutes; American release date: July 6, 2007.

### Cast

Sam Worthington (Macbeth); Victoria Hill (Lady Macbeth); Lachy Hulme (Macduff); Gary Sweet (Duncan); Steve Bastoni (Banquo); Mick Molloy (Murderer in Brown); Kat Stewart (Lady Macduff); Matt Doran (Malcolm); Damian Walshe-Howling (Ross); Jonny Pasvolsky (Lennox); Rel Hunt (Angus); John Molloy (Murderer in Black); Chloe Armstrong, Kate Bell, Miranda Nation (Witches); Bob Franklin (Siward); Simon Scott (Zapata); Nash Edgerton (Macdonwald); Lance Anderson (Henchman with Glasses); Kevin Tran (Macdonwald's Bagman); Samuel Twe (Goateed Gunman); Christopher Shen (Smirk); Anna Anderson (Shy Girl); Hai Ha (Skinny Girl); Nikon Souphan (Elevator Gunman); Ri-Jie Kwok (Getaway Driver); George Vidalis (Cawdor); Terry Lim (Chinese Businessman); Norman Keller (Duncan's Bald Bodyguard); Charles Lavea-Williams (Duncan's Bearded Bodyguard); Socratis Otto (Det. Mentieth); Christopher Kirby (Seton); Ruby O'Rourke (Singer on TV); Katherine Tonkin (Lady Macbeth's Maid); Craig Stott (Fleance); Corinne Davies (Ross' Girl); Saskia Sansom (Angus' Girl); Edwina Wren (Malcolm's Girl); Louis Corbett (Macduff's Son); Chris Vance (Det. Caithness); Jamie-Lee Wilson (Constable); Peter Davenport (Constable Michael); Esther Usher, Katie James (Barmaids); Inouk Arnall (Reporter on TV); Siros Niaros (Scar-Mouthed Henchman); Jarrah Cocks (One-Eyed Henchman); Robert Shook (Long-Haired Henchman); Kym Gyngell (Doctor); Haiha Le (Skinny Girl).

# CZECH DREAM

*Czech Dream* © SMITH/TASKOVSKI

(SCHWARZ SMITH & TASKOVSKI FILMS) Executive Producers, Morgan Spurlock, Filip Cermák; Directors/Screenplay/Photography, Vit Klusák, Filip Remunda; Music, Varhan Ochestratovich Bauer; Editor, Zdenek Marek; a Ceská Televize, FAMU, Hypermarket Film production; Czech, 2004; Color; Not rated; 90 minutes; American release date: June 15, 2007. Documentary on two Czech film students' promotional campaign for a nonexistent supermarket, Czech Dream.

# STRIKE

(LAEMMLE/ZELLER FILMS) aka *Strajk: Die Heldin von Danzig*; Producer, Juergen Haase; Executive Producer, Wolfgang Plehn; Director, Volker Schloendorff; Screenplay, Andreas Pflueger, Sylke Rene Meyer; Photography, Andreas Hoefer; Editors, Peter Przygodda, Wanda Zeman; Music, Jean Michel Jarre; Designer, Robert Czesak; a Provobis Film, Mediopolis, BR, ARTE (Germany), PAISA Film (Warsaw) production; German-Polish; Dolby; Color/B&W; Not rated; 111 minutes; American release date: June 15, 2007.

### Cast

Katharina Thalbach (Agnieszka), Dominique Horwitz (Kazimierz), Andrzej Chyra (Lech Walesa), Dariusz Kowalski (Bochnak), Krzysztof Kiersznowski (Mateusz), Ewa Telega (Mirka), Wojciech Pszoniak (Kaminski), Wojciech Solarz (Krystian as Youngster), Barbara Kurzaj (Elwira), Maria Maj (Chomska), Jowita Budnik (Dobrowolska), Joanna Bogacka (Szymborska), Henryk Golebiewski (Marek), Marta Kalmus (Worker), Dorota Kolak (Kaminska), Magdalena Smalara (Renata).

# BEYOND HATRED

(FIRST RUN FEATURES) aka *Au-delà de la haine*; Producers, Christophe Girard, Katherina Marx; Director, Olivier Meyrou; Photography, Jean Marc Bouzou; Editor, Cathie Dambel; Music, Francois-Eudes Chanfrault; a Hold Up Films, Miss Luna Films production, with the support of France 5, France 2, and CNC. French; Color, 16mm-to-35mm; Not rated; 90 minutes; American release date: June 15, 2007. Documentary on the efforts of Francois Chenu's family to find forgiveness after he was murdered by homophobic skinheads in 2002; with Jean-Paul Chenu, Marie-Cecile Chenu.

# MANUFACTURED LANDSCAPES

(ZEITGEIST) Producers, Nick de Pencier, Daniel Iron, Jennifer Baichwal; Director, Jennifer Baichwal; Photography, Peter Mettler; Editor, Roland Schlimme; Music, Dan Driscoll; Associate Producers, Jeff Powis, Lucas Lackner; a Mercury Films and Foundry Films co-production with the National Film Board of Canada in association with TV Ontario; Canadian; Dolby; Color/B&W; 16mm-to-35mm; Not rated; 86 minutes; American release date: June 20, 2007. Documentary recording photographer Edward Burtynsky's glimpse into China's modern-day industrial revolution.

# WHITE PALMS

(STRAND) aka *Fehér Tenyér*; Producers, Ivan Angelusz, Gabor Kovacs, Agi Pataki, Peter Reich; Executive Producers, Fellegi Thomas, Mathieu Kassovitz, Peter Kassovitz, Zsofia Kende, Kornel Sipos; Director/Screenplay, Szabolcs Hajdu; Photography, Andras Nagy; Editor, Peter Politzer; Music, Peace Orchestra, Gail McDermot, Ferenc Darvas, Rimsky-Korsakov; Designer, Monika Esztan; Costumes, Krisztina Berzsenyi; a Katapult Films, Filmpartners production; Hungarian, 2006; Color; Not rated; 103 minutes; American release date: June 20, 2007.

## Cast

Zoltán Miklós Hajdu (Mikló Dongó); Orion Radies (10-year-old Dongó); Silas Wind Radies (13-year-old Dongó); Gheorghe Dinica (Ferenc Sz-abó, "Puma"); Kyle Shewfelt (Kyle Manjak); Oana Pellea (Mom); Andor Lukáts (Dad); Dávid Horváth (10-year-old Józsi); Dávid Vecsernyés (10-year-old Bakos); Péter Déri (10-year-old Fónyi); Krisztián Oltyán (10-year-old Csaba); Illés Vér (10-year-old Miki); Csaba Mészáros (10-year-old Sztelek); Tibor Géza Papp (10-year-old Váganyik); Olivér Bajnóczi (10-year-old Vágó); Ábel Dénes, Bence Ladóczky, Zsolt Lengyel, Bence Tálas, Gergely Fanó, Dávid Göbölös, Gergely Romhányi (10-year-old Gymnasts); Zsolt Virág (13-year-old Bakos); Róbert Heitzmann (13-year-old Fónyi); Gyula Tamás Pénzes (13-year-old Józsi); Gábor Kentner (13-year-old Váganyik); Csaba Nyers (13-year-old Vágó); Gyula Benedek (13-year-old Gymnast); Valter Csonka (Józsi's Dad); Alexander Brousnikin (Pavel Bazarov); Artyom Brousnikin (Andrei Bazarov); Tibor Mészáros (Ippolo); Alexandru Repan (Repan).

# KLIMT

Saffron Burrows, John Malkovich in *Klimt* © OUTSIDER PICTURES

(OUTSIDER PICTURES) Producers, Dieter Pochlatko, Arno Ortmair, Matthew Justice, Andreas Schmid; Co-Producers, Ira Zloczower, Paolo Branco; Direc-tor/Screenplay, Raul Ruiz; English Screenplay Adaptation, Gilbert Adair; Photography, Ricardo Aronovich; Editor, Valeria Sarmiento; Music, Jorge Arriagada; Designers, Rudi Czettel, Katharina Woeppermann; Costumes, Bir-git Hutter; Line Producer, Dieter Limbek; Casting, Fleischhacker/Englander (Austria), Baumueller/Schottldreier (Germany), Sue Jones (U.K.). An EPO Film (Austria)/Film-Line (Germany)/Lunar Films (U.K.)/Gemini Films (France) production, in association with Andreas Schmid; Austrian-German-British-French; Dolby; Color; Not rated; 96 minutes (also shown at 130 minutes); American release date: June 22, 2007.

## Cast

John Malkovich (Gustav Klimt), Veronica Ferres (Emilie Flöge), Saffron Burrows (Lea de Castro), Stephen Dillane (Secretary), Paul Hilton (Octave Herzog), Sandra Ceccarelli (Serena Lederer), Karl Fischer (August Lederer), Irina Wanka (Berta Zuckerkandl), Antje Charlotte Sieglin (Vally), Nikolai Kinski (Egon Schiele), Joachim Bissmeier (Hugo Moritz), Peter Appiano (Carl Moll), Mark Zak (Hevesi), Gunther Gillian (Georges Méliès), Alexander Strobele (Hermann Bahr), Dennis Petkovic (Adolf Loos), Annemarie Düringer (Klimt's Mother), Marion Mitterham-mer (Hermine Klimt), Nicole Beutler (English Lady), Miguel Herz-Kestranek (Dr. Stein), Aglaia Szyszykowitz (Mizzi), Alexandra Hilverth (Madame), Miriam Heard (Kranehschwester), Rose-Lise Bonin (Young Sylvia), Martin Brambach (Thomas), Julie Bräuning (Lissie), Georg Friedrich (Kellner), Ariella Hirschfeld (Kati), Erwin Ledger (Kranken-pfleger), Katie Pfleghar (Prostitute), Tom Trambow (Photographer), Susanne Wolhsein (Girl with Opera Glass).

# YELLOW

(SONY PICTURES) Producers, Stephen J. Brown, Dennis Murphy; Executive Producers, Donald A. Barton, Jeff Golenberg, Sam Maydew, Nat Moss, Richard Rionda Del Castro; Director, Alfredo de Villa; Screenplay, Roselyn Sanchez, Nacoma Whobrey; Photography, Claudio Chea; Editors, John Coniglio, Richard Halsey; Music, Andre Abujamra; Designer, Charlotte Bourke; Costumes, Julia Michelle Santiago; Choreographer, Carlton Wilburn; Casting, Michelle Morris; a Hannibal Pictures presentation of a Yellow Prods. Production; Puerto Rican-American; Dolby; Widescreen; Color; Rated R; 93 minutes; American release date: June 22, 2007.

### Cast

Roselyn Sanchez (Amaryllis Campos), D.B. Sweeney (Christian Kile), Bill Duke (Miles Emory), Manny Perez (Angelo), Jaime Tirelli (Franco Campos), Eric Michels Brown (Elizabeth), Richard Petrocelli (Jack Frawley), Sammi Rotibi (Red), Sully Diaz (Carmen Campos), Nancy Millan (Hilda), Jorge R. Calderon (Joeli), Carlton Wilborn (Broadway Choreographer), Ricardo Alvarez Santiago (Johnny Cantu), Sorely Muentes (Dancer).

# LONGING

(ANTHOLOGY FILM ARCHIVES) aka *Sehnsucht*; Producer, Peter Rommel; Co-Producer, David Groenewold; Executive Producer, Jutta Frech; Director/Screenplay, Valeska Grisebach; Photography, Bernhard Keller; Editors, Bettina Boehler, Grisebach, Natali Barrey; Music Adviser, Martin Hossbach; Art Director, Beatrice Schultz; Costumes, Birte Meesmann; Casting, Christiane Lilge, Hannah Marquardt; a Rommel Film, GFP Medienfonds production, in association with ZDF (Das Kleine Fernsehspiel), ZDF/3sat; German, 2006; Color; Not rated; 85 minutes; American release date: June 22, 2007.

### Cast

Andreas Müller (Markus); Ilka Welz (Ella); Anett Dornbusch (Rose); Erika Lemke (Oma); Markus Werner (Neighbor Boy); Doritha Richter (Mother); Detlef Baumann (Neighbor); Ilse Lausch (Aunt); Jan Günzel, Bernd Liske, Bern Wachsmuth (Friends); Hartmut Schliephacke (Burgermeister).

# GHOSTS OF CITÉ SOLEIL

(THINKFILM/SONY BMG) Producers, Mikael Chr. Rieks, Tomas Radoor, Seth Kanegis; Executive Producers, Kim Magnusson, Cary Woods, George Hickenlooper, Jerry Duplessis, Wyclef Jean; Director/Screenplay, Asger Leth; Co-Director/Photography, Milos Loncarevic; Editor, Adam Nielsen; Music, Wyclef Jean, Jerry Duplessis; a Nordisk Film A/S, Sakpase Films, Sunset Prods. Independent Pictures production in association with the Danish Film Institute; Danish-American; Dolby; Color/B&W, 16mm/DV-to-35mm; Not rated; 88 minutes; American release date: June 27, 2007. Documentary on the Chimeres, a gang allegedly employed and armed by President Jean-Bertrand Aristide in Haiti's worst slum, Cite Soleil.

# FALLING

Ursula Strauss, Georg Friedrich in *Falling* © KINO

(KINO) aka *Fallen*; Producers, Antonin Svoboda, Martin Gschlacht, Bruno Wagner, Barbara Albert; Director/Screenplay, Barbara Albert; Photography, Bernhard Keller; Editor, Karina Ressler; Art Director, Katharina Woeppermann; Costumes, Veronika Albert; a coop99 filmproduktion production, in association with ORF, ZDF/Arte; German-Austrian, 2006; Color; Not rated; 88 minutes; American release date: June 29, 2007.

### Cast

Nina Proll (Nina), Birgit Minichmayr (Brigitte), Ursula Strauss (Alex), Kathrin Resetarits (Carmen), Gabriela Hegedüs (Nicole), Kellie Jaxson (Waitresss), Katie Pfleghar (Barmaid), Ina Strnad, Georg Friedrich, Darina Dujmic, Angelika Niedetzky, Simon Hatzl, Christian Strasser, Erich Knoth, Noemi Fischer.

# FLYING: CONFESSIONS OF A FREE WOMAN

(ZOHEN FILM PRODUCTION) Producers, Claus Ladegaard, Jennifer Fox; Co-Producers, Kerthy Fix, Amy Foote, Mette Mailand, Elizabeth Mandel; Director/Screenplay, Jennifer Fox; Photography, Jennifer Fox and Cast; Music, Jan Tilman Schade; Editor, Niels Pagh Anderson; Associate Producer, Ariel Amsalem; an Easy Films presentation in association with Zohe Film Prods.; Danish-American; Color; Not rated; 353 minutes; American release date: July 4, 2007. Documentary in which Jennifer Fox explores today's women dealing with life, sex, work, and love. Originally broadcast in Denmark as a miniseries.

## DYNAMITE WARRIOR

Dan Chupong in *Dynamite Warrior* © MAGNOLIA PICTURES

(MAGNOLIA) aka *Khon fai bin*; Producers, Prachya Pinkaew, Sukanya Vongsthapat; Executive Producer, Somsak Techaratanaprasert; Director, Chalerm Wongpim; Screenplay, Chalerm Wongpim, Yuthapong Pirayuthapon; Photography, Thanachat Bunlah, Chalerm Wongpim; Art Director, Thanom Nantaworaphongsaa; Costumes, Keattichai Keereesri; Editors, Chalerm Wongpim, Wichit Wattananon, Triple-X CG Co.; Music, Theppanom Piriya-worakul; Visual Effects, It-Ti-Rit House Co.; Stunts, Satit Vosbein; Action Choreographer, Somjai Junmoontree; Action Supervisor, Panna Rittikrai; Associate Producer, Vosbein; Line Producer, Thanapop Bhaibulaya; Casting, Hengsawast, Wattananon, Phithan Chokkitchakarn; a Sahamongkolfilm Intl. presentation of a Baa-Ram-Ewe production; Thai, 2006; Dolby; Color; Not rated; 103 minutes; American release date: July 6, 2007.

**Cast**

Dan Chupong (Jone Bang Fai), Leo Putt (Lord Wang), Panna Rittikrai (Nai Hoi Dam), Samart Payakarun (Nai Hoi Singh), Kanyapak Su-worakood (E-sao), Somdet Kaew-ler (The Thief), Ampon Rattanawong (Khan), Wichai Prommajan (Phaen), Jaran Ngamdee (Naai Jan).

## THE METHOD

(PALM PICTURES) aka *El Método* and *The Gronholm Method*; Producers, Francisco Ramos, Gerardo Herrero; Executive Producer, Ricardo Garcia Arrojo; Director, Marcelo Pineyro; Screenplay, Mateo Gil, Marcelo Pineyro, based on the play by Jordi Galceran Ferrer; Photography, Alfredo Mayo; Editor, Ivan Aledo; Music, Frederic Begin; Production Costume Designer, Veronica Toledo; Sound (Dolby Digital), Eduardo Noriega, Polo Aledo; Assistant Director, Javier Petit; an Alquimia Cinema/Tornasol Films/Arena Films/Cattleya presentation of a Francisco Ramos production; Spanish-Argentine-Italian, 2005; Dolby; Widescreen; Color; Not rated; 115 minutes; American release date: July 6, 2007.

**Cast**

Eduardo Noriega (Carlos), Najwa Nimri (Nieves), Eduard Fernández (Fernando), Pablo Echarri (Ricardo), Ernesto Alterio (Enrique), Carmelo Gómez (Julio), Adriana Ozores (Ana), Natalia Verbeke (Montse).

## SHADOW COMPANY

*Shadow Company* © PURPOSE FILMS

(PURPOSE FILMS) Producers, Nick Bicanic, Remy Kozak; Directors/Screenplay, Nick Bicanic, Jason Bourque; Photography, Jason Bourque, Jarred Land; Editor, Les Lukacs; Music, Andrew Wanliss-Orlebar; a Purpose Built production; Canadian; Color; HD; Not rated; 85 minutes; Release date: July 6, 2007. Documentary on private military companies that fight for financial gain during the Iraq War; with James Ashcroft, Alan Bell, Rob McKintyre, Phil Lancaster, Madelaine Drohan, Robert Young Pelton, Peter Singer, Doug Brooks, Stephen J. Cannell, Cobus Claassens, Slavko Ilic, Neall Ellis, Frances Stonor Saunders, John F. Mullins, Eike Kluge, Tasha Bradsell.

## DRAMA/MEX

Diana Garcia in *Drama/Mex* © IFC FIRST TAKE

(IFC FIRST TAKE) Producers, Gabriel Garcia, Santiago Paredes, Miriana Moro; Executive Producers, Gabriel Garcia, Renato Ornelas, Yibran Asuad, Kyzza Terrazas, Diego Luna, Gael Garcia Bernal, Pablo Cruz; Director/Screenplay, Gerardo Naranjo; Photography, Tobias Datum; Designer, Claudio Castelli; Costumes, Annai Ramos; Editor, Yibran Asuad; Music, Julio Preciado, Chimo Bayo; Music Supervisor, Lynn Fainchtein; Casting, Alejandro Reza; an El Revolcadero, "La Bella Sobriedad" presentation of a Revolcadero Films, Canana, IMCINE production; Mexican, 2006; Dolby; Cinemascope; Super-16-to-35mm; Not rated; 105 minutes; American release date: July 11, 2007.

**Cast**

Fernando Becerril (Jaime), Diana Garcia (Fernanda), Miriana Moro (Tigrillo), Juan Pablo Castaneda (Gonzalo), Emilio Valdés (Chano Cuerpiperro).

# TIME

Park Ji-yeon in *Time* © LIFESIZE

(LIFESIZE) aka *Shi gan*; Producer/Director/Screenplay, Kim Ki-duk; Executive Producer, Michio Suzuki; Co-Producer, Kang Yeong-gu; Photography, Seong Jong-mu; Editor, Kim; Music, Noh Hyeong-woo; Art Director, Choi Geun-woo; Costumes, Lee Da-yeon; a Happinet Pictures (Japan)/Kim Ki Duk Film Co. (South Korea) presentation of a Kim Ki Duk Film Co. production; Japanese-South Korean, 2006; Dolby; Color; Not rated; 97 minutes; American release date: July 13, 2007.

### Cast

Ha Jung-woo (Ji-woo), Park Ji-yeon (See-hee Before Plastic Surgery), Kim Seong-min (Plastic Surgeon), Seong Hyeon-a (See-hee), Kim Ji-hyeon, Kim Bo-na, Hong Jeong-yeon, Seo Yeong-hwa, Jang Jun-yeong.

# TEKKONKINKREET

(DESTINATION FILMS) aka *Tekon kinkurîto*; Producers, Eiko Tanaka, Eiichi Kamagata, Masao Teshima, Ayako Ueda; Executive Producers, Naoki Kitagawa, Yasushi Shiina, Osamu Teshima, Eiko Tanaka; Director, Michael Arias; Co-Director, Himaki Ando; Screenplay, Anthony Weintraub, based on the manga by Taio Matsumoto; Editor, Mutsumi Takemiya; Music, Plaid; Art Director, Shinji Kimura; CGI Director, Takuma Sakamoto; Animation, Shojiro Nishimi, Chie Uratan, Masahiko Kubo; Character Design, Shojiro Nishimi; an Aniplex, Asmik Ace Entertainment, Beyond C, Shogakukan production of a Studio 4 Degree C film; Japanese; Dolby; Color; Rated R; 100 minutes; American release date: July 13, 2007. Animated.

# LIVE-IN MAID

(KOCH LORBER/THE FILM SALES COMPANY) aka *Cama adentro*; Producers, Anton Reixa, Diego Mas Trellis, Veronica Cura; Director/Screenplay, Jorge Gaggero; Photography, Javier Julia; Editor, Guillermo Represa; Designer, Marcela Bazzano; a Filmanova Invest (Spain)/Aquafilms, Libidofilms (Argentina) production; Spanish-Argentine; Dolby; Color; Not rated; 85 minutes; American release date: July 18, 2007.

### Cast

Norma Aleandro (Beba Pujol), Norma Argentina (Dora), Marcos Mundstock (Victor), Raul Panguinao (Miguel), Susana Lanteri (Memé), Claudia Lapacó (Perla), Eduardo Rodriguez (Lusito), Monica Gonzaga (Irma), Elsa Berenguer (Sara).

# THE SUGAR CURTAIN

*The Sugar Curtain* © FIRST RUN/ICARUS

(FIRST RUN/ICARUS) aka *El Telón de azúcar*; Producer/ Director/Screenplay/ Photography, Camila Guzmán Urzúa; Executive Producer, Nathalie Trafford; Editors, Claudio Martinez, Camila Guzmán Urzúa; Music, Omar Sosa; a Luz Film/Paraiso Production Diffusion production; French-Spanish; Color; DV Betacam; Not rated; 80 minutes; American release date: July 25, 2007. Documentary in which Camila Guzmán Urzúa returns to her Cuban homeland only to experience the modern-day poverty of so many of its inhabitants.

## SUMMER '04

(THE CINEMA GUILD) aka *Sommer '04 an der schlei*; Producers, Katrin Schloesser, Frank Loeprich; Co-Producers, Sabine Holtgreve, Bettina Reitz, Barbara Buhl, Georg Steinert; Director, Stefan Krohmer; Screenplay, Daniel Nocke; Photography, Patrick Orth; Editor, Gisela Zick; Art Director, Silke Fischer; Costumes, Silke Sommer; Casting, Nina Haun; an Oe Filmproduktion production, in association with SWR, BR, WDR, Arte; German, 2006; DTS Stereo; Color; Not rated; 97 minutes; Release date: August 1, 2007.

### Cast

Martina Gedeck (Mirjam), Robert Seeliger (Bill), Peter Davor (Andre), Svea Lohde (Livia), Lucas Kotaranin (Nils), Nicole Marischka (Grietje), Gábor Altorjay (Daniel), Michael Benthin (Arzt).

## THE WILLOW TREE

(NEW YORKER) aka *Beed-e majnoon*; Producer/Director/Idea, Majid Majidi; Executive Producer, Seyyed Saeed Seyedzadeh; Screenplay, Majid Majidi, Fouad Nahas, Nasser Hashemzadeh; Photography, Mahmoud Kalari; Designer, Behzad Kazzazi; Music, Ahmad Pezhman; Editor, Hassan Hassandoost; a Majid Majidi Film production; Iranian, 2005; Dolby; Kodak color; Not rated; 96 minutes; American release date: August 3, 2007.

### Cast

Parviz Parastui (Youssef), Roya Taymourian (Roya), Afarin Obeisi (Mother), Mohammad Amir Naji (Morteza), Melika Eslafi (Mariam), Leila Outsadi (Pari), Mahmoud Behraznia (Mahmood), Dawlat Asadi (Puya), Melika Aslafi (Maryam), Ahmad Gavaheri (Cashani), Fouad Nahas (Dr. Roque).

## COLOSSAL YOUTH

(INDEPENDENT/ANTHOLOGY FILM ARCHVIES) aka *Juventude em Marcha*; Producer, Francisco Villa-Lobos; Co-Producers, Philippe Avril, Andres Pfaffli, Elda Guidinetti; Director, Pedro Costa; Photography, Pedro Costa, Leonardo Simoes; Editor, Pedro Marques; a Contracosta Producoes (Portugal)/Les Films de l'Etranger (France)/Unlimited (France)/Ventura Film (Switzerland)/ RTP (Portugal)/RTSI (Switzerland)/Arte (France) production; Portuguese-French-Swiss, 2006; Dolby; Color; DV-to-35mm; Not rated; 155 minutes; American release date: August 3, 2007.

### Cast

Ventura (Ventura), Vanda Duarte (Vanda), Isabel Cardoso (Clotilde), Alberto Barros (Lento), Beatriz Duarte, Gustavo Sumpta, Cila Cardoso, Antonio Semedo "Nhurro," Paulo Nunes, Jose Maria Pina, Andre Semedo, Alexandre Silva, Paula Barrulas.

## SKIN WALKERS

Matthew Knight, Rhona Mitra in *Skin Walkers* © LIONSGATE

(LIONSGATE) Producers, Don Carmody, Dennis Berardi; Executive Producers, Robert Kulzer, Brian Gilbert; Director, James Isaac; Screenplay, James DeMonaco, James Roday, Todd Harthan; Photography, Adam Kane, David A. Armstrong; Editor, Allan Lee; Music, Andrew Lockington; Designer, David Hackl; Costumes, Antoinette Messam; Creature Effects, Stan Winston; Casting, Deirdre Brown; a Lionsgate, After Dark Films (U.S.) presentation, in association with Constantin Film (Germany)/Stan Winston Prods. (U.S.), of a Skinwalkers DCP (Canada) production, in association with Red Moon Films (Canada); Canadian-German-American; Dolby; Panavision; Color; Rated PG-13; 110 minutes; American release date: August 10, 2007.

### Cast

Jason Behr (Varek); Elias Koteas (Jonas); Rhona Mitra (Rachel); Kim Coates (Zo); Natassia Malthe (Sonja); Matthew Knight (Timothy); Sarah Carter (Katherine); Lyriq Bent (Dorak); Tom Jackson (Will); Rogue Johnston (Grenier); Barbara Gordon (Nana); Shawn Roberts (Adam); Christine Brubaker (Justine); Roman Podhora (Ralph); Wayne Ward (Justine's Husband); Scott Anderson (Courtney); Caroline Mangosing (Receptionist); Everton Lawrence (Paramedic); Patriz Quas (Waitress); James Kirchner (Motel Clerk); Jessica Huras (Bar Girl); Matt Hopkins (Gas Station Attendant); Jasmin Geljo, Charmine Hamp (Cabin People); David Sparrow (Manny the Butcher); Carl Marotte (Sheriff John Kilmer); Todd William Schroeder, Tig Fong (Red Necks); L.J. Vasilantonakis (Bartender); Wayne Downer (Bar Patron); Derek Kealey (Grim Reaper); Wendy Crewson (Leader); Wesley French (Native American); Julian Richings (Sad-Looking Man).

# CUT SLEEVE BOYS

(REGENT/HERE!) Producers, Chowee Leow, Ray Yeung; Director/Screenplay, Ray Yeung; Photography, Patrick Duval; Editors, Anuree De Silva, Catherine Fletcher; Music, Paul Turner; Designer, Malin Lindholm; Costumes, Maria Papandrea; a Rice Is Nice production; British-Hong Kong, 2006; Dolby; Color; Not rated; 86 minutes; American release date: August 10, 2007.

## Cast

Chowee Leow (Ashley Wang), Steven Lim (Melvin Shu), Gareth Rhys Davies (Todd Charrington), Neil Collie (Ross Foreman), John "Ebon-knee" Campbell (Diane/Dan), Mark Hampton (Gavin Chan), Paul Cox (Brad), David Cary (Ian, Trannie Club Cashier), David Tse (Pastor Joseph Szeto), Michelle Lee (Choi Lin Cheung), Shirley Chantrell (Mrs. Chan), Paul Courtenay Hyu (Kelvin Chan), Robert Leigh (Master Bates), Mark Wakeling (Antoine), James Bridgeman (Cheeky Workman), Ian Campbell (Gay Cafe Waiter), Kai Ting Chiang (Lucy in Charity Shop), Gerard Canning (Bald Man in Toilet), Rob Prewett (Taxi Driver), Susan Hodgetts (Girlfriend at Hammersmith Bridge), Michael Onder (Man at Hammersmith Bridge), Stephen Carlill (Solicitor), Naveen Mann (Workman #2), Eric Way (Man in Soho).

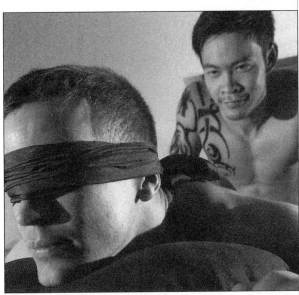

Garreth Rhys Davies, Steven Lim in *Cut Sleeve Boys* © HERE!/REGENT

# CROSSING THE LINE

James Dresnok in *Crossing the Line* © KINO

(KINO) Producers, Daniel Gordon, Nicholas Bonner; Director, Daniel Gordon; Photography, Nick Bennet; Editor, Peter Haddon; Music, Craig Armstrong; Narrator, Christian Slater; a VeryMuchSo (cq) presentation of a VeryMuchSo Passion Pictures production, in association with BBC, E Pictures, Koryo Tours, Dongsoong Art Center; British; B&W/Color; HD; Not rated; 91 minutes; American release date: August 10, 2007. Documentary on former GI James Dresnok, who defected to North Korea in 1962; with James Dresnok, Charles Robert Jenkins.

# ZEBRAMAN

(MEDIA BLASTERS) aka *Zeburaman*; Producers, Kumi Fukuchi, Shigeyuki Endo; Executive Producers, Mitsuru Kurosawa, Takashi Hirano; Co-Producers, Makoto Okada, Tsuguo Hattori; Director, Takashi Miike; Screenplay, Kankuro Kudo; Photography, Kaz Tanaka; Editor, Taiji Shimamura; Music, Kozy Endo; Designer, Akira Sakamoto; CGI producer, Misako Saka; a Toei Co. Production; Japanese, 2004; Dolby; Color; Not rated; 111 minutes; American release date: August 15, 2007.

## Cast

Show Aikawa (Shinichi/Zebraman), Kyoka Suzuki (Kana), Atsuro Watabe (Oikawa at the Defence Agency), Teruyoshi Uchimura (Ippongi), Yui Ichikawa (Midori), Kouen Kondo (Segawa), Akira Emoto (Kani-Otoko), Ryo Iwamatsu (Kanda), Ren Osugi (Kuroda).

## LOVE FOR SALE

Hermila Guedes in *Love for Sale* © STRAND RELEASING

(STRAND) aka *O Céu de Suely*; Producers, Walter Salles, Mauricio Andrade Ramos, Hengameh Panahi, Thomas Haberle, Peter Rommel; Executive Producer, Joao Vieira Jr.; Director, Karim Ainouz; Screenplay, Mauricio Zacharias, Felipe Braganca, Karim Ainouz; Photography, Walter Carvalho; Editor, Isabela Monteiro de Castro, Tina Baz Le Gal; Music, Berna Ceppas, Kamal Kassin; Designer/Costumes, Marcos Pedroso; Associate Producers, Christian Baute, Luis Galvao Teles; a Videofilmes/Celluloid Dreams/Shotgun pictures/Fado Filmes coproduction; Brazilian-German-Portuguese-French, 2006; Dolby; Color; Not rated; 88 minutes; American release date: August 15, 2007.

### Cast

Hermila Guedes (Hermila), Maria Menezes (Maria), Zezita Matos (Zezita), João Miguel (João), Georgina Castro (Georgina), Claudio Jaborandy (Claudio), Marcelia Cartaxo (Marcelia), Flavio Bauraqui (Balconista).

## THEM

(SLOWHAND CINEMA) aka *Ils*; Producer, Richard Grandpierre; Executive Producer, Fred Doniguian; Directors/Screenplay, David Moreau, Xavier Palud; Photography, Axel Cosnefroy; Editor, Nicolas Sarkissian; Music, Rene Marc Bini; Costumes, Elisabeth Mehu; Casting, Guillaume Moulin, David Bertrand; a Richard Grandpierre presentation of an Eskwad, StudioCanal, Castelfilm co-production; French, 2006; Digital Video, Widescreen; Color; Not rated; 74 minutes; American release date: August 17, 2007.

### Cast

Olvia Bonamy (Clémentine); Michaël Cohen (Lucas); Adriana Moca (Ilona); Maria Roman (Sanda); Camelia Maxim (Maria); Alexandrau Boghiu (Child); Emanuel Stefanuc, Horia Ioan, Stefan Comic, George Iulian (Adolescents).

## THE LAST LEGION

Aishwarya Rai, Colin Firth in *The Last Legion* © MGM/WEINSTEIN CO.

(MGM/WEINSTEIN CO.) Producers, Dino De Laurentiis, Martha De Laurentiis, Raffaella De Laurentiis, Tarak Ben Ammar; Executive Producers, Harvey Weinstein, James Clayton, Duncan Reid; Co-Producers, Chris Curling, Philip Robertson, Taoufik Guiga, Lorenzo De Maio, Iveta Hrdlovicova; Co-Executive Producer, Salvatore Morello; Director, Doug Lefler; Screenplay, Jez Butterworth, Tom Butterworth; Story, Carlo Carlei, Peter Rader, Valerio Manfredi, based in part on the novel by Valerio Manfredi; Photography, Marco Pontecorvo; Designer, Carmelo Argate; Costumes, Paolo Scalabrino; Editor, Simon Cozens; Music, Patrick Doyle; Line Producer, Hester Hargett-Aupetit; Casting, Lucy Ewan; a Dino De Laurentiis (Italy) production in association with Quinta Communications (France)/Ingenious Film Partners (U.K.); British-French-Italian; Dolby; Super 35 Widescreen; Color; Rated PG-13; 102 minutes; American release date: August 17, 2007.

### Cast

Colin Firth (Aurelius), Ben Kingsley (Ambrosinus/Merlin), Aishwarya Rai (Mira), Peter Mullan (Odoacer), Kevin McKidd (Wulfilla), John Hannah (Nestor), Thomas Sangster (Romulus Augustus), Iain Glen (Orestes), Rupert Friend (Demetrius), Nonso Anozie (Batiatus), Owen Teale (Vatrenus), Alexander Siddig (Theodorus Andronikus), Robert Pugh (Kustennin), James Cosmo (Hrothgar), Harry Van Gorkum (Vortgyn), Beata Sonczuk-Ben Ammar (Flavia), Murray McArthur (Tertius), Ferdinand Kingsley (Young Druid), Rory James (Young Arthur), Lee Ingleby (Germanus), Andrew Westfield (Marcallis), Alexandra Thomas-Davies (Ygraine), Zarrouk Brahim (Slave), Robert Brazil (Scorpion Commander), Querghi Chedly (Fisherman), Kathleen Segal (Flirting Girl).

# PRIMO LEVI'S JOURNEY

(THE CINEMA GUILD) aka *La Strada di Levi*; Producer/ Director, Davide Ferrario; Executive Producer, Ladis Zanini; Screenplay, Davide Ferrario, Marco Belpoliti; Photography, Gherardo Gossi, Massimiliano Trevis; Editor, Claudio Cormio; Music, Daniele Sepe; Associate Producer, Francesca Bocca; a Rosso-fuoco, RaiCinema production; Italian, 2006; Dolby; Widescreen; Color/B&W; 35mm, Mini-DV-to-35mm; Not rated; 93 minutes; American release date: August 17, 2007. Documentary tracing Italian chemist Primo Levi's journey through Europe following his release from Auschwitz; with Andrzej Wajda, Ruslana Bilozir, Modesto Ferrarini, Mario Rigoni Stern.

# SUNFLOWER

(NEW YORKER) aka *Xiangrikui*; Producers, Peter Loehr, Han Sanping; Executive Producer, Yang Buting; Co-Producers, Michael Werner, Wouter Barendrecht; Co-Executive Producer, Jiang Tao; Director, Zhang Yang; Screenplay, Zhang Yang, Cai Shangjun, Huo Xin; Photography, Jong Lin; Editor, Yang Hongyu; Music, Lin Hai; Art Directors, An Bin, Huang Xinming; Costumes, Xiang Honghui; Visual Consultant, Christopher Doyle; A Fortissimo Films presentation of a Ming Prods., Beijing Film Studio of a China Film Corp. (China)/Fortissimo Films (H.K.) production; Chinese-Hong Kong; Dolby; Color; Not rated; 132 minutes; American release date: August 17, 2007.

### Cast

Joan Chen (Xiuqing), Sun Haiying (Gengnian), Liu Zifeng (Old Liu), Zhang Fan (9-year-old Xiangyang), Gao Ge (19-year-old Xiangyang), Wang Haidi (30-year-old Xiangyang).

# DEEP WATER

(IFC) Producers, Al Morrow, John Persey, John Smithson; Executive Producers, Francoi Ivernel, Ralph Lee, Cameron McCracken, Paul Trijbits; Co-Producer, Steward le Marechal; Director/Screenplay, Louise Osmond, Jerry Rothwell; Photography, Nina Kellgren; Editors, Justine Wright, Ben Lester; Music, Molly Nyman, Harry Escott; Designer, Jane Linz Roberts; Narrator, Tilda Swinton; a Pathe Prods./UK Film Council/FilmFour presentation of an APT Films/Stir Fried Films production, in association with Darlow Smithson Prods.; British; Dolby; Color/B&W; Rated PG; 93 minutes; Release date: August 24, 2007. Documentary on amateur yachtsman Donald Crowhurst's participation in a 1968 sailing race around the world; with Clare Crowhurst, Simon Crowhurst, Francoise Moitessier de Cazalet, Ted Hynds, Santiago Franchessie, Donald Kerr, Robin Knox-Johnston, Ron Winspear; and Simon Russell Beale (Voice of Donald Crowhurst), Jean Badin (Voice of Bernard Moitessier).

# ANGER ME

(FACETS MULTIMEDIA) Producers, Varlo Vitali, Elio Gemini; Director, Elio Gemini; Photography, J.P. Locherer; Editors, Varlo Vitali, Elio Gemini, Dennis Day; Music, Steven Brown, Nikolas Klau, Trevor Turesky, Richard Sacks; a Signale Digitale, Few Steps production, with the assistance of the Canada Council for the Arts, Ontario Arts Council; Canadian; Color; DV; Not rated; 73 minutes; American release date: August 24, 2007. Documentary in which experimental filmmaker Kenneth Anger talks about his career; with Jonas Mekas.

# THE BOTHERSOME MAN

Trond Fausa Aurvag in *The Bothersome Man* © FILM MOVEMENT

(FILM MOVEMENT) aka *Den Brysomme mannen*; Producer, Jorgen Storm Rosenberg; Director, Jens Lien; Screenplay, Per Schreiner, based on his radio play; Photography, John Christian Rosenlund; Editor, Vidar Flataukan; Music, Ginge; Designer, Are Sjaastad; Costumes, Anne Pedersen; a Tordenfilm production, in association with the Icelandic Film Co., with the support of the Norsk Filmfond, Sandrew Metronome, Norsk Filmstudio, Icelandic Film Centre, TV 2; Norwegian, 2006; Dolby; Widescreen; Kodak color; Not rated; 95 minutes; American release date: August 24, 2007.

### Cast

Trond Fausa Aurvag (Andreas), Petronella Barker (Anne Britt), Per Schaaning (Hugo), Birgitte Larsen (Ingeborg), Johannes Joner (Håvard), Ellen Horn (Trulsen), Anders. T Andersen (Harald).

# THE MONASTERY: MR. VIG AND THE NUN

(KOCH LORBER) Producer, Sigrid Helene Dyekjaer; Executive Producer, Michael Fleischer; Director/Photography, Pernille Rose Gronkjaer; Screenplay, Jens Arentzen, Per K. Kirkegaard, Pernille Rose Gronkjaer; Editors, Pernille Bech Christensen, Theis Schmidt; Music, Johan Soderqvist; a Tju-Bang Film A/S production in association with the Danish Film Institute, Nordic Film & TV Fund in co-production with DR TV, YLE TV2 Documentaries; Danish, 2006; Color; 16mm-to-35mm; Not rated; 84 minutes; American release date: August 29, 2007. Documentary in which elderly Jorgen Lauersen donates his Danish castle to the Russian Orthodox Church, only to clash with religious officials; with Jorgen Lauersen Vig, Sister Amvrosya, Pernille Rose Gronkjaer.

# EXILED

(MAGNOLIA) aka *Fong juk*; Producer/Director, Johnnie To; Executive Producer, John Chong; Associate Director, Law Wing-cheong; Screenplay, Szeto Kam-yuen, Yip Tin-shing, Milkyway Creative Team; Photography, Cheng Siu-keung; Editor, David Richardson; Music, Guy Zerafa; Art Director, Tony Yu; Costumes, Stanley Cheung; Special Visual Effects, Brilliant Genesis; Visual Effects Supervisor, Stephen Ma; Stunts, Ling Chun-pong; Action Director, Wong Chi-wai; a Media Asia presentation of a Milkyway Image production; Hong Kong, 2006; Dolby; Super 35 Widescreen; Color; Rated R; 108 minutes; American release date: August 31, 2007.

### Cast

Anthony Wong (Blaze), Francis Ng (Tai), Nick Cheung (Wo), Simon Yam (Boss Fay), Josie Ho (Jin), Roy Cheung (Cat), Lam Suet (Fat), Richie Jen (Sgt. Chen), Lam Ka Tung (Boss Keung), Cheung Siu Fai (Jeff), Tam Ping Man (Uncle Fortune), Hui Siu Hung (Sgt. Shan), Ellen Chan (Hooker), Wong Wah Wo (Darkie).

# VANAJA

(EMERGING PICTURES) Producer, Latha R. Domalapalli; Executive Producer, Andrew Lund; Director/Screenplay, Rajnesh Domalpalli; Photography, Milton Kam; Editors, Robert Q. Lovett, Rajnesh Domalpalli; Music, Indira Amperian, Bhaskara S. Narayanan; Designers, Babu Rao Murugula, Nagulu Busigampala, Krishna Bolagani, Brahmam Atigadda, Sati Devi Tacchota, Krishna Garlapati; Costumes, Sati Devi Tacchota, Brahmam Atigadda; Dance Director, Srinivas Devarakonda; Line Producers, Sarju Patel, Vijay Santosh; a Varija Films production; Indian; Dolby; Color; Not rated; 111 minutes; American release date: August 31, 2007.

### Cast

Mamatha Bhukya (Vanaja), Urmila Dammannagari (Rama Devi), Karan Singh (Shekhar), Ramachandriah Marikanti (Somayya), Krishna Garlapati (Ram Babu), Krishnamma Gundimalla (Radhamma), Bhavani Renukunta (Lacchi), Veeramma Sadula (Padma), Prabhu Garlapati (Yadigiri), Ram Babu Tarra (Yagnesh).

# THE INNER LIFE OF MARTIN FROST

David Thewlis, Irène Jacob in *The Inner Life of Martin Frost* © NEW YORKER FILMS

(NEW YORKER) Producers, Paulo Branco, Paul Auster, Yael Melamede; Executive Producers, Eva Kolodner, Greg Johnson, Peter Newman; Director/Screenplay, Paul Auster; Photography, Christophe Beaucarne; Editor, Tim Squyres; Music, Laurent Petitgand; a Clap Filmes (Portugal), Salty Features (U.S.), Alma Films (France), Tornasol Films (Spain) production; Portuguese-American-French-Spanish; Dolby; Color; Not rated; 93 minutes; American release date: September 7, 2007.

### Cast

David Thewlis (Martin Frost), Irène Jacob (Claire Martin), Michael Imperioli (Jim Fortunato), Sophie Auster (Anna James).

# IN THE SHADOW OF THE MOON

Neil Armstrong, Michael Collins, Buzz Aldrin in *In the Shadow of the Moon* © THINKFILM

(THINKFILM) Producer, Duncan Copp; Executive Producer, John Battsek, Julie Goldman, Simon Andreae; Co-Producer, Christopher Riley; Director, David Sington; Photography, Clive North; Editor, David Fairhead; Music, Philip Sheppard; Associate Producer, Sarah Kinsella; a Discovery Film Channel presentation of a DOX production in association with Passion Pictures; British; Color/B&W; HD; Rated; 96 minutes; American release date: September 7, 2007. Documentary on the U.S. space program during the 1960s and early 1970s; with Buzz Aldrin, Alan Bean, Eugene Cernan, Michael Collins, Charlie Duke, Jim Lovell, Edgar D. Mitchell, Dave Scott, Harrison Schmitt, John Young.

# THE UNKNOWN SOLDIER

(FIRST RUN FEATURES) aka *Der Unbekannte Soldat*; Producers, Michael Verhoeven, Ernst Ludwig Ganzert; Director/Screenplay, Michael Verhoeven; Photography, Stefan Schindler, Valentin Kurz, Knut Muhaik, Uwe Ahlborn, Britta Becker, Holger Hahn, Joerg Hieronymus, Peter Petridis, Christoph Wirsing; Editor, Gabriele Kroeber; Music, Martin Grubinger, Art Percussion; a Sentana Filmproduktion production, in association with Eikon; German; Color/B&W; DV; Not rated; 97 minutes; American release date: September 7, 2007. Documentary on the controversial Holocaust exhibition *Crimes of the German Wehrmacht*; with Hannes Heer, Dieter Pohl, Myriam Y. Arani, Dirk Rupnow, Rudolf Moessner.

# MILAREPA

(LUMINOUS VELOCITY) Producer, Raymond Steiner; Co-Producer, Norbu Wangmo Gyari; Director, Neten Chokling; Screenplay, Neten Chokling, Choyang Gyari; Camera (color, Super-16-to-35mm), Paul Warren; Editor, Suzy Elmiger; Music, Joel Diamond; Designer, Orgyen Tobgyal; Costumes, Francois Perez; Visual Effects, John P. Nugent; Associate Producers, Edwina Hayes, Jill Heald, Mumta Ito, Isabel Pedrosa, Isaiah Seret; a Shining Moon production; Bhutanese; Dolby; Color; Super-16-to-35mm; Not rated; 94 minutes; American release date: September 7, 2007.

### Cast

Jamyang Lodro (Thopaga, age 16), Kelsang Chukie Tethtong (Kargyen), Orgyen Tubgyal (Yongten Trugyel), Dechen Wangmo (Thopaga, age 7), Gonpo (Uncle Gyalsten), Tsamchoe (Aunt Peydon), Tashi Lhamo (Peta), Tashi Choedon Gyari (Zesay), Gimyan Lodro (Milarepa).

# FOREVER

David Pouly in *Forever* © FIRST RUN/ICARUS

(FIRST RUN/ICARUS) Producer, Carmen Cobos; Director, Heddy Honigmann; Screenplay, Heddy Honigmann, Ester Gould, Judith Vreriks; Photography, Robert Alazraki; Editor, Danniel Danniel; Associate Producer, Judith Vreriks; a Cobos Films production in association with NPS; Dutch, 2006; Dolby; Color; Not rated; 98 minutes; American release date: September 12, 2007. Documentary on Paris' Père-Lachaise cemetery; with Leone Desmasures, Yoshino Kimura, Stephane Heuet, Reza Khoddam, Bertrand Beyern, Valerie Bajou, David Pouly.

# DRAGON WARS: D-WAR

*Dragon Wars: D-War* © FREESTYLE RELEASING

(FREESTYLE) Producers, Choi Sung-ho, James B. Kang, Jeong Tae-sung; Executive Producers, Kim Woo-taek, Shim Hyung-Correa; Director/Screenplay, Shim Heung-rae; Photography, Hubert Taczanowski; Designers, Kim Yong-suk, Shim Jong-nam; Costumes, Niklas J. Palm; Editor, Tim Alverson; Music, Steve Jablonsky; Visual Effects, Younggu Art Studios; Visual Effects Supervisor, Shim Ki-wook; Stunts, Bud Davis, Dennis Scott; Casting, Christine Sheaks; a Showbox presentation of a Younggu Art production; South Korean; Dolby; Super 35 Widescreen; Deluxe Color; Rated PG-13; 100 minutes; American release date: September 14, 2007.

### Cast

Jason Behr (Ethan); Amanda Brooks (Sarah); Robert Forster (Jack); Aimee Garcia (Brandy); Craig Robinson (Bruce); Elizabeth Peña (Agent Linda Perez); Chris Mulkey (Agent Frank Pinsky); John Ales (Agent Judah Campbell); Billy Gardell (Zoo Guard); Holmes Osborne (Hypnotherapist); NiCole Robinson (Psychiatrist); Geoffrey Pierson (Secretary of Defense); Cody Arens (Young Ethan); Kevin Breznahan (Reporter); Jody L. Carlson (Sarah's Mother); Dominic Olivier (Head Doctor); Craig Anton (Dr. Austin); Patricia Lee (Sarah's Nurse); Jody Carlson (Sarah's Mother); Eloy Casados (Homeless Native American); Alexa Motley (Mystery Driver); Matthias Hues, Gregory Hinton, Derek Mears, Gerard Griesbaum (Bounty Hunters); Retta (Receptionist Nurse); Jane Silvia (Nurse #1); Cheyenne Alexis Dean (Young Sarah); Enci (Screaming Office Worker); Roberta Farkas (Narrator); Rob Roy Fitzgerald (Detective); Ethan Grant (FBI Agent); Joe Don Harris (LA SWAT); James Intveld (Homeless Man); Kerry Liu (Christine Shim); Scott Lunsford (Police Officer); Nathan Mills (Pizza Delivery Guy); Anthony Molinari (Dude #1); Art Oughton (Hospital Guard); Richard Steen (Ethan's Dad); Michael Shamus Wiles (Evil General).

# BEAUTY REMAINS

Zhou Xun, Vivian Wu in *Beauty Remains* © EMERGING PICTURES

(EMERGING PICTURES) aka *Mei Ren Yi Jiu*; Producers, Ira Deutchman, Ann Hu, Han San Ping, Ren Zhong Lun; Executive Producers, Lisa Lu, Adam Zhu, Nina Wang, Erik Siao; Director, Ann Hu; Screenplay, Beth Schacter, Michael Eldridge, Wang Bin; Photography, Scott Kevan; Designers, Carol Wells, Feng Li Gang; Costumes, Li Lu, Gu Lin; Editor, Sara Thorson; Music, Sasha Gordon; Associate Producers, Scott Karpf, Josh Green, Song Zhen Shan; an Emerging Pictures presentation in association with Media Asia/China Film Group/Shanghai Film Group; Chinese, 2005; Dolby; Color; Not rated; 86 minutes; American release date: September 19, 2007.

### Cast

Zhou Xun (Fei), Vivian Wu (Ying), Wang Zhi Wen (Huang), Lisa Lu (The Woman Gambler), Zhu Man Fang (Bai), Shen Chang (Xiao Tian), Wang Jian Jun (Li Zhu), Xu Jing (Niu Niu), Jin Hong Wen (Lawyer).

# HONOR DE CAVALLERIA

(NOTRO FILMS) Producer/Director/Screenplay, Albert Serra, based on *El ingenioso hidalgo Don Quixote de la Mancha* by Miguel de Cervantes; Executive Producers, Montse Triola, Lluis Minarro, Alvaro Blanco; Photography, Christophe Farnarier, Eduard Grau; Editor, Angel Martin; Music, Ferrant Font; Art Director, Jimmy Gimferrer; an Andergraun Films, Eddie Saeta, Notro Films production, with participation of TVE, TVC; Spanish, 2006; Dolby; Color; DV-to-35mm; Not rated; 111 minutes; American release date: September 21, 2007.

### Cast

Lluis Carbó (Quixot), Lluís Serrat (Sancho), Glynn Bruce, Lluis Cardenal, Bartomeu Casellas, Jimmy Gimferrer, Xavier Gratacós, Eliseu Huertas, Enric Junca, Josep Pages, Jordi Pau, Rufino Pijoan, Eduard Sancho, Jordi Sancho, Albert Pla.

# ANTONIA

Leilah Moreno, Negra Li, Quelynah, Cindy Mendes in *Antonia* © ANYWHERE ROAD ENTERTAINMENT

(ANYWHERE ROAD ENTERTAINMENT/RED ENVELOPE) Producers, Georgia Costa Araujo, Tata Amaral; Co-Producers, Andrea Barata Ribeiro, Bel Berlinck, Fernando Meirelles; Director, Tata Amaral; Screenplay, Roberto Moreira, Tata Amaral; Photography, Jacob Sarmento Solitrenick; Editor, Ide Lacreta; Music, Beto Villares, Parteum; Designer, Rafael Ronconi; Casting, Patricia Faria; a Petrobras and ENDES presentation of a Coracao da Selva/O2 Filmes/Tangerina Entertainment/Globo Filmes production; Brazilian; Dolby; Color; Rated PG-13; 89 minutes; American release date: September 21, 2007.

### Cast

Negra Li (Preta), Leilah Moreno (Barbarah), Quelynah (Maya), Cindy Mendes (Lena), Thaide (Marcelo Diamante), Fernando Macário (Ermano), Chico Andrade (Duda), Nathalye Cris (Emilia), Thobias da Vai-Vai (João), Sandra de Sá (Maria), Odara Carvalho (Roberta), Ezequiel da Silva (Robinho), Mercilio Duarte (Delegado), Claudio Galperin (Doctor), Hadji (DC Cocáo), Hébanco (Talarico), Kamau (Dante), Giulio Lopes (Antenor), Rubinho Louzada (Caixa), Júlio Machado (Noivo), Maionezi (JP), Negro Rico (DJ Anjo).

# THE MAN OF MY LIFE

(STRAND) aka *L'Homme de sa vie*; Producer, Philippe Godeau; Executive Producer, Jean-Yves Asselin; Director, Zabou Breitman; Screenplay, Zabou Breitman, Agnes de Sacy; Photography, Michel Amathieu; Editor, Richard Marizy; Music, Laurent Korcia, Liviu Badiu; a Pan-Europeene, France 3 Cinema, Rhones-Alpes Cinema, StudioUrania production in association with Sofica Europacorp, Carrimages 2, with participation of Canal Plus, CineCinema, Region Rhone-Alpes, Centre National de la Cinematographie; French-Italian, 2006; Dolby; Color; Not rated; 112 minutes; American release date: September 21, 2007.

### Cast

Bernard Campan (Frédéric), Charles Berling (Hugo), Léa Drucker (Frédérique), Jacqueline Jehanneuf (Jacqueline), Eric Prat (Guillaume), Niels Lexcellent (Arthur), Anna Chalon (Capucine), Antonin Chalon (Mathieu), Léocadia Rodriguez-Henocq (Jeanne), Caroline Gonce (Ilse), Aurélie Guichard (Lucinda), Philippe Lefebvre (Benoît), Angie David (Anne-Sophie), Gabrielle Atger (Pauline).

# THE MAN WHO SOULED THE WORLD

(WHYTE HOUSE PRODS.) Producers, Matt Hill, Jason Boulter; Director, Mike Hill; Photography, Sue Collins, Socrates Leal; Music, Adam Starr; Editor, Cindy Clarkson; Australian-American; Color; Not rated; 87 minutes; American release date: October 5, 2007. Documentary on influential skateboarder Steve Rocco; with Steve Rocco, Rodney Mullen, Jesse Martinez, Marc McKee, Daewon Song, Jeremy Klein, Jason Lee, Mike Vallely, Danny Way, Natas Kaupas, Shiloh Greathouse, Kris Markovich, Mike Carroll, John Lucero, Richard Novak, Bod Boyle, Per Holknekt, Salvador Barbier, Chris Pastras, Jacob Rosenberg, Sean Cliver, Jovontae Turner, James Craig, Ron Chatman II, Pat Duffy, Daniel Castillo, Douglas J Winbury II, Clyde Singleton, Steve Berra, Tim Gavin, Rudy Johnson, Randy Colvin, Steve Hill, Jeff Tremaine, Ed Templeton, Jason "Wee Man" Acuna, Tony Magnussen, Ryan Sheckler, Colin McKay, Chico Brenes, Brian Lotti, Paul Machnau, Paul Rafferty, Chet Thomas, Per Welinder, Fausto Vitello, Steve Douglas, Matt Hill, Don Brown, Kevin Harris, Luis Cruz, Keith Cochrane, Jeremy Fox, Mark Oblow, Mitsuaki Kizaki, Tom Schmitt, Earl Parker, Rick Kosick, Dave Swift, John Casement, John Kirby, Charlie Thomas, Scott Droulliard, Frank Messman, Socrates Leal, Matt Pritchard, Ron Jeremy, Fletcher Dragge, Johnny Knoxville, Larry Flynt, Peter Hill, Mark Gonzales, Paul Schmitt, Ronnie Creager, Larry Balma, Bill Weiss, Tod Swank, Mike Smith, Ray Flores.

# WEIRDSVILLE

Scott Speedman, Wes Bentley in *Weirdsville* © THINKFILM

(THINKFILM) Producer, Nicholas D. Tabarrok; Executive Producers, Perry Zimel, Michael Baker, Jeff Sackman, Morris Ruskin; Director, Allan Moyle; Screenplay, Willem Wennekers; Photography, Adam Swica; Editor, Michael Doherty; Music, John Rowley; Designer, Oleg Savytski; a Shoreline Entertainment presentation of a Darius Films production with the participation of Telefilm Canada and Astral Media; Canadian; Dolby; Color; Not rated; 90 minutes; American release date: October 5, 2007.

### Cast

Scott Speedman (Dexter), Wes Bentley (Royce), Taryn Manning (Matilda), Matt Frewer (Jason Taylor), Greg Bryk (Abel), Maggie Castle (Treena), Raoul Bhaneja (Omar), Joe Dinicol (Jeremy), Jordan Prentice (Martin), Dax Ravina (Seamus), Joey Beck (Sheldon), Raoul Bhaneja (Omar), Randy Butcher (Hockey Goalie), Derek Gilroy (Squinty), James McQuade (Gary), Mark Parr (Anthony), Allan Redford (Theo), Shane Wyler (Todd).

# TERROR'S ADVOCATE

(MAGNOLIA) aka *L'Avocat de la terreur*; Producer, Rita Dagher; Co-Producer, Brahim Chioua, Vincent Maraval; Director, Barbet Schroeder; Photography, Caroline Champetier, Jean-Luc Perreard; Editor, Nelly Quettier; Music, Jorge Arriagada; a Rita Dagher presentation of a Yalla Films, Wild Bunch production with the participation of CanalPlus, CNC, in association with Sofica Uni Etoile 3; French; Dolby; Color; Not rated; 138 minutes; American release date: October 12, 2007. Documentary on Frenchman Jacques Verges, who has served as legal counsel for several notorious criminals; with Jacques Verges, Bachir Boumaza, Yacef Saadi, Sine, Magdalena Kopp, Anis Naccache, Lionel Duroy, Maher Souleiman, Hans Joachim Klein, Carlos, Neda Vidakovic, Louis Caprioli, Jean-Paul Dolle, Claude Faure, David Fechheimer, Horst Franz, Claude Moniquet, Olivier Schrom, Patricia Tourancheau, Tobias Wunschik, Milous Brahimi, Nuon Chea, Isabelle Coutant-Peyre, Zohra Drif, Rolande Girard-Arnaud, Gilles Menage, Alain Marsaud, Martine Tigrane.

# KHADAK

(LIFESIZE) Producer, Heino Deckert; Director/Screenplay, Peter Brosens, Jessica Woodworth; Photography, Rimvydas Leipus; Editor, Nico Leunen; Music, Altan Urag, Dominique Lawalree, Michel Schoepping, Christian Fennesz; Designer/Costumes, Agi Dawaachu; a Bo Films, Motion Investment Group (Belgium)/Ma.Ja.De Filmproduktion (Germany)/Lemming Film (Netherlands) production, with the support of Vlaams Audiovisueel Fonds, Medienboard Berlin-Brandenburg, Mitteldeutsch Medienfoerderung, Netherlands Film Fund, Centre du Cinema et de l'Audiovisuel de la Communaute Francaise de Belgique et des teledistrbuteurs wallons, Cineart, Cineworx, Contact Film, NPS, Telenet, VRT, ZDF/Arte, i2i; Belgian-German-Dutch; Dolby; Color; Not rated; 104 minutes; American release date: October 12, 2007.

## Cast

Batzul Khayankhyarvaa (Bagi), Tsetsegee Byamba (Zolzaya), Damchaa Banzar, Tserendarizav Dashnyam, Dugarsuren Dagvadorj, Uuriintuya Enkhtaivan, Bat-Erdene Damdinsuren.

# SUMMER LOVE

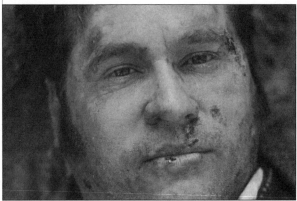

Val Kilmer in *Summer Love* © BARNHOLTZ ENTERTAINMENT

(BARNHOLTZ ENTERTAINMENT) aka *Dead Man's Bounty*; Producers, Hamish Skeggs, Piotr Uklanski, Staffan Ahrenberg; Director/Screenplay, Piotr Uklanski; Photography, Jacek Petrycki; Designer, Ewa Skoczkowska; Costumes, Ewa Helman-Szczerbic; Editor, Mike Horton; Music, Karel Holas, India Czajkowska; a Polski Western presentation; Polish; Widescreen; Color; Not rated; 94 minutes; Release date: October 17, 2007.

## Cast

Boguslaw Linda (The Sheriff), Karel Roden (The Stranger), Katarzyna Figura (The Woman), Val Kilmer (The Wanted Man), Krzytof Zaleski (Zawiadowca), Rafal Mohr (The Shop Assistant), Jerzy Rogalski (The Shopkeeper), Miroslaw Zbrojewicz (The Boxer), Bartosz Zukowski (The Blond Man).

# OUT OF THE BLUE

Paul Glover, Karl Urban in *Out of the Blue* © IFC FIRST TAKE

(IFC FIRST TAKE) Producers, Tim White, Steven O'Meagher; Director, Robert Sarkies; Screenplay, Graham Tetley, Robert Sarkies, based on the book *Aramoana: 22 Hours of Terror* by Bill O'Brien; Photography, Greig Fraser; Designer, Phil Ivey; Costumes, Lesley Burkes-Harding; Editor, Annie Collins; Music, Victoria Kelly; Casting, Rachel Bullock; a New Zealand Film Commission presentation in association with NZ On Air and TV3 of a Southern Light Films and Desert Road Films production; New Zealand, 2006; Dolby; Color; Not rated; 102 minutes; American release date: October 19, 2007.

## Cast

Karl Urban (Nick Harvey), Matthew Sunderland (David Gray), Lois Lawn (Helen Dickson), Simon Ferry (Garry Holden), Tandi Wright (Julie-Anne Bryson), Paul Glover (Paul Knox), William Kircher (Stu Guthrie), Georgina Fabish (Chiquita Holden), Fayth Rasmussen (Stacey Percy), Timothy Bartlett (Jimmy Dickson), Tony Bishop (Ross Percy), Baxter Cannell (Dion Percy), Murray Davidson (Bank Manager), Dave Dudfield (AOS/ATS Officer), Nick Duval-Smith (Brian Wilson), Natalie Ellis (Dorothy Crimp), Fatu Ioane (Aleki Tali), Brenda Kendall (Garry Holden's Mother), Richard Knowles (Rene Aarsen), Thomas Lee-Batley (Leo Wilson), Finn Liddell (Jordan Harvey), Stuart Mathieson (Vic Crimp), Dra McKay (Heather Dickson), Steven Moore (Ron Braithwaite), Ryan O'Kane (Darren Buist), Patrick Paynter (Tim Jamieson), Bruce Phillips (Chris Cole), Vaughan Slinn (Russell Anderson), Phoebe Smith (Jenny Austin), Vanessa Stacey (Vanessa Percy), Claire Waldron (Fiona Harvey), Kerrie Waterworth (Bank Teller), Jacinta Wawatai (Rewa Bryson), Richard West (Warren Wilson), Michael Whalley (Darren Gibbs), Danaka Wheeler (Jasmine Holden), Ashley Wilson (Gunshop Owner).

# LAGERFELD CONFIDENTIAL

(KOCH LORBER) Producer, Gregory Bernard; Director/Screenplay/Photography, Rodolphe Marconi; a Realitism Films production, in association with Backup Films; French; Color; DV- and Super-8-to-35mm; Not rated; 89 minutes; American release date: October 24, 2007. Documentary on designer Karl Lagerfeld; with Karl Lagerfeld, Anna Wintour, Nicole Kidman, Baz Luhrmann. French, English dialogue.

# HOW TO COOK YOUR LIFE

Edward Espe Brown in *How to Cook Your Life* © ROADSIDE ATTRACTIONS

(ROADSIDE ATTRACTIONS) Producers, Franz X. Gernstl, Fidelis Mager; Director/Screenplay, Doris Doerrie; Photography, Joerg Jeshel, Doris Doerrie; Editor, Suzi Giebler; Music, B:sides music production (Sven Faller, Mathias Goetz, Martin Kolb, Florian Riedl); a Megaherz production; German; Dolby; Color; HDCam; HDV-to-35mm; Rated PG-13; 93 minutes; American release date: October 26, 2007. Documentary on Zen priest and cook Edward Espe Brown; with Edward Espe Brown, Doris Dörrie.

# LYNCH

(ABSURDA) Producers, Jon Nguyen, Jason S., Brynn McQuade, Soren Larsen; Executive Producers, Slin Almquist, Rips Penderis, Matt Semi; Director/Editor, blackANDwhite; Photography, Morton Soborg, Jason S.; Music, Sune Martin; Associate Producers, Jay Aaseng, Erik Crary, Ole J. Roska, Anges Wasiak; an Absurda (Denmark) production; Danish; Color/B&W; DV; Not rated; 82 minutes; American release date: October 26, 2007. Documentary looking at filmmaker David Lynch during production of *Inland Empire*; with David Lynch, Laura Dern, Krzysztof Majchrazk, Phillip Patela, Weronika Rosati.

# JOE STRUMMER: THE FUTURE IS UNWRITTEN

Joe Strummer in *Joe Strummer: The Future is Unwritten* © IFC FIRST TAKE

(IFC FIRST TAKE) Producers, Amanda Temple, Anna Campeau, Alan Moloney; Executive Producer, Jeremy Thomas; Co-Producers, Orlagh Collins, Susan Mullen, Stephan Mallmann; Director, Julien Temple; Photography, Ben Cole; Editors, Mark Reynolds, Tobias Zaldua, Niven Howie; Music Supervisor, Ian Neil; Animation, Tim Standard; Artwork, Joe Strummer; Archive Producer, Sam Dwyer; a Film 4/Sony BMG film/Parallel Films/HanWay Films presentation of a Nitrate Film and Parallel Films production; Irish-British; Dolby; Color; DV; Not rated; 125 minutes; American release date: November 2, 2007. Documentary on the late punk rocker Joe Strummer; with Mick Jones, Topper Headon, Terry Chimes, Iain Gillis, Alasdair Gillis, Luce Mellor, Bono, John Cusack, Johnny Depp, Matt Dillon, Jim Jarmusch, Steve Buscemi, John Cooper Clarke, Dick Evans, Topper Headon, Steve Jones, Anthony Kiedis, Don Letts, Bernie Rhodes.

# SHARKWATER

(SHARKWATER PRODS.) Producer/Director/Screenplay, Rob Stewart; Executive Producers, Brian Stewart, Sandra Campbell, Alexandra Stewart; Photography, Rob Stewart; Underwater Camera, Brian Stewart, David Hannan; Editors, Ric Morden, Jeremy Stuart; Supervising Editor, Michael Clarke; Music, Jeff Rona; Music Supervisor, Androo Mitchell; Visual Research; Gina Cali; a Diatribe production; Canadian; Color; HD; Not rated; 89 minutes; American release date: November 2, 2007. Documentary on the indiscriminate killing of sharks for their fins; with Patrick Moore, Erich Ritter, Rob Stewart, Pal Watson, Boris Worm.

## GLASS LIPS

(IFC) aka *Blood of a Poet*; Producer/Director/Screenplay/Photography, Lech Majewski; Editors, Eliot Ems, Norbert Rudzik; Music, Lech Majewski, Jozef Skrzek; Designers, Joanna Macha, Leon Herlig; Costumes, Dorota Lis; an Angelus Silesius production; Polish; Color; Not rated; 99 minutes; American release date: November 7, 2007.

**Cast**

Patryk Czajka (Patient), Joanna Litwin (Mother), Grzegorz Przybyl (Father).

## MY NAME IS ALBERT AYLER

Albert Ayler in *My Name is Albert Ayler*

(INDEPENDENT) Director, Kasper Collin; No other credits available; Swedish; B&W/color; Not rated; 79 minutes; American release date: November 8, 2007. Documentary on musician Albert Ayler.

## COCALERO

(CINEMA TROPICAL) Producers, Julia Solomonoff, Alejandro Landes; Executive Producer, Ellyn Daniels; Director, Alejandro Landes; Photography, Jorge Manrique Behrens; Editors, Kate Taverna, Jorge Manrique Behrens, Lorenzo Bombicci, Jacopo Quadri; Music, Leo Heiblum, Jacobo Lieberman; Archival Researcher, Monica Machicao; Field Producer, Machicao; Associate Producers, Roberto Alem, Jorge Manrique Behrens, Paula Alvarez Vaccaro; a Fall Line Films presentation; Bolivian-Argentine; Alta Definicion Argentina color, DV; Not rated; 97 minutes; American release date: November 9, 2007. Documentary on Evo Morales' campaign for president of Bolivia; with Evo Morales, Leonilda Zurita, Alvaro Garcia Linera, Javier Escalas, Alex Contreras.

## THE SACRED FAMILY

(GLOBAL FILM INITIATIVE) aka *La Sagrada familia*; Producer, Ursula Budnik; Executive Producer, Antonino Ballestrazzi; Director/Screenplay/Editor, Sebastián Campos; Photography, Sebastián Campos, Gabriel Díaz; Music, Javiera y los Imposibles; Art Director, Antonia Hernández; an Horamagica/Zoofilms production with the participation of TVE, Canal Plus; Chilean, 2005; Dolby; Color; DV-35mm; Not rated; 99 minutes; American release date: November 9, 2007.

**Cast**

Sergio Hernández (Marco, father), Coca Guazzini (Soledad), Néstor Cantillana (Marco, son), Patricia López (Sofia), Macarena Teke (Rita), Mauricio Diocares (Aldo), Juan Pablo Miranda (Pedro).

## SAAWARIYA

(SONY PICTURES ENTERTAINMENT) Producer/Director/Editor, Sanjay Leela Bhansali; Executive Producers, Kuldeep Singh Rathore, Deepak Sharma; Screenplay, Prakash Kapadia, Sanjay Leela Bhansali, based on Fyodor Dostoyevsky's short story *White Nights;* Photography, Ravi K. Chandran; Music, Monty; Lyrics, Sameer; Choreographers, Shiamak Davar, Pappu Mallu; Art Directors, Omung Kumar Bhandula, Vanita Omung Kumar; Costumes, Anuradha Vakil, Bhansali, Rajesh Pratap Singh, Reza Shariffi; Visual Effects Supervisor, Merzin Tavaria; Visual Effects, Prime Focus VFX; Casting, Amita Sehgal; a Columbia Pictures, SPE Films India presentation of an SPE Films India, SLB Films production; Indian; Color; Widescreen; Rated PG; 137 minutes; American release date: November 9, 2007.

**Cast**

Ranbir Kapoor (Ranbir Raj), Sonam Kapoor (Sakina), Rani Mukherjee (Gulabji), Salman Khan (Imaan), Zohra Segal (Raj's Grandmom), Begum Para (Sakina's Grandmother).

Rani Mukherjee in *Saawariya* © SONY PICTURES ENTERTAINMENT

# ELEVEN MEN OUT

Jóhann G. Jóhannson in *Eleven Men Out* © HERE!/REGENT

(HERE!/REGENT) aka *Strakarnir Okkar*; Producers, Julius Kemp, Ingvar Thorolarson; Co-Producers, Sam Taylor, Mike Downey, Markus Selin, Jukka Helle; Director, Robert I. Douglas; Screenplay, Jon Atli Jonasson, Douglas; Photography, G. Magni Agustsson; Designer, Konrad Haller; Costumes, Linda Bjorg Arnadottir; Editor, Asta Briem; Music, Bardi Johannsson & Minus; an Icelandic Film Co., F&ME, Solarfilms production in association with Icelandic Film Center and Invicta Capital; Icelandic-Finnish-British, 2005; Dolby; Color; Not rated; 86 minutes; American release date: November 16, 2007.

## Cast

Björn Hlynur Haraldsson (Ottar Thor), Lilja Nótt (Gugga), Arnmundur Ernst (Magnus), Helgi Björnsson (Pétur), Sigurdur Skúlason (Eiríkur), Thorstein Bachmann (Georg), Björk Jakobsdóttir (Lára), Pattra Sriyanonge (Goth Girl), Marius Sverrisson (Starri), Jón Atli Jónasson (Orri), Damon Younger (Brósi), Nanna Ósk Jónsdóttir (Sigga), Hilmar Jonsson (Viktor Ingi), Pétur Einarsson (Björgvin), Felix Bergsson (Dómari), Erlendur Eiríksson (Alfreð), Valdimar Örn Flygenring (Valdi), Davið Guðbrandsson (Ingvar), Jóhann G. Jóhannsson (Matthias), Magnús Jónsson (Logi), Stefán Jónsson (Ási Sálfræðingur), Ingibjörg Reynisdóttir (Blaðakona), Jón Jósep Snæbjörnsson (Stebbi).

# NINA'S HEAVENLY DELIGHTS

(HERE!/REGENT) Producers, Pratibha Parmar, Chris Atkins, Marion Pilowsky; Executive Producers, Colin Leventhal, Margaret Matheson, Scott Meek; Director, Pratibha Parmar; Screenplay, Andrea Gibb; Photography, Simon Dennis; Editor, Mary Finlay; Art Director, Margaret Horspool; Costumes, Louise Allen; Choreographer, Piers Gielgud; Associate Producers, Neil Chordia, Megan Davis; a Fortissimo Films presentation of a Scion Films, Scottish Screen, Kali Films, Priority Pictures production in association with Sky Movies; British; Dolby; Widescreen; Color; Not rated; 96 minutes; American release date: November 21, 2007.

## Cast

Shelley Conn (Nina Shah), Laura Fraser (Lisa Mackinlay), Raji James (Sanjay Khanna), Ronny Jhutti (Bobbi), Art Malik (Raj Khanna), Kulvinder Ghir (TV Presenter), Veena Sood (Suman Shah), Atta Yaqub (Kary Shah), Zoe Henretty (Priya Shah), Raad Rawi (Mohan Shan), Kathleen McDermott (Janice), Adam Sinclair (Fish), Rita Wolf (Auntie Tumi), Francisco Bosch (Shriv), Umar Ahmed (Ghandi), Tariq Mullan (Ravi), Elaine C. Smith (Auntie Mamie), Hritika Thaker (Young Nina).

Shelley Conn, Laura Fraser in *Nina's Heavenly Delights* © HERE!/REGENT

## YIDDISH THEATER: A LOVE STORY

Roni Neuman in *Yiddish Theater: A Love Story* © NEW LINE FILMS

(NEW LOVE FILMS) Producers, Ravit Marksu, Yael Katzir, Dan Katzir; Director/Photography, Dan Katzir; Screenplay, Dan Katzir, Ravit Markus; Editor, Neta Dvorkis; Israeli; Color; DV; Not rated; 77 minutes; Release date: November 21, 2007. Documentary on actress Zypora Spaisman's efforts to keep Yiddish theatre alive and active in the 21st Century; with Zypora Spaisman, David Romeo, Felix Fibich, Shifra Lerer, Seymour Rechzeit, Sally Dobekire, Jechiel Dobekire, Roni Neuman, Joad Kohn.

## MIDNIGHT EAGLE

Yoshihiko Hakamada in *Midnight Eagle* © STRAND RELEASING

(STRAND) aka *Middonaito Îguru*; Producers, Michihiko Umezawa, Masakazu Yoda, Teruo Noguchi, Tomiyasu Moriya, Kei Fujiki; Director, Izuru Narushima; Screenplay, Yasuo Hasegawa, Kenzaburo Iida; Story, Tetsuo Takashima; Photography, Hideo Yamamoto; Designer, Hajime Oikawa; Music, Takeshi Kobayashi; Editor, William Anderson; a Shochiku Pictures presentation; Japanese; Dolby; Color; Not rated; 131 minutes; American release date: November 23, 2007.

### Cast

Tatsuya Fuji (Prime Minister Watarase), Yoshihiko Hakamada (Toshimitsu Fuyuki), Ken Ishiguro (Tadao Miyata), Nao Omori (Kensuke Saito), Takao Osawa (Yuji Nishizaki), Yuko Takeuchi (Keiko Arisawa), Hiroshia Tamaki (Shinichiro Ochiai), A-Saku Yoshida (Akihiko Saeki).

## CHRONICLE OF AN ESCAPE

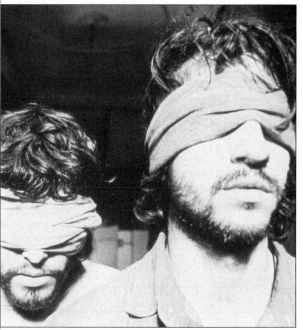

Nazareno Casero, Alfonso Tor in *Chronicle of an Escape* © IFC FIRST TAKE

(IFC FIRST TAKE) aka *Crónica de una fuga* and *Buenos Aires, 1977*; Producers, Óscar Kramer, Hugo Sigman; Director, Israel Adrian Caetano; Screenplay, Israel Adrian Caetano, Esteban Student, Julian Loyola, based on a book by Claudio Tamburrini; Photography, Julián Apezteguía; Designers, Juan Mario Roust, Jorge Ferrari; Costumes, Julio Suárez; Editor, Alberto Ponce; Music, Iván Wyzsogrod; a K&S Films production; Argentine; Color; Not rated; 104 minutes; American release date: November 28, 2007.

### Cast

Rodrigo De La Serna (Claudio Tamburrini), Nazareno Casero (Guillermo Fernández), Lautaro Delgado (El Gallego), Matias Marmorato (El Vasco), Pablo Echarri (Huguito), Guillermo Fernandez (Judge), Martin Urruty (El Tano), Diego Alonso (Lucas), Leonardo Bargiga (Capt. Almagro), Luis Enrique Caetano (Taxi Driver), Alfredo Castellani (Trainer), Daniel Di Blase (Gallego's Father), Rito Fernández (Rito), Pacho Guerty (Raviol), Julián Krakov (Mario), Rubén Nocedal (Tanito), Erasmo (Tucumano), Silivia Ribe (Vecina), Alfonso Tor (Jorge).

# THE ROCKET

(PALM PICTURES) aka *Maurice Richard*; Producers, Denise Robert, Daniel Louis; Director, Charles Binamé; Screenplay, Ken Scott; Photography, Pierre Gill; Designer, Michel Proulx; Costumes, Francesca Chamberland; Music, Michel Cusson; Editor, Michel Arcand; Casting, Lucie Robitaille; Canadian, 2005; CinemaScope; Color; Rated PG; 124 minutes; American release date: November 30, 2007.

### Cast

Roy Dupuis (Maurice Richard); Stephen McHattie (Dick Irvin); Julie Le Breton (Lucille Richard); Philip Craig (Tommy Gorman); Patrice Robitaille (Emile "Butch" Bouchard); Michel Barrette (Mr. Norchet); Diane Lavallée (Alice Norchet); Tony Calabretta (Frank Selke); François Langolis Vallières (Maurice at 16 years old); Pierre-François Legendre (Georges Norchet); Mario Jean (Paul Stuart); Robert Brouillette (Enthusiastic Fan); Benoît Girard (Paul St-Georges); Paul Doucet (Camil Desroches); Normand Chouinard (Sports Commentator); Randy Thomas (Hector "Toe" Blake); Mike Ricci (Elmer Lach); René Arbour (Bob Filion); Sean Avery (Bob Dill); Rick Bramucci (Bodyguard); Tedd Dillon (Clarence Campbell); André-Sébastien Dorion (Referee); Pascal Dupuis (Milt Schmidt); Rémy Girard (Tony Bergeron); Terry Haig (Dr. Walter McKay); Serge Houde (Conn Smythe); Mario Jean (Paul Stuart); Ian Laperrière (Bernard "Boom Boom" Geoffrion); Vincent Lecavalier (Jean Beliveau); John Maclaren (Anglophone Journalist); Mathieu Morin, Steven Petitpas, Marc Tanguay (Referees); Stéphane Quintal (Dollard St-Laurent); Amélie Richer (Lucille Morchet); Sebastien Roberts (Bob Fillion); Howard Rosenstein (Ken Reardon); Philippe Sauvé (Jim Henry); Mylène St-Sauveur (Irma Daigle);  Allen Zarnett (Henchman).

Roy Dupuis in *The Rocket* © PALM PICTURES

# THE VIOLIN

*The Violin* © FILM MOVEMENT

(FILM MOVEMENT) aka *El Violin*; Producer/Director/Screenplay, Francisco Vargas; Photography, Martin Boege Pare; Editors, Francisco Vargas Quevedo, Ricardo Garfias; Music, Cuauhtemoc Tavira, Armando Rosas; Designer, Claudio "Pache" Contreras; Costumes, Rafael Ravello; Casting, Natalia Beristain, Isabel Cortazar; a Camara Carnal Films presentation in association with Fidecine-Mexico and Centro de Capacitacion Cinematografica; Mexican, 2005; Dolby; B&W; Not rated; 98 minutes; American release date: December 5, 2007.

### Cast

Ángel Tavira (Don Plutarco), Dagoberto Gama (The Captain), Fermín Martinez (The Lieutenant), Gerardo Taracena (Genaro), Mario Garibaldi (Lucio), Silverio Palacios (Commander Cayetano), Octavio Castro (Zacarías), Mercedes Hernández (Jacinta), Gerardo Juárez (Pedro), Ariel Galvan (Joaquin), Amorita Rasgado (Joven Prostituta), María Elena Olivares (Doña Lupe), Esteban Castellanos (Manuel).

## LOOKING FOR CHEYENNE

(HERE!/REGENT) aka *Oublier Cheyenne*; Producer, Dominique Crevecoeur; Director, Valerie Minetto; Screenplay, Valerie Minetto, Cecile Vargaftig; Photography, Stephan Massis; Editor, Tina Baz-Le-Gal; Music, Christophe Chevalier; a Dominique Crevecoeur presentation of a Bandoneon production, with participation of CNC; French; Dolby: Color; Not rated; 87 minutes; American release date: December 7, 2007.

### Cast

Mila Dekker (Cheyenne); Aurélia Petit (Sonia); Laurence Côte (Edith); Malik Zidi (Pierre); Guilaine Londez (Béatrice); Éléonore Michelin (Sandy); Miglen Mirtchev (Vladimir); Luc Leclerc Du Sablon, Christine Dory (The Neighbors), Pierre Hiessler (Professor); Aurélie Léon (Cindy); Michèle Humbert (SDF); Max Athanase (Farmer).

# STRENGTH AND HONOR

(SLOWHAND RELEASING/MARON PICTURES) Producer/Director/Screenplay, Mark Mahon; Executive Producer, Olann Kelleher; Photography, Alan Almond; Designer, Eleanor Wood; Costumes, Eimer Ni Mhaoldomhnaigh; Editor, Kate Coggins; Music, Ilan Eshkeri; Casting, Carmel O'Connor; a Maron Pictures presentation of a Mahon production; Irish; Dolby; Arriflex Widescreen; Deluxe Color; Rated R; 92 minutes; American release date: December 7, 2007.

## Cast

Michael Madsen (Sean Kelleher); Vinnie Jones (Smasher O'Driscoll); Patrick Bergin (Papa Boss); Richard Chamberlain (Denis O'Leary); Michael Rawley (Chaser McGrath); Gail Fitzpatrick (Mammy); Luke Whelton (Michael Kelleher); Sheridan Mahon (Coco McGrath); Finbar Furey (Chosky Boss); Myles Horgan (Barry Lacey); Pat Shortt (Wheeler McCoy); Krystal Mahon (Baby McGrath); Michael John Galvin (Fixer Ward); Joe O'Gorman (Michael Murphy); Norma Sheahan (Shannon Kelleher); Lesley Conroy (Ciara Lacey); Kevin McCormack (Neiler); David Keelan (Barman); James Brown (Cathal Murphy); Paul Valentine, Liam Heffernan, Paul Creighton (Travellers); Hilary O'Shaughnessy (Waitress); Debbie Byrne (District Nurse); Cora Fenton (Dr. McCarthy); Denis Touhy (James O'Shea); Michelle Forde (Journalist); Fiona Condon (Nurse, Kids Ward); Mary Mooney (Nurse, ICU); Neil Prendeville (Surgeon McGrath); Michael Collins (Frankie O'Neill); Conor Dwane (Desmond Curran); Alf McCarthy (Dr. Sheridan); Geraldine McLoughlin (Mary Murphy); Pascal Scott (Postman).

# HALF MOON

(STRAND) aka *Niewmang*; Producer/Director, Bahman Ghobadi; Executive Producers, Simon Field, Keith Griffiths; Screenplay, Bahman Ghobadi, Behnam Behzadi; Camera (color, widescreen), Nigel Bluck; Additional Camera, Crighton Bone; Editor, Hayedeh Safiyari; Music, Hossein Alizadeh; Production Designers, Mansooreh Yazdanjoo, Bahman Ghobadi; a Mij Film (Iran-Iraq)/New Crowned Hope (Austria)/Silkroad (France) production; Iranian-Iraqi-Austrian-French; Dolby; Widescreen; Color; Not rated; 113 minutes; American release date: December 14, 2007.

## Cast

Ismail Ghaffari (Mamo), Allah Morad Rashtiani (Kako), Hedieh Tehrani (Hesho), Golshifteh Farahani (Niwemang), Hassan Poorshirazi (Border Policeman), Sadiq Behzadpoor (Shouan).

# THE DISTRICT!

*The District!* © ATOPIA

(ATOPIA) aka *Nyócker!*; Producers, Erik Novak, Robert Hamori; Director, Aron Gauder; Screenplay, Viktor Nagy, Laszlo Jakab Orsos, Damage; Photography, Krisztian Viktorin; Editor, Kincso Palotas; Art Director, Igor Boka; a Lichtof production; Hungarian, 2005; Color; DV; Not rated; 88 minutes; American release date: December 19, 2007. Animated.

# PROMISING NEW

## ACTORS
### 2007

**NIKKI BLONSKY**
(Hairspray)

**ZAC EFRON**
(Hairspray)

**IDRIS ELBA**
(Daddy's Little Girls, The Reaping, American Gangster, This Christmas)

**ALICE BRAGA**
(I Am Legend)

**ANNASOPHIA ROBB**
(Bridge to Terabithia, The Reaping)

**ANDREW GARFIELD**
(Lions for Lambs)

**ELIJAH KELLEY**
(Hairspray)

**SAOIRSE RONAN**
(Atonement)

**KRISTEN STEWART**
(The Messengers, In the Land of Women, Fierce People, Into the Wild)

**JIM STURGESS**
(Across the Universe)

**ANTON YELCHIN**
(Alpha Dog, Fierce People)

**OLIVIA THIRLBY**
(Juno)

# ACADEMY AWARD

## BEST PICTURE
# NO COUNTRY FOR OLD MEN

Josh Brolin

(MIRAMAX/PARAMOUNT VANTAGE) Producers, Scott Rudin, Ethan Coen, Joel Coen; Executive Producers, Robert Graf, Mark Roybal; Directors/Screenplay, Joel Coen, Ethan Coen, based on the novel by Cormac McCarthy; Photography, Roger Deakins; Designer, Jess Gonchor; Costumes, Mary Zophres; Editor, Roderick Jaynes; Music, Carter Burwell; Associate Producer, David Diliberto; Casting, Ellen Chenoweth; a Scott Rudin/Mike Zoss production; Dolby; Super 35 Widescreen; Deluxe color; Rated R; 122 minutes; Release date: November 9, 2007

### Cast

Sheriff Ed Tom Bell **Tommy Lee Jones**
Anton Chigurh **Javier Bardem**
Llewelyn Moss **Josh Brolin**
Carson Wells **Woody Harrelson**
Carla Jean Moss **Kelly Macdonald**
Deputy Wendell **Garret Dillahunt**
Loretta Bell **Tess Harper**
Ellis **Barry Corbin**
Man Who Hires Wells **Stephen Root**
El Paso Sheriff **Rodger Boyce**
Carla Jean's Mother **Beth Grant**
Poolside Woman **Ana Reeder**
Molly, Bell's Secretary **Kit Gwin**
Strangled Deputy **Zach Hopkins**
Man in Ford **Chip Love**
"Agua" Man **Eduardo Antonio Garcia**
Gas Station Proprietor **Gene Jones**
"Managerial" Victims **Myk Watford, Boots Southerland**
Desert Aire Manager **Kathy Lamkin**
Cabbie at Bus Station **Johnnie Hector**
Del Rio Motel Clerk **Margaret Bowman**
Boot Salesman **Thomas Kopache**
Cabbie at Motel **Jason Douglas**
Waitress **Doris Hargrave**
Gun Store Clerk **Rutherford Cravens**
Sporting Goods Clerk **Matthew Posey**
Mexican in Bathtub **George Adelo**
Hitchhiking Driver **Mathew Greer**
Nervous Accountant **Trent Moore**
Hotel Eagle Clerk **Marc Miles**
Pickup Driver **Luce Rains**
Border Bridge Youths **Philip Bentham, Eric Reeves, Josh Meyer**
Flatbed Driver **Chris Warner**
INS Official **Brandon Smith**
Well-Dressed Mexican **H. Roland Uribe**
Chicken Farmer **Richard Jackson**
Boys on Bikes **Josh Blaylock, Caleb Jones**
Odessa Cabbie **Dorsey Ray**
Norteño Band Members **Angel H. Alvarado Jr., David A. Gomez, Milton Hernandez, John Mancha**
Cab Driver **Scott Flick**

After Llewelyn Moss takes off with the money found at the site of a drug deal gone wrong, he is relentlessly pursued by a psychopathic hitman who has no qualms about who he must kill to get his job done.

2007 Academy Award winner for Best Picture, Best Supporting Actor (Javier Bardem), Best Directors, and Best Adapted Screenplay. This film received additional nominations for Cinematography, Sound Mixing, and Sound Editing.

Javier Bardem © MIRAMAX/PARAMOUNT VANTAGE

Javier Bardem

Tommy Lee Jones

Josh Brolin

Kelly Macdonald

BEST ANIMATED FEATURE
# RATATOUILLE

Remy

**Voice Cast**

Remy ("Little Chef")  **Patton Oswalt**
Skinner  **Ian Holm**
Linguini  **Lou Romano**
Django  **Brian Dennehy**
Emile  **Peter Sohn**
Anton Ego  **Peter O'Toole**
Gusteau  **Brad Garrett**
Colette  **Janeane Garofalo**
Horst  **Will Arnett**
Lalo and Francois  **Julius Callahan**
Larousse  **James Remar**
Mustafa  **John Ratzenberger**
Lawyer (Talon Labarthe)  **Teddy Newton**
Pompidou and Health Inspector  **Tony Fucile**
Git (Lab Rat)  **Jake Steinfeld**
Ambrister Minion  **Brad Bird**
Narrator  **Stéphane Roux**

(WALT DISNEY PICTURES) Producer, Brad Lewis; Executive Producers, John Lasseter, Andrew Stanton; Director/Screenplay, Brad Bird; Original Story, Jan Pinkava, Jim Capobianco, Brad Bird; Associate Producer, Galyn Sussman; Music, Michael Giacchino; Song: "Le Festin" by Michael Giacchino, performed by Camille; Story Supervisor, Mark Andrews; Editor, Darren Holmes; Supervising Technical Director, Michael Fong; Designer, Harley Jessup; Supervising Animators, Dylan Brown, Mark Walsh; Director of Photography/Lighting, Sharon Calahan; Director of Photography/Camera, Robert Anderson; Character Design, Jason Deamer, Greg Dykstra, Carter Goodrich, Dan Lee; Character Supervisor, Brian Green; Co-Director, Jan Pinkava; a Pixar Animation Studios film; Distributed by Buena Vista Pictures; Dolby; Technicolor; Rated G; 110 minutes; Release date: June 29, 2007

Django, Emile

Skinner © WALT DISNEY PICTURES

Inspired by Gusteau's proclamation that "anyone can cook," a rat ends up at the late chef's Paris restaurant, where he fulfills his lifelong dream of becoming a master culinary wizard through the help of kitchen worker Linguini.

Ratatouille received additional nominations for Original Screenplay, Original Score, Sound Mixing, and Sound Editing.

Pompidou, Colette, Larousse, Lalo, Horst

Anton Ego

Remy

Linguini, Colette

# BEST FEATURE DOCUMENTARY
## TAXI TO THE DARK SIDE

(THINKFILM) Producers, Alex Gibney, Eva Orner, Susannah Shipman; Executive Producers, Don Glascoff, Robert Johnson, Sidney Blumenthal, Jedd Wider, Todd Wider; Co-Producers, Martin Fisher, Blair Foster, Sloane Klevin; Director/Screenplay/ Narrator, Alex Gibney; Photography, Maryse Alberti, Greg Andracke; Editor, Sloane Klevin; Music, Ivor Guest; a Jigsaw Prods. presentation of a Jigsaw Prods., X-Ray Prods. production, in association with Tall Woods, Wider Film Project; Color/Black and white; Not rated; 106 minutes; Release date: January 18, 2008. Documentary on the abusive interrogation practices used by American military forces at Bagram Air Force Base.

**With**

Brian Keith Allen, Moazzam Begg, Willie Brand, Jack Cloonan, Damien Corsetti, Thomas Curtis, Greg D'Agostino, Carlotta Gall, Tim Golden, Gita Gutierrez, Scott Horton, John Hutson, Maan Kaassamani, Carl Levin, Alfred W. McCoy, Alberto J. Mora, Anthony Morden, Karyn Plonsky, Clive Stafford Smith, Lawrence Wilkerson, Tom Wilner, John Yoo.

© THINKFILM

# BEST FOREIGN LANGUAGE FILM
## THE COUNTERFEITERS

August Diehl

Marie Bäumer

(SONY CLASSICS) a.k.a. *Die Falscher*; Producers, Josef Aichholzer, Nina Bohlmann, Babette Schroeder; Director/Screenplay, Stefan Ruzowitzky; Based on the book *The Devil's Workshop*, by Adolf Burger; Photography, Benedict Neunfels; Designer, Isidor Wimmer; Costumes, Nicole Fishcnaller; Music, Marius Ruhland; Editor, Britta Nahler; a Beta Cinema presentation of an Aichholzer Film (Austria), Magnolia Film (Germany) production, in co-production with Studio Babelsberg Motion Pictures/Babelsberg Film, ZDF; German-Austrian; Dolby SRD & SR; Color; Rated ; 99 minutes; American release date: February 22, 2008

### Cast

Salomon Sorowitsch **Karl Markovics**
Adolf Burger **August Diehl**
Friedrich Herzog **David Striesow**
Holst **Martin Brambach**
Woman in Casino **Dolores Chaplin**
Dr. Klinger **August Zirner**
Aglaia **Marie Bäumer**
Atze **Veit Stübner**
Kolya Karloff **Sebastian Urzendowsky**
Zilinski **Andreas Schmidt**
Dr. Viktor Hahn **Tilo Prückner**
Loszek **Lenn Kudrjawizki**
Abramovic **Norman Stoffregena**
and Bernd Raucamp (KZ- Inmate, Showers), Gode Benedix, Oliver Kanter (Inmates), Dirk Prinz (SS), Hille Beseler (Grete Herzog), Erik Jan Rippmann (Bank Director), Tim Breyvogel (Agent), Louie Austen (Poker Player), Michael Blohn (Croupier   Monte Carlo), Arndt Schwering-Sohnrey (Hans), Jan Pohl (Sascha), Matthias Lühne (Ganove), Holger Schober (Troop Leader), Peter Strauss (SS Officer), Werner Daehn (Rosenthal), Leander Modersohn (SS Platoon Soldier)

Karl Markovics, Devid Striesow, Martin Brambach

During World War II a group of con artists incarcerated by the Nazis are forced to forge millions of dollars in currency in order to assist the German war effort.

Dolores Chaplin, Karl Markovics © SONY CLASSICS

ACADEMY AWARD FOR **BEST ACTOR**

**DANIEL DAY-LEWIS** in *There Will Be Blood*

ACADEMY AWARD FOR **BEST ACTRESS**

**MARION COTILLARD** in *La Vie en Rose*

ACADEMY AWARD FOR **BEST SUPPORTING ACTOR**

**JAVIER BARDEM** in *No Country for Old Men*

ACADEMY AWARD FOR **BEST SUPPORTING ACTRESS**

TILDA SWINTON in *Michael Clayton*

## ACADEMY AWARD NOMINEES FOR **BEST ACTOR**

George Clooney in *Michael Clayton*

Johnny Depp in *Sweeney Todd: The Demon Barber of Fleet Street*

Tommy Lee Jones in *In the Valley of Elah*

Viggo Mortensen in *Eastern Promises*

ACADEMY AWARD NOMINEES FOR **BEST ACTRESS**

Cate Blanchett in *Elizabeth: The Golden Age*

Julie Christie in *Away from Her*

Laura Linney in *The Savages*

Ellen Page in *Juno*

ACADEMY AWARD NOMINEES FOR **BEST SUPPORTING ACTOR**

Casey Affleck in *The Assassination of Jesse James by the Coward Robert Ford*

Philip Seymour Hoffman in *Charlie Wilson's War*

Hal Holbrook in *Into the Wild*

Tom Wilkinson in *Michael Clayton*

## ACADEMY AWARD NOMINEES FOR BEST SUPPORTING ACTRESS

Cate Blanchett in *I'm Not There*

Ruby Dee in *American Gangster*

Saoirse Ronan in *Atonement*

Amy Ryan in *Gone Baby Gone*

# TOP BOX OFFICE

## STARS AND FILMS
### 2007

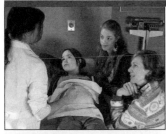

## TOP BOX OFFICE STARS OF 2007

(Clockwise from top left corner)

1. JOHNNY DEPP

2. WILL SMITH

3. GEORGE CLOONEY

4. MATT DAMON

5. DENZEL WASHINGTON

6. RUSSELL CROWE

7. TOM CRUISE

8. NICOLAS CAGE

9. WILL FERRELL

10. TOM HANKS

# TOP 100
# BOX OFFICE FILMS OF 2007

Josh Duhamel, Shia LaBeouf in *Transformers* © DREAMWORKS/PARAMONT

1. **Spider-Man 3** (Columbia)  $335,440,000
2. **Shrek the Third** (DW)  $319,210,000
3. **Transformers** (Par/DW)  $318,350,000
4. **Pirates of the Caribbean: At World's End** (Disney)  $307,600,000
5. **Harry Potter and the Order of the Phoenix** (WB)  $291,100,000
6. **I Am Legend** (WB)  $256,400,000
7. **The Bourne Ultimatum** (Univ)  $227,440,000
8. **National Treasure: Book of Secrets** (BV)  $219,950,000
9. **Alvin and the Chipmunks** (20th)  $217,330,000
10. **300** (WB)  $208,100,000
11. **Ratatouille** (BV)  $204,400,000
12. **The Simpsons Movie** (20th)  $182,520,000
13. **Wild Hogs** (BV)  $163,270,000
14. **Knocked Up** (Univ)  $148,740,000
15. **Juno** (Fox Searchlight)  $143,480,000
16. **Rush Hour** 3 (New Line)  $138,250,000
17. **Live Free or Die Hard** (20th)  $134,500,000
18. **4: Rise of the Silver Surfer** (20th)  $131,930,000
19. **American Gangster** (Univ)  $130,130,000
20. **Enchanted** (BV)  $127,810,000
21. **Bee Movie** (DW)  $126,640,000
22. **Superbad** (Columbia)  $121,140,000
23. **I Now Pronounce You Chuck & Larry** (Univ)  $119,690,000
24. **Hairspray** (New Line)  $118,880,000
25. **Blades of Glory** (BV)  $117,520,000
26. **Ocean's Thirteen** (WB)  $116,270,000
27. **Ghost Rider** (Columbia)  $114,830,000
28. **Evan Almighty** (Univ)  $100,190,000
29. **Meet the Robinsons** (Disney)  $97,700,000
30. **Norbit** (DW)  $95,370,000
31. **The Bucket List** (WB)  $93,470,000
32. **The Game Plan** (Disney)  $90,430,000
33. **Beowulf** (Par)  $82,200,000
34. **Bridge to Terabithia** (Disney)  $81,260,000
35. **Disturbia** (DW)  $78,550,000
36. **No Country for Old Men** (Miramax)  $74,290,000
37. **Fred Claus** (WB)  $72,100,000

38. **1408** (MGM/Weinstein)  $71,980,000
39. **The Golden Compass** (New Line)  $70,110,000
40. **Charlie Wilson's War** (Univ)  $66,670,000
41. **Saw IV** (Lionsgate)  $62,170,000
42. **Stomp the Yard** (Screen Gems)  $61,360,000
43. **Surf's Up** (Columbia)  $58,370,000
44. **Halloween** (Weinstein/MGM)  $57,780,000
45. **Why Did I Get Married?** (Lionsgate)  $55,110,000
46. **P.S. I Love You** (WB)  $53,700,000
47. **TMNT** (WB)  $53,300,000
48. **Sweeney Todd: The Demon Barber of Fleet Street** (DW)  $52,900,000
49. **3:10 to Yuma** (Lionsgate)  $52,710,000
50. **Music and Lyrics** (WB)  $51,540,000
51. **Atonement** (Focus)  $50,930,000
52. **Resident Evil: Extinction** (Screen Gems)  $50,100,000
53. **This Christmas** (Screen Gems)  $49,130,000
54. **Michael Clayton** (WB)  $49,100,000
55. **Premonition** (TriStar)  $47,860,000
56. **Dan in Real Life** (BV)  $47,560,000
57. **The Kingdom** (Univ)  $47,460,000
58. **Are We Done Yet?** (Columbia)  $47,360,000

Bart Simpson, Homer Simpson in *The Simpsons Movie* © 20TH CENTURY FOX

Rowena King, Morgan Freeman in *The Bucket List* © WARNER BROTHERS

Alex Etel, Crusoe, Priyanka Xi in *The Water Horse* © COLUMBIA PICTURES

59. **Shooter** (Paramount) $46,300,000
60. **License to Wed** (WB) $42,900,000
61. **Underdog** (Disney) $42,890,000
62. **Because I Said So** (Universal) $42,680,000
63. **No Reservations** (WB) $42,550,000
64. **Alien vs. Predator: Requiem** (20th) $41,800,000
65. **The Water Horse** (Columbia) $40,410,000
66. **There Will Be Blood** (Paramount Vantage/Miramax) $40,230,000
67. **Hitman** (Fox) $39,690,000
68. **Epic Movie** (20th Century Fox) $39,500,000
69. **30 Days of Night** (Columbia) $39,150,000
70. **Stardust** (Paramount) $38,640,000
71. **Fracture** (New Line) $37,130,000
72. **Freedom Writers** (Paramount) $36,310,000
73. **Smokin' Aces** (Universal) $35,400,000
74. **The Messengers** (Screen Gems) $35,380,000
75. **The Number 23** (New Line) $35,200,000

76. **The Brave One** (WB) $34,390,000
77. **Good Luck Chuck** (Lionsgate) $34,210,000
78. **Breach** (Universal) $33,100,000
79. **Zodiac** (Paramount/DW) $32,830,000
80. **Balls of Fury** (Rogue) $32,730,000
81. **Mr. Bean's Holiday** (Univ) $32,300,000
82. **The Heartbreak Kid** (DW) $32,120,000
83. **Mr. Magorium's Wonder Emporium** (20th) $32,100,000
84. **August Rush** (WB) $31,670,000
85. **Daddy's Little Girls** (Lionsgate) $31,370,000
86. **The Great Debaters** (MGM) $30,230,000
87. **28 Weeks Later** (Fox Searchlight) $28,640,000
88. **We Own the Night** (Columbia) $28,570,000
89. **Mr. Brooks** (MGM) $28,480,000
90. **Hannibal Rising** (Weinstein/MGM) $27,590,000
91. **The Nanny Diaries** (MGM) $25,780,000
92. **The Mist** (MGM/Weinstein) $25,600,000
93. **Nancy Drew** (WB) $25,360,000
94. **Mr. Woodcock** (MGM/Weinstein) $25,150,000
95. **Grindhouse** (Weinstein Co.) $25,100,000
96. **The Reaping** (WB) $24,780,000
97. **Sicko** (Lionsgate) $24,520,000
98. **Hot Fuzz** (Rogue) $23,620,000
99. **Perfect Stranger** (Columbia) $22,900,000
100. **WAR** (Lionsgate) $22,360,000

Freddie Highmore, Robin Williams in *August Rush* © WARNER BROTHERS

Rose McGowan, Marley Shelton in *Grindhouse* © DIMENSION FILMS

# BIOGRAPHICAL DATA

2007

**Aames, Willie** (William Upton) Los Angeles, CA, July 15, 1960.
**Aaron, Caroline** Richmond, VA, Aug. 7, 1954. Catholic U.
**Abbott, Diahnne** New York, NY, 1945.
**Abraham, F. Murray** Pittsburgh, PA, Oct. 24, 1939. U Texas.
**Ackland, Joss** London, England, Feb. 29, 1928.
**Adams, Amy** Vicenza, Italy, Aug. 20, 1975.
**Adams, Brooke** New York, NY, Feb. 8, 1949. Dalton.
**Adams, Catlin** Los Angeles, CA, Oct. 11, 1950.
**Adams, Edie** (Elizabeth Edith Enke) Kingston, PA, Apr. 16, 1927. Juilliard, Columbia.
**Adams, Jane** Washington, DC, Apr. 1, 1965.
**Adams, Joey Lauren** Little Rock, AR, Jan. 6, 1971.
**Adams, Julie** (Betty May) Waterloo, IA, Oct. 17, 1926. Little Rock, Jr. College.
**Adams, Maud** (Maud Wikstrom) Lulea, Sweden, Feb. 12, 1945.
**Adjani, Isabelle** Paris, France, June 27, 1955.
**Affleck, Ben** Berkeley, CA, Aug. 15, 1972.
**Affleck, Casey** Falmouth, MA, Aug. 12, 1975.
**Aghdashloo, Shohreh** Tehran, Iran, May 11, 1952.
**Agutter, Jenny** Taunton, England, Dec. 20, 1952.
**Aiello, Danny** New York, NY, June 20, 1933.
**Aiken, Liam** New York, NY, Jan. 7, 1990.
**Aimee, Anouk** (Dreyfus) Paris, France, Apr. 27, 1934. Bauer Therond.
**Akers, Karen** New York, NY, Oct. 13, 1945, Hunter College.
**Alba, Jessica** Pomona, CA, Apr. 28, 1981.
**Alberghetti, Anna Maria** Pesaro, Italy, May 15, 1936.
**Albright, Lola** Akron, OH, July 20, 1925.
**Alda, Alan** New York, NY, Jan. 28, 1936. Fordham.
**Aleandro, Norma** Buenos Aires, Argentina, Dec. 6, 1936.
**Alejandro, Miguel** New York, NY, Feb. 21, 1958.
**Alexander, Jane** (Quigley) Boston, MA, Oct. 28, 1939. Sarah Lawrence.
**Alexander, Jason** (Jay Greenspan) Newark, NJ, Sept. 23, 1959. Boston U.
**Alice, Mary** Indianola, MS, Dec. 3, 1941.
**Allen, Debbie** (Deborah) Houston, TX, Jan. 16, 1950. Howard U.
**Allen, Joan** Rochelle, IL, Aug. 20, 1956. East Illinois U.
**Allen, Karen** Carrollton, IL, Oct. 5, 1951. U Maryland.
**Allen, Nancy** New York, NY, June 24, 1950.
**Allen, Tim** Denver, CO, June 13, 1953. Western Michigan U.
**Allen, Woody** (Allan Stewart Konigsberg) Brooklyn, NY, Dec. 1, 1935.
**Alley, Kirstie** Wichita, KS, Jan. 12, 1955.
**Alonso, Maria Conchita** Cuba, June 29, 1957.
**Alt, Carol** Queens, NY, Dec. 1, 1960. Hofstra U.
**Alvarado, Trini** New York, NY, Jan. 10, 1967.
**Amalric, Mathieu** Neuilly-sur-Seine, France, Oct. 25, 1965.
**Ambrose, Lauren** New Haven, CT, Feb. 20, 1978.
**Amis, Suzy** Oklahoma City, OK, Jan. 5, 1958. Actors Studio.
**Amos, John** Newark, NJ, Dec. 27, 1940. Colorado U.
**Anderson, Anthony** Los Angeles, CA, Aug. 15, 1970.
**Anderson, Gillian** Chicago, IL, Aug. 9, 1968. DePaul U.
**Anderson, Kevin** Waukeegan, IL, Jan. 13, 1960.
**Anderson, Loni** St. Paul, MN, Aug. 5, 1946.
**Anderson, Melissa Sue** Berkeley, CA, Sept. 26, 1962.
**Anderson, Melody** Edmonton, Canada, Dec. 3, 1955. Carlton U.
**Anderson, Michael, Jr.** London, England, Aug. 6, 1943.
**Anderson, Richard Dean** Minneapolis, MN, Jan. 23, 1950.

**Andersson, Bibi** Stockholm, Sweden, Nov. 11, 1935. Royal Dramatic School.
**Andress, Ursula** Bern, Switzerland, Mar. 19, 1936.
**Andrews, Anthony** London, England, Dec. 1, 1948.
**Andrews, Julie** (Julia Elizabeth Wells) Surrey, England, Oct. 1, 1935.
**Andrews, Naveen** London, England, Jan. 17, 1969.
**Angarano, Michael** Brooklyn, NY, Dec. 3, 1987.
**Anglim, Philip** San Francisco, CA, Feb. 11, 1953.
**Aniston, Jennifer** Sherman Oaks, CA, Feb. 11, 1969.
**Ann-Margret** (Olsson) Valsjobyn, Sweden, Apr. 28, 1941. Northwestern.
**Ansara, Michael** Lowell, MA, Apr. 15, 1922. Pasadena Playhouse.
**Anspach, Susan** New York, NY, Nov. 23, 1945.
**Anthony, Lysette** London, England, Sept. 26, 1963.
**Anthony, Marc** New York, NY, Sept. 16, 1968.
**Anthony, Tony** Clarksburg, WV, Oct. 16, 1937. Carnegie Tech.
**Anton, Susan** Yucaipa, CA, Oct. 12, 1950. Bernardino College.
**Antonelli, Laura** Pola, Italy, Nov. 28, 1941.
**Anwar, Gabrielle** Laleham, England, Feb. 4, 1970.
**Applegate, Christina** Hollywood, CA, Nov. 25, 1972.
**Archer, Anne** Los Angeles, CA, Aug. 25, 1947.
**Ardant, Fanny** Monte Carlo, Monaco, Mar 22, 1949.
**Arkin, Adam** Brooklyn, NY, Aug. 19, 1956.
**Arkin, Alan** New York, NY, Mar. 26, 1934. LACC.
**Armstrong, Bess** Baltimore, MD, Dec. 11, 1953.
**Arnaz, Desi, Jr.** Los Angeles, CA, Jan. 19, 1953.
**Arnaz, Lucie** Hollywood, CA, July 17, 1951.
**Arness, James** (Aurness) Minneapolis, MN, May 26, 1923. Beloit College.
**Arnett, Will** Toronto, ON, Canada, May 5, 1970.
**Arquette, David** Winchester, VA, Sept. 8, 1971.
**Arquette, Patricia** New York, NY, Apr. 8, 1968.
**Arquette, Rosanna** New York, NY, Aug. 10, 1959.
**Arthur, Beatrice** (Frankel) New York, NY, May 13, 1924. New School.
**Asher, Jane** London, England, Apr. 5, 1946.
**Ashley, Elizabeth** (Elizabeth Ann Cole) Ocala, FL, Aug. 30, 1939.
**Ashton, John** Springfield, MA, Feb. 22, 1948. USC.
**Asner, Edward** Kansas City, KS, Nov. 15, 1929.
**Assante, Armand** New York, NY, Oct. 4, 1949. AADA.
**Astin, John** Baltimore, MD, Mar. 30, 1930. U Minnesota.
**Astin, MacKenzie** Los Angeles, CA, May 12, 1973.
**Astin, Sean** Santa Monica, CA, Feb. 25, 1971.
**Atherton, William** Orange, CT, July 30, 1947. Carnegie Tech.
**Atkins, Christopher** Rye, NY, Feb. 21, 1961.
**Atkins, Eileen** London, England, June 16, 1934.
**Atkinson, Rowan** Consett, England, Jan. 6, 1955. Oxford.
**Attenborough, Richard** Cambridge, England, Aug. 29, 1923. RADA.
**Auberjonois, Rene** New York, NY, June 1, 1940. Carnegie Tech.
**Audran, Stephane** Versailles, France, Nov. 8, 1932.
**Auger, Claudine** Paris, France, Apr. 26, 1942. Dramatic Cons.
**Aulin, Ewa** Stockholm, Sweden, Feb. 14, 1950.
**Auteuil, Daniel** Alger, Algeria, Jan. 24, 1950.
**Avalon, Frankie** (Francis Thomas Avallone) Philadelphia, PA, Sept. 18, 1939.
**Aykroyd, Dan** Ottawa, Canada, July 1, 1952.
**Azaria, Hank** Forest Hills, NY, Apr. 25, 1964. AADA, Tufts U.
**Aznavour, Charles** (Varenagh Aznourian) Paris, France, May 22, 1924.
**Azzara, Candice** Brooklyn, NY, May 18, 1947.

**Bacall, Lauren** (Betty Perske) New York, NY, Sept. 16, 1924. AADA.
**Bach, Barbara** Queens, NY, Aug. 27, 1946.
**Bach, Catherine** Warren, OH, Mar. 1, 1954.
**Backer, Brian** New York, NY, Dec. 5, 1956. Neighborhood Playhouse.
**Bacon, Kevin** Philadelphia, PA, July 8, 1958.
**Bain, Barbara** Chicago, IL, Sept. 13, 1934. U Illinois.
**Baio, Scott** Brooklyn, NY, Sept. 22, 1961.
**Baker, Blanche** New York, NY, Dec. 20, 1956.
**Baker, Carroll** Johnstown, PA, May 28, 1931. St. Petersburg, Jr. College.
**Baker, Diane** Hollywood, CA, Feb. 25, 1938. USC.
**Baker, Dylan** Syracuse, NY, Oct. 7, 1959.
**Baker, Joe Don** Groesbeck, TX, Feb. 12, 1936.
**Baker, Kathy** Midland, TX, June 8, 1950. UC Berkley.
**Baker, Simon** Launceston, Tasmania, July 30, 1969.
**Bakula, Scott** St. Louis, MO, Oct. 9, 1955. Kansas U.
**Balaban, Bob** Chicago, IL, Aug. 16, 1945. Colgate.
**Baldwin, Adam** Chicago, IL, Feb. 27, 1962.
**Baldwin, Alec** Massapequa, NY, Apr. 3, 1958. NYU.
**Baldwin, Daniel** Massapequa, NY, Oct. 5, 1960.
**Baldwin, Stephen** Massapequa, NY, May 12, 1966.
**Baldwin, William** Massapequa, NY, Feb. 21, 1963.
**Bale, Christian** Pembrokeshire, West Wales, Jan. 30, 1974.
**Balk, Fairuza** Point Reyes, CA, May 21, 1974.
**Ballard, Kaye** Cleveland, OH, Nov. 20, 1926.
**Bana, Eric** Melbourne, Australia, Aug. 9, 1968.
**Banderas, Antonio** Malaga, Spain, Aug. 10, 1960.
**Banerjee, Victor** Calcutta, India, Oct. 15, 1946.
**Banes, Lisa** Chagrin Falls, OH, July 9, 1955. Juilliard.
**Banks, Elizabeth** Pittsfield, MA, Feb. 19, 1974. U of PA.
**Baranski, Christine** Buffalo, NY, May 2, 1952. Juilliard.
**Barbeau, Adrienne** Sacramento, CA, June 11, 1945. Foothill College.
**Bardem, Javier** Gran Canaria, Spain, May 1, 1969.
**Bardot, Brigitte** Paris, France, Sept. 28, 1934.
**Barkin, Ellen** Bronx, NY, Apr. 16, 1954. Hunter College.
**Barnes, Christopher Daniel** Portland, ME, Nov. 7, 1972.
**Barnett, Samuel** Whitby, No. Yorkshire, England, Apr. 25, 1980.
**Baron Cohen, Sacha** London, England, Oct. 13, 1971.
**Barr, Jean-Marc** Bitburg, Germany, Sept. 27, 1960.
**Barr, Roseanne** Salt Lake City, UT, Nov. 3, 1952.
**Barrault, Marie-Christine** Paris, France, Mar. 21, 1944.
**Barraza, Adriana** Toluca, Mexico, March 5, 1956.
**Barrett, Majel** (Hudec) Columbus, OH, Feb. 23, 1939. Western Reserve U.
**Barrie, Barbara** Chicago, IL, May 23, 1931.
**Barry, Gene** (Eugene Klass) New York, NY, June 14, 1919.
**Barry, Neill** New York, NY, Nov. 29, 1965.
**Barrymore, Drew** Los Angeles, CA, Feb. 22, 1975.
**Bart, Roger** Norwalk, CT, Sept. 29, 1962.
**Bartha, Justin** West Bloomfield, MI, July 21, 1978.
**Baruchel, Jay** Ottawa, Canada, Apr. 9, 1982.
**Baryshnikov, Mikhail** Riga, Latvia, Jan. 27, 1948.
**Basinger, Kim** Athens, GA, Dec. 8, 1953. Neighborhood Playhouse.
**Bassett, Angela** New York, NY, Aug. 16, 1958.
**Bateman, Jason** Rye, NY, Jan. 14, 1969.

**Bateman, Justine** Rye, NY, Feb. 19, 1966.
**Bates, Jeanne** San Francisco, CA, May 21, 1918. RADA.
**Bates, Kathy** Memphis, TN, June 28, 1948. S. Methodist U.
**Bauer, Steven** (Steven Rocky Echevarria) Havana, Cuba, Dec. 2, 1956. U Miami.
**Baxter, Keith** South Wales, England, Apr. 29, 1933. RADA.
**Baxter, Meredith** Los Angeles, CA, June 21, 1947. Interlochen Academy.
**Baye, Nathalie** Maineville, France, July 6, 1948.
**Beach, Adam** Winnipeg, Manitoba, Canada, Nov. 11, 1972.
**Beacham, Stephanie** Casablanca, Morocco, Feb. 28, 1947.
**Beals, Jennifer** Chicago, IL, Dec. 19, 1963.
**Bean, Orson** (Dallas Burrows) Burlington, VT, July 22, 1928.
**Bean, Sean** Sheffield, Yorkshire, England, Apr. 17, 1958.
**Béart, Emmanuelle** Gassin, France, Aug. 14, 1965.
**Beatty, Ned** Louisville, KY, July 6, 1937.
**Beatty, Warren** Richmond, VA, Mar. 30, 1937.
**Beck, John** Chicago, IL, Jan. 28, 1943.
**Beck, Michael** Memphis, TN, Feb. 4, 1949. Millsap College.
**Beckinsale, Kate** London, England, July 26, 1974.
**Bedelia, Bonnie** New York, NY, Mar. 25, 1946. Hunter College.
**Begley, Ed, Jr.** New York, NY, Sept. 16, 1949.
**Belafonte, Harry** New York, NY, Mar. 1, 1927.
**Bell, Jamie** Billingham, England, Mar. 14, 1988.
**Bell, Tobin** Queens, NY, Aug. 7, 1942.
**Beller, Kathleen** New York, NY, Feb. 10, 1957.
**Bello, Maria** Norristown, PA, Apr. 18, 1967.
**Bellucci, Monica** Citta di Castello, Italy, Sept. 30, 1964.
**Bellwood, Pamela** (King) Scarsdale, NY, June 26, 1951.
**Belmondo, Jean Paul** Paris, France, Apr. 9, 1933.
**Belushi, James** Chicago, IL, June 15, 1954.
**Belzer, Richard** Bridgeport, CT, Aug. 4, 1944.
**Benedict, Dirk** (Niewoehner) White Sulphur Springs, MT, March 1, 1945. Whitman College.
**Benedict, Paul** Silver City, NM, Sept. 17, 1938.
**Benigni, Roberto** Tuscany, Italy, Oct. 27, 1952.
**Bening, Annette** Topeka, KS, May 29, 1958. San Francisco State U.
**Benjamin, Richard** New York, NY, May 22, 1938. Northwestern.
**Bennent, David** Lausanne, Switzerland, Sept. 9, 1966.
**Bennett, Alan** Leeds, England, May 9, 1934. Oxford.
**Bennett, Hywel** Garnant, South Wales, Apr. 8, 1944.
**Benson, Robby** Dallas, TX, Jan. 21, 1957.
**Bentley, Wes** Jonesboro, AR, Sept. 4, 1978.
**Berenger, Tom** Chicago, IL, May 31, 1950, U Missouri.
**Berenson, Marisa** New York, NY, Feb. 15, 1947.
**Berg, Peter** New York, NY, March 11, 1964. Malcalester College.
**Bergen, Candice** Los Angeles, CA, May 9, 1946. U Pennsylvania.
**Bergen, Polly** Knoxville, TN, July 14, 1930. Compton, Jr. College.
**Berger, Helmut** Salzburg, Austria, May 29, 1942.
**Berger, Senta** Vienna, Austria, May 13, 1941. Vienna School of Acting.
**Berger, William** Austria, Jan. 20, 1928. Columbia.
**Bergerac, Jacques** Biarritz, France, May 26, 1927. Paris U.
**Bergin, Patrick** Dublin, Ireland, Feb. 4, 1951.
**Berkley, Elizabeth** Detroit, MI, July 28, 1972.

Berkoff, Steven  London, England, Aug. 3, 1937.
Berlin, Jeannie  Los Angeles, CA, Nov. 1, 1949.
Berlinger, Warren  Brooklyn, NY, Aug. 31, 1937. Columbia U.
Bernal, Gael García  Guadalajara, Mexico, Oct. 30, 1978.
Bernhard, Sandra  Flint, MI, June 6, 1955.
Bernsen, Corbin  Los Angeles, CA, Sept. 7, 1954. UCLA.
Berri, Claude  (Langmann) Paris, France, July 1, 1934.
Berridge, Elizabeth  Westchester, NY, May 2, 1962. Strasberg Institute.
Berry, Halle  Cleveland, OH, Aug. 14, 1968.
Berry, Ken  Moline, IL, Nov. 3, 1933.
Bertinelli, Valerie  Wilmington, DE, Apr. 23, 1960.
Best, James  Corydon, IN, July 26, 1926.
Bettany, Paul  London, England, May 27, 1971.
Bey, Turhan  Vienna, Austria, Mar. 30, 1921.
Beymer, Richard  Avoca, IA, Feb. 21, 1939.
Bialik, Mayim  San Diego, CA, Dec. 12, 1975.
Biehn, Michael  Anniston, AL, July 31, 1956.
Biel, Jessica  Ely, MN, Mar. 3, 1982.
Biggerstaff, Sean  Glasgow, Scotland, Mar. 15, 1983.
Biggs, Jason  Pompton Plains, NJ, May 12, 1978.
Bikel, Theodore  Vienna, Austria, May 2, 1924. RADA.
Billingsley, Peter  New York, NY, Apr. 16, 1972.
Binoche, Juliette  Paris, France, Mar. 9, 1964.
Birch, Thora  Los Angeles, CA, Mar. 11, 1982.
Birkin, Jane  London, England, Dec. 14, 1947.
Birney, David  Washington, DC, Apr. 23, 1939. Dartmouth, UCLA.
Birney, Reed  Alexandria, VA, Sept. 11, 1954. Boston U.
Bishop, Kevin  Kent, England, June 18, 1980.
Bisset, Jacqueline  Waybridge, England, Sept. 13, 1944.
Black, Jack (Thomas Black)  Edmonton, Alberta, Canada, Apr. 7, 1969.
Black, Karen  (Ziegler) Park Ridge, IL, July 1, 1942. Northwestern.
Black, Lewis  Silver Spring, MD, Aug. 30, 1948.
Black, Lucas  Speake, AL, Nov. 29, 1982.
Blackman, Honor  London, England, Aug. 22, 1926.
Blades, Ruben  Panama City, FL, July 16, 1948. Harvard.
Blair, Betsy  (Betsy Boger) New York, NY, Dec. 11, 1923.
Blair, Linda  Westport, CT, Jan. 22, 1959.
Blair, Selma  Southfield, MI, June 23, 1972.
Blake, Robert  (Michael Gubitosi) Nutley, NJ, Sept. 18, 1933.
Blakely, Susan  Frankfurt, Germany, Sept. 7, 1950. U Texas.
Blakley, Ronee  Stanley, ID, 1946. Stanford U.
Blanchett, Cate  Melbourne, Australia, May 14, 1969.
Bledel, Alexis  Houston, TX, Sept. 16, 1981.
Blethyn, Brenda  Ramsgate, Kent, England, Feb. 20, 1946.
Blonsky, Nikki  Great Neck, NY, Nov. 9, 1988.
Bloom, Claire  London, England, Feb. 15, 1931. Badminton School.
Bloom, Orlando  Canterbury, England, Jan. 13, 1977.
Bloom, Verna  Lynn, MA, Aug. 7, 1939. Boston U.
Blount, Lisa  Fayettville, AK, July 1, 1957. U Arkansas.
Blum, Mark  Newark, NJ, May 14, 1950. U Minnesota.
Blunt, Emily  London, England, Feb. 23, 1983.
Blyth, Ann  Mt. Kisco, NY, Aug. 16, 1928. New Waybum Dramatic School.
Bochner, Hart  Toronto, ON, Canada, Oct. 3, 1956. U San Diego.

Bogosian, Eric  Woburn, MA, Apr. 24, 1953. Oberlin College.
Bohringer, Richard  Paris, France, Jan. 16, 1941.
Bolkan, Florinda  (Florinda Soares Bulcao) Ceara, Brazil, Feb. 15, 1941.
Bologna, Joseph  Brooklyn, NY, Dec. 30, 1938. Brown U.
Bonet, Lisa  San Francisco, CA, Nov. 16, 1967.
Bonham-Carter, Helena  London, England, May 26, 1966.
Boone, Pat  Jacksonville, FL, June 1, 1934. Columbia U.
Boothe, Powers  Snyder, TX, June 1, 1949. Southern Methodist U.
Borgnine, Ernest  (Borgnino) Hamden, CT, Jan. 24, 1917. Randall School.
Bosco, Philip  Jersey City, NJ, Sept. 26, 1930. Catholic U.
Bosley, Tom  Chicago, IL, Oct. 1, 1927. DePaul U.
Bostwick, Barry  San Mateo, CA, Feb. 24, 1945. NYU.
Bosworth, Kate  Los Angeles, CA, Jan. 2, 1983.
Bottoms, Joseph  Santa Barbara, CA, Aug. 30, 1954.
Bottoms, Sam  Santa Barbara, CA, Oct. 17, 1955.
Bottoms, Timothy  Santa Barbara, CA, Aug. 30, 1951.
Boulting, Ingrid  Transvaal, South Africa, 1947.
Boutsikaris, Dennis  Newark, NJ, Dec. 21, 1952. Catholic U.
Bowie, David  (David Robert Jones) Brixton, South London, England, Jan. 8, 1947.
Bowker, Judi  Shawford, England, Apr. 6, 1954.
Boxleitner, Bruce  Elgin, IL, May 12, 1950.
Boyd, Billy  Glasgow, Scotland, Aug. 28, 1968.
Boyle, Lara Flynn  Davenport, IA, Mar. 24, 1970.
Bracco, Lorraine  Brooklyn, NY, Oct. 2, 1949.
Bradford, Jesse  Norwalk, CT, May 27, 1979.
Braeden, Eric  (Hans Gudegast) Kiel, Germany, Apr. 3, 1942.
Braff, Zach  South Orange, NJ, Apr. 6, 1975.
Braga, Alice  São Paolo, Brazil, Apr. 15, 1983.
Braga, Sonia  Maringa, Brazil, June 8, 1950.
Branagh, Kenneth  Belfast, Northern Ireland, Dec. 10, 1960.
Brandauer, Klaus Maria  Altaussee, Austria, June 22, 1944.
Brandon, Clark  New York, NY, Dec. 13, 1958.
Brandon, Michael  (Feldman) Brooklyn, NY, Apr. 20, 1945.
Brantley, Betsy  Rutherfordton, NC, Sept. 20, 1955. London Central School of Drama.
Bratt, Benjamin  San Francisco, CA, Dec. 16, 1963.
Brennan, Eileen  Los Angeles, CA, Sept. 3, 1935. AADA.
Brenneman, Amy  Glastonbury, CT, June 22, 1964.
Breslin, Abigail  New York, NY, Apr. 14, 1996.
Brialy, Jean-Claude  Aumale, Algeria, 1933. Strasbourg Cons.
Bridges, Beau  Los Angeles, CA, Dec. 9, 1941. UCLA.
Bridges, Chris "Ludacris"  Champagne, IL, Sept. 11, 1977.
Bridges, Jeff  Los Angeles, CA, Dec. 4, 1949.
Bright, Cameron  Victoria, BC, Canada, Jan. 26, 1993.
Brimley, Wilford  Salt Lake City, UT, Sept. 27, 1934.
Brinkley, Christie  Malibu, CA, Feb. 2, 1954.
Britt, May  (Maybritt Wilkins) Stockholm, Sweden, Mar. 22, 1936.
Brittany, Morgan  (Suzanne Cupito) Los Angeles, CA, Dec. 5, 1950.
Britton, Tony  Birmingham, England, June 9, 1924.
Broadbent, Jim  Lincoln, England, May 24, 1959.
Broderick, Matthew  New York, NY, Mar. 21, 1962.
Brody, Adrien  New York, NY, Dec. 23, 1976.

**Brolin, James** Los Angeles, CA, July 18, 1940. UCLA.
**Brolin, Josh** Los Angeles, CA, Feb. 12, 1968.
**Bron, Eleanor** Stanmore, England, Mar. 14, 1934.
**Brookes, Jacqueline** Montclair, NJ, July 24, 1930. RADA.
**Brooks, Albert** (Einstein) Los Angeles, CA, July 22, 1947.
**Brooks, Mel** (Melvyn Kaminski) Brooklyn, NY, June 28, 1926.
**Brosnan, Pierce** County Meath, Ireland. May 16, 1952.
**Brown, Blair** Washington, DC, Apr. 23, 1947. Pine Manor.
**Brown, Bryan** Panania, Australia, June 23, 1947.
**Brown, Georg Stanford** Havana, Cuba, June 24, 1943. AMDA.
**Brown, James** Desdemona, TX, Mar. 22, 1920. Baylor U.
**Brown, Jim** St. Simons Island, NY, Feb. 17, 1935. Syracuse U.
**Browne, Leslie** New York, NY, 1958.
**Bruckner, Agnes** Hollywood, CA, Aug. 16, 1985.
**Brühl, Daniel** (Daniel Domingo) Barcelona, Spain, June 16, 1978.
**Buckley, Betty** Big Spring, TX, July 3, 1947. Texas Christian U.
**Bujold, Genevieve** Montreal, Quebec, Canada, July 1, 1942.
**Bullock, Sandra** Arlington, VA, July 26, 1964.
**Burghoff, Gary** Bristol, CT, May 24, 1943.
**Burgi, Richard** Montclair, NJ, July 30, 1958.
**Burke, Paul** New Orleans, LA, July 21, 1926. Pasadena Playhouse.
**Burnett, Carol** San Antonio, TX, Apr. 26, 1933. UCLA.
**Burns, Catherine** New York, NY, Sept. 25, 1945. AADA.
**Burns, Edward** Valley Stream, NY, Jan. 28, 1969.
**Burrows, Darren E.** Winfield, KS, Sept. 12, 1966.
**Burrows, Saffron** London, England, Jan. 1, 1973.
**Burstyn, Ellen** (Edna Rae Gillhooly) Detroit, MI, Dec. 7, 1932.
**Burton, Kate** Geneva, Switzerland, Sept. 10, 1957.
**Burton, LeVar** Los Angeles, CA, Feb. 16, 1958. UCLA.
**Buscemi, Steve** Brooklyn, NY, Dec. 13, 1957.
**Busey, Gary** Goose Creek, TX, June 29, 1944.
**Busfield, Timothy** Lansing, MI, June 12, 1957. East Tennessee State U.
**Butler, Gerard** Glasgow, Scotland, Nov. 13, 1969.
**Buzzi, Ruth** Westerly, RI, July 24, 1936. Pasadena Playhouse.
**Bygraves, Max** London, England, Oct. 16, 1922. St. Joseph's School.
**Bynes, Amanda** Thousand Oaks, CA, Apr. 3, 1986.
**Byrne, David** Dumbarton, Scotland, May 14, 1952.
**Byrne, Gabriel** Dublin, Ireland, May 12, 1950.
**Byrnes, Edd** New York, NY, July 30, 1933.

**Caan, James** Bronx, NY, Mar. 26,1939.
**Caesar, Sid** Yonkers, NY, Sept. 8, 1922.
**Cage, Nicolas** (Coppola) Long Beach, CA, Jan. 7, 1964.
**Cain, Dean** (Dean Tanaka) Mt. Clemens, MI, July 31, 1966.
**Caine, Michael** (Maurice Micklewhite) London, England, Mar. 14, 1933.
**Caine, Shakira** (Baksh) Guyana, Feb. 23, 1947. Indian Trust College.
**Callan, Michael** (Martin Calinieff) Philadelphia, PA, Nov. 22, 1935.
**Callow, Simon** London, England, June 15, 1949. Queens U.
**Cameron, Kirk** Panorama City, CA, Oct. 12, 1970.
**Camp, Colleen** San Francisco, CA, June 7, 1953.
**Campbell, Bill** Chicago, IL, July 7, 1959.
**Campbell, Glen** Delight, AR, Apr. 22, 1935.
**Campbell, Neve** Guelph, ON, Canada, Oct. 3, 1973.

**Campbell, Tisha** Oklahoma City, OK, Oct. 13, 1968.
**Canale, Gianna Maria** Reggio Calabria, Italy, Sept. 12, 1927.
**Cannon, Dyan** (Samille Diane Friesen) Tacoma, WA, Jan. 4, 1937.
**Capshaw, Kate** Ft. Worth, TX, Nov. 3, 1953. U Misourri.
**Cara, Irene** New York, NY, Mar. 18, 1958.
**Cardellini, Linda** Redwood City, CA, June 25, 1975.
**Cardinale, Claudia** Tunis, North Africa. Apr. 15, 1939. College Paul Cambon.
**Carell, Steve** Concord, MA, Aug. 16, 1962.
**Carey, Harry, Jr.** Saugus, CA, May 16, 1921. Black Fox Military Academy.
**Carey, Philip** Hackensack, NJ, July 15, 1925. U Miami.
**Cariou, Len** Winnipeg, Manitoba, Canada, Sept. 30, 1939.
**Carlin, George** New York, NY, May 12, 1938.
**Carlyle, Robert** Glasgow, Scotland, Apr. 14, 1961.
**Carmen, Julie** Mt. Vernon, NY, Apr. 4, 1954.
**Carmichael, Ian** Hull, England, June 18, 1920. Scarborough College.
**Carne, Judy** (Joyce Botterill) Northampton, England, 1939. Bush-Davis Theatre School.
**Caron, Leslie** Paris, France, July 1, 1931. Nationall Conservatory, Paris.
**Carpenter, Carleton** Bennington, VT, July 10, 1926. Northwestern.
**Carradine, David** Hollywood, CA, Dec. 8, 1936. San Francisco State.
**Carradine, Keith** San Mateo, CA, Aug. 8, 1950. Colo. State U.
**Carradine, Robert** San Mateo, CA, Mar. 24, 1954.
**Carrel, Dany** Tourane, Indochina, Sept. 20, 1932. Marseilles Cons.
**Carrera, Barbara** Managua, Nicaragua, Dec. 31, 1945.
**Carrere, Tia** (Althea Janairo) Honolulu, HI, Jan. 2, 1965.
**Carrey, Jim** Jacksons Point, ON, Canada, Jan. 17, 1962.
**Carriere, Mathieu** Hannover, West Germany, Aug. 2, 1950.
**Carroll, Diahann** (Johnson) New York, NY, July 17, 1935. NYU.
**Carroll, Pat** Shreveport, LA, May 5, 1927. Catholic U.
**Carson, John David** Los Angeles, CA, Mar. 6, 1952. Valley College.
**Carsten, Peter** (Ransenthaler) Weissenberg, Bavaria, Apr. 30, 1929. Munich Akademie.
**Cartwright, Veronica** Bristol, England, Apr 20, 1949.
**Caruso, David** Forest Hills, NY, Jan. 7, 1956.
**Carvey, Dana** Missoula, MT, Apr. 2, 1955. San Francisco State U.
**Casella, Max** Washington D.C, June 6, 1967.
**Casey, Bernie** Wyco, WV, June 8, 1939.
**Cassavetes, Nick** New York, NY, 1959, Syracuse U, AADA.
**Cassel, Seymour** Detroit, MI, Jan. 22, 1935.
**Cassel, Vincent** Paris, France, Nov. 23, 1966.
**Cassidy, David** New York, NY, Apr. 12, 1950.
**Cassidy, Joanna** Camden, NJ, Aug. 2, 1944. Syracuse U.
**Cassidy, Patrick** Los Angeles, CA, Jan. 4, 1961.
**Castellaneta, Dan** Chicago, IL, Oct. 29, 1957.
**Cates, Phoebe** New York, NY, July 16, 1962.
**Cattrall, Kim** Liverpool, England, Aug. 21, 1956. AADA.
**Caulfield, Maxwell** Glasgow, Scotland, Nov. 23, 1959.
**Cavani, Liliana** Bologna, Italy, Jan. 12, 1933. U Bologna.
**Cavett, Dick** Gibbon, NE, Nov. 19, 1936.
**Caviezel, Jim** Mt. Vernon, WA, Sept. 26, 1968.
**Cedric the Entertainer** (Cedric Kyles) Jefferson City, MO, Apr. 24, 1964.
**Cera, Michael** Brampton, ON, Canada, June 7, 1988.

**Chakiris, George** Norwood, OH, Sept. 16, 1933.
**Chamberlain, Richard** Beverly Hills, CA, March 31, 1935. Pomona.
**Champion, Marge** (Marjorie Belcher) Los Angeles, CA, Sept. 2, 1923.
**Chan, Jackie** Hong Kong, Apr. 7, 1954.
**Chandler, Kyle** Buffalo, NY, Sept. 17, 1965
**Channing, Carol** Seattle, WA, Jan. 31, 1921. Bennington.
**Channing, Stockard** (Susan Stockard) New York, NY, Feb. 13, 1944. Radcliffe.
**Chapin, Miles** New York, NY, Dec. 6, 1954. HB Studio.
**Chaplin, Ben** London, England, July 31, 1970.
**Chaplin, Geraldine** Santa Monica, CA, July 31, 1944. Royal Ballet.
**Chaplin, Sydney** Los Angeles, CA, Mar. 31, 1926. Lawrenceville.
**Charisse, Cyd** (Tula Ellice Finklea) Amarillo, TX, Mar. 3, 1922. Hollywood Professional School.
**Charles, Josh** Baltimore, MD, Sept. 15, 1971.
**Charles, Walter** East Strousburg, PA, Apr. 4, 1945. Boston U.
**Chase, Chevy** (Cornelius Crane Chase) New York, NY, Oct. 8, 1943.
**Chatwin, Justin** Nanaimo, BC, Canada, Oct. 31, 1982.
**Chaves, Richard** Jacksonville, FL, Oct. 9, 1951. Occidental College.
**Chaykin, Maury** Brooklyn, NY, July 27, 1949.
**Cheadle, Don** Kansas City, MO, Nov. 29, 1964.
**Chen, Joan** (Chen Chung) Shanghai, China, Apr. 26, 1961. Cal State.
**Chenoweth, Kristin** Broken Arrow, OK, July 24, 1968.
**Cher** (Cherilyn Sarkisian) El Centro, CA, May 20, 1946.
**Chiklis, Michael** Lowell, MA, Aug. 30, 1963.
**Chiles, Lois** Alice, TX, Apr. 15, 1947.
**Cho, John** Seoul, Korea, June 16, 1972.
**Cho, Margaret** San Francisco, CA, Dec. 5, 1968.
**Chong, Rae Dawn** Vancouver, BC, Canada, Feb. 28, 1962.
**Chong, Thomas** Edmonton, Alberta, Canada, May 24, 1938.
**Christensen, Erika** Seattle, WA, Aug. 19, 1982.
**Christensen, Hayden** Vancouver, BC, Canada, Apr. 19, 1981.
**Christian, Linda** (Blanca Rosa Welter) Tampico, Mexico, Nov. 13, 1923.
**Christie, Julie** Chukua, Assam, India, Apr. 14, 1941.
**Christopher, Dennis** (Carrelli) Philadelphia, PA, Dec. 2, 1955. Temple U.
**Christopher, Jordan** Youngstown, OH, Oct. 23, 1940. Kent State.
**Church, Thomas Haden** El Paso, TX, June 17, 1961.
**Cilento, Diane** Queensland, Australia, Oct. 5, 1933. AADA.
**Clark, Candy** Norman, OK, June 20, 1947.
**Clark, Dick** Mt. Vernon, NY, Nov. 30, 1929. Syracuse U.
**Clark, Matt** Washington, DC, Nov. 25, 1936.
**Clark, Petula** Epsom, England, Nov. 15, 1932.
**Clark, Susan** Sarnid, ON, Canada, Mar. 8, 1943. RADA.
**Clarkson, Patricia** New Orleans, LA, Dec. 29, 1959.
**Clay, Andrew Dice** (Andrew Silverstein) Brooklyn, NY, Sept. 29, 1957, Kingsborough College.
**Clayburgh, Jill** New York, NY, Apr. 30, 1944. Sarah Lawrence.
**Cleese, John** Weston-Super-Mare, England, Oct. 27, 1939, Cambridge.
**Clooney, George** Lexington, KY, May 6, 1961.
**Close, Glenn** Greenwich, CT, Mar. 19, 1947. William & Mary College.
**Cochrane, Rory** Syracuse, NY, Feb. 28, 1972.
**Cody, Kathleen** Bronx, NY, Oct. 30, 1953.
**Coffey, Scott** Honolulu, HI, May 1, 1967.

**Cole, George** London, England, Apr. 22, 1925.
**Coleman, Dabney** Austin, TX, Jan. 3, 1932.
**Coleman, Gary** Zion, IL, Feb. 8, 1968.
**Coleman, Jack** Easton, PA, Feb. 21, 1958. Duke U.
**Colin, Margaret** New York, NY, May 26, 1957.
**Collet, Christopher** New York, NY, Mar. 13, 1968. Strasberg Institute.
**Collette, Toni** Sydney, Australia, Nov. 1, 1972.
**Collins, Clifton, Jr.** Los Angeles, CA, June 16, 1970.
**Collins, Joan** London, England, May 21, 1933. Francis Holland School.
**Collins, Pauline** Devon, England, Sept. 3, 1940.
**Collins, Stephen** Des Moines, IA, Oct. 1, 1947. Amherst.
**Colon, Miriam** Ponce, PR., Aug. 20, 1936. UPR.
**Coltrane, Robbie** Ruthergien, Scotland, Mar. 30, 1950.
**Combs, Sean "Puffy"** New York, NY, Nov. 4, 1969.
**Comer, Anjanette** Dawson, TX, Aug. 7, 1942. Baylor, Texas U.
**Conant, Oliver** New York, NY, Nov. 15, 1955. Dalton.
**Conaway, Jeff** New York, NY, Oct. 5, 1950. NYU.
**Connelly, Jennifer** New York, NY, Dec. 12, 1970.
**Connery, Jason** London, England, Jan. 11, 1963.
**Connery, Sean** Edinburgh, Scotland, Aug. 25, 1930.
**Connick, Harry, Jr.** New Orleans, LA, Sept. 11, 1967.
**Connolly, Billy** Glasgow, Scotland, Nov. 24, 1942.
**Connors, Mike** (Krekor Ohanian) Fresno, CA, Aug. 15, 1925. UCLA.
**Conrad, Robert** (Conrad Robert Falk) Chicago, IL, Mar. 1, 1935. Northwestern.
**Considine, Paddy** Burton-on-Trent, England, Sept. 5, 1974.
**Constantine, Michael** Reading, PA, May 22, 1927.
**Conti, Tom** Paisley, Scotland, Nov. 22, 1941.
**Converse, Frank** St. Louis, MO, May 22, 1938. Carnegie Tech.
**Conway, Gary** Boston, MA, Feb. 4, 1936.
**Conway, Kevin** New York, NY, May 29, 1942.
**Conway, Tim** (Thomas Daniel) Willoughby, OH, Dec. 15, 1933. Bowling Green State.
**Coogan, Keith** (Keith Mitchell Franklin) Palm Springs, CA, Jan. 13, 1970.
**Coogan, Steve** Manchester, England, Oct. 14, 1965.
**Cook, Dane** Boston, MA, March 18, 1972.
**Cook, Rachael Leigh** Minneapolis, MN, Oct. 4, 1979.
**Coolidge, Jennifer** Boston, MA, Aug. 28, 1963.
**Cooper, Ben** Hartford, CT, Sept. 30, 1930. Columbia U.
**Cooper, Chris** Kansas City, MO, July 9, 1951. U Misourri.
**Cooper, Dominic** London, England, June 2, 1978.
**Cooper, Jackie** Los Angeles, CA, Sept. 15, 1921.
**Copeland, Joan** New York, NY, June 1, 1922. Brooklyn, NY College, RADA.
**Corbett, Gretchen** Portland, OR, Aug. 13, 1947. Carnegie Tech.
**Corbett, John** Wheeling, WV, May 9, 1961.
**Corbin, Barry** Dawson County, TX, Oct. 16, 1940. Texas Tech. U.
**Corcoran, Donna** Quincy, MA, Sept. 29, 1942.
**Cord, Alex** (Viespi) Floral Park, NY, Aug. 3, 1931. NYU, Actors Studio.
**Corday, Mara** (Marilyn Watts) Santa Monica, CA, Jan. 3, 1932.
**Cornthwaite, Robert** St. Helens, OR, Apr. 28, 1917. USC.
**Corri, Adrienne** Glasgow, Scotland, Nov. 13, 1933. RADA.
**Cort, Bud** (Walter Edward Cox) New Rochelle, NY, Mar. 29, 1950. NYU.
**Cortesa, Valentina** Milan, Italy, Jan. 1, 1924.
**Cosby, Bill** Philadelphia, PA, July 12, 1937. Temple U.

**Coster, Nicolas** London, England, Dec. 3, 1934. Neighborhood Playhouse.
**Costner, Kevin** Lynwood, CA, Jan. 18, 1955. California State U.
**Cotillard, Marion** Paris, France, Sept. 30, 1975.
**Courtenay, Tom** Hull, England, Feb. 25, 1937. RADA.
**Courtland, Jerome** Knoxville, TN, Dec. 27, 1926.
**Cox, Brian** Dundee, Scotland, June 1, 1946. LAMDA.
**Cox, Charlie** London, England, Dec. 21, 1982.
**Cox, Courteney** Birmingham, AL, June 15, 1964.
**Cox, Ronny** Cloudcroft, NM, Aug. 23, 1938.
**Coyote, Peter** (Cohon) New York, NY, Oct. 10, 1941.
**Craig, Daniel** Chester, England, Mar. 2, 1968. Guildhall.
**Craig, Michael** Poona, India, Jan. 27, 1929.
**Craven, Gemma** Dublin, Ireland, June 1, 1950.
**Crawford, Michael** (Dumbel-Smith) Salisbury, England, Jan. 19, 1942.
**Cremer, Bruno** Saint-Mande, Val-de-Varne, France, Oct. 6, 1929.
**Cristal, Linda** (Victoria Moya) Buenos Aires, Argentina, Feb. 25, 1934.
**Cromwell, James** Los Angeles, CA, Jan. 27, 1940.
**Crosby, Denise** Hollywood, CA, Nov. 24, 1957.
**Crosby, Harry** Los Angeles, CA, Aug. 8, 1958.
**Crosby, Mary Frances** Los Angeles, CA, Sept. 14, 1959.
**Cross, Ben** London, England, Dec. 16, 1947. RADA.
**Cross, Joseph** New Brunswick, NJ, May 28, 1986.
**Crouse, Lindsay** New York, NY, May 12, 1948. Radcliffe.
**Crowe, Russell** New Zealand, Apr. 7, 1964.
**Crowley, Pat** Olyphant, PA, Sept. 17, 1932.
**Crudup, Billy** Manhasset, NY, July 8, 1968. UNC, Chapel Hill.
**Cruise, Tom** (T. C. Mapother, IV) July 3, 1962, Syracuse, NY.
**Cruz, Penélope** (P.C. Sanchez) Madrid, Spain, Apr. 28, 1974.
**Cruz, Wilson** Brooklyn, NY, Dec. 27, 1973.
**Cryer, Jon** New York, NY, Apr. 16, 1965, RADA.
**Crystal, Billy** Long Beach, NY, Mar. 14, 1947. Marshall U.
**Culkin, Kieran** New York, NY, Sept. 30, 1982.
**Culkin, Macaulay** New York, NY, Aug. 26, 1980.
**Culkin, Rory** New York, NY, July 21, 1989.
**Cullum, John** Knoxville, TN, Mar. 2, 1930. U Tennessee.
**Cullum, John David** New York, NY, Mar. 1, 1966.
**Culp, Robert** Oakland, CA, Aug. 16, 1930. U Washington.
**Cumming, Alan** Perthshire, Scotland, Jan. 27, 1965.
**Cummings, Quinn** Hollywood, CA, Aug. 13, 1967.
**Cummins, Peggy** Prestatyn, North Wales, Dec. 18, 1926. Alexandra School.
**Curry, Tim** Cheshire, England, Apr. 19, 1946. Birmingham U.
**Curtin, Jane** Cambridge, MA, Sept. 6, 1947.
**Curtis, Jamie Lee** Los Angeles, CA, Nov. 22, 1958.
**Curtis, Tony** (Bernard Schwartz) New York, NY, June 3, 1924.
**Curtis-Hall, Vondie** Detroit, MI, Sept. 30, 1956.
**Cusack, Joan** Evanston, IL, Oct. 11, 1962.
**Cusack, John** Chicago, IL, June 28, 1966.
**Cusack, Sinead** Dalkey, Ireland, Feb. 18, 1948.

**Dafoe, Willem** Appleton, WI, July 22, 1955.
**Dahl, Arlene** Minneapolis, MN, Aug. 11, 1928. U Minnesota.
**Dale, Jim** Rothwell, England, Aug. 15, 1935.
**Dallesandro, Joe** Pensacola, FL, Dec. 31, 1948.

**Dalton, Timothy** Colwyn Bay, Wales, Mar. 21, 1946. RADA.
**Daltrey, Roger** London, England, Mar. 1, 1944.
**Daly, Tim** New York, NY, Mar. 1, 1956. Bennington College.
**Daly, Tyne** Madison, WI, Feb. 21, 1947. AMDA.
**Damon, Matt** Cambridge, MA, Oct. 8, 1970.
**Damone, Vic** (Vito Farinola) Brooklyn, NY, June 12, 1928.
**Dance, Charles** Plymouth, England, Oct. 10, 1946.
**Dancy, Hugh** Stoke-on-Trent, England, June 19, 1975.
**Danes, Claire** New York, NY, Apr. 12, 1979.
**D'Angelo, Beverly** Columbus, OH, Nov. 15, 1953.
**Daniels, Jeff** Athens, GA, Feb. 19, 1955. Central Michigan U.
**Daniels, William** Brooklyn, NY, Mar. 31, 1927. Northwestern.
**Danner, Blythe** Philadelphia, PA, Feb. 3, 1944. Bard College.
**Danning, Sybil** (Sybille Johanna Danninger) Vienna, Austria, May 4, 1949.
**Dano, Paul** Wilton, CT, June 19, 1983.
**Danson, Ted** San Diego, CA, Dec. 29, 1947. Stanford, Carnegie Tech.
**Dante, Michael** (Ralph Vitti) Stamford, CT, 1935. U Miami.
**Danza, Tony** Brooklyn, NY, Apr. 21, 1951. U Dubuque.
**D'arbanville, Patti** New York, NY, May 25, 1951.
**Darby, Kim** (Deborah Zerby) North Hollywood, CA, July 8, 1948.
**Darcel, Denise** (Denise Billecard) Paris, France, Sept. 8, 1925. U Dijon.
**Darren, James** Philadelphia, PA, June 8, 1936. Stella Adler School.
**Darrieux, Danielle** Bordeaux, France, May 1, 1917. Lycee LaTour.
**Davenport, Jack** Suffolk, England, March 1, 1973.
**Davenport, Nigel** Cambridge, England, May 23, 1928. Trinity College.
**David, Keith** New York, NY, June 4, 1954. Juilliard.
**Davidovich, Lolita** Toronto, ON, Canada, July 15, 1961.
**Davidson, Jaye** Riverside, CA, Mar. 21, 1968.
**Davidson, John** Pittsburgh, PA, Dec. 13, 1941. Denison U.
**Davidtz, Embeth** Lafayette, IN, Jan. 1, 1966.
**Davies, Jeremy** (Boring) Rockford, IA, Oct. 28, 1969.
**Davis, Clifton** Chicago, IL, Oct. 4, 1945. Oakwood College.
**Davis, Geena** Wareham, MA, Jan. 21, 1957.
**Davis, Hope** Tenafly, NJ, Mar. 23, 1964.
**Davis, Judy** Perth, Australia, Apr. 23, 1955.
**Davis, Mac** Lubbock, TX, Jan. 21,1942.
**Davis, Nancy** (Anne Frances Robbins) New York, NY, July 6, 1921. Smith College.
**Davis, Sammi** Kidderminster, Worcestershire, England, June 21, 1964.
**Davison, Bruce** Philadelphia, PA, June 28, 1946.
**Dawber, Pam** Detroit, MI, Oct. 18, 1954.
**Dawson, Rosario** New York, NY, May 9, 1979.
**Day, Doris** (Doris Kappelhoff) Cincinatti, OH, Apr. 3, 1924.
**Day-Lewis, Daniel** London, England, Apr. 29, 1957. Bristol Old Vic.
**Dayan, Assi** Israel, Nov. 23, 1945. U Jerusalem.
**Deakins, Lucy** New York, NY, 1971.
**Dean, Jimmy** Plainview, TX, Aug. 10, 1928.
**Dean, Loren** Las Vegas, NV, July 31, 1969.
**De Bankole, Isaach** Abidjan, Ivory Coast, Aug. 12, 1957.
**Dee, Joey** (Joseph Di Nicola) Passaic, NJ, June 11, 1940. Patterson State College.
**Dee, Ruby** Cleveland, OH, Oct. 27, 1924. Hunter College.
**DeGeneres, Ellen** New Orleans, LA, Jan. 26, 1958.

**DeHaven, Gloria** Los Angeles, CA, July 23, 1923.

**DeHavilland, Olivia** Tokyo, Japan, July 1, 1916. Notre Dame Convent School.

**Delair, Suzy** (Suzanne Delaire) Paris, France, Dec. 31, 1917.

**Delany, Dana** New York, NY, March 13, 1956. Wesleyan U.

**Delon, Alain** Sceaux, France, Nov. 8, 1935.

**Delorme, Daniele** Paris, France, Oct. 9, 1926. Sorbonne.

**Delpy, Julie** Paris, France, Dec, 21, 1969.

**Del Toro, Benicio** Santurce, Puerto Rico, Feb. 19, 1967.

**DeLuise, Dom** Brooklyn, NY, Aug. 1, 1933. Tufts College.

**DeLuise, Peter** New York, NY, Nov. 6, 1966.

**Demongeot, Mylene** Nice, France, Sept. 29, 1938.

**DeMornay, Rebecca** Los Angeles, CA, Aug. 29, 1962. Strasberg Institute.

**Dempsey, Patrick** Lewiston, ME, Jan. 13, 1966.

**DeMunn, Jeffrey** Buffalo, NY, Apr. 25, 1947. Union College.

**Dench, Judi** York, England, Dec. 9, 1934.

**Deneuve, Catherine** Paris, France, Oct. 22, 1943.

**De Niro, Robert** New York, NY, Aug. 17, 1943. Stella Adler.

**Dennehy, Brian** Bridgeport, CT, July 9, 1938. Columbia U.

**Depardieu, Gérard** Chateauroux, France, Dec. 27, 1948.

**Depp, Johnny** Owensboro, KY, June 9, 1963.

**Derek, Bo** (Mary Cathleen Collins) Long Beach, CA, Nov. 20, 1956.

**Dern, Bruce** Chicago, IL, June 4, 1936. UPA.

**Dern, Laura** Los Angeles, CA, Feb. 10, 1967.

**DeSalvo, Anne** Philadelphia, PA, Apr. 3, 1949.

**Deschanel, Zooey** Los Angeles, CA, Jan. 17, 1980.

**Devane, William** Albany, NY, Sept. 5, 1939.

**Devine, Loretta** Houston, TX, Aug. 21, 1949.

**DeVito, Danny** Asbury Park, NJ, Nov. 17, 1944.

**Dey, Susan** Pekin, IL, Dec. 10, 1953.

**DeYoung, Cliff** Los Angeles, CA, Feb. 12, 1945. California State U.

**Diamond, Neil** New York, NY, Jan. 24, 1941. NYU.

**Diaz, Cameron** Long Beach, CA, Aug. 30, 1972.

**DiCaprio, Leonardo** Hollywood, CA, Nov. 11, 1974.

**Dickinson, Angie** (Angeline Brown) Kulm, ND, Sept. 30, 1932. Glendale College.

**Diesel, Vin** (Mark Vincent) New York, NY, July 18, 1967.

**Diggs, Taye** (Scott Diggs) Rochester, NY, Jan. 2, 1972.

**Dillahunt, Garret** Castro Valley, CA Nov. 24, 1964.

**Diller, Phyllis** (Driver) Lima, OH, July 17, 1917. Bluffton College.

**Dillman, Bradford** San Francisco, CA, Apr. 14, 1930. Yale.

**Dillon, Kevin** Mamaroneck, NY, Aug. 19, 1965.

**Dillon, Matt** Larchmont, NY, Feb. 18, 1964. AADA.

**Dillon, Melinda** Hope, AR, Oct. 13, 1939. Goodman Theatre School.

**Dinklage, Peter** Morristown, NJ, June 11, 1969.

**Dixon, Donna** Alexandria, VA, July 20, 1957.

**Dobson, Kevin** New York, NY, Mar. 18, 1944.

**Doherty, Shannen** Memphis, TN, Apr. 12, 1971.

**Dolan, Michael** Oklahoma City, OK, June 21, 1965.

**Donat, Peter** Nova Scotia, Canada, Jan. 20, 1928. Yale.

**Donnelly, Donal** Bradford, England, July 6, 1931.

**D'Onofrio, Vincent** Brooklyn, NY, June 30, 1959.

**Donohoe, Amanda** London, England, June 29 1962.

**Donovan, Martin** Reseda, CA, Aug. 19, 1957.

**Donovan, Tate** New York, NY, Sept. 25, 1963.

**Dooley, Paul** Parkersburg WV, Feb. 22, 1928. U West Virginia.

**Dorff, Stephen** Atlanta, GA, July 29, 1973.

**Doug, Doug E.** (Douglas Bourne) Brooklyn, NY, Jan. 7, 1970.

**Douglas, Donna** (Dorothy Bourgeois) Baywood, LA, Sept. 26, 1935.

**Douglas, Illeana** Quincy, MA, July 25, 1965.

**Douglas, Kirk** (Issur Danielovitch) Amsterdam, NY, Dec. 9, 1916. St. Lawrence U.

**Douglas, Michael** New Brunswick, NJ, Sept. 25, 1944. U California.

**Douglass, Robyn** Sendai, Japan, June 21, 1953. UC Davis.

**Dourif, Brad** Huntington, WV, Mar. 18, 1950. Marshall U.

**Down, Lesley-Anne** London, England, Mar. 17, 1954.

**Downey, Robert, Jr.** New York, NY, Apr. 4, 1965.

**Drake, Betsy** Paris, France, Sept. 11, 1923.

**Drescher, Fran** Queens, NY, Sept. 30, 1957.

**Dreyfuss, Richard** Brooklyn, NY, Oct. 19, 1947.

**Drillinger, Brian** Brooklyn, NY, June 27, 1960. SUNY/Purchase.

**Driver, Minnie** (Amelia Driver) London, England, Jan. 31, 1971.

**Duchovny, David** New York, NY, Aug. 7, 1960. Yale.

**Dudikoff, Michael** Torrance, CA, Oct. 8, 1954.

**Duff, Hilary** Houston, TX, Sept. 28, 1987.

**Dugan, Dennis** Wheaton, IL, Sept. 5, 1946.

**Duhamel, Josh** Minot, ND, Nov. 14, 1972.

**Dukakis, Olympia** Lowell, MA, June 20, 1931.

**Duke, Bill** Poughkeepsie, NY, Feb. 26, 1943. NYU.

**Duke, Patty** (Anna Marie) New York, NY, Dec. 14, 1946.

**Dullea, Keir** Cleveland, OH, May 30, 1936. San Francisco State College.

**Dunaway, Faye** Bascom, FL, Jan. 14, 1941, Florida U.

**Duncan, Lindsay** Edinburgh, Scotland, Nov. 7, 1950.

**Duncan, Sandy** Henderson, TX, Feb. 20, 1946. Len Morris College.

**Dunne, Griffin** New York, NY, June 8, 1955. Neighborhood Playhouse.

**Dunst, Kirsten** Point Pleasant, NJ, Apr. 30, 1982.

**Duperey, Anny** Paris, France, June 28, 1947.

**Durbin, Deanna** (Edna) Winnipeg, Manitoba, Canada, Dec. 4, 1921.

**Duris, Romain** Paris, France, May 28, 1974.

**Durning, Charles** Highland Falls, NY, Feb. 28, 1923. NYU.

**Dushku, Eliza** Boston, MA, Dec. 30, 1980.

**Dussollier, André** Annecy, France, Feb. 17, 1946.

**Dutton, Charles** Baltimore, MD, Jan. 30, 1951. Yale.

**DuVall, Clea** Los Angeles, CA, Sept. 25, 1977.

**Duvall, Robert** San Diego, CA, Jan. 5, 1931. Principia College.

**Duvall, Shelley** Houston, TX, July 7, 1949.

**Dysart, Richard** Brighton, ME, Mar. 30, 1929.

**Dzundza, George** Rosenheim, Germany, July 19, 1945.

**Easton, Robert** Milwaukee, WI, Nov. 23, 1930. U Texas.

**Eastwood, Clint** San Francisco, CA, May 31, 1931. LACC.

**Eaton, Shirley** London, England, Jan. 12, 1937. Aida Foster School.

**Eckemyr, Agneta** Karlsborg, Sweden, July 2, 1950 Actors Studio.

**Eckhart, Aaron** Santa Clara, CA, Mar. 12, 1968.

**Edelman, Gregg** Chicago, IL, Sept. 12, 1958. Northwestern.

**Eden, Barbara** (Huffman) Tucson, AZ, Aug. 23, 1934.

**Edwards, Anthony** Santa Barbara, CA, July 19, 1962. RADA.

Edwards, Luke  Nevada City, CA, Mar. 24, 1980.
Efron, Zac  San Luis Obispo, CA, Oct. 18, 1987.
Eggar, Samantha  London, England, Mar. 5, 1939.
Eichhorn, Lisa  Reading, PA, Feb. 4, 1952. Queens Ont. U RADA.
Eikenberry, Jill  New Haven, CT, Jan. 21, 1947.
Eilber, Janet  Detroit, MI, July 27, 1951. Juilliard.
Eisenberg, Jesse  New York, NY, Oct. 5, 1983.
Ejiofor, Chiwitel  London, England, July 10, 1974.
Ekberg, Anita  Malmo, Sweden, Sept. 29, 1931.
Ekland, Britt  Stockholm, Sweden, Oct. 6, 1942.
Eldard, Ron  Long Island, NY, Feb. 20, 1965.
Elfman, Jenna  (Jennifer Mary Batula) Los Angeles, CA, Sept. 30, 1971.
Elise, Kimberly  Minneapolis, MN, Apr. 17, 1967.
Elizondo, Hector  New York, NY, Dec. 22, 1936.
Elliott, Alison  San Francisco, CA, May 19, 1970.
Elliott, Chris  New York, NY, May 31, 1960.
Elliott, Patricia  Gunnison, CO, July 21, 1942. U Colorado.
Elliott, Sam  Sacramento, CA, Aug. 9, 1944. U Oregon.
Elwes, Cary  London, England, Oct. 26, 1962.
Ely, Ron  (Ronald Pierce) Hereford, TX, June 21, 1938.
Embry, Ethan  (Ethan Randall) Huntington Beach, CA, June 13, 1978.
Englund, Robert  Glendale, CA, June 6, 1949.
Epps, Mike  Indianapolis, IN, Nov. 18, 1970.
Epps, Omar  Brooklyn, NY, July 23, 1973.
Erbe, Kathryn  Newton, MA, July 2, 1966.
Erdman, Richard  Enid, OK, June 1, 1925.
Ericson, John  Dusseldorf, Germany, Sept. 25, 1926. AADA.
Ermey, R. Lee  (Ronald) Emporia, KS, Mar. 24, 1944.
Esposito, Giancarlo  Copenhagen, Denmark, Apr. 26, 1958.
Estevez, Emilio  New York, NY, May 12, 1962.
Estrada, Erik  New York, NY, Mar. 16, 1949.
Etel, Alex  Manchester, England, Sept. 19, 1994.
Evans, Chris  Sudbury, MA, June 13, 1981.
Evans, Josh  New York, NY, Jan. 16, 1971.
Evans, Linda  (Evanstad) Hartford, CT, Nov. 18, 1942.
Everett, Chad  (Ray Cramton) South Bend, IN, June 11, 1936.
Everett, Rupert  Norfolk, England, May 29, 1959.
Evigan, Greg  South Amboy, NJ, Oct. 14, 1953.

Fabares, Shelley  Los Angeles, CA, Jan. 19, 1944.
Fabian  (Fabian Forte) Philadelphia, PA, Feb. 6, 1943.
Fabray, Nanette  (Ruby Nanette Fabares) San Diego, Oct. 27, 1920.
Fahey, Jeff  Olean, NY, Nov. 29, 1956.
Fairchild, Morgan  (Patsy McClenny) Dallas, TX, Feb. 3, 1950. UCLA.
Falco, Edie  Brooklyn, NY, July 5, 1963.
Falk, Peter  New York, NY, Sept. 16, 1927. New School.
Fallon, Jimmy  Brooklyn, NY, Sept. 19, 1974.
Fanning, Dakota  Conyers, GA, Feb. 23, 1994.
Farentino, James  Brooklyn, NY, Feb. 24, 1938. AADA.
Fargas, Antonio  Bronx, NY, Aug. 14, 1946.
Farina, Dennis  Chicago, IL, Feb. 29, 1944.
Faris, Anna  Baltimore, MD, Nov. 29, 1976. Univ of Washington.
Farmiga, Vera  Passaic, NJ, Aug. 6, 1973.

Farr, Felicia  Westchester, NY, Oct. 4. 1932. Penn State College.
Farrell, Colin  Castleknock, Ireland, Mar. 31, 1976.
Farrow, Mia  (Maria) Los Angeles, CA, Feb. 9, 1945.
Faulkner, Graham  London, England, Sept. 26, 1947. Webber-Douglas.
Favreau, Jon  Queens, NY, Oct. 16, 1966.
Fawcett, Farrah  Corpus Christie, TX, Feb. 2, 1947. Texas U.
Feinstein, Alan  New York, NY, Sept. 8, 1941.
Feldman, Corey  Encino, CA, July 16, 1971.
Feldon, Barbara  (Hall) Pittsburgh, PA, Mar. 12, 1941. Carnegie Tech.
Feldshuh, Tovah  New York, NY, Dec. 27, 1953, Sarah Lawrence College.
Fellows, Edith  Boston, MA, May 20, 1923.
Fenn, Sherilyn  Detroit, MI, Feb. 1, 1965.
Ferrell, Conchata  Charleston, WV, Mar. 28, 1943. Marshall U.
Ferrell, Will  Irvine, CA, July 16, 1968.
Ferrer, Mel  Elbeton, NJ, Aug. 25, 1912. Princeton.
Ferrer, Miguel  Santa Monica, CA, Feb. 7, 1954.
Ferrera, America  Los Angeles, CA, Apr. 18, 1984.
Ferris, Barbara  London, England, July 27, 1942.
Fey, Tina  (Elizabeth Stamatina Fey) Upper Darby, PA, May 18, 1970.
Field, Sally  Pasadena, CA, Nov. 6, 1946.
Field, Shirley-Anne  London, England, June 27, 1938.
Field, Todd  (William Todd Field) Pomona, CA, Feb. 24, 1964.
Fiennes, Joseph  Salisbury, Wiltshire, England, May 27, 1970.
Fiennes, Ralph  Suffolk, England, Dec. 22, 1962. RADA.
Fierstein, Harvey  Brooklyn, NY, June 6, 1954. Pratt Institute.
Finch, Jon  Caterham, England, Mar. 2, 1941.
Finlay, Frank  Farnworth, England, Aug. 6, 1926.
Finney, Albert  Salford, Lancashire, England, May 9, 1936. RADA.
Fiorentino, Linda  Philadelphia, PA, Mar. 9, 1960.
Firth, Colin  Grayshott, Hampshire, England, Sept. 10, 1960.
Firth, Peter  Bradford, England, Oct. 27, 1953.
Fishburne, Laurence  Augusta, GA, July 30, 1961.
Fischer, Jenna  Ft. Wayne, IN, Mar. 7, 1974.
Fisher, Carrie  Los Angeles, CA, Oct. 21, 1956. London Central School of Drama.
Fisher, Eddie  Philadelphia, PA, Aug. 10, 1928.
Fisher, Frances  Milford-on-the-Sea, England, May 11, 1952.
Fisher, Isla  Muscat, Oman, Feb. 3, 1976.
Fitzgerald, Tara  London, England, Sept. 17, 1968.
Flagg, Fannie  Birmingham, AL, Sept. 21, 1944. U Alabama.
Flanagan, Fionnula  Dublin, Ireland, Dec. 10, 1941.
Flannery, Susan  Jersey City, NJ, July 31, 1943.
Fleming, Rhonda  (Marilyn Louis) Los Angeles, CA, Aug. 10, 1922.
Fletcher, Louise  Birmingham, AL, July 22 1934.
Flockhart, Calista  Stockton, IL, Nov. 11, Rutgers U.
Foch, Nina  Leyden, Holland, Apr. 20, 1924.
Fogler, Dan  Brooklyn, NY, Oct. 20, 1976.
Foley, Dave  Toronto, ON, Canada, Jan. 4, 1963.
Follows, Megan  Toronto, ON, Canada, Mar. 14, 1968.
Fonda, Bridget  Los Angeles, CA, Jan. 27, 1964.
Fonda, Jane  New York, NY, Dec. 21, 1937. Vassar.
Fonda, Peter  New York, NY, Feb. 23, 1939. U Omaha.
Fontaine, Joan  Tokyo, Japan, Oct. 22, 1917.

**Foote, Hallie** New York, NY, 1953. U New Hampshire.
**Ford, Harrison** Chicago, IL, July 13, 1942. Ripon College.
**Forlani, Claire** London, England, July 1, 1972.
**Forrest, Frederic** Waxahachie, TX, Dec. 23, 1936.
**Forrest, Steve** Huntsville, TX, Sept. 29, 1924. UCLA.
**Forslund, Connie** San Diego, CA, June 19, 1950. NYU.
**Forster, Robert** (Foster, Jr.) Rochester, NY, July 13, 1941. Rochester U.
**Forsythe, John** (Freund) Penns Grove, NJ, Jan. 29, 1918.
**Forsythe, William** Brooklyn, NY, June 7, 1955.
**Fossey, Brigitte** Tourcoing, France, Mar. 11, 1947.
**Foster, Ben** Boston, MA, Oct. 29, 1980.
**Foster, Jodie** (Alicia Christian Foster) Los Angeles, CA, Nov. 19, 1962. Yale.
**Foster, Meg** Reading, PA, May 14, 1948.
**Fox, Edward** London, England, Apr. 13, 1937. RADA.
**Fox, James** London, England, May 19, 1939.
**Fox, Megan** Rockwood, TN, May 16, 1986.
**Fox, Michael J.** Vancouver, BC, Canada, June 9, 1961.
**Fox, Vivica A.** Indianapolis, July 30, 1964.
**Foxworth, Robert** Houston, TX, Nov. 1, 1941. Carnegie Tech.
**Foxx, Jamie** Terrell, TX, Dec. 13, 1967.
**Frain, James** Leeds, England, Mar. 14, 1969.
**Frakes, Jonathan** Bethlehem, PA, Aug. 19, 1952. Harvard.
**Francis, Anne** Ossining, NY, Sept. 16, 1932.
**Francis, Arlene** (Arlene Kazanjian) Boston, MA, Oct. 20, 1908. Finch School.
**Francis, Connie** (Constance Franconero) Newark, NJ, Dec. 12, 1938.
**Francks, Don** Vancouver, BC, Canada, Feb. 28, 1932.
**Franco, James** Palo Alto, CA, Apr. 19, 1978.
**Franklin, Pamela** Tokyo, Japan, Feb. 4, 1950.
**Franz, Dennis** Chicago, IL, Oct. 28, 1944.
**Fraser, Brendan** Indianapolis, IN, Dec. 3, 1968.
**Frazier, Sheila** New York, NY, Nov. 13, 1948.
**Frechette, Peter** Warwick, RI, Oct. 1956. U Rhoad Island.
**Freeman, Al, Jr.** San Antonio, TX, Mar. 21, 1934. CCLA.
**Freeman, Martin** Aldershot, England, Sept. 8, 1971.
**Freeman, Mona** Baltimore, MD, June 9, 1926.
**Freeman, Morgan** Memphis, TN, June 1, 1937. LACC.
**Frewer, Matt** Washington, DC, Jan. 4, 1958, Old Vic.
**Fricker, Brenda** Dublin, Ireland, Feb. 17, 1945.
**Friel, Anna** Rochdale, England, July 12, 1976.
**Friels, Colin** Glasgow, Scotland, Sept. 25, 1952.
**Frost, Nick** Essex, England, Mar. 28, 1972.
**Fry, Stephen** Hampstead, London, England, Aug. 24, 1957.
**Fuller, Penny** Durham, NC, July 21, 1940. Northwestern.
**Funicello, Annette** Utica, NY, Oct. 22, 1942.
**Furlong, Edward** Glendale, CA, Aug. 2, 1977.
**Furneaux, Yvonne** Lille, France, May 11, 1928. Oxford U.
**Futterman, Dan** Silver Spring, MD, June 8, 1967.

**Gable, John Clark** Los Angeles, CA, Mar. 20, 1961. Santa Monica College.
**Gabor, Zsa Zsa** (Sari Gabor) Budapest, Hungary, Feb. 6, 1917.
**Gail, Max** Derfoil, MI, Apr. 5, 1943.
**Gaines, Boyd** Atlanta, GA, May 11, 1953. Juilliard.
**Gainsbourg, Charlotte** London, England, July 21, 1971.

**Galecki, Johnny** Bree, Belgium, Apr. 30, 1975.
**Gallagher, Peter** New York, NY, Aug. 19, 1955. Tufts U.
**Galligan, Zach** New York, NY, Feb. 14, 1963. Columbia U.
**Gallo, Vincent** Buffalo, NY, Apr. 11, 1961.
**Gam, Rita** Pittsburgh, PA, Apr. 2, 1928.
**Gamble, Mason** Chicago, IL, Jan. 16, 1986.
**Gambon, Michael** Dublin, Ireland, Oct. 19, 1940.
**Gandolfini, James** Westwood, NJ, Sept. 18, 1961.
**Ganz, Bruno** Zurich, Switzerland, Mar. 22, 1941.
**Garai, Romola** Hong Kong, Aug. 6, 1982.
**Garber, Victor** Montreal, Quebec, Canada, Mar. 16, 1949.
**Garcia, Adam** Wahroonga, New So. Wales, Australia, June 1, 1973.
**Garcia, Andy** Havana, Cuba, Apr. 12, 1956. FlaInt.
**Garfield, Allen** (Allen Goorwitz) Newark, NJ, Nov. 22, 1939. Actors Studio.
**Garfunkel, Art** New York, NY, Nov. 5, 1941.
**Garland, Beverly** Santa Cruz, CA, Oct. 17, 1926. Glendale College.
**Garlin, Jeff** Chicago, IL, June 5, 1962.
**Garner, James** (James Baumgarner) Norman, OK, Apr. 7, 1928. Oklahoma U.
**Garner, Jennifer** Houston, TX, Apr. 17, 1972.
**Garner, Kelli** Bakersfield, CA, Aprl. 11, 1984.
**Garofalo, Janeane** Newton, NJ, Sept. 28, 1964.
**Garr, Teri** Lakewood, OH, Dec. 11, 1949.
**Garrett, Betty** St. Joseph, MO, May 23, 1919. Annie Wright Seminary.
**Garrison, Sean** New York, NY, Oct. 19, 1937.
**Gary, Lorraine** New York, NY, Aug. 16, 1937.
**Gavin, John** Los Angeles, CA, Apr. 8, 1935. Stanford U.
**Gaylord, Mitch** Van Nuys, CA, Mar. 10, 1961. UCLA.
**Gaynor, Mitzi** (Francesca Marlene Von Gerber) Chicago, IL, Sept. 4, 1930.
**Gazzara, Ben** New York, NY, Aug. 28, 1930. Actors Studio.
**Geary, Anthony** Coalsville, UT, May 29, 1947. U Utah.
**Gedrick, Jason** Chicago, IL, Feb. 7, 1965. Drake U.
**Geeson, Judy** Arundel, England, Sept. 10, 1948. Corona.
**Gellar, Sarah Michelle** New York, NY, Apr. 14, 1977.
**Geoffreys, Stephen** (Miller) Cincinnati, OH, Nov. 22, 1959. NYU.
**George, Susan** West London, England, July 26, 1950.
**Gerard, Gil** Little Rock, AR, Jan. 23, 1940.
**Gere, Richard** Philadelphia, PA, Aug. 29, 1949. U Mass.
**Gerroll, Daniel** London, England, Oct. 16, 1951. Central.
**Gershon, Gina** Los Angeles, CA, June 10, 1962.
**Gertz, Jami** Chicago, IL, Oct. 28, 1965.
**Gervais, Ricky** Reading, England, June 25, 1961.
**Getty, Balthazar** Los Angeles, CA, Jan. 22, 1975.
**Getty, Estelle** New York, NY, July 25, 1923. New School.
**Gholson, Julie** Birmingham, AL, June 4, 1958.
**Giamatti, Paul** New York, NY, June 6, 1967. Yale.
**Giannini, Giancarlo** Spezia, Italy, Aug. 1, 1942. Rome Academy of Drama.
**Gibb, Cynthia** Bennington, VT, Dec. 14, 1963.
**Gibson, Henry** Germantown, PA, Sept. 21, 1935.
**Gibson, Mel** Peekskill, NY, Jan. 3, 1956. NIDA.
**Gibson, Thomas** Charleston, SC, July 3, 1962.
**Gibson, Tyrese** Los Angeles, CA, Dec. 30, 1978.
**Gift, Roland** Birmingham, England, May 28 1962.
**Gilbert, Melissa** Los Angeles, CA, May 8, 1964.

**Giles, Nancy** New York, NY, July 17, 1960, Oberlin College.
**Gillette, Anita** Baltimore, MD, Aug. 16, 1938.
**Gilliam, Terry** Minneapolis, MN, Nov. 22, 1940.
**Gillis, Ann** (Alma O'Connor) Little Rock, AR, Feb. 12, 1927.
**Ginty, Robert** New York, NY, Nov. 14, 1948. Yale.
**Girardot, Annie** Paris, France, Oct. 25, 1931.
**Gish, Annabeth** Albuquerque, NM, Mar. 13, 1971. Duke U.
**Givens, Robin** New York, NY, Nov. 27, 1964.
**Glaser, Paul Michael** Boston, MA, Mar. 25, 1943. Boston U.
**Glass, Ron** Evansville, IN, July 10, 1945.
**Gleason, Joanna** Winnipeg, Manitoba, Canada, June 2, 1950. UCLA.
**Gleeson, Brendan** Belfast, Northern Ireland, Nov. 9, 1955.
**Glenn, Scott** Pittsburgh, PA, Jan. 26, 1942. William and Mary College.
**Glover, Crispin** New York, NY, Sept 20, 1964.
**Glover, Danny** San Francisco, CA, July 22, 1947. San Francisco State U.
**Glover, John** Kingston, NY, Aug. 7, 1944.
**Glynn, Carlin** Cleveland, OH, Feb. 19, 1940. Actors Studio.
**Goldberg, Adam** Santa Monica, CA, Oct. 25, 1970.
**Goldberg, Whoopi** (Caryn Johnson) New York, NY, Nov. 13, 1949.
**Goldblum, Jeff** Pittsburgh, PA, Oct. 22, 1952. Neighborhood Playhouse.
**Golden, Annie** Brooklyn, NY, Oct. 19, 1951.
**Goldstein, Jenette** Beverly Hills, CA, Feb. 4, 1960.
**Goldthwait, Bob** Syracuse, NY, May 1, 1962.
**Goldwyn, Tony** Los Angeles, CA, May 20, 1960. LAMDA.
**Golino, Valeria** Naples, Italy, Oct. 22, 1966.
**Gonzalez, Cordelia** San Juan, PR Aug. 11, 1957,. UPR.
**Good, Meagan** Panorama City, CA, Aug. 8, 1981.
**Goodall, Caroline** London, England, Nov. 13, 1959. Bristol U.
**Goode, Matthew** Exeter, England, Apr. 3, 1978.
**Gooding, Cuba, Jr.** Bronx, NY, Jan. 2, 1968.
**Goodman, Dody** Columbus, OH, Oct. 28, 1915.
**Goodman, John** St. Louis, MO, June 20, 1952.
**Gordon, Keith** New York, NY, Feb. 3, 1961.
**Gordon-Levitt, Joseph** Los Angeles, CA, Feb. 17, 1981.
**Gortner, Marjoe** Long Beach, CA, Jan. 14, 1944.
**Gosling, Ryan** London, ON, Canada, Nov. 12, 1980.
**Goss, Luke** London, England, Sept. 28, 1968.
**Gossett, Louis, Jr.** Brooklyn, NY, May 27, 1936. NYU.
**Gould, Elliott** (Goldstein) Brooklyn, NY, Aug. 29, 1938. Columbia U.
**Gould, Harold** Schenectady, NY, Dec. 10, 1923. Cornell.
**Gould, Jason** New York, NY, Dec. 29, 1966.
**Grace, Topher** New York, NY, July 12, 1978.
**Graf, David** Lancaster, OH, Apr. 16, 1950. Ohio State U.
**Graff, Todd** New York, NY, Oct. 22, 1959. SUNY/Purchase.
**Graham, Heather** Milwaukee, WI, Jan. 29, 1970.
**Grammer, Kelsey** St. Thomas, Virgin Islands, Feb. 21, 1955.
**Granger, Farley** San Jose, CA, July 1, 1925.
**Grant, David Marshall** Westport, CT, June 21, 1955. Yale.
**Grant, Hugh** London, England, Sept. 9, 1960. Oxford.
**Grant, Kathryn** (Olive Grandstaff) Houston, TX, Nov. 25, 1933. UCLA.
**Grant, Lee** New York, NY, Oct. 31, 1927. Juilliard.
**Grant, Richard E.** Mbabane, Swaziland, May 5, 1957. Cape Town U.
**Graves, Peter** (Aurness) Minneapolis, MN, Mar. 18, 1926. U Minnesota.

**Graves, Rupert** Weston-Super-Mare, England, June 30, 1963.
**Gray, Coleen** (Doris Jensen) Staplehurst, NB, Oct. 23, 1922. Hamline.
**Gray, Linda** Santa Monica, CA, Sept. 12, 1940.
**Grayson, Kathryn** (Zelma Hedrick) Winston-Salem, NC, Feb. 9, 1922.
**Green, Eva** Paris, France, July 5, 1980.
**Green, Kerri** Fort Lee, NJ, Jan. 14, 1967. Vassar.
**Green, Seth** Philadelphia, PA, Feb. 8, 1974.
**Greene, Ellen** New York, NY, Feb. 22, 1950. Ryder College.
**Greene, Graham** Six Nations Reserve, ON, Canada, June 22, 1952.
**Greenwood, Bruce** Quebec, Canada, Aug. 12, 1956.
**Greer, Michael** Galesburg, IL, Apr. 20, 1943.
**Greist, Kim** Stamford, CT, May 12, 1958.
**Grenier, Adrian** Brooklyn, NY, July 10, 1976.
**Grey, Jennifer** New York, NY, Mar. 26, 1960.
**Grey, Joel** (Katz) Cleveland, OH, Apr. 11, 1932.
**Grieco, Richard** Watertown, NY, Mar. 23, 1965.
**Grier, David Alan** Detroit, MI, June 30, 1955. Yale.
**Grier, Pam** Winston-Salem, NC, May 26, 1949.
**Griffin, Eddie** Kansas City, MO, July 15, 1968.
**Griffith, Andy** Mt. Airy, NC, June 1, 1926. U North Carolina.
**Griffith, Melanie** New York, NY, Aug. 9, 1957. Pierce Collge.
**Griffith, Thomas Ian** Hartford, CT, Mar. 18, 1962.
**Griffiths, Rachel** Melbourne, Australia, June 4, 1968.
**Griffiths, Richard** Tornaby-on-Tees, England, July 31, 1947.
**Grimes, Gary** San Francisco, CA, June 2, 1955.
**Grimes, Scott** Lowell, MA, July 9, 1971.
**Grimes, Tammy** Lynn, MA, Jan. 30, 1934. Stephens College.
**Grint, Rupert** Watton-at-Stone, England, Aug. 24, 1988.
**Grodin, Charles** Pittsburgh, PA, Apr. 21, 1935.
**Groh, David** New York, NY, May 21, 1939. Brown U, LAMDA.
**Gross, Mary** Chicago, IL, Mar. 25, 1953.
**Gross, Michael** Chicago, IL, June 21, 1947.
**Gruffudd, Ioan** Cardiff, Wales, Oct. 6, 1973.
**Guest, Christopher** New York, NY, Feb. 5, 1948.
**Guest, Lance** Saratoga, CA, July 21, 1960. UCLA.
**Guillaume, Robert** (Williams) St. Louis, MO, Nov. 30, 1937.
**Guiry, Thomas** Trenton, NJ, Oct. 12, 1981.
**Gulager, Clu** Holdenville, OK, Nov. 16 1928.
**Guttenberg, Steve** Massapequa, NY, Aug. 24, 1958. UCLA.
**Guy, Jasmine** Boston, MA, Mar. 10, 1964.
**Guzman, Luis** Cayey, Puerto Rico, Jan. 1, 1957.
**Gyllenhaal, Jake** Los Angeles, CA, Dec. 19, 1980.
**Gyllenhaal, Maggie** Los Angeles, CA, Nov. 16, 1977.

**Haas, Lukas** West Hollywood, CA, Apr. 16, 1976.
**Hack, Shelley** Greenwich, CT, July 6, 1952.
**Hackman, Gene** San Bernardino, CA, Jan. 30, 1930.
**Hagerty, Julie** Cincinnati, OH, June 15, 1955. Juilliard.
**Hagman, Larry** (Hageman) Weatherford, TX, Sept. 21, 1931. Bard.
**Haid, Charles** San Francisco, CA, June 2, 1943. Carnegie Tech.
**Haim, Corey** Toronto, ON, Canada, Dec. 23, 1972.
**Hale, Barbara** DeKalb, IL, Apr. 18, 1922. Chicago Academy of Fine Arts.
**Haley, Jackie Earle** Northridge, CA, July 14, 1961.

**Hall, Albert** Boothton, AL, Nov. 10, 1937. Columbia U.
**Hall, Anthony Michael** Boston, MA, Apr. 14, 1968.
**Hall, Arsenio** Cleveland, OH, Feb. 12, 1959.
**Hall, Philip Baker** Toledo, OH, Sept. 10, 1931.
**Hamel, Veronica** Philadelphia, PA, Nov. 20, 1943.
**Hamill, Mark** Oakland, CA, Sept. 25, 1952. LACC.
**Hamilton, George** Memphis, TN, Aug. 12, 1939. Hackley.
**Hamilton, Josh** New York, NY, June 9, 1969.
**Hamilton, Linda** Salisbury, MD, Sept. 26, 1956.
**Hamlin, Harry** Pasadena, CA, Oct. 30, 1951.
**Hampshire, Susan** London, England, May 12, 1941.
**Hampton, James** Oklahoma City, OK, July 9, 1936. Northern Texas State U.
**Han, Maggie** Providence, RI, 1959.
**Handler, Evan** New York, NY, Jan. 10, 1961. Juillard.
**Hanks, Colin** Sacramento, CA, Nov. 24, 1977.
**Hanks, Tom** Concord, CA, July 9, 1956. California State U.
**Hannah, Daryl** Chicago, IL, Dec. 3, 1960. UCLA.
**Hannah, Page** Chicago, IL, Apr. 13, 1964.
**Harden, Marcia Gay** La Jolla, CA, Aug. 14, 1959.
**Hardin, Ty** (Orison Whipple Hungerford, II) New York, NY, June 1, 1930.
**Harewood, Dorian** Dayton, OH, Aug. 6, 1950. U Cinncinatti.
**Harmon, Mark** Los Angeles, CA, Sept. 2, 1951. UCLA.
**Harper, Jessica** Chicago, IL, Oct. 10, 1949.
**Harper, Tess** Mammoth Spring, AK, 1952. South Western Misourri State.
**Harper, Valerie** Suffern, NY, Aug. 22, 1940.
**Harrelson, Woody** Midland, TX, July 23, 1961. Hanover College.
**Harrington, Pat** New York, NY, Aug. 13, 1929. Fordham U.
**Harris, Barbara** (Sandra Markowitz) Evanston, IL, July 25, 1935.
**Harris, Ed** Tenafly, NJ, Nov. 28, 1950. Columbia U.
**Harris, Jared** London, England, Aug. 24, 1961.
**Harris, Julie** Grosse Point, MI, Dec. 2, 1925. Yale Drama School.
**Harris, Mel** (Mary Ellen) Bethlehem, PA, 1957. Columbia U.
**Harris, Neil Patrick** Albuquerque, NM, June 15, 1973.
**Harris, Rosemary** Ashby, England, Sept. 19, 1930. RADA.
**Harrison, Gregory** Catalina Island, CA, May 31, 1950. Actors Studio.
**Harrison, Noel** London, England, Jan. 29, 1936.
**Harrold, Kathryn** Tazewell, VA, Aug. 2, 1950. Mills College.
**Harry, Deborah** Miami, IL, July 1, 1945.
**Hart, Ian** Liverpool, England, Oct. 8, 1964.
**Hart, Roxanne** Trenton, NJ, July 27, 1952. Princeton.
**Hartley, Mariette** New York, NY, June 21, 1941.
**Hartman, David** Pawtucket, RI, May 19, 1935. Duke U.
**Hartnett, Josh** San Francisco, CA, July 21, 1978.
**Hassett, Marilyn** Los Angeles, CA, Dec. 17, 1947.
**Hatcher, Teri** Sunnyvale, CA, Dec. 8, 1964.
**Hathaway, Anne** Brooklyn, NY, Nov. 12, 1982.
**Hatosy, Shawn** Fredrick, MD, Dec. 29, 1975.
**Hauer, Rutger** Amsterdam, Holland, Jan. 23, 1944.
**Hauser, Cole** Santa Barbara, CA, Mar. 22, 1975.
**Hasuer, Wings** (Gerald Dwight Hauser) Hollywood, CA, Dec. 12, 1947.
**Havoc, June** (Hovick) Seattle, WA, Nov. 8, 1916.
**Hawke, Ethan** Austin, TX, Nov. 6, 1970.

**Hawn, Goldie** Washington, DC, Nov. 21, 1945.
**Hayek, Salma** Coatzacoalcos, Veracruz, Mexico, Sept. 2, 1968.
**Hayes, Isaac** Covington, TN, Aug. 20, 1942.
**Hayes, Sean** Chicago, IL, June 26, 1970.
**Hays, Robert** Bethesda, MD, July 24, 1947. South Dakota State College.
**Haysbert, Dennis** San Mateo, CA, June 2, 1954.
**Headey, Lena** Bermuda, Oct. 3, 1973.
**Headly, Glenne** New London, CT, Mar. 13, 1955. AmCollege.
**Heald, Anthony** New Rochelle, NY, Aug. 25, 1944. Michigan State U.
**Heard, John** Washington, DC, Mar. 7, 1946. Clark U.
**Heatherton, Joey** New York, NY, Sept. 14, 1944.
**Heche, Anne** Aurora, OH, May 25, 1969.
**Hedaya, Dan** Brooklyn, NY, July 24, 1940.
**Heder, Jon** Fort Collins, CO, Oct. 26, 1977.
**Hedison, David** Providence, RI, May 20, 1929. Brown U.
**Hedren, Tippi** (Natalie) Lafayette, MN, Jan. 19, 1931.
**Hegyes, Robert** Metuchen, NJ, May 7, 1951.
**Heigl, Katherine** Washington, DC, Nov. 24, 1978.
**Helmond, Katherine** Galveston, TX, July 5, 1934.
**Hemingway, Mariel** Ketchum, ID, Nov. 22, 1961.
**Hemsley, Sherman** Philadelphia, PA, Feb. 1, 1938.
**Henderson, Florence** Dale, IN, Feb. 14, 1934.
**Hendry, Gloria** Winter Haven, FL, Mar. 3, 1949.
**Henner, Marilu** Chicago, IL, Apr. 6, 1952.
**Henriksen, Lance** New York, NY, May 5, 1940.
**Henry, Buck** (Henry Zuckerman) New York, NY, Dec. 9, 1930. Dartmouth.
**Henry, Justin** Rye, NY, May 25, 1971.
**Henstridge, Natasha** Springdale, Newfoundland, Canada, Aug. 15, 1974.
**Hernandez, Jay** (Javier Hernandez, Jr.) Montebello, CA, Feb. 20, 1978.
**Herrmann, Edward** Washington, DC, July 21, 1943. Bucknell, LAMDA.
**Hershey, Barbara** (Herzstein) Hollywood, CA, Feb. 5, 1948.
**Hesseman, Howard** Lebanon, OR, Feb. 27, 1940.
**Heston, Charlton** Evanston, IL, Oct. 4, 1922. Northwestern.
**Hewitt, Jennifer Love** Waco, TX, Feb. 21, 1979.
**Hewitt, Martin** Claremont, CA, Feb. 19, 1958. AADA.
**Heywood, Anne** (Violet Pretty) Birmingham, England, Dec. 11, 1932.
**Hickey, John Benjamin** Plano, TX, June 25, 1963.
**Hickman, Darryl** Hollywood, CA, July 28, 1933. Loyola U.
**Hickman, Dwayne** Los Angeles, CA, May 18, 1934. Loyola U.
**Hicks, Catherine** New York, NY, Aug. 6, 1951. Notre Dame.
**Higgins, Anthony** (Corlan) Cork City, Ireland, May 9, 1947. Birmingham Dramatic Arts.
**Higgins, John Michael** Boston, MA, Feb. 12, 1963.
**Higgins, Michael** Brooklyn, NY, Jan. 20, 1921. AmThWing.
**Highmore, Freddie** London, England, Feb. 14, 1992.
**Hill, Bernard** Manchester, England, Dec. 17, 1944.
**Hill, Jonah** Los Angeles, CA, Dec. 20, 1983.
**Hill, Steven** Seattle, WA, Feb. 24, 1922. U Wash.
**Hill, Terrence** (Mario Girotti) Venice, Italy, Mar. 29, 1941. U Rome.
**Hillerman, John** Denison, TX, Dec. 20, 1932.
**Hinds, Ciaran** Belfast, Northern Ireland, Feb. 9, 1953.
**Hingle, Pat** Denver, CO, July 19, 1923. Texas U.
**Hirsch, Emile** Topanga Canyon, CA, Mar. 13, 1985.

**Hirsch, Judd** New York, NY, Mar. 15, 1935. AADA.
**Hobel, Mara** New York, NY, June 18, 1971.
**Hodge, Patricia** Lincolnshire, England, Sept. 29, 1946. LAMDA.
**Hoffman, Dustin** Los Angeles, CA, Aug. 8, 1937. Pasadena Playhouse.
**Hoffman, Philip Seymour** Fairport, NY, July 23, 1967. NYU.
**Hogan, Jonathan** Chicago, IL, June 13, 1951.
**Hogan, Paul** Lightning Ridge, Australia, Oct. 8, 1939.
**Holbrook, Hal** (Harold) Cleveland, OH, Feb. 17, 1925. Denison.
**Hollander, Tom** Oxford, England, 1967.
**Holliman, Earl** Tennesas Swamp, Delhi, LA, Sept. 11, 1928. UCLA.
**Holm, Celeste** New York, NY, Apr. 29, 1919.
**Holm, Ian** Ilford, Essex, England, Sept. 12, 1931. RADA.
**Holmes, Katie** Toledo, OH, Dec. 18, 1978.
**Homeier, Skip** (George Vincent Homeier) Chicago, IL, Oct. 5, 1930. UCLA.
**Hooks, Robert** Washington, DC, Apr. 18, 1937. Temple.
**Hopkins, Anthony** Port Talbot, So. Wales, Dec. 31, 1937. RADA.
**Hopper, Dennis** Dodge City, KS, May 17, 1936.
**Horne, Lena** Brooklyn, NY, June 30, 1917.
**Horrocks, Jane** Rossendale Valley, England, Jan. 18, 1964.
**Horsley, Lee** Muleshoe, TX, May 15, 1955.
**Horton, Robert** Los Angeles, CA, July 29, 1924. UCLA.
**Hoskins, Bob** Bury St. Edmunds, England, Oct. 26, 1942.
**Houghton, Katharine** Hartford, CT, Mar. 10, 1945. Sarah Lawrence.
**Hoult, Nicholas** Wokingham, England, Dec. 7, 1989.
**Hounsou, Djimon** Benin, West Africa, Apr. 24, 1964.
**Houser, Jerry** Los Angeles, CA, July 14, 1952. Valley, Jr. College.
**Howard, Arliss** Independence, MO, 1955. Columbia College.
**Howard, Bryce Dallas** Los Angeles, CA, March 2, 1981.
**Howard, Ken** El Centro, CA, Mar. 28, 1944. Yale.
**Howard, Ron** Duncan, OK, Mar. 1, 1954. USC.
**Howard, Terrence** Chicago, IL, Mar. 11, 1969. Pratt Inst.
**Howell, C. Thomas** Los Angeles, CA, Dec. 7, 1966.
**Howes, Sally Ann** London, England, July 20, 1930.
**Howland, Beth** Boston, MA, May 28, 1941.
**Hubley, Season** New York, NY, May 14, 1951.
**Huddleston, David** Vinton, VA, Sept. 17, 1930.
**Hudson, Ernie** Benton Harbor, MI, Dec. 17, 1945.
**Hudson, Jennifer** Chicago, IL, Sept. 12, 1981.
**Hudson, Kate** Los Angeles, CA, Apr. 19, 1979.
**Huffman, Felicity** Bedford, NY, Dec. 9, 1962. NYU.
**Hughes, Kathleen** (Betty von Gerkan) Hollywood, CA, Nov. 14, 1928. UCLA.
**Hulce, Tom** Plymouth, MI, Dec. 6, 1953. North Carolina School of Arts.
**Hunnicut, Gayle** Ft. Worth, TX, Feb. 6, 1943. UCLA.
**Hunt, Helen** Los Angeles, CA, June 15, 1963.
**Hunt, Linda** Morristown, NJ, Apr. 1945. Goodman Theatre.
**Hunt, Marsha** Chicago, IL, Oct. 17, 1917.
**Hunter, Holly** Atlanta, GA, Mar. 20, 1958. Carnegie-Mellon.
**Hunter, Tab** (Arthur Gelien) New York, NY, July 11, 1931.
**Huntington, Sam** Peterborough, NH, Apr. 1, 1982.
**Huppert, Isabelle** Paris, France, Mar. 16, 1955.
**Hurley, Elizabeth** Hampshire, England, June 10, 1965.
**Hurt, John** Lincolnshire, England, Jan. 22, 1940.
**Hurt, Mary Beth** (Supinger) Marshalltown, IA, Sept. 26, 1948. NYU.

**Hurt, William** Washington, DC, Mar. 20, 1950. Tufts, Juilliard.
**Huston, Anjelica** Santa Monica, CA, July 9, 1951.
**Huston, Danny** Rome, Italy, May 14, 1962.
**Hutcherson, Josh** Union, KY, Oct. 12, 1992.
**Hutton, Lauren** (Mary) Charleston, SC, Nov. 17, 1943. Newcomb College.
**Hutton, Timothy** Malibu, CA, Aug. 16, 1960.
**Hyer, Martha** Fort Worth, TX, Aug. 10, 1924. Northwestern.

**Ice Cube** (O'Shea Jackson) Los Angeles, CA, June 15, 1969.
**Idle, Eric** South Shields, Durham, England, Mar. 29, 1943. Cambridge.
**Ifans, Rhys** Ruthin, Wales, July 22, 1968.
**Ingels, Marty** Brooklyn, NY, Mar. 9, 1936.
**Ireland, Kathy** Santa Barbara, CA, Mar. 8, 1963.
**Irons, Jeremy** Cowes, England, Sept. 19, 1948. Old Vic.
**Ironside, Michael** Toronto, ON, Canada, Feb. 12, 1950.
**Irving, Amy** Palo Alto, CA, Sept. 10, 1953. LADA.
**Irwin, Bill** Santa Monica, CA, Apr. 11, 1950.
**Isaak, Chris** Stockton, CA, June 26, 1956. U of Pacific.
**Ivanek, Zeljko** Lujubljana, Yugoslavia, Aug. 15, 1957. Yale, LAMDA.
**Ivey, Judith** El Paso, TX, Sept. 4, 1951.
**Izzard, Eddie** Aden, Yemen, Feb. 7, 1962.

**Jackson, Anne** Allegheny, PA, Sept. 3, 1926. Neighborhood Playhouse.
**Jackson, Glenda** Hoylake, Cheshire, England, May 9, 1936. RADA.
**Jackson, Janet** Gary, IN, May 16, 1966.
**Jackson, Joshua** Vancouver, BC, Canada, June 11, 1978.
**Jackson, Kate** Birmingham, AL, Oct. 29, 1948. AADA.
**Jackson, Michael** Gary, IN, Aug. 29, 1958.
**Jackson, Samuel L.** Atlanta, GA, Dec. 21, 1948.
**Jackson, Victoria** Miami, FL, Aug. 2, 1958.
**Jacobi, Derek** London, England, Oct. 22, 1938. Cambridge.
**Jacobi, Lou** Toronto, ON, Canada, Dec. 28, 1913.
**Jacobs, Lawrence-Hilton** Virgin Islands, Sept. 14, 1953.
**Jacoby, Scott** Chicago, IL, Nov. 19, 1956.
**Jagger, Mick** Dartford, Kent, England, July 26, 1943.
**James, Clifton** New York, NY, May 29, 1921. Oregon U.
**James, Kevin** Stony Brook, NY, Apr. 26, 1965.
**Jane, Thomas** Baltimore, MD, Jan. 29, 1969.
**Janney, Allison** Dayton, OH, Nov. 20, 1960. RADA.
**Janssen, Famke** Amsterdam, Holland, Nov. 5, 1965.
**Jarman, Claude, Jr.** Nashville, TN, Sept. 27, 1934.
**Jean, Gloria** (Gloria Jean Schoonover) Buffalo, NY, Apr. 14, 1927.
**Jeffreys, Anne** (Carmichael) Goldsboro, NC, Jan. 26, 1923. Anderson College.
**Jeffries, Lionel** London, England, June 10, 1926. RADA.
**Jillian, Ann** (Nauseda) Cambridge, MA, Jan. 29, 1951.
**Johansen, David** Staten Island, NY, Jan. 9, 1950.
**Johansson, Scarlett** New York, NY, Nov. 22, 1984.
**John, Elton** (Reginald Dwight) Middlesex, England, Mar. 25, 1947. RAM.
**Johns, Glynis** Durban, S. Africa, Oct. 5, 1923.
**Johnson, Don** Galena, MO, Dec. 15, 1950. U Kansas.
**Johnson, Page** Welch, WV, Aug. 25, 1930. Ithaca.
**Johnson, Rafer** Hillsboro, TX, Aug. 18, 1935. UCLA.

**Johnson, Richard** Essex, England, July 30, 1927. RADA.
**Johnson, Robin** Brooklyn, NY, May 29, 1964.
**Johnson, Van** Newport, RI, Aug. 28, 1916.
**Jolie, Angelina** (Angelina Jolie Voight) Los Angeles, CA, June 4, 1975.
**Jones, Cherry** Paris, France, TN, Nov. 21, 1956.
**Jones, Christopher** Jackson, TN, Aug. 18, 1941. Actors Studio.
**Jones, Dean** Decatur, AL, Jan. 25, 1931. Actors Studio.
**Jones, Grace** Spanishtown, Jamaica, May 19, 1952.
**Jones, Jack** Bel Air, CA, Jan. 14, 1938.
**Jones, James Earl** Arkabutla, MS, Jan. 17, 1931. U Michigan
**Jones, Jeffrey** Buffalo, NY, Sept. 28, 1947. LAMDA.
**Jones, Jennifer** (Phyllis Isley) Tulsa, OK, Mar. 2, 1919. AADA.
**Jones, L.Q.** (Justice Ellis McQueen) Beaumont, TX, Aug 19, 1927.
**Jones, Orlando** Mobile, AL, Apr. 10, 1968.
**Jones, Sam J.** Chicago, IL, Aug. 12, 1954.
**Jones, Shirley** Smithton, PA, March 31, 1934.
**Jones, Terry** Colwyn Bay, Wales, Feb. 1, 1942.
**Jones, Toby** Oxford, England, Sept. 7, 1967.
**Jones, Tommy Lee** San Saba, TX, Sept. 15, 1946. Harvard.
**Jourdan, Louis** Marseilles, France, June 19, 1920.
**Jovovich, Milla** Kiev, Ukraine, Dec. 17, 1975.
**Joy, Robert** Montreal, Quebec, Canada, Aug. 17, 1951. Oxford.
**Judd, Ashley** Los Angeles, CA, Apr. 19, 1968.

**Kaczmarek, Jane** Milwaukee, WI, Dec. 21, 1955.
**Kane, Carol** Cleveland, OH, June 18, 1952.
**Kaplan, Marvin** Brooklyn, NY, Jan. 24, 1924.
**Kapoor, Shashi** Calcutta, India, Mar. 18, 1938.
**Kaprisky, Valerie** (Cheres) Paris, France, Aug. 19, 1962.
**Karras, Alex** Gary, IN, July 15, 1935.
**Kartheiser, Vincent** Minneapolis, MN, May 5, 1979.
**Karyo, Tcheky** Istanbul, Oct. 4, 1953.
**Kassovitz, Mathieu** Paris, France, Aug. 3, 1967.
**Katt, Nicky** South Dakota, May 11, 1970.
**Katt, William** Los Angeles, CA, Feb. 16, 1955.
**Kattan, Chris** Mt. Baldy, CA, Oct. 19, 1970.
**Kaufmann, Christine** Lansdorf, Graz, Austria, Jan. 11, 1945.
**Kavner, Julie** Burbank, CA, Sept. 7, 1951. UCLA.
**Kazan, Lainie** (Levine) Brooklyn, NY, May 15, 1942.
**Kazurinsky, Tim** Johnstown, PA, March 3, 1950.
**Keach, Stacy** Savannah, GA, June 2, 1941. U California, Yale.
**Keaton, Diane** (Hall) Los Angeles, CA, Jan. 5, 1946. Neighborhood Playhouse.
**Keaton, Michael** Coraopolis, PA, Sept. 9, 1951. Kent State U.
**Keegan, Andrew** Los Angeles, CA, Jan. 29, 1979.
**Keener, Catherine** Miami, FL, Mar. 26, 1960. Wheaton College.
**Keeslar, Matt** Grand Rapids, MI, Oct. 15, 1972.
**Keitel, Harvey** Brooklyn, NY, May 13, 1939.
**Keith, David** Knoxville, TN, May 8, 1954. U Tennessee.
**Keller, Marthe** Basel, Switzerland, 1945. Munich Stanislavsky School.
**Kellerman, Sally** Long Beach, CA, June 2, 1936. Actors Studio West.
**Kelley, Elijah** LaGrange, GA, Aug. 1, 1986.
**Kelly, Moira** Queens, NY, Mar. 6, 1968.

**Kemp, Jeremy** (Wacker) Chesterfield, England, Feb. 3, 1935. Central School.
**Kennedy, George** New York, NY, Feb. 18, 1925.
**Kennedy, Jamie** Upper Darby, PA, May 25, 1970.
**Kennedy, Leon Isaac** Cleveland, OH, Jan. 1, 1949.
**Kensit, Patsy** London, England, Mar. 4, 1968.
**Kerr, John** New York, NY, Nov. 15, 1931. Harvard, Columbia.
**Kerwin, Brian** Chicago, IL, Oct. 25, 1949.
**Keyes, Evelyn** Port Arthur, TX, Nov. 20, 1919.
**Kidder, Margot** Yellow Knife, Canada, Oct. 17, 1948. U British Columbia.
**Kidman, Nicole** Honolulu, HI June 20, 1967.
**Kiel, Richard** Detroit, MI, Sept. 13, 1939.
**Kier, Udo** Koeln, Germany, Oct. 14, 1944.
**Kikuchi, Rinko** Kanagawa, Japan, Jan. 6, 1981.
**Kilmer, Val** Los Angeles, CA, Dec. 31, 1959. Juilliard.
**Kincaid, Aron** (Norman Neale Williams, III) Los Angeles, CA, June 15, 1943. UCLA.
**Kind, Richard** Trenton, NJ, Nov. 22, 1956.
**King, Perry** Alliance, OH, Apr. 30, 1948. Yale.
**Kingsley, Ben** (Krishna Bhanji) Snaiton, Yorkshire, England, Dec. 31, 1943.
**Kinnear, Greg** Logansport, IN, June 17, 1963.
**Kinski, Nastassja** Berlin, Germany, Jan. 24, 1960.
**Kirk, Justin** Salem, OR, May 28, 1969.
**Kirk, Tommy** Louisville, KY, Dec. 10 1941.
**Kirkland, Sally** New York, NY, Oct. 31, 1944. Actors Studio.
**Kitt, Eartha** North, SC, Jan. 26, 1928.
**Klein, Chris** Hinsdale, IL, March 14, 1979.
**Klein, Robert** New York, NY, Feb. 8, 1942. Alfred U.
**Kline, Kevin** St. Louis, MO, Oct. 24, 1947. Juilliard.
**Klugman, Jack** Philadelphia, PA, Apr. 27, 1922. Carnegie Tech.
**Knight, Michael E.** Princeton, NJ, May 7, 1959.
**Knight, Shirley** Goessel, KS, July 5, 1937. Wichita U.
**Knightley, Keira** Teddington, England, Mar. 26, 1985.
**Knox, Elyse** Hartford, CT, Dec. 14, 1917. Traphagen School.
**Knoxville, Johnny** (Phillip John Clapp) Knoxville, TN, March 11, 1971.
**Koechner, David** Tipton, MO, Aug. 24, 1962.
**Koenig, Walter** Chicago, IL, Sept. 14, 1936. UCLA.
**Kohner, Susan** Los Angeles, CA, Nov. 11, 1936. U California.
**Korman, Harvey** Chicago, IL, Feb. 15, 1927. Goodman.
**Korsmo, Charlie** Minneapolis, MN, July, 20, 1978.
**Koteas, Elias** Montreal, Quebec, Canada, 1961. AADA.
**Kotto, Yaphet** New York, NY, Nov. 15, 1937.
**Kozak, Harley Jane** Wilkes-Barre, PA, Jan. 28, 1957. NYU.
**Krabbe, Jeroen** Amsterdam, The Netherlands, Dec. 5, 1944.
**Krasinski, John** Newton, MA, Oct. 20, 1979.
**Krause, Peter** Alexandria, MN, Aug. 12, 1965.
**Kretschmann, Thomas** Dessau, East Germany, Sept. 8, 1962.
**Kreuger, Kurt** St. Moritz, Switzerland, July 23, 1917. U London.
**Krige, Alice** Upington, South Africa, June 28, 1955.
**Kristel, Sylvia** Amsterdam, The Netherlands, Sept. 28, 1952.
**Kristofferson, Kris** Brownsville, TX, June 22, 1936. Pomona College.
**Kruger, Diane** Algermissen, Germany, July 15, 1976.
**Kruger, Hardy** Berlin, Germany, April 12, 1928.
**Krumholtz, David** New York, NY, May 15, 1978.

**Kudrow, Lisa** Encino, CA, July 30, 1963.
**Kurtz, Swoosie** Omaha, NE, Sept. 6, 1944.
**Kutcher, Ashton** (Christopher Ashton Kutcher) Cedar Rapids, IA, Feb. 7, 1978.
**Kwan, Nancy** Hong Kong, May 19, 1939. Royal Ballet.

**LaBelle, Patti** Philadelphia, PA, May 24, 1944.
**LaBeouf, Shia** Los Angeles, CA, June 11, 1986.
**Lacy, Jerry** Sioux City, IA, Mar. 27, 1936. LACC.
**Ladd, Cheryl** (Stoppelmoor) Huron, SD. July 12, 1951.
**Ladd, Diane** (Ladner) Meridian, MS, Nov. 29, 1932. Tulane U.
**Lahti, Christine** Detroit, MI, Apr. 4, 1950. U Michigan.
**Lake, Ricki** New York, NY, Sept. 21, 1968.
**Lamas, Lorenzo** Los Angeles, CA, Jan. 28, 1958.
**Lambert, Christopher** New York, NY, Mar. 29, 1958.
**Landau, Martin** Brooklyn, NY, June 20, 1931. Actors Studio.
**Lane, Abbe** Brooklyn, NY, Dec. 14, 1935.
**Lane, Diane** New York, NY, Jan. 22, 1963.
**Lane, Nathan** Jersey City, NJ, Feb. 3, 1956.
**Lang, Stephen** New York, NY, July 11, 1952. Swarthmore College.
**Lange, Jessica** Cloquet, MN, Apr. 20, 1949. U Minnesota
**Langella, Frank** Bayonne, NJ, Jan. 1, 1940. Syracuse U.
**Lansbury, Angela** London, England, Oct. 16, 1925. London Academy of Music.
**LaPaglia, Anthony** Adelaide, Australia. Jan 31, 1959.
**Larroquette, John** New Orleans, LA, Nov. 25, 1947.
**Lasser, Louise** New York, NY, Apr. 11, 1939. Brandeis U.
**Lathan, Sanaa** New York, NY, Sept. 19, 1971.
**Latifah, Queen** (Dana Owens) East Orange, NJ, Mar. 18, 1970.
**Laughlin, John** Memphis, TN, Apr. 3.
**Laughlin, Tom** Minneapolis, MN, 1938.
**Lauper, Cyndi** Astoria, Queens, New York, NY, June 20, 1953.
**Laure, Carole** Montreal, Quebec, Canada, Aug. 5, 1951.
**Laurie, Hugh** Oxford, England, June 11, 1959.
**Laurie, Piper** (Rosetta Jacobs) Detroit, MI, Jan. 22, 1932.
**Lauter, Ed** Long Beach, NY, Oct. 30, 1940.
**Lavin, Linda** Portland, ME, Oct. 15 1939.
**Law, John Phillip** Hollywood, CA, Sept. 7, 1937. Neighborhood Playhouse, U Hawaii.
**Law, Jude** Lewisham, England, Dec. 29, 1972.
**Lawrence, Barbara** Carnegie, OK, Feb. 24, 1928. UCLA.
**Lawrence, Carol** (Laraia) Melrose Park, IL, Sept. 5, 1935.
**Lawrence, Martin** Frankfurt, Germany, Apr. 16, 1965.
**Lawrence, Vicki** Inglewood, CA, Mar. 26, 1949.
**Lawson, Leigh** Atherston, England, July 21, 1945. RADA.
**Leachman, Cloris** Des Moines, IA, Apr. 30, 1930. Northwestern.
**Leal, Sharon** Tuscon, AZ, Oct. 17, 1972.
**Leary, Denis** Boston, MA, Aug. 18, 1957.
**Léaud, Jean-Pierre** Paris, France, May 5, 1944.
**LeBlanc, Matt** Newton, MA, July 25, 1967.
**Ledger, Heath** Perth, Australia, Apr. 4, 1979.
**Lee, Christopher** London, England, May 27, 1922. Wellington Col.
**Lee, Jason** Huntington Beach, CA, Apr. 25, 1970.

**Lee, Mark** Sydney, Australia, 1958.
**Lee, Michelle** (Dusiak) Los Angeles, CA, June 24, 1942. LACC.
**Lee, Sheryl** Augsburg, Germany, Arp. 22, 1967.
**Lee, Spike** (Shelton Lee) Atlanta, GA, Mar. 20, 1957.
**Legge, Michael** Newry, Northern Ireland, 1978.
**Legros, James** Minneapolis, MN, Apr. 27, 1962.
**Leguizamo, John** Colombia, July 22, 1965. NYU.
**Leibman, Ron** New York, NY, Oct. 11, 1937. Ohio Wesleyan.
**Leigh, Jennifer Jason** Los Angeles, CA, Feb. 5, 1962.
**Le Mat, Paul** Rahway, NJ, Sept. 22, 1945.
**Lemmon, Chris** Los Angeles, CA, Jan. 22, 1954.
**Leno, Jay** New Rochelle, NY, Apr. 28, 1950. Emerson Col.
**Lenz, Kay** Los Angeles, CA, Mar. 4, 1953.
**Lenz, Rick** Springfield, IL, Nov. 21, 1939. U Michigan.
**Leonard, Robert Sean** Westwood, NJ, Feb. 28, 1969.
**Leoni, Téa** (Elizabeth Téa Pantaleoni) New York, NY, Feb. 25, 1966.
**Lerman, Logan** Beverly Hills, Jan. 19, 1992.
**Lerner, Michael** Brooklyn, NY, June 22, 1941.
**Leslie, Joan** (Joan Brodell) Detroit, MI, Jan. 26, 1925. St. Benedict's.
**Lester, Mark** Oxford, England, July 11, 1958.
**Leto, Jared** Bossier City, LA, Dec. 26, 1971.
**Leung, Tony** Hong Kong, June 27, 1962.
**Levels, Calvin** Cleveland. OH, Sept. 30, 1954. CCC.
**Levin, Rachel** (Rachel Chagall) New York, NY, Nov. 24, 1954. Goddard College.
**Levine, Jerry** New Brunswick, NJ, Mar. 12, 1957, Boston U.
**Levy, Eugene** Hamilton, Canada, Dec. 17, 1946. McMaster U.
**Lewis, Charlotte** London, England, Aug. 7, 1967.
**Lewis, Damian** London, England, Feb. 11, 1971. Guildhall.
**Lewis, Geoffrey** San Diego, CA, Jan. 1, 1935.
**Lewis, Jerry** (Joseph Levitch) Newark, NJ, Mar. 16, 1926.
**Lewis, Juliette** Los Angeles, CA, June 21, 1973.
**Li, Jet** Beijing, China, Apr. 26, 1963.
**Ligon, Tom** New Orleans, LA, Sept. 10, 1945.
**Lillard, Matthew** Lansing, MI, Jan. 24, 1970.
**Lincoln, Abbey** (Anna Marie Woolridge) Chicago, IL, Aug. 6, 1930.
**Linden, Hal** Bronx, NY, Mar. 20, 1931. City College of NY.
**Lindo, Delroy** London, England, Nov. 18, 1952.
**Lindsay, Robert** Ilketson, Derbyshire, England, Dec. 13, 1951, RADA.
**Linn-Baker, Mark** St. Louis, MO, June 17, 1954. Yale.
**Linney, Laura** New York, NY, Feb. 5, 1964.
**Liotta, Ray** Newark, NJ, Dec. 18, 1955. U Miami.
**Lisi, Virna** Rome, Italy, Nov. 8, 1937.
**Lithgow, John** Rochester, NY, Oct. 19, 1945. Harvard.
**Liu, Lucy** Queens, NY, Dec. 2, 1967.
**Livingston, Ron** Cedar Rapids, IA, June 5, 1968.
**LL Cool J** (James Todd Smith) Queens, NY, Jan. 14, 1968.
**Lloyd, Christopher** Stamford, CT, Oct. 22, 1938.
**Lloyd, Emily** London, England, Sept. 29, 1970.
**Locke, Sondra** Shelbyville, TN, May, 28, 1947.
**Lockhart, June** New York, NY, June 25, 1925. Westlake School.
**Lockwood, Gary** Van Nuys, CA, Feb. 21, 1937.
**Loggia, Robert** Staten Island, NY, Jan. 3, 1930. U Missouri.

Lohan, Lindsay New York, NY, July 2, 1986.
Lohman, Alison Palm Springs, CA, Sept. 18, 1979.
Lollobrigida, Gina Subiaco, Italy, July 4, 1927. Rome Academy of Fine Arts.
Lom, Herbert Prague, Czech Republic, Jan. 9, 1917. Prague U.
Lomez, Celine Montreal, Quebec, Canada, May 11, 1953.
Lone, John Hong Kong, Oct 13, 1952. AADA.
Long, Justin Fairfield, CT, June 2, 1978.
Long, Nia Brooklyn, NY, Oct. 30, 1970.
Long, Shelley Ft. Wayne, IN, Aug. 23, 1949. Northwestern.
Lopez, Jennifer Bronx, NY, July 24, 1970.
Lopez, Perry New York, NY, July 22, 1931. NYU.
Lords, Tracy (Nora Louise Kuzma) Steubenville, OH, May 7, 1968.
Loren, Sophia (Sophia Scicolone) Rome, Italy, Sept. 20, 1934.
Louis-Dreyfus, Julia New York, NY, Jan. 13, 1961.
Louise, Tina (Blacker) New York, NY, Feb. 11, 1934, Miami U.
Love, Courtney (Love Michelle Harrison) San Francisco, CA, July 9, 1965.
Lovett, Lyle Klein, TX, Nov. 1, 1957.
Lovitz, Jon Tarzana, CA, July 21, 1957.
Lowe, Chad Dayton, OH, Jan. 15, 1968.
Lowe, Rob Charlottesville, VA, Mar. 17, 1964.
Lucas, Josh Little Rock, AR, June 20, 1971.
Luckinbill, Laurence Fort Smith, AK, Nov. 21, 1934.
Luft, Lorna Los Angeles, CA, Nov. 21, 1952.
Luke, Derek Jersey City, NJ, Apr. 24, 1974.
Lulu (Marie Lawrie) Glasgow, Scotland, Nov. 3, 1948.
Luna, Barbara New York, NY, Mar. 2, 1939.
Luna, Diego Mexico City, Mexico, Dec. 29, 1979.
Lundgren, Dolph Stockolm, Sweden, Nov. 3, 1959. Royal Institute.
LuPone, Patti Northport, NY, Apr. 21, 1949, Juilliard.
Lydon, James Harrington Park, NJ, May 30, 1923.
Lynch, Jane Dolton, IL, July 14, 1960.
Lynch, Kelly Minneapolis, MN, Jan. 31, 1959.
Lynley, Carol (Jones) New York, NY, Feb. 13, 1942.
Lyon, Sue Davenport, IA, July 10, 1946.
Lyonne, Natasha (Braunstein) New York, NY, Apr. 4, 1979.

Mac, Bernie (Bernard Jeffrey McCollough) Chicago, IL, Oct. 5, 1958.
MacArthur, James Los Angeles, CA, Dec. 8, 1937. Harvard.
Macchio, Ralph Huntington, NY, Nov. 4, 1961.
MacCorkindale, Simon Cambridge, England, Feb. 12, 1953.
Macdonald, Kelly Glasgow, Scotland, Feb. 23, 1976.
MacDowell, Andie (Rose Anderson MacDowell) Gaffney, SC, Apr. 21, 1958.
MacFadyen, Angus Glasgow, Scotland, Oct. 21, 1963.
MacGinnis, Niall Dublin, Ireland, Mar. 29, 1913. Dublin U.
MacGraw, Ali New York, NY, Apr. 1, 1938. Wellesley.
MacLachlan, Kyle Yakima, WA, Feb. 22, 1959. U Washington.
MacLaine, Shirley (Beaty) Richmond, VA, Apr. 24, 1934.
MacLeod, Gavin Mt. Kisco, NY, Feb. 28, 1931.
MacNaughton, Robert New York, NY, Dec. 19, 1966.
Macnee, Patrick London, England, Feb. 6, 1922.
MacNicol, Peter Dallas, TX, Apr. 10, 1954. U Minnesota.
MacPherson, Elle Sydney, Australia, Mar. 29, 1963.
MacVittie, Bruce Providence, RI, Oct. 14, 1956. Boston U.

Macy, William H. Miami, FL, Mar. 13, 1950. Goddard College.
Madigan, Amy Chicago, IL, Sept. 11, 1950. Marquette U.
Madonna (Madonna Louise Veronica Cicone) Bay City, MI, Aug. 16, 1958. U Michigan.
Madsen, Michael Chicago, IL, Sept. 25, 1958.
Madsen, Virginia Winnetka, IL, Sept. 11, 1963.
Magnuson, Ann Charleston, WV, Jan. 4, 1956.
Maguire, Tobey Santa Monica, CA, June 27, 1975.
Maharis, George Astoria, NY, Sept. 1, 1928. Actors Studio.
Mahoney, John Manchester, England, June 20, 1940. Western Illinois U.
Mailer, Stephen New York, NY, Mar. 10, 1966. NYU.
Majors, Lee Wyandotte, MI, Apr. 23, 1940. Eastern Kentucky State College.
Makepeace, Chris Toronto, ON, Canada, Apr. 22, 1964.
Malden, Karl (Mladen Sekulovich) Gary, IN, Mar. 22, 1914.
Malkovich, John Christopher, IL, Dec. 9, 1953, Illinois State U.
Malone, Dorothy Chicago, IL, Jan. 30, 1925.
Malone, Jena Lake Tahoe, NV, Nov. 21, 1984.
Mann, Leslie San Francisco, CA, Mar. 26, 1972.
Mann, Terrence Kentucky, July 1, 1951. NC School Arts.
Manoff, Dinah New York, NY, Jan. 25, 1958. Cal Arts.
Mantegna, Joe Chicago, IL, Nov. 13, 1947. Goodman Theatre.
Manz, Linda New York, NY, 1961.
Marceau, Sophie (Maupu) Paris, France, Nov. 17, 1966.
Marcovicci, Andrea New York, NY, Nov. 18, 1948.
Margulies, Julianna Spring Valley, NY, June 8, 1966.
Marin, Cheech (Richard) Los Angeles, CA, July 13, 1946.
Marinaro, Ed New York, NY, Mar. 31, 1950. Cornell.
Mars, Kenneth Chicago, IL, Apr. 14, 1936.
Marsden, James Stillwater, OK, Sept. 18, 1973.
Marsh, Jean London, England, July 1, 1934.
Marshall, Ken New York, NY, June 27, 1950. Juilliard.
Marshall, Penny Bronx, NY, Oct. 15, 1942. UN. Mex.
Martin, Andrea Portland, ME, Jan. 15, 1947.
Martin, Dick Battle Creek, MI Jan. 30, 1923.
Martin, George N. New York, NY, Aug. 15, 1929.
Martin, Millicent Romford, England, June 8, 1934.
Martin, Pamela Sue Westport, CT, Jan. 15, 1953.
Martin, Steve Waco, TX, Aug. 14, 1945. UCLA.
Martin, Tony (Alfred Norris) Oakland, CA, Dec. 25, 1913. St. Mary's College.
Martindale, Margo Jacksonsville, TX, July 18, 1951.
Martinez, Olivier Paris, France, Jan. 12, 1966.
Mason, Marsha St. Louis, MO, Apr. 3, 1942. Webster College.
Masters, Ben Corvallis, OR, May 6, 1947. U Oregon.
Masterson, Mary Stuart Los Angeles, CA, June 28, 1966, NYU.
Masterson, Peter Angleton, TX, June 1, 1934. Rice U.
Mastrantonio, Mary Elizabeth Chicago, IL, Nov. 17, 1958. U Illinois.
Masur, Richard New York, NY, Nov. 20, 1948.
Matheson, Tim Glendale, CA, Dec. 31, 1947. Cal State.
Mathis, Samantha New York, NY, May 12, 1970.
Matlin, Marlee Morton Grove, IL, Aug. 24, 1965.
Matthews, Brian Philadelphia, PA, Jan. 24. 1953. St. Olaf.
Maura, Carmen Madrid, Spain, Sept. 15, 1945.
May, Elaine (Berlin) Philadelphia, PA, Apr. 21, 1932.

**Mayron, Melanie** Philadelphia, PA, Oct. 20, 1952. AADA.
**Mazursky, Paul** Brooklyn, NY, Apr. 25, 1930. Brooklyn, NY College.
**Mazzello, Joseph** Rhinebeck, NY, Sept. 21, 1983.
**McAdams, Rachel** London, ON, Canada, Oct. 7, 1976.
**McAvoy, James** Glasgow, Scotland, Jan. 1, 1979.
**McBride, Chi** Chicago, IL, Sept. 23, 1961.
**McCallum, David** Scotland, Sept. 19, 1933. Chapman College.
**McCarthy, Andrew** New York, NY, Nov. 29, 1962, NYU.
**McCarthy, Kevin** Seattle, WA, Feb. 15, 1914. Minnesota U.
**McCartney, Paul** Liverpool, England, June 18, 1942.
**McClanahan, Rue** Healdton, OK, Feb. 21, 1934.
**McClure, Marc** San Mateo, CA, Mar. 31, 1957.
**McClurg, Edie** Kansas City, MO, July 23, 1950.
**McCormack, Catherine** Alton, Hampshire, England, Jan. 1, 1972.
**McCowen, Alec** Tunbridge Wells, England, May 26, 1925. RADA.
**McCrane, Paul** Philadelphia, PA, Jan. 19. 1961.
**McCrary, Darius** Walnut, CA, May 1, 1976.
**McDermott, Dylan** Waterbury, CT, Oct. 26, 1962. Neighborhood Playhouse.
**McDonald, Christopher** New York, NY, Feb. 15, 1955.
**McDonnell, Mary** Wilkes Barre, PA, Apr. 28, 1952.
**McDonough, Neal** Dorchester, MA, Feb. 13, 1966.
**McDormand, Frances** Illinois, June 23, 1957. Yale.
**McDowell, Malcolm** (Taylor) Leeds, England, June 19, 1943. LAMDA.
**McElhone, Natascha** (Natasha Taylor) London, England, Mar. 23, 1971.
**McEnery, Peter** Walsall, England, Feb. 21, 1940.
**McEntire, Reba** McAlester, OK, Mar. 28, 1955. Southeastern St. U.
**McGill, Everett** Miami Beach, FL, Oct. 21, 1945.
**McGillis, Kelly** Newport Beach, CA, July 9, 1957. Juilliard.
**McGinley, John C.** New York, NY, Aug. 3, 1959. NYU.
**McGoohan, Patrick** New York, NY, Mar. 19, 1928.
**McGovern, Elizabeth** Evanston, IL, July 18, 1961. Juilliard.
**McGovern, Maureen** Youngstown, OH, July 27, 1949.
**McGowan, Rose** Florence, Italy, Sept. 5, 1973.
**McGregor, Ewan** Perth, Scotland, March 31, 1971.
**McGuire, Biff** New Haven, CT, Oct. 25. 1926. Mass. State College.
**McHattie, Stephen** Antigonish, Nova Scotia, Feb. 3, 1947. Acadia U AADA.
**McKean, Michael** New York, NY, Oct. 17, 1947.
**McKee, Lonette** Detroit, MI, July 22, 1955.
**McKellen, Ian** Burnley, England, May 25, 1939.
**McKenna, Virginia** London, England, June 7, 1931.
**McKenzie, Ben** (Benjamin Schenkkan) Austin, TX, Sept. 12, 1978. U Virginia.
**McKeon, Doug** Pompton Plains, NJ, June 10, 1966.
**McLerie, Allyn Ann** Grand Mere, Canada, Dec. 1, 1926.
**McMahon, Ed** Detroit, MI, Mar. 6, 1923.
**McMahon, Julian** Sydney, Australia, July 27, 1968.
**McNamara, William** Dallas, TX, Mar. 31, 1965.
**McNichol, Kristy** Los Angeles, CA, Sept. 11, 1962.
**McQueen, Armelia** North Carolina, Jan. 6, 1952. Bklyn Consv.
**McQueen, Chad** Los Angeles, CA, Dec. 28, 1960. Actors Studio.
**McRaney, Gerald** Collins, MS, Aug. 19, 1948.
**McShane, Ian** Blackburn, England, Sept. 29, 1942. RADA.
**McTeer, Janet** York, England, May 8, 1961.

**Meadows, Jayne** (Jayne Cotter) Wuchang, China, Sept. 27, 1924. St. Margaret's.
**Meaney, Colm** Dublin, Ireland, May 30, 1953.
**Meara, Anne** Brooklyn, NY, Sept. 20, 1929.
**Meat Loaf** (Marvin Lee Aday) Dallas, TX, Sept. 27, 1947.
**Mechlowicz, Scott** New York, NY, Jan. 17, 1981.
**Medwin, Michael** London, England, July 18, 1923. Instut Fischer.
**Mekka, Eddie** Worcester, MA, June 14, 1952. Boston Cons.
**Melato, Mariangela** Milan, Italy, Sept. 18, 1941. Milan Theatre Acad.
**Mendes, Eva** Los Angeles, CA, Mar. 5, 1974.
**Menzel, Idina** Syosset, NY, May 30, 1971. NYU.
**Meredith, Lee** (Judi Lee Sauls) River Edge, NJ, Oct. 22, 1947. AADA.
**Merkerson, S. Epatha** Saganaw, MI, Nov. 28, 1952. Wayne St. Univ.
**Merrill, Dina** (Nedinia Hutton) New York, NY, Dec. 29, 1925. AADA.
**Messing, Debra** Brooklyn, NY, Aug. 15, 1968.
**Metcalf, Laurie** Edwardsville, IL, June 16, 1955. Illinois State U.
**Metzler, Jim** Oneonta, NY, June 23, 1955. Dartmouth.
**Meyer, Breckin** Minneapolis, MN, May 7, 1974.
**Michell, Keith** Adelaide, Australia, Dec. 1, 1926.
**Midler, Bette** Honolulu, HI, Dec. 1, 1945.
**Mihok, Dash** New York, NY, May 24, 1974.
**Mikkelsen, Mads** Copenhagen, Denmark, Nov. 22, 1965.
**Milano, Alyssa** Brooklyn, NY, Dec. 19, 1972.
**Miles, Joanna** Nice, France, Mar. 6, 1940.
**Miles, Sarah** Ingatestone, England, Dec. 31, 1941. RADA.
**Miles, Sylvia** New York, NY, Sept. 9, 1934. Actors Studio.
**Miles, Vera** (Ralston) Boise City, OK, Aug. 23, 1929. UCLA.
**Miller, Barry** Los Angeles, CA, Feb. 6, 1958.
**Miller, Dick** New York, NY, Dec. 25, 1928.
**Miller, Jonny Lee** Surrey, England, Nov. 15, 1972.
**Miller, Linda** New York, NY, Sept. 16, 1942. Catholic U.
**Miller, Penelope Ann** Santa Monica, CA, Jan. 13, 1964.
**Miller, Rebecca** Roxbury, CT, Sept. 15, 1962. Yale.
**Miller, Sienna** New York, NY, Dec. 28, 1981.
**Mills, Donna** Chicago, IL, Dec. 11, 1945. U Illinois.
**Mills, Hayley** London, England, Apr. 18, 1946. Elmhurst School.
**Mills, Juliet** London, England, Nov. 21, 1941.
**Milner, Martin** Detroit, MI, Dec. 28, 1931.
**Mimieux, Yvette** Los Angeles, CA, Jan. 8, 1941. Hollywood High.
**Minnelli, Liza** Los Angeles, CA, Mar. 19, 1946.
**Miou-Miou** (Sylvette Henry) Paris, France, Feb. 22, 1950.
**Mirren, Helen** (Ilynea Mironoff) London, England, July 26, 1946.
**Mistry, Jimi** Scarborough, England, 1973.
**Mitchell, James** Sacramento, CA, Feb. 29, 1920. LACC.
**Mitchell, John Cameron** El Paso, TX, Apr. 21, 1963. Northwestern.
**Mitchell, Radha** Melbourne, Australia, Nov. 12, 1973.
**Mitchum, James** Los Angeles, CA, May 8, 1941.
**Modine, Matthew** Loma Linda, CA, Mar. 22, 1959.
**Moffat, Donald** Plymouth, England, Dec. 26, 1930. RADA.
**Moffett, D. W.** Highland Park, IL, Oct. 26, 1954. Stanford U.
**Mohr, Jay** Verona, NJ, Aug. 23, 1971.
**Mokae, Zakes** Johannesburg, South Africa, Aug. 5, 1935. RADA.
**Mol, Gretchen** Deep River, CT, Nov. 8, 1972.

**Molina, Alfred** London, England, May 24, 1953. Guildhall.
**Moll, Richard** Pasadena, CA, Jan. 13, 1943.
**Monaghan, Dominic** Berlin, Germany, Dec. 8, 1976.
**Monaghan, Michelle** Winthrop, IA, March 23, 1976.
**Mo'Nique (Monique Imes)** Woodland, MD, Dec. 11, 1967.
**Monk, Debra** Middletown, OH, Feb. 27, 1949.
**Montalban, Ricardo** Mexico City, Mexico, Nov. 25, 1920.
**Montenegro, Fernanda** (Arlete Pinheiro) Rio de Janiero, Brazil, 1929.
**Montgomery, Belinda** Winnipeg, Manitoba, Canada, July 23, 1950.
**Moody, Ron** London, England, Jan. 8, 1924. London U.
**Moore, Demi** (Guines) Roswell, NM, Nov. 11, 1962.
**Moore, Dick** Los Angeles, CA, Sept. 12, 1925.
**Moore, Julianne** (Julie Anne Smith) Fayetteville, NC, Dec. 30, 1960.
**Moore, Mandy** Nashua, NH, Apr. 10, 1984.
**Moore, Mary Tyler** Brooklyn, NY, Dec. 29, 1936.
**Moore, Roger** London, England, Oct. 14, 1927. RADA.
**Moore, Stephen Campbell** (Stephen Thorpe) London, England, 1979.
**Moore, Terry** (Helen Koford) Los Angeles, CA, Jan. 7, 1929.
**Morales, Esai** Brooklyn, NY, Oct. 1, 1962.
**Moranis, Rick** Toronto, ON, Canada, Apr. 18, 1954.
**Moreau, Jeanne** Paris, France, Jan. 23, 1928.
**Moreno, Catalina Sandino** Bogota, Colombia, Apr. 19, 1981.
**Moreno, Rita** (Rosita Alverio) Humacao, P.R., Dec. 11, 1931.
**Morgan, Harry** (Henry) (Harry Bratsburg) Detroit, MI, Apr. 10, 1915. U Chicago.
**Morgan, Michele** (Simone Roussel) Paris, France, Feb. 29, 1920. Paris Dramatic School.
**Moriarty, Cathy** Bronx, NY, Nov. 29, 1960.
**Moriarty, Michael** Detroit, MI, Apr. 5, 1941. Dartmouth.
**Morison, Patricia** New York, NY, Mar. 19, 1915.
**Morris, Garrett** New Orleans, LA, Feb. 1, 1937.
**Morrow, Rob** New Rochelle, NY, Sept. 21, 1962.
**Morse, David** Hamilton, MA, Oct. 11, 1953.
**Morse, Robert** Newton, MA, May 18, 1931.
**Mortensen, Viggo** New York, NY, Oct. 20, 1958.
**Mortimer, Emily** London, England, Dec. 1, 1971.
**Morton, Joe** New York, NY, Oct. 18, 1947. Hofstra U.
**Morton, Samantha** Nottingham, England, May 13, 1977.
**Mos Def** (Dante Beze) Brooklyn, NY, Dec. 11, 1973.
**Moses, William** Los Angeles, CA, Nov. 17, 1959.
**Moss, Carrie-Anne** Vancouver, BC, Canada, Aug. 21, 1967.
**Mostel, Josh** New York, NY, Dec. 21, 1946. Brandeis U.
**Mouchet, Catherine** Paris, France, 1959. Ntl. Consv.
**Moynahan, Bridget** Binghamton, NY, Sept. 21, 1972.
**Mueller-Stahl, Armin** Tilsit, East Prussia, Dec. 17, 1930.
**Muldaur, Diana** New York, NY, Aug. 19, 1938. Sweet Briar College.
**Mulgrew, Kate** Dubuque, IA, Apr. 29, 1955. NYU.
**Mulhern, Matt** Philadelphia, PA, July 21, 1960. Rutgers U.
**Mull, Martin** N. Ridgefield, OH, Aug. 18, 1941. RI School of Design.
**Mulroney, Dermot** Alexandria, VA, Oct. 31, 1963. Northwestern.
**Mumy, Bill** (Charles William Mumy, Jr.) San Gabriel, CA, Feb. 1, 1954.
**Muniz, Frankie** Ridgewood, NJ, Dec. 5, 1985.
**Murphy, Brittany** Atlanta, GA, Nov. 10, 1977.

**Murphy, Cillian** Douglas, Ireland, March 13, 1974.
**Murphy, Donna** Queens, NY, March 7, 1958.
**Murphy, Eddie** Brooklyn, NY, Apr. 3, 1961.
**Murphy, Michael** Los Angeles, CA, May 5, 1938. U Arizona.
**Murray, Bill** Wilmette, IL, Sept. 21, 1950. Regis College.
**Murray, Don** Hollywood, CA, July 31, 1929.
**Musante, Tony** Bridgeport, CT, June 30, 1936. Oberlin College.
**Myers, Mike** Scarborough, Canada, May 25, 1963.

**Nabors, Jim** Sylacauga, GA, June 12, 1932.
**Nader, Michael** Los Angeles, CA, Feb. 19, 1945.
**Namath, Joe** Beaver Falls, PA, May 31, 1943. U Alabama.
**Naughton, David** Hartford, CT, Feb. 13, 1951.
**Naughton, James** Middletown, CT, Dec. 6, 1945.
**Neal, Patricia** Packard, KY, Jan. 20, 1926. Northwestern.
**Neeson, Liam** Ballymena, Northern Ireland, June 7, 1952.
**Neill, Sam** Northern Ireland, Sept. 14, 1947. U Canterbury.
**Nelligan, Kate** London, ON, Canada, Mar. 16, 1951. U Toronto.
**Nelson, Craig T.** Spokane, WA, Apr. 4, 1946.
**Nelson, David** New York, NY, Oct. 24, 1936. USC.
**Nelson, Judd** Portland, ME, Nov. 28, 1959, Haverford College.
**Nelson, Lori** (Dixie Kay Nelson) Santa Fe, NM, Aug. 15, 1933.
**Nelson, Tim Blake** Tulsa, OK, Nov. 5, 1964.
**Nelson, Tracy** Santa Monica, CA, Oct. 25, 1963.
**Nelson, Willie** Abbott, TX, Apr. 30, 1933.
**Nemec, Corin** Little Rock, AK, Nov. 5, 1971.
**Nero, Franco** (Francisco Spartanero) Parma, Italy, Nov. 23, 1941.
**Nesmith, Michael** Houston, TX, Dec. 30, 1942.
**Nettleton, Lois** Oak Park, IL, 1931. Actors Studio.
**Neuwirth, Bebe** Princeton, NJ, Dec. 31, 1958.
**Newhart, Bob** Chicago, IL, Sept. 5, 1929. Loyola U.
**Newman, Barry** Boston, MA, Nov. 7, 1938. Brandeis U.
**Newman, Laraine** Los Angeles, CA, Mar. 2, 1952.
**Newman, Nanette** Northampton, England, May 29, 1934.
**Newman, Paul** Cleveland, OH, Jan. 26, 1925. Yale.
**Newmar, Julie** (Newmeyer) Los Angeles, CA, Aug. 16, 1933.
**Newton, Thandie** Zambia, Nov. 16, 1972.
**Newton-John, Olivia** Cambridge, England, Sept. 26, 1948.
**Nguyen, Dustin** Saigon, Vietnam, Sept. 17, 1962.
**Nicholas, Denise** Detroit, MI, July 12, 1945.
**Nicholas, Paul** Peterborough, Cambridge, England, Dec. 3, 1945.
**Nichols, Nichelle** Robbins, IL, Dec. 28, 1933.
**Nicholson, Jack** Neptune, NJ, Apr. 22, 1937.
**Nicholson, Julianne** Medford, MA, July 1, 1971.
**Nickerson, Denise** New York, NY, Apr. 1, 1959.
**Nielsen, Brigitte** Denmark, July 15, 1963.
**Nielsen, Connie** Elling, Denmark, July 3, 1965.
**Nielsen, Leslie** Regina, Saskatchewan, Canada, Feb. 11, 1926. Neighborhood Playhouse.
**Nighy, Bill** Caterham, England, Dec. 12, 1949. Guildford.
**Nimoy, Leonard** Boston, MA, Mar. 26, 1931. Boston College, Antioch College.
**Nivola, Alessandro** Boston, MA, June 28, 1972. Yale.

**Nixon, Cynthia** New York, NY, Apr. 9, 1966. Columbia U.
**Noble, James** Dallas, TX, Mar. 5, 1922, SMU.
**Nolan, Kathleen** St. Louis, MO, Sept. 27, 1933. Neighborhood Playhouse.
**Nolte, Nick** Omaha, NE, Feb. 8, 1940. Pasadena City College.
**Norris, Bruce** Houston, TX, May 16, 1960. Northwestern.
**Norris, Christopher** New York, NY, Oct. 7, 1943. Lincoln Square Acad.
**Norris, Chuck** (Carlos Ray) Ryan, OK, Mar. 10, 1940.
**North, Heather** Pasadena, CA, Dec. 13, 1950. Actors Workshop.
**Northam, Jeremy** Cambridge, England, Dec. 1, 1961.
**Norton, Edward** Boston, MA, Aug. 18, 1969.
**Norton, Ken** Jacksonville, IL, Aug. 9, 1945.
**Noseworthy, Jack** Lynn, MA, Dec. 21, 1969.
**Nouri, Michael** Washington, DC, Dec. 9, 1945.
**Novak, Kim** (Marilyn Novak) Chicago, IL, Feb. 13, 1933. LACC.
**Novello, Don** Ashtabula, OH, Jan. 1, 1943. U Dayton.
**Nuyen, France** (Vannga) Marseilles, France, July 31, 1939. Beaux Arts School.

**O'Brian, Hugh** (Hugh J. Krampe) Rochester, NY. Apr. 19, 1928. Cincinnati U.
**O'Brien, Clay** Ray, AZ, May 6, 1961.
**O'Brien, Margaret** (Angela Maxine O'Brien) Los Angeles, CA, Jan. 15, 1937.
**O'Connell, Jerry** (Jeremiah O'Connell) New York, NY, Feb. 17, 1974.
**O'Connor, Glynnis** New York, NY, Nov. 19, 1955. NYSU.
**O'Donnell, Chris** Winetka, IL, June 27, 1970.
**O'Donnell, Rosie** Commack, NY, March 21, 1961.
**Oh, Sandra** Nepean, ON, Canada, Nov. 30, 1970.
**O'Halloran, Brian** Old Bridge, NJ, Sept. 1, 1965.
**O'Hara, Catherine** Toronto, ON, Canada, Mar. 4, 1954.
**O'Hara, Maureen** (Maureen Fitzsimons) Dublin, Ireland, Aug. 17, 1920.
**O'Hare, Dennis** Kansas City, MO, Jan. 17, 1962.
**O'Keefe, Michael** Larchmont, NY, Apr. 24, 1955. NYU, AADA.
**Okonedo, Sophie** London, England, Jan. 1, 1969.
**Oldman, Gary** New Cross, South London, England, Mar. 21, 1958.
**O'Leary, Matt** Chicago, IL, July 6, 1987.
**Olin, Ken** Chicago, IL, July 30, 1954. U Pa.
**Olin, Lena** Stockholm, Sweden, Mar. 22, 1955.
**Olmos, Edward James** Los Angeles, CA, Feb. 24, 1947. CSLA.
**O'Loughlin, Gerald S.** New York, NY, Dec. 23, 1921. U Rochester.
**Olson, James** Evanston, IL, Oct. 8, 1930.
**Olson, Nancy** Milwaukee, WI, July 14, 1928. UCLA.
**Olyphant, Timothy** Honolulu, HI, May 20, 1968.
**O'Neal, Griffin** Los Angeles, CA, Oct. 28, 1964.
**O'Neal, Ryan** Los Angeles, CA, Apr. 20, 1941.
**O'Neal, Tatum** Los Angeles, CA, Nov. 5, 1963.
**O'Neil, Tricia** Shreveport, LA, Mar. 11, 1945. Baylor U.
**O'Neill, Ed** Youngstown, OH, Apr. 12, 1946.
**O'Neill, Jennifer** Rio de Janeiro, Brazil, Feb. 20, 1949. Neighborhood Playhouse.
**Ontkean, Michael** Vancouver, BC, Canada, Jan. 24, 1946.
**O'Quinn, Terry** Newbury, MI, July 15, 1952.
**Ormond, Julia** Epsom, England, Jan. 4, 1965.
**O'Shea, Milo** Dublin, Ireland, June 2, 1926.
**Osment, Haley Joel** Los Angeles, CA, Apr. 10, 1988.

**O'Toole, Annette** (Toole) Houston, TX, Apr. 1, 1953. UCLA.
**O'Toole, Peter** Connemara, Ireland, Aug. 2, 1932. RADA.
**Otto, Miranda** Brisbane, Australia, Dec. 16, 1967.
**Overall, Park** Nashville, TN, Mar. 15, 1957. Tusculum College.
**Owen, Clive** Keresley, England, Oct. 3, 1964.
**Oz, Frank** (Oznowicz) Hereford, England, May 25, 1944.

**Pace, Lee** Chickasha, OK, Mar. 25, 1979.
**Pacino, Al** New York, NY, Apr. 25, 1940.
**Pacula, Joanna** Tamaszow Lubelski, Poland, Jan. 2, 1957. Polish Natl. Theatre Sch.
**Page, Ellen** Hallifax, Nova Scotia, Feb. 21, 1987.
**Paget, Debra** (Debralee Griffin) Denver, CO, Aug. 19, 1933.
**Paige, Janis** (Donna Mae Jaden) Tacoma, WA, Sept. 16, 1922.
**Palin, Michael** Sheffield, England, May 5, 1943, Oxford.
**Palmer, Betsy** East Chicago, IN, Nov. 1, 1926. DePaul U.
**Palmer, Gregg** (Palmer Lee) San Francisco, CA, Jan. 25, 1927. U Utah.
**Palminteri, Chazz** (Calogero Lorenzo Palminteri) New York, NY, May 15, 1952.
**Paltrow, Gwyneth** Los Angeles, CA, Sept. 28, 1973.
**Pampanini, Silvana** Rome, Italy, Sept. 25, 1925.
**Panebianco, Richard** New York, NY, 1971.
**Pankin, Stuart** Philadelphia, PA, Apr. 8, 1946.
**Pantoliano, Joe** Jersey City, NJ, Sept. 12, 1954.
**Papas, Irene** Chiliomodion, Greece, Mar. 9, 1929.
**Paquin, Anna** Winnipeg, Manitoba, Canada, July, 24, 1982.
**Pardue, Kip** (Kevin Ian Pardue) Atlanta, GA, Sept. 23, 1976. Yale.
**Pare, Michael** Brooklyn, NY, Oct. 9, 1959.
**Parker, Corey** New York, NY, July 8, 1965. NYU.
**Parker, Eleanor** Cedarville, OH, June 26, 1922. Pasadena Playhouse.
**Parker, Fess** Fort Worth, TX, Aug. 16, 1925. USC.
**Parker, Jameson** Baltimore, MD, Nov. 18, 1947. Beloit College.
**Parker, Mary-Louise** Ft. Jackson, SC, Aug. 2, 1964. Bard College.
**Parke, Nate** Norfolk, VA, Nov. 18, 1979.
**Parker, Nathaniel** London, England, May 18, 1962.
**Parker, Sarah Jessica** Nelsonville, OH, Mar. 25, 1965.
**Parker, Trey** Auburn, AL, May 30, 1972.
**Parkins, Barbara** Vancouver, BC, Canada, May 22, 1943.
**Parks, Michael** Corona, CA, Apr. 4, 1938.
**Parsons, Estelle** Lynn, MA, Nov. 20, 1927. Boston U.
**Parton, Dolly** Sevierville, TN, Jan. 19, 1946.
**Pascal, Adam** Bronx, NY, Oct. 25, 1970.
**Patinkin, Mandy** Chicago, IL, Nov. 30, 1952. Juilliard.
**Patric, Jason** New York, NY, June 17, 1966.
**Patrick, Robert** Marietta, GA, Nov. 5, 1958.
**Patterson, Lee** Vancouver, BC, Canada, Mar. 31, 1929. Ontario College.
**Patton, Will** Charleston, SC, June 14, 1954.
**Paulik, Johan** Prague, Czech Republic, Mar. 14, 1975.
**Paulson, Sarah** Tampa, FL, Dec. 17, 1975.
**Pavan, Marisa** (Marisa Pierangeli) Cagliari, Sardinia, June 19, 1932. Torquado Tasso College.
**Paxton, Bill** Fort Worth, TX, May. 17, 1955.
**Paymer, David** Oceanside, Long Island, NY, Aug. 30, 1954.

**Pays, Amanda** Berkshire, England, June 6, 1959.
**Peach, Mary** Durban, South Africa, Oct. 20, 1934.
**Pearce, Guy** Ely, England, Oct. 5, 1967.
**Pearson, Beatrice** Dennison, TX, July 27, 1920.
**Peet, Amanda** New York, NY, Jan. 11, 1972.
**Pegg, Simon** Gloucester, England, Feb. 14, 1970.
**Peña, Elizabeth** Elizabeth, NJ, Sept. 23, 1961.
**Peña, Michael** Chicago, IL, Jan. 13, 1976.
**Pendleton, Austin** Warren, OH, Mar. 27, 1940. Yale.
**Penhall, Bruce** Balboa, CA, Aug. 17, 1960.
**Penn, Kal** Montclair, NJ, Apr. 23, 1977.
**Penn, Sean** Burbank, CA, Aug. 17, 1960.
**Pepper, Barry** Campbell River, BC, Canada, Apr. 4, 1970.
**Perabo, Piper** Toms River, NJ, Oct. 31, 1976.
**Perez, Jose** New York, NY, 1940.
**Perez, Rosie** Brooklyn, NY, Sept. 6, 1964.
**Perkins, Elizabeth** Queens, NY, Nov. 18, 1960. Goodman School.
**Perkins, Millie** Passaic, NJ, May 12, 1938.
**Perlman, Rhea** Brooklyn, NY, Mar. 31, 1948.
**Perlman, Ron** New York, NY, Apr. 13, 1950. U Mn.
**Perreau, Gigi** (Ghislaine) Los Angeles, CA, Feb. 6, 1941.
**Perrine, Valerie** Galveston, TX, Sept. 3, 1943. U Ariz.
**Perry, Luke** (Coy Luther Perry, III) Fredricktown, OH, Oct. 11, 1966.
**Perry, Tyler** New Orleans, LA, Sept. 13, 1969.
**Pesci, Joe** Newark, NJ. Feb. 9, 1943.
**Pescow, Donna** Brooklyn, NY, Mar. 24, 1954.
**Peters, Bernadette** (Lazzara) Jamaica, NY, Feb. 28, 1948.
**Petersen, Paul** Glendale, CA, Sept. 23, 1945. Valley College.
**Petersen, William** Chicago, IL, Feb. 21, 1953.
**Peterson, Cassandra** Colorado Springs, CO, Sept. 17, 1951.
**Pettet, Joanna** London, England, Nov. 16, 1944. Neighborhood Playhouse.
**Petty, Lori** Chattanooga, TN, Mar. 23, 1963.
**Pfeiffer, Michelle** Santa Ana, CA, Apr. 29, 1958.
**Phifer, Mekhi** New York, NY, Dec. 12, 1975.
**Phillippe, Ryan** (Matthew Phillippe) New Castle, DE, Sept. 10, 1975.
**Phillips, Lou Diamond** Phillipines, Feb. 17, 1962, U Tx.
**Phillips, MacKenzie** Alexandria, VA, Nov. 10, 1959.
**Phillips, Michelle** (Holly Gilliam) Long Beach, CA, June 4, 1944.
**Phillips, Sian** Bettws, Wales, May 14, 1934. U Wales.
**Phoenix, Joaquin** San Juan, Puerto Rico, Oct. 28, 1974.
**Picardo, Robert** Philadelphia, PA, Oct. 27, 1953. Yale.
**Picerni, Paul** New York, NY, Dec. 1, 1922. Loyola U.
**Pidgeon, Rebecca** Cambridge, MA, Oct. 10, 1965.
**Pierce, David Hyde** Saratoga Springs, NY, Apr. 3, 1959.
**Pigott-Smith, Tim** Rugby, England, May 13, 1946.
**Pinchot, Bronson** New York, NY, May 20, 1959. Yale.
**Pine, Phillip** Hanford, CA, July 16, 1920. Actors' Lab.
**Pinsent, Gordon** Grand Falls, Newfoundland, July 12, 1930.
**Piscopo, Joe** Passaic, NJ, June 17, 1951.
**Pisier, Marie-France** Dalat, Vietnam, May 10, 1944. U Paris.
**Pitillo, Maria** Elmira, NY, Jan. 8, 1965.
**Pitt, Brad** (William Bradley Pitt) Shawnee, OK, Dec. 18, 1963.
**Pitt, Michael** West Orange, NJ, Apr. 10, 1981.

**Piven, Jeremy** New York, NY, July 26, 1965.
**Place, Mary Kay** Tulsa OK, Sept. 23, 1947. U Tulsa.
**Platt, Oliver** Windsor, ON, Canada, Oct. 10, 1960.
**Playten, Alice** New York, NY, Aug. 28, 1947. NYU.
**Pleshette, Suzanne** New York, NY, Jan. 31, 1937. Syracuse U.
**Plimpton, Martha** New York, NY, Nov. 16, 1970.
**Plowright, Joan** Scunthorpe, England, Oct. 28, 1929. Old Vic.
**Plumb, Eve** Burbank, CA, Apr. 29, 1958.
**Plummer, Amanda** New York, NY, Mar. 23, 1957. Middlebury College.
**Plummer, Christopher** Toronto, ON, Canada, Dec. 13, 1927.
**Podesta, Rossana** Tripoli, Libya, June 20, 1934.
**Poehler, Amy** Burlington, MA, Sept. 16, 1971.
**Poitier, Sidney** Miami, FL, Feb. 27, 1927.
**Polanski, Roman** Paris, France, Aug. 18, 1933.
**Polito, Jon** Philadelphia, PA, Dec. 29, 1950. Villanova U.
**Polito, Lina** Naples, Italy, Aug. 11, 1954.
**Pollack, Sydney** South Bend, IN, July 1, 1934.
**Pollak, Kevin** San Francisco, CA, Oct. 30, 1958.
**Pollan, Tracy** New York, NY, June 22, 1960.
**Pollard, Michael J.** Passaic, NJ, May 30, 1939.
**Polley, Sarah** Toronto, ON, Canada, Jan. 8, 1979.
**Portman, Natalie** Jerusalem, Israel, June 9, 1981.
**Posey, Parker** Baltimore, MD, Nov. 8, 1968.
**Postlethwaite, Pete** London, England, Feb. 7, 1945.
**Potente, Franka** Dulmen, Germany, July 22, 1974.
**Potter, Monica** Cleveland, OH, June 30, 1971.
**Potts, Annie** Nashville, TN, Oct. 28, 1952. Stephens College.
**Powell, Jane** (Suzanne Burce) Portland, OR, Apr. 1, 1928.
**Powell, Robert** Salford, England, June 1, 1944. Manchester U.
**Power, Taryn** Los Angeles, CA, Sept. 13, 1953.
**Power, Tyrone, IV** Los Angeles, CA, Jan. 22, 1959.
**Powers, Stefanie** (Federkiewicz) Hollywood, CA, Oct. 12, 1942.
**Prentiss, Paula** (Paula Ragusa) San Antonio, TX, Mar. 4, 1939. Northwestern.
**Presle, Micheline** (Micheline Chassagne) Paris, France, Aug. 22, 1922. Rouleau Drama School.
**Presley, Priscilla** Brooklyn, NY, May 24, 1945.
**Presnell, Harve** Modesto, CA, Sept. 14, 1933. USC.
**Preston, Kelly** Honolulu, HI, Oct. 13, 1962. USC.
**Preston, William** Columbia, PA, Aug. 26, 1921. Pennsylvania State U.
**Price, Lonny** New York, NY, Mar. 9, 1959. Juilliard.
**Priestley, Jason** Vancouver, BC, Canada, Aug, 28, 1969.
**Primus, Barry** New York, NY, Feb. 16, 1938. CCNY.
**Prince** (P. Rogers Nelson) Minneapolis, MN, June 7, 1958.
**Principal, Victoria** Fukuoka, Japan, Jan. 3, 1945. Dade, Jr. College.
**Prinze, Freddie, Jr.,** Los Angeles, CA, March 8, 1976.
**Prochnow, Jurgen** Berlin, Germany, June 10, 1941.
**Prosky, Robert** Philadelphia, PA, Dec. 13, 1930.
**Proval, David** Brooklyn, NY, May 20, 1942.
**Provine, Dorothy** Deadwood, SD, Jan. 20, 1937. U Washington.
**Pryce, Jonathan** Wales, June 1, 1947, RADA.
**Pucci, Lou Taylor** Seaside Heights, NJ, July 27, 1985.
**Pullman, Bill** Delphi, NY, Dec. 17, 1954. SUNY/Oneonta, U Mass.
**Purcell, Lee** Cherry Point, NC, June 15, 1947. Stephens.

**Purdom, Edmund** Welwyn Garden City, England, Dec. 19, 1924. St. Ignatius College.
**Pyle, Missi** Houston, TX, Nov. 16, 1972.

**Quaid, Dennis** Houston, TX, Apr. 9, 1954.
**Quaid, Randy** Houston, TX, Oct. 1, 1950. U Houston.
**Qualls, DJ** (Donald Joseph) Nashville, TN, June 12, 1978.
**Quinlan, Kathleen** Mill Valley, CA, Nov. 19, 1954.
**Quinn, Aidan** Chicago, IL, Mar. 8, 1959.

**Radcliffe, Daniel** London, England, July 23, 1989.
**Raffin, Deborah** Los Angeles, CA, Mar. 13, 1953. Valley Col.
**Ragsdale, William** El Dorado, AK, Jan. 19, 1961. Hendrix Col.
**Railsback, Steve** Dallas, TX, Nov. 16, 1948.
**Rainer, Luise** Vienna, Austria, Jan. 12, 1910.
**Ramis, Harold** Chicago, IL, Nov. 21, 1944. Washington U.
**Rampling, Charlotte** Surmer, England, Feb. 5, 1946. U Madrid.
**Rapaport, Michael** New York, NY, March 20, 1970.
**Rapp, Anthony** Chicago, IL, Oct. 26, 1971.
**Rasche, David** St. Louis, MO, Aug. 7, 1944.
**Rea, Stephen** Belfast, Northern Ireland, Oct. 31, 1949.
**Reason, Rex** Berlin, Germany, Nov. 30, 1928. Pasadena Playhouse.
**Reddy, Helen** Melbourne, Australia, Oct. 25, 1942.
**Redford, Robert** Santa Monica, CA, Aug. 18, 1937. AADA.
**Redgrave, Corin** London, England, July 16, 1939.
**Redgrave, Lynn** London, England, Mar. 8, 1943.
**Redgrave, Vanessa** London, England, Jan. 30, 1937.
**Redman, Joyce** County Mayo, Ireland, Dec. 9, 1918. RADA.
**Reed, Nikki** W. Los Angeles, CA, May 17, 1988.
**Reed, Pamela** Tacoma, WA, Apr. 2, 1949.
**Rees, Roger** Aberystwyth, Wales, May 5, 1944.
**Reese, Della** Detroit, MI, July 6, 1932.
**Reeves, Keanu** Beiruit, Lebanon, Sept. 2, 1964.
**Regehr, Duncan** Lethbridge, Canada, Oct. 5, 1952.
**Reid, Elliott** New York, NY, Jan. 16, 1920.
**Reid, Tara** Wyckoff, NJ, Nov. 8, 1975.
**Reid, Tim** Norfolk, VA, Dec, 19, 1944.
**Reilly, John C.** Chicago, IL, May 24, 1965.
**Reiner, Carl** New York, NY, Mar. 20, 1922. Georgetown.
**Reiner, Rob** New York, NY, Mar. 6, 1947. UCLA.
**Reinhold, Judge** (Edward Ernest, Jr.) Wilmington, DE, May 21, 1957. NC
**Reinking, Ann** Seattle, WA, Nov. 10, 1949.
**Reiser, Paul** New York, NY, Mar. 30, 1957.
**Remar, James** Boston, MA, Dec. 31, 1953. Neighborhood Playhouse.
**Renfro, Brad** Knoxville, TN, July 25, 1982.
**Reno, Jean** (Juan Moreno) Casablanca, Morocco, July 30, 1948.
**Reubens, Paul** (Paul Reubenfeld) Peekskill, NY, Aug. 27, 1952.
**Revill, Clive** Wellington, NZ, Apr. 18, 1930.
**Rey, Antonia** Havana, Cuba, Oct. 12, 1927.
**Reynolds, Burt** Waycross, GA, Feb. 11, 1935. Florida State U.
**Reynolds, Debbie** (Mary Frances Reynolds) El Paso, TX, Apr. 1, 1932.
**Reynolds, Ryan** Vancouver, BC, Can, Oct. 23, 1976.
**Rhames, Ving** (Irving Rhames) New York, NY, May 12, 1959.

**Rhoades, Barbara** Poughkeepsie, NY, Mar. 23, 1947.
**Rhodes, Cynthia** Nashville, TN, Nov. 21, 1956.
**Rhys, Paul** Neath, Wales, Dec. 19, 1963.
**Rhys-Davies, John** Salisbury, England, May 5, 1944.
**Rhys Meyers, Jonathan** Cork, Ireland, July 27, 1977.
**Ribisi, Giovanni** Los Angeles, CA, Dec. 17, 1974.
**Ricci, Christina** Santa Monica, CA, Feb. 12, 1980.
**Richard, Cliff** (Harry Webb) India, Oct. 14, 1940.
**Richards, Denise** Downers Grove, IL, Feb. 17, 1972.
**Richards, Michael** Culver City, CA, July 14, 1949.
**Richardson, Joely** London, England, Jan. 9, 1965.
**Richardson, Miranda** Southport, England, Mar. 3, 1958.
**Richardson, Natasha** London, England, May 11, 1963.
**Rickles, Don** New York, NY, May 8, 1926. AADA.
**Rickman, Alan** Hammersmith, England, Feb. 21, 1946.
**Riegert, Peter** New York, NY, Apr. 11, 1947. U Buffalo.
**Rifkin, Ron** New York, NY, Oct. 31, 1939.
**Rigg, Diana** Doncaster, England, July 20, 1938. RADA.
**Ringwald, Molly** Rosewood, CA, Feb. 16, 1968.
**Rivers, Joan** (Molinsky) Brooklyn, NY, June 8, 1933.
**Roache, Linus** Manchester, England, Feb. 1, 1964.
**Robards, Sam** New York, NY, Dec. 16, 1963.
**Robb, AnnaSophia** Denver, CO, Dec. 8, 1993.
**Robbins, Tim** New York, NY, Oct. 16, 1958. UCLA.
**Roberts, Dallas** Houston, TX, May 10, 1970.
**Roberts, Eric** Biloxi, MS, Apr. 18, 1956. RADA.
**Roberts, Julia** Atlanta, GA, Oct. 28, 1967.
**Roberts, Tanya** (Leigh) Bronx, NY, Oct. 15, 1954.
**Roberts, Tony** New York, NY, Oct. 22, 1939. Northwestern.
**Robertson, Cliff** La Jolla, CA, Sept. 9, 1925. Antioch College.
**Robertson, Dale** Oklahoma City, OK, July 14, 1923.
**Robinson, Chris** West Palm Beach, FL, Nov. 5, 1938. LACC.
**Robinson, Jay** New York, NY, Apr. 14, 1930.
**Robinson, Roger** Seattle, WA, May 2, 1940. USC.
**Rochefort, Jean** Paris, France, Apr. 29, 1930.
**Rochon, Lela** Los Angeles, CA, Apr. 17, 1964.
**Rock, The** (Dwayne Johnson) Hayward, CA, May 2, 1972.
**Rock, Chris** Brooklyn, NY, Feb. 7, 1966.
**Rockwell, Sam** Daly City, CA, Nov. 5, 1968.
**Rodriguez, Freddy** Chicago, IL, Jan. 17, 1975.
**Rodriguez, Michelle** Bexar County, TX, July 12, 1978.
**Rogen, Seth** Vancouver, BC, Canada, Apr. 14, 1982.
**Rogers, Mimi** Coral Gables, FL, Jan. 27, 1956.
**Rogers, Wayne** Birmingham, AL, Apr. 7, 1933. Princeton.
**Romano, Ray** Queens, NY, Dec. 21, 1957.
**Romijn, Rebecca** Berkeley, CA, Nov. 6, 1972.
**Ronan, Saoirse** New York, NY, Apr. 12, 1994.
**Ronstadt, Linda** Tucson, AZ, July 15, 1946.
**Rooker, Michael** Jasper, AL, Apr. 6, 1955.
**Rooney, Mickey** (Joe Yule, Jr.) Brooklyn, NY, Sept. 23, 1920.
**Rose, Reva** Chicago, IL, July 30, 1940. Goodman.
**Ross, Diana** Detroit, MI, Mar. 26, 1944.
**Ross, Justin** Brooklyn, NY, Dec. 15, 1954.

**Ross, Katharine** Hollywood, CA, Jan. 29, 1943. Santa Rosa College.
**Rossellini, Isabella** Rome, Italy, June 18, 1952.
**Rossovich, Rick** Palo Alto, CA, Aug. 28, 1957.
**Rossum, Emmy** New York, NY, Sept. 12, 1986.
**Roth, Tim** London, England, May 14, 1961.
**Roundtree, Richard** New Rochelle, NY, Sept. 7, 1942. Southern Il.
**Rourke, Mickey** (Philip Andre Rourke, Jr.) Schenectady, NY, Sept. 16, 1956.
**Routh, Brandon** Des Moines, IA, Oct. 9, 1979.
**Rowe, Nicholas** London, England, Nov. 22, 1966, Eton.
**Rowlands, Gena** Cambria, WI, June 19, 1934.
**Rubin, Andrew** New Bedford, MA, June 22, 1946. AADA.
**Rubinek, Saul** Fohrenwold, Germany, July 2, 1948.
**Rubinstein, John** Los Angeles, CA, Dec. 8, 1946. UCLA.
**Ruck, Alan** Cleveland, OH, July 1, 1960.
**Rucker, Bo** Tampa, FL, Aug. 17, 1948.
**Rudd, Paul** Boston, MA, May 15, 1940.
**Rudd, Paul** Passaic, NJ, Apr. 6, 1969.
**Rudner, Rita** Miami, FL, Sept. 17, 1955.
**Ruehl, Mercedes** Queens, NY, Feb. 28, 1948.
**Ruffalo, Mark** Kenosha, WI, Nov. 22, 1967.
**Rule, Janice** Cincinnati, OH, Aug. 15, 1931.
**Rupert, Michael** Denver, CO, Oct. 23, 1951. Pasadena Playhouse.
**Rush, Barbara** Denver, CO, Jan. 4, 1927. U California.
**Rush, Geoffrey** Toowoomba, Australia, July 6, 1951. U Queensland.
**Russell, Jane** Bemidji, MI, June 21, 1921. Max Reinhardt School.
**Russell, Keri** Fountain Valley, CA, Mar. 23, 1976.
**Russell, Kurt** Springfield, MA, Mar. 17, 1951.
**Russell, Theresa** (Paup) San Diego, CA, Mar. 20, 1957.
**Russo, James** New York, NY, Apr. 23, 1953.
**Russo, Rene** Burbank, CA, Feb. 17, 1954.
**Rutherford, Ann** Toronto, ON, Canada, Nov. 2, 1920.
**Ryan, Amy** Queens, NY, Nov. 30, 1969.
**Ryan, Meg** Fairfield, CT, Nov. 19, 1961. NYU.
**Ryder, Winona** (Horowitz) Winona, MN, Oct. 29, 1971.

**Sacchi, Robert** Bronx, NY, 1941. NYU.
**Sägebrecht, Marianne** Starnberg, Bavaria, Aug. 27, 1945.
**Saint, Eva Marie** Newark, NJ, July 4, 1924. Bowling Green State U.
**Saint James, Susan** (Suzie Jane Miller) Los Angeles, CA, Aug. 14, 1946. Conn. College.
**St. John, Betta** Hawthorne, CA, Nov. 26, 1929.
**St. John, Jill** (Jill Oppenheim) Los Angeles, CA, Aug. 19, 1940.
**Sala, John** Los Angeles, CA, Oct. 5, 1962.
**Saldana, Theresa** Brooklyn, NY, Aug. 20, 1954.
**Salinger, Matt** Windsor, VT, Feb. 13, 1960. Princeton, Columbia.
**Salt, Jennifer** Los Angeles, CA, Sept. 4, 1944. Sarah Lawrence College.
**Samms, Emma** London, England, Aug. 28, 1960.
**San Giacomo, Laura** Orange, NJ, Nov. 14, 1961.
**Sanders, Jay O.** Austin, TX, Apr. 16, 1953.
**Sandler, Adam** Bronx, NY, Sept. 9, 1966. NYU.
**Sands, Julian** Yorkshire, England, Jan 15, 1958.
**Sands, Tommy** Chicago, IL, Aug. 27, 1937.
**San Juan, Olga** New York, NY, Mar. 16, 1927.

**Sara, Mia** (Sarapocciello) Brooklyn, NY, June 19, 1967.
**Sarandon, Chris** Beckley, WV, July 24, 1942. U West Virginia., Catholic U.
**Sarandon, Susan** (Tomalin) New York, NY, Oct. 4, 1946. Catholic U.
**Sarrazin, Michael** Quebec City, Canada, May 22, 1940.
**Sarsgaard, Peter** Scott Air Force Base, Illinois, Mar. 7, 1971. Washington U St. Louis
**Savage, Fred** Highland Park, IL, July 9, 1976.
**Savage, John** (Youngs) Long Island, NY, Aug. 25, 1949. AADA.
**Saviola, Camille** Bronx, NY, July 16, 1950.
**Savoy, Teresa Ann** London, England, July 18, 1955.
**Sawa, Devon** Vancouver, BC, Canada, Sept. 7, 1978.
**Saxon, John** (Carmen Orrico) Brooklyn, NY, Aug. 5, 1935.
**Sbarge, Raphael** New York, NY, Feb. 12, 1964.
**Scacchi, Greta** Milan, Italy, Feb. 18, 1960.
**Scalia, Jack** Brooklyn, NY, Nov. 10, 1951.
**Scarwid, Diana** Savannah, GA, Aug. 27, 1955, AADA. Pace U.
**Scheider, Roy** Orange, NJ, Nov. 10, 1932. Franklin-Marshall.
**Schell, Maximilian** Vienna, Austria, Dec. 8, 1930.
**Schlatter, Charlie** Englewood, NJ, May 1, 1966. Ithaca College.
**Schneider, John** Mt. Kisco, NY, Apr. 8, 1960.
**Schneider, Maria** Paris, France, Mar. 27, 1952.
**Schneider, Paul** Asheville, NC, Mar. 16, 1976.
**Schreiber, Liev** San Francisco, CA, Oct. 4, 1967.
**Schroder, Rick** Staten Island, NY, Apr. 13, 1970.
**Schuck, John** Boston, MA, Feb. 4, 1940.
**Schultz, Dwight** Baltimore, MD, Nov. 24, 1947.
**Schwartzman, Jason** Los Angeles, CA, June 26, 1980.
**Schwarzenegger, Arnold** Austria, July 30, 1947.
**Schwimmer, David** Queens, NY, Nov. 12, 1966.
**Schygulla, Hanna** Katlowitz, Germany, Dec. 25, 1943.
**Sciorra, Annabella** New York, NY, Mar. 24, 1964.
**Scofield, Paul** Hurstpierpoint, England, Jan. 21, 1922. London Mask Theatre School.
**Scoggins, Tracy** Galveston, TX, Nov. 13, 1959.
**Scolari, Peter** Scarsdale, NY, Sept. 12, 1956. New York, NYC.
**Scott, Campbell** South Salem, NY, July 19, 1962. Lawrence.
**Scott, Debralee** Elizabeth, NJ, Apr. 2, 1953.
**Scott, Lizabeth** (Emma Matso) Scranton, PA, Sept. 29, 1922.
**Scott, Seann William** Cottage Grove, MN, Oct. 3, 1976.
**Scott Thomas, Kristin** Redruth, Cornwall, England, May 24, 1960.
**Seagal, Steven** Detroit, MI, Apr. 10, 1951.
**Sears, Heather** London, England, Sept. 28, 1935.
**Sedgwick, Kyra** New York, NY, Aug. 19, 1965. USC.
**Segal, George** New York, NY, Feb. 13, 1934. Columbia U.
**Seinfeld, Jerry** Brooklyn, NY, Apr. 29, 1954.
**Selby, David** Morganstown, WV, Feb. 5, 1941. U West Virginia.
**Sellars, Elizabeth** Glasgow, Scotland, May 6, 1923.
**Selleck, Tom** Detroit, MI, Jan. 29, 1945. USC.
**Sernas, Jacques** Lithuania, July 30, 1925.
**Seth, Roshan** New Delhi, India, Aug. 17, 1942.
**Sevigny, Chloë** Springfield, MA, Nov. 18, 1974.
**Sewell, Rufus** Twickenham, England, Oct. 29, 1967.
**Seymour, Jane** (Joyce Frankenberg) Hillingdon, England, Feb. 15, 1952.

**Shalhoub, Tony** Green Bay, WI, Oct. 9, 1953.

**Shandling, Garry** Chicago, IL, Nov. 29, 1949.

**Shannon, Molly** Shaker Heights, OH, Sept. 16, 1964.

**Sharif, Omar** (Michel Shalhoub) Alexandria, Egypt, Apr. 10, 1932. Victoria College.

**Shatner, William** Montreal, Quebec, Canada, Mar. 22, 1931. McGill U.

**Shaver, Helen** St. Thomas, ON, Canada, Feb. 24, 1951.

**Shaw, Fiona** Cork, Ireland, July 10, 1955. RADA.

**Shaw, Stan** Chicago, IL, July 14, 1952.

**Shawn, Wallace** New York, NY, Nov. 12, 1943. Harvard.

**Shea, John** North Conway, NH, Apr. 14, 1949. Bates, Yale.

**Shearer, Harry** Los Angeles, CA, Dec. 23, 1943. UCLA.

**Sheedy, Ally** New York, NY, June 13, 1962. USC.

**Sheen, Charlie** (Carlos Irwin Estevez) Santa Monica, CA, Sept. 3, 1965.

**Sheen, Martin** (Ramon Estevez) Dayton, OH, Aug. 3, 1940.

**Sheen, Michael** Newport, Wales, Feb. 5, 1969.

**Sheffer, Craig** York, PA, Apr. 23, 1960. E. Stroudsberg U.

**Sheffield, John** Pasadena, CA, Apr. 11, 1931. UCLA.

**Shelley, Carol** London, England, Aug. 16, 1939.

**Shelton, Marley** Los Angeles, CA, Apr. 12, 1974.

**Shepard, Dax** Milford, MI, Jan. 2, 1975.

**Shepard, Sam** (Rogers) Ft. Sheridan, IL, Nov. 5, 1943.

**Shepherd, Cybill** Memphis, TN, Feb. 18, 1950. Hunter, NYU.

**Sher, Antony** Cape Town, South Africa, June 14, 1949.

**Sherbedgia, Rade** Korenica, Croatia, July 27, 1946.

**Sheridan, Jamey** Pasadena, CA, July 12, 1951.

**Shields, Brooke** New York, NY, May 31, 1965.

**Shire, Talia** Lake Success, NY, Apr. 25, 1946. Yale.

**Short, Martin** Toronto, ON, Canada, Mar. 26, 1950. McMaster U.

**Shue, Elisabeth** S. Orange, NJ, Oct. 6, 1963. Harvard.

**Siemaszko, Casey** Chicago, IL, March 17, 1961.

**Sikking, James B.** Los Angeles, CA, Mar. 5, 1934.

**Silva, Henry** Brooklyn, NY, Sept. 15, 1928.

**Silver, Ron** New York, NY, July 2, 1946. SUNY.

**Silverman, Jonathan** Los Angeles, CA, Aug. 5, 1966. USC.

**Silverman, Sarah** Bedford, NH, Dec. 1, 1970.

**Silverstone, Alicia** San Francisco, CA, Oct. 4, 1976.

**Silverstone, Ben** London, England, Apr. 9, 1979.

**Simmons, Jean** London, England, Jan. 31, 1929. Aida Foster School.

**Simon, Paul** Newark, NJ, Nov. 5, 1942.

**Simpson, O.J.** (Orenthal James) San Francisco, CA, July 9, 1947. UCLA.

**Sinbad** (David Adkins) Benton Harbor, MI, Nov. 10, 1956.

**Sinden, Donald** Plymouth, England, Oct. 9, 1923. Webber-Douglas.

**Singer, Lori** Corpus Christi, TX, May 6, 1962. Juilliard.

**Sinise, Gary** Chicago, IL, Mar. 17, 1955.

**Sizemore, Tom** Detroit, MI, Sept. 29, 1964.

**Skarsgård, Stellan** Gothenburg, Sweden, June 13, 1951.

**Skerritt, Tom** Detroit, MI, Aug. 25, 1933. Wayne State U.

**Skye, Ione** (Leitch) London, England, Sept. 4, 1971.

**Slater, Christian** New York, NY, Aug. 18, 1969.

**Slater, Helen** New York, NY, Dec. 15, 1965.

**Slattery, John** Boston, MA, Aug. 13, 1963.

**Smart, Amy** Topanga Canyon, CA, Mar. 26, 1976.

**Smith, Charles Martin** Los Angeles, CA, Oct. 30, 1953. Cal State U.

**Smith, Jaclyn** Houston, TX, Oct. 26, 1947.

**Smith, Jada Pinkett** Baltimore, MD, Sept. 18, 1971.

**Smith, Kerr** Exton, PA, Mar. 9, 1972.

**Smith, Kevin** Red Bank, NJ, Aug. 2, 1970.

**Smith, Kurtwood** New Lisbon, WI, July 3, 1942.

**Smith, Lewis** Chattanooga, TN, 1958. Actors Studio.

**Smith, Lois** Topeka, KS, Nov. 3, 1930. U Washington.

**Smith, Maggie** Ilford, England, Dec. 28, 1934.

**Smith, Roger** South Gate, CA, Dec. 18, 1932. U Arizona.

**Smith, Will** Philadelphia, PA, Sept. 25, 1968.

**Smithers, William** Richmond, VA, July 10, 1927. Catholic U.

**Smits, Jimmy** Brooklyn, NY, July 9, 1955. Cornell U.

**Smollett, Jurnee** New York, NY, Oct. 1, 1986.

**Snipes, Wesley** New York, NY, July 31, 1963. SUNY/Purchase.

**Snoop Dogg** (Calvin Broadus) Long Beach, CA, Oct. 20, 1971.

**Snow, Brittany** Tampa, FL, Mar. 9, 1986.

**Sobieksi, Leelee** (Liliane Sobieski) New York, NY, June 10, 1982.

**Solomon, Bruce** New York, NY, Aug. 12, 1944. U Miami, Wayne State U.

**Somerhalder, Ian** Covington, LA, Dec. 8, 1978.

**Somers, Suzanne** (Mahoney) San Bruno, CA, Oct. 16, 1946. Lone Mt. College.

**Sommer, Elke** (Schletz) Berlin, Germany, Nov. 5, 1940.

**Sommer, Josef** Greifswald, Germany, June 26, 1934.

**Sorvino, Mira** Tenafly, NJ, Sept. 28, 1967.

**Sorvino, Paul** New York, NY, Apr. 13, 1939. AMDA.

**Soto, Talisa** (Miriam Soto) Brooklyn, NY, Mar. 27, 1967.

**Soul, David** Chicago, IL, Aug. 28, 1943.

**Spacek, Sissy** Quitman, TX, Dec. 25, 1949. Actors Studio.

**Spacey, Kevin** So. Orange, NJ, July 26, 1959. Juilliard.

**Spade, David** Birmingham, MS, July 22, 1964.

**Spader, James** Buzzards Bay, MA, Feb. 7, 1960.

**Spall, Timothy** London, England, Feb. 27, 1957.

**Spano, Vincent** Brooklyn, NY, Oct. 18, 1962.

**Spenser, Jeremy** London, England, July 16, 1937.

**Spinella, Stephen** Naples, Italy, Oct. 11, 1956. NYU.

**Springfield, Rick** (Richard Spring Thorpe) Sydney, Australia, Aug. 23, 1949.

**Stadlen, Lewis J.** Brooklyn, NY, Mar. 7, 1947. Neighborhood Playhouse.

**Stahl, Nick** Dallas, TX, Dec. 5, 1979.

**Stallone, Frank** New York, NY, July 30, 1950.

**Stallone, Sylvester** New York, NY, July 6, 1946. U Miami.

**Stamp, Terence** London, England, July 23, 1939.

**Stanford, Aaron** Westford, MA, Dec. 18, 1977.

**Stang, Arnold** Chelsea, MA, Sept. 28, 1925.

**Stanton, Harry Dean** Lexington, KY, July 14, 1926.

**Stapleton, Jean** New York, NY, Jan. 19, 1923.

**Starr, Ringo** (Richard Starkey) Liverpool, England, July 7, 1940.

**Statham, Jason** London, England, Sept. 12, 1972.

**Staunton, Imelda** London, England, Jan. 9, 1956.

**Steele, Barbara** England, Dec. 29, 1937.

**Steele, Tommy** London, England, Dec. 17, 1936.

**Steenburgen, Mary** Newport, AR, Feb. 8, 1953. Neighborhood Playhouse.

**Stern, Daniel** Bethesda, MD, Aug. 28, 1957.

**Sternhagen, Frances** Washington, DC, Jan. 13, 1932.

**Stevens, Andrew** Memphis, TN, June 10, 1955.

**Stevens, Connie** (Concetta Ann Ingolia) Brooklyn, NY, Aug. 8, 1938. Hollywood Professional School.

**Stevens, Fisher** Chicago, IL, Nov. 27, 1963. NYU.

**Stevens, Stella** (Estelle Eggleston) Hot Coffee, MS, Oct. 1, 1936.

**Stevenson, Juliet** Essex, England, Oct. 30, 1956.

**Stevenson, Parker** Philadelphia, PA, June 4, 1953. Princeton.

**Stewart, Alexandra** Montreal, Quebec, Canada, June 10, 1939. Louvre.

**Stewart, Elaine** (Elsy Steinberg) Montclair, NJ, May 31, 1929.

**Stewart, French** (Milton French Stewart) Albuquerque, NM, Feb. 20, 1964.

**Stewart, Jon** (Jonathan Stewart Liebowitz) Trenton, NJ, Nov. 28, 1962.

**Stewart, Kristen** Los Angeles, CA, Apr. 9, 1990.

**Stewart, Martha** (Martha Haworth) Bardwell, KY, Oct. 7, 1922.

**Stewart, Patrick** Mirfield, England, July 13, 1940.

**Stiers, David Ogden** Peoria, IL, Oct. 31, 1942.

**Stiles, Julia** New York, NY, Mar. 28, 1981.

**Stiller, Ben** New York, NY, Nov. 30, 1965.

**Stiller, Jerry** New York, NY, June 8, 1931.

**Sting** (Gordon Matthew Sumner) Wallsend, England, Oct. 2, 1951.

**Stockwell, Dean** Hollywood, CA, Mar. 5, 1935.

**Stockwell, John** (John Samuels, IV) Galveston, TX, Mar. 25, 1961. Harvard.

**Stoltz, Eric** Whittier, CA, Sept. 30, 1961. USC.

**Stone, Dee Wallace** (Deanna Bowers) Kansas City, MO, Dec. 14, 1948. UKS.

**Storm, Gale** (Josephine Cottle) Bloomington, TX, Apr. 5, 1922.

**Stowe, Madeleine** Eagle Rock, CA, Aug. 18, 1958.

**Strassman, Marcia** New York, NY, Apr. 28, 1948.

**Strathairn, David** San Francisco, CA, Jan. 26, 1949.Williams Col.

**Strauss, Peter** New York, NY, Feb. 20, 1947.

**Streep, Meryl** (Mary Louise) Summit, NJ, June 22, 1949 Vassar, Yale.

**Streisand, Barbra** Brooklyn, NY, Apr. 24, 1942.

**Stritch, Elaine** Detroit, MI, Feb. 2, 1925. Drama Workshop.

**Stroud, Don** Honolulu, HI, Sept. 1, 1937.

**Struthers, Sally** Portland, OR, July 28, 1948. Pasadena Playhouse.

**Studi, Wes** (Wesley Studie) Nofire Hollow, OK, Dec. 17, 1947.

**Summer, Donna** (LaDonna Gaines) Boston, MA, Dec. 31, 1948.

**Sumpter, Jeremy** Monterey, CA, Feb. 5, 1989.

**Sutherland, Donald** St. John, New Brunswick, Canada, July 17, 1935. U Toronto.

**Sutherland, Kiefer** Los Angeles, CA, Dec. 18, 1966.

**Suvari, Mena** Newport, RI, Feb. 9, 1979.

**Svenson, Bo** Goreborg, Sweden, Feb. 13, 1941. UCLA.

**Swank, Hilary** Bellingham, WA, July 30, 1974.

**Swayze, Patrick** Houston, TX, Aug. 18, 1952.

**Sweeney, D. B.** (Daniel Bernard Sweeney) Shoreham, NY, Nov. 14, 1961.

**Swinton, Tilda** London, England, Nov. 5, 1960.

**Swit, Loretta** Passaic, NJ, Nov. 4, 1937, AADA.

**Sykes, Wanda** Portsmouth, VA, Mar. 7, 1964.

**Symonds, Robert** Bistow, AK, Dec. 1, 1926. Texas U.

**Syms, Sylvia** London, England, June 1, 1934. Convent School.

**Szarabajka, Keith** Oak Park, IL, Dec. 2, 1952. U Chicago.

**T, Mr.** (Lawrence Tero) Chicago, IL, May 21, 1952.

**Tabori, Kristoffer** (Siegel) Los Angeles, CA, Aug. 4, 1952.

**Takei, George** Los Angeles, CA, Apr. 20, 1939. UCLA.

**Talbot, Nita** New York, NY, Aug. 8, 1930. Irvine Studio School.

**Tamblyn, Amber** Santa Monica, CA, May 14, 1983.

**Tamblyn, Russ** Los Angeles, CA, Dec. 30, 1934.

**Tambor, Jeffrey** San Francisco, CA, July 8, 1944.

**Tarantino, Quentin** Knoxville, TN, Mar. 27, 1963.

**Tate, Larenz** Chicago, IL, Sept. 8, 1975.

**Tautou, Audrey** Beaumont, France, Aug. 9, 1978.

**Taylor, Elizabeth** London, England, Feb. 27, 1932. Byron House School.

**Taylor, Lili** Glencoe, IL, Feb. 20, 1967.

**Taylor, Noah** London, England, Sept. 4, 1969.

**Taylor, Renée** New York, NY, Mar. 19, 1935.

**Taylor, Rod** (Robert) Sydney, Australia, Jan. 11, 1929.

**Taylor-Young, Leigh** Washington, DC, Jan. 25, 1945. Northwestern.

**Teefy, Maureen** Minneapolis, MN, Oct. 26, 1953, Juilliard.

**Temple, Shirley** Santa Monica, CA, Apr. 23, 1927.

**Tennant, Victoria** London, England, Sept. 30, 1950.

**Tenney, Jon** Princeton, NJ, Dec. 16, 1961.

**Terzieff, Laurent** Paris, France, June 25, 1935.

**Tewes, Lauren** Braddock, PA, Oct. 26, 1954.

**Thacker, Russ** Washington, DC, June 23, 1946. Montgomery College.

**Thaxter, Phyllis** Portland, ME, Nov. 20, 1921. St. Genevieve.

**Thelen, Jodi** St. Cloud, MN, June 12, 1962.

**Theron, Charlize** Benoni, South Africa, Aug. 7, 1975.

**Thewlis, David** Blackpool, England, Mar. 20, 1963.

**Thieriot, Max** Los Altos Hills, CA, Oct. 14, 1988.

**Thomas, Henry** San Antonio, TX, Sept. 8, 1971.

**Thomas, Jay** New Orleans, LA, July 12, 1948.

**Thomas, Jonathan Taylor** (Weiss) Bethlehem, PA, Sept. 8, 1981.

**Thomas, Marlo** (Margaret) Detroit, MI, Nov. 21, 1937. USC.

**Thomas, Philip Michael** Columbus, OH, May 26, 1949. Oakwood College.

**Thomas, Richard** New York, NY, June 13, 1951. Columbia.

**Thompson, Emma** London, England, Apr. 15, 1959. Cambridge.

**Thompson, Fred Dalton** Sheffield, AL, Aug. 19, 1942.

**Thompson, Jack** (John Payne) Sydney, Australia, Aug. 31, 1940.

**Thompson, Lea** Rochester, MN, May 31, 1961.

**Thompson, Rex** New York, NY, Dec. 14, 1942.

**Thompson, Sada** Des Moines, IA, Sept. 27, 1929. Carnegie Tech.

**Thornton, Billy Bob** Hot Spring, AR, Aug. 4, 1955.

**Thorson, Linda** Toronto, ON, Canada, June 18, 1947. RADA.

**Thurman, Uma** Boston, MA, Apr. 29, 1970.

**Ticotin, Rachel** Bronx, NY, Nov. 1, 1958.

**Tierney, Maura** Boston, MA, Feb. 3, 1965.

**Tiffin, Pamela** (Wonso) Oklahoma City, OK, Oct. 13, 1942.

**Tighe, Kevin** Los Angeles, CA, Aug. 13, 1944.

**Tilly, Jennifer** Los Angeles, CA, Sept. 16, 1958.

**Tilly, Meg** Texada, Canada, Feb. 14, 1960.

**Timberlake, Justin** Memphis, TN, Jan. 31, 1981.

**Tobolowsky, Stephen** Dallas, TX, May 30, 1951. Southern Methodist U.

**Todd, Beverly** Chicago, IL, July 1, 1946.

**Todd, Richard** Dublin, Ireland, June 11, 1919. Shrewsbury School.

**Todd, Tony** Washington, DC, Dec. 4, 1954.

**Tolkan, James** Calumet, MI, June 20, 1931.

**Tomei, Marisa** Brooklyn, NY, Dec. 4, 1964. NYU.
**Tomlin, Lily** Detroit, MI, Sept. 1, 1939. Wayne State U.
**Topol** (Chaim Topol) Tel Aviv, Israel, Sept. 9, 1935.
**Torn, Rip** Temple, TX, Feb. 6, 1931. U Texas.
**Torres, Liz** New York, NY, Sept. 27, 1947. NYU.
**Totter, Audrey** Joliet, IL, Dec. 20, 1918.
**Towsend, Robert** Chicago, IL, Feb. 6, 1957.
**Townsend, Stuart** Dublin, Ireland, Dec. 15, 1972.
**Trachtenberg, Michelle** New York, NY, Oct. 11, 1985.
**Travanti, Daniel J.** Kenosha, WI, Mar. 7, 1940.
**Travis, Nancy** Astoria, NY, Sept. 21, 1961.
**Travolta, Joey** Englewood, NJ, Oct. 14, 1950.
**Travolta, John** Englewood, NJ, Feb. 18, 1954.
**Trejo, Danny** Los Angeles, CA, May 16, 1944.
**Trintignant, Jean-Louis** Pont-St. Esprit, France, Dec. 11, 1930. DullinBala-chova Drama School.
**Tripplehorn, Jeanne** Tulsa, OK, June 10, 1963.
**Tsopei, Corinna** Athens, Greece, June 21, 1944.
**Tubb, Barry** Snyder, TX, 1963. Am Consv Th.
**Tucci, Stanley** Katonah, NY, Jan. 11, 1960.
**Tucker, Chris** Decatur, GA, Aug. 31, 1972.
**Tucker, Jonathan** Boston, MA, May 31, 1982.
**Tucker, Michael** Baltimore, MD, Feb. 6, 1944.
**Tudyk, Alan** El Paso, TX, March 16, 1971.
**Tune, Tommy** Wichita Falls, TX, Feb. 28, 1939.
**Tunney, Robin** Chicago, IL, June 19, 1972.
**Turner, Janine** (Gauntt) Lincoln, NE, Dec. 6, 1963.
**Turner, Kathleen** Springfield, MO, June 19, 1954. U Maryland.
**Turner, Tina** (Anna Mae Bullock) Nutbush, TN, Nov. 26, 1938.
**Turturro, John** Brooklyn, NY, Feb. 28, 1957. Yale.
**Tushingham, Rita** Liverpool, England, Mar. 14, 1940.
**Twiggy** (Lesley Hornby) London, England, Sept. 19, 1949.
**Twomey, Anne** Boston, MA, June 7, 1951. Temple U.
**Tyler, Liv** Portland, ME, July 1, 1977.
**Tyrrell, Susan** San Francisco, CA, Mar. 18, 1945.
**Tyson, Cathy** Liverpool, England, June 12, 1965. Royal Shake. Co.
**Tyson, Cicely** New York, NY, Dec. 19, 1933. NYU.

**Uggams, Leslie** New York, NY, May 25, 1943. Juilliard.
**Ulliel, Gaspard** Boulogne-Billancourt, France, Nov. 25, 1984.
**Ullman, Tracey** Slough, England, Dec. 30, 1959.
**Ullmann, Liv** Tokyo, Japan, Dec. 10, 1938. Webber-Douglas Acad.
**Ulrich, Skeet** (Bryan Ray Ulrich) North Carolina, Jan. 20, 1969.
**Underwood, Blair** Tacoma, WA, Aug. 25, 1964. Carnegie-Mellon U.
**Unger, Deborah Kara** Victoria, BC, Canada, May 12, 1966.
**Union, Gabrielle** Omaha, NE, Oct. 29, 1973.

**Vaccaro, Brenda** Brooklyn, NY, Nov. 18, 1939. Neighborhood Playhouse.
**Van Ark, Joan** New York, NY, June 16, 1943. Yale.
**Van Damme, Jean-Claude** (J-C Vorenberg) Brussels, Belgium, Apr. 1, 1960.
**Van De Ven, Monique** Zeeland, Netherlands, July 28, 1952.
**Van Der Beek, James** Chesire, CT, March 8, 1977.

**Van Devere, Trish** (Patricia Dressel) Englewood Cliffs, NJ, Mar. 9, 1945. Ohio Wesleyan.
**Van Dien, Casper** Ridgefield, NJ, Dec. 18, 1968.
**Van Doren, Mamie** (Joan Lucile Olander) Rowena, SD, Feb. 6, 1933.
**Van Dyke, Dick** West Plains, MO, Dec. 13, 1925.
**Vanity** (Denise Katrina Smith) Niagara, ON, Can, Jan. 4, 1959.
**Van Pallandt, Nina** Copenhagen, Denmark, July 15, 1932.
**Van Patten, Dick** New York, NY, Dec. 9, 1928.
**Van Patten, Joyce** New York, NY, Mar. 9, 1934.
**Van Peebles, Mario** New York, NY, Jan. 15, 1958. Columbia U.
**Van Peebles, Melvin** Chicago, IL, Aug. 21, 1932.
**Vance, Courtney B.** Detroit, MI, Mar. 12, 1960.
**Vardalos, Nia** Winnipeg, Manitoba, Canada, Sept. 24, 1962.
**Vartan, Michael** Boulogne-Billancourt, France, Nov. 27, 1968.
**Vaughn, Robert** New York, NY, Nov. 22, 1932. USC.
**Vaughn, Vince** Minneapolis, MN, Mar. 28, 1970.
**Vega, Isela** Hermosillo, Mexico, Nov. 5, 1940.
**Veljohnson, Reginald** New York, NY, Aug. 16, 1952.
**Vennera, Chick** Herkimer, NY, Mar. 27, 1952. Pasadena Playhouse.
**Venora, Diane** Hartford, CT, Aug. 10, 1952. Juilliard.
**Vereen, Ben** Miami, FL, Oct. 10, 1946.
**Victor, James** (Lincoln Rafael Peralta Diaz) Santiago, D.R., July 27, 1939. Haaren HS/New York, NY.
**Vincent, Jan-Michael** Denver, CO, July 15, 1944. Ventura.
**Violet, Ultra** (Isabelle Collin-Dufresne) Grenoble, France, Sept. 6, 1935.
**Visnjic, Goran** Sibenik, Yugoslavia, Sept. 9, 1972. .
**Voight, Jon** Yonkers, NY, Dec. 29, 1938. Catholic U.
**Von Bargen, Daniel** Cincinnati, OH, June 5, 1950. Purdue.
**Von Dohlen, Lenny** Augusta, GA, Dec. 22, 1958. U Texas.
**Von Sydow, Max** Lund, Sweden, July 10, 1929. Royal Drama Theatre.

**Wagner, Lindsay** Los Angeles, CA, June 22. 1949.
**Wagner, Natasha Gregson** Los Angeles, CA, Sept. 29, 1970.
**Wagner, Robert** Detroit, MI, Feb. 10, 1930.
**Wahl, Ken** Chicago, IL, Feb. 14, 1953.
**Waite, Genevieve** Cape Town, South Africa, Feb. 19, 1948.
**Waite, Ralph** White Plains, NY, June 22, 1929. Yale.
**Waits, Tom** Pomona, CA, Dec. 7, 1949.
**Walken, Christopher** Astoria, NY, Mar. 31, 1943. Hofstra.
**Walker, Clint** Hartfold, IL, May 30, 1927. USC.
**Walker, Paul** Glendale, CA, Sept. 12, 1973.
**Wallach, Eli** Brooklyn, NY, Dec. 7, 1915. CCNY, U Texas.
**Wallach, Roberta** New York, NY, Aug. 2, 1955.
**Wallis, Shani** London, England, Apr. 5, 1941.
**Walsh, Dylan** Los Angeles, CA, Nov. 17, 1963.
**Walsh, M. Emmet** Ogdensburg, NY, Mar. 22, 1935. Clarkson College, AADA.
**Walter, Jessica** Brooklyn, NY, Jan. 31, 1944 Neighborhood Playhouse.
**Walter, Tracey** Jersey City, NJ, Nov. 25, 1942.
**Walters, Julie** London, England, Feb. 22, 1950.
**Walton, Emma** London, England, Nov. 1962. Brown U.
**Wanamaker, Zoë** New York, NY, May 13, 1949.
**Ward, Burt** (Gervis) Los Angeles, CA, July 6, 1945.
**Ward, Fred** San Diego, CA, Dec. 30, 1942.

**Ward, Rachel** London, England, Sept. 12, 1957.
**Ward, Sela** Meridian, MS, July 11, 1956.
**Ward, Simon** London, England, Oct. 19, 1941.
**Warner, David** Manchester, England, July 29, 1941. RADA.
**Warner, Malcolm-Jamal** Jersey City, NJ, Aug. 18, 1970.
**Warren, Jennifer** New York, NY, Aug. 12, 1941. U Wisc.
**Warren, Lesley Ann** New York, NY, Aug. 16, 1946.
**Warren, Michael** South Bend, IN, Mar. 5, 1946. UCLA.
**Washington, Denzel** Mt. Vernon, NY, Dec. 28, 1954. Fordham.
**Washington, Kerry** Bronx, NY, Jan. 31, 1977.
**Wasson, Craig** Ontario, OR, Mar. 15, 1954. U Oregon.
**Watanabe, Ken** Koide, Japan, Oct. 21, 1959.
**Waterston, Sam** Cambridge, MA, Nov. 15, 1940. Yale.
**Watson, Emily** London, England, Jan. 14, 1967.
**Watson, Emma** Oxford, England, Apr. 15, 1990.
**Watts, Naomi** Shoreham, England, Sept. 28, 1968.
**Wayans, Damon** New York, NY, Sept. 4, 1960.
**Wayans, Keenen Ivory** New York, NY, June 8, 1958. Tuskegee Inst.
**Wayans, Marlon** New York, NY, July 23, 1972.
**Wayans, Shawn** New York, NY, Jan. 19, 1971.
**Wayne, Patrick** Los Angeles, CA, July 15, 1939. Loyola.
**Weathers, Carl** New Orleans, LA, Jan. 14, 1948. Long Beach CC.
**Weaver, Fritz** Pittsburgh, PA, Jan. 19, 1926.
**Weaver, Sigourney** (Susan) New York, NY, Oct. 8, 1949. Stanford, Yale.
**Weaving, Hugo** Austin, Nigeria, Apr. 4, 1960. NIDA.
**Webber, Mark** Minneapolis, MN, July 19, 1980.
**Weber, Steven** Queens, NY, March 4, 1961.
**Wedgeworth, Ann** Abilene, TX, Jan. 21, 1935. U Texas.
**Weisz, Rachel** London, England, Mar. 7, 1971. Cambridge.
**Welch, Raquel** (Tejada) Chicago, IL, Sept. 5, 1940.
**Weld, Tuesday** (Susan) New York, NY, Aug. 27, 1943. Hollywood Professional School.
**Weldon, Joan** San Francisco, CA, Aug. 5, 1933. San Francisco Conservatory.
**Weller, Peter** Stevens Point, WI, June 24, 1947. Am. Th. Wing.
**Welling, Tom** New York, NY, Apr. 26, 1977.
**Wendt, George** Chicago, IL, Oct. 17, 1948.
**West, Adam** (William Anderson) Walla Walla, WA, Sept. 19, 1929.
**West, Dominic** Sheffield, England, Oct. 15, 1969.
**West, Shane** Baton Rouge, LA, June 10, 1978.
**Westfeldt, Jennifer** Guilford, CT, Feb. 2, 1971.
**Wettig, Patricia** Cincinatti, OH, Dec. 4, 1951. Temple U.
**Whaley, Frank** Syracuse, NY, July 20, 1963. SUNY/Albany.
**Whalley-Kilmer, Joanne** Manchester, England, Aug. 25, 1964.
**Wheaton, Wil** Burbank, CA, July 29, 1972.
**Whishaw, Ben** Clifton, England, Oct. 14, 1980.
**Whitaker, Denzel** Torrance, CA, June 15, 1990.
**Whitaker, Forest** Longview, TX, July 15, 1961.
**Whitaker, Johnny** Van Nuys, CA, Dec. 13, 1959.
**White, Betty** Oak Park, IL, Jan. 17, 1922.
**White, Charles** Perth Amboy, NJ, Aug. 29, 1920. Rutgers U.
**White, Julie** San Diego, CA, June 4, 1961.
**Whitelaw, Billie** Coventry, England, June 6, 1932.
**Whitman, Stuart** San Francisco, CA, Feb. 1, 1929. CCLA.

**Whitmore, James** White Plains, NY, Oct. 1, 1921. Yale.
**Whitney, Grace Lee** Detroit, MI, Apr. 1, 1930.
**Whitton, Margaret** Philadelphia, PA, Nov. 30, 1950.
**Widdoes, Kathleen** Wilmington, DE, Mar. 21, 1939.
**Widmark, Richard** Sunrise, MN, Dec. 26, 1914. Lake Forest.
**Wiest, Dianne** Kansas City, MO, Mar. 28, 1948. U Maryland.
**Wilby, James** Burma, Feb. 20, 1958.
**Wilcox, Colin** Highlands, NC, Feb. 4, 1937. U Tennessee.
**Wilder, Gene** (Jerome Silberman) Milwaukee, WI, June 11, 1935. U Iowa.
**Wilkinson, Tom** Leeds, England, Dec. 12, 1948. U Kentucky.
**Willard, Fred** Shaker Heights, OH, Sept. 18, 1939.
**Williams, Billy Dee** New York, NY, Apr. 6, 1937.
**Williams, Cara** (Bernice Kamiat) Brooklyn, NY, June 29, 1925.
**Williams, Cindy** Van Nuys, CA, Aug. 22, 1947. KACC.
**Williams, Clarence, III** New York, NY, Aug. 21, 1939.
**Williams, Esther** Los Angeles, CA, Aug. 8, 1921.
**Williams, JoBeth** Houston, TX, Dec 6, 1948. Brown U.
**Williams, Michelle** Kalispell, MT, Sept. 9, 1980.
**Williams, Olivia** London, England, Jan. 1, 1968.
**Williams, Paul** Omaha, NE, Sept. 19, 1940.
**Williams, Robin** Chicago, IL, July 21, 1951. Juilliard.
**Williams, Treat** (Richard) Rowayton, CT, Dec. 1, 1951.
**Williams, Vanessa** Tarrytown, NY, Mar. 18, 1963.
**Williamson, Fred** Gary, IN, Mar. 5, 1938. Northwestern.
**Williamson, Nicol** Hamilton, Scotland, Sept. 14, 1938.
**Willis, Bruce** Penns Grove, NJ, Mar. 19, 1955.
**Willison, Walter** Monterey Park, CA, June 24, 1947.
**Wilson, Demond** New York, NY, Oct. 13, 1946. Hunter College.
**Wilson, Elizabeth** Grand Rapids, MI, Apr. 4, 1925.
**Wilson, Lambert** Neuilly-sur-Seine, France, Aug. 3, 1958.
**Wilson, Luke** Dallas, TX, Sept. 21, 1971.
**Wilson, Owen** Dallas, TX, Nov. 18, 1968.
**Wilson, Patrick** Norfolk, VA, July 3, 1973.
**Wilson, Rainn** Seattle, WA, Jan. 20, 1966.
**Wilson, Scott** Atlanta, GA, Mar. 29, 1942.
**Wilson, Stuart** Guildford, England, Dec. 25, 1946.
**Wincott, Jeff** Toronto, ON, Canada, May 8, 1957.
**Wincott, Michael** Toronto, ON, Canada, Jan. 6, 1959. Juilliard.
**Windom, William** New York, NY, Sept. 28, 1923. Williams College.
**Winfrey, Oprah** Kosciusko, MS, Jan. 29, 1954. Tennessee State U.
**Winger, Debra** Cleveland, OH, May 17, 1955. Cal State.
**Winkler, Henry** New York, NY, Oct. 30, 1945. Yale.
**Winn, Kitty** Washington, DC, Feb, 21, 1944. Boston U.
**Winningham, Mare** Phoenix, AZ, May 6, 1959.
**Winslet, Kate** Reading, England, Oct. 5, 1975.
**Winslow, Michael** Spokane, WA, Sept. 6, 1960.
**Winstone, Ray** London, England, Feb. 19, 1957.
**Winter, Alex** London, England, July 17, 1965. NYU.
**Winters, Jonathan** Dayton, OH, Nov. 11, 1925. Kenyon College.
**Withers, Googie** Karachi, India, Mar. 12, 1917. Italia Conti.
**Withers, Jane** Atlanta, GA, Apr. 12, 1926.
**Witherspoon, Reese** (Laura Jean Reese Witherspoon) Nashville, TN, Mar. 22, 1976.

**Wolf, Scott** Newton, MA, June 4, 1968.
**Wong, B.D.** San Francisco, CA, Oct. 24,1962.
**Wong, Russell** Troy, NY, Mar. 1, 1963. Santa Monica College.
**Wood, Elijah** Cedar Rapids, IA, Jan 28, 1981.
**Wood, Evan Rachel** Raleigh, NC, Sept. 7, 1987.
**Woodard, Alfre** Tulsa, OK, Nov. 2, 1953. Boston U.
**Woodlawn, Holly** (Harold Ajzenberg) Juana Diaz, PR, 1947.
**Woods, James** Vernal, UT, Apr. 18, 1947. MIT.
**Woodward, Edward** Croyden, Surrey, England, June 1, 1930.
**Woodward, Joanne** Thomasville, GA, Feb. 27, 1930. Neighborhood Playhouse.
**Woronov, Mary** Brooklyn, NY, Dec. 8, 1946. Cornell.
**Wright, Amy** Chicago, IL, Apr. 15, 1950.
**Wright, Jeffrey** Washington, DC, Dec. 7, 1965. Amherst Col.
**Wright, Max** Detroit, MI, Aug. 2, 1943. Wayne State U.
**Wright, Robin** Dallas, TX, Apr. 8, 1966.
**Wuhl, Robert** Union City, NJ, Oct. 9, 1951. U Houston.
**Wyle, Noah** Los Angeles, CA, June 2, 1971.
**Wymore, Patrice** Miltonvale, KS, Dec. 17, 1926.
**Wynn, May** (Donna Lee Hickey) New York, NY, Jan. 8, 1930.
**Wynter, Dana** (Dagmar) London, England, June 8. 1927. Rhodes U.

**Yelchin, Anton** St. Petersburg, Russia, March 11, 1989.
**Yoba, Malik** Bronx, NY, Sept. 17, 1967.
**York, Michael** Fulmer, England, Mar. 27, 1942. Oxford.
**York, Susannah** London, England, Jan. 9, 1941. RADA.
**Young, Alan** (Angus) North Shield, England, Nov. 19, 1919.
**Young, Burt** Queens, NY, Apr. 30, 1940.
**Young, Chris** Chambersburg, PA, Apr. 28, 1971.
**Young, Sean** Louisville, KY, Nov. 20, 1959. Interlochen.
**Yulin, Harris** Los Angeles, CA, Nov. 5, 1937.
**Yun-Fat, Chow** Lamma Island, Hong Kong, May 18, 1955.

**Zacharias, Ann** Stockholm, Sweden, Sept. 19, 1956.
**Zadora, Pia** Hoboken, NJ, May 4, 1954.
**Zahn, Steve** Marshall, MN, Nov. 13, 1968.
**Zegers, Kevin** Woodstock, ON, Canada, Sept. 19, 1984.
**Zellweger, Renée** Katy, TX, Apr. 25, 1969.
**Zerbe, Anthony** Long Beach, CA, May 20, 1939.
**Zeta-Jones, Catherine** Swansea, Wales, Sept. 25, 1969.
**Zimbalist, Efrem, Jr.** New York, NY, Nov. 30, 1918. Yale.
**Zuniga, Daphne** Berkeley, CA, Oct. 28, 1963. UCLA

# OBITUARIES

2007

Michaelangelo Antonioni

Ingmar Bergman

Joey Bishop

Janet Blair

Yvonne de Carlo

Kitty Carlisle

Betty Hutton

Deborah Kerr

Michael Kidd

Barry Nelson

Miyoshi Umuki

Jane Wyman

TIGE ANDREWS, **86,** Brooklyn-born character actor, best known for playing Capt. Adam Greer on the ABC series *The Mod Squad*, died of cardiac arrest on Jan. 27, 2007 in Encino, CA. His film credits include *Mister Roberts, Imitation General, Onionhead, A Private's Affair,* and *The Last Tycoon.* Survived by six children and eleven grandchildren.

MICHELANGELO ANTONIONI, **94,** one of the foremost figures of modern Italian cinema, best known in the U.S. for his 1966 film *Blowup* (for which he earned two Oscar nominations, as writer and director), died in Rome on July 30, 2007. His other films as director-writer include *L'Avventura, La Notte, Eclipse, Red Desert, Zabriskie Point, The Passenger,* and *Beyond the Clouds.* Survived by his wife.

BRUCE BENNETT **(Herman Brix), 100,** Tacoma-born Olympic athlete-turned-actor, died of complications of a broken hip on Feb. 24, 2007 in Los Angeles, CA. Under his real name he appeared in such films as *The New Adventures of Tarzan, Million Dollar Racket,* and *The Fighting Devil Dogs.* His credits after changing his name to Bruce Bennett include *Atlantic Convoy, The More the Merrier, Sahara, There's Something About a Soldier, Mildred Pierce, A Stolen Life, Nora Prentiss, Dark Passage, The Treasure of the Sierra Madre, The Younger Brothers, Task Force, The Great Missouri Raid, Sudden Fear, Strategic Air Command, Love Me Tender, The Alligator People,* and *Fiend of Dope Island* (which he also co-wrote). Survived by his son, daughter, three grandchildren, and two great-grandchildren.

INGMAR BERGMAN **(Ernst Ingmar Bergman), 89,** Sweden's most revered and notable filmmaker, whose worldwide acclaim came with the 1956 drama *The Seventh Seal,* died in his sleep on July 30, 2007 at his home in Faro, Sweden. In addition to three of his films (*The Virgin Spring, Through a Glass Darkly,* and *Fanny and Alexander*) receiving the Academy Award for Best Foreign Language Film, he was nominated for directing Oscars for *Cries and Whispers* (also screenplay and picture nominations), *Face to Face,* and *Fanny and Alexander* (also screenplay nomination), and for writing *Wild Strawberries, Through a Glass Darkly,* and *Autumn Sonata.* Other films include *Smiles of a Summer Night, Brink of Life, The Magician* (1959), *Winter Light, Persona, Hour of the Wolf, Shame, The Passion of Anna, The Touch, Scenes from a Marriage, The Magic Flute, The Serpent's Egg,* and *From the Life of Marionettes.* Survivors include his fifth wife and nine children from various wives and relationships.

JOEY BISHOP **(Joseph Abraham Gottlieb), 89,** Bronx-born comedian-actor, the last surviving member of Frank Sinatra's fabled "Rat Pack," known for his deadpan delivery, died of multiple causes at his home in Newport Beach, CA on Oct. 17, 2007. He could be seen in such films as *The Deep Six, The Naked and the Dead, Onionhead, Ocean's Eleven* (1960), *Sergeants 3, Texas Across the River, A Guide for the Married Man, Who's Minding the Mint?, Valley of the Dolls, The Delta Force, Betsy's Wedding,* and *Mad Dog Time* (written and directed by his son, Larry). His wife of 58 years died in 1999. He is survived by his son, two grandchildren, and his companion.

JANET BLAIR **(Martha Janet Lafferty), 85,** Pennsylvania-born screen, television, and stage actress who dabbled in both dramatic and musical roles, died from complications of pneumonia on Feb. 19, 2007 in Santa Monica. Her films include *Three Girls About Town* (her debut, in 1941), *Broadway, My Sister Eileen* (1942), *Something to Shout About, Once Upon a Time, Tonight and Every Night, Tars and Spars, The Fabulous Dorseys, The Black Arrow, The Fuller Brush Man, Boys' Night Out, Burn Witch Burn, The One and Only Genuine Original Family Band,* and *Won Ton Ton the Dog Who Saved Hollywood.* She is survived by her two children.

MICHAEL BLODGETT, **68,** Minneapolis-born actor-writer, died of a heart attack on Nov. 14, 2007 in Los Angeles, CA. He appeared in such films as *The Trip, Catalina Caper, Beyond the Valley of the Dolls,* and *There Was a Crooked Man…* before becoming a writer. His script credits including *Rent-a-Cop, Hero and the Terror* (from his novel), *Turner & Hooch,* and *Run.* He is survived by three daughters.

ROSCOE LEE BROWNE, **81,** New Jersey–born character actor, died of cancer in Los Angeles, CA on April 11, 2007. His film credits include *Black Like Me, Topaz, Cisco Pike, The Cowboys, The World's Greatest Athlete, Logan's Run, Legal Eagles, Jumpin' Jack Flash, The Mambo Kings, Last Summer in the Hamptons,* and *Babe* (narrator). On television he won an Emmy for guesting on *The Cosby Show.* He is survived by two brothers and a sister.

CAROL BRUCE **(Shirley Levy), 87,** Long Island–born screen, stage, and television actress-singer, died in Woodland Hills, CA on October 9, 2007 of chronic obstructive pulmonary disease. Her film credits include *Keep 'em Flying; Behind the Eight Ball; American Gigolo;* and *Planes, Trains, & Automobiles.* Survived by her daughter.

SONNY BUPP **(Moyer MacClendon Bupp), 79,** New York City–born child bit player whose one notable role was portraying Orson Welles' son in the 1941 classic *Citizen Kane,* died on Nov. 1, 2007 in Henderson, NV. He could be seen in such other films as *Swing Your Lady, Angels with Dirty Faces, Boy Trouble, The Renegade Trail, Parole Fixer, Abe Lincoln in Illinois, Three Faces West,* and *Tennessee Johnson.* Survivors include his wife.

LEO BURMESTER, **62,** screen, stage, and television character actor, died on June 28, 2007 in New York. His film credits include *Cruising, Daniel, Sweet Liberty, Big Business, The Last Temptation of Christ, The Abyss, Innocent Blood, Passion Fish, A Perfect World, Lone Star, Limbo,* and *City by the Sea.* Survived by his wife, son, and daughter.

RON CAREY **(Ronald Joseph Cicenia), 71,** Newark-born character player–comedian best known for his role as Officer Carl Levitt on the sitcom *Barney Miller,* died in Los Angeles, CA of a stroke on Jan. 19, 2007. His films include *The Out-of-Towners, Silent Movie, High Anxiety, Fatso, History of the World Part 1,* and *Johnny Dangerously.* He is survived by his wife and his brother.

**KITTY CARLISLE HART** (Catherine Conn), **96,** New Orleans-born actress-singer who appeared opposite the Marx Brothers in the 1935 comedy classic *A Night at the Opera*, died at her home in Manhattan on April 17, 2007 of heart failure. In addition to appearing in such films as *Murder at the Vanities, She Loves Me Not, Here is My Heart, Hollywood Canteen, Radio Days,* and *Six Degrees of Separation*, she served as chairman of the New York Council on the Arts and appeared as a panelist on the long-running game show *To Tell the Truth*. Survivors include two children from her marriage to writer-director Moss Hart (who died in 1961) and three grandchildren.

**AJ CAROTHERS, 75,** Houston-born screenwriter, died on April 9, 2007 in Los Angeles, CA of cancer. He scripted the films *Miracle of the White Stallions, Emil and the Detectives* (1964), *The Happiest Millionaire, Never a Dull Moment, Hero at Large,* and *The Secret of My Success* (1987).

**JEAN-PIERRE CASSEL** (Jean-Pierre Crochon), **74,** French actor, died of cancer on April 19, 2007. Among his many films are *The Lovers, The Seven Deadly Sins, Those Magnificent Men in Their Flying Machines, Is Paris Burning?, Anyone Can Play, Army of Shadows, Baxter!, The Three Musketeers* (1974), *Murder on the Orient Express, Who is Killing the Great Chefs of Europe, Vincent & Theo, The Favor the Watch & the Very Big Fish,* and *The Diving Bell and the Butterfly*. Survived by his two sons and a daughter.

**LONNY CHAPMAN, 87,** Tulsa-born character actor, died of heart disease on Oct. 12, 2007 in Studio City, CA. His films include *East of Eden, The Stalking Moon, The Reivers, I Walk the Line, The Cowboys, Norma Rae, The Border, 52 Pick-Up,* and *The Hunted*.

**BOB CLARK** (Benjamin Clark), **67,** Louisiana-born filmmaker who directed, wrote, and produced the 1982 hit comedy *Porky's*, died on Apr. 4, 2007 in Pacific Palisades, CA in a head-on collision with a drunk driver. His son was also killed in the crash. His other films include *Children Shouldn't Play with Dead Things, Murder by Decree, Tribute, A Christmas Story, Rhinestone, Turk 182!, From the Hip,* and *It Runs in the Family*.

**LARAINE DAY** (Laraine Johnson), **87 or 90,** Utah-born actress perhaps best known for playing Nurse Mary Lamont in seven Dr. Kildare dramas for MGM, died on Nov. 10, 2007 in Irvine, UT. Her other films include *Stella Dallas* (1937), *Tarzan Finds a Son, Foreign Correspondent, My Son My Son, Mr. Lucky, Fingers at the Window, Unholy Partners, A Yank on the Burma Road, The Story of Dr. Wassell, Tycoon, The High and the Mighty,* and *The Third Voice*. She is survived by a son and daughter from her first marriage, to baseball manager Leo Durocher; two daughters from her second marriage, to producer Michel M. Grilikhes; her twin brother; and several grandchildren.

**YVONNE DE CARLO** (Peggy Yvonne Middleton), **84,** Vancouver-born screen, stage, and television actress whose film assignments included playing Sephora, the wife of Moses, in the 1956 blockbuster *The Ten Commandments*, died on January 8, 2007 in Woodland Hills, CA of natural causes. Launching her career in the early 1940s as a unbilled bit player in such movies as *This Gun for Hire* and *Road to Morroco*, she later appeared as a star in such pictures as *Song of Scheherazade; Brute Force; Black Bart; Casbah; Criss Cross; Calamity Jane and Sam Bass; Buccaneer's Girl; Silver City; Hurricane Smith; Sombrero; The Captain's Paradise; Flame of the Islands; Band of Angels; Timbuktu; McLintock!; A Global Affair; Munster Go Home; Arizona Bushwhackers; The Seven Minutes; Won Ton Ton, the Dog Who Saved Hollywood; The Man with Bogart's Face; American Gothic;* and *Oscar*. On television she became best known for playing Lily Munster on *The Munsters*, while she made her mark on Broadway introducing the song "I'm Still Here" in *Follies*. No reported survivors.

**DONFELD** (Donald Lee Feld), **72,** Los Angeles-born costume designer, died of natural causes in Los Angeles, CA on Feb. 3, 2007. He earned Oscar nominations for his work on *Days of Wine and Roses, They Shoot Horses Don't They?, Tom Sawyer,* and *Prizzi's Honor*. His many other credits include *Mr. Hobbs Takes a Vacation, Under the Yum Yum Tree, Viva Las Vegas, The Great Race, The Phynx, Fun with Dick and Jane* (1977), *The China Syndrome,* and *Brainstorm*. Survivors include his brother, an aunt, and several cousins.

**PETER ELLENSHAW, 93,** London-born matte artist, art director-production designer and special effects creator for Disney Studios, died on Feb. 12, 2007 in Santa Barbara, CA of natural causes. He won an Academy Award for his work on *Mary Poppins* and received additional Oscar nominations for *Bedknobs and Broomsticks, The Island at the Top of the World,* and *The Black Hole*.

**MICHAEL EVANS** (John Michael Evans), **87,** British screen, stage, and television actor best known to American audiences for playing Col. Douglas Austin on *The Young and the Restless*, died in Los Angeles, CA on Sept. 4, 2007. He could also be seen in such films as *Island Rescue (Appointment with Venus), Bye Bye Birdie, Riot on Sunset Strip, The Love-Ins,* and *Time After Time*. Survived by two sons and two sisters.

**MALI FINN, 69,** Illinois-born casting director, died of melanoma on Nov. 28, 2007 in Sonoma, CA. Her credits include *The Untouchables, Hot Shots!, Batman Forever, L.A. Confidential, Titanic* (1997), *The Matrix, The Green Mile, Wonder Boys, 8 Mile, North Country, Running with Scissors, Shooter,* and *The Assassination of Jesse James*.

**JOHN FLYNN, 75,** Chicago-born film director, died on April 4, 2007 of natural causes. His movies include *The Sergeant, The Outfit* (which he also wrote), *Rolling Thunder, Best Seller, Lock Up,* and *Out for Justice*.

FREDDIE FRANCIS, **89,** British cinematographer, who won Academy Awards for his work on *Sons and Lovers* and *Glory,* died on March 17, 2007 in Ilseworth, England. He photographed such other films as *Room at the Top, Saturday Night and Sunday Morning, The Innocents, The Elephant Man, Cape Fear* (1991), *School Ties,* and *The Straight Story,* as well as directing several horror thrillers including *Dr. Terror's House of Horrors, Torture Garden, Dracula Has Risen from the Grave, Trog, Tales That Witness Madness,* and *The Doctor and the Devils.* He is survived by his second wife and three children.

RICHARD FRANKLIN, **58,** Australian filmmaker, died in his native Melbourne on July 11, 2007. His films include *Patrick* (also prod.), *Roadgames* (also prod.), *Psycho II, Cloak & Dagger* (1984), and *FX2.*

ALICE GHOSTLEY, **81,** Missouri-born character player, best known for her roles on the series *Bewitched* and *Designing Women,* died of cancer at her home in Studio City, CA on Sept. 21, 2007. Among her films were *New Faces, To Kill a Mockingbird, My Six Loves, The Flim-Flam Man, The Graduate, With Six You Get Eggroll, Viva Max!, Rabbit Test,* and *Grease.* On Broadway she won a Tony Award for her performance in *The Sign in Sidney Brustein's Window.* Survived by her sister.

BERNARD GORDON, **88,** Connecticut-born screenwriter who became one of the Hollywood Ten when he was blacklisted in the 1950s, died of bone cancer on May 11, 2007 in Hollywood. His credits include *Flesh and Fury, Lawless Breed, Earth vs. the Flying Saucers, Hellcats of the Navy, Escape from San Quentin* (the last three billed under the pseudonym "Raymond T. Marcus"), *The Day of the Triffids, Circus World, Battle of the Bulge* (the last three fronted by Phillip Yordan), and *Krakatoa East of Java.* Survived by his daughter.

ROBERT GOULET, **73,** Massachusetts-born, Canadian-raised singer-actor who launched his career singing "If Ever I Would Leave You" in the 1960 Broadway musical *Camelot,* died on October 30, 2007 in Los Angeles, CA while awaiting a lung transplant. He had been diagnosed with interstitial pulmonary fibrosis. Among his films were *Gay Purr-ee* (voice), *Honeymoon Hotel, I'd Rather Be Rich, Atlantic City, Beetlejuice,* and *The Naked Gun 2 1/2: The Smell of Fear.* He is survived by his third wife; a daughter from his first marriage; two sons, from his marriage to actress Carol Lawrence; and two grandchildren.

DABBS GREER **(Robert William Greer), 90,** Missouri-born character actor, died on April 28, 2007 in Pasadena, CA following a battle with kidney and heart disease. His many credits include *Devil's Doorway, Room for One More, House of Wax* (1953), *Riot in Cell Block 11, Invasion of the Body Snatchers* (1956), *Baby Face Nelson, It! The Terror from Beyond Space, Shenandoah, The Cheyenne Social Club, Two Moon Junction, Pacific Heights,* and *The Green Mile.*

MERV GRIFFIN, **82,** California-born TV host, entrepreneur, actor, and singer, died of prostate cancer on Aug. 12, 2007 in Los Angeles, CA. In addition to hosting the syndicated *Merv Griffin Show* for over twenty years, he created the long-running game shows *Jeopardy* and *Wheel of Fortune.* He was seen in such movies as *Cattle Town, By the Light of the Silvery Moon, So This is Love, Phantom of the Rue Morgue, Hello Down There, Two Minute Warning, The Seduction of Joe Tynan, The Man with Two Brains,* and *The Lonely Guy.* Survived by his son and two grandchildren.

CHARLES B. GRIFFITH, **77,** Chicago-born screenwriter whose work for filmmaker Roger Corman included the 1960 cult classic *The Little Shop of Horrors,* died in San Diego, CA on Sept. 28, 2007. Among his other credits are *It Conquered the World, Attack of the Crab Monsters, Bucket of Blood, Rock All Night, The Wild Angels,* and *Death Race 2000.* Survived by his wife, a daughter, and four grandchildren.

GEORGE GRIZZARD, **79,** North Carolina–born screen, stage, and television actor, who won a Tony for his performance in the revival of Edward Albee's *A Delicate Balance,* died on Oct. 2, 2007 in New York of complications resulting from lung cancer. His films include *From the Terrace, Advise & Consent, Warning Shot, Comes a Horseman, Seems Like Old Times, Wrong is Right, Bachelor Party, Wonder Boys,* and *Flags of Our Fathers.* He is survived by his partner.

CURTIS HARRINGTON, **80,** Los Angeles–born filmmaker who specialized in such macabre films as *Night Tide* and *What's the Matter with Helen?,* died on May 6, 2007 at his home in the Hollywood Hills. His other movies include *Games, Whoever Slew Auntie Roo?, The Killing Kind,* and *Ruby.* No immediate survivors.

BETTY HUTTON **(Elizabeth June Thornberg), 86,** Michigan-born screen, stage, and television actress-singer, whose brash personality carried such motion pictures as *The Miracle of Morgan's Creek* and *Annie Get Your Gun,* died from complications of colon cancer on March 12, 2007 in Palm Springs, CA. Following her film debut in *The Fleet's In,* she appeared in such movies as *Star Spangled Rhythm, Let's Face It, Happy Go Lucky, And the Angels Sing, Here Come the Waves, Incendiary Blonde, The Stork Club, Duffy's Tavern, The Perils of Pauline* (1947), *The Greatest Show on Earth, Somebody Loves Me,* and *Spring Reunion.* She is survived by three daughters.

RICHARD JENI, **49,** Brooklyn-born standup comedian-actor, died on March 11, 2007 in West Hollywood, CA from a self-inflicted gunshot wound. He was seen in such movies as *The Mask, An Allan Smithee Film: Burn Hollywood Burn,* and *The Aristocrats.*

MARCIA MAE JONES, **82,** Los Angeles–born actress, died of pneumonia on Sept. 2, 2007 in Woodland Hills, CA. Her credits include *The Champ* (1931), *The Life of Emile Zola, Heidi* (1937), *The Adventures of Tom Sawyer* (1938), *The Little Princess* (1939), *First Love* (1939), *Anne of Windy Poplars, The Gang's All Here, The Youngest Profession, The Daughter of Rosie O'Grady,* and *The Way We Were.*

**DEBORAH KERR**, **86 (Deborah Kerr-Trimmer),** Scottish actress, who went from stardom in British films to become one of the best known and most acclaimed international performers of the 1950s, died on Oct. 16, 2007 in Suffolk, England, having suffered for years from Parkinson's disease. She earned six Oscar nominations for her performances in the films *Edward, My Son; From Here to Eternity; The King and I; Heaven Knows, Mr. Allison; Separate Tables;* and *The Sundowners* (1960). Following her debut in *Major Barbara* in 1940, she was seen in such other pictures as *Hatter's Castle, The Life and Death of Colonel Blimp, The Adventuress (I See a Dark Stranger), Vacation from Marriage (Perfect Strangers), Black Narcissus, The Hucksters* (her U.S. debut, in 1947), *King Solomon's Mines* (1950), *Quo Vadis, The Prisoner of Zenda* (1952), *Young Bess, Julius Caesar* (1953), *The End of the Affair* (1955), *The Proud and the Profane, Tea and Sympathy, An Affair to Remember, Bonjour Tristesse, The Journey, Beloved Infidel, The Grass is Greener, The Naked Edge, The Innocents, The Chalk Garden, The Night of the Iguana, Casino Royale* (1967), *Prudence and the Pill, The Gypsy Moths,* and *The Assam Garden.* At the 1994 Academy Award ceremony she was given a special Oscar for her contributions to film. Her second husband, writer Peter Viertel, survived her only to pass away less than a month later. Her other survivors were two daughters and three grandchildren.

**MICHAEL KIDD** **(Milton Greenwald), 92,** Brooklyn-born choreographer, perhaps best known to film audiences for his exuberant dances in *Seven Brides for Seven Brothers,* died of cancer on Dec. 23, 2007 in Los Angeles, CA. His other film credits include *Where's Charley?; The Band Wagon; Guys and Dolls; Merry Andrew* (which he also directed); *Li'l Abner; Star!; Hello, Dolly!;* and *Movie, Movie* (also actor), in addition to acting in *It's Always Fair Weather, Smile,* and *Skin Deep.* He was given an honorary Academy Award in 1997. On Broadway he won Tony Awards for *Finian's Rainbow, Guys and Dolls, Can-Can, Li'l Abner,* and *Destry Rides Again.* He is survived by his second wife and four children.

**LASZLO KOVACS**, **74,** Hungarian cinematographer, who achieved fame through his work on the influential 1969 film *Easy Rider,* died in his sleep on July 21, 2007. His other movies include *Psych-Out, Targets, Getting Straight, Five Easy Pieces, The Last Movie, What's Up Doc?, The King of Marvin Gardens, Paper Moon, At Long Last Love, Shampoo, Nickelodeon, New York New York, Frances, Ghostbusters, Mask, Say Anything…, Radio Flyer, Copycat,* and *Two Weeks Notice.* He is survived by his wife and two daughters.

**BERNARD L. KOWALSKI**, **78,** Texas-born screen and television director, died on Oct. 26, 2007 in Los Angeles, CA. He directed the theatrical features *Night of the Blood Beast, Hot Car Girl, Blood and Steel, Krakatoa East of Java, Stiletto, Macho Callahan,* and *SSSSSSS.*

**FRANKIE LAINE** **(Francisco Paolo LoVecchio), 93,** Chicago-born singer, whose hit songs included "Mule Train" and "High Noon (Do Not Forsaken Me Oh My Darlin')," died of cardiovascular disease on Feb. 6, 2007 in San Diego. He appeared in the films *Make Believe Ballroom, When You're Smiling, Sunny Side of the Street, Bring Your Smile Along, Meet Me in Las Vegas,* and *He Laughed Last,* and was heard singing the title songs of such movies as *Man without a Star, 3:10 to Yuma* (1957), *Gunfight at the O.K. Corral,* and *Blazing Saddles.* His forty-year marriage to actress Nan Grey ended with her death in 1993. He is survived by his second wife, a brother, his stepdaughters, and two grandsons.

**CHARLES LANE** **(Charles Gerstle Levison), 102,** San Francisco-born character actor, whose ubiquitous appearances in films and television made him one of the most familiar of all faces, died on July 9, 2007 in Los Angeles, CA. His many film credits include *Smart Money, 42nd Street, Twentieth Century, Mr. Deeds Goes to Town, Kentucky, You Can't Take it With You, Mr. Smith Goes to Washington, Johnny Apollo, Rhythm on the River, Buy Me That Town, Ball of Fire, Arsenic and Old Lace, It's a Wonderful Life, Call Northside 777, State of the Union, Apartment for Peggy, I Can Get it for You Wholesale, The Affairs of Dobie Gillis, It's a Mad Mad Mad Mad World, Good Neighbor Sam, The Ugly Dachshund, The Gnome-Mobile, Get to Know Your Rabbit, Movie Movie,* and *Murphy's Romance.* He is survived by his two children and a grandchild.

**MOIRA LISTER**, **84,** Cape Town-born screen, stage, and television actress, died on Oct. 27, 2007 in Cape Town, South Africa. She appeared in such British films as *So Evil My Love, A Run for Your Money, The Cruel Sea, The Deep Blue Sea, Abandon Ship (Seven Waves Away), The Yellow Rolls-Royce,* and *The Double Man.* She is survived by two daughters.

**CALVIN LOCKHART**, **72,** Bahamian screen, stage, and television actor, died on March 29, 2007 in Nassau of complications from a stroke. His films include *A Dandy in Aspic, Dark of the Sun, Salt and Pepper, Joanna, Halls of Anger, Cotton Comes to Harlem, Myra Breckinridge, Melinda, Uptown Saturday Night, Let's Do It Again, The Baltimore Bullet, Coming to America,* and *Wild at Heart.* Survived by his wife and two sons.

**SALEM LUDWIG**, **91,** Brooklyn-born character actor, died on April 1, 2007 in New York. He could be seen in such pictures as *Never Love a Stranger, America America, I Love You Alice B. Toklas, Endless Love, Heartburn, Family Business, I'm Not Rappaport, The Object of My Affection,* and *The Savages.*

**NORMAN MAILER**, **84,** New Jersey-born author of such acclaimed and influential works as *The Naked and the Dead* and *The Executioner's Song,* died of renal failure in New York on Nov. 10, 2007. He directed and wrote the films *Beyond the Law* (also prod.), *Wild 90, Maidstone* (also prod.), and *Tough Guys Don't Dance,* in addition to appearing in such pictures as *Diaries Notes and Sketches, Ragtime, King Lear* (1987), *When We Were Kings,* and *Inside Deep Throat.* He is survived by his sixth wife and eight children, including actors Stephen and Kate, and producer Michael Mailer.

**DELBERT MANN** (Delbert Martin Mann, Jr.), **87,** Kansas-born director, who won an Academy Award for his debut film *Marty*, the 1955 Oscar-winner for Best Picture, died of pneumonia in Los Angeles, CA on November 11, 2007. His other films include *The Bachelor Party, Desire Under the Elms, Separate Tables, Middle of the Night, The Dark at the Top of the Stairs, Lover Come Back* (1961), *The Outsider* (1961), *That Touch of Mink, A Gathering of Eagles, Dear Heart, Mister Buddwing, Fitzwilly,* and *Night Crossing*. Survivors include his two sons and seven grandchildren.

**MARTIN MANULIS, 92,** New York City–born producer, best known for his work on the acclaimed 1950s series *Playhouse 90*, died at his Los Angeles, CA home on Sept. 28, 2007. He also produced the theatrical features *Days of Wine and Roses, Dear Heart, Luv,* and *Duffy*. He is survived by two daughters, a son, a grandson, and two great-grandchildren.

**MARCEL MARCEAU** (Marcel Mangel), **84,** France's foremost mime, best known for his character of Bip, died on September 22, 2007 in Cahors, France. Although principally a stage performer, he could be seen in such films as *Barbarella, Shanks,* and *Silent Movie*. He is survived by two sons and two daughters.

**KERWIN MATHEWS, 81,** Seattle-born actor, best known for his starring roles in the Ray Harryhausen fantasies *The 7th Voyage of Sinbad* and *The 3 Worlds of Gulliver*, died of a heart attack on July 5, 2007 at his home in San Francisco, CA. His other films include *Five Against the House, The Garment Jungle, Tarawa Beachhead, The Devil at 4 O'Clock, Jack the Giant Killer, Barquero,* and *The Boy Who Cried Werewolf*. He is survived by his partner of 46 years, Tom Nicoll.

**BOBBY MAUCH, 86,** Peoria-born actor, best known for starring opposite his twin brother Billy in the 1937 version of *The Prince and the Pauper*, died of complications from a heart condition in Santa Rosa, CA on Oct. 15, 2007. He was also seen in *Penrod's Twin Brother* and *Penrod's Double Trouble*, with his sibling. His brother had died the previous year.

**LOIS MAXWELL** (Lois Hooker), **80,** Ontario-born actress, best known for her fourteen appearances as M's secretary Miss Moneypenny in the James Bond films, died near her home in Perth, Australia on Sept. 29, 2007. She had been suffering from cancer. Aside from appearing in all the 007 adventures from *Dr. No* to *A View to a Kill*, she was seen in such films as *That Hagen Girl, The Dark Past, Scotland Yard Inspector, Aida, Time without Pity, Lolita, The Haunting* (1963), and *Operation Kid Brother*. She is survived by her daughter and her son.

**BARBARA MCNAIR, 72,** Wisconsin-born singer-actress, died on Feb. 4, 2007 in Los Angeles, CA after a long battle with throat cancer. She could be seen in such films as *Spencer's Mountain, If He Hollers Let Him Go, Change of Habit, They Call Me MISTER Tibbs!,* and *The Organization*. Survivors include her sister and her fourth husband.

**BILL MOOR, 76,** Ohio-born character player, died in Englewood, NJ on Nov. 27, 2007. He could be seen in such films as *The Seduction of Joe Tynan, Kramer vs. Kramer, Hanky Panky, Ishtar, The House on Carroll Street, New York Stories, Quiz Show,* and *The Devil's Advocate*.

**KIERON MOORE** (Kieron O'Hanrahan), **82,** Irish character actor, died on July 15, 2007 in France. His films include *Mine Own Executioner, David and Bathsheba, Ten Tall Men, The Key, Darby O'Gill and the Little People, The League of Gentlemen, The Day They Robbed the Bank of England, The Day of the Triffids, The 300 Spartans, The Thin Red Line* (1964), *Crack in the World,* and *Arabesque*. Survived by his wife of sixty years, former actress Barbara White; a daughter; and two sons.

**BARRY NELSON** (Robert Haakon Nielsen), **86 or 89,** San Francisco–born screen, stage, and television actor, died in Bucks County, PA, on April 7, 2007. He could be seen in such motion pictures as *Shadow of the Thin Man* (debut, 1941), *Johnny Eager, The Human Comedy, Bataan, A Guy Named Joe, Winged Victory, The Beginning or the End, Tenth Avenue Angel, The First Traveling Saleslady, Mary Mary* (repeating his Broadway role), *Airport, Pete 'n' Tillie,* and *The Shining*. Survived by his second wife.

**BOBBY PICKETT, 69,** Massachusetts born musician-entertainer-actor who, as Bobby "Boris" Pickett, became a pop cult figure with his 1962 novelty record "Monster Mash," which landed on the charts on no less than three separate occasions, died of leukemia on April 25, 2007 in West Los Angeles, CA. He appeared in such movies as *It's a Bikini World, The Babymaker, Strange Invaders,* and *Sister Sister*. Survived by his daughter, a sister, and two grandchildren.

**ANNE PITONIAK, 85,** Massachusetts-born character actress, whose career was launched with her 1981 Tony-nominated performance in the Broadway drama *'night, Mother*, died of cancer on Apr. 22, 2007 in Manhattan, NY. Among her films were *The Survivors, Agnes of God, The Wizard of Loneliness, Old Gringo, The Ballad of the Sad Café, A Thousand Acres, Where the Money Is,* and *Unfaithful*. She is survived by her son, her daughter, a brother, a sister, and a grandson.

**CARLO PONTI, 94,** Italian producer, best known for his collaborations with his wife of 41 years, actress Sophia Loren, died on Jan. 10, 2007 in Geneva of natural causes. In addition to receiving an Oscar nomination for *Doctor Zhivago*, his other credits include *Mambo, La Strada, The Miller's Beautiful Wife, War and Peace* (1956), *The Black Orchid, That Kind of Woman, Two Women* (for which Loren won an Oscar), *Boccaccio '70, The Condemned of Altona, Yesterday Today and Tomorrow* (the Academy Award–winner for Best Foreign Language Film of 1964), *Marriage Italian Style, Operation Crossbow, Casanova '70, Kiss the Other Sheik, Blowup, More Than a Miracle, Lady Liberty, The Priest's Wife, Andy Warhol's Frankenstein,* and *The Cassandra Crossing*. Although Ponti and Loren had first wed in 1957, the marriage was annulled; their official union came in 1966. In addition to Loren, he is survived by their two sons and two children from a previous marriage.

**TOM POSTON, 85,** Columbus-born character actor-comedian, best known for his roles on the series *The Steve Allen Show* and *The Bob Newhart Show*, died on April 30, 2007 at his home in Los Angeles, CA. His films include *Zotz!*, *The Old Dark House* (1963), *Soldier in the Rain*, *Cold Turkey*, *The Happy Hooker*, *Carbon Copy*, *Krippendorf's Tribe*, and *Christmas with the Kranks*. He is survived by his son and daughter and his third wife, actress Suzanne Pleshette.

**MALA POWERS, 75,** San Francisco–born actress, who played Roxanne opposite Jose Ferrer in the 1950 film of *Cyrano de Bergerac*, died on June 11, 2007 in Santa Monica, CA of complications of leukemia. Her other films include *Tough as They Come*, *Edge of Doom*, *Rose of Cimarron*, *City Beneath the Sea*, *Bengazi*, and *The Storm Rider*. She is survived by her son from her first marriage.

**CHARLES NELSON REILLY, 76,** Bronx-born actor-director, best known for his frequent television work, including appearances on game shows, talk-variety guest spots, and voice work, died on May 25, 2007 at his Beverly Hills, CA home, of pneumonia. His films include *Two Tickets for Paris*, *The Tiger Makes Out*, *Cannonball Run II*, *Body Slam*, and *The First of May*, as well as voices for *All Dogs Go to Heaven* and *Rock-a-Doodle*. On stage, he won a Tony Award for the musical *How to Succeed in Business Without Really Trying*. Survived by his partner of many years.

**CAROL RICHARDS (Carol Swiedler), 84,** singer, died on March 16, 2007 in Vero Beach, CA of complications from pneumonia. She was called on to dub dancer-actress Cyd Charisse on four occasions, in the films *Brigadoon*, *Deep in My Heart*, *It's Always Fair Weather*, and *Silk Stockings*, and was best known for her duet with Bing Crosby on the hit recording "Silver Bells." She is survived by her husband, her twelve children and stepchildren, nineteen grandchildren, and eight great-grandchildren.

**IAN RICHARDSON, 72,** Edinburgh-born screen, stage, and television actor, died on Feb. 9, 2007 in London. His films include *The Persecution and Assassination of Jean-Paul Marat . . .* (as Marat, repeating his stage role), *Man of La Mancha*, *Brazil*, *The Fourth Protocol*, *Cry Freedom*, *Rosencrantz and Guildenstern Are Dead*, *M. Butterfly*, *From Hell*, and *Joyeux Noel*. He is survived by his wife and two sons.

**ANTON RODGERS, 74,** British actor, who sang the Oscar-nominated "Thank You Very Much" in the musical *Scrooge*, died in Reading, England on Dec. 1, 2007. Among his other films are *Rotten to the Core*, *Where Eagles Dare*, *The Fourth Protocol*, *Dirty Rotten Scoundrels*, *Son of the Pink Panther*, and *The Merchant of Venice*.

**STUART ROSENBERG, 79,** Brooklyn-born director, best known for the 1967 Paul Newman drama *Cool Hand Luke*, died of a heart attack on March 15, 2007 at his home in Beverly Hills, CA. His other films include *Murder, Inc.* (co-directed with Burt Balaban), *Question 7*, *The April Fools*, *WUSA*, *Pocket Money*, *The Laughing Policeman*, *The Amityville Horror* (1979), *Brubaker*, *The Pope of Greenwich Village*, and *My Heroes Have Always Been Cowboys*. He is survived by his wife; his son; his daughter-in-law; and four grandchildren.

**AARON RUSSO, 64,** Brooklyn-born movie producer, died of bladder cancer on Aug. 24, 2007 in Los Angeles, CA. His films include *The Rose* (starring Bette Midler, whom Russo once managed), *Partners*, *Trading Places*, *Teachers*, *Wise Guys*, and *Rude Awakening*.

**JOHN P. RYAN, 70,** New York City–born character actor, best known for villainous roles, died on March 27, 2007 in Los Angeles, CA from a stroke. He was seen in such pictures as *A Lovely Way to Die*, *Five Easy Pieces*, *The King of Marvin Gardens*, *It's Alive*, *The Missouri Breaks*, *The Postman Always Rings Twice* (1981), *Breathless* (1983), *The Right Stuff*, *The Cotton Club*, *Runaway Train*, *Hoffa*, and *Bound*. Survived by two daughters.

**GORDON SCOTT (Gordon Merrill Werschkul), 81,** Oregon-born actor best known for portraying Tarzan in six films, starting with *Tarzan's Hidden Jungle* (1955), died in Baltimore on April 30, 2007 of post-heart surgery complications. Other films include *Duel of the Titans* and *Gladiator of Rome*. Survivors include two sisters and a brother.

**MICHEL SERRAULT, 79,** French actor, best known to American audiences for playing cross-dressing Albin in the international hit *La Cage aux Folles*, died of cancer at his home in Honfleur, France on July 29, 2007. Among his many other films were *Three Fables of Love*, *The Annuity*, *Get Out Your Handkerchiefs*, *Garde a vue*, *Nelly and Mr. Arnaud*, *Beaumarchais the Scoundrel*, *The Butterfly*, and *Joyeux Noel*. Survived by his wife and daughter.

**MELVILLE SHAVELSON, 90,** New York City–born writer-director, who received Oscar nominations for his scripts for *The Seven Little Foys* (which he also directed) and *Houseboat* (also director), died of natural causes on Aug. 8, 2007 in Studio City, CA. His other films as writer include *The Princess and the Pirate*, *Wonder Man*, *Sorrowful Jones*, *On Moonlight Bay*, *Room for One More* (*The Easy Way*), *Living it Up*, and, as writer-director, *Beau James*, *The Five Pennies*, *It Started in Naples*, *The Pigeon That Took Rome* (also producer), *A New Kind of Love* (also producer), *Cast a Giant Shadow* (also producer), and *Yours, Mine and Ours*. He is survived by his second wife and his son and daughter from his first marriage.

**SIDNEY SHELDON, 89,** Chicago-born screenwriter and novelist, who won an Academy Award for writing the 1947 comedy *The Bachelor and the Bobby-Soxer*, died of complications of pneumonia on Jan. 30, 2007 in Rancho Mirage, CA. His other script credits include *Easter Parade*, *The Barkleys of Broadway*, *Annie Get Your Gun*, *Nancy Goes to Rio*, *Rich Young and Pretty*, *Dream Wife* (which he also directed), *You're Never Too Young*, *The Buster Keaton Story* (also director, producer), and *Billy Rose's Jumbo*. He later created the television series *The Patty Duke Show* and *I Dream of Jeannie* and became a best-selling novelist of such books as *The Other Side of Midnight* and *Bloodline*, both of which became movies. Survivors include his second wife, his daughter, a brother, and two grandchildren.

**ANNA NICOLE SMITH (Vicky Lynn Hogan), 39,** Houston-born tabloid celebrity, died on Feb. 8, 2007 in Hollywood, CA of a drug overdose. She appeared in two theatrical features, *The Hudsucker Proxy* and *Naked Gun 33 1/3: The Final Insult*. Survived by her daughter.

IRMA ST. PAULE, **approximately 80,** Ukrainian character actress, died in New York on January 9, 2007. Among her films were *The Cemetery Club, Household Saints, Party Girl, Jeffrey, Twelve Monkeys, Trees Lounge, Thinner, Where the Money Is,* and *Duane Hopwood.* No reported survivors.

WILLIAM TUTTLE, **95,** Florida-born makeup artist, who received the very first Academy Award bestowed upon this craft, for the 1964 fantasy *7 Faces of Dr. Lao,* died of natural causes at his home in Pacific Palisades, CA on July 27, 2007. His many other credits include *The Red Badge of Courage, Singin' in the Rain, Julius Caesar* (1953), *Brigadoon, Kismet, Blackboard Jungle, Lust for Life, The Teahouse of the August Moon, The Brothers Karamazov, North by Northwest, The Time Machine* (1960), *The Wonderful World of the Brothers Grimm, Viva Las Vegas, Young Franken- stein, Logan's Run,* and *Love at First Bite.* He is survived by his fifth wife and a daughter from his second marriage.

MIYOSHI UMEKI, **78,** Japanese actress-singer, who became the first Asian performer to win an Academy Award, for her debut performance in the 1957 film *Sayonara,* died of cancer in Licking, MO, on Aug. 28, 2007. Her other films were *Flower Drum Song* (repeating her Broadway role), *Cry for Happy, The Horizontal Lieutenant,* and *A Girl Named Tamiko.* After her role in the early 1970s series *The Courtship of Eddie's Father* she retired from show business. Survived by her son from her second marriage and two grandchildren.

JOSE LUIS DE VILLALONGA, **87,** Spanish actor, best known to American audiences for his role as Audrey Hepburn's fiancé in *Breakfast at Tiffany's,* died of natural causes on Aug. 30, 2007 in Mallorca in the Balearic Islands. His other films include *Any Number Can Win, Behold a Pale Horse, Darling, Juliet of the Spirits,* and *The Burglars.*

FRED "RED CROW" WESTERMAN, **71,** South Dakota–born actor, who appeared as "Ten Bears" in the 1990 Oscar-winner *Dances with Wolves,* died in Los Angeles, CA of complications from leukemia on Dec. 13, 2007. His other films include *Powwow Highway, Renegades, The Doors,* and *Clearcut.* Survivors include his wife, four daughters, his son, and several grandchildren.

DICK WILSON, **91,** British-born, Ontario-raised character actor best known for his twenty-one year stint as "Mr. Whipple" on the "Please don't squeeze the Charmin" bathroom tissue ads, died on November 19, 2007 in Woodland Hills, CA. He could be seen in small roles in such films as *Diary of a Madman, Our Man Flint, Caprice, The Shakiest Gun in the West, The World's Greatest Athlete,* and *The Incredible Shrinking Woman.* He is survived by his wife, a son, two daughters, and five grandchildren.

GRETCHEN WYLER **(Gretchen Patricia Wienecke), 75,** Okla- homa-born screen, stage, and television actress, died on May 27, 2007 at her home in Camarillo, CA, of complications from breast cancer. Her handful of films include *The Devil's Brigade, Private Benjamin,* and *The Marrying Man.* Survived by a sister and a brother.

JANE WYMAN **(Sarah Jane Mayfield), 90,** Missouri-born actress who won an Academy Award for her portrayal of a deaf woman in *Johnny Belinda,* died on Sept. 10, 2007 at her home in Palm Springs, CA of natural causes. Following several bit parts under her real name, she first appeared as Jane Wyman in the 1936 release *Stage Struck.* Over the next 33 years she appeared in such films as *Gold Diggers of 1937, The King and the Chorus Girl, Public Wedding, The Crowd Roars, Wide Open Faces, Brother Rat, Torchy Blane ... Playing with Dynamite, An Angel from Texas, My Love Came Back, You're in the Army Now, Larceny Inc., Princess O'Rourke, Make Your Own Bed, The Doughgirls, Footlight Serenade, The Lost Weekend, Night and Day, The Yearling* (Oscar nomination), *A Kiss in the Dark, The Glass Menagerie* (1950), *Stage Fright, Three Guys Named Mike, Here Comes the Groom, The Blue Veil* (Oscar nomination), *The Story of Will Rogers, Just for You, So Big* (1953), *Magnificent Obsession* (Oscar nomination), *All That Heaven Allows, Lucy Gallant, Miracle in the Rain, Holiday for Lovers, Pollyanna* (1960), *Bon Voyage,* and *How to Commit Marriage.* She is survived by her son from her third marriage, to actor Ronald Reagan, and two grandchildren.

# INDEX